PRAISE FOR *CODEBREAKING*

"One of the most helpful guides outside the N
if you don't become a codebreaker, this book

—STEVEN LE
AUTHOR OF
THE INSIDE STORY

"Another kind of *Applied Cryptography*."

—WHITFIELD DIFFIE, TURING LAUREATE AND
CREATOR OF PUBLIC-KEY CRYPTOGRAPHY

"A compendium of historical cryptography. Approachable, accessible, this book brings back the joy I felt when I first read about these things as a kid."

—PHIL ZIMMERMANN, CREATOR OF PGP
ENCRYPTION AND INDUCTEE INTO THE
INTERNET HALL OF FAME

"*Codebreaking: A Practical Guide* is quite the best book on codebreaking I have read: clear, engaging, and fun. A must for would-be recruits to GCHQ and the NSA!"

—SIR DERMOT TURING, AUTHOR OF *PROF*, THE
BIOGRAPHY OF HIS UNCLE, ALAN TURING

"Riveting. Dunin and Schmeh show us that we each have our own inner code-breaker yearning to be set free. *Codebreaking* isn't just for super-geniuses with supercomputers; it's something we were all born to do."

—MIKE GODWIN, CREATOR OF GODWIN'S LAW
AND FORMER GENERAL COUNSEL FOR THE
WIKIMEDIA FOUNDATION

"This is THE book about codebreaking. Very concise, very inclusive, and easy to read. Good references for those who would make codes, too, like *Kryptos*."

—ED SCHEIDT, CIA

"This is the book of my dreams. Super-clear, super-fun guide for solving secret messages of all kinds."

—JASON FAGONE, AUTHOR OF THE
BESTSELLING BOOK *THE WOMAN WHO
SMASHED CODES*

"Kool dnoces a htrow era snootrac eht fo ynam."

—SUOMYNONA ECILA

"A wonderful mix of ciphers, both famous and little-known, solved and unsolved. Beginners will be hooked on exploring the world of secrets in cipher, and those who have already been introduced to the field will find much that is new."

—CRAIG BAUER, EDITOR IN CHIEF OF
CRYPTOLOGIA AND AUTHOR OF *UNSOLVED!:*
THE HISTORY AND MYSTERY OF THE WORLD'S
GREATEST CIPHERS

"Pdqb ri wkh fduwrrqv duh zruwk d vhfrqg orrn."

—DQRQBPRXV

"Cryptography? Ciphers? I thought this would be an easy book to put down. I was very wrong."

—STEVE MERETZKY, CO-AUTHOR WITH
DOUGLAS ADAMS OF *THE HITCHHIKER'S GUIDE*
TO THE GALAXY COMPUTER GAME

CODEBREAKING

Also by Elonka Dunin

The Mammoth Book of Secret Codes and Cryptograms
Secrets of the Lost Symbol (with Daniel Burstein and Arne de Keijzer)
Codebreaking: A Practical Guide (UK edition)

Also by Klaus Schmeh

Cryptography and Public Key Infrastructure on the Internet
Codebreaking: A Practical Guide (UK edition)

In German:

Codeknacker gegen Codemacher
Chief Security Officer (comic)
Versutus (comic)
Versteckte Botschaften
Kryptografie—Verfahren, Protokolle, Infrastrukturen
Nicht zu knacken
Die Erben der Enigma
Elektronische Ausweisdokumente
Die Welt der geheimen Zeichen
Kryptografie und Public-Key-Infrastrukturen im Internet
Safer Net

CODEBREAKING
A Practical Guide

Expanded Edition

by Elonka Dunin
and Klaus Schmeh

no starch
press®

San Francisco

Codebreaking: A Practical Guide was first published in the United Kingdom by Robinson, an imprint of Little, Brown Book Group Limited, © 2020 by Elonka Dunin and Klaus Schmeh.

Printed in the United States of America

First printing

27 26 25 24 23   1 2 3 4 5

ISBN-13: 978-1-7185-0272-7 (print)
ISBN-13: 978-1-7185-0273-4 (ebook)

Publisher: William Pollock
Managing Editor: Jill Franklin
Production Manager: Sabrina Plomitallo-González
Production Editor: Jennifer Kepler
Developmental Editor: Frances Saux
Cover Illustrator: Gina Redman
Interior Design: Octopod Studios
Copyeditor: Doug McNair
Compositor: Maureen Forys, Happenstance Type-O-Rama
Proofreader: Elizabeth Littrell

The cryptogram used in the background on the cover is courtesy of Andrew Furlong; see page 50.

For information on distribution, bulk sales, corporate sales, or translations, please contact No Starch Press® directly at info@nostarch.com or:

No Starch Press, Inc.
245 8th Street, San Francisco, CA 94103
phone: 1.415.863.9900
www.nostarch.com

Library of Congress Cataloging-in-Publication Data

```
Names: Dunin, Elonka, author. | Schmeh, Klaus, author.
Title: Codebreaking : a practical guide / by Elonka Dunin and Klaus Schmeh.
Description: San Francisco, CA : No Starch Press, [2023] | Includes
    bibliographical references and index.
Identifiers: LCCN 2023002094 (print) | LCCN 2023002095 (ebook) | ISBN
    9781718502727 (paperback) | ISBN 9781718502734 (ebook)
Subjects: LCSH: Cryptography. | Ciphers.
Classification: LCC Z103 .D86 2023  (print) | LCC Z103  (ebook) | DDC
    652/.8--dc23/eng/20230322
LC record available at https://lccn.loc.gov/2023002094
LC ebook record available at https://lccn.loc.gov/2023002095
```

For Thomas Ernst
—Klaus Schmeh

For cryptophiles everywhere
—Elonka Dunin

About the Authors

Elonka Dunin is an American video game developer, management consultant, and cryptologist. Bestselling author Dan Brown named Nola Kaye, a character in his novel *The Lost Symbol*, after her. Elonka maintains cryptography-related websites about topics such as the world's most famous unsolved codes and *Kryptos*, a sculpture at the Central Intelligence Agency containing an encrypted message. She is considered the leading *Kryptos* expert in the world. Elonka was a member of the United States National Cryptologic Foundation's Board from 2012 to 2022 and frequently gives lectures on the subject of cryptography. She has published multiple books and articles on classical cryptography, including "How We Set New World Records in Breaking Playfair Ciphertexts" with Klaus Schmeh in the academic journal *Cryptologia*. She also gives talks on her favorite subjects: games, Wikipedia, Agile, medieval history, and geocaching. She lives in Rockville, Maryland, with her cat, Crypto Kitty.

Klaus Schmeh, of Gelsenkirchen, Germany, is one of the world's leading experts on the history of encryption. He has published 15 books about encryption technology (mostly written in German), as well as over 250 articles, 30 research papers, and 1,600 blog posts, which makes him the most published cryptology author in the world. He is a member of the editorial board of the scientific magazine *Cryptologia* and a frequent speaker at encryption conferences in Europe and the United States. He has given presentations at the NSA Symposium on Cryptologic History, the Charlotte International Cryptologic Symposium, the RSA Conference in San Francisco, DEF CON, HOPE, Dragon Con, and many more. He is known for his entertaining presentation style involving self-drawn cartoons and LEGO models.

BRIEF CONTENTS

CONTENTS IN DETAIL

4
SIMPLE SUBSTITUTION CIPHERS WITHOUT SPACES
BETWEEN WORDS: PATRISTOCRATS   51

5
SIMPLE SUBSTITUTION CIPHERS IN NON-ENGLISH LANGUAGES   65

6
HOMOPHONIC CIPHERS   85

7
CODES AND NOMENCLATORS   113

14
DICTIONARY CODES AND BOOK CIPHERS   285

15
ADDITIONAL ENCRYPTION METHODS   303

16
SOLVING CIPHERS WITH HILL CLIMBING   329

PREFACE

We both have an interest in classical ciphers and codebreaking, so it was pretty much inevitable that our paths would cross someday. This happened in October 2009, when we attended the NSA Symposium on Cryptologic History in Laurel, Maryland. During the first networking session, we realized that we had much in common. This was the start of a friendship that is still enduring, although we live in different parts of the world and are separated by about 4,000 miles, as well as lots of water (the Atlantic Ocean), with Elonka in Rockville, Maryland, near Washington, DC, and Klaus in Gelsenkirchen, Germany. We still meet regularly in Maryland at the biennial NSA Symposium on Cryptologic History and other events.

In 2017, on one such visit, we took a spur-of-the-moment, multi-hour road trip down to southern Virginia in order to explore a famous cipher mystery: the Beale ciphers (see Chapter 6). This story, about a hidden treasure and three encrypted messages that describe its location, is probably a mere hoax, but at least it's a tantalizing one. We went to Bedford, Virginia, to conduct research at its library, which had a collection of Beale memorabilia. Then, we ate dinner at Beale's Beer restaurant, sitting next to a large map that showed the notable places of the Beale story (Figure 1).

Figure 1: Klaus and Elonka in front of a map showing notable places related to the Beale treasure and the three encrypted notes allegedly describing its location

On our five-hour return trip from Bedford to Washington, DC, by car, we talked, among other things, about codebreaking literature and the regrettable fact that no up-to-date book about this topic was available. What we wished for was a work that covered the solving of authentic ciphertexts, which we kept encountering in the form of encrypted postcards, letters, telegrams, diaries, journals, and other documents from the past few hundred years. Deciphering such cryptograms always provides a firsthand glimpse into a moment of history—something even the best crossword puzzle or Rubik's Cube cannot do.

In addition, we lamented the lack of a codebreaking book that was computer aware and covered the numerous software programs and websites available today for solving ciphertexts. We also wanted such a book to include the recent codebreaking research and fascinating new methods of solving ciphers. No book on the market came even close to our expectations. The only ones we could think of were the pre–computer age 1939 classic by Helen Fouché Gaines, *Cryptanalysis*, and bits and pieces of other books and journals. None of these really scratched the itch by pulling everything together.

By the time we arrived back in Maryland, we had decided we were going to change this by co-authoring such a book. The rest is history. The first edition was published in 2020, and here we are, years later, putting the finishing touches on the expanded edition of *Codebreaking: A Practical Guide*.

Writing a book was nothing new for either of us. Elonka, a game developer by trade, has written about cryptography in the past, notably in *The Mammoth Book of Secret Codes and Cryptograms* in 2006 and two articles in the 2009 bestseller *Secrets of the Lost Symbol*, about Dan Brown's *Da Vinci Code* sequel. She has also created multiple web pages concerning ciphers and codebreaking that have received millions of page views on the internet.

Klaus has authored some 25 books in German (over half of which are about encryption technology), along with 250 magazine articles, 30 research papers, and 1,600 posts on his *Cipherbrain* blog. All of that makes him the most prolific crypto author in the world.

Despite our experience, co-writing this book was far from a routine project. We both had busy day jobs and speaking schedules, which had us constantly traveling. Also, as there was an ocean between us, we had to remotely sync our schedules to communicate via Skype and Zoom calls across a time difference of five to nine hours, depending on which part of the world we were in. We did have two in-person meetings, though, to be honest, we did not really use them to work on our book; the time was filled with research in libraries, interviewing crypto people, and other field trips. We even made a second visit to the home of the Beale ciphers in Bedford, Virginia, and a pilgrimage to the George C. Marshall Library in Lexington, Virginia, to research the history of the United States's most famous cryptanalytic couple, Elizebeth and William Friedman.

Still, working on our codebreaking book was a rewarding task. We put on paper what had occupied us for over two decades, and it felt gratifying to finally give these thoughts a home. The book you are holding draws from many sources, including other codebreaking books from the pre-computer era, articles in the academic journal *Cryptologia*, and Klaus's hundreds of relevant blog posts, many of which had been commented upon by some of the best codebreakers in the world. In addition to describing solving methods, we include numerous success stories that show that, when it comes to cracking ciphers, devotion, imagination, and luck are sometimes just as helpful as expertise and years of experience.

As one of our few setbacks, we had to accept that there is much more interesting material about codebreaking than we could fit into a book of 500+ pages. With the first edition, we had no other choice than (with a great amount of screaming and gnashing of teeth) to narrow our scope, which meant that dozens of codebreaking methods, unsolved crypto mysteries, cipher challenges, and success stories we would have loved to include didn't make it into the final manuscript. However, now that we have an expanded edition, we have put many of them back in!

And then, toward the end of our (first) book-writing project, the entire world took a bizarre turn when COVID-19 surfaced. It was the start of a crisis that affected both of our lives and, of course, the rest of the world. Elonka was in San Francisco when this occurred, and the initial "shelter in place" order and advice to avoid airports meant she was unable to return to her home in Maryland for months. She continued working on the book while perched in a guest room at the home of her Bay Area friends, Jon and Beth Leonard. Klaus spent the coronavirus time in his apartment in Gelsenkirchen, Germany.

Surviving the COVID crisis, we successfully turned in our manuscript, and the first edition of our book was published in the United Kingdom on December 10, 2020. But then, on December 11, we were contacted by our colleague Dave Oranchak, who told us that we were going to need to rework the book! As was later reported in the news, he and two others had just cracked a legendary unsolved code: the fifty-year-old Zodiac Z340. So, we knew almost immediately that our book needed a new edition.

This version includes, of course, all the latest details on the Z340 solve, plus more information about other codes that (as of this nanosecond) are unsolved. For example, we have expanded the sections on two different sculptures on either side of the equator: *Kryptos* in the Northern Hemisphere and the Australian *NKRYPT* in the Southern. Reaching back to the nineteenth century, we've added more about both the Furlong postcard and the Collinson newspaper ads. We've also provided updates on the recently exhumed Somerton Man; the message from the World War II carrier pigeon that was found in a chimney in 1982; the Dorabella Cipher of 1897; and the Chinese Gold Bars, from our conversation with Peter Bisno, Esq., in December 2020.

Other additions include a nomenclator message sent by Charles I of England that we found in the archives and more information about other ciphers and cipher solvers. Drawing from our article in the academic journal *Cryptologia*, "How We Set New World Records in Breaking Playfair Ciphertexts," we've added more information about the hot cryptanalytic technique of hill climbing and how it is being used to solve older ciphers left and right. Also, we've fixed several errors that crept into the first edition. Thank you to all our eagle-eyed readers!

You'll find an appendix with a Morse code table (we were astonished to learn we missed that in the 2020 edition!); a new section on the Voynich manuscript that shows the results of our comparing its traits with similar encrypted books from the last 600 years; many new references; an updated metapuzzle (with a fresh hint or two); and an expanded reading list of additional titles of use to codebreakers, including several new biographies of Elizebeth Friedman.

As before and always, we wish you the most fun in reading our book.

Elonka Dunin and Klaus Schmeh
Rockville, Maryland, and Gelsenkirchen, Germany, 2023
codebreaking.guide@gmail.com
http://codebreaking-guide.com

1

HOW CAN I BREAK AN ENCRYPTED MESSAGE? AND OTHER INTRODUCTORY QUESTIONS

The postcard in Figure 1-1 (provided to us by Karsten Hansky) was sent in 1904.[1] As can be easily seen, the message written on it is encrypted.

Figure 1-1: Apparently, the sender of this postcard didn't want the letter carrier or the family of the recipient to read it. So, they chose to encrypt the message.

Decades- or even centuries-old encrypted messages are far from unusual. Countless encrypted diaries, letters, notebooks, radio messages, newspaper ads, and telegrams are known to exist—not to mention numerous encrypted postcards, such as the one in Figure 1-1. Encrypted documents can also be found in archives, private collections, and flea markets, as well as on internet auction portals, websites, and mailing lists. Many more encrypted messages are printed in books, newspapers, and magazines, both old and new.

Before computers became popular, encryption was mainly performed by hand, usually with pencil and paper (hence the term *pencil-and-paper encryption*). Sometimes, cryptographers also employed simple equipment such as leather strips or wooden and metallic implements, like disks or slides. Starting in the late 1920s, mechanical and electrical encryption machines came into use, the most famous of which was the German Enigma machine (see Chapter 15). As encryption machines were expensive, they saw widespread use primarily in the military, intelligence organizations, and diplomatic services. Those with fewer financial resources tended to continue using pencil-and-paper systems.

With the advent of modern digital technology around 1970, commercial and military encryption began using computer hardware and software. Nevertheless, pencil-and-paper encryption endured and is still relevant today. It is used by a wide cross section of the population: criminals protecting illegal activities, friends and lovers exchanging secret messages, and others who use it in various recreational activities. For example, geocachers, escape room aficionados, and those involved with other kinds of high-tech scavenger hunts might use cryptography to hide latitude and longitude coordinates.

What is this book about?

We will show you historical examples of real messages, such as postcards, diaries, letters, and telegrams, that were encrypted with pencil and paper or other manual methods. We will also teach you methods for breaking them. Although manual encryption and decryption have lost much of their importance due to the widespread use of computer technology, many people are still interested in deciphering encrypted messages for several reasons:

- Families may want to read encrypted postcards, letters, or diaries they have inherited from their ancestors.

- Historians endeavor to decipher encrypted documents they have encountered during their research in order to gain insight into previous eras.

- Police officers may want to break enciphered messages written by criminals.

- Geocachers want to solve puzzle caches.

- Decryption enthusiasts take delight in deciphering encrypted documents that were created decades or even centuries ago; many of these enthusiasts regard solving an unsolved cipher to be as exciting a task as climbing Mount Everest or making a new archaeological discovery.

- Students try to solve challenges from their cryptography classes. Most classes focus on computer-based encryption, but they usually include the study of pencil-and-paper methods as well.

While some solvers are mainly interested in historical encrypted messages, others enjoy encryption puzzles created as recreation, like those found in Elonka's book *The Mammoth Book of Secret Codes and Cryptograms*[2] or in the regular publications of the American Cryptogram Association. This book mainly deals with historical encryption. The postcard from 1904 shown at the beginning of this chapter is the first example we provide. In Chapter 5, we will explain how it can be deciphered.

Which technical terms do I need to know?

A text that is to be encrypted is termed a *plaintext*. The result of an encryption is the *ciphertext*. Sometimes, the ciphertext may be embedded in other readable text, which is called the *cleartext* to distinguish it from the ciphertext that appears within it.

Many encryption methods are based on some secret information that may only be known to the sender and the receiver—the *key*. A typical example of a key is a *substitution table* that replaces every letter of the alphabet for another one. Sometimes, the key is represented by a word, the *keyword*.

There are two kinds of encryption methods: ciphers and codes. The easiest way to describe the difference is that a *cipher* (sometimes spelled "cypher") generally works on letters, while a *code* works on words or phrases. The problem with using a code is that you often need to first think of nearly every word you want to use and then generate a codebook that has an equivalent for each one. Since a language can have thousands of words, such codebooks could be quite large! But a cipher, which operates only on letters, can be a much more compact system. Pretty much anything can be encrypted with a cipher, as long as both the sender and receiver know the system; no hefty codebook is required. Most of the encryption methods covered in this book are ciphers. Codes will be addressed in Chapter 7.

Unfortunately, these terms can be confusing because many other meanings of the term *code* are in general use. For instance, a ZIP code or a code of conduct has nothing to do with encryption. Even if we restrict ourselves to the field of encryption technology, the use of the word *code* is ambiguous, as it sometimes refers to encryption in general (for example, in the expression *codebreaking*). Even professional cryptographers, when speaking casually, may use the terms *code* and *cipher* interchangeably. In this book, we will use the term *code* only in the way we defined it in the previous paragraph (i.e., as a method of encrypting messages at the level of words and phrases). There is only one exception: when we say *codebreaking*, we refer to all kinds of encryption, not only codes.

If we have the key, we can *decrypt* a ciphertext to obtain the plaintext. If we try to derive a plaintext from a ciphertext without knowing the key, we usually speak of *breaking* the encryption. An encrypted message we want to break we refer to as a *cryptogram*.

While the art and craft of encryption is referred to as *cryptography*, the breaking of cryptograms is called *cryptanalysis*. *Codebreaking* is another word for cryptanalysis. Also, the term *cryptology* often means cryptography and cryptanalysis but can also mean the study of everything encryption related, including people, machines, systems, and history. The term *crypto* can be used as a catchall term to apply to many items on this list.

Generally, *cryptology* refers to messages that are encrypted, but sometimes, *steganography*, the hiding of information (see Chapter 15), is included in cryptology as well.

When breaking a cryptogram, it is usually helpful to know or to guess a word or phrase that appears in the plaintext. Such a word or phrase is called a *crib*.

In addition, several characters are frequently referenced in the literature on cryptography (though they don't play a major role in this book): *Alice* and *Bob* are often used as placeholder names when it comes to explaining encryption methods. Usually, the sender of an encrypted message is referred to as Alice and the receiver is referred to as Bob. Sometimes, additional characters appear, such as *Carol* (another crypto user), *Eve* (an eavesdropper), and *Mallory* (a malicious person). These characters do not necessarily stand for humans; they might also refer to computer programs or hardware components.

See the glossary in Appendix C for definitions of these and other terms.

How can I break an encrypted text?

You've come to the right place! The purpose of our book is exactly to help you with this question, especially in regard to classical ciphers. We introduce the main pencil-and-paper encryption techniques encountered in practice and then describe how to solve them.

For impatient readers, we provide our first codebreaking example in the following cryptogram: an encrypted advertisement published in the London newspaper *The Times* on August 1, 1873. This and some other encrypted newspaper ads we will be referring to later are from Jean Palmer's 2005 book *The Agony Column Codes & Ciphers*. (Jean Palmer is a pen name of London-based codebreaking expert Tony Gaffney.)[3]

HFOBWDS wtbsfdoeskejd ji ijs mjiae (dai ditwy). Afods ks rofed dpficqp Hcqp. Toeqfwus yic lsrd vspojt uwjjid qsd ibsf. Aoll sjtswbicf di edwy apsfs yic lsrd ce doll 0 pswf rfik yic, qobs yicf wtbous. Ylcf cjpwhhy aors jd asll.

Here's the ciphertext written in a more readable way:

HFOBWDS wtbsfdoesksjd ji ijs mjiae (dai ditwy). Afods ks rofed
dpficqp licqp. Toeqfwus yic lsrd vspojt uwjjid qsd ibsf. Aoll
sjtswbicf di edwy apsfs yic lsrd ce doll 0 pswf rfik yic, qobs
yicf wtbous. Yicf cjpwhhy aors jid asll.

A good first step in codebreaking is to count the letters in the message. This technique, called *frequency analysis*, lets us make educated guesses about what each letter represents, based on how often it appears in the text:

A B C D E F G H I J K L M N O P Q R S T U V W X Y Z

(frequency analysis tally chart for each letter of the alphabet)

As can be seen, the ciphertext letter s is the most frequent. It probably stands for the plaintext letter **e**, which is the most frequent letter in virtually every English text. After **e**, the letters **t**, **a**, and **o** are the next most frequent ones in the English language, although it is difficult to identify these based on their frequencies alone. However, there is another letter we can easily guess by looking at the ciphertext: the word 0 must stand for **I**, as there is no other word in the English language that consists of only one capitalized letter (unless it is at the beginning of a sentence, in which case, the letter **A** would fit).

Further analysis shows that the ciphertext contains the word yic three times and the word yicf twice. The plaintext words **the** and **them** would be good guesses, but we've already determined that s (not c) stands for **e**. So, **you** and **your** make sense.

Knowing the ciphertext equivalents of the six plaintext letters **e**, **i**, **y**, **o**, **u**, and **r** makes it easy to guess more words. For instance, ijs decrypts to **o*e** (with the asterisk standing for an unknown letter), which likely means **one**. In the end, we receive the following plaintext:

> PRIVATE advertisement no one knows (two today). Write me first through lough. Disgrace you left behind cannot get over. Will endeavour to stay where you left us till I hear from you, give your advice. Your unhappy wife not well.

If we have access to a computer and a program such as CrypTool 2 (free open source software available at *https://cryptool.org*), we can use an even more efficient method to break the encrypted advertisement in *The Times*: we look for a word in the ciphertext that has a distinctive letter pattern. The best candidate we can find is wtbsfdoesksjd—it contains the same letter (s) at the fourth, ninth, and eleventh position, and the sixth and the last letter (d) are the same, too. All other letters in this word are different. CrypTool 2 provides a tool that searches for words with a given repetition pattern in a large database. For wtbsfdoesksjd, we receive only one hit: **advertisement**. This is certainly a common word in a newspaper ad.

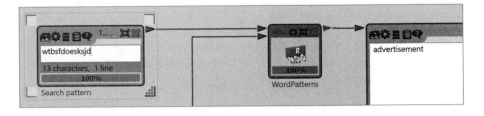

Assuming that **advertisement** is correct, we can determine the meaning of the following letters:

```
Plaintext:  a d e i m n r s t v
Ciphertext: w t s o k j f e d b
```

This information enables us to identify or guess more words. For instance, the first word, HFOBWDS, represents *R*VATE, which can be solved as **PRIVATE**. Now we know that the ciphertext letters H and O stand for **P** and **I**. The ciphertext wtbous decrypts to **advi*e**, which should be **advice**. (It can't be **advise**, as the **s** is already attributed to another letter.) This also shows that ciphertext u corresponds to plaintext **c**. We have identified enough letters now that we should be able to decipher more words. In the end, we get the plaintext given above.

This advertisement appears to be a message from a woman to her husband, who has left her. We will probably never learn who created it and why—after all, this ad was published 150 years ago. However, from a codebreaker's point of view, the mystery is solved.

That was not very difficult, was it? In the course of this book, you will get to know more complicated encryption methods, along with more sophisticated techniques for breaking them.

How do I know what kind of encryption I am dealing with?

Breaking a ciphertext usually requires knowing what kind of encryption method has been used. In addition to cipher-breaking methods, we therefore introduce in this book several cipher-detecting techniques. Identifying the cipher in use can be quite simple or very difficult. It is helpful to know that most messages encountered in practice have been encrypted with one of about a dozen methods that can usually be distinguished from each other with some analysis.

If you want to identify a particular cipher without reading the whole book, the following paragraphs will give you some guidance.

If the encrypted text you want to solve looks like this[4] . . .

. . . or like this[5] . . .

. . . or like this . . .

. . . or like this . . .

```
SIAA ZQ LKBA. VA ZOA RFPBLUAOAR!
```

. . . the cipher is likely substitution, and you should read Chapters 3, 4, and 5.
If the cryptogram you want to solve looks like this[6] . . .

to communicate 3693: 2517. 65. 3423. 576. 1100.
47. 1765. 3000. 259. 3032. 57. 66. 1795. 19. 211.
46. 1038. 1637. 970. 2609. 3369. 696. 3696. 427. 118.
3364. 1362. 456. 111. 566. 77. 1551. 29 61. 1504. 1437.

. . . check out Chapter 7 (on codes and nomenclators).
    If your ciphertext looks like this[7] . . .

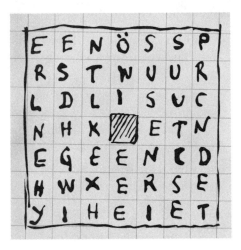

. . . it is likely a turning grille encryption, which is covered in Chapter 11.
    If the encrypted text you want to solve looks like this[8] . . .

. . . or like this . . .

. . . check Chapter 13 (abbreviation ciphers).

If the encrypted text you want to solve looks like this . . .

```
218.57 106.11 8.93 17.61 223.64 146.7 244.53 224.21 20 192.5 160.19
99.39 No. 8 251.70 1 223.64 58.89 151.79 226.69 8.93 40.12 149.9
248.101 167.12 252.35 12.31 135.100 149.9 145.76 225.53 212.25 20
241.6 222.22 78.45 12.31 66.28 252.33 158.33 6.65 20 2 11.50 142.37
223.87 12.31 142.37 105.33 142.37 157.20 58.62 133.89 250.86.
```

. . . read Chapter 14 (on dictionary codes and book ciphers).

If you are dealing with five-letter groups . . .

. . . there are several possibilities, the most likely being a code (Chapter 7), a transposition cipher (Chapters 9 and 10), a digraph substitution (Chapter 12), or a machine cipher (Chapter 15).

If your cryptogram doesn't look like any of these, or if you are not sure which category fits best, we're afraid you may need to read one chapter after another until you find what you are looking for.

I have found an encrypted text in the attic; can you decipher it for me?

Maybe! Did you find an encrypted postcard from your great-grandfather? Did you purchase an encrypted notebook at a flea market? Do you still own a cipher message your best friend sent you back in your childhood days? If so, you can try to break the message with one of the techniques described in this book.

If you are not successful, or if you simply do not want to invest the time to solve a cryptogram yourself, feel free to send it to us. (Our email addresses are in the "I have a comment" section at the end of this chapter.) Of course, we can't investigate every crypto mystery we receive, but in many cases, we can help. We are particularly interested in historical examples, less so in systems someone has invented in the modern day. Klaus is always searching for interesting encrypted texts he can write about, and Elonka has a website for famous unsolved codes. We don't guarantee anything, let alone that your mystery will be solved, but we will at least look at it.

If you send us a cryptogram you have found, please provide the following information:

- Tell us what you know about the cryptogram's background. Where did you find it? Who created it? Do you have any other information, such as the time period when it was created? Was it sent to or from someone you know? Which languages did this person speak? Information of this kind can be extremely helpful for a codebreaker.

- Tell us if we may publish this cryptogram (such as on the internet or in a book like this) or if you want to keep it confidential. Of course, we won't publish anything without the consent of the sender.

- In case you allow us to publish a cryptogram, tell us if you would like credit for it and/or if we may mention your name.

I have encrypted a text myself; can you break it?

While we are always very interested in genuine historical and classical ciphers, we generally cannot help with newer items. This is in large part because of the quantity of mail that we get; plus, it is far too easy for someone to compile a bunch of random text and proclaim, "Break my code!"

We make exceptions when a particular cipher has been drawing a great deal of public interest. For instance, if an encrypted message is presented in an artwork, as an inscription on a building, on a gravestone, or in some other unusual way, it might be intriguing to a larger audience. In addition, offering a cash reward or some other prize for solving a crypto puzzle is a good way to make a new puzzle more attractive. We might also take interest in crypto challenges published by the NSA or another organization with a relationship to codebreaking.

If you like to design encryption challenges, we recommend joining the American Cryptogram Association, which is always looking for people to craft puzzles for their regular newsletter. You may also wish to visit the crypto puzzle platform MysteryTwister (*https://mysterytwister.org*) and submit a challenge.

I have invented a new encryption method; can you take a look at it?

Like everyone who has a certain level of prominence on the crypto scene, we often receive communications from people who have invented their own encryption method and want us to review or crack it. To be honest, we have never been sent such a system that was solid or seemed a good use of our time, so in all seriousness, it is probably not a good idea to do this.

If you have created a method that is related to one of the many manual ciphers we cover in this book, it is likely very crackable, as there are many methods, especially with modern computers, to take these apart. New ciphers must compete with state-of-the-art crypto algorithms such as AES, Diffie-Hellman, and RSA (which are not within the scope of this book). Designing an encryption algorithm that can play in the big leagues is a difficult task, and even highly trained experts usually need several years of effort to create a good encryption algorithm.

So, if you are new to the field of encryption technology and really want to design a new system, we recommend first getting a good cryptography book and studying encryption algorithms that already exist. For example, *CryptoSchool* (2015) by Joachim von zur Gathen[9] is a comprehensive introduction, while *Serious Cryptography* (2017), written by Jean-Philippe Aumasson,[10] is a shorter alternative. If you can read German, you should try Klaus's book *Kryptografie—Verfahren, Protokolle, Infrastrukturen* (2016).[11]

For a related opinion on this phenomenon of crypto experts continually receiving examples of crackable systems, we strongly recommend Bruce Schneier's 1998 essay "Memo to the Amateur Cipher Designer."[12] It's over two decades old but still relevant. In a nutshell, Schneier says (and we agree) that to attempt to create a new cipher system, it is first essential to have substantial experience in breaking existing systems.

I have solved a famous unsolved cryptogram; what should I do?

In this book, we introduce dozens of unsolved cryptograms. Some of them, such as the Voynich manuscript, are quite famous, while others, such as the cigarette case cryptogram, have not received much attention yet. (Both of these cryptograms can be seen in Chapter 5.) A list of famous cryptograms is available on Elonka's website,[13] and Klaus has published his top-fifty unsolved cryptograms on his own blog.[14]

Virtually every popular unsolved ciphertext has received numerous dubious solutions. The more famous a cryptogram is, the more people claim to have solved it. At least sixty "solutions" to the Voynich manuscript have been published. Other favorites include the two remaining Zodiac Killer cryptograms, the Dorabella cryptogram, and the fourth *Kryptos* message. (We will come back to these mysteries later.) The internet is littered with doubtful solutions to famous cryptograms.

If you are a serious codebreaker and believe you have found the solution to an unsolved cryptogram, the first thing to do is challenge your own solution. Could you describe the method simply enough that a third party could use it and generate the same result? Ask yourself if the decryption process you have discovered is straightforward and does not involve too many tweaks and exceptions. Check if the resulting plaintext is meaningful without requiring dozens of alterations and interpretations. Finally, read Ryan Garlick's 2014 essay "How to Know That You Haven't Solved the Zodiac-340 Cipher."[15] (It's about alleged solutions to the second Zodiac cryptogram, but most of the content can be generalized to other cipher mysteries.)

If your solution does make sense, we are, of course, extremely interested in learning about it. If you have solved a cryptogram that is mentioned on Elonka's list, you can even expect to become a famous codebreaker.

Before you tackle one of the "Mount Everests" of codebreaking, we recommend, dear reader, that you start with cryptograms that have already been solved, of which you will find many in this book. Then, perhaps, proceed to the lesser-known unsolved ones. Some of these have not yet received much attention in the research community, so your chances of success are improved. The codebreaking methods you will learn about in this book might help you succeed. And who knows? One day, you might even master one of the world's most famous unsolved cipher challenges!

What tools do I need for codebreaking?

This book focuses on breaking pencil-and-paper ciphers, not on modern computer-based encryption. However, this doesn't mean that we don't use computers for our codebreaking work. Here are the three most important computer utilities we use in this book (all of which are available for free):

- CrypTool 2 (*https://cryptool.org*) is a crypto learning program developed by an international team headed by Bernhard Esslinger. Among other things, it supports many helpful codebreaking tools. The CrypTool project also offers e-learning programs for cryptography and cryptanalysis, such as CrypTool 1, JCrypTool, and CrypTool-Online.

- The website dCode (*https://dcode.fr/en*), operated by an anonymous group of crypto-enthusiasts, provides numerous helpful codebreaking and statistics tools.

- Cipher Tools (*https://rumkin.com/tools/cipher/*) is a large collection of classical cryptanalysis tools maintained by Tyler Akins.

Looking for more utilities? Check our codebreaking tools list in Chapter 17.

How can I encrypt my files and email?

Please note that the encryption techniques covered in this book should not be used to encrypt valuable secrets. This book deals with pencil-and-paper (i.e., manual) encryption. While studying manual encryption is interesting and important for several reasons, using this kind of encryption for sensitive data is completely outdated. If you need a tool to encrypt your computer files, look for a good encryption program such as the open source VeraCrypt or Philip Zimmermann's well-known PGP. Programs of this kind use modern encryption algorithms, including AES, Diffie-Hellman, and RSA, which can't be broken with today's technology.

I have a comment on this book; what should I do?

If you like this book, don't like it, have found a mistake, or just have a comment, please send us an email at *codebreaking.guide@gmail.com*. You may also wish to check the errata page at *https://codebreaking-guide.com/errata* to see if a mistake has already been reported. Feedback is extremely important for us.

Who contributed to this book?

We want to express special thanks to Tyler Akins, Michelle Barette, Kent D. Boklan, Bill Briere, Magnus Ekhall, Zachary Epstein, Thomas Ernst, Bernhard Esslinger, Dan Fretwell, Lawrence McElhiney, Dave Oranchak, Tobias Schrödel, Dale Sibborn, Gerhard Strasser, Erica Swearingen, and Satoshi Tomokiyo for their enthusiastic and comprehensive proofreading.

We would also like to thank John Allman; Christiane Angermayr; Lucia Angermayr (RIP); Nicolay Anitchkin; Eugen Antal; Philip Aston; Guy Atkins; Leopold Auer; Marc Baldwin; Paul Barron; Max Bärtl; Craig Bauer; Christian Baumann; Richard Bean; Stefan Beck; Arianna Benini; Neal Bennett; Yudhijit Bhattacharjee; Norbert Biermann; Peter Bisno; Sam Blake; Bob Bogart; Paolo Bonavoglia; Raymond Borges; Thomas Bosbach; Gert Brantner; Dan Brown (yes, *the* Dan Brown!); Ralf Bülow; Chris Christensen; Frank Corr; Nicolas Courtois; Carola Dahlke; Jason Davidson; Melissa Davis; Deb Desch; Whitfield Diffie; Jörg Drobick; Stanley Dunin; Ralph Erskine (RIP); Jarl Van Eycke; Jason Fagone; Cheri Farnsworth; Nick Fawcett; Gérard Fetter; Heathyr Fields; Frank Förster; Andrew Furlong; Tom (Monty) Fusco; Tony Gaffney; Jim Gandy; Joachim von zur Gathen; Declan Gilligan; Jim Gillogly; Dan Girard; Nicole Glücklich; Frank Gnegel; Marek Grajek; Joel Greenberg; Jackie Griffith; Marc Gutgesell; Sandi Hackney; Karsten Hansky; Louie Helm; Lonnie Henderson; Jürgen Hermes; Jan Henrik Holst; Michael Hörenberg; Günter Hütter; A.J. Jacobs; Ralf Jäger; JannaK; David Kahn; Bryan Kesselman; Manfred Kienzle; Michael Kirk; Gary Klivans; Oliver Knörzer; Stuart Kohlhagen; Daniel Kolb; Anatoly Kolker; Klaus Kopacz; Nils Kopal; Armin Krauß; Teresa Kuhl; Oliver Kuhlemann; Benedek Láng; Jew-Lee Lann-Briere; George Lasry; Karl de Leeuw (RIP); Jon, Beth, Peter, and Amber Leonard; Peter Lichtenberger; Greg Lloyd; Joe Loera; Krista van Loon; Tom Mahon; Denny McDaniels (RIP); Glenn McIntosh; John McVey; Hans van der Meer; Beáta Megyesi; Glen Miranker; Didier Müller; Wolfgang Müller; Walter C. Newman; Jim Oram; Olaf Ostwald; Nick Pelling; Klaus Pommerening; Beryl Pratt; Duncan Proudfoot; Katja Rasch; Jim Reeds; Paul Reuvers; Dirk Rijmenants; Sara Rivers-Cofield; Richard SantaColoma; D.P.J.A. Scheers; Volker Schmeh; Wolfgang Schmidt; Leon Schulman; Dale Sibborn; Linda Silverman; Marc Simons; Ralph Simpson; Rob Simpson; Dale Speirs; Rene Stein; Moritz Stocker; Christoph Tenzer; Satoshi Tomokiyo; Dermot Turing; Alexander Uliyanenkov; Ilona Sofia Vine; TJ Dunin Vine; Arno Wacker; Rich Wales; Frode Weierud; Meg Welch; Bart Wenmeckers; Bart Wessel; David Allen Wilson; Richard van de Wouw; Ruth Wüst; YefimShifrin; Gordon Young; DeEva Zabylivich; René Zandbergen; and Philip Zimmermann for their contributions, either to the book or to relevant discussions.

In addition, we appreciate the support of the Aargau Cantonal Library in Switzerland; the American Cryptogram Association; the Beale's Beer restaurant; the British Library; the dCode group; the Deutsches Museum (Munich, Germany); the Franz Steiner Verlag; the George C. Marshall Foundation (Lexington, VA); the Heinz Nixdorf MuseumsForum (Paderborn, Germany); the John F. Kennedy Presidential Library and Museum; the Kryptologikum (Karlsruhe, Germany); the Lehrsammlung für Nachrichten-, Fernmelde- und Informationstechnik der Bundeswehr (Feldafing, Germany); the Louis Round Wilson Special Collections Library at the University of North Carolina, Chapel Hill; the Museum für Kommunikation (Frankfurt, Germany); the Museum of Freemasonry, London; the National Cryptologic Museum (Fort Meade, MD); the New York Chancellor Robert R. Livingston Masonic Library and Museum; the New York State Archives; the New York State Military Museum; the Niedersächsisches Landesarchiv Abteilung Wolfenbüttel; the Royal Collection, The Netherlands; the Schreibmaschinenmuseum Beck (Pfäffikon, Switzerland); Touchstone Films; and Walt Disney Pictures; along with all of our internet friends: blog readers, friends, and participants from Facebook, Reddit, the Kryptos Group, and others around the World Wide Web.

2

THE CAESAR CIPHER

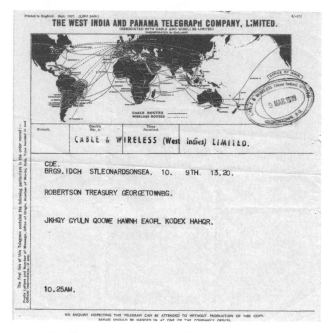

Figure 2-1: The message on this 1939 telegram is encrypted
with a Caesar cipher.

The telegram depicted in Figure 2-1 (and provided to us by Karsten Hansky)
was sent from St Leonards-on-Sea, United Kingdom, to Georgetown, British
Guyana, in 1939.[1] The message on this telegram is partially encrypted. In
the following transcript, the ciphertext is printed in bold on the fourth line:

CDE.
BRG9.IDCH. STLEONARDSONSEA. 10. 9th. 13.20.
ROBERTSON TREASURY GEORGETOWNBG.
JKHQY GYULN QOOWE HAWNH EAOPL KODEX HAHQR.
10.25AM.

The encryption method used here, called the Caesar cipher, is quite
simple, so it will serve as a good starting point for our discussion of encryption techniques. We dedicate this chapter to it.

How the Caesar cipher works

The Caesar cipher shifts each letter of the alphabet by a certain number
of characters. We can consider the cipher's key to be a number that determines the shift offset.

In the telegram shown in Figure 2-1, the key is 4, as visualized in the following table:

Plaintext: **ABCDEFGHIJKLMNOPQRSTUVWXYZ**
Ciphertext: EFGHIJKLMNOPQRSTUVWXYZABCD

Here's a different way to represent this key. This diagram shows that **A** is replaced by E, **B** by F, **C** by G, **D** by H, and so on:

A B C D E F G H I J K L M N O P Q R S T U V W X Y Z

A B C D E F G H I J K L M N O P Q R S T U V W X Y Z

When we apply the key to the encrypted telegram line in reverse, we get the following plaintext: **NOLUC KCYPR USSAI LEARL IESTP OSHIB LELUV**. If we put the blanks in the right places, the message might then say, **NO LUCK CYPRUS SAIL EARLTEST POSHIBLE LUV.**

We still don't know exactly what this message means. **POSHIBLE** is probably an incorrect spelling of **POSSIBLE**, while **CYPRUS** might refer to a ship of that name. **LUV** could be an acronym for the sender's initials or simply an abbreviation for **LOVE**.

If we used the Caesar cipher with an alphabet of twenty-six letters, there would be twenty-five (useful) different keys. That's because a shift of zero would not change the text, as every letter would shift to itself. A shift of twenty-six would do the same thing.

To apply a Caesar cipher, you can use a cipher disk or a cipher slide (see Figure 2-2). A Caesar cipher with the key 13, also referred to as ROT-13, is a *self-inverting cipher*—if you use it twice, you get the plaintext again.

Figure 2-2: A cipher disk or a cipher slide can be used to apply a Caesar cipher.

ROT-13 is often used on geocaching websites to encrypt spoilers.

How to detect a Caesar cipher

If you want to check whether a certain cryptogram has been created with a Caesar cipher, counting the letters (i.e., performing a frequency analysis) is helpful. To see why this is the case, let's first look at the letter frequencies in a typical English text:

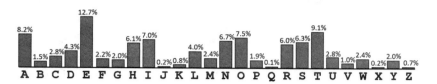

We see that **E** is the most frequent letter, and that it is surrounded by much less frequent ones. **R**, **S**, and **T** are three frequent letters in a row. The last five letters, **V**, **W**, **X**, **Y**, and **Z**, are all quite rare. If we apply a Caesar cipher to an English text, we'll notice the bars of this diagram move by a certain number of steps. For instance, if K is the letter with the highest bar, we should see it surrounded by far less frequent letters on each side, indicating that it corresponds to **E**. We can use this fact to detect a Caesar cipher.

Look now at the following two newspaper ads, which were both published in the London newspaper *The Times* in 1853:[2]

2 February 1853:

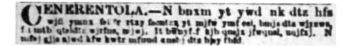

CENERENTOLA.–N bnxm yt ywd nk dtz hfs wjfi ymnx fsi fr rtxy
fscntzx yt mjfw ymfy fsi, bmjs dtz wjyzws, fsi mtb qtsl dtz
wjrfns, mjwj. It bwnyj f kjb qnsjx ifwqnsl, uqjfxj. N mfaj gjjs
ajwd kfw kwtr mfuud xnshj dtz bjsy fbfd.

11 February 1853:

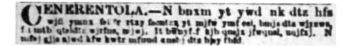

CENERENTOLA.–Zsynq rd mjfwy nx xnhp mfaj n ywnji yt kwfrj fs
jcuqfsfynts ktw dtz, gzy hfssty. Xnqjshj nx xfkjxy nk ymj ywzj
hfzxj nx sty xzxujhyji: nk ny nx, fqq xytwnjx bnqq gj xnkkyji yt
ymj gtyytr. It dtz wjrjrgjw tzw htzxns'x knwxy uwtutxnynts: ymnsp
tk ny.

We assume that both ads were encrypted the same way. **CENERENTOLA** (Italian for "Cinderella") is probably the pseudonym of the sender or recipient. As it is not encrypted, we can omit it from our examinations.

A good way to proceed is to perform a frequency count of the two cryptograms combined. We could count the letters manually or use computer assistance, such as with CrypTool 2 or a web-based tool such as *https://dcode .fr/en*. Here is a chart we made ourselves:

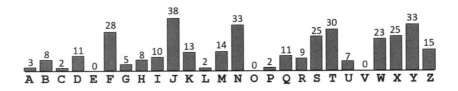

We see in Figure 2-3 that j is the most frequently used letter and is surrounded by less frequent ones. The letters w, x, and y form a block of three consecutive letters of high frequency. a, b, c, d, and e make up five letters of low frequency in a row.

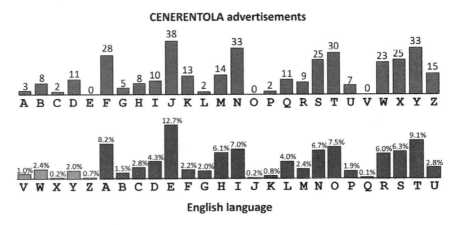

Figure 2-3: Comparing the letter frequencies of the CENERENTOLA ads with the letter frequencies of the English language suggests that we are dealing with a Caesar cipher.

All in all, the frequency analysis of our ciphertexts looks very similar to the frequencies of the English language, except that the bars are all shifted by five steps (**A** = **F**, **B** = **G**, **C** = **H** . . .). This suggests that we are dealing with a Caesar cipher. In fact, by applying this exact five-step shift, we can derive the following plaintexts:

```
CENERENTOLA.—I wish to try if you can read this and am most
anxious to hear that and, when you return, and how long you
remain, here. Do write a few lines darling, please. I have been
very far from happy since you went away.
```

CENERENTOLA.—Until my heart is sick have i tried to frame an explanation for you, but cannot. Silence is safest if the true cause is not suspected: If it is, all stories will be siffted to the bottom. Do you remember our cousin's first proposition: think of it.

Apparently, these two messages were written by a romantic couple. This is no surprise, as encrypted newspaper ads were a popular means of secret communication between lovers in Victorian England.

How to break a Caesar cipher

As should have become clear, a Caesar cipher is easily broken once identified. If you know the ciphertext letter that stands for, say, **E**, you can easily figure out the key.

Of course, there are other ways to solve a Caesar cryptogram. We can try all possible keys, checking for a plaintext that makes sense. This approach is referred to as *brute-force* or *exhaustive key search*. As there are only twenty-five keys, a brute-force attack on a Caesar cipher isn't too difficult. Let's perform one on the following advertisement, published in the London *Standard* on May 26, 1888:[3]

A frequency analysis of the ciphertext reveals that a Caesar cipher is very likely. To break it, let's write the message's first two words in the first row of a table, then fill in the table by shifting each letter by one in each subsequent row. When we reach Z, we'll wrap back around to A. We recommend writing this table column-wise:

0 URNYGU ORGGRE
1 VSOZHV PSHHSF
2 WTPAIW QTIITG
3 XUQBJX RUJJUH
4 YVRCKY SVKKVI
5 ZWSDLZ TWLLWJ
6 AXTEMA UXMMXK
7 BYUFNB VYNNYL
8 CZVGOC WZOOZM
9 DAWHPD XAPPAN

```
10 EBXIQE YBQQBO
11 FCYYRF ZCRRCP
12 GDZKSG ADSSDQ
13 HEALTH BETTER
14 IFBMUI CFUUFS
. . .
```

It is immediately clear that line 13, HEALTH BETTER, is the correct one. This means the text used ROT-13. Usually, creating such a table for only one word is enough.

Brute-forcing becomes even easier if we use CrypTool 2 to perform the twenty-five Caesar decryptions. The CrypTool 2 template "Caesar Brute-Force Analysis" provides the functionality we need for this purpose. Let's apply it to the following ciphertext taken from Elonka's *The Mammoth Book of Secret Codes and Cryptograms*:[4]

Devhqfh vkdushqv oryh, suhvhqfh vwuhqjwkhqv lw. Ehqmdplq Iudqnolq

Here's an excerpt from the twenty-five decryptions CrypTool 2 performs:

```
1 Wxoajya odwnlajo hkra, lnaoajya opnajcpdajo ep. Xajfwiej Bnwjghej
2 Xypbkzb pexombkp ilsb, mobpbkzb pqobkdqebkp fq. Ybkgxjfk Coxkhifk
3 Yzqclac qfypnclq jmtc, npcqclac qrpclerfclq gr. Zclhykgl Dpylijgl
4 Zardmbd rgzqodmr knud, oqdrdmbd rsqdmfsgdmr hs. Admizlhm Eqzmjkhm
5 Absence sharpens love, presence strengthens it. Benjamin Franklin
6 Bctfodf tibsqfot mpwf, qsftfodf tusfohuifot ju. Cfokbnjo Gsbolmjo
7 Cdugpeg ujctrgpu nqxg, rtgugpeg uvtgpivjgpu kv. Dgplcokp Htcpmnkp
8 Devhqfh vkdushqv oryh, suhvhqfh vwuhqjwkhqv lw. Ehqmdplq Iudqnolq
. . .
```

It is not very difficult to see that line 5 is correct:

Absence sharpens love, presence strengthens it. Benjamin Franklin

Success stories

A prison inmate's cipher

Our colleague Gary Klivans, a retired police captain from New York State, is a prominent expert on encryption methods used by gangs and prison inmates.[5] His fascinating 2016 book *Gang Secret Codes: Deciphered* is a must-read for everybody interested in codebreaking.[6] As of 2023, Gary works as a forensics consultant specializing in gang codes. He is also a frequent writer and lecturer in the field of forensic codebreaking. Gary provided us with an undated encrypted message from a prison inmate, shown in Figure 2-4.[7]

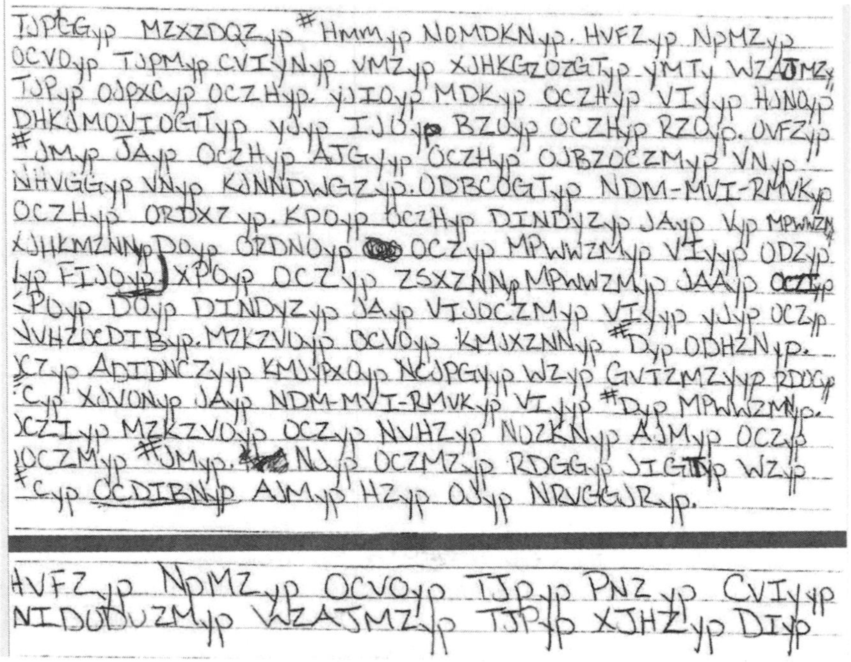

Figure 2-4: An encrypted message from a prison inmate. The plaintext proved quite interesting.

Every word in this message ends with yp. It was clear to Gary that these two-letter suffixes had no meaning and were included to confuse the code-breaker. Using frequency analysis (ignoring the yp's), Gary saw that this cryptogram had most likely been created with a Caesar cipher. As z is the most frequent letter, finding the solution was quite simple. Here's the substitution table the prison inmate used (the key is 21):

```
Plaintext:  ABCDEFGHIJKLMNOPQRSTUVWXYZ
Ciphertext: VWXYZABCDEFGHIJKLMNOPQRSTU
```

Based on this table, the following plaintext can be retrieved:

```
YOU'LL RECEIVE # MRR STRIPS MAKE SURE
THAT YOUR HANDS ARE COMPLETELY DRY BEFORE
YOU TOUCH THEM. DON'T RIP THEM AND MOST
IMPORTANTLY DO NOT GET THEM WET. TAKE
# OR OF THEM FOLD THEM TOGETHER AS
SMALL AS POSSIBLE TIGHTLY SIR-RAN-WRAP
THEM TWICE. PUT THEM INSIDE OF A RUBBER
COMPRESS IT TWIST THE RUBBER AND TIE
A KNOT. CUT THE EXCESS RUBBER OFF THEN
PUT IT INSIDE OF ANOTHER AND DO THE
SAME THING. REPEAT THAT PROCESS # I TIMES
THE FINISHED PRODUCT SHOULD BE LAYERED WITH
#H COATS OF SIR-RAN-WRAP #I RUBBERS
```

```
THEN REPEAT THE SAME STEPS FOR THE
OTHER # OR SO THERE WILL ONLY BE
#H THINGS FOR ME TO SWALLOW.
MAKE SURE THAT YOU USE HAND
SANITIZER BEFORE YOU COME IN
```

This message proved quite interesting. A prison inmate seems to be explaining to the recipient (perhaps his wife) how to pack drugs (MRR STRIPS) into a condom and Saran Wrap (SIR-RAN-WRAP). He advises this person to hand him these drug packages during a visit so that he can immediately swallow them, smuggling the drugs into his prison cell.

A spy's encrypted sheet

Brian Regan (not to be confused with the comedian of the same name) used to work as a master sergeant in the US Air Force. In 1999, he began trying to sell highly classified documents, videotapes, and storage media to foreign governments, hoping to receive over $10 million. In 2001, before he was able to succeed, he was arrested, convicted of espionage, and sentenced to life in prison.

Regan, who had been trained in cryptography, used several encryption methods to conceal banking codes, addresses, and other information. The FBI's codebreaking unit, called the Cryptanalysis and Racketeering Records Unit (CRRU), was able to break most of Regan's ciphertexts thanks to its master codebreaker, Dan Olson. The following was one of the easier ones:

As Olson found out (probably by brute force), this note is encrypted using a Caesar cipher with a key of 1. The numbers are shifted by one, too. We can easily decrypt the first two lines:

```
Ciphertext: MM-56NVOAIPG CBIOIPG-TUS VCT-AV-533341011943418
Plaintext:  LL-45MUNZHOF BAHNHOF-STR UBS-ZU-422230900832307
```

This message refers to the Union Bank of Switzerland (UBS), located in a building named Münzhof at Bahnhofstrasse 45 in Zurich, Switzerland. (Regan evidently used the codename LL for this bank.) The number 422230900832307 is a bank account number. Lines 3 and 4 are encrypted in the same way:

```
Ciphertext: SS-CVOEFTQMBUA3CFSO-576795218837795
Plaintext:  RR-BUNDESPLATZ2BERN-465684107726684
```

Bundesplatz 2 in Bern, Switzerland, is the address of another major Swiss bank, Credit Suisse (codenamed **RR** by Regan). Once again, **465684107726684** is a bank account number.

If you want to know more about the Brian Regan spy case, you should read the highly recommended 2016 book *The Spy Who Couldn't Spell* by Yudhijit Bhattacharjee.[8]

An encrypted journal from the movie The Prestige

The movie *The Prestige* (2006) is about two London stage magicians in the late nineteenth century who engage in a deadly rivalry. One magician, Alfred Borden, uses cryptography to protect his magic secrets. Excerpts from his journal can be seen several times during the movie. Here's an example (shown about eight minutes into the film):

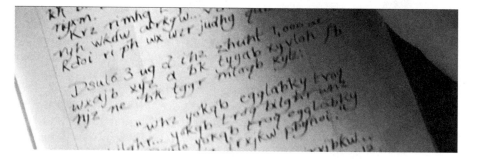

Crypto enthusiasts soon found out that this journal contained real encrypted text.[9] The cipher used turned out to be a Caesar cipher with the key 23, and the plaintext proved to contain numerous nonsense words. For instance, the line . . .

```
Dsulo 3 ug d ihz zhunt 1,000 ae
```

. . . decrypts to . . .

```
April 3 rd a few werkq 1,000 xb
```

We have no idea what werkq and xb were intended to mean.

Challenges

For hints to help you solve all of the challenges in this book, along with the solutions, see *https://codebreaking-guide.com/challenges/*.

Herbert Yardley's first challenge

Herbert Yardley (1889–1958) was a successful codebreaker working for the US Department of State. He is best known for his whistleblowing 1931 book, *The American Black Chamber*.[10] A lesser-known book of his is the 1932

Ciphergrams, which provides a collection of encryption puzzles (Yardley calls them "ciphergrams") along with fictional background stories.[11] The first ciphergram (see Figure 2-5) is encrypted using the Caesar cipher.

"Each night we recorded the signals on a phonograph record which was played over and over again in an effort to catch some inkling of the nature of the code. But we had absolutely no results. Then, one day, the machine happened to run down and, to our astonishment, the jargon resolved itself into a perfectly intelligible sequence of letters. I'm going to give you the very last message we received and let you try your skill," Crossle concluded. "Here it is."

snszk kxchr zakdc knmfh stcde nqsxk
zshst cdrdu dmsxs gqdd

Figure 2-5: One of Herbert Yardley's ciphergrams. It is encrypted using the Caesar cipher.

Can you solve it?

A series of newspaper advertisements from 1900

Here are four more newspaper advertisements we found in *The Agony Column*.[12] They were originally published in the British newspaper the *Evening Standard* in 1900.

ALICE R.P. Qcbufohizohs mci. I do not tcfush but hvwby of you jsfm aiqv and kcbrsf if we gvozzassh wbgwl cfgsjsb kssyg. Tuesday, March 27, 1900

ALICE R.P. How nice of you to remember. Will certainly meet you. Always thinking of you. Thursday, March 29, 1900

ALICE R.P. Am so looking forward to it. Kobhhc gssmci acfs hvob wqob hszzmci. Will zsh ybck in opcih twjs kssyg hwas. Monday, April 2, 1900

ALICE R.P. Gvozz kowh dcfhzobr rd ghohwcb hvifgrom twjs qzcqy gvcizr aiqv zwys gssmci. Thursday, May 17, 1900

As can be seen, the second ad is written completely in cleartext. The other three are partially encrypted with the Caesar cipher. Can you break these cryptograms?

3

SIMPLE SUBSTITUTION CIPHERS

Anybody interested in encryption and codebreaking should visit a museum of cryptology. In the United States, the best one is the National Cryptologic Museum, which is the doorway to NSA's headquarters in Fort Meade, Maryland. If you are in the United Kingdom, go to Bletchley Park, and in Germany, visit the Heinz Nixdorf MuseumsForum in Paderborn or the Deutsches Museum in Munich. These institutions exhibit fascinating cipher machines, such as the Enigma (see Chapter 15), as well as other crypto-related items.

Let's turn our attention now to an object we found in the National Cryptologic Museum's gift shop: a mug bearing an encrypted inscription (see Figure 3-1).

Figure 3-1: The inscription on these NSA mugs is encrypted in a pigpen cipher.

The encryption algorithm used here is a variant of the so-called *pigpen cipher*. Also known in the last few centuries as the Freemason's cipher, it is a very old and widespread enciphering technique.[1] The following diagram shows how the pigpen cipher turns every letter of the alphabet into a symbol consisting of lines and dots:

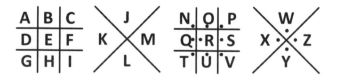

Using this diagram, it becomes clear that the mug inscription decrypts to **NATEONAL SECURITY AGENCY**. (Yes, the first word contains a typo. Things like this happen, even at the NSA!)

There are many other variants of the pigpen cipher. For instance, the following text, written on a tombstone[2] from 1796 in New York City . . .

. . . turns out to be encrypted in the following scheme:

A	B	C		K	L	M		T	U	V
D	E	F		N	O	P		W	X	Y
G	H	I		Q	R	S		Z		

The plaintext is **REMEMBER DEAAH**.

Of course, that second **A** should be a **T**, as clearly, the intended message was **REMEMBER DEATH**. Evidently, the stonecutter (or the tombstone designer) made a small typo, omitting the two dots! This is common in cryptography. Consider how easy it is to make typos in nonencrypted English text. The problem becomes even more pronounced with ciphertext, because it is more difficult to proofread. This can both add to and subtract from the level of difficulty for codebreakers.

There are many other pigpen cipher variations, such as those that change the order of the letters in the tables. For another variant, see the glossary in Appendix C of this book. For an overview of crypto museums and other cryptologic sites around the world, check out the Cryptologic Travel Guide, a website operated by Klaus and the Austrian IT expert Christian Baumann, at *https://cryptologictravelguide.com*.

How simple substitution ciphers work

The pigpen cipher and Caesar cipher are each examples of encryption methods that replace every letter of the alphabet with another letter or symbol. Ciphers of this kind are referred to as *simple substitution ciphers* or *monoalphabetic substitution ciphers (MASCs)*. A simple substitution cipher provides exactly one ciphertext letter for each plaintext letter.

There are two main types of simple substitution ciphers: one makes substitutions within the original alphabet, and the other transfers plaintext letters to characters in a different alphabet, which could be anything from a writing system such as the Cyrillic alphabet, to one invented by the user of the cipher, to a series of numbers, to a set of unusual symbols. The pigpen cipher is a simple substitution cipher of the *different-alphabet* type. So is the cipher that was used for the following text from *The Book of Woo*, as introduced in the webcomic *Sandra and Woo* in 2013:[3, 4]

By contrast, the left-hand side of Figure 3-2 shows a message of the *same-alphabet* type. This is the title page of an encrypted book published in London in 1835.[5]

EBPOB ES LYO UTLUB,	ORDER OF THE ALTAR,
UMGJOML NÝFLOBJOF	**ANCIENT MYSTERIES**
LE VYJGY	TO WHICH
SONUTOF VOBO UTEMO UPNJFFJRTO:	FEMALES WERE ALONE ADMISSABLE:
ROJMC DUBL LYO SJBFL	BEING PART THE FIRST
ES LYO	OF THE
FOGBOLF DBOFOBWOP	SECRETS PRESERVED
JM LYO	IN THE
UFFEGJULJEM	**ASSOCIATION**
ES	OF
NUJPOM AMJLH UNP ULLUGYNOML.	MAIDEN UNITY AND ATTACHMENT.
„Vonon ubo fibemcofl."—Ofpb. 3.11.	„Wemem are sjrongest."—Esdr. 3.11.
LONDON	LONDON
M.DCCC.XXXV.	M.DCCC.XXXV.

Figure 3-2: The book UMGJOML NÝFLOBJOF (left) was published by a women's secret order in London in 1835. It is encrypted with a simple substitution cipher. The right side shows the decrypted version.

Using the following decryption table . . .

```
Ciphertext: ABCDEFGHIJKLMNOPQRSTUVWXYÝZ
Plaintext:  URGPOSC-JIKTNMEDQBFLAWVXHYZ
```

. . . this title decrypts to the text shown on the right side of the figure.

There are also mixtures of the two schemes. For instance, the following letter (sent in 1841 by one W.B. Tyler to Edgar Allan Poe,[6] whom we will come back to in Chapter 6) is written in both standard and nonstandard characters:

A different-alphabet simple substitution cipher can easily be changed into one of the same-alphabet type by randomly substituting every non-standard character with a letter from the ordinary alphabet. This process is referred to as *transcription*, and the resulting text is called a *transcript*. For instance, the Voynich manuscript (covered in Chapter 5), which uses a unique set of symbols ("Voynichese"), has been transcribed into the standard alphabet by several researchers in different ways.[7]

As an example of transcription, we can use the following message, which was published in Reddit's Unsolved Codes forum in 2018 by a user named RetroSA, who said that he found it in his family's personal effects.[8] (It is still unsolved, by the way.)

Another Reddit reader named NickSB2013 provided a transcript based on the following table:

Here's the transcribed version of the cryptogram:

```
ABCDE ABFGH ABIJKLMNO OPBD
OPNQAQRS ATRDH NVRDF: OSGA OQCEWKF T VFKO: PGA
DRQAPF OBRSADF EQWXF
```

Don't be confused by the fact that the transcribed cryptogram starts with ABCDE. This is only because the Reddit reader transcribed the first letter appearing in the message as A, the second as B, and so on.

A transcribed message can be examined more easily than the original, especially if one uses a computer program. As it is possible to transfer a different-alphabet simple substitution cipher into a same-alphabet one, cryptanalysts usually don't distinguish between the two. The methods used to attack a simple substitution cipher cryptogram do not depend on whether the ciphertext is written with standard letters or an alternate alphabet.

The American Cryptogram Association calls any same-alphabet simple substitution cipher that includes spaces (i.e., boundaries between words) an *Aristocrat*. Every issue of its newsletter, *The Cryptogram*, contains a number of Aristocrats for the user to solve. Other newspapers and magazines publish Aristocrats along with crossword puzzles and chess problems. In addition, books have been published that contain nothing but Aristocrats. Plenty of people seem to enjoy solving this kind of puzzle!

How to detect a simple substitution cipher

There is an easy, yet very useful, rule of thumb: in the overwhelming majority of cases, if a ciphertext is written in a nonstandard alphabet, its author used a simple substitution cipher (sometimes with a few additional tweaks). For instance, all the texts written in a pigpen alphabet we have ever encountered are encrypted this way—although it would be easy to use a pigpen alphabet along with another encryption method. Apparently, people who are clever enough to avoid a simple substitution cipher, opting for a more complex encryption system instead, also realize that using a nonstandard alphabet does not increase security.

There is, of course, no guarantee that a text written in a nonstandard alphabet is a simple substitution cipher. In order to make a more accurate diagnosis, we need frequency analysis and possibly other statistical methods. We'll demonstrate this process with the encrypted postcard from 1909 depicted in Figure 3-3.[9]

Figure 3-3: A 1909 postcard encrypted in a simple substitution cipher of the different-alphabet type

Using the following table . . .

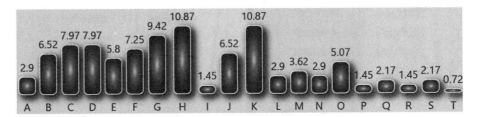

| A | B | C | D | E | F | G | H | I | J | K | L | M | N | O | P | Q | R | S | T |

. . . we create a transcribed version of the cryptogram. Note that the letters U, V, W, X, Y, and Z don't appear in the transcript, as the alphabet used on the postcard only has eighteen letters:

```
ABC DCEFG
FHI JBK LHM KGFKN
OMPPHOK LHM JBK
OGQLCDE GH DCEFG
C FJRK SKKD GBLCDE
GH ANHMBCOF J
NCGGNK. FJRK
SKKD HMG SBKJTCDE
BHJQO GFCO
JAGKBDHHD AHB GFK
IJEHDO. EHHQ DCEFG
```

Next, we perform frequency analysis. The following report was created with the computer program CrypTool 2, but you can also figure out these frequencies manually or use the website *https://dcode.fr/en*. In this case, we are only interested in the percentage frequencies:

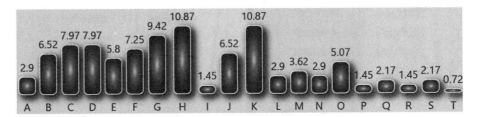

For comparison, here is a percentage frequency analysis of an ordinary English text:

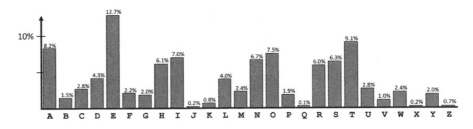

If we look at the four most frequent and least frequent letters of the two texts, we get the following:

```
Ciphertext:    10.87, 10.87, 9.42, 7.97 / 0.00, 0.00, 0.00, 0.00
Plain English: 12.7,   9.1,  8.2, 7.5  / 0.75, 0.25, 0.25, 0.25
```

As you can see, there are some differences. For instance, the most frequent letter of the ciphertext has a share of 10.87%, compared to 12.7% in plain English. Apart from this, however, the numbers are quite similar. Overall, the encrypted text on the postcard is consistent with a simple substitution cipher applied to an English plaintext. Further examination shows that this is the case. This postcard is included as one of the challenges at the end of this chapter. Can you solve it?

Example of a cipher that is not a simple substitution cipher

Let's now look at the ciphertext in Figure 3-4. This message is the first half of the encrypted inscription on the famous *Kryptos* sculpture at CIA headquarters, which we know does not use a simple substitution cipher (see Chapter 8 and Appendix A).

```
EMUFPHZLRFAXYUSDJKZLDKRNSHGNFIVJ
YQTQUXQBQVYUVLLTREVJYQTMKYRDMFD
VFPJUDEEHZWETZYVGWHKKQETGFQJNCE
GGWHKK?DQMCPFQZDQMMIAGPFXHQRLG
TIMVMZJANQLVKQEDAGDVFRPJUNGEUNA
QZGZLECGYUXUEENJTBJLBQCRTBJDFHRR
YIZETKZEMVDUFKSJHKFWHKUWQLSZFTI
HHDDUVH?DWKBFUFPWNTDFIYCUQZERE
EVLDKFEZMOQQJLTTUGSYQPFEUNLAVIDX
FLGGTEZ?FKZBSFDQVGOGIPUFXHHDRKF
FHQNTGPUAECNUVPDJMQCLQUMUNEDFQ
ELZZVRRGKFFVOEEXBDMVPNFQXEZLGRE
DNQFMPNZGLFLPMRJQYALMGNUVPDXVKP
DQUMEBEDMHDAFMJGZNUPLGEWJLLAETG
```

Figure 3-4: The first half of the famous Kryptos sculpture does not have the statistical properties of a simple substitution cipher.

To prove this, here's the percentage frequency analysis of this cryptogram:

Again, we look at the four most and least frequent letters and compare their frequencies to those in plain English:

```
Ciphertext:    7.18, 7.18, 6.71, 6.48 / 0.69, 1.39, 1.62, 1.85
Plain English: 12.7, 9.1,  8.2,  7.5  / 0.75, 0.25, 0.25, 0.25
```

As you can see, the differences are now a lot greater. Compared to plain English, the most frequent letters of this cryptogram are too rare, while the rare ones are too frequent. The cryptogram's frequency distribution is a lot flatter than that of English text in general. This indicates that the first half of the *Kryptos* inscription is not encrypted using a simple substitution cipher. We will come back to this famous cryptogram in Chapter 8.

Index-of-coincidence technique

Whenever we have access to a computer, we can use another statistical method to make an educated guess about whether a certain ciphertext was created with a simple substitution cipher or not: the *index of coincidence (IC)*, which we define as the probability of two randomly chosen letters from a text being the same. (Other sources may describe IC differently.) The details of this important codebreaking tool are in Appendix B. For the time being, know that the IC of an English plaintext encrypted using a simple substitution cipher is usually about 6.7%, while for pure random text, it is about 3.8%.

As calculating the IC is a laborious process to do by hand, in this example, we use the website *https://dcode.fr/en*, which provides an IC calculator. Applying this tool on the postcard message . . .

Cryptanalysis using Index of Coincidence

✳ MESSAGE TO ANALYSE

```
ABC DCEFG
FHI JBK LHM KGKN
OMPPHOK LHM JBK
OGQLCDEG HDCEFG
C FJRK SKKD GBLCDE
GH ANHMBCOF J
NCCCNK FJRK
```

CALCULATE IC

. . . and on the *Kryptos* text, we receive the following values:

Index of coincidence of the postcard message: 6.4%

Index of coincidence of the *Kryptos* text: 4.5%

The IC of the postcard text (6.4%) is pretty close to what we would expect for English text encrypted with a simple substitution cipher (6.7%), while the IC of the *Kryptos* text (4.5%) is further from it. This confirms the (correct) conjecture that the postcard is encrypted with a simple substitution cipher, while the *Kryptos* encryption is not.

How to break a simple substitution cipher

There are two basic tools for deciphering a simple substitution cipher: guessing words and frequency analysis.[10] Usually, combining these two approaches works best, so we'll do this in the following example. You can usually guess both frequent words and words with unusual letter patterns. We demonstrate these techniques with the ciphertext in Figure 3-5 (taken from the 2015 computer game *Call of Duty: Black Ops III*), which is written in a pigpen variant.

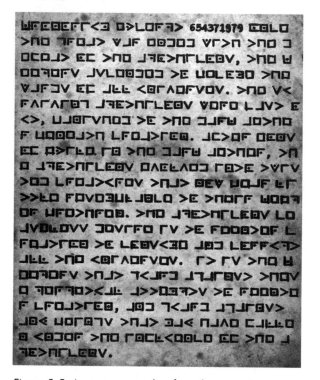

Figure 3-5: A cryptogram taken from the computer game Call of Duty: Black Ops III (2015)

To transcribe this message, let's use the pigpen variant shown in the following diagram:

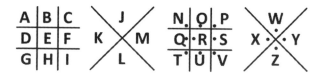

This gives us the following transcript. Now that we've converted the symbols into letters, we can more easily review the text:

```
OVSRSVIMQ EXCEVTK 654371979 SRCE KHE GVEAK WAV ERDED WIKH KHE
DEFEAK SF KHE ATSKHICSRJ, KHE OEETEVJ AJCERDED KS BECSQE KHE WAVDJ
SF APP MRI LEVJEJ. KHE JMVLILIRG ATSKHICSRJ WEVE CAJK SMK, BARIJHED
KS KHE DAVO AEKHEV BEREAKH CVEAKISR. AFKEV ESRJ SF EXIPE IR KHE
DAVO AEKHEV, KHE ATSKHICSRJ ELSPLED IRKS KWIJKED CVEAKMVEJ KHAK RSW
BEAV PIKKPE VEJEQBPARCE KS KHEIV OEETEV BVEKHVER. KHE ATSKHICSRJ
CEAJEPEJJ DEJIVE IJ KS VEERKEV CVEAKISR KS CSRJMQE ARD CSVVMTK APP
KHE MRILEVJEJ. IK IJ KHE OEETEVJ KHAK GMAVD AGAIRJK KHEJE TEVTEKMAP
AKKEQTKJ KS VEERKEV CVEAKISR, ARD GMAVD AGAIRJK ARY BEIRGJ KHAK QAY
HALE FAPPER MRDEV KHE IRFPMERCE SF KHE ATSKHICSRJ.
```

Performing a frequency analysis

We start our analysis by counting the letters (either by hand or with software such as CrypTool 2):

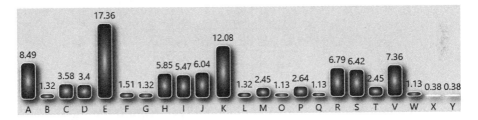

Apparently, E is the ciphertext's most frequent letter. Assuming that the plaintext is in English, E might stand for **E**. Sometimes, things are that simple.

Guessing frequent words

Now, let's try to guess a few words:

- The word KHE (which we can also write as KH**E**, as we already know that E probably stands for **E**) appears fourteen times in the cryptogram. It can only stand for **THE**. This means that we have identified the letters **E**, **H**, and **T**.

- The word KHAK (**THAT**) must stand for **THAT**, as **THET**, **THIT**, **THOT**, **THUT**, and **THYT** don't make sense.

- The word KS (**T**S) appears five times in the text. Provided that there is no word in the English language that consists of only two consonants (*Scrabble* experts may quibble about this for certain archaic forms), this word must be **TA**, **TE**, **TI**, **TO**, **TU**, or **TY**. Only **TO** makes sense. So, we have now identified **A**, **E**, **H**, **O**, and **T**.

- SMK (**O**T) likely stands for **OUT**.

- AEKHEV (**AETHE**V) apparently stands for **AETHER**.

- APP (**A**PP) stands for **ALL**.

The remaining letters are easily found in a similar way. We get the following plaintext:

```
KRONORIUM EXCERPT 654371979 ONCE THE GREAT WAR ENDED WITH THE
DEFEAT OF THE APOTHICONS THE KEEPERS ASCENDED TO BECOME THE WARDS
OF ALL UNIVERSES THE SURVIVING APOTHICONS WERE CAST OUT BANISHED
TO THE DARK AETHER BENEATH CREATION AFTER EONS OF EXILE IN THE
DARK AETHER THE APOTHICONS EVOLVED INTO TWISTED CREATURES THAT NOW
BEAR LITTLE RESEMBLANCE TO THEIR KEEPER BRETHREN THE APOTHICONS
CEASELESS DESIRE IS TO REENTER CREATION TO CONSUME AND CORRUPT ALL
THE UNIVERSES IT IS THE KEEPERS THAT GUARD AGAINST THESE PERPETUAL
ATTEMPTS TO REENTER CREATION AND GUARD AGAINST ANY BEINGS THAT MAY
HAVE FALLEN UNDER THE INFLUENCE OF THE APOTHICONS.
```

Using our results, we can reconstruct the pigpen diagram in use. It is slightly different from the one applied on the NSA mug:

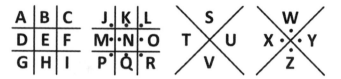

Guessing words with unusual letter patterns

For a second approach to deciphering a simple substitution cipher, we can try to guess words by their letter patterns. Until a few decades ago, code-breakers had to employ word pattern lists for this task, which was quite laborious,[11] but today, we can use computer programs to perform fast searches.

First, we need to check the ciphertext for words with rare letter patterns. Our ciphertext includes the word VEERKEV, which is a good candidate. The first and last letter are the same; in addition, this word has a pattern of three identical letters. When we enter this word in CrypTool 2's word pattern analyzer, we get the following results, showing which common words have letters with that same pattern:

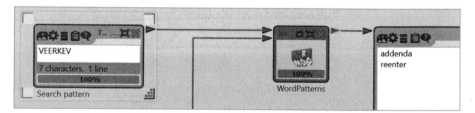

As you can see, among all the words contained in an English dictionary, only **ADDENDA** and **REENTER** fit this pattern. Which one might be correct? We can answer this question by looking at the frequency analysis calculated above. If **ADDENDA** were correct, **D** would be the most frequent letter in our text. In the case of **REENTER**, it would be **E**. The latter is by far the more likely case.

Knowing that VEERKEV stands for **REENTER** thus gives us the potential plaintext equivalents of four letters. We could then substitute those potential plaintext equivalents throughout the ciphertext, then proceed to guess short words such as **THE**, **TO**, and **OUT** or look for more words with rare letter patterns.

Success stories

How Gary Klivans broke a prison inmate's code

Gary Klivans, our colleague and an expert on encryption methods used by gangs and prison inmates (see Chapter 2), is the author of the fascinating 2016 book *Gang Secret Codes: Deciphered*.[12] Gary provided us with an interesting encrypted note—a letter written by a New Jersey prison inmate to his girlfriend (see Figure 3-6).[13] We have no further information about the background of this message.

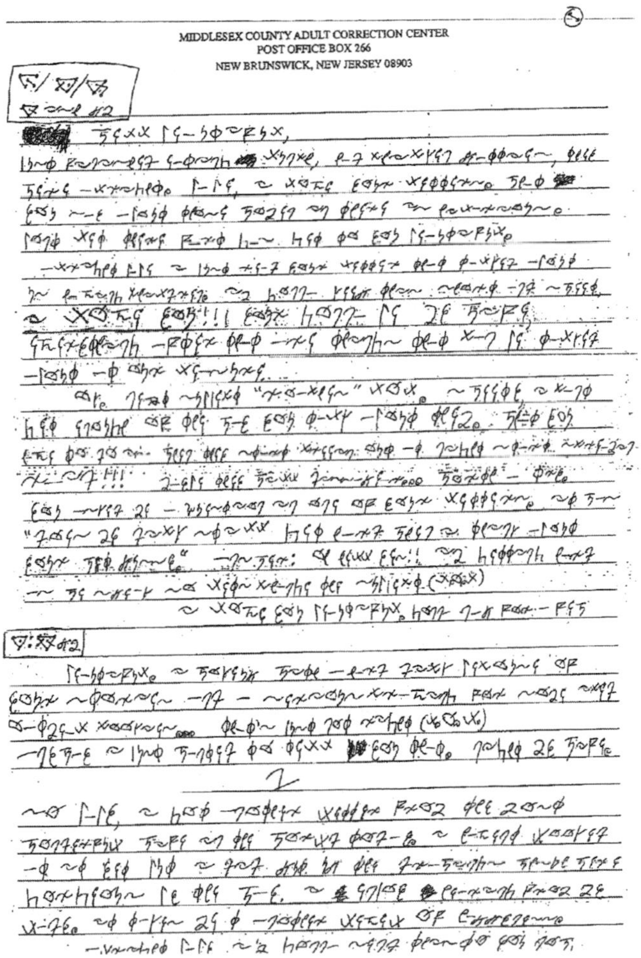

Figure 3-6: This encrypted letter, written by a New Jersey prison inmate to his girlfriend, was broken by cipher expert Gary Klivans.

As can be seen, the sender of this note used a nonstandard alphabet (probably of his own invention). Provided that this letter is likely encrypted using a simple substitution cipher, transcribing the text and performing a frequency analysis might be a good start to breaking it. However, Gary usually avoids the tedious process of transcribing and prefers guessing words based on letter patterns. When he combed through the ciphertext, he found the following word, which appears twice and seemed like a good candidate:

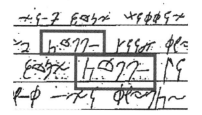

Gary's guess was that it stood for **HOLLA** (a slang word with a similar meaning to "hello"). We will see that his suspicion was not entirely correct, but it proved helpful anyway. Based on his assumption, Gary could immediately identify the indefinite article **A**, which appears a few times in the text. As there is only one other common English word consisting of one letter, the pronoun **I**, the symbol representing it was easy to find, too (see the framed symbols in lines 1, 6, and 9):

Gary then tried to guess the following pair of words:

Transcribed, the symbols are **OA***A* *OO****, a unique pattern. Gary's guess was that these were the words **OATMEAL COOKIES**, which proved correct. At this point he knew enough letters to easily decipher the whole text (which was when he realized that the word he had first tried to decipher was not **HOLLA**, but **GONNA**). Gary finally came up with the following substitution table:

A B C D E F G H I J K L M N O P Q R S T U V W X Y 1 2

This leads to the following plaintext (note the two appearances of GONNA in the seventh and eighth lines):

```
WELL BEAUTIFUL,

JUST FINISHED EATING LUNCH, HAD CHICKEN PATTIES, THEY
WERE ALRIGHT. BABE, I LOVE YOUR LETTERS. WHAT
YOU SAY ABOUT THESE WOMEN IN HERE IS HILARIOUS.
BONT LET THEIR FART GAS GET TO YOU BEAUTIFUL.

ALRIGHT, BABE, I JUST READ YOUR LETTER THAT TALKED ABOUT
US HAVING CHILDREN. IM GONNA KEEP THIS SHORT AND SWEET
I LOVE YOU!!! YOUR GONNA BE MY WIFE,

. . .
```

As far as we can tell, this is an ordinary love letter without any criminal content. The sender probably encrypted it because it contains intimate information—not because he wanted to hide something illegal.

How Kent Boklan broke encrypted diary entries from the Civil War

Our colleague Kent D. Boklan is a New York–based professor of computer science and a successful codebreaker focusing on US encryptions from the nineteenth century. In addition to several Civil War ciphertexts from the 1860s, he has deciphered encrypted passages from a diary written by a doctor during the War of 1812.[14] These successes are all described in articles Kent published in the scientific journal *Cryptologia*. Another broken cipher he reported in 2014 came once again from a diary.[15] This diary was written by a Confederate soldier named James Malbone during the US Civil War. While most of Malbone's diary is in cleartext, a few passages are encrypted. Here is one of the encrypted parts:

Between the cleartext expressions **Three** and **March 11th 1863**, Malbone wrote a few lines of ciphertext in a nonstandard (probably self-invented) alphabet. Kent supposed that Malbone had used a simple substitution cipher. The first ciphertext word consists of three letters: *.£. On a different page, Kent found a similar word at the end of a paragraph: ?*.£. (In the picture below, the cleartext in the two lines above this expression is **May the Lord bless + be with you in my prayer.**)

If we transcribe these two words (ignoring the rest of the ciphertext), we get BCD and ABCD. Kent realized that **AMEN** might be a good candidate for the last word of a paragraph that talks about a prayer. If this assumption were correct, the first plaintext word in the cryptogram would be **MEN** and the text would start with **Three MEN**. This made sense.

Knowing the letters **A**, **M**, **E**, and **N**, Kent could easily decipher the rest of the encrypted passages. The two ciphertexts shown above decrypted to the following plaintexts:

```
Three MEN WERE PUPLICLY WHIPT @ WHIPPING
POST BEFOR THE WHOLE BRIGADE March 11th, 1863
```

```
May the Lord bless + be with
you in my prayer. FOR
CHRIST SAKE AMEN
```

Beatrix Potter's diary

Beatrix Potter (1866–1943) was an English writer and illustrator best known for her classic 1902 children's book *The Tale of Peter Rabbit*. Around the age of fourteen, she began to keep an encrypted diary, using a monoalphabetic cipher of her own devising. She wrote in this diary for fifteen years.

In 1952, nine years after Potter's death, a relative of hers found the encrypted diary.[16] As she couldn't make sense of it, she consulted Beatrix Potter enthusiast Leslie Linder, who immediately became interested and started to work on deciphering the diary. Though Potter's encryption method was a pure monoalphabetic cipher, the codebreaking work proved difficult. Potter's writing was small, sometimes tiny, with thousands of words squeezed onto some of the pages (see Figure 3-7).

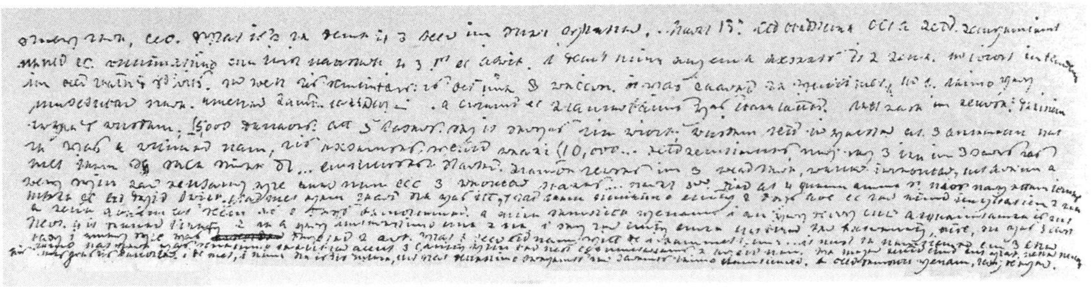

Figure 3-7: Beatrix Potter, author of the famous 1902 children's book The Tale of Peter Rabbit, kept an encrypted diary.

On one page, Linder found two cleartext (unencrypted) expressions that proved very helpful: the Roman numeral **XVI** and the year **1793**. In a history book, he read that the French king Louis XVI was guillotined in 1793. This enabled him to decrypt a word he found nearby as **execution**. Linder then knew the symbols for eight letters of the alphabet, including four vowels. By the end of the same day, he had solved practically the whole of Potter's cipher alphabet. The real labor, however, had just begun. It took Linder thirteen years to decode all the diaries.

Linder was painstaking in his work, careful to decipher everything correctly. If Potter wrote of a plant, Linder checked with a botanist. When she described a work of art, he verified her thoughts by consulting art books and exhibition catalogs. In addition, he would trace Potter's journeys on a map or even travel to the particular places himself. In 1966, Linder's results were published in a book titled *The Journal of Beatrix Potter: 1881–1897*.[17] Here's the substitution table he derived:

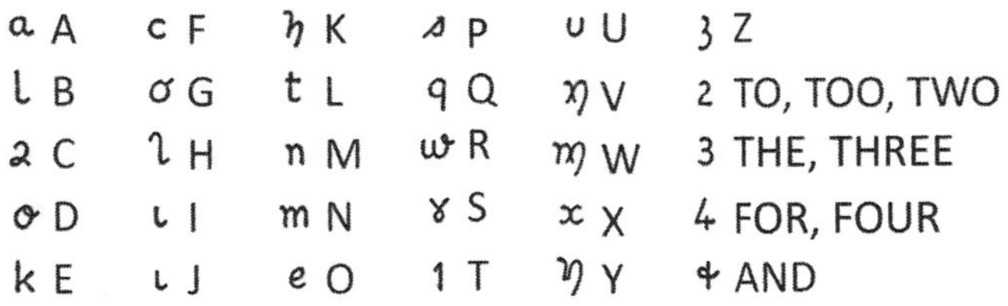

a A	c F	ꜧ K	ꝑ P	ʋ U	ꝫ Z
↳ B	ơ G	t L	q Q	ŋ V	2 TO, TOO, TWO
ꝛ C	↰ H	n M	ꙍ R	ꙡ W	3 THE, THREE
ơ D	↳ I	m N	ꝕ S	x X	4 FOR, FOUR
k E	↳ J	e O	1 T	ꝺ Y	ꝗ AND

In his book, Linder writes that the excerpt shown in Figure 3-7, from April 9, 1886, decrypts as follows:

Snow here. fog. What is to be done for the poor in such weather? Sunday March 13th.-Old Gladstone got a cold. Convenient method of ruminating on Irish measure for the 1st. of April. I don't think any one expects it to come. Mr. Bright in London, in good health and spirits. Mr. Roth his son-in-law got into the Reform, it was feared he would not, Mr. Bright being very unpopular there.

Potter was far from the only person to keep an encrypted diary.[18] One thing of note for those who may wish to crack a diary belonging to their own ancestors is that it is very difficult to write large amounts of text with a complicated cipher. It therefore comes as no surprise that nearly all of the encrypted diaries we know of used simple substitution ciphers, though perhaps with some additional expressions here and there to make writing easier. In Potter's case, she used 2 for the words **to** and **too**, as well as 3 for **the**. As a rule of thumb, the more handwritten encrypted text you see, the easier it will be to solve.

Challenges

A prison code

The fragment of a message depicted in Figure 3-8 was sent by an unknown person to a prison inmate in Montgomery, Pennsylvania, in December 2013.[19] The prison staff did not deliver this message to the intended recipient. Instead, they forwarded it to Gary Klivans, the forensic codebreaker mentioned earlier, who deciphered it using techniques described in this chapter, especially word guessing. Later, it became clear to him that the text was written in a well-known *Star Wars* writing system named Aurebesh. With knowledge of this symbol set, the deciphering is quite straightforward.

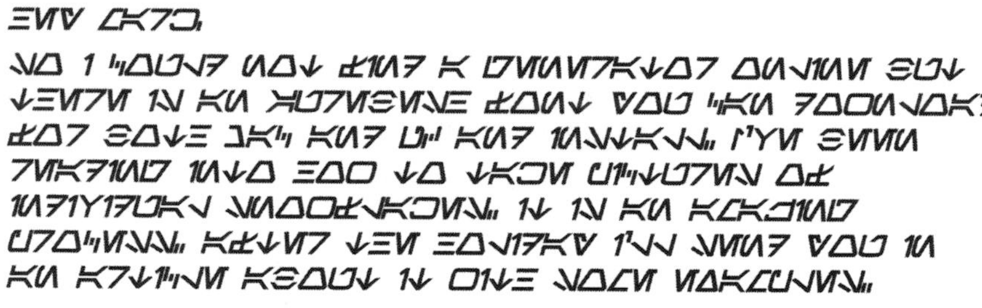

Figure 3-8: This message sent to a prison inmate in 2013 turned out to be written in a Star Wars font.

Can you break it, like Gary Klivans, with frequency analysis and word guessing only?

A postcard

Solve the postcard from 1909 shown earlier in this chapter, in Figure 3-3. You can use the transcript and the frequency analysis we provided.

Another postcard

Can you decipher the postcard in Figure 3-9 (provided to us by Raymond Borges), which is encrypted in a pigpen variant?[20]

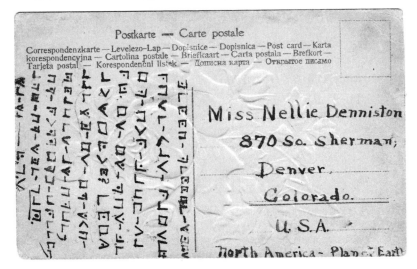

Figure 3-9: Another postcard encrypted using a pigpen variant

The Friedmans' wedding centennial nickel

Copies of the "wooden nickel" shown in Figure 3-10 were given out by Bill Briere and Jew-Lee Lann-Briere at the 2017 Symposium on Cryptologic History in Fort Meade, Maryland, to honor the centennial of the wedding of Elizebeth and William Friedman, the legendary couple who created the field of American cryptology. The nickel's inscription is encrypted using a simple substitution cipher.

Figure 3-10: An encrypted message on a wooden nickel

Here's a transcript. On the reverse side of the nickel are a pair of wedding bells.

```
UWCKWCCBSD EX KZW OWVVBCY
EX WDBRWTWKZ SCV OBDDBSJ
1917 * XHBWVJSC * 2017
```

Can you break it?

An Aristocrat from the ACA

The following Aristocrat was published in a 2018 issue of *The Cryptogram*, the newsletter of the American Cryptogram Association:[21]

```
WNO ZA JYV YVA YNKHV RAU WNO XKRGUZAX JYV YVA YNKHV RGV JYV HRIV.
JYKH, YV MYN NMAH JYV YVA YNKHV IKHJ SV UVRW, SBZAU, NG SNJY.
```

Unsolved cryptograms

Numerous unsolved cryptograms appear to have been created with simple substitution ciphers (although, of course, these are only guesses, as the solutions are not known). Here are a few of the most interesting ones.

An encrypted newspaper ad from 1888

The encrypted newspaper advertisement depicted in Figure 3-11 was published in the London *Daily Chronicle* on February 13, 1888.[22, 23]

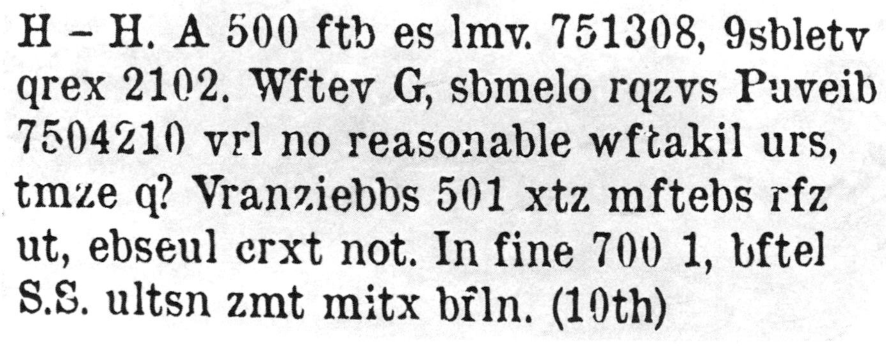

H – H. A 500 ftb es lmv. 751308, 9sbletv qrex 2102. Wftev G, sbmelo rqzvs Puveib 7504210 vrl no reasonable wftakil urs, tmze q? Vranziebbs 501 xtz mftebs rfz ut, ebseul crxt not. In fine 700 1, bftel S.S. ultsn zmt mitx bfln. (10th)

Figure 3-11: This is a reproduction of an encrypted newspaper ad that was published in 1888. The plaintext is unknown.

Here's a transcript:

```
H–H. A 500 ftb es lmv. 751308, 9sbletv qrex 2102. Wftev G, sbmelo
rqzvs Puveib 7504210 vrl no reasonable wftakil urs, tmze q?
Vranziebbs 501 xtz mftebs rfz ut, ebseul crxt not. In fine 700 1,
bftel S.S. ultsn zmt mitx bfln. (10th)
```

To our knowledge, this cryptogram has never been deciphered. Can you solve it?

The Zodiac Celebrity Cypher

On September 25, 1990, an unknown person sent the postcard depicted in Figure 3-12 to the *Vallejo Times-Herald*, a newspaper in the San Francisco area. The message on the postcard imitates the style of the Zodiac Killer, a serial murderer who sent encrypted letters to regional newspapers in the late 1960s.[24] (The Zodiac murder case and the cryptograms connected to it are explained in Chapter 6.) The identity of the postcard's author is not known, but it is not likely the Zodiac Killer himself.[25] This means that we are dealing with a Zodiac copycat cryptogram (of which you will see more over the course of this book).

Figure 3-12: This postcard was written by a Zodiac Killer copycat.

The three lines of cleartext on the card contain the name and the location of the newspaper, as well as the expression **CELEBRITY CYPHER**. A *celebrity cypher* (today usually spelled *celebrity cipher*) is a crypto puzzle (typically an Aristocrat) that, once deciphered, turns out to be a quote by a famous person. Celebrity ciphers are quite popular among the members of the American Cryptogram Association and other puzzle enthusiasts. There are entire books and web pages dedicated to celebrity ciphers. Elonka's book *The Mammoth Book of Secret Codes and Cryptograms* contains scores of them.[26]

The copycat postcard message (referred to as the Zodiac Celebrity Cypher) has never been solved. It is, of course, possible that it encrypts a quote by a famous person, but we don't know this for sure.

It goes without saying that codebreakers have checked whether the creator of the Zodiac Celebrity Cypher message might have used the encryption systems found in the first two Zodiac cryptograms (which are solved), to no avail. There are several web pages providing information about the Zodiac Celebrity Cypher, some of which even suggest alleged solutions. However, from what we have seen so far, none of these makes sense.

The Furlong postcard

The postcard depicted in Figure 3-13 was written by soccer official George Furlong (1843-1911) from Luton, United Kingdom, to his sister Lizzie in 1873.[27] Unlike most of the encrypted postcards of the time that we know about, this one hasn't been solved.

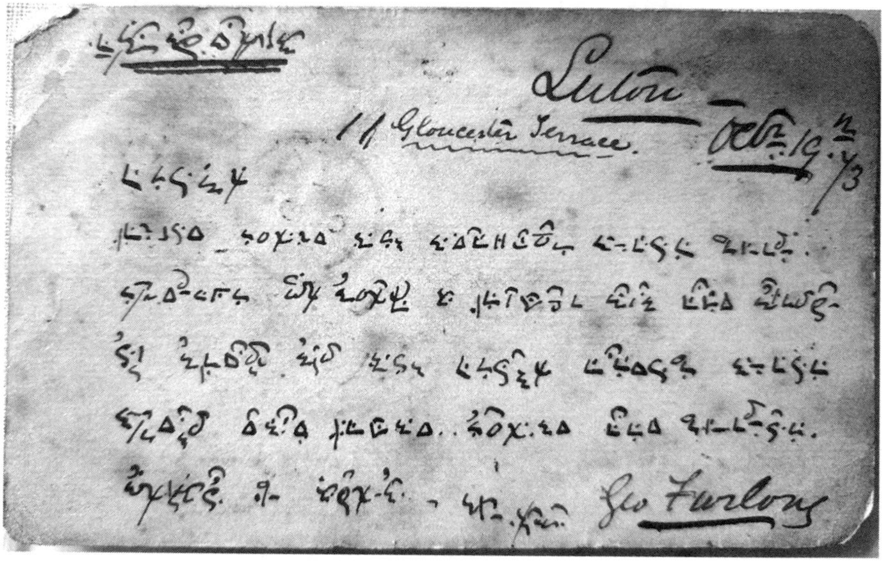

Figure 3-13: This British postcard from 1873 has never been deciphered.

The script in which this postcard is written is a mystery of its own. It could be an ordinary, yet rarely used, writing system or an invented, secret script. It could also be a kind of shorthand, except that some of the letters (e.g., the triangle-shaped symbol) are not well suited for speedy writing. At least we can tell that the author wrote fluently and was practiced in using these glyphs. Transcribing this cryptogram is difficult, as some letters are written on top of each other. Numerous skilled codebreakers, including fans of Klaus's blog, tried their luck on this message without success. Perhaps a reader can shed light on this unusual secret?

4

SIMPLE SUBSTITUTION CIPHERS WITHOUT SPACES BETWEEN WORDS: PATRISTOCRATS

The message shown in Figure 4-1 was sent to the *New York Post* by a copycat of the infamous Zodiac Killer (see Chapter 6) in 1994—about twenty-five years after the killer's last original message had appeared.[1] It is encrypted with the substitution table provided in the same figure and decrypts to the following plaintext (which includes a few spelling mistakes): `THIS IS THE ZODIAC SPEUKING. I AM IN CONTROL. THO' MASTERY, BE READY FOR MORE. YOURS TRLIY.`

How a Patristocrat, a simple substitution cipher without spaces, works

As you will certainly have noticed, this Zodiac copycat cryptogram was encrypted with a monoalphabetic substitution cipher of the different-alphabet type. However, unlike the ciphertexts we saw in Chapter 3, this one doesn't contain spaces between the words. Crypto puzzle fans and members of the American Cryptogram Association typically use the term *Patristocrat* to refer to monoalphabetic substitution ciphers without spaces, especially ones that use Latin letters.

Figure 4-1: This message by an alleged murderer is encrypted in a monoalphabetic substitution cipher. It doesn't contain spaces.

It should be clear that the absence of spaces makes a Patristocrat more difficult to break than an Aristocrat cipher. However, Patristocrats are more difficult for the legitimate recipient to handle, too, because it is sometimes hard to correctly determine the word boundaries when decrypting the message. Ambiguities may appear. For instance, `YOUDONTGETMEAPARTOFTHEUNION` may mean "You don't get me, a part of the union," or "You don't get me apart of the union."

For this reason, we encounter Patristocrat ciphers a lot less in practice than ordinary simple substitution ciphers. Still, this kind of encryption is far from infrequent and therefore should be studied by everybody interested in codebreaking.

How to detect a Patristocrat

If the text you are looking at has no pattern of word breaks, or if this pattern is too regular (consisting, for instance, of groups of five characters), you may be dealing with a Patristocrat. A Patristocrat will generally have the same letter variety as other simple substitution cryptograms, which means that frequency analysis and the index of coincidence are helpful tools to detect it.

As an example, let's look at a cryptogram published by the NSA. As many readers might know, the NSA is quite active on social media, publishing crypto puzzles on Facebook (NSAUSGov) and Twitter (@NSAUSGov). If you're interested in a career at this agency, solving these challenges might be a good way to get their attention. The ciphertext in Figure 4-2 is the first of four challenge ciphers that the NSA announced via Twitter in May 2014. Because each cipher was tweeted on a Monday, they are referred to as the "NSA Monday Challenges."[2]

NSA Careers
@NSACareers

tpfccdlfdtte pcaccplircdt dklpcfrp?qeiq
lhpqlipqeodf gpwafopwprti izxndkiqpkii
krirrifcapnc dxkdciqcafmd vkfpcadf.
#MissionMonday #NSA #news

Figure 4-2: First of the four NSA Monday
Challenges in 2014

Here's a transcript of the first NSA Monday Challenge:

```
tpfccdlfdtte pcaccplircdt dklpcfrp?qeiq
lhpqlipqeodf gpwafopwprti izxndkiqpkii
krirrifcapnc dxkdciqcafmd vkfpcadf.
```

Don't let the spaces confuse you. They separate blocks of twelve letters and do not correspond to the word separations in the plaintext. Here's a frequency analysis:

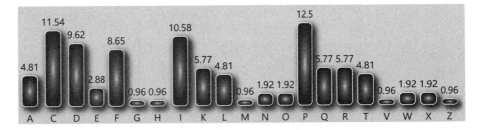

The frequencies are consistent with a simple substitution cipher. The index of coincidence of the ciphertext is 6.7%, which is exactly the expected value of an English text. So, it makes sense to assume that this first NSA Monday Challenge is a Patristocrat.

How to break a Patristocrat

The first NSA Monday Challenge can be solved within seconds by a computer, using techniques such as hill climbing (see Chapter 16). To do so, you could use the cryptogram solver available as a part of Tyler Akins' Cipher Tools at *https://rumkin.com/tools/cipher/* or CrypTool 2. For those who prefer to solve cryptograms by hand, read on.

Frequency analysis using digraphs

Clearly, frequency analysis can be very helpful for breaking a Patristocrat, but we can use a few additional statistics in our analyses. The first involves *digraphs*, or consecutive letter pairs, that appear in the text. Here is a frequency analysis of digraphs in the first NSA Monday Challenge:

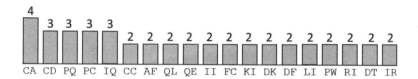

To make use of these statistics, we need a few further facts about the English language:

- The most frequent digraph in the English language is *EN*.

- The digraph *ER* is frequent in both directions: *ER/RE*.

- The most frequent digraph consisting of doubled letters is *LL*, followed by *TT* and *SS*.

- The digraphs *AA* and *II* are very rare in English, although *A* and *I* are frequent standalone letters.

You can find more information about English digraphs in Appendix B.

You might initially assume that the most frequent digraph in the ciphertext corresponds to the most frequent one in the English language. However, this assumption doesn't work very well for a ciphertext of only about a hundred letters. Nevertheless, knowledge of digraph frequencies can be helpful, as will become clear.

Before we move on, let's also perform a triple-letter (trigraph) analysis of the ciphertext. This analysis reveals that the trigraphs PQE and PCA appear twice, while all other groupings of three letters have a frequency of one. The most frequent trigraph in the English language is *THE*, followed by *AND*, *ING*, *ENT*, *ION*, *HER*, *FOR*, and *THA* (see Appendix B for additional trigraph statistics).

Trigraph frequencies may be quite helpful for breaking longer ciphertexts, but they are not relevant here because only two trigraphs appear more than once in the challenge. For similar reasons, tetragraph (four-letter), pentagraph (five-letter), and hexagraph (six-letter) frequencies are of no use in this context, though, believe it or not, they all have been used by codebreakers. In general, a group of *n* letters is referred to as an *n-graph*.

Let's now try to apply the statistics we have computed. As shown in our initial frequency analysis, the most frequent letter in the first NSA Monday Challenge ciphertext is P (12.5%), followed by C (11.54%) and I (10.58%). So, let's assume that these letters stand for **E**, **T**, and **A**, the most frequent letters in the English language. There are several possibilities for how to map P, C, and I onto **E**, **T**, and **A**, starting with the following option:

```
A B C D E F G H I J K L M N O P Q R S T U V W X Y Z
* * T * * * * * A * * * * * * E * * * * * * * * * *
```

We could check the plausibility of this assumption by taking a look at the resulting digraphs, either by hand or by using modern tools such as Cipher Tools or CrypTool 2, which produces the following:

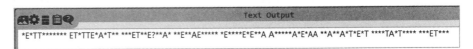

It is immediately clear that a few things don't look plausible. For example, the digraph **AA** (which appears twice) and the digraph **AE** are not very common in English. We're probably on the wrong track.

We therefore try another assumption:

```
A B C D E F G H I J K L M N O P Q R S T U V W X Y Z
* * A * * * * * T * * * * * * E * * * * * * * * * *
```

This renders the following plaintext candidate:

*E*AA*******EA*AAE*T*A*****EA**E?**T***E**TE******E****E*E**TT****
*T*E*TT**T**T*A*E*A****AT*A*******EA***

Again, we have two **AA**s, which is not very likely. Moreover, the trigraph **AAE** appears in the plaintext but is very rare in the English language. Our guess was apparently wrong again.

Now, let's try a third assumption:

```
A B C D E F G H I J K L M N O P Q R S T U V W X Y Z
* * T * * * * * E * * * * * * A * * * * * * * * * *
```

This renders as follows:

*A*TT*******AT*TTA*E*T*****AT**A?**E***A**EA*******A****A*A**EE****
*E*A*EE**E**E*T*A*T****TE*T*******AT***

This is the best result so far, so let's stick with it.

Examining the results further, it becomes apparent that the missing letter (a ciphertext A) in **AT*TTA** is probably a vowel. As **A** and **E** are already in use, this letter can only be **I**, **O**, **U**, or **Y**. If **I** is correct, we get the digraph **IT**, which is a frequent English word. Let's try this:

```
A B C D E F G H I J K L M N O P Q R S T U V W X Y Z
I * T * * * * * E * * * * * * A * * * * * * * * * *
```

This renders as the following:

```
*A*TT********ATITTA*E*T*****AT**A?**E***A**EA******A*I**A*A**EE****
*E*A*EE**E**E*TIA*T****TE*TI******ATI**
```

This looks good; it could be English, and there is nothing that shows up as a red flag. What can we try next? The string **ATI**** at the end might stand for **ATING**, as in **RATING** or **SKATING**. Let's add **N** and **G** to our table:

```
A B C D E F G H I J K L M N O P Q R S T U V W X Y Z
I * T N * G * * E * * * * * * A * * * * * * * * * *
```

We now get this:

```
*AGTTN*GN***ATITTA*E*TN*N**ATG*A?**E***A**EA***NG*A*IG*A*A**EE***N
*E*A*EE**E**EGTIA*TN**NTE*TIG*N**GATING
```

AGTTN and **GTIA** are not very likely in an English text. Moreover, the word **GATING** at the end doesn't make much sense. *EN*, the most frequent English digraph, doesn't appear at all in this plaintext candidate. Altogether, this means that our assumption concerning **N** and **G** is probably wrong.

Perhaps the last five letters are not **ATING**, but **ATION**. There are many words with this ending, for instance, **STATION**, **RELATION**, and **FRUSTRATION**. Let's check this guess:

```
A B C D E F G H I J K L M N O P Q R S T U V W X Y Z
I * T O * N * * E * * * * * * A * * * * * * * * * *
```

Here is our plaintext candidate:

```
*ANTTO*NO***ATITTA*E*TO*O**ATN*A?**E***A**EA***ON*A*IN*A*A**EE***O
*E*A*EE**E**ENTIA*TO**OTE*TIN*O**NATION
```

This looks pretty good. **NATION** as the last word in an NSA cryptogram is quite plausible. The digraph **EN**, which we expect to be frequent, shows up once. Also, we can now guess several additional words: **O**NATION** probably means **OUR NATION**; **E**ENTIA*** could stand for **ESSENTIAL**; and ***ANTTO** most likely represents **WANT TO**. This gives us several more letters:

```
A B C D E F G H I J K L M N O P Q R S T U V W X Y Z
I * T O * N * * E * R * * L * A * S * W * U * * * *
```

Here is our next plaintext candidate:

```
WANTTO*NOWW*ATITTA*ESTOWOR*ATNSA?**E***A**EA***ON*A*IN*A*ASWEE**LO
RE*AREERSESSENTIALTO*ROTE*TIN*OURNATION
```

Guessing the remaining letters is straightforward. Here's the plaintext of the first NSA Monday Challenge:

WANT TO KNOW WHAT IT TAKES TO WORK AT NSA? CHECK BACK EACH MONDAY IN MAY AS WE EXPLORE CAREERS ESSENTIAL TO PROTECTING OUR NATION.

Here's the substitution table (ciphertext letters marked with ? are those for which the corresponding plaintext letter does not exist):

```
Plaintext:   A B C D E F G H I J K L M N O P Q R S T U V W X Y Z
Ciphertext:  P H Q G I ? M E A ? L N O F D X ? K S C V ? T Z W ?
```

Word guessing

Other techniques can help us decipher Patristocrats. Let's look at the first NSA Monday Challenge (including the frequency chart) again:

```
tpfccdlfdtte pcaccplircdt dklpcfrp?qeiq lhpqlipqeodf gpwafopwprti
izxndkiqpkii krirrifcapnc dxkdciqcafmd vkfpcadf.
```

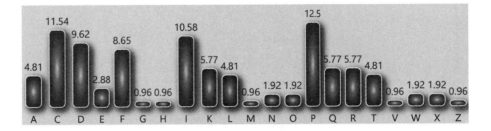

One possibility is to start by guessing a word. This would be a lot easier if we knew the positions of the spaces, but this is not the case here. Still, word guessing may work. We know that the NSA is the sender of the message, so searching for the trigraph **NSA** seems like a good idea. This search won't work, however, as this set of letters is hard to spot in the more than one hundred trigraphs we would have to check.

Let's assume that we know from some source that the word **CAREER** appears in the plaintext (after all, **CAREER** is a likely word in an NSA challenge cryptogram made to attract talented codebreakers). Now we can use it as a crib. The word **CAREER** contains the string **REER**, which has a letter pattern of type 1221. If we search for this pattern in the ciphertext, we find two strings of this kind:

- KIIK: This looks like a good candidate.
- IRRI: There's an R left of the first I, so the letter pattern is actually 21221. This doesn't fit with **CAREER**.

This means that KIIK is the only string that fits. If our guess is correct, QPKIIK stands for **CAREER**. The identified letters **A**, **C**, **E**, and **R** should be enough to determine the remaining letters. We leave the rest of the deciphering process to the reader.

Success stories

A prison message

The note depicted in Figure 4-3 was sent in 2012 by an inmate of a prison in Manchester, UK, to his sister.[3] According to the sender of the message, the numbers represented a puzzle for his sister to solve. Police of course immediately suspected an encrypted message, so they asked British forensic linguist John Olsson to take a look at the note.

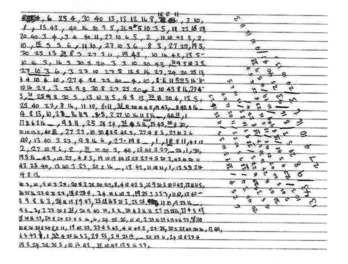

Figure 4-3: This encrypted message sent in 2012 by a British prison inmate doesn't contain spaces.

Olsson saw that the cryptogram contained twenty-three distinct numbers. A frequency analysis revealed that it was consistent with a simple substitution ciphertext. To break the cipher, Olsson first tried to guess words—a difficult task, as the message didn't contain spaces. Following a systematic approach, Olsson analyzed 840 letter combinations of various lengths in the ciphertext and checked each one to see if it could represent a certain word. The breakthrough came when he assumed that the sequence 38, 9, 5, 10, 3, 5 stood for **PLEASE**—a guess that proved correct. Knowing five letters, Olsson could then identify all the others. Here are the first eight lines of the plaintext. (It contains many mistakes and unusual spellings.)

```
KOH C U M M A x I WID SA
xY UNCLE PLEASE I
RUSH SHUD TAKE 2 DAYS 2
A WEK DA TASK IS TO BE
COMPLETED BY ANY ME-
ANS NECERSSARY PLEASE
TASK STATEMENT FROM
SHAKA THROUGH INDECEND-
```

One potential way to interpret this plaintext is this:

Kohcumma and I would say, "Uncle, please don't rush. Should take two days to a week." The task is to be completed by any means necessary. Please task statement from Shaka through indecent . . .

The rest of the message is available online at Klaus's blog.[4]

The Cheltenham Number Stone

The British Government Communications Headquarters (GCHQ) is one of the most powerful surveillance organizations in the world, comparable to the American NSA. It is located in a large, round building ("The Doughnut") on the outskirts of Cheltenham, UK. A side exit of this building leads to Hester's Way Park, where a set of nine stone sculptures, the *Listening Stones*, created in 2004 by artist Gordon Young, are exhibited.[5]

Each of the *Listening Stones* has a set of carvings consisting of letters, numbers, or symbols. Two of these inscriptions are encrypted messages. Because one of these ciphertexts consists of numbers while the other is composed of letters, we refer to them as the "Number Stone" and the "Letter Stone," respectively (though these are not their official names). The Letter Stone will be covered in Chapter 16.

Figure 4-4 shows the Number Stone, which bears a cryptogram consisting of about 1,300 two-digit numbers, all between 01 and 66.

Figure 4-4: The Number Stone is one of the Listening Stones created in 2004 by British artist Gordon Young. The inscribed numbers represent an encrypted message.

Here are the first hundred numbers of the message:

```
23 02 13 22 25 33 02 14 33 25 02 21 16 26 10 03 06 33 04 13 21 16
01 15 26 25 33 47 44 33 26 10 12 15 16 11 10 05 10 33 10 20 13 22
```

```
16 33 30 53 46 64 33 46 33 42 51 57 54 37 53 64 33 54 64 33 54 63
33 30 53 51 43 33 40 43 33 64 53 51 33 47 46 60 47 40 40 33 60 46
64 64 54 43 37 33 16 43 33 60 44 33
```

In 2015, Klaus published an article about this cryptogram on his *Cipherbrain* blog.[6] After only a few hours, a blog reader named Robert posted a (correct) solution in the comments section. It turned out that the creator of the message had used a simple substitution cipher. We don't know exactly how Robert broke this ciphertext, but we assume that he used frequency analysis. Considering that the message is quite long, it was certainly possible to identify a few letters based solely on their frequency. In addition, the substitution table shows some regularities, as the letters of the alphabet are sorted using the artist's name, Gordon Young, as the keyword. Here's the table:

G	O	R	D	N	Y	U	A	B	C	E	F	H	I	J	K	L	M	P	Q	S	T	V	W	X	Z
01	02	03	04	05	06	07	10	11	12	13	14	15	16	17	20	21	22	23	24	25	26	27	30	31	32

_	.	,	'
33	34	35	36

g	o	r	d	n	y	u	a	b	c	e	f	h	I	j	k	l	m	p	q	s	t	v	w	x	z
37	40	41	42	43	44	45	46	47	50	51	52	53	54	55	56	57	60	61	62	63	64	65	66	67	70

Here are the first lines of the plaintext:

```
POEMS OF SOLITARY DELIGHTS by
TACHIBANA AKEMI What a delight it
is When on the bamboo matting
In my grassthatched hut,
All on my own, I make myself at
ease. What a delight it is
When, borrowing Rare writings
from a friend, I open out The
first sheet. What a delight
it is When, spreading paper,
I take my brush And find my
hand Better than I thought.
```

Challenges

Rudyard Kipling's encrypted message

Rudyard Kipling was the author of many famous tales, such as those found in *The Jungle Book* (1894). Within his considerable body of work are the *Just So Stories* (1902) for children, one of which is "How the First Letter Was Written." The story's original print included an illustration between two sequences of symbols (Figure 4-5). These symbols are a message encrypted in a Patristocrat style. Can you break it?

Figure 4-5: The symbols on the left and right of this illustration in a 1902 Rudyard Kipling story represent a message encrypted in a substitution cipher.

Hint: This is not as difficult as it appears! Look carefully, and you will see that the first word is **THIS**. For more hints, just as for everything in our Challenges sections, check out *https://codebreaking-guide.com/challenges/*.

NSA's second Monday Challenge

Earlier in this chapter, we introduced the first NSA Monday Challenge released in 2014. Here's the second one:

```
Rimfinnpeqcnvqauuagcrdokvdisndrdcrpigaisacpsdffaicvhakcfdqfpqdetrk
ilfa ecnpqacakqisacpfampoacfimannicfakdumfalddnraprf
```

This cryptogram needs to be read backward. Apart from this, it's an ordinary substitution cipher without spaces.

Unsolved cryptograms

Several unsolved cryptograms appear to be English texts encrypted with substitution ciphers without spaces. We'll introduce three of them.

The Dorabella cryptogram

The Dorabella cryptogram is extremely well known. It is covered in everything from David Kahn's 1967 classic *The Codebreakers* (including the 1996 edition),[7] to Elonka's "Famous Unsolved Codes and Ciphers" page,[8] to Klaus's "Top 50 Unsolved Cryptograms" list.[9]

British composer Edward Elgar (1857–1934) not only created famous music pieces, such as the early twentieth-century march "Pomp and Circumstance," but also was fond of cryptography. In 1897, when his wife Alice sent a thank-you letter to the Penny family, he included an encrypted note to his friend, the twenty-three-year-old Dora Penny (Figure 4-6).[10] This ciphertext is referred to as the Dorabella cryptogram, and despite analysis by many people (from amateurs to renowned codebreakers) for over a century, it has never been solved.

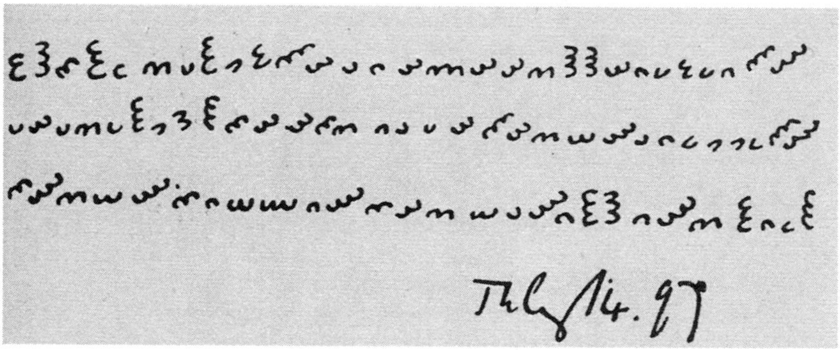

Figure 4-6: The Dorabella cryptogram is one of the most famous unsolved crypto mysteries.

The frequency distribution of the Dorabella cryptogram fits well with a monoalphabetic substitution cipher, but this has not led to the solution. There are many ways to explain this. Elgar might have deliberately avoided words containing Es. Others have suggested that the Dorabella cryptogram might encrypt a melody (i.e., musical notes), rather than a text. It is also possible that the plaintext is in a language other than English. Or, of course, the Dorabella cryptogram may not be a simple substitution cipher at all. If you want to dig deeper, check out Craig Bauer's 2017 book *Unsolved!*[11] It provides a comprehensive analysis of the Dorabella cryptogram.

The Chinese gold bars mystery

Another well-known unsolved cryptogram is inscribed on seven Chinese gold bars, as described on the International Association for Cryptologic Research website in 1996.[12] These gold bars were allegedly issued to a General Wang in Shanghai, China, in 1933. They appear to represent metal certificates related to a bank deposit with a US bank. The gold bars bear pictures, Chinese writing, some form of script writing, and cryptograms in Latin letters. The Chinese writing discusses a transaction in excess of

$300 million. The cryptograms consist of sixteen encrypted lines, some of which are repeated:

```
SKCDKJCDJCYQSZKTZJPXPWIRN
MQOLCSJTLGAJOKBSSBOMUPCE
RHZVIYQIYSXVNQXQWIOVWPJO
FEWGDRHDDEEUMFFTEEMJXZR
XLYPISNANIRUSFTFWMIY
HFXPCQYZVATXAWIZPVE
YQHUDTABGALLOWLS
UGMNCBXCFLDBEY
ABRYCTUGVZXUPB
JKGFIJPMCWSAEK
KOWVRSRKWTMLDH
HLMTAHGBGFNIV
MVERZRLQDBHQ
VIOHIKNNGUAB
GKJFHYXODIE
ZUQUPNZN
```

It is difficult to know how to categorize this cryptogram, as it is unsolved. We are making a guess that it might be a Patristocrat, but of course, it might be some other system.

There has been an update to this mystery since the publication of this book's first edition: on December 10, 2020, we attempted to contact the owner of the bars but found the phone number disconnected. We had more luck contacting the listed attorney, Peter Bisno. He confirmed that he had seen the bars themselves and that they were "large," around the size of television remote controls. He informed us that there had been some effort to contact banks about them in the 1990s, but that it hadn't gone anywhere and that he had dropped his research. He did not know anything more about the current location of the bars.

James Hampton's notebook

Another difficult-to-categorize unsolved crypto mystery is by US amateur artist James Hampton (1909–1964), who left behind an artwork known as *The Throne of the Third Heaven of the Nations' Millennium General Assembly*. He created this massive, altar-like installation over several years, starting in 1950, out of cardboard, aluminum foil, and other cheap materials. Today, it is on display in the Smithsonian American Art Museum in Washington, DC. Hampton was also the author of manually encrypted notes, including a notebook with over a hundred pages of ciphertext (Figure 4-7).[13] None of his notes have ever been deciphered. Scans of all the pages are available online.[14]

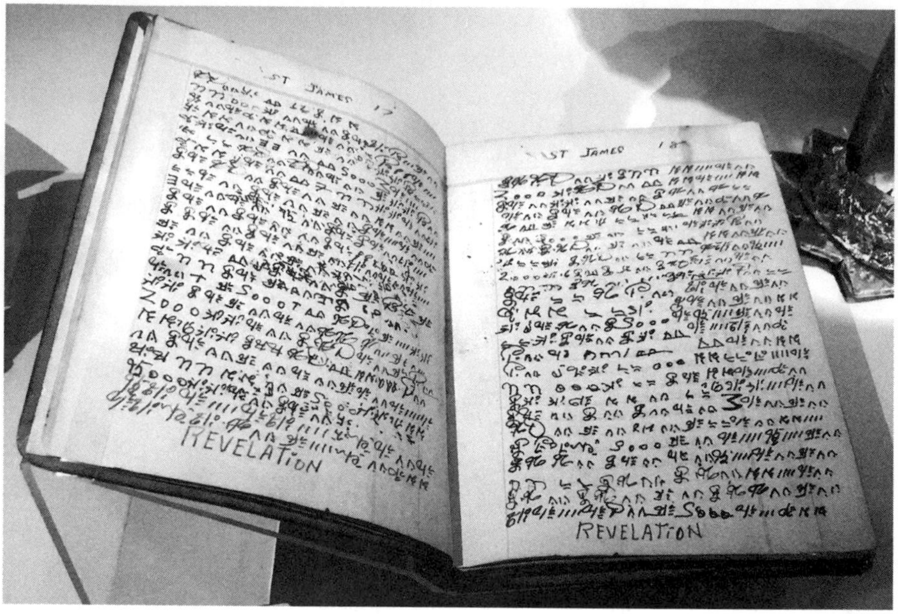

Figure 4-7: The encrypted notebook of amateur artist James Hampton has never been deciphered.

5

SIMPLE SUBSTITUTION CIPHERS IN NON-ENGLISH LANGUAGES

The world's most famous unsolved cryptogram, the Voynich manuscript, is a 230-page document in the Beinecke Rare Book & Manuscript Library at Yale University in Connecticut. From cover to cover, this probably 600-year-old, handwritten book is filled with incomprehensible text. The writing looks like a simple substitution cipher with spaces of the different-alphabet type, and the plaintext appears to have been written in an unknown language (but could also be an ordinary text written in a lost writing system, or completely meaningless nonsense). We will revisit the Voynich manuscript at the end of this chapter.

Let's take a look at the postcard in Figure 5-1 (provided to us by Richard SantaColoma), which was sent in 1912.[1] Because at least 90% of the encrypted postcards we have seen are encrypted with a simple substitution cipher, we can assume that we are dealing with one here. In addition, the sender used a nonstandard alphabet, which is also typical for a simple substitution cipher.

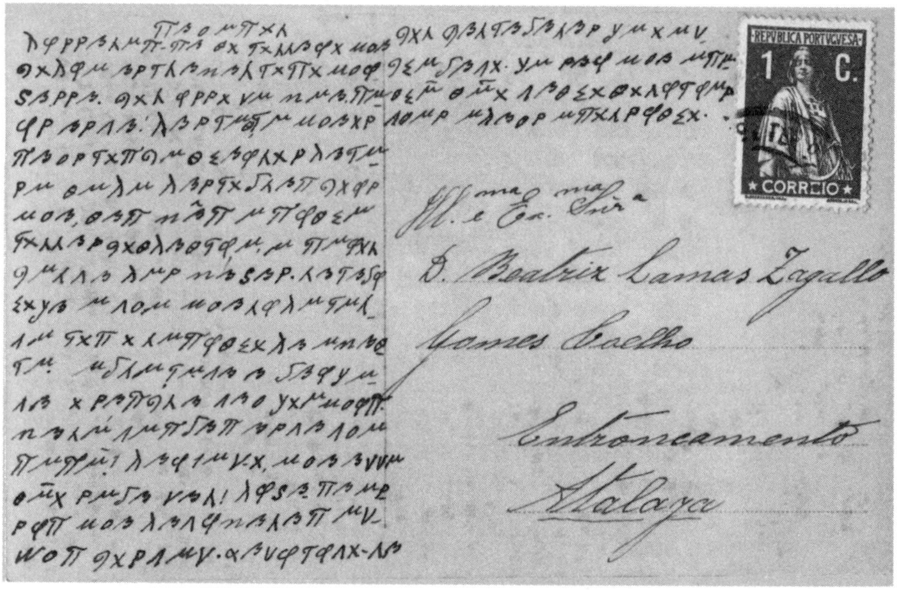

Figure 5-1: The plaintext of this 1912 encrypted postcard is in Portuguese.

It is unlikely, however, that this postcard was written in English. As the card bears a Portuguese stamp and was sent to a woman with a Portuguese surname living in Portugal, we can guess that the plaintext is written in Portuguese.

We can try to solve this postcard with the codebreaking methods discussed in Chapters 2 through 4; however, we must adapt our word guessing, frequency analysis, and word pattern searches to the Portuguese language.

You don't speak Portuguese? Don't hesitate to try breaking this message anyway. Experience shows that breaking an encrypted message does not necessarily require command of the language used. Letter frequencies and other information about non-English languages are available in Appendix B and on numerous web pages.

Detecting the language used

Identifying the postcard's likely language was not very difficult. However, things are not always that simple. In fact, detecting a cryptogram's plaintext language may be a major challenge, which is why it is always a good idea to learn an item's context. Before examining a ciphertext, figure out where it comes from and which languages its author spoke.

We can also apply statistical techniques to detect the language of a cryptogram. Take a look at the postcard reproduced in Figure 5-2, which was written in 1906 and provided to us by Tobias Schrödel.[2] Again, the non-standard alphabet makes a simple substitution cipher very likely. The spaces between the words are indicated by commas.

Figure 5-2: A 1906 Russian postcard sent to a woman in Finland. Which language might the sender have used?

Which language might have been used? The postcard itself, just like the stamp, is Russian. The recipient, a certain Inkeri Wink, lived in Vaasa, Finland. The main language spoken there is Finnish, but Swedish is also common. Other Scandinavian and Baltic languages are encountered in Finland as well. The surname Wink could be English or German. Let's start our analysis, as usual, with a transcript (provided to us by Thomas Bosbach):

A B C D E F G H I J K L M N O P Q R S T
\ ∾ ┼ ⏀ — = | ☺ ∨ ▽ O ⊂ ⌗ ⊗ ∞ § || / •

```
ABCDB JORB ATOG
SBCDBD NCBFBD GHIËDBD
FKCBL FBMEAABD STDM
IBKPNCHIBD STDM
CDJKCS CHI FCD GE
JNÖHMNCHI ACR LKBOSCJBA
IBKPBD KBCGB CHI DTHI ITOGB
CHI MTDD DEHI DCHIR GTJBD QTDD
SO FBMEAAGR BKGR DEHI BCDBD FKCB
IBKPNCHI GBC JBJKÖGGR ODS
JBMÖGGR QED SBCDBA ITDG
```

Frequency analysis might help us once again. Here are the letter frequencies of the postcard message:

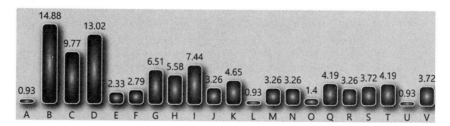

How well do these frequencies match the five languages most likely to have been used on the postcard (Finnish, Russian, Swedish, English, and German)? Here are the most frequent and the second-most frequent letters in each:

Language	Most frequent letter	Frequency	Second-most frequent letter	Frequency
Finnish	A	12%	I	11%
Russian	O	11%	E	9%
Swedish	A	10%	E	10%
English	E	12%	T	9%
German	E	16%	N	10%

With respect to the most frequent letter, German is the best fit. We see that the most frequent letter in the postcard has a frequency of 14.88%, while the most frequent letter in the German alphabet has a frequency of 16%. But the second-most frequent letter in the postcard fits best with Finnish (13.02% and 11%). Here are a few more statistical indicators that may help detect the language (see Appendix B for more information):

- No one-letter word appears in the cryptogram. This is consistent with German and Finnish, which do not have one-letter words either. As there are one-letter words in English, Swedish, and Russian, these languages are therefore less likely candidates.

- The average word length in the postcard message is 5.0 letters. This fits best with German (6.0 letters) and Swedish (6.0). The average word lengths of English, Russian, and Finnish are 6.2, 6.6, and 7.6.

- If we have a computer available, we can compute the index of coincidence of the cryptogram (see Appendix B). The result is 7.2%. Here are the relevant comparison values for the index of coincidence in other languages: Finnish: 7.0%, Russian: 5.3%, English: 6.7%, Swedish: 6.8%, and German: 7.3%. German again delivers the best match.

If we look at the alphabet the sender used, we note something else interesting: this character set contains two letters . . .

. . . that each bear two dots at the top in some (but not all) cases. We have transcribed these letters using E and O; the dots are also present in the transcript. Dots like these sometimes appear on the letters *A*, *O*, and *U* in certain languages, as with *Ä*, *Ö*, and *Ü*. These dots are called umlauts. Finnish, Swedish, and German (among others) have umlauts, but English doesn't. In the Russian alphabet, only one double-dotted letter exists.

As can be seen, German is the best fit with respect to the most frequent letter, the average word length, and the index of coincidence. In addition, German has umlauts, and there are no one-letter words in the German language. Overall, German is by far the most likely language used on the postcard. Considering that this message was sent from Russia to Finland, this is certainly a surprise!

How to break a non-English simple substitution cipher

Now that we have guessed the postcard message's language, we can apply the methods we covered in Chapter 3 by adapting these techniques to the German language.

Frequency analysis and word guessing

Frequency analysis is even more effective in German than in English, as the most frequent letter (*E*) is easier to distinguish from the others due to the larger margin between it and the second-most frequent letter: *E* has a frequency of 16%, followed by *N* with 10% (see Appendix B). The most frequent German digraphs (letter pairs) are *EN* and *ER*.

On this postcard, B is the most frequent letter and therefore probably stands for **E**, while D (the second-most frequent) might represent **N**. These guesses are confirmed by the fact that BD is the most frequent letter pair in the ciphertext, which is consistent with *EN* being the most frequent German digraph.

Good words to search for in a German text are the commonly used indefinite articles *EIN, EINE, EINEN, EINER*, and *EINES*. These are helpful for a codebreaker because they appear often, consist of frequent letters, and (with the exception of *EIN*) contain letter repetitions. (*EINEN* even contains two.) In fact, the word BCDBD in the third-to-last line of the transcript is easily identified as **EINEN**. Knowing this, we can guess that the first word in the letter, ABCDB, is **MEINE** (**my** in English). With some basic knowledge of German, the rest can be solved as well.

Word pattern guessing

Another way to decipher this postcard is to search for words with rare letter patterns. The CrypTool 2 software supports this technique for many languages, including German. So, our next step might be to check the ciphertext for a word with many letter repetitions. JNÖHMNCHI, which has the pattern 123452647, looks like a good candidate. At first glance, CrypTool 2 delivers disappointing results, as it gives us twenty-six different matches for this pattern (Figure 5-3). Even if we discard words such as **PIPELINES**, **MACULATURE**, and **GOLDBONDS**, which are not very likely to appear on a 1906 postcard, we are left with many choices.

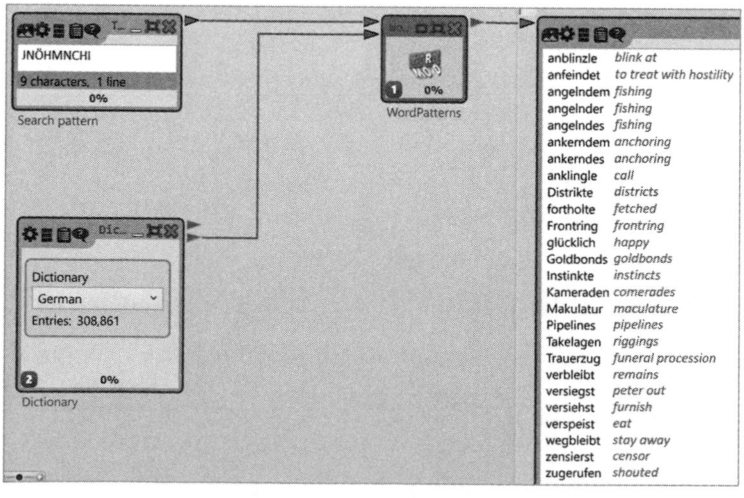

anblinzle	blink at
anfeindet	to treat with hostility
angelndem	fishing
angelnder	fishing
angelndes	fishing
ankerndem	anchoring
ankerndes	anchoring
anklingle	call
Distrikte	districts
fortholte	fetched
Frontring	frontring
glücklich	happy
Goldbonds	goldbonds
Instinkte	instincts
Kameraden	comerades
Makulatur	maculature
Pipelines	pipelines
Takelagen	riggings
Trauerzug	funeral procession
verbleibt	remains
versiegst	peter out
versiehst	furnish
verspeist	eat
wegbleibt	stay away
zensierst	censor
zugerufen	shouted

Search pattern — JNÖHMNCHI — 9 characters, 1 line — 0%

WordPatterns

Dictionary — German — Entries: 308,861

Figure 5-3: CrypTool 2 can be used to search for word patterns in many different languages.

However, one word stands out: **GLÜCKLICH**, which means "happy." First, this word seems a good fit for a postcard that apparently contains a love message. And second, if we look at the following word . . .

. . . (transcribed as JNÖHMNCHI), we see that the third letter has two dots on it (i.e., it has an umlaut, provided that our assumption with respect to umlauts is correct). The word **GLÜCKLICH** has an umlaut at the third position, as well.

Having identified **GLÜCKLICH**, we have seven letters we can use to guess the rest of the text:

```
Plaintext:      I    CHG KLU
Ciphertext:  ABCDEFGHIJKLMNOPQRST
```

With a basic knowledge of German, it is not very difficult to guess more words. For instance, we already know that the middle three letters of the ciphertext word DCHIR stand for *ICH*. This expression can be identified as the common word **NICHT** (**not**).

If you don't speak German, you can boost the process by combining the word pattern search with frequency analysis. The seven letters we know (**I**, **C**, **H**, **G**, **K**, **L**, **U**), along with the assumption that B stands for **E** (because it's the most frequent letter) and D stands for **N** (because it's the second-most frequent), go a long way. Next, look for the indefinite articles *EIN*, *EINE*, *EINEN*, *EINER*, *EINES*, and *EINES*, as described above. With over ten letters identified, the rest of the codebreaking job should be easy.

This key recovers the following plaintext:

```
MEINE GUTE MAUS
DEINEN LIEBEN SCHÖNEN
BRIEF BEKOMMEN. DANK
HERZLICHEN DANK.
INGRID ICH BIN SO
GLÜCKLICH. MIT FREUDIGEM
HERZEN REISE ICH NACH HAUSE.
ICH KANN NOCH NICHT SAGEN WANN.
DU BEKOMMST ERST NOCH EINEN BRIE[F.]
HERZLICH SEI GEGRÜSST UND
GEKÜSST VON DEINEM HANS.
```

This translates to:

```
My dear mouse
I have received your nice and beautiful letter. Thanks, many
thanks. Ingrid, I'm so happy. I will travel home with a joyful
heart. I can't say when yet. You will receive a letter first.
Cordial greetings and kisses from your Hans.
```

Success stories

A girl's pigpen cipher (Spanish)

The ciphertext depicted in Figure 5-4 is described in one of the books Klaus often recommends, the 1922 *Cryptography* by André Langie (1871–1961).[3] According to Langie, a wealthy man found this encrypted note in his son's textbook. Wondering why his offspring wrote or received such a message, he asked crypto-specialist Langie to break it.

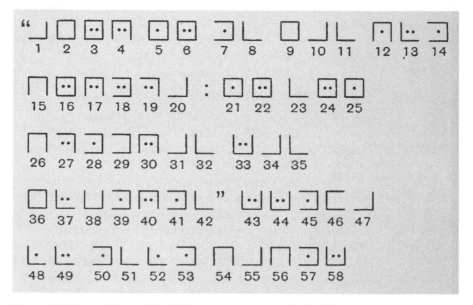

Figure 5-4: A wealthy man found this message in a textbook of his son's. (The numbers were added later by a cryptanalyst.)

Langie saw that the encryption system was a variant of the pigpen cipher. The note also included spaces and punctuation marks between the words, which always makes guessing the words considerably easier. As you can see, symbols 1–42 are enclosed between quotation marks, and there is a colon after symbol 20. The most frequently occurring character is symbol 7, which is repeated nine times.

Langie first tried to determine the plaintext language. Because the story about the man and his son took place in the French-speaking part of Switzerland, French was the most likely option. However, the word starting at symbol 43 begins with a double letter, which hardly ever happens in a French text. Langie then assumed that the plaintext might be written in Spanish, a language spoken by the client's son. The only double letter encountered at the beginning of Spanish words is *L* (for instance, in *LLEVAR* or *LLAMARSE*).

If this assumption were correct, symbol 45, the most frequent one in the cryptogram, is likely to be an **A** or an **E** (in Spanish, a double *L* is always followed by a vowel, and *A* and *E* are frequent letters). The two letters **L** and **A/E** occur again at the end of the last word of the text, but in reverse order. This is a five-letter word whose first letter is the same as the third, so it must be **PAPEL** (**paper**).

Knowing the letters **A**, **E**, **L**, and **P**, Langie could easily guess a few more. He finally derived the following substitution diagram. In this elegant system, the alphabet is drawn from left to right, one grid at a time:

It generates the following plaintext:

```
"AMOR NO ES MAS QUE PORFIA:
NO SON PIEDRAS LAS MUJERES"
LLEVA TU ESTE PAPEL
```

This translates to:

```
"Love is nothing more than a squabble:
Women are not stones."
Keep this paper.
```

Apparently, this note was a girl's enciphered rejection.

The La Buse cryptogram (French)

French pirate Olivier Levasseur (ca. 1690–1730), also known as "La Buse," or "The Buzzard," seized many a richly loaded ship in the Indian Ocean during the early eighteenth century. He was captured in 1729 and executed one year later on the French island of La Réunion, off the coast of Madagascar.[4] Legend has it that, with the gallows rope around his neck, Levasseur threw a parchment bearing an encrypted message into the crowd and shouted, "Mon trésor à qui saura le prendre!" ("My treasure for the one who will know how to take it!") The message is depicted in Figure 5-5.

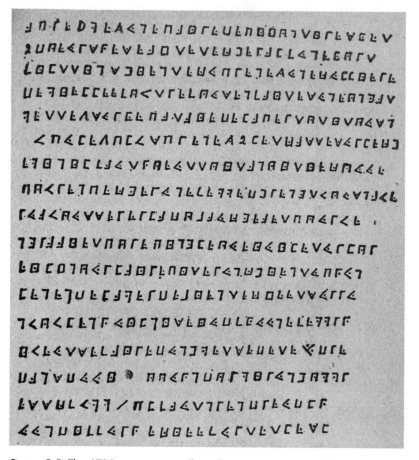

Figure 5-5: This 1730 cryptogram, allegedly created by pirate Olivier Levasseur, is said to reveal the location of a treasure. The message has been deciphered, but the treasure has never been found.

This ciphertext message used a pigpen cipher. In 1947, an Englishman named Reginald Cruise-Wilkins broke this encryption (most likely with frequency analysis).

The French plaintext was published on Nick Pelling's blog in 2013.[5]

```
aprè jmez une paire de pijon tiresket
2 doeurs sqeseaj tête cheral funekort
filttinshientecu prenez une cullière
de mielle ef ovtre fous en faites une ongat
mettez sur ke patai de la pertotitousn
vpulezolvs prenez 2 let cassé sur le che
min il faut qoe ut toit a noitie couue
povr en pecger une femme dhrengt vous n ave
eua vous serer la dobaucfea et pour ve
ngraai et por epingle oueiuileturlor
eiljn our la ire piter un chien tupqun
lenen de la mer de bien tecjeet sur ru
```

```
nvovl en quilnise iudf kuue femm rq
i veut se faire dun hmetsedete s/u dre
dans duui ooun dormir un homm r
esscfvmm / pl faut n rendre udlq
u un diffur qecieefurtetlesl
```

Even if you speak French, this text doesn't make much sense. So far, nobody seems to have found a treasure based on it, but at least the cryptographic part of this mystery is solved.

A postcard with a love message (German)

In 1901, a young man sent an encrypted postcard from Iserlohn, Germany, to nearby Arnsberg (Figure 5-6).[6] The encryption system looks like a simple substitution cipher similar to a pigpen, with spaces indicated by colons. The most likely plaintext language is German. The recipient listed on the address side of the card, a woman named Helene, is probably the sender's lover. Here's a transcript of the ciphertext:

```
ABCD:ACEB!
ÜDCH:ICBECE:ABCDCE:DHBCJ:KCLH:MCJHCFN.:IF:OFEICKN:IBPL:ÜDCH:QCBEC:R
SCKBC:.ICBE:KPLTNU:QFKK:TAACK:VÖEECE:ITQBN:IF:QBN:KCBECE:ACBKNFEMCE
:UF=JHBCICE:DBKN.:IBH:HÄFQC:BPL:ITK:HCPLN:CBE:,ITKK:IF:CENUÜPVCEI:
ABCDCE:VTEEKN:OBH:DCBIC:VCHKNCLCE:FEK:VSH=NHCJJABPL:.FEKCH:UFKTQQC
EKCBE:KSAA:KRÄNCH:CBE:RTHTTBCK:KCBE,:QCBE:KÜKKCH:CEMCA!!!MFKNTV:KT
MNC:TQ:KSEENTM:TEEC:VTQC:BE:ETPLKNCE:NTMCE:KPLSE:OBCICH.:VBCA=ACBP-
LN:KBEI:OBH:KSEENTM:ISHN.:KPLHCBDC:IBH:VSHLCH:QCBE:ABCD:ACECVCE.LCH
UABPL:MHFKKN:FEI:VFKKN:IBPL:BQQCH:ICBE:IBPL:NHCF:ABCDCEICH:JHBNUC.
```

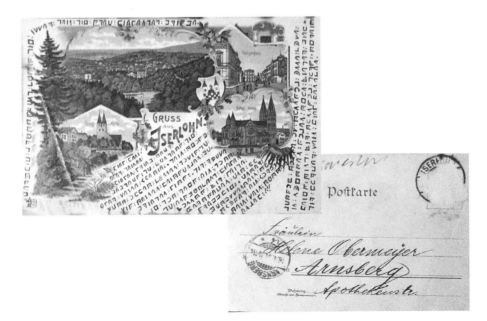

Figure 5-6: This German postcard from 1901 bears an encrypted love message.

Tobias Schrödel provided this postcard to Klaus in 2018. Klaus posted a picture of the postcard on his blog, and Thomas Bosbach, an experienced codebreaker, had little trouble solving the cryptogram. As ciphertext C is the most frequent letter, Thomas concluded that C stands for plaintext E. The letters B and E are also very frequent in the ciphertext, which makes them candidates for the plaintext letters N, I, S, and R.

After some trial and error, Thomas found that the first line (ABCD:ACEB!) stands for LIEB LENI. LIEB means "dear," while LENI is a common abbreviation of the female name Helene. Knowing five letters, Thomas could then guess the rest of the message. The plaintext turned out to be a sweet love letter. This is not surprising, as most encrypted postcards appear to have been sent by young men (and sometimes young women) to their lovers:

```
LIEB LENI,

ÜBER DEINEN LIEBEN BRIEF SEHR GEFREUT. DU WUNDE(R)ST DICH ÜBER
MEINE POESIE. DEIN SCHATZ MUSS ALLES KÖNNEN DAMIT DU MIT SEINEN
LEISTUNGEN ZUFRIEDEN BIST. DIR RÄUME ICH DAS RECHT EIN, DASS DU
ENTZÜCKEND LIEBEN KANNST. WIR BEIDE VERSTEHEN UNS VORTREFFLICH.
UNSER ZUSAMMENSEIN SOLL SPÄTER EIN PARADIES SEIN, MEIN SÜSSER
ENGEL!

GUSTAV SAGTE AM SONNTAG, ÄNNE KÄME IN NÄCHSTEN TAGEN SCHON WIEDER.
VIELLEICHT SIND WIR SONNTAG DORT. SCHREIBE DIR VORHER, MEIN LIEB
LENEKEN.

HERZLICH GRÜSST UND KÜSST DICH IMMER DEIN DICH TREU LIEBENDER
FRITZE.
```

Substituting some names (Leneken is another nickname for Helene, Änne is a female name, and Fritze is the name of the sender), we can derive a translation:

```
Dear Leni,

Very happy to have your last letter. You wonder about my poetry.
Your darling needs to be capable of doing everything in order to
make you satisfied. I allow you to love in a pleasing way. The
two of us get along with each other very well. Our being together
shall be a paradise later, my sweet angel!

Gustav said last Sunday that Änne will already return over the
next days. Perhaps, we'll be there on Sunday. I will write you
before, dear Leneken.

Cordial greetings and kisses from your always faithfully loving
Fritze.
```

A Mafia message (Italian)

During a Mafia raid in 2013, Italian police found a three-page-long encrypted document. Figure 5-7 shows an excerpt.[7] Investigators had no codebreaking unit they could consult, so they asked several policemen who were crossword puzzle enthusiasts to break the cryptogram. They were successful, though regretfully, press reports did not reveal how the cipher was broken. We can assume that the policemen worked with frequency analysis and word guessing. The excerpt in the figure decrypts as follows:

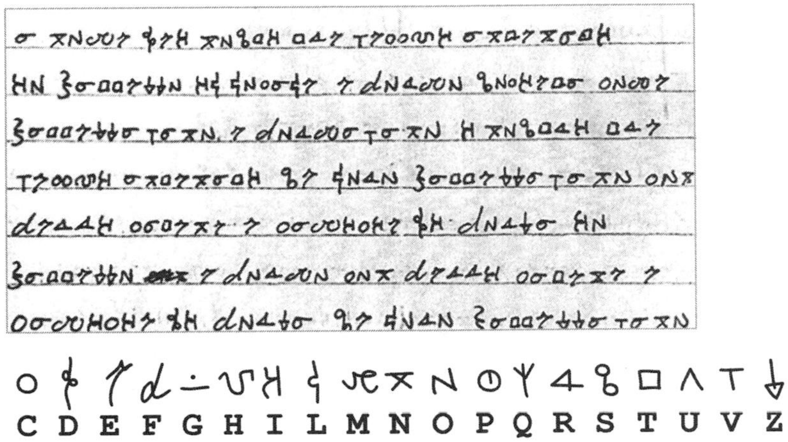

Figure 5-7: This message was created by a Mafia member in Italy. Police broke it and derived the key shown below the text.

```
A NOME DEI NOSTRI TRE VECCHI ANTENATI, IO BATTEZZO IL LOCALE E
FORMO SOCIETÀ COME BATTEZZAVANO E FORMAVANO I NOSTRI TRE VECCHI
ANTENATI, SE LORO BATTEZZAVANO CON FERRI, CATENE E CAMICIE DI
FORZA IO BATTEZZO E FORMO CON FERRI, CATENE E CAMICIE DI FORZA, SE
LORO FORMAVANO
```

This translates as follows:

```
In the name of our three old ancestors, I baptize the place
and form companies as they baptized and formed our three old
ancestors, if they baptized with irons, chains and straitjackets
I baptize and form with irons, chains and straitjackets, if they
formed
```

This message describes a Mafia initiation ritual. As it does not contain any references to criminal offences or persons, its content did not prove helpful for the investigating officers, but at least a Mafia mystery had been solved.

Challenges

An encrypted postcard

The French postcard shown in Figure 5-8 (provided to us by Karsten Hansky) is encrypted with a Caesar cipher.[8] The plaintext is French. Can you decipher it?

Figure 5-8: Can you decipher this French postcard from 1904?

The third NSA Monday Challenge

As mentioned in Chapter 4, the NSA published four crypto challenges on Twitter in May 2014: the NSA Monday Challenges. The following ciphertext was the third in this series:[9]

    nbylcrhspclbyxrnmlbzevsmlchscrhrhnmbebfs
    vhcxmxxrmzencmfyvychclcmscgmyimkcncxm
    xrydsmnrhsbyemfmmefrhxrfdyrfczmtchmscgby

The encryption system used turns out to be a simple substitution cipher, and the plaintext is written in a non-English language. Can you solve it?

Christlieb Funk's challenge cryptogram

The 1783 book *Natürliche Magie* (*Natural Magic*) by German author Christlieb Benedict Funk (1736–1786) is unusual for its time in that it expresses a high degree of skepticism concerning psychic phenomena.[10] It debunks all kinds of allegedly supernatural activities, such as fortune-telling, dousing, and astrology, in a way that is similar to how James Randi, Michael Shermer, and other skeptics have unmasked these practices in modern times.

One chapter of *Natürliche Magie* covers people who break encrypted texts while pretending that their ability involves supernatural powers, rather than frequency analysis and word guessing. As a challenge for his readers, Funk introduces the cryptogram in Figure 5-9. We leave it to the reader to decipher it with either conventional or psychic codebreaking techniques.

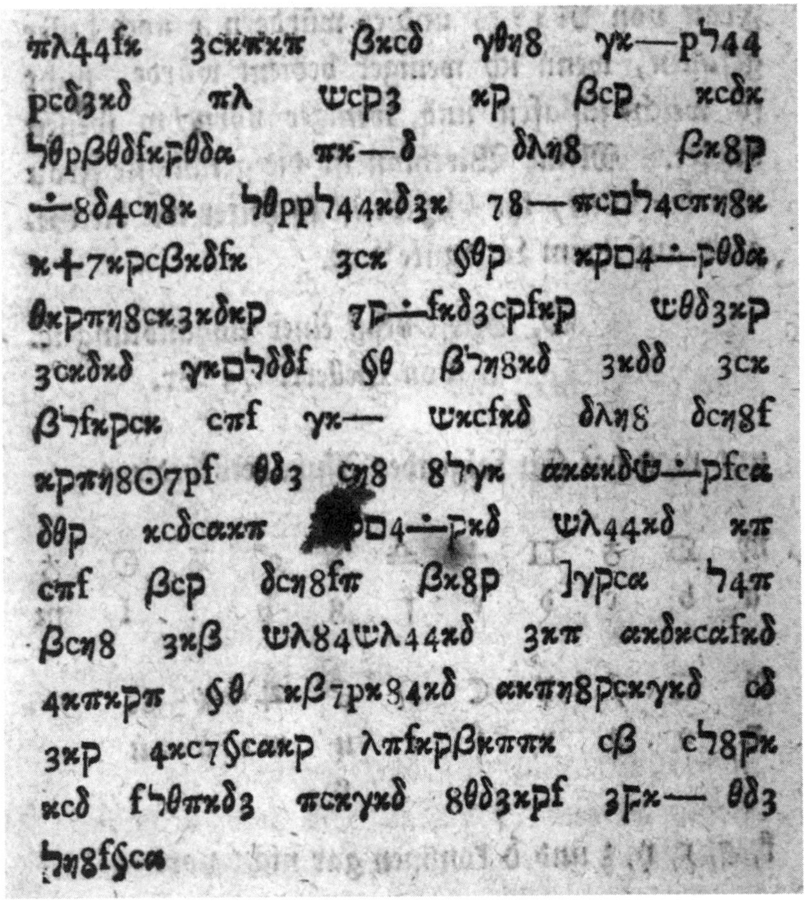

Figure 5-9: Contrary to beliefs of the era, no psychic powers are necessary to decipher this cryptogram from 1783.

Unsolved cryptograms

Numerous unsolved cryptograms look like simple substitution ciphertexts and are unlikely to have English plaintexts. In the following sections, we introduce a few.

The Voynich manuscript

One of the most famous unsolved cryptograms in the world, the centuries-old Voynich manuscript is a handwritten collection of unknown text and cryptic illustrations. The manuscript is named after book dealer Wilfrid Voynich (1865–1930), who reportedly purchased it in 1912 from an Italian Jesuit college. Today, the manuscript is owned by the Beinecke Rare Book & Manuscript Library at Yale University in Connecticut, where it is known as Beinecke MS 408.

The manuscript uses an alphabet that consists of approximately twenty-five symbols. Through radiocarbon analysis, the vellum (calfskin) it is written upon was dated to the early fifteenth century. Hundreds of experts and generations of hobbyist researchers have examined the manuscript in great detail, but their main questions remain unanswered. We do not know where, when, and by whom it was written, despite the radiocarbon dating. The purpose of the manuscript is also unclear. Theories have proposed that it is an herbal or religious text, an alchemical tome, or a sales catalog for medicinal ointments. Forgery and fraud have been suggested, as well. The plants depicted cannot be identified with certainty, and most look like mere fantasy images, containing no clear relationship to any specific place, time, religion, or ideology.

Over the last several decades, at least sixty alleged solutions to the Voynich manuscript have been published, but none have been accepted by experts. Naturally, researchers have applied to the text all codebreaking methods described in our book, including frequency analysis, word guessing, and the index of coincidence, to no avail. It is also unclear in which language the plaintext was written (if in any at all). People have argued in favor of Italian, Latin, Greek, English, German, and many others.

Klaus has compiled an extensive list of other encrypted books on his website. Elonka encouraged him to formalize the list, and it is now formally known as "Klaus Schmeh's Encrypted Books List," or EBL for short. Grouping the 125-odd books (and counting!) into categories, sorted by quantity, Klaus came up with the following:[11]

- Diaries
- Secret society books
- Knowledge books
- Literature
- Puzzle books
- Art books
- Hoaxes

- Religious books
- Notebooks
- Unable to categorize

After examining the traits of each category and then comparing those traits with the Voynich manuscript (Figure 5-10), our conclusion is that, provided that the manuscript was not created by someone who was mentally ill, it is most likely either a book of knowledge or a hoax.

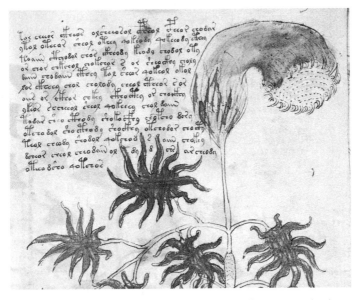

Figure 5-10: The Voynich manuscript is the most famous unsolved cryptogram in the world.

In the internet age, when the Voynich manuscript's mysterious images have become available to a wider audience, an already thriving subculture of Voynichologists has grown even larger. A Voynich manuscript conference held in Italy in 2012 attracted scores of researchers, including both authors of this book.[12] Another (virtual) conference was held ten years later, on the island of Malta, where the authors presented a new paper outlining their categorization findings.[13]

There are many websites dedicated to the manuscript, and the most comprehensive is operated by René Zandbergen (*https://voynich.nu*). Moreover, the text has inspired many books[14, 15, 16, 17] and the discussion forums at *https://voynich.ninja* and *https://voynich.net*. The latter is operated by Richard SantaColoma, who also maintains a Voynich manuscript mailing list. Whoever finally provides an accepted decipherment of the manuscript will be considered one of the greatest codebreakers ever.

The cigarette case cryptogram

In 2017, we were contacted by the owner of an antique cigarette case that bears an encrypted inscription (see Figure 5-11).[18] This message looks like an ordinary simple substitution cipher of the different-alphabet type—which any good cryptanalyst can usually decipher easily. Klaus shared this cryptogram with his online community of avid codebreakers, but surprisingly, nobody came up with a solution.

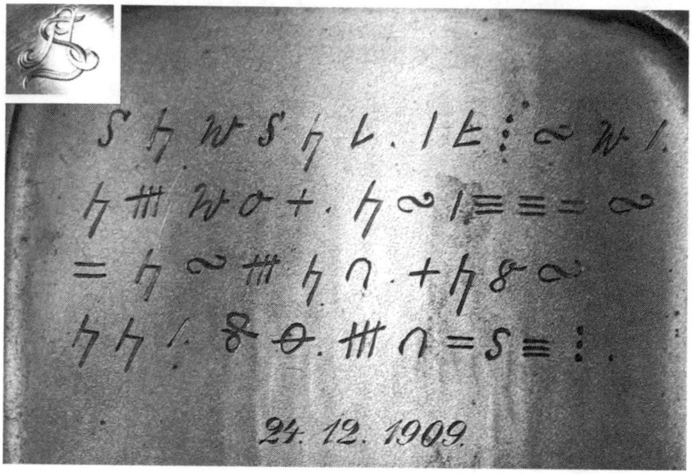

Figure 5-11: This inscription on a German cigarette case has yet to be deciphered. On the front side, the letters AS are engraved (upper left).

The cigarette case cryptogram consists of four encrypted lines. Below the text is a date written in a standard German format (dd.mm.yyyy), dated 24 December, 1909. This suggests that the case was a Christmas present. (Gifts are typically exchanged on December 24 in Germany.) The owner said it had been in his family for generations. He inherited it from his father but did not know much about its origin. His ancestry mainly stems from ancient Thuringia (Thüringen), now a region in central Germany, and his family has always spoken German. A symbol on the front side of the case depicts the letters *AS*. These are probably the initials of the original owner.

The cigarette case cryptogram is a relative newcomer among the most famous unsolved ciphertexts. If you are an ambitious codebreaker, you might choose to study this crypto mystery.

NSA's fourth Monday Challenge

Though the first three NSA Monday Challenges are not terribly difficult (all are simple substitution cipher cryptograms that were solved within a day), the fourth one, released on May 26, 2014, proved to be a different matter:[19]

```
pjbbfcklerfebjppjjlboumcuppelqpfezbjruoqlerdjbcuddbu
kulfjojprfebjbjzfrtmloupraublxpepkurtppdbjcbelfrfebkj
```

The letter frequencies and the index of coincidence (6.7%) are consistent with a simple substitution cipher. (Remember that the English index of coincidence is 6.7%.) Nevertheless, to our knowledge, the solution is still unknown.

As with all unsolved challenges, it is difficult to say for certain which type of system was used or what the plaintext language is. However, we are including this one in our non-English substitution chapter, as we think it's a good possibility that the plaintext is not in English. Of course, we may be wrong!

The Moustier altar inscriptions

Moustier, a district of the small town of Frasnes-lez-Anvaing in eastern Belgium, is the home of an unsolved crypto mystery: the two encrypted altar inscriptions in St Martin's church (see Figure 5-12).[20] The Moustier altar inscriptions became known to crypto history enthusiasts when, in 2013, the NSA declassified 136 editions of its internal newsletter *Cryptolog*. When British crypto-researcher Nick Pelling read through these publications, he found an article from 1974 introducing the cryptograms.[21] He had never heard of them before, and he wrote about them in his blog *Cipher Mysteries* to inform the codebreaking community of his find.[22]

Figure 5-12: The encrypted altar inscriptions of Moustier, Belgium

The first Moustier cryptogram is on the church's St Martin's Altar, the second on its Virgin's Altar. These altars, including the encrypted inscriptions, were probably built in the first half of the nineteenth century, but we do not know who created these messages or what intentions the creator had. Compared to other crypto mysteries, such as the Dorabella cryptogram and the Zodiac Killer messages, the Moustier altar inscriptions have received considerably less attention from cipher experts. They are still unsolved.

6

HOMOPHONIC CIPHERS

Among the best-known cryptograms in the world are three ciphertexts published in an 1885 pamphlet titled *The Beale Papers.*[1] Referred to as the "Beale ciphers," they were allegedly created by a Virginian buffalo hunter named Thomas Beale in the 1820s to conceal the location of a gold treasure buried somewhere in Bedford County, Virginia.

Although we and many other crypto experts believe that the whole Beale story is a mere hoax (Thomas Beale, let alone his treasure, probably never existed), the three ciphertexts are interesting to study. Messages #1 and #3 are unsolved and, therefore, covered in the "Unsolved cryptograms" section of this chapter. The second Beale cryptogram is solvable using the Declaration of Independence, a version of which is reproduced in the pamphlet.

The encrypted version of the second message reads as follows:

115, 73, 24, 807, 37, 52, 49, 17, 31, 62, 647, 22, 7, 15, 140, 47,
29, 107, 79, 84, 56, 239, 10, 26, 811, 5, 196, 308, 85, 52, 160,
136, 59, 211, 36, 9, 46, 316, 554, 122, 106, 95, 53, 58, 2, 42,
7, 35, 122, 53, 31, 82, 77, 250, 196, 56, 96, 118, 71, 140, 287,
28, 353, 37, 1005, 65, 147, 807, 24, 3, 8, 12, 47, 43, 59, 807,
45, 316, 101, 41, 78, 154, 1005, 122, 138, 191, 16, 77, 49, 102,
57, 72, 34, 73, 85, 35, 371, 59, 196, 81, 92, 191, 106, 273, 60,
394, 620, 270, 220, 106, 388, 287, 63, 3, 6, 191, 122, 43, 234,
400, 106, 290, 314, 47, 48, 81, 96, 26, 115, 92, 158, 191, 110,
77, 85, 197, 46, 10, 113, 140, 353, 48, 120, 106, 2, 607, 61, 420,
811, 29, 125, 14, 20, 37, 105, 28, 248, 16, 159, 7, 35, 19, 301,
125, 110, 486, 287, 98, 117, 511, 62, 51, 220, 37, 113, 140, 807,
138, 540, 8, 44, 287, 388, 117, 18, 79, 344, 34, 20, 59, 511, 548,
107, 603, 220, 7, 66, 154, 41, 20, 50, 6, 575, 122, 154, 248, 110,
61, 52, 33, 30, 5, 38, 8, 14, 84, 57, 540, 217, 115, 71, 29, 84,
63, 43, 131, 29, 138, 47, 73, 239, 540, 52, 53, 79, 118, 51, 44,
63, 196, 12, 239, 112, 3, 49, 79, 353, 105, 56, 371, 557, 211,
505, 125, 360, 133, 143, 101, 15, 284, 540, 252, 14, 205, 140,
344, 26, 811, 138, 115, 48, 73, 34, 205, 316, 607, 63, 220, 7,
52, 150, 44, 52, 16, 40, 37, 158, 807, 37, 121, 12, 95, 10, 15,
35, 12, 131, 62, 115, 102, 807, 49, 53, 135, 138, 30, 31, 62, 67,
41, 85, 63, 10, 106, 807, 138, 8, 113, 20, 32, 33, 37, 353, 287,
140, 47, 85, 50, 37, 49, 47, 64, 6, 7, 71, 33, 4, 43, 47, 63, 1,
27, 600, 208, 230, 15, 191, 246, 85, 94, 511, 2, 270, 20, 39, 7,
33, 44, 22, 40, 7, 10, 3, 811, 106, 44, 486, 230, 353, 211, 200,
31, 10, 38, 140, 297, 61, 603, 320, 302, 666, 287, 2, 44, 33, 32,
511, 548, 10, 6, 250, 557, 246, 53, 37, 52, 83, 47, 320, 38, 33,
807, 7, 44, 30, 31, 250, 10, 15, 35, 106, 160, 113, 31, 102, 406,
230, 540, 320, 29, 66, 33, 101, 807, 138, 301, 316, 353, 320, 220,
37, 52, 28, 540, 320, 33, 8, 48, 107, 50, 811, 7, 2, 113, 73, 16,
125, 11, 110, 67, 102, 807, 33, 59, 81, 158, 38, 43, 581, 138, 19,
85, 400, 38, 43, 77, 14, 27, 8, 47, 138, 63, 140, 44, 35, 22, 177,
106, 250, 314, 217, 2, 10, 7, 1005, 4, 20, 25, 44, 48, 7, 26, 46,
110, 230, 807, 191, 34, 112, 147, 44, 110, 121, 125, 96, 41, 51,

```
50, 140, 56, 47, 152, 540, 63, 807, 28, 42, 250, 138, 582, 98,
643, 32, 107, 140, 112, 26, 85, 138, 540, 53, 20, 125, 371, 38,
36, 10, 52, 118, 136, 102, 420, 150, 112, 71, 14, 20, 7, 24, 18,
12, 807, 37, 67, 110, 62, 33, 21, 95, 220, 511, 102, 811, 30, 83,
84, 305, 620, 15, 2, 108, 220, 106, 353, 105, 106, 60, 275, 72, 8,
50, 205, 185, 112, 125, 540, 65, 106, 807, 138, 96, 110, 16, 73,
33, 807, 150, 409, 400, 50, 154, 285, 96, 106, 316, 270, 205, 101,
811, 400, 8, 44, 37, 52, 40, 241, 34, 205, 38, 16, 46, 47, 85,
24, 44, 15, 64, 73, 138, 807, 85, 78, 110, 33, 420, 505, 53, 37,
38, 22, 31, 10, 110, 106, 101, 140, 15, 38, 3, 5, 44, 7, 98, 287,
135, 150, 96, 33, 84, 125, 807, 191, 96, 511, 118, 40, 370, 643,
466, 106, 41, 107, 603, 220, 275, 30, 150, 105, 49, 53, 287, 250,
208, 134, 7, 53, 12, 47, 85, 63, 138, 110, 21, 112, 140, 485, 486,
505, 14, 73, 84, 575, 1005, 150, 200, 16, 42, 5, 4, 25, 42, 8, 16,
811, 125, 160, 32, 205, 603, 807, 81, 96, 405, 41, 600, 136, 14,
20, 28, 26, 353, 302, 246, 8, 131, 160, 140, 84, 440, 42, 16, 811,
40, 67, 101, 102, 194, 138, 205, 51, 63, 241, 540, 122, 8, 10, 63,
140, 47, 48, 140, 288.
```

As can be seen, it consists of a series of numbers between 1 and 1005. The encryption method used is quite simple: every number stands for a certain letter and several numbers may represent the same letter. Here's an excerpt from the substitution table:

A: 24, 27, 28, 36, 45, 81, 83 . . .
B: 9, 77, 90 . . .
C: 21, 84, 92, 94 . . .
D: 15, 52, 63 . . .

Using this excerpt, we can encrypt the plaintext string **ABC** in many different ways. For example, 24, 9, 21 is a valid encryption of **ABC**, as are 27, 9, 92 and 45, 77, 21.

The substitution table of the second Beale cryptogram was created with one of the versions of the Declaration of Independence. [1]Thomas [2]Beale ([3]or [4]whoever [5]the [6]real [7]author [8]was) [9]numbered [10]each [11]word [12]of [13]it, [14]just [15]like [16]we [17]have [18]done [19]in [20]this [21]sentence. Afterward, he used each number as a potential replacement for the starting letter of the word to which it refers. For example, the message **WE ARE THE WORLD** can be encrypted to the following: 11 10, 7 6 10, 20 17 10, 4 3 6 15 18.

When we use the Declaration of Independence in the way we've described, the second Beale cryptogram decrypts to the following:

```
I have deposited in the county of Bedford, about four miles from
Buford's, in an excavation or vault, six feet below the surface
of the ground, the following articles, belonging jointly to the
parties whose names are given in number three, herewith:

The first deposit consisted of ten hundred and fourteen pounds
of gold, and thirty-eight hundred and twelve pounds of silver,
deposited Nov. eighteen nineteen. The second was made Dec.
```

eighteen twenty-one, and consisted of nineteen hundred and seven pounds of gold, and twelve hundred and eighty-eight of silver; also jewels, obtained in St. Louis in exchange to save transportation, and valued at thirteen thousand dollars.

The above is securely packed in iron pots, with iron covers. The vault is roughly lined with stone, and the vessels rest on solid stone, and are covered with others. Paper number one describes the exact locality of the vault, so that no difficulty will be had in finding it.

Since the publication of the Beale pamphlet in 1885, countless treasure hunters have descended upon the Bedford, Virginia, area with pickaxes, shovels, and bulldozers at the ready. Many holes have been dug, but no treasure has been found. Although we believe the pamphlet was most likely a hoax, a Masonic fable, or simply a way to raise money for a failing newspaper, the story of the Beale cryptograms and their idea of unfound treasure remains one of the most famous cipher mysteries in the world.

How homophonic ciphers work

Several ciphertext letters, numbers, or symbols that represent the same plaintext letter are called *homophones*. A cipher that substitutes letters and uses homophones is referred to as a *homophonic cipher*. The second Beale cryptogram is encrypted in a homophonic cipher. (It is also a book cipher, as will be shown in Chapter 14.)

Of course, one does not need a source text such as the Declaration of Independence to create a homophonic cipher. Instead, one can simply assign several ciphertext letters to a plaintext letter and list them in a table. Here is a seventeenth-century example[2] in which multiple symbols could be used to encipher each letter of the alphabet in the top row:

A	B	C	D	E	F	G	H	I	K	L	M	N	O	P	Q	R	S	T	U	W	X	Y	Z
2	7	9	11	13	10	20	22	27	29	31	33	32	30	28	23	21	19	17	12	10	8	3	1
4	⌐	‡	I	♄	○	♂	φ	↔	♣	⚹	♀	♀	♃	⊗	▽	♃	‡	Γ	⅃	⊔	⊔	⊹	¥
37		30					76	71			77		70				72	73	39				
8		ᵐ	84				♂	18					8				88	181					

Homophonic ciphers have been used since the Middle Ages to beat frequency analysis.

The size of the alphabet used in a homophonic cipher may vary considerably. Some ciphers employ homophones only for the more frequent letters, as in the following eighteenth-century example:[3]

A	B	C	D	E	F	G	H	I	K	L	M	N	O	P	Q	R	S	T	V	W	X	Y	Z
44	45	46	47	48	49	50	51	52	53	54	55	33	34	35	36	37	38	39	40	41	42	43	32
56			57					58				59					60						

Most homophonic ciphers use a larger alphabet than this one. In our experience, homophonic ciphers usually use fifty to one hundred cipher-text letters to encrypt the original alphabet. Each ciphertext letter consists of a combination of letters, numbers, and symbols.

Ideally, the number of homophones assigned to a letter would be proportional to its frequency in the respective language; the more frequent letters, such as *E* and *T*, should receive more homophones than the less frequent ones, like *Q* and *X*. However, experience shows that most homophonic ciphers used in practice were not constructed in such a sophisticated way.

How to detect a homophonic cipher

To identify a homophonic cipher, it is often necessary to distinguish it from a simple substitution cipher. If there are spaces in the ciphertext, it could simply be an Aristocrat. If there are no spaces, we need to distinguish it from a Patristocrat.

There is one obvious difference between any simple substitution cipher and a homophonic cipher: the latter requires a larger ciphertext alphabet. If you encounter a ciphertext written in the standard alphabet or another alphabet with about twenty-six letters, you can assume that it is not a homophonic cipher (or, if nothing else, that the message will not contain very many homophones). If the alphabet contains, say, fifty letters, a homophonic cipher becomes much more likely.

Figure 6-1 shows a message that is partially encrypted in a homophonic cipher used by Benjamin Franklin, among others.[4] The ciphertext alphabet used here consists of numbers, the highest of which in this excerpt is 227. This means that plenty of homophones can be assigned to each character, **A** through **Z**.

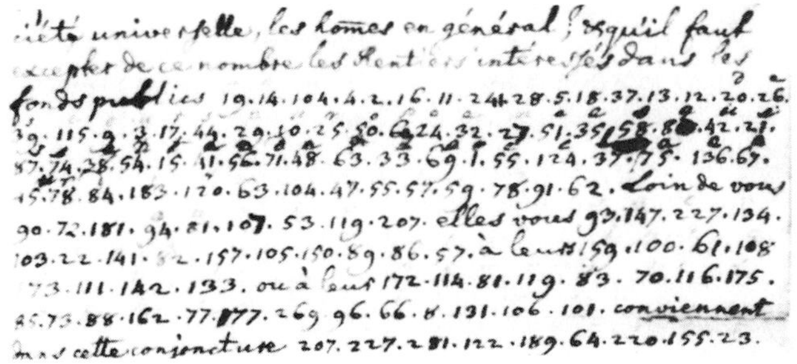

Figure 6-1: A sample of a message encrypted with a homophonic cipher, recorded in the Papers of the Continental Congress of the United States.

Some homophonic ciphers we have encountered use an alphabet that consists of both ordinary and invented letters. Figure 6-2 shows an example. It's a challenge cipher message sent to the Zodiac Killer via a newspaper advertisement in 1969.[5] We will come back to this cryptogram in the "Challenges" section of this chapter. An alphabet like this is ideal for a homophonic cipher with a few dozen homophones. However, it would be difficult to write the second Beale cryptogram this way, as inventing hundreds of different symbols is an arduous task.

Figure 6-2: This 1969 newspaper advertisement, provided to us by Zodiac expert Dave Oranchak, shows a ciphertext that was meant to challenge the Zodiac Killer. It is encrypted in a homophonic cipher.

The matter of how to distinguish a homophonic cipher from systems other than simple substitutions remains an issue. The Vigenère cipher and many other encryption methods described in this book typically use an alphabet consisting of about twenty-six letters, which separates them from homophonic ciphers. However, a homophonic cipher can easily be confused with a *nomenclator*, which is a hybrid of codes and ciphers and consists of a collection of names (see Chapter 7 for full details on nomenclators). Differentiating between these two methods is sometimes tricky, as many nomenclators include homophones. So, in a way, a nomenclator can be regarded as a generalization of a homophonic cipher.

However, there is one important difference between nomenclators and homophonic ciphers: the former are encountered much more often in practice. In fact, in the course of history, the use of homophonic ciphers was much less common than the use of nomenclators. If you examine an original ciphertext (one that is not a manufactured puzzle) based on a large alphabet, the chances are extremely high that you are dealing with a nomenclator.

There is another way to distinguish a homophonic cipher from a nomenclator: homophonic ciphers rarely use an alphabet of more than 200 letters. The second Beale cryptogram, with its over 1,000-letter alphabet, is an exception, possibly because it is also a book cipher (see Chapter 14). If you encounter a ciphertext that contains 1,000 or more distinct numbers or letter sequences, chances are that you are dealing with a nomenclator or a code. If the alphabet is smaller, a homophonic cipher becomes more likely.

How to break a homophonic cipher

Today, the best approach to solving a homophonic cipher—like for many other encryption systems—is the computer-based, computationally intensive method of hill climbing. Several software programs support this technique; enter "homophonic solver" in a search engine to find one. These programs can break some homophonic cryptograms within seconds (see Chapter 16).

If you want to solve a homophonic cipher without computer support, your chances of success heavily depend on whether the spaces between the words are visible. If they aren't, the task becomes very difficult unless you have a very long ciphertext to analyze. If, however, the word boundaries are apparent, your chances are quite good as long as there aren't too many homophones in play. We'll demonstrate the breaking of a homophonic cipher with the following text, which you might encounter at a geocaching event:

```
U3EI0 RH84 MB9Y B3 0GN DEIYP1C DZEX5 KJB4 7ELN1SB XI5JY 3NK AP95U 1F40O HT XFHZSKC0F1 FK IHEL 3MF
0MJ13R TH9ZFM 3GN THH0DBEO KF40G 3OIH8CG 3OJ TFI5U0 ET054 E7H83 F1J YP9HAN05I 3BYN B 4SCG0 EKL MBZY
E9F1C 3OJ T5KXN BT05I USQ 081L4JL AN05IU RH8 MP99 4NEXG B DPX1SX DZBXJ MP3O E D9ERCIF8KL SK 0G5
XN13N4 HT 0O5 DPXKSX DZBXJ 3G5IN PU E 0B0 S1 3G5 9FM54 DBI0 HT 3GJ 4NE4 MB9Z FT 0OJ OB3 7JGSKL 0O5
7N1XG RH8 MPZ9 TS1L E UABZ9 D9BU3PX 7FQ XHK0ESKP1C T8I3O5I SKU0I8X3SF1U CFHL Z8XY
```

Here's a transcript:

```
U3EI0 RH84 MB9Y B3 0GN DEIYP1C DZEX5 KJB4 7ELN1SB XI5JY 3NK AP95U
1F40O HT XFHZSKC0F1 FK IHEL 3MF 0MJ13R TH9ZFM 3GN THH0DBEO KF40G
3OIH8CG 3OJ TFI5U0 ET054 E7H83 F1J YP9HAN05I 3BYN B 4SCG0 EKL MBZY
E9F1C 3OJ T5KXN BT05I USQ 081L4JL AN05IU RH8 MP99 4NEXG B DPX1SX
DZBXJ MP3O E D9ERCIF8KL SK 0G5 XN13N4 HT 0O5 DPXKSX DZBXJ 3G5IN
PU E 0B0 S1 3G5 9FM54 DBI0 HT 3GJ 4NE4 MB9Z FT 0OJ OB3 7JGSKL
0O5 7N1XG RH8 MPZ9 TS1L E UABZ9 D9BU3PX 7FQ XHK0ESKP1C T8I3O5I
SKU0I8X3SF1U CFHL Z8XY
```

The ciphertext alphabet used here has thirty-six characters (A–Z and 0–9). A plausible explanation for this is that it uses a homophonic cipher employing about ten homophones. Frequency analysis . . .

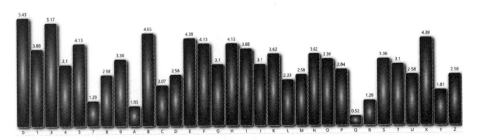

. . . shows that no letter makes up more than 5.4% of the ciphertext, despite the fact that several letters, especially E, T, A, O, and I, appear far more often in the English language. This might be because the author used homophones for the most frequent letters in order to make them harder to spot—which is exactly what a homophonic cipher is for.

As our cryptogram contains spaces (provided that these spaces mark the boundaries between the words correctly), we can make use of the frequency distribution of each word's initial and final letters, which is different from the frequency distribution of all letters in a text. Before we take a closer look at our geocaching cryptogram, we need some statistics about the English language in general. Figure 6-3 (a) shows the frequency distribution of an ordinary English text. Next, let's assume that, in an ordinary English text, there are two different representations of each of the letters *A, E, I, O,* and *T* (i.e., homophones). We'll call these A1 and A2, E1 and E2, I1 and I2, O1 and O2, and T1 and T2. We have chosen to focus on *A, E, I, O,* and *T* because they are the most frequent letters in English. If we replace each of these letters with the corresponding homophones and use the two representations of each letter roughly equally often, the frequency distribution of a typical English text will look as shown in Figure 6-3 (b).

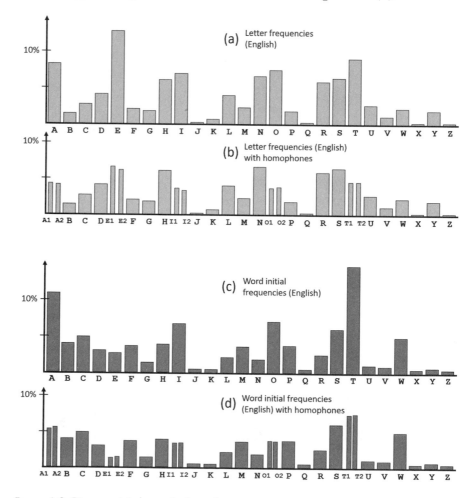

Figure 6-3: Diagram (a) shows the letter frequencies in a typical English text, diagram (b) introduces homophones, and diagrams (c) and (d) display the same statistics for the frequencies of initial letters.

To generate another reference statistic, let's look solely at the initial letters of the words in a typical English text. Figure 6-3 (c) shows initial-letter frequencies without homophones, while Figure 6-3 (d) displays initial-letter frequencies after introducing the same A1/A2, E1/E2, and so on homophones as above.

Many of the differences between the overall letter frequencies with homophones (b) and initial frequencies with homophones (d) might be helpful for a codebreaker. However, for us, it is sufficient to know one specific difference: *T* is one of the most common letters in English (9%), and if we consider how often it is used as the initial letter of a word, it has an even higher frequency (14%). Because of this increase, there is a good chance that the *T* homophones have the highest initial-letter frequency in an English homophonic ciphertext. This may help us identify the plaintext **T** in a cryptogram of this kind.

The situation is similar if we look at the frequency of the final letters in each word of an English text. In particular, *I* is a frequent letter in English in general, but it almost never appears at the end of a word. This may help us identify the plaintext **I** in a homophonic cryptogram.

With this background information, let's return to the geocaching text. We need to take a look at the frequencies of the letters in total, of the initial letters, and of the final letters of each word. We have done this using CrypTool 2, which supports initial- and final-letter counting, and we have compiled the results in Figure 6-4. (We are not aware of a computer program that does this entire job automatically.)

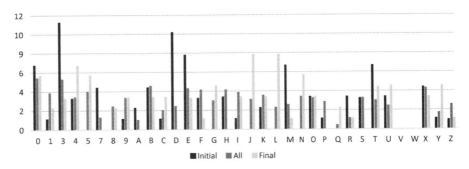

Figure 6-4: The bars in this diagram show the frequencies of all letters (the middle bars), as well as the initial and final letters of each word in the ciphertext we are examining.

Here are a few observations:

- The ciphertext letter 3 is the most frequent initial letter. It is less common elsewhere in the text. So, 3 could be a homophone standing for **T**.

- There must be at least one more **T** homophone (otherwise, we would expect the ciphertext letter 3 to have an initial-letter frequency of about 15%). **E** appears to be a good candidate, because, like 3, it has a very high initial-letter frequency despite lower overall and final-letter frequencies.

- The ciphertext letters H and S each have about the same overall and initial-letter frequencies but don't appear as the final letter of a word. They could stand for the letter I.

Let's now proceed with a letter-pair (digraph) frequency analysis. We will only consider digraphs without spaces between the letters. Here are all the digraphs that appear more than once. We used the website *http://dcode .fr/en* for this analysis:

Four appearances	Three appearances	Two appearances
O5	KL, H8, 3O	FH, OO, HT, AN, F1, OB, 4O, O5, U3, G5, SX, XJ, 1L, YP, ZB, SK, EI, DP

Here are a few digraph-related facts that might be helpful:

- The most frequent digraphs in the English language are *TH, HE,* and *IN.*
- The most frequent reversed digraph is *ER/RE.* (Unfortunately, no reversed digraph appears more than once in our ciphertext.)
- Our cryptogram contains two words that consist of only one letter: B (which appears twice) and E (which appears three times). There are only two common English one-letter words: A and I.
- The following two-letter words appear in the ciphertext: B3, HT (which appears three times), FK, SK, BU, S1, and FT. Frequent English two-letter words are OF, TO, IN, IT, IS, BE, AS, AT, and SO.

How do we proceed? We know that the ciphertext letters B and E (which both appear as one-letter words) stand for either A or I (the only common one-letter words in English). We also know that the letter I very rarely appears as the final letter of a word. Looking at the frequency chart, we see that the ciphertext letters B and E both appear at the end of a word several times. We can therefore conclude that neither B nor E decrypts to I, which means that both stand for A.

What else can we find out? As we discussed, the ciphertext letter 3 is a good candidate for the plaintext T. If so, the fourth word in the cryptogram (B3) is AT, which makes sense. Note that we find the digraph 3O among the most frequent ones in the ciphertext. Does 3O stand for TH, which is one of the most frequent digraphs in the English language? Probably.

Looking at the cryptogram, we see that the word 3OJ appears twice. If our assumption that 3O stands for TH is correct, then 3OJ must stand for THE, as no other common three-letter word starts with TH. This means J decrypts to E.

The ciphertext contains the word 3GJ, which decrypts to T*E. It is likely that G, like O, stands for H.

Now that we know ciphertext equivalents of A, E, H, and T, we can guess others. For instance, the ciphertext word MP3O, which decrypts to **TH, might stand for WITH. The word MP99 should be WILL. MPZ9 probably has the same meaning, suggesting that Z and 9 are homophones. Now look at MB9Y, which must be WAL*. WALK is a good guess.

Let's skip the rest of this guessing exercise and provide the plaintext:

```
START YOUR WALK AT THE PARKING PLACE NEAR BADENIA CREEK TEN MILES
NORTH OF COOLINGTON ON ROAD TWO TWENTY FOLLOW THE FOOTPATH NORTH
THROUGH THE FOREST AFTER ABOUT ONE KILOMETER TAKE A RIGHT AND WALK
ALONG THE FENCE AFTER SIX HUNDRED METERS YOU WILL REACH A PICNIC
PLACE WITH A PLAYGROUND IN THE CENTER OF THE PICNIC PLACE THERE
IS A HAT IN THE LOWER PART OF THE REAR WALL OF THE HAT BEHIND
THE BENCH YOU WILL FIND A SMALL PLASTIC BOX CONTAINING FURTHER
INSTRUCTIONS GOOD LUCK
```

Success stories

The first Zodiac message (Z408)

The Zodiac Killer was a serial killer who operated in Northern California in the late 1960s and early 1970s. He killed at least five people and severely injured two. In a series of taunting letters sent to local newspapers, he made fun of the police and announced his intent to engage in more murders and mayhem. The identity of the Zodiac Killer remains unknown. What makes this case interesting for codebreakers is that some of the killer's letters contained encrypted messages.[6] Altogether, four cryptograms can be attributed to the Zodiac Killer.

The first Zodiac Killer cryptogram, also known as Z408 because of the number of characters it contains, can be seen in Figure 6-5. It was originally divided into three parts, each of which was sent to a different newspaper. The police consulted professional codebreakers but did not hear back quickly. With a sense of urgency, each of the newspapers published the cryptograms within a few days.

Donald and Bettye Harden, a puzzle-loving couple living in Salinas, California, read about Z408 in a newspaper and decided to try to decipher it. Bettye tested the assumption that the Zodiac Killer, perhaps a self-centered and pretentious person, would start the message with the plaintext word **I**, and that maybe the word **KILL** might appear in the text as well. Her guess that the first plaintext words were **I LIKE KILLING** was the breakthrough.

Bettye Harden soon found out that the Zodiac Killer had used a homophonic cipher to encrypt this message. Here's the (rather gruesome) plaintext, spelling errors and all:

```
I LIKE KILLING PEOPLE BECAUSE IT IS SO MUCH FUN IT IS MORE FUN
THAN KILLING WILD GAME IN THE FORREST BECAUSE MAN IS THE MOST
DANGEROUE ANAMAL OF ALL TO KILL SOMETHING GIVES ME THE MOST
THRILLING EXPERENCE IT IS EVEN BETTER THAN GETTING YOUR ROCKS
OFF WITH A GIRL THE BEST PART OF IT IS THAE WHEN I DIE I WILL BE
REBORN IN PARADICE AND ALL THEI HAVE KILLED WILL BECOME MY SLAVES
I WILL NOT GIVE YOU MY NAME BECAUSE YOU WILL TRY TO SLOI DOWN OR
ATOP MY COLLECTIOG OF SLAVES FOR MY AFTERLIFE. EBEORIETEMETHHPITI
```

Figure 6-5: The first message from the Zodiac Killer was broken by Donald and Bettye Harden.

The Zodiac Killer's second message (Z340)

Figure 6-6 shows the second of the Zodiac Killer's four messages, which had been sent to local newspapers. It was mailed on November 8, 1969. This cryptogram consists of 340 characters and is therefore referred to as Z340. Contrary to the aforementioned Z408, it wasn't solved right away. Over the decades, Z340, which is long enough to allow for meaningful frequency analysis and other statistical examinations, became one of the most famous unsolved crypto mysteries in the world. In the first edition of this book, released on December 10, 2020, Z340 was even listed in the "Unsolved cryptograms" section of this chapter.

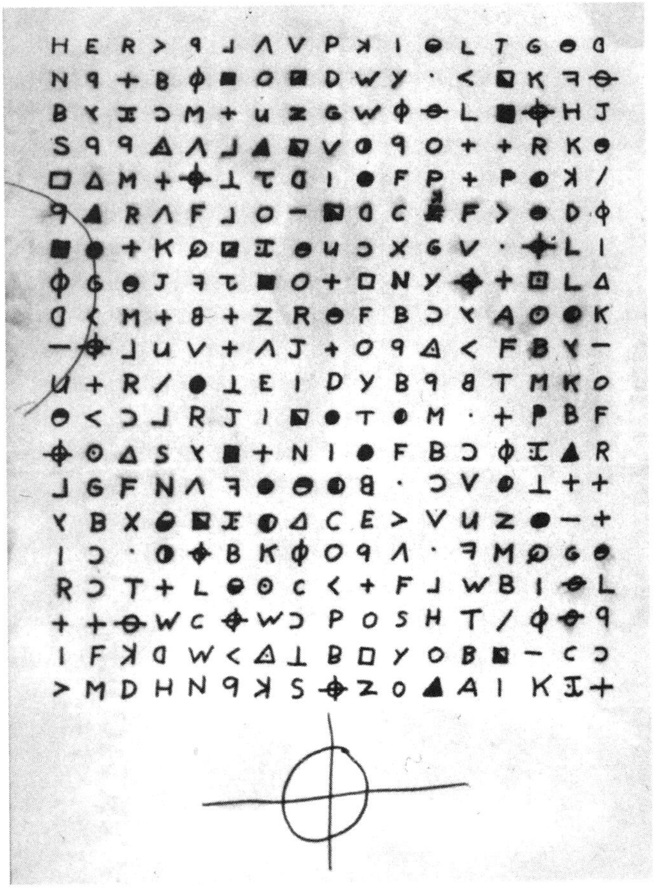

Figure 6-6: The second encrypted message from the Zodiac Killer remained unsolved for decades.

However, on December 11, 2020, only one day after publication of the first edition, we received a message from our friend, Zodiac Killer expert Dave Oranchak. What he wrote was hard to believe: he claimed that Z340 had been solved! According to his message, this success had been achieved by a team of three experts consisting of Dave himself, Belgian codebreaking specialist Jarl Van Eycke, and Australian mathematician Sam Blake (Figure 6-7).

Figure 6-7: From left: Dave Oranchak, Jarl Van Eycke, and Sam Blake broke the Z340 message.

Of course, we were skeptical, as many bogus decipherments of this famous ciphertext had been published before. However, a video Dave published about the solution that he and his colleagues had found appeared to make sense.[7] Several cipher experts mentioned in our own book, including Nils Kopal,[8] Nick Pelling,[9] Joachim von zur Gathen,[10] and George Lasry (via email), confirmed the correctness of Dave, Jarl, and Sam's decipherment. To really clinch things, the FBI published an official statement via Twitter, saying, "A cipher attributed to the Zodiac Killer was recently solved by private citizens."[11] There could be no doubt: Z340 had been broken!

Dave and Jarl had originally connected in 2014, which led to Jarl's creation of the AZDecrypt software in 2015 to break homophonic ciphers. Then Dave and Sam connected in 2019 through Dave's YouTube channel, *Let's Crack Zodiac*. They jointly examined Z340 for months, suspecting that the Zodiac Killer had used a combination of two ciphers: a homophonic substitution similar to the one employed for Z408, and a transposition cipher (see Chapter 9).[12, 13]

As there is a mind-boggling quantity of possible transpositions that could be applied to a text of this length—in fact, the options are seemingly infinite—the three codebreakers had to limit their examinations to the most likely ones. So, they assumed that the message had been split up in a simple way—horizontally, vertically, or both. Among other possibilities, they considered the following:

- It might have been split into one horizontal section with two vertical sections.

- It might have been split into two horizontal sections with three vertical sections.

In 2015, Jarl and an anonymous forum user nicknamed "daikon" had already discovered that the digraph frequencies of Z340 had some interesting statistical properties when every nineteenth symbol was read. This suggested that leaping through the ciphertext in steps of nineteen was a part of the process that led to the plaintext.

Even within these constraints, sifting through all the substitution and transposition candidates still meant searching for a needle in a gigantic haystack. Dave, Jarl, and Sam tested no fewer than 650,000 transposition variants. When at first they didn't find anything close to a solution to Z340, they decided to shift their focus to re-examining the top 10% of the candidate transpositions, as scored by AZDecrypt. This time, they also gave the software more time to search.

The breakthrough came on December 3, 2020, when, in one of the numerous deciphering attempts, the expressions HOPE YOU ARE, TRYING TO CATCH ME and THE GAS CHAMBER appeared. When Dave configured these text fragments as cribs, AZDecrypt suddenly produced meaningful sentences.

An even more exciting development was that this plaintext candidate contained the phrase THAT WASNT ME ON THE TV SHOW, which Dave immediately recognized as an allusion to a man who had called in to a TV show pretending to be the perpetrator two weeks before the encrypted message was sent in 1969. This strongly implied that they had the solution to the first nine lines of the ciphertext!

However, applying that technique to the rest of the message still didn't result in a meaningful plaintext. The team needed two further breakthroughs to bring the whole plaintext into view. First, Dave discovered that in the last two lines, a few words were written backward, with no other transposition being used. Second, Jarl figured out a few mistakes or disrupted transpositions in the second section. Now, the successful codebreakers could finally determine the following plaintext (a few errors are corrected):

```
I HOPE YOU ARE HAVING LOTS OF FUN IN TRYING TO CATCH ME   THAT
WASNT ME ON THE TV SHOW  WHICH BRINGS UP A POINT ABOUT ME  I AM
NOT AFRAID OF THE GAS CHAMBER BECAUSE IT WILL SEND ME TO PARADICE
ALL THE SOONER BECAUSE I NOW HAVE ENOUGH SLAVES TO WORK FOR ME
WHERE EVERYONE ELSE HAS NOTHING WHEN THEY REACH PARADICE SO THEY
ARE AFRAID OF DEATH  I AM NOT AFRAID BECAUSE I KNOW THAT MY NEW
LIFE IS DEATH LIFE WILL BE AN EASY ONE IN PARADICE
```

Unfortunately, the plaintext does not contain any information that directly suggests the identity of the Zodiac Killer. During the deciphering process, it became clear that the message was divided into three sections. This means that the codebreakers' hypothesis that the text was split up in a simple way proved correct. This is the kind of lucky guesswork one needs to break a difficult cipher!

Figure 6-8 shows the homophonic cipher table the Zodiac Killer used. As one would expect, the number of homophones available for each letter is roughly proportional to the letter's frequency. *E* and *T*, the most common letters in the English language, can be mapped to six different symbols, respectively.

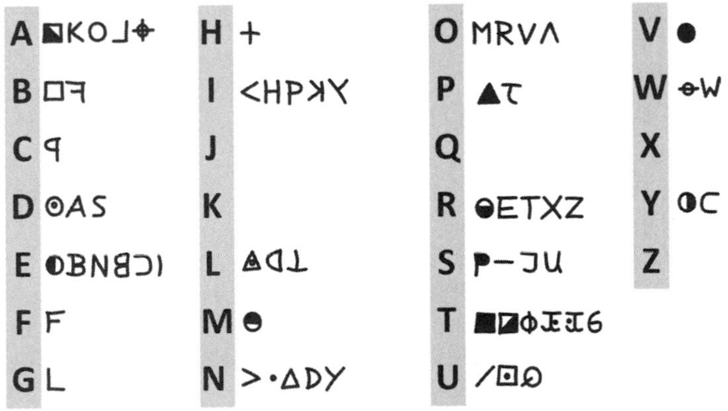

Figure 6-8: The substitution table used for Z340 represents a homophonic cipher.

The transposition cipher that Z340 is based on is explained in Figure 6-9. As can be seen, the message needs to be divided into two large sections (of nine lines each) and one small section (of two lines). To decrypt the two large sections, one starts in each section's upper-left-hand corner and works through the message with knight moves (two steps to the right, one step down). Once the right-hand edge of the section is reached, one repeats the pattern, starting with the second symbol in the first row. When all symbols in the upper-right-hand half of the block have been visited, the path continues in the lower-left-hand one. Note that in many cases, a leap of symbols (e.g., from the first symbol in the first line to the third symbol in the second line) is necessary, as suggested by "daikon" and Jarl.

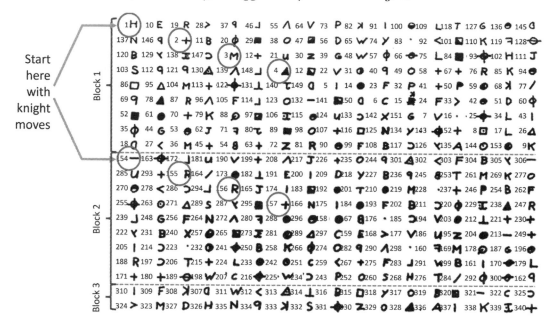

Figure 6-9: The transposition the Zodiac Killer used for the upper two blocks of Z340 is mainly based on knight moves (two steps to the right, one step down).

In the third section, no knight moves are used. Instead, the message is written from left to right and top to bottom, with some words written backward. It seems possible that, in addition, the expressions **LIFE IS**, **LIFE WILL**, and **DEATH** need to be shifted elsewhere. To date, several possible suggestions have been made.[14]

Did the Zodiac Killer want Z340 to be deciphered? The phrase **THAT WASN'T ME ON THE TV SHOW** suggests that he did because it contains information he probably wanted to be known relatively quickly. This leads to the question of whether the killer underestimated the difficulty of his cipher. Could we extrapolate that he had never tried to solve such a system? What types of ciphers had he tried to solve in the past that would lead him to think this cipher was solvable with the technology of the time?

It goes without saying that Dave, Jarl, and Sam did a tremendous job in combing through countless potential substitution tables and transposition patterns to identify the correct one. In our opinion, this proved to be one of the greatest nonmilitary codebreaking successes in generations!

Ferdinand III's letters

Ferdinand III (1608–57), a Holy Roman emperor from the House of Habsburg, played an important role in the Thirty Years' War, one of the most devastating wars in Europe. When researching his life, historians such as Leopold Auer from Vienna repeatedly encountered encrypted letters. The system Ferdinand III used was based on numbers and simple geometric symbols arranged in pairs. As can be seen in Figure 6-10, Ferdinand's letters were a mixture of encrypted and cleartext passages, but they remained unsolved by historians.

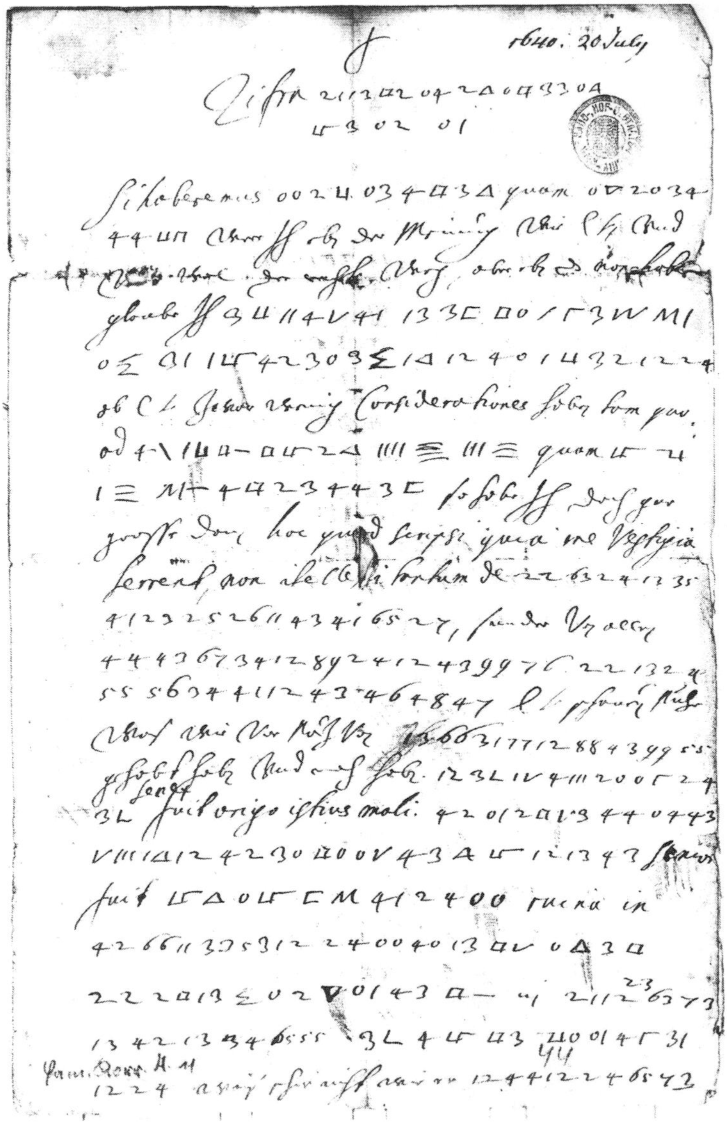

Figure 6-10: The first page of an encrypted letter written by Holy Roman Emperor Ferdinand III to his brother Leopold Wilhelm in 1640. German philologist and historian Thomas Ernst broke it.

Thomas Ernst, a German scientist who teaches in the United States, tried his luck on this mystery.[15] Ernst had already made a name for himself in the 1990s when he deciphered the third book of the *Steganographia* by Johannes Trithemius (1462–1516) (see Chapter 15).

Parts of Ferdinand's letter had already been transcribed: a mixture of the cleartext letters and words, combined with encrypted portions that were a jumble of numbers and symbols.

As a scholar of languages and a historian, Ernst could easily read the emperor's cleartext passages, which were a mixture of seventeenth-century German and Latin. On the remaining portions, Ernst tested several hypotheses. His central discovery was that each geometric symbol represented the number of lines or semicircles it consisted of. For example, a square, with its four sides, stood for the number 4, a triangle for the number 3, and so forth. Using these numbers, Ernst constructed the following transcript:

```
1640, 20 July /
Zifra 21 13 42 04 23 14 33 13 / 43 02 01
Si haberemus 00 23 03 44 33 quam 13 20 34 / 44 33 were Ich eben der
meinung wie E L vnd / were wol der rechte weg, aber eben das non
habere / glaube Ich 33 11 42 41 13 33 41 12 34 41 / 14 31 14 42 30
34 13 12 40 13 32 12 24 / ob E L zwar wenig Considerationes haben
tam quo: / ad 41 13 41 44 23 44 33 quam 44 / 13 41 44 23 44 33 / so
habe Ich doch gar grosse Dann hoc quod scripsi quia me Vestigia /
terrent, non intellexi tantum de 22 63 24 13 35 / 41 23 25 25 11 43
41 65 27, sunder von allen / 44 43 67 34 12 89 24 12 43 99 76 22 13
24 / 55 56 34 41 12 43 46 48 47 E L schauen nuhr / was wir vor nuz
von 13 66 31 77 12 88 43 99 55 / gehabt haben Vnd noch haben. 12 32
12 43 20 12 24 / 32 senex fuit origo istius mali. 42 01 24 23 44 04
43 / 23 13 12 42 30 41 12 43 34 12 13 43 / fuit 43 14 34 41 24 00
ruina in / 42 66 11 33 53 12 24 00 40 13 42 13 34 / 22 24 13 41 23
01 43 41 in 21 12 23 63 73 / 13 42 13 34 65 55 32 44 43 41 01 42 31
/ 12 24 wais schir nicht wie er 12 44 12 24 65 73
```

The second breakthrough occurred when he realized that the Habsburg motto "AEIOU" played a role in the cipher. One interpretation of the motto is "Austria erit in orbe ultima," which translates to "Austria will exist until the end of the world." From the "AEIOU" motto, Ernst derived the following mappings in Ferdinand's cipher:

```
A: 01, 11
E: 02, 12
I: 03, 13
O: 04, 14
```

When he looked at the sequence 21 13 42 04 23 04 33 03 43 02 01 at the beginning of the letter, he identified the following vowels: **I – O – O – I – E A**, where the dashes stood for missing consonants. The vowel pattern suggested an adjective that could only be **PICOLOMINEA**. Octavio Piccolomini, along with the emperor's brother Leopold Wilhelm, was the chief commander of the imperial army at the time. **PICOLOMINEA** was encrypted without the double **C. Zifra PICCOLOMINEA** meant an enciphered letter with Piccolomini as the name of the cipher.

Next, Ernst guessed that the missing word in **fuit** 43 04 34 41 24 00 **ruina** was **NOSTRA** (Latin for **OUR**). He could then derive the remaining letters easily, constructing the following substitution table:

A	B,W,P	C,K,Z	E	F	G	H	I/J	K	L	M	N	O	P	R	S	D,T	U/V	Z
00	20	42	02	22	32	30	03	30	23	33	43	04	21	24	34	40	44	10
01	21		12			31	13					14				41		
11																		

Here is the plaintext of the first part of the letter, according to Ernst's decryption:

```
Zifra PICOLOMINEA
Si haberemus ALIUM quam IPS
UM were Ich eben der Meinung wie E L Vnd
Were Wol der rehte Weg, aber eben das non habere
glaube Ich MAC<H>T IM DEST
O HOCHSIEDIGER
ob E L zwar wenig Considerationes haben tam quo:
ad TITULUM quam U
ITULUM so habe Ich doch gar
grosse Dann hoc quod scripsi quia me Vestigia
terrent, non intellexi tantum de FRI
DLANT, sunder Von allen
UNSEREN FIR
STEN E L schauen Nuhr
Was wir vor nuz von IH<N>EN
gehabt haben Vnd noch haben. EGENBER
G senex fuit origo istius mali. CARL UON
LIECHTENS<T>EIN senior
fuit NOSTRA ruina in
CAMERADICIS
FRIDLAND in BEL
ICIS<.> GUNDACK
[. . .]
```

It's written in a difficult-to-understand mixture of old German and Latin, including abbreviations and spelling errors. Here is a rough annotated translation that Ernst has provided:

```
Zifra picolominea
If we had someone else [for the position of commander-in-chief]
but him [field marshal Ottavio Piccolomini]
I would share your opinion,
and it would be the right way, but it is this not having
anyone else [no other viable choice for commander-in-chief] that
makes him [Piccolomini]
even more high-handed.
```

```
While you may have few reservations with regard
to another title [rewarding Piccolomini with an imperial
princicipality],
I have quite a few [reservations].
That which haunts me are not just what Fridland
. . .
```

A postcard from Hawaii

The cryptogram shown in Figure 6-11 was written on a postcard sent from Hawaii in 1886.[16] It was provided to us by the National Cryptologic Museum in Maryland and solved by our colleague Armin Krauß, a very skilled German codebreaker. Armin knew that most encrypted postcards are encoded in simple substitution ciphers—but usually ones that include spaces, which is not the case here. That means this is a Patristocrat cipher, not Aristocrat. So, Armin suspected that one of the symbols represented the space character. After some analysis, Armin realized that there were, in fact, two symbols representing spaces (i.e., homophones): T and its upside-down version. Next, he identified that the one-letter word that appeared four times in the text was **I**.

Armin then tried to identify **E**, the most frequent letter in the English language. However, none of the symbols appeared as frequently as one would expect if they stood for **E**, so he made another guess: perhaps two symbols stood for **E**. This hypothesis proved correct. Based on frequency analysis and some guessing, Armin saw that both X and the symbol that consists of three parallel horizontal lines stood for **E**. The rest of the decryption was routine. Here is the plaintext Armin recovered:

```
FEBRUARY TWENTY-EIGHTH.
THANKS FOR YOUR LETTER
WHICH I RECEIVED LAST W
EDNESDAY. I AM VERY GLAD
INDEED CHURCHILL HAS G
OT SOME WORK TO DO. YOU
R LETTER HAD SEVERAL
WISTAKES IN IT , BU
T I DARESAY MINE HA
S A NUMBER TOO. I SH
OT A BIG GOAT UP THE
MOUNTAIN YESTERDAY , W
EIGHING ABOUT ONE HUN
DRED AND TMENTY POUNDS.
DONT BEGIN YOUR LETT
ER "MY DEAR", BECAUSE
IF ANY ONE GOT HOLD OF
ONE, THEY MIGHT GUESS SOME
OF THE ALPHABET.
ALOHA OE.
```

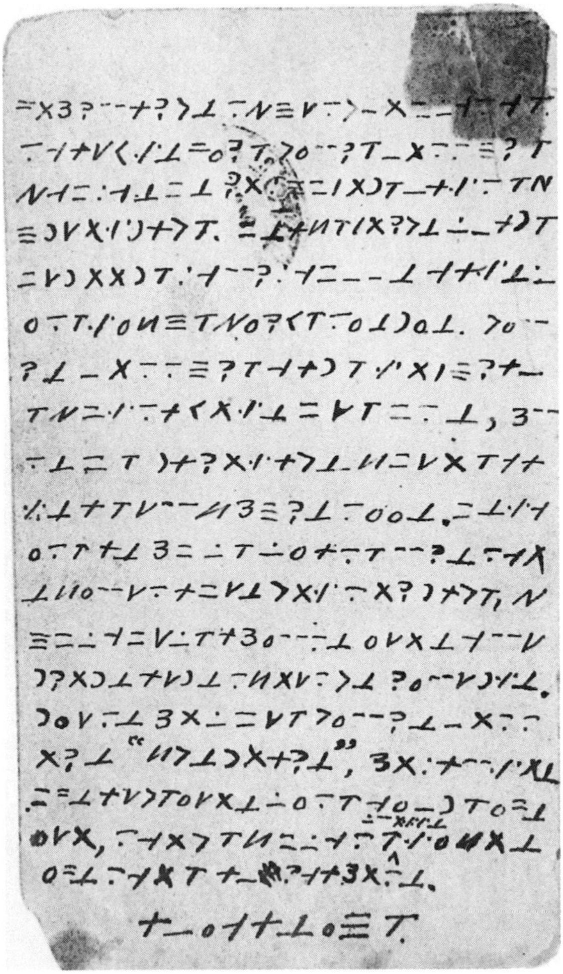

Figure 6-11: This 1886 postcard from Hawaii is encrypted with a letter substitution that includes homophones for the space character and *E*.

Challenges

A message to the Zodiac Killer

Earlier in this chapter, we introduced a Zodiac-style cipher message (see Figure 6-2) published by the police in California newspaper advertisements around the time of the Zodiac murders in the late 1960s. The message is encrypted with a simple homophonic cipher, and the plaintext contains a telephone number. Police hoped that the killer would succeed in deciphering the message and then call the number to demonstrate his superiority. The plan failed, but at least the cryptogram makes a nice cipher challenge. Can you solve it?

Edgar Allan Poe's second challenge

American author Edgar Allan Poe had a long fascination with cryptology. His 1843 short story "The Gold-Bug" is the most famous work of fiction that describes codebreaking. (The system broken in the story is a simple substitution cipher.) A few years earlier, in 1839, when Poe wrote for *Alexander's Weekly Messenger*, he initiated a cryptography contest that challenged his readers to send him ciphertexts to break.[17] As a result, his readers sent him simple substitution ciphertexts, which, as we know now, are fairly simple to solve. He made a similar call in 1841 in *Graham's Magazine*, for which he received about a hundred cryptograms that he allegedly solved. To conclude the *Messenger* contest around 1840, he published two ciphertexts (supposedly submitted by a W.B. Tyler) that remained unsolved for over 150 years.

In 1985, Louis Renza, professor of English at Dartmouth College, proposed that this W.B. Tyler had never existed and that Poe had created the messages himself. Renza's writings brought the two challenge ciphertexts to new public attention, and in the 1990s, the first of these messages was solved independently by Terence Whalen and John Hodgson (see Chapter 9).

The second ciphertext is depicted in Figure 6-12. In 2000, Canadian software engineer Gil Broza found the correct decryption, and it turned out that a homophonic cipher had been used.[18] As you can guess from the fact that it took 160 years for the ciphertext to be solved, this cryptogram is not necessarily a beginner's challenge!

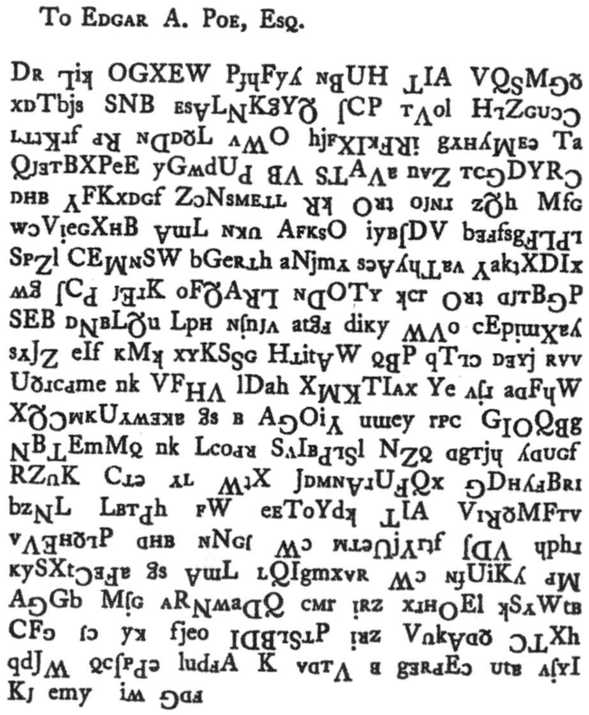

Figure 6-12: This homophonic cryptogram left behind by Edgar Allan Poe was solved 160 years after its creation.

For a transcript of this challenge and some hints, check out *http://codebreaking-guide.com/challenges/*.

Unsolved cryptograms

Beale Papers #1 and #3

As discussed earlier in this chapter, a nineteenth-century Virginian adventurer named Thomas Beale allegedly described a treasure and its location in three encrypted notes. This story is likely mere fiction, but the encrypted notes are worth studying. While the second message has been broken, the two other cryptograms have yet to be deciphered. Beale Paper #1 reportedly contains the location of the treasure, while #3 contains the names and residences of Beale's associates and their families.

Here is Beale Paper #1, "The Locality of the Vault":

71, 194, 38, 1701, 89, 76, 11, 83, 1629, 48, 94, 63, 132, 16, 111, 95, 84, 341, 975, 14, 40, 64, 27, 81, 139, 213, 63, 90, 1120, 8, 15, 3, 126, 2018, 40, 74, 758, 485, 604, 230, 436, 664, 582, 150, 251, 284, 308, 231, 124, 211, 486, 225, 401, 370, 11, 101, 305, 139, 189, 17, 33, 88, 208, 193, 145, 1, 94, 73, 416, 918, 263, 28, 500, 538, 356, 117, 136, 219, 27, 176, 130, 10, 460, 25, 485, 18, 436, 65, 84, 200, 283, 118, 320, 138, 36, 416, 280, 15, 71, 224, 961, 44, 16, 401, 39, 88, 61, 304, 12, 21, 24, 283, 134, 92, 63, 246, 486, 682, 7, 219, 184, 360, 780, 18, 64, 463, 474, 131, 160, 79, 73, 440, 95, 18, 64, 581, 34, 69, 128, 367, 460, 17, 81, 12, 103, 820, 62, 116, 97, 103, 862, 70, 60, 1317, 471, 540, 208, 121, 890, 346, 36, 150, 59, 568, 614, 13, 120, 63, 219, 812, 2160, 1780, 99, 35, 18, 21, 136, 872, 15, 28, 170, 88, 4, 30, 44, 112, 18, 147, 436, 195, 320, 37, 122, 113, 6, 140, 8, 120, 305, 42, 58, 461, 44, 106, 301, 13, 408, 680, 93, 86, 116, 530, 82, 568, 9, 102, 38, 416, 89, 71, 216, 728, 965, 818, 2, 38, 121, 195, 14, 326, 148, 234, 18, 55, 131, 234, 361, 824, 5, 81, 623, 48, 961, 19, 26, 33, 10, 1101, 365, 92, 88, 181, 275, 346, 201, 206, 86, 36, 219, 324, 829, 840, 64, 326, 19, 48, 122, 85, 216, 284, 919, 861, 326, 985, 233, 64, 68, 232, 431, 960, 50, 29, 81, 216, 321, 603, 14, 612, 81, 360, 36, 51, 62, 194, 78, 60, 200, 314, 676, 112, 4, 28, 18, 61, 136, 247, 819, 921, 1060, 464, 895, 10, 6, 66, 119, 38, 41, 49, 602, 423, 962, 302, 294, 875, 78, 14, 23, 111, 109, 62, 31, 501, 823, 216, 280, 34, 24, 150, 1000, 162, 286, 19, 21, 17, 340, 19, 242, 31, 86, 234, 140, 607, 115, 33, 191, 67, 104, 86, 52, 88, 16, 80, 121, 67, 95, 122, 216, 548, 96, 11, 201, 77, 364, 218, 65, 667, 890, 236, 154, 211, 10, 98, 34, 119, 56,216, 119, 71, 218, 1164, 1496, 1817, 51, 39, 210, 36, 3, 19, 540, 232, 22, 141, 617, 84, 290, 80, 46, 207, 411, 150, 29, 38, 46, 172, 85, 194, 39, 261, 543, 897, 624, 18, 212, 416, 127, 931, 19, 4, 63, 96, 12, 101, 418, 16, 140, 230, 460, 538, 19, 27, 88, 612, 1431, 90, 716, 275, 74, 83, 11, 426, 89, 72, 84, 1300, 1706, 814, 221, 132, 40, 102, 34, 868, 975, 1101,

84, 16, 79, 23, 16, 81, 122, 324, 403, 912, 227, 936, 447, 55, 86, 34, 43, 212, 107, 96, 314, 264, 1065, 323, 428, 601, 203, 124, 95, 216,814, 2906, 654, 820, 2, 301, 112, 176, 213, 71, 87, 96, 202, 35, 10, 2, 41, 17, 84, 221, 736, 820, 214, 11, 60, 760.

And here is Beale Paper #3, "Names and Residences":

317, 8, 92, 73, 112, 89, 67, 318, 28, 96, 107, 41, 631, 78, 146, 397, 118, 98, 114, 246, 348, 116, 74, 88, 12, 65, 32, 14, 81, 19, 76, 121, 216, 85, 33, 66, 15, 108, 68, 77, 43, 24, 122, 96, 117, 36, 211, 301, 15, 44, 11, 46, 89, 18, 136, 68, 317, 28, 90, 82, 304, 71, 43, 221, 198, 176, 310, 319, 81, 99, 264, 380, 56, 37, 319, 2, 44, 53, 28, 44, 75, 98, 102, 37, 85, 107, 117, 64, 88, 136, 48, 154, 99, 175, 89, 315, 326,78, 96, 214, 218, 311, 43, 89, 51, 90, 75, 128, 96, 33, 28, 103, 84, 65, 26, 41, 246, 84, 270, 98, 116, 32, 59, 74, 66, 69, 240, 15, 8, 121, 20, 77, 89, 31, 11, 106, 81, 191, 224, 328, 18, 75, 52, 82, 117, 201, 39, 23, 217, 27, 21, 84, 35, 54, 109, 128, 49, 77, 88, 1, 81, 217, 64, 55, 83, 116, 251, 269, 311, 96, 54, 32, 120, 18, 132, 102, 219, 211, 84, 150, 219, 275, 312, 64, 10, 106, 87, 75, 47, 21, 29, 37, 81, 44, 18, 126, 115, 132, 160, 181, 203, 76, 81, 299, 314, 337, 351, 96, 11, 28, 97, 318, 238, 106, 24, 93, 3, 19, 17, 26, 60, 73, 88, 14, 126, 138, 234, 286, 297, 321, 365, 264, 19, 22, 84, 56, 107, 98, 123, 111, 214, 136, 7, 33, 45, 40, 13, 28, 46, 42, 107, 196, 227, 344, 198, 203, 247, 116, 19, 8, 212, 230, 31, 6, 328, 65, 48, 52, 59, 41, 122, 33, 117, 11, 18, 25, 71, 36, 45, 83, 76, 89, 92, 31, 65, 70, 83, 96, 27, 33, 44, 50, 61,24, 112, 136, 149, 176, 180, 194, 143, 171, 205, 296, 87, 12, 44, 51, 89, 98, 34, 41, 208, 173, 66, 9, 35, 16, 95, 8, 113, 175, 90, 56, 203, 19, 177, 183, 206, 157, 200, 218, 260, 291, 305, 618, 951, 320, 18, 124, 78, 65, 19, 32, 124, 48, 53, 57, 84, 96, 207, 244, 66, 82, 119, 71, 11, 86, 77, 213, 54, 82, 316, 245, 303, 86, 97, 106, 212, 18, 37, 15, 81, 89, 16, 7, 81, 39, 96, 14, 43, 216, 118, 29, 55, 109, 136, 172, 213,64, 8, 227, 304, 611, 221, 364, 819, 375, 128, 296, 1, 18, 53, 76, 10, 15, 23, 19, 71, 84, 120, 134, 66, 73, 89, 96, 230, 48, 77, 26, 101, 127, 936, 218, 439, 178, 171, 61, 226, 313, 215, 102, 18, 167, 262, 114, 218, 66, 59, 48, 27, 19, 13, 82, 48, 162, 119, 34, 127, 139, 34, 128, 129, 74, 63, 120, 11, 54, 61, 73, 92, 180, 66, 75, 101, 124, 265, 89, 96, 126, 274, 896, 917, 434, 461, 235, 890, 312, 413, 328, 381, 96, 105, 217, 66, 118, 22, 77, 64, 42, 12, 7, 55, 24, 83, 67, 97, 109, 121, 135, 181, 203, 219, 228, 256, 21, 34, 77, 319, 374, 382, 675, 684, 717, 864, 203, 4, 18, 92, 16, 63, 82, 22, 46, 55, 69, 74, 112, 134, 186, 175, 119, 213, 416, 312, 343, 264, 119, 186, 218, 343, 417, 845, 951, 124, 209, 49, 617, 856, 924, 936, 72, 19, 28, 11, 35, 42, 40, 66, 85, 94, 112, 65, 82, 115, 119, 236, 244, 186, 172, 112, 85, 6, 56, 38, 44, 85, 72, 32, 47, 73, 96, 124, 217, 314, 319, 221, 644, 817, 821, 934, 922, 416, 975, 10, 22,18, 46, 137, 181, 101, 39, 86, 103, 116, 138, 164, 212, 218, 296, 815, 380, 412, 460, 495, 675, 820, 952.

If you find the treasure, please let us know.

The Zodiac Killer's third message (Z13)

On April 20, 1970, the Zodiac Killer sent his third cryptogram (today called Z13) to a newspaper. It consists of only thirteen letters.

Allegedly, this short ciphertext contains the name of the killer. It is unsolved.

The Zodiac Killer's fourth message (Z32)

The fourth and last message from the Zodiac Killer (Z32) consists of thirty-two letters and was sent on June 26, 1970. Along with Z32, the killer sent a map of the San Francisco area and the following cleartext words: The map coupled with this code will tell you where the bomb is set.[19]

The solution is unknown.

The Scorpion cryptograms

In the 1990s, John Walsh, best known as the host of *America's Most Wanted*, received a series of letters signed SCORPION.[20] Some of these messages contained encrypted messages and are usually referred to as the Scorpion cryptograms.[21] Only two of these ciphertexts and a few pages of unencrypted text have so far been released. Figure 6-13 shows one of the publicly circulated ciphertexts.

As can be seen, the sender of this note imitated the Zodiac Killer. The solution to the Scorpion cryptograms is unknown.

Figure 6-13: The Scorpion cryptograms (of which this is only an excerpt) were created by a Zodiac Killer copycat.

Henry Debosnys's messages

In 1882, a man named Henry Debosnys (1836–1883) settled in Essex County, New York.[22] He soon started courting a widow named Elizabeth Wells, and after only a few weeks, the two married. A few months later, Elizabeth was found murdered, and Debosnys was arrested as the alleged perpetrator. It became clear that two earlier wives of Debosnys had also died at a young age under similarly strange circumstances. While in prison, Debosnys, who was a knowledgeable and well-educated man, created drawings, wrote poems, and also authored a few texts that appear to be encrypted (see Figure 6-14). In 1883, he was condemned to death and subsequently hanged. The Adirondack History Museum in Elizabethtown, New York, has many interesting exhibits about the execution, as well as the actual ciphers created by Debosnys.

The story of Henry Debosnys has been best documented by Cheri Farnsworth in her 2010 book *Adirondack Enigma*.[23] There are many open questions about this case, including more reliable information about the deaths of his two earlier wives.

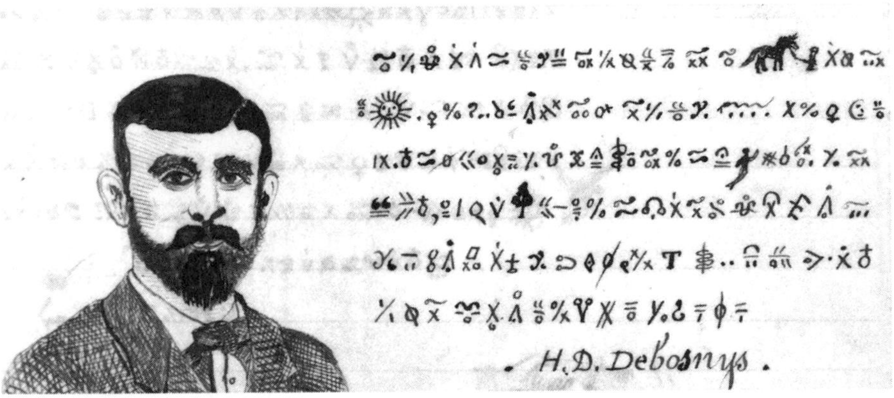

Figure 6-14: The cryptograms of condemned wife-murderer Henry Debosnys have never been solved.

The four known cryptograms Debosnys left behind might shed light on these questions, but they have never been deciphered. Debosnys, an accomplished artist, used a large set of pictogram-style symbols to encode his messages, which suggests the application of a homophonic cipher. Although the Debosnys cryptograms are a spectacular crypto mystery, they have not received much attention in the international codebreaking community so far. Perhaps you, dear reader, might be able to solve them!

7

CODES AND NOMENCLATORS

The 1917 Zimmermann Telegram (Figure 7-1), whose solving changed the course of World War I, was a secret diplomatic note sent by the German secretary of state, Arthur Zimmermann, to Mexico in January 1917. It proposed a military alliance between Germany and Mexico in the event that the United States entered the war against the Germans.[1] The telegram was surreptitiously intercepted in England and forwarded to British cryptanalysts, who succeeded in breaking it. Revelation of the contents enraged Americans and helped generate support within the United States (which had thus far been neutral) for declaring war on Germany.

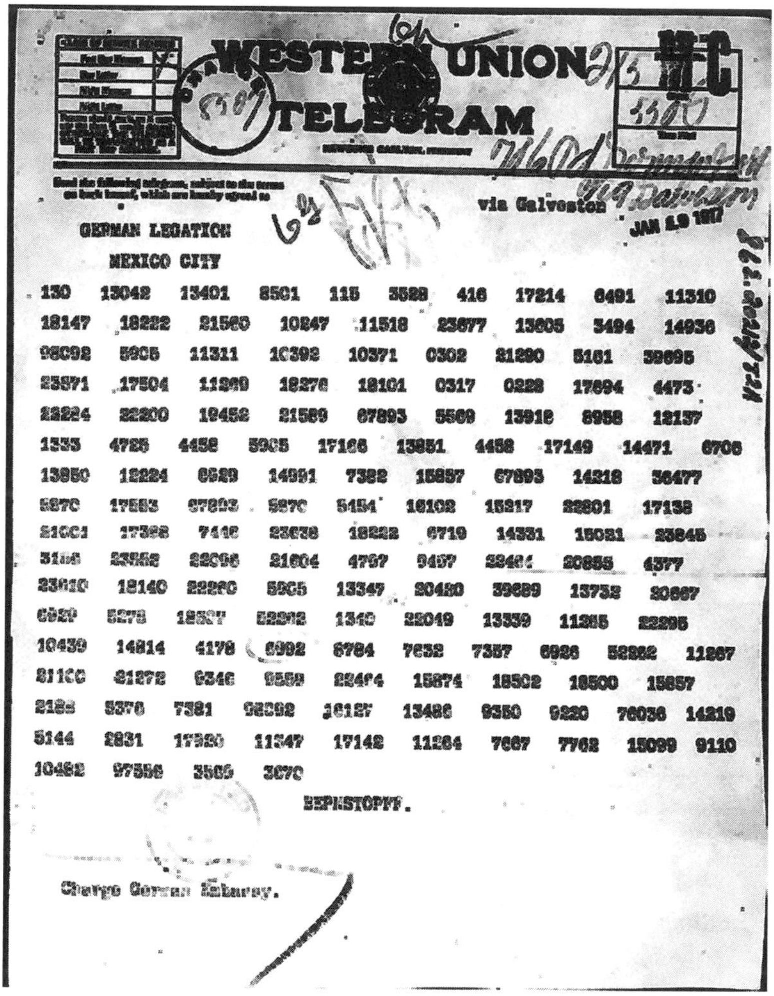

WESTERN UNION TELEGRAM

via Galveston

JAN 19 1917

GERMAN LEGATION

MEXICO CITY

130 13042 13401 8501 115 3528 416 17214 6491 11310
18147 18222 21560 10247 11518 23677 13605 3494 14936
98092 5905 11311 10392 10371 0302 21290 5161 39695
23571 17504 11269 18276 18101 0317 0228 17694 4473
22284 22200 19452 21589 67893 5569 13918 8958 12137
1333 4725 4458 5905 17166 13851 4458 17149 14471 6706
13850 12224 6929 14991 7382 15857 67893 14218 36477
5870 17553 67893 5870 5454 16102 15217 22801 17138
21001 17388 7446 23638 18222 6719 14331 15021 23845
3156 23552 22096 21604 4797 9497 22464 20855 4377
23610 18140 22260 5905 13347 20420 39689 13732 20667
6929 5275 18507 52262 1340 22049 13339 11265 22295
10439 14814 4178 6992 8784 7632 7357 6926 52262 11267
21100 21272 9346 9559 22464 15874 18502 18500 15857
2188 5376 7381 98092 16127 13486 9350 9220 76036 14219
5144 2831 17920 11347 17142 11264 7667 7762 15099 9110
10482 97556 3569 3670

BERNSTORFF.

Charge German Embassy.

Figure 7-1: The Zimmermann Telegram, a secret diplomatic note sent by the German secretary of state in 1917, is encrypted in a code.

As can be seen, the text of the Zimmermann Telegram consists of numbers, most of which have five digits. Each number stands for a word. For instance, 4458 means **`zusammen`** (**`together`**), 13850 stands for **`finanziell`** (**financial**), and 36477 represents **Texas**. To encrypt the message, the Germans used a kind of dictionary with thousands of entries for every common word of their language. Decrypted and translated, the Zimmermann Telegram reads as follows:

```
On the first of February we intend to begin submarine warfare
unrestricted. In spite of this, it is our intention to endeavor to
keep neutral the United States of America.

If this attempt is not successful, we propose an alliance on the
following basis with Mexico: that we shall make war together and
together make peace. We shall give general financial support, and
it is understood that Mexico is to reconquer the lost territory in
New Mexico, Texas, and Arizona. The details are left to you for
settlement . . .

You are instructed to inform the President of Mexico of the above
in the greatest confidence as soon as it is certain that there
will be an outbreak of war with the United States and suggest that
the President of Mexico, on his own initiative, should communicate
with Japan suggesting adherence at once to this plan; at the same
time, offer to mediate between Germany and Japan.

Please call to the attention of the President of Mexico that the
employment of ruthless submarine warfare now promises to compel
England to make peace in a few months.

Zimmermann (Secretary of State)
```

Codes

An encryption method that replaces entire words or phrases with single numbers, letter groups, or symbols is referred to as a *code*. Codes were especially popular in the days of telegraphy, when—as will be pointed out below—many were used not only for secrecy but also for shortening messages.

In the case of the Zimmermann Telegram, secrecy, not condensing a message, was the main goal. The Germans introduced the system used, named Code 13040, in 1916. It was partially based on earlier codes already known to the British cryptanalysts. By analyzing dozens of telegrams in Code 13040, codebreakers in London could improve their knowledge of it, and in early 1917, when they were ordered to decipher the Zimmermann Telegram, they were well prepared. They could immediately solve parts of the message and later broke it completely.

Most encryption methods described in this book are not technically codes, but *ciphers*, because they work on single letters, not on words. Simple substitution ciphers such as the Caesar cipher (or ROT-13), the polyalphabetic Vigenère system, and the digraph-swapping Playfair methodology are all ciphers. The systems used for the Zimmermann Telegram, a dictionary code (see Chapter 14), and Navajo code talking (see Chapter 15) are all codes. To say it in a different way: a code is an encryption method that typically operates at the level of words or phrases, while a cipher generally encrypts messages at the level of individual letters.

We must briefly touch on some additional terminology. A *codegroup* is a number, letter group, or symbol that represents a word in a code. Any code designed for encrypting arbitrary texts needs to provide a codegroup for every single common word of a language. This could mean thousands of entries and is why writing a code usually requires creating a whole book, called a *codebook*. A code, as defined here, can therefore also be called a *codebook code*. Figures 7-2 and 7-3 show pages from codebooks printed in 1911 and 1892.[2, 3]

While some codes were used for all kinds of messages, others provided special-purpose vocabulary for use in telegrams. Among others, there were timber, cotton, railway, machinery, and chess codes. Some companies created codes based on their sales catalogs, with codegroups for every product. Stockbroker codes provided codegroups for words such as **sell** and **buy**, as well as company names and numbers. Codes of this kind allowed for telegraphy-based trading, the forerunner of today's online trading.

A distinction needs to be made between one-part and two-part codes. In a *one-part code*, the plaintext units and the codegroups are assigned according to some order (such as the alphabetical sorting in **A** = 1, **AM** = 2, **AND** = 3, **ARMY** = 4, **AT** = 5, **AUSTRIA** = 6 . . .). In a *two-part code*, no such sorting is possible (such as in **A** = 1523, **AM** = 912, **AND** = 2303, **ARMY** = 809, **AT** = 1825, **AUSTRIA** = 145 . . .). Code 13040, the one used in the Zimmermann Telegram, is a two-part code.

A two-part code usually requires two substitution tables—one sorted by words and letters (for encryption) and another sorted by codegroups (for decryption). Decrypting a two-part code message without access to a table sorted by codegroups is laborious unless the code is very short. Likewise, Code 13040, which filled a whole book, would have been effectively unusable with a table sorted by codegroups only. Decryption would have been easy, but encryption would have been extremely time-consuming due to the difficulty of finding the words that needed to be encrypted.

The additional substitution table makes a two-part code more cumbersome to design than a one-part code. On the other hand, a two-part code is much more secure because a cryptanalyst can't take advantage of the relationships between related code expressions and codegroups. For instance, if a codebreaker dealing with a one-part code knows that 1 stands for **A** and 3 stands for **AND**, they can guess that 2 represents a word located in the codebook between **A** and **AND**: for instance, **AM**. We will come back to this weakness later.

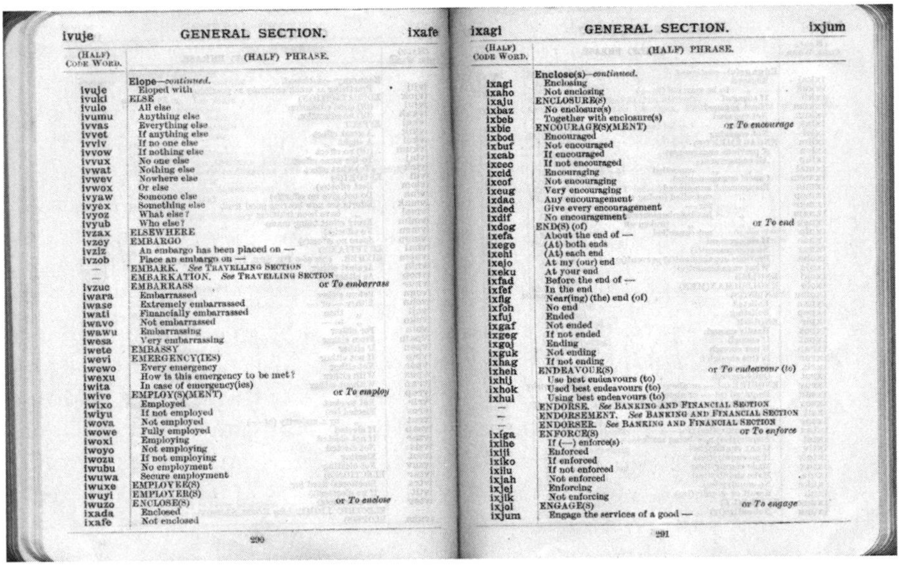

(HALF) CODE WORD	(HALF) PHRASE
	Elope—continued.
ivuje	Eloped with
ivuki	ELSE
ivulo	All else
ivumu	Anything else
ivvas	Everything else
ivvet	If anything else
ivviv	If no one else
ivvow	If nothing else
ivvux	No one else
ivvwat	Nothing else
ivvwv	Nowhere else
ivvwox	Or else
ivyaw	Someone else
ivyex	Something else
ivyoz	What else?
ivyub	Who else?
ivzax	ELSEWHERE
ivzoy	EMBARGO
—	An embargo has been placed on —
—	Place an embargo on —
—	EMBARK. See TRAVELLING SECTION
—	EMBARKATION. See TRAVELLING SECTION
ivzuc	EMBARRASS or To embarrass
iwara	Embarrassed
iwase	Extremely embarrassed
iwati	Financially embarrassed
iwavo	Not embarrassed
iwawu	Embarrassing
iwesa	Very embarrassing
iweto	EMBASSY
iwevi	EMERGENCY(IES)
iwewo	Every emergency
iwexu	How is this emergency to be met?
iwtta	In case of emergency(ies)
iwive	EMPLOY(S)(MENT) or To employ
iwixo	Employed
iwiyu	If not employed
iwova	Not employed
iwowe	Fully employed
iwoxi	Employing
iwoyo	Not employing
iwozu	If not employing
iwubu	No employment
iwuwa	Secure employment
iwuxe	EMPLOYEE(S)
iwuyi	EMPLOYER(S)
iwuzo	ENCLOSE(S) or To enclose
ixada	Enclosed
ixafe	Not enclosed

290

(HALF) CODE WORD	(HALF) PHRASE
	Enclose(s)—continued.
ixagi	Enclosing
ixaho	Not enclosing
ixaju	ENCLOSURE(S)
ixbaz	No enclosure(s)
ixbeb	Together with enclosure(s)
ixbie	ENCOURAG(ES)(MENT) or To encourage
ixbod	Encouraged
ixbuf	Not encouraged
ixeab	If encouraged
ixeec	If not encouraged
ixeid	Encouraging
ixeof	Not encouraging
ixeug	Very encouraging
ixdac	Any encouragement
ixded	Give every encouragement
ixdif	No encouragement
ixdog	END(S) (of) or To end
ixefa	About the end of —
ixego	(At) both ends
ixehi	(At) each end
ixejo	At my (our) end
ixeku	At your end
ixfad	Before the end of —
ixfef	In the end
ixfig	Near(ing) (the) end (of)
ixfoh	No end
ixfuj	Ended
ixgaf	Not ended
ixgeg	Ending
ixgoj	If not ended
ixguk	Not ending
ixhag	If not ending
ixheh	ENDEAVOUR(S) or To endeavour (to)
ixhlj	Use best endeavours (to)
ixhok	Used best endeavours (to)
ixhul	Using best endeavours (to)
—	ENDORSE. See BANKING AND FINANCIAL SECTION
—	ENDORSEMENT. See BANKING AND FINANCIAL SECTION
—	ENDORSER. See BANKING AND FINANCIAL SECTION
ixiga	ENFORCE(S) or To enforce
ixihe	If (—) enforce(s)
ixiji	Enforced
ixiko	If enforced
ixilu	If not enforced
ixjah	Not enforced
ixjel	Enforcing
ixjik	Not enforcing
ixjol	ENGAGE(S) or To engage
ixjum	Engage the services of a good —

291

Figure 7-2: A page from a 1911 codebook, which shows how words and phrases are replaced. In this case, the codegroups consist of five letters.

No.	CIPHER.	DEFINITION.
1795	earth.	deprived.
1796	easter.	depriving.
1797	easy.	describe-s.
1798	eatable.	described.
1799	eating.	describing.
1800	ebbing.	description.
1801	ebony.	desert-s.
1802	eclipse.	deserted.
1803	economist.	deserting.
1804	economy.	design-s.
1805	edgar.	deserve-s.
1806	edible.	deserved.
1807	edifice.	deserving.
1808	edify.	desirable.
1809	edifying.	desire-s.
1810	edited.	desired.
1811	editing.	desiring.
1812	edition.	desirous.
1813	edmund.	despatch.
1814	educate.	desperate-ly.
1815	educating.	desperation.
1816	education.	despise-d-s.
1817	edward.	destination.
1818	edwin.	destined.
1819	efface.	destroy-s.
1820	effacing.	destroyed.
1821	effective.	destroying.
1822	effectual.	destruction.
1823	efficient.	detach.
1824	effigy.	detached.
1825	effort.	detaching.
1826	effulgent.	detail-s.
1827	effusive.	detain-s.
1828	egotism.	detained.
1829	egregious.	detaining.
1830	elaborate.	detect-s.
1831	elapse.	detected.
1832	elastic.	detecting.
1833	elated.	detection.
1834	elation.	detective.

61

Figure 7-3: This 1892 work, Sheahan's Telegraphic Cipher Code, lists numbers and meaningful words as codegroups for every plaintext word.

Nomenclators

Now let's look at a system that constitutes a sort of hybrid between two systems: the *nomenclator*. This system includes both a code, as in numbers representing different words; and a cipher, with numbers or other symbols representing letters or letter combinations. The term itself is derived from the fact that these often consisted of a collection of names. At large events, there would be a person, called a nomenclator, who would announce the names of arrivals. The word *nomen* means "name" in Latin—specifically, a person's second name, which designated their clan.

No exact border can be drawn between a code and a nomenclator. Most would consider any codebook with 50,000 entries to be a code, even if it contains codegroups for the letters of the alphabet. (Most codebooks do, as it is impossible to list all words and names a potential user might want to encrypt.) Most authors use the term *code* if an encryption table contains at least a few thousand words or phrases. If it contains fewer, the table is usually referred to as a nomenclator.

Nomenclator encryption systems were most commonly used between the fourteenth and nineteenth centuries. For example, Figure 7-4 shows an excerpt from a letter written by a William Perwich in 1670.[4, 5] It starts with some fifteen words in cleartext (**But now whilst all the world was in . . .**), followed by several lines of numbers beginning with 76 and interrupted by a few more plaintext words.

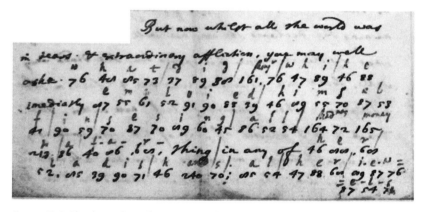

Figure 7-4: This letter from the seventeenth century is partially encrypted with a nomenclator.

We are dealing here with a message that is partially encrypted. An unknown person (hopefully the recipient!) wrote the plaintext equivalent above each number. The message reads as follows (bold has been removed from the parts that were originally encrypted):

```
But now whilst all the world was
in tears & extraordinary affliction, you may well
aske what did Monsieur whi he
imediatly emploied himsel
f in sesing all Madame's money
```

to a far**thing in any of** her
ladis hands al her Jewels

While most of the numbers (codegroups) in this message stand for letters, like in a cipher, some replace complete words, like in a code. For instance, 76 stands for **W**, 23 for **T**, and 47 for **H**. On the other hand, 161 is the equivalent of **Monsieur**, 164 of **Madame**, 165 of **money**, and 240 of **and**.

The following is a very simple example of a nomenclator:

A = 1, **B** = 2, **C** = 3, . . . **Z** = 26

London = 27, **Paris** = 28; **Rome** = 29; **today** = 30; **tomorrow** = 31

Using this nomenclator, the plaintext **WILL TRAVEL FROM LONDON TO PARIS TOMORROW** encrypts to 23 9 12 12 / 20 18 1 21 5 12 / 6 18 15 13 / 27 / 20 15 / 28 / 31.

Now lost, the nomenclator used for encrypting the Perwich letter probably included a few dozen words. Apart from **Monsieur**, **Madame**, **money**, and **and**, it might have contained names and places. The sender of a message could have then encrypted the most commonly used words of the English language with a single number while enciphering less common expressions letter by letter with one number each.

Figure 7-5 shows a nomenclator used by Italian scientist and military officer Luigi Marsigli (1658–1730). He began using it in 1691, while in service to the Holy Roman emperor.[6] As can be seen, this nomenclator provides three numbers to choose from (homophones) for every letter of the alphabet. In addition, there are two homophones for many common letter pairs. Finally, there is a group of 130 words, each of which has a codegroup of its own.

Figure 7-5: This nomenclator used by an Italian scientist in the late seventeenth century contains some 130 words.

Just as there are one-part and two-part codes, there are also one-part and two-part nomenclators. In a *one-part nomenclator*, the codegroups and the letters, words, or phrases they represent are assigned according to some system; but in a *two-part nomenclator*, this is not the case. The seventeenth-century nomenclator shown above is a mixture of the two variants. While the letter codegroups are unsorted, the word codegroups are assigned in alphabetical order: `Ablegat` = 216, `Adrianopol` = 217, `Agri` = 219, `Allianz` = 220, etc.

One-part codes and nomenclators are more common than their two-part equivalents. This is because sorted codegroups make a code or nomenclator easier to design and more convenient to use. On the other hand, one-part schemes are less secure. As soon as a codebreaker knows, say, that 4523 stands for `Washington`, they can be sure that 4524 represents another word starting with a `W`. Similarly, once they realize that `A` = 44, `B` = 45, and `C` = 46, all the other letters become easy to guess, as well.

Terminology

Nomenclators and codes are an active field of inquiry. Many interesting papers have been published in recent years in the journal *Cryptologia*, in the proceedings of the HistoCrypt symposium,[7, 8] and in other conference proceedings.[9, 10]

At the HistoCrypt 2018 conference, which took place in Uppsala, Sweden, with some fifty crypto-historians, Dutch crypto history expert Karl de Leeuw initiated a workshop about codes and nomenclators.[11] One of the goals of this session was to establish a consistent terminology, as different terms are sometimes used for the same thing. For example, "nulls" are also named "non-valeurs" or "blenders." The terminology developed in this workshop has been documented online.[12]

The history of codes and nomenclators

Nomenclators emerged centuries before codes were invented. The oldest known one was used in the fourteenth century at the Vatican.[13] They were probably introduced by cipher clerks, who extended simple substitution ciphers or simple homophonic ciphers by adding a number of symbols for common words to save encryption and decryption time. Later, encryption specialists created nomenclators systematically.

Nomenclators soon became very popular.[14] If you encounter an encrypted document written before 1800, the chances are very high that it was encrypted with a nomenclator. Crypto history experts who do research in archives, such as Anne-Simone Rous, Karl de Leeuw, Beáta Megyesi, and Paolo Bonavoglia, encounter this type of encrypted message quite often. There may be tens of thousands of these documents in European archives, consisting mainly of messages sent by aristocrats, diplomats, and soldiers. Only a small fraction of these encrypted documents has ever been published for a larger audience. Figure 7-6 shows an example of a message sent by James Madison, one of the Founders and eventually president of the United States, in the eighteenth century.[15]

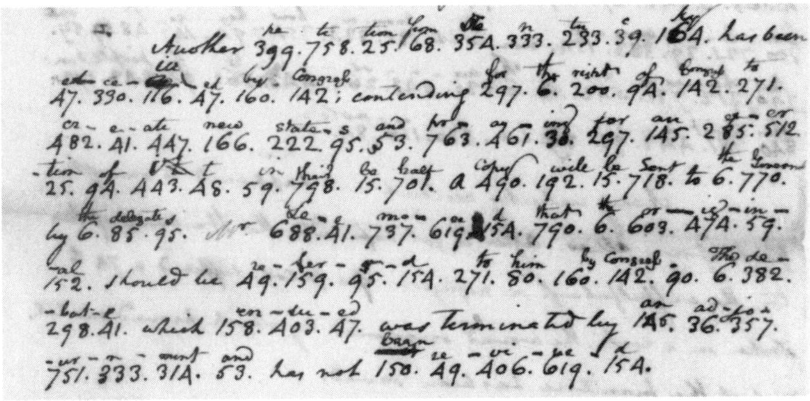

Figure 7-6: This 1782 letter from James Madison shows a nomenclator message with a mixture of encrypted letters and words.

Figure 7-7 provides another example. In 2021, while doing research on documents in the British Library, we came across this nomenclator-encrypted message from King Charles I of England in a letter he wrote on August 1, 1648, to his son.[16, 17]

Figure 7-7: This 1648 letter by King Charles I used a nomenclator cipher, alternating between cleartext and ciphertext.

The first nomenclators, generated in the Middle Ages, tended to have only a few dozen codegroups that stood for words. The others stood for letters.[18] Over the centuries, larger and larger nomenclator tables were constructed. Many of these included *homophones* (different codegroups standing for the same plaintext item), *nulls* (codegroups without a meaning) and *nullifiers* (codegroups making other, nearby codegroups meaningless). In addition to letters and words, letter pairs, syllables, and common phrases entered nomenclators.

The nomenclator table shown in Figure 7-8 is a simple one.[19] As can be seen, it contains two or three homophones for every letter (for instance, 2, 12, and 22 for **E**). The number 8 is used as a null (seen in the last line as a "chiffre non-valeur," or "symbol without value"). In addition, it provides some thirty-five codegroups standing for words. This nomenclator is two-part, as the codegroups are not sorted.

Buchstaben		Nomenclator			
a	01, 03, 05	S. Stä, N. Sre	90	avviso	97
b	07, 09	imperatore	70	havere	25
c	02, 04	re Catholico	50	havendo	35
d	06, 0i	cardinale Lorena	23	essere	45
e	2, 12, 22	concilio	30	essendo	55
f	32, 42	Trento	20	quì	73
g	52, 62	Germania	10	questo	93
i	6, 16, 26	Francia	11	quello	15
l	36, 46	Spagna	21	che	65
m	56, 66	vescovo	71	per	75
n	76, 96	monsignore	91	quà	53
o	4, 14, 24	duca	61	que	63
p	34, 44	V. Srìa Illma	37	come	95
r	54, 64	S. Srìa Illma	47	non	39
s	74, 94	legati	57	quando	17
t	72, 92	negocio	19	et	04
u	05, 07, 09	risposta	29	con	
z	02	corriere	59		
Chiffre non-valeur					8

Figure 7-8: A nineteenth-century reprint of a nomenclator used by the Vatican in the sixteenth century

The eighteenth-century nomenclator depicted in Figure 7-9 is one-part, as the entries are partially sorted.[20] For instance, the first half of the alphabet is assigned to the following numbers: A = 44, B = 45, C = 46, D = 47 . . . The second half is N = 33, O = 34, P = 35, Q = 36 . . . The words are sorted, too: **Aquaviva** = 100, **Abbate** = 101, **Althann** = 102, **Antonio** = 103, **Ascanio** = 104 . . .

Figure 7-9: Like many others of its kind, this eighteenth-century nomenclator is partially sorted. For instance, the first half of the alphabet is assigned to the numbers A = 44, B = 45, C = 46, D = 47, . . . , M = 55.

With the advent of the telegraph in the nineteenth century, the number of messages sent grew considerably, which caused an increasing demand for both encryption technology and cost-effective means of sending long messages. Thus began the era of codes, with codebooks that grew to over 50,000 entries,[21] containing codegroups that typically consisted of five- or six-digit numbers. As telegraph companies charged by the number of words transmitted, many codebooks primarily served to shorten messages. For most, making the text harder to read was not even a goal. To conserve words and therefore cost, these codes replaced not only single expressions but also common phrases with codegroups. The telegraph companies reacted to this development by charging higher fees for nonreadable (i.e., coded) messages, which caused the codebook producers to include additional and longer phrases.

During World War II, codes remained in use, though usually not at the highest security level. The popularity of codes and nomenclators came to an end in the middle of the twentieth century, when encryption machines (which work on letters, applying ciphers rather than codes) became widely available. Since the advent of electronics and computer technology, codes and nomenclators have served little purpose.

Although codes and nomenclators were the most popular kind of encryption for about 500 years, with hundreds of thousands of messages encrypted, this branch of cryptography has not received as much attention from crypto-historians as ciphers. Some renowned codebreaking books, such as those by Helen Fouché Gaines[22] and Abraham Sinkov,[23] cover the topic only very briefly or not at all. Nor have codes and nomenclators generally played a role in recreational codebreaking, because the solver would have to see the codebooks to have a chance of solving them. We are also unaware of any computer program designed primarily for analyzing and breaking codes and nomenclators. Most cryptogram books, puzzle columns, and cryptographic challenges tend to ignore codes and nomenclators entirely.

Recently, though, these types of systems have become an active field of historical research. Historians, who have encountered piles of encrypted documents in archives, have begun working with codebreaking experts trying to solve these. (Of course, not all archived encrypted messages are code- or nomenclator-encrypted.) A few examples are shown in the following sections. We are confident that historians will continue to publish many more cryptograms of this kind, along with efforts to solve them.

Superencryption of codes and nomenclators

One simple technique to make a code or nomenclator more secure is *superencryption*, or adding a second encryption step to a message that has already been encrypted with a code, nomenclator, or some other system. The second encryption step used for this purpose could be quite simple. For instance, if the codegroups consist of digits, you could add a number derived from the current date to the codegroups. On October 16, for example, the number 1016 might be added to every codegroup, so that 1234 becomes 2250. While the recipient—who knows the superencryption method applied—has no trouble subtracting 1016 from every number they encounter in the ciphertext, a cryptanalyst's work becomes much harder, as every codegroup has a different meaning on a different day of the year. Among other things, frequency analysis is almost useless if applied to messages sent on different days.

How to detect a code or nomenclator

In many cases, it is quite easy to recognize a ciphertext encrypted using a code or nomenclator rather than a cipher system. Before 1800, nomenclator messages were typically handwritten texts consisting of numbers with several digits, often interrupted by plaintext passages. The message from 1783 depicted in Figure 7-10 (a) is quite typical, and we will come back to it in the "Unsolved cryptograms" section of this chapter. No other crypto system in frequent use at that time produced ciphertexts of this kind. The same is true of the example in Figure 7-10 (b), from 1702.[24] While systems such as a book cipher (see Chapter 14) or a digraph substitution (see Chapter 12) may produce similar-looking ciphertexts, they were uncommon at that time.

If we look at messages created in the nineteenth or twentieth century, things get a little more complex. Some codebooks from this era use random words from different languages as codegroups. The cryptogram from 1898 in Figure 7-10 (c) is an example. Words such as CRAQUEREZ or IMPAZZAVA are most likely codegroups and potentially superencrypted.

The message in Figure 7-10 (d) was sent by telegram in 1911.[25] We can assume that it was created with a code or a nomenclator, as few other encryption methods in use in the early twentieth century produced number sequences of this kind.

In other cases, however, code and nomenclator messages from the last 200 years are hard to distinguish from ciphertexts created with other methods (e.g., an encryption machine such as the Enigma). This is especially the case if the codewords consist of five-letter groups; since the early twentieth century, it has been common practice to write ciphertexts of all kinds in letter groups of five. For instance, the following consular message from 1940 (provided to us by Enigma expert Frode Weierud) is a code cryptogram, though it may look similar to ciphertext produced by an encryption machine (see Chapter 15) or some other system:[26]

```
BBBTT YIXBA YIVYL OXUAB ARPBO UJTNU ASZAF UKURL YORAY MAXAD EWDKY
IBEKY WITOS WIYVU MAMAN REKTI ASTCA EUKIM IVYDE UCHRE CEXLO HUNAL
OXUAB ARXPU WIFOH IGAEB
```

A typical property of a nomenclator or code cryptogram is that parts of the message are left in cleartext. Most of the code and nomenclator messages shown in this chapter are of this kind. Of course, it is also possible to leave words in cleartext when applying a cipher, but this is less common, especially if an encryption machine was utilized.

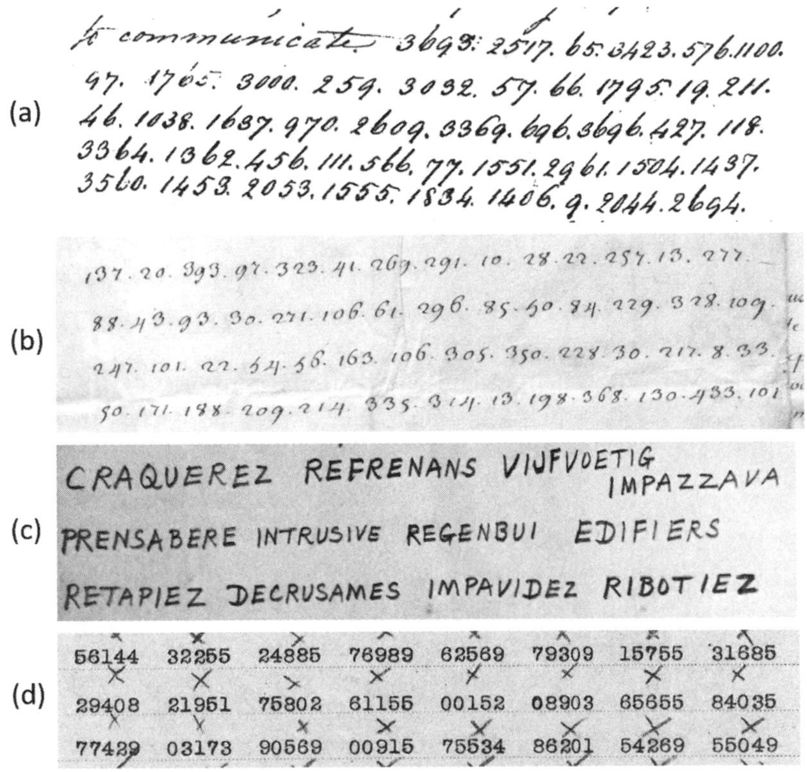

Figure 7-10: Codes and nomenclator messages are often, yet not always, easy to detect.

Statistical evidence can also be used to detect a code or nomenclator. For instance, repetitions among the letter or number groups of a message, such as OXUAB in the first and third lines of the consular message above, indicate either a relatively weak cipher (like simple substitution or a Vigenère cipher) or a code or nomenclator. This is because the ciphertext produced by a strong cipher system such as the Enigma appears visually similar to a random sequence, which makes it very unlikely that, say, a five-letter group would appear twice in a message of a few hundred characters—let alone several times.

How to break a code or nomenclator

A code or nomenclator that is constructed and used properly is very difficult, if not impossible, to break. Nevertheless, skilled codebreakers have solved a surprising number of cryptograms of this kind. There are several reasons for this:

- It is sometimes possible to locate the table or codebook.
- The meanings of some of the codegroups might be known to the codebreaker and can be used as cribs.
- Many nomenclators are poorly constructed. For instance, letter/number combinations are often sorted in an easy-to-determine alphabetical or numerical order. It might also be possible to tell the difference between letter and word codegroups. For example, if two-digit numbers tended to occur one after another, they might be letter groups. If these letter groups can be broken with the usual cryptanalytic techniques, they might provide cribs to solve the other codegroups.
- Historically, many cipher clerks didn't use codes and nomenclators properly; for instance, they always chose the same homophone when several others were available.

These weaknesses play an important role in the methods for solving nomenclators that we will introduce now.

Finding the nomenclator table or codebook

One disadvantage of a code or nomenclator is that changing the key (i.e., the codebook or table used) is a costly process. Assembling a new nomenclator table is laborious, as is rewriting a whole codebook. For this reason, codes and nomenclators typically used the same table or codebook for long periods, even years, without being changed. This fact, of course, is helpful for codebreakers.

When trying to break a code or nomenclator message, it is therefore a good idea to search for the codebook or nomenclator table used. This approach works especially well for messages created after about 1850, when telegraphy was booming. Nomenclator tables began falling out of favor, but the number of encrypted texts and the size of the codebooks rose considerably. Hundreds of old codebooks from this time are available online today. A good starting point is to look at the websites maintained by Japanese cipher expert Satoshi Tomokiyo[27] and John McVey,[28] each of which lists hundreds of telegraphic codebooks, many of which are available for download. It is also worth remembering that many of these codebooks were not used primarily for secrecy but for shortening messages. Codebooks of this kind were sold in large quantities and not kept secret.

As an example, look at the nineteenth-century telegram depicted in Figure 7-11, which was provided to us by blog reader Karsten Hansky.[29] The sender of this note, a US astronomer named John Ritchie, transmitted it from Boston, Massachusetts, to the Chamberlain Observatory in Denver, Colorado, on September 7, 1896. Some of the words in the telegram, such as **COMET** and **USUAL**, are obviously in cleartext. Readers knowledgeable about astronomy might recognize that **BROOKS** and **GIACOBINI** are names of comets and that **LICK** and **HUSSEY** refer to astronomical observatories in the USA. Other words, such as BOUCHETROU, CALIMA, and FACILENESS, don't make sense. They could be codegroups. If so, we are dealing with a code based on made-up words.

Solving this short message with conventional codebreaking techniques would be extremely difficult, if not impossible. Finding the codebook is the only realistic option. Karsten tried his luck and was successful. On the Internet Archive website (*https://archive.org*), he found the matching codebook, *The Science Observer Code*, from 1885.[30] Ritchie, the sender of the telegram, is one of the authors of this codebook, which made Karsten's search a little easier!

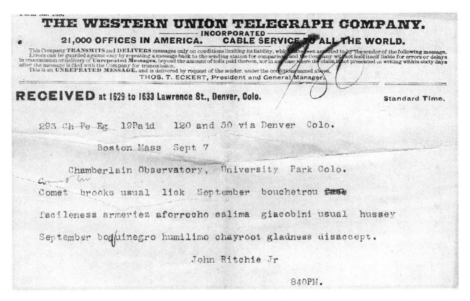

Figure 7-11: This 1896 telegram, sent by astronomer John Ritchie, contains a number of codewords. After the codebook used was identified, the message could be read.

Figure 7-12 shows a page from this codebook—and it's quite a special one. It was meant to transmit the plaintext numbers **0** to **39,999**. Astronomers could use these codegroups to encode positions, orbits, and other astronomical data. This code was probably not designed to keep messages secret but to avoid errors in the transmission of numbers. BOUCHETROU, for example, stands for **6835**. The other codegroups appearing in the telegram have the following meanings: FACILENESS = **20756**, ARMERIEZ = **3435**, AFORRECHO = **1085**, CALIMA = **8085**, BOQUINEGRO = **6691**, HUMILIMO = **25844**, CHAYROOT = **9752**, GLADNESS = **23266**, and DISACCEPT = **16388**.

14		15	
00 AISLAR	50 ALAMBIQUE	00 ALBERCA	50 ALCAIDIAS
01 AITCHBONE	51 ALAMBRADO	01 ALBERGADA	51 ALCALAINO
02 AJADAS	52 ALAMBRERA	02 ALBERGADOR	52 ALCALDADA
03 AJAMAR	53 ALAMOS	03 ALBERGAR	53 ALCALDIA
04 AJAQUEFA	54 ALAMPARSE	04 ALBERGARIA	54 ALCALIZADO
05 AJAQUEINTO	55 ALAMUD	05 ALBERGIERS	55 ALCALIZAR
06 AJEDREA	56 ALANAS	06 ALBERO	56 ALCALLERIA
07 AJENADO	57 ALANCEADOR	07 ALBESCENT	57 ALCAMIZ
08 AJENISIMO	58 ALANTINE	08 ALBESTOR	58 ALCAMONIAS
09 AJENTE	59 ALAQUECA	09 ALBICANTE	59 ALCANCE
10 AJENUZ	60 ALARDE	10 ALBIDRADO	60 ALCANCIAS
11 AJESUITADO	61 ALARDEAR	11 ALBIGENSES	61 ALCANCIAZO
12 AJEVIO	62 ALARDOSO	12 ALBIHAR	62 ALCANFOR
13 AJIACEITE	63 ALARGADAS	13 ALBILLA	63 ALCANNA
14 AJICOLA	64 ALARGADERA	14 ALBINISM	64 ALCANTARAS
15 AJIMEZ	65 ALARGAMA	15 ALBINOES	65 ALCANZANTE
16 AJIPUERRO	66 ALARGUEZ	16 ALBITANA	66 ALCAPARRON
17 AJOBILLA	67 ALARIFES	17 ALBOGUE	67 ALCARACENO
18 AJOLINO	68 ALARMANTE	18 ALBOGUEAR	68 ALCARAVAN
19 AJOMATE	69 ALARMING	19 ALBOGUERO	69 ALCARRAZA
20 AJONJE	70 ALARMINGLY	20 ALBONDIGON	70 ALCATIFA
21 AJONJOLI	71 ALASTRAR	21 ALBOQUERON	71 ALCATIFERO
22 AJOQUESO	72 ALATONERO	22 ALBORECER	72 ALCAUDON
23 AJORARE	73 ALAUDA	23 ALBORNEZ	73 ALCHEMICAL
24 AJORCA	74 ALAVES	24 ALBORNO	74 ALCHEMIQUE
25 AJOURNANT	75 ALBACORA	25 ALBOROCERA	75 ALCHEMIST
26 AJOURNERA	76 ALBAHACA	26 ALBORONIA	76 ALCHYMY
27 AJUAGAS	77 ALBAIDA	27 ALBOROQUE	77 ALCINA
28 AJUDIADO	78 ALBAIRE	28 ALBOROTADO	78 ALCIONIO
29 AJUICIAR	79 ALBANARSE	29 ALBOROTAR	79 ALCMANIAN
30 AJUSTERA	80 ALBANDOS	30 ALBOROTO	80 ALCOBA
31 AJUTAGES	81 ALBANEGA	31 ALBOTIN	81 ALCOBAZA
32 ALABANDINA	82 ALBANIANS	32 ALBRICIAR	82 ALCOCARRA
33 ALABARDA	83 ALBANIL	33 ALBUFERA	83 ALCOHOL
34 ALABARDAZO	84 ALBAQUIA	34 ALBUGO	84 ALCOHOLERA
35 ALABASTER	85 ALBARAN	35 ALBUMENIZE	85 ALCOHOLIC
36 ALABASTRUM	86 ALBARAZADO	36 ALBUMINEUX	86 ALCOLLA
37 ALABEOS	87 ALBARDANIA	37 ALBUMINOID	87 ALCOMENIAS
38 ALABIADO	88 ALBARDERIA	38 ALBURNOUS	88 ALCOMETER
39 ALACIAR	89 ALBARDIN	39 ALCABALERO	89 ALCONCILLA
40 ALACRIOUS	90 ALBARICO	40 ALCABOR	90 ALCORAN
41 ALACRITY	91 ALBATOZA	41 ALCABOTA	91 ALCORANIST
42 ALADIERNA	92 ALBATROSS	42 ALCACHOFA	92 ALCORCI
43 ALADINIST	93 ALBAYALDE	43 ALCAHAZ	93 ALCORNOCAL
44 ALADO	94 ALBAZO	44 ALCAHAZADA	94 ALCORNOQUE
45 ALADRADA	95 ALBEDRIO	45 ALCAHEST	95 ALCOROVIA
46 ALAGADIZO	96 ALBEITERIA	46 ALCAHUETE	96 ALCORQUE
47 ALAGARTADO	97 ALBELLON	47 ALCAIC	97 ALCOTAN
48 ALAHILCA	98 ALBENDERA	48 ALCAIDESA	98 ALCOVES
49 ALAMBICAR	99 ALBENGALA	49 ALCAIDIADO	99 ALCREBITE

Figure 7-12: A page from The Science Observer Code *from 1885. Astronomer John Ritchie used this code for his telegram.*

Even once we know the meanings of these codegroups, the content of the telegram is difficult to understand. This is because the sender encoded dates and astronomical information in a way that made the messages shorter. The methods he used are explained in the codebook's introduction. Applying these methods, Karsten reconstructed the following plaintext:

```
Boston Mass, September 7th
Comet Brooks was observed by Lick (observatory) on September
6.8355 at the following
position:
RA: 207° 56' 01" ' 13h 51m 44.1s
Dec: 55° 24' 52"
Giacobini was observed by Hussey on September 6.6916 at the
following position:
RA: 258° 44' ' 17h 14m 58.3s
Dec: -7° 52' 26"
John Ritchie Jr
```

The purpose of the telegram was to inform the receiver (an astronomical observatory in Denver, Colorado) of the coordinates of the comets Brooks and Giacobini measured in Boston on September 6, 1896.

Exploiting weaknesses of codes and nomenclators

If we can't find the substitution table used, we'll need to employ code-breaking methods to decipher a code or nomenclator message. As mentioned, this is an extremely difficult task if the code or nomenclator is well constructed and used properly. Computer algorithms that perform such cryptanalysis constitute an active field of research. Hill climbing (see Chapter 16), the seemingly omnipotent tool in historical codebreaking, is not very helpful here, as there are too many potential words and phrases. So far, there are no available computer programs for solving codes and nomenclators. This may change, but for the time being, solving a code or nomenclator message is mainly a matter of human intelligence, not computer intelligence.

Luckily for us, many codes and nomenclators are of poor quality. For instance, a one-part code or nomenclator is a lot easier to break than a two-part code or nomenclator. Even in two-part specimens, we can expect regularities in the way the codegroups are ordered, which makes breaking a message a lot easier.

Let's break a nomenclator message written by a spy in Great Britain in the seventeenth century. Both the cryptogram and the solution we present are described by mathematician and crypto-historian Peter P. Fagone in *Cryptologia*.[31] Here is an excerpt from the message:

```
. . . 44, 38, 62, 39, I send you my 34, 74, 58, 44, 38, 62, with
116, 66, 57, give him selfe 50, 38, 30, 64, 67, 42, 50, 30, 54,
38, have, 51, 56, 64, 66, 46, 67, 26 &, I, 42, 30, 68, 38, 125,
the 36, 57, 68, 32, 50, 38, of it to lett him see that I deale
```

```
fairly what comes, 40, 62, 56, 52, 26, 116, must come, 66, 56,
27, 125, tell 103, that hee must 70, 62, 46, 66, 39, 54, 56, 38,
52, 57, 63, 38 . . .
```

This ciphertext consists of (mostly two-digit) numbers separated by commas. Some passages are written in cleartext. In all, the message consists of about a thousand numbers and an alphabet of ninety different numbers. Based on the criteria discussed earlier in this chapter, we can assume that this cryptogram was created with a nomenclator.

As a first step, we count the codegroups to perform frequency analysis. This reveals that the numbers 30 through 77 are much more frequent than the others, which raises a suspicion: those forty-eight numbers might stand for letters, while the remaining ones might encode complete words. Since the alphabet used in the seventeenth century contained twenty-four letters (*U* and *V*, as well as *I* and *J*, were not distinguished), we can appropriately hypothesize that there are two numbers (homophones) for each letter of the alphabet. We first try the following scheme:

```
A: 30/31
B: 32/33
C: 34/35
D: 36/37
E: 38/39
. . .
```

As it turns out, we get a meaningful text. The developer of the nomenclator could not have made it easier for us!

Here is the excerpt shown above with the letter codegroups decrypted:

```
. . . here i send you my cypher with 116, to give him selfe least
g lane have lost it, 26, &, i gaue 125, the double of it to lett
him see that i deal fairely what comes from 26, 116, must come to
27, 125, tell 103, that he must writ c noe more . . .
```

Can we guess the remaining codegroups, too? They probably stand for words, phrases, or syllables. It turns out that the numbers between 11 and 30 can simply be omitted. Most or all of them are probably nulls. The numbers 1 through 10 probably stand for numbers. As the nomenclator is poorly designed, we can assume 1 = **1**, 2 = **2**, 3 = **3**, and so on. The three-digit numbers most likely represent names and places. We can't determine their meanings without having detailed background information.

The content of the message does, however, confirm that a spy had indeed been at work, talking about bribery and other covert actions. Perhaps the sender of the message was a British spy in Ireland at the time of the Irish Confederate Wars (1641–1653). Their identity will probably remain a mystery forever.

Next, let's look at a papal cipher from the sixteenth century. Figure 7-13 shows a nomenclator message sent by the Vatican to a papal diplomat in Poland in 1573. This message was originally broken by crypto-historian Albert Leighton in 1969.[32]

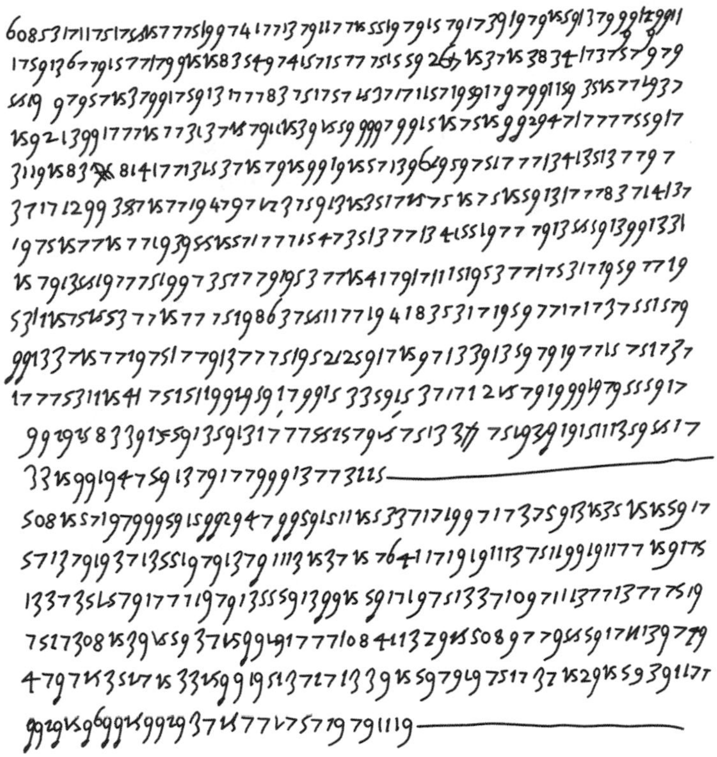

Figure 7-13: This sixteenth-century nomenclator message was broken because the nomenclator used was a very simple one.

The ciphertext consists of an unbroken series of numbers. Closer inspection reveals a tendency for the numbers to be linked in pairs. There are exceptions, such as a few three-figure groups and dots over the first digits of certain pairs. Here's a transcript of the first two lines. The dotted digits are transcribed as underlined digits:

608 53 17 11 75 17 55 25 77 75 29 97 41 77 13 79 11 77 15 59 19 79 15 79 17 39 19 79 15 59 13 79 99 58 99 11
17 59 13 <u>67</u> 79 15 77 17 99 15 15 83 <u>54</u> 97 41 57 15 77 75 15 59 26 99 15 37 <u>15</u> 38 34 17 37 57 19 79

Considering the era when this was written, and knowing that the Vatican used an abundance of nomenclators during the Renaissance, we can assume that the text is nomenclator-encrypted. If we are dealing with a poorly constructed nomenclator, it seems possible that the three-digit numbers and the dotted numbers stand for words, while all other digit pairs represent letters. Here is a frequency analysis of the supposed letters:

25	29	17	77	13	79	59	99	37	75	11	55	57	97	41	27	39	53	35	19	83	23	31	15	33	86	91	10	51	96
78	45	43	42	38	33	32	29	25	24	21	15	12	12	11	10	9	9	8	7	6	5	4	4	3	1	1	1	1	1

As can be seen, thirty two-digit numbers are used. If they really stand for the letters of the alphabet, there are enough numbers to encode the letters **A** through **Z**, as well as a few nulls. Four of the five most frequent numbers start with 1 or 2 (25, 29, 17, and 13) and these do not form longer sequences in the ciphertext. They might stand for vowels. In the Italian language, the vowels *E*, *A*, *I*, and *O* all have nearly the same frequency (between 10% and 12%), while *U* (usually identical to the *V* in old texts) makes up only about 3% of text (see Appendix B). It is therefore likely that there is only one codegroup representing **U** and that this is the rarest vowel codegroup, namely 11.

The most common non-vowel is 77. This number must stand for **N**, the most common consonant in Italian. The next three consonants are 59, 79, and 99. They might stand for the letters **R**, **S**, and **T**. Trial and error confirms that 59 = **R**, 79 = **S**, and 99 = **T** are valid. Knowing these consonants and the most frequent Italian digraphs (also described in Appendix B), it is possible to derive the meaning of vowels 25, 29, 17, and 13: **A** = 25, **E** = 13, **I** = 17, and **O** = 29. What we have found out so far is sufficient to decipher most of the message:

> (608) giudicando che con nessuna cosa si possa restituire piu sanita
> a questo regno che con mandar costoro a la guerra ricuperation
> de' beni regii il mosco per smaltire in questo modo i mali umori
> turbano la religion cattolica et inanz(i) la sua partita ha dato
> molto indrizzo a questo consiglio et ne ha lassato a me particolar
> ordine et benche li heretici temano molto che il re abbia da dare
> in questo sua santita et lo dannano nondimeno cammina molto bene et
> con sucretezza secondo che bisogna et si va ogni giorno guadagnando
> qualcuno con questi giorni il castellano di sendomiria que e'
> persona di lingua et d'autorita' fra li heretici ha sottoscritto a
> questo parere in casa de' ? dopo averci fatto molto resistenza
>
> (508). ha mostrato molto travaglio que il re abbia rimesso le cose
> sue a la dieta et io ho veduto una lettera del basino secretario
> del re christianissimo che venendo di (308) ha parlato in (108)
> con essa (508) che scrive che per molto che abbia fatto non li e
> parso di lassar punto aquetato l'animo suo

The numbers 608, 508, 308, and 108 cannot be solved in the same way since they probably refer to specific names or places.

Here's a translation of the first few sentences:

> (608) judging that by no other means it is possible to restore
> sanity to this kingdom than by sending a deputation to the war
> [for the] recovery of the royal goods, IL MOSCO, to purge in this
> way the evil honors that disturb the Catholic faith and before
> his departure, did much to implement this decision and left to me
> particular responsibility for its implementation; and although
> the heretics are afraid that the king may thus have to forfeit his
> sanctity and blame him for it, none the less it is going very well
> and with the necessary secrecy and each day we win over someone.

Many other code and nomenclator cryptograms have been solved in a similar way.

Solving codes and nomenclators with cribs

Sometimes, it helps to know the meaning of codegroups from related codes or nomenclators that were used in the same environment as the one you are trying to decode. You may even have a ciphertext-plaintext pair with which to reconstruct the related code. Reports on successful codebreaking efforts of this kind have been published by Paolo Bonavoglia,[33] George Lasry, and Luigi Sacco,[34] among others. This technique can also be helpful with many cipher types.[35] Researching the context in which a cipher was created can be a very powerful tool.

Success stories

A telegram sent to Tel Aviv

The encrypted telegram in Figure 7-14, provided to us by Karsten Hansky,[36] was sent from New York, via London, to Tel Aviv, on June 5, 1948. The recipient listed on the telegram form is **GOVTT MEMISRAEL TEL AVIV**, the government of Israel. As the state of Israel formed on May 14, 1948, in Tel Aviv, this telegram was sent at an interesting time and to an interesting place. The ciphertext contains a few cleartext words, such as **VERTICALLY**, **BANK**, **ANGLO**, and **PALESTINE**.

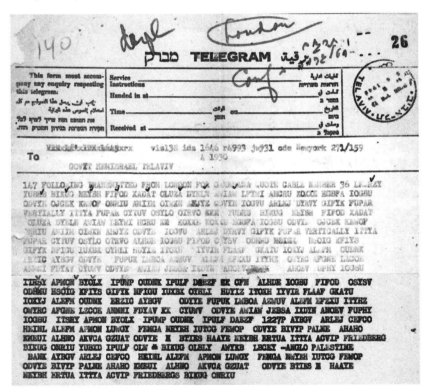

Figure 7-14: An encrypted telegram sent from New York to Tel Aviv in 1948. As the codebook used is available online, it is not very difficult to decrypt this message.

Provided that the government of Israel used a well-made code, the codebreakers' only chance of solving this cryptogram was finding the codebook used, which is, in fact, what happened. Codebook expert John McVey discovered that the authors had applied *Peterson International Code*, 3rd edition (1929).[37] Richard van de Wouw came to the same conclusion. Hansky derived the following plaintext (which omits several parts, as they are redundant):

```
Cable sent from Haifa, Palestine 28th May Currency of board
regrets unable to agree with proposal destruction of notes—They
are prepared to accept the following arrangements—Notes to be
cut in half vertically, one half consigned uninsured to us and
if notes from unissued stocks are preserved in serial orders with
labels on parcel giving indication of serial numbers and values,
each bundle is to be retained by you and dispatched only when
advice received from safe arrival of first consignment—Board will
pay out on arrival of first half of notes on our bank certificates
of the value of contents 1127P bundles to be checked later and
bank is responsible for shortage or forgery—Cable whether you
agree this procedure and if so exact amount of involved—This cable
is being sent in duplicate of one in accordance with FRIEDBERGS
cable to ANGLO PALESTINE BANK.
```

Encrypted messages by Mary, Queen of Scots

Sixteenth-century solution

In 1569, Queen Elizabeth I of England had her cousin Mary, Queen of Scots, imprisoned. Mary was known to communicate frequently in cipher with her supporters.

Among her allies was a group of English Catholics who attempted to murder Elizabeth I in order to put Mary on the English throne. Mary and the conspirators communicated via encrypted letters hidden in a beer barrel cork. Unfortunately for her, the servant who transported the messages was an agent who worked for the English spymaster Francis Walsingham, who in turn provided copies of the encrypted letters to his codebreaker, Thomas Phelippes.

Phelippes noticed that Mary and the conspirators wrote their encrypted letters in an alphabet consisting of about forty symbols. His guess was that he was dealing with a nomenclator comprising about twenty-five letter symbols, with around fifteen standing for words or nulls. Nomenclators consisting of only forty codegroups were quite common in the sixteenth century. Later, they grew much larger.

A forty-codegroup nomenclator can be solved with frequency analysis. We don't know exactly how Phelippes worked, but he probably assumed that the most frequent symbols stood for the most frequent letters of the English language, though he may have been confused by a few nulls. After some analysis, Phelippes was able to reconstruct the whole nomenclator, as shown in Figure 7-15.[38]

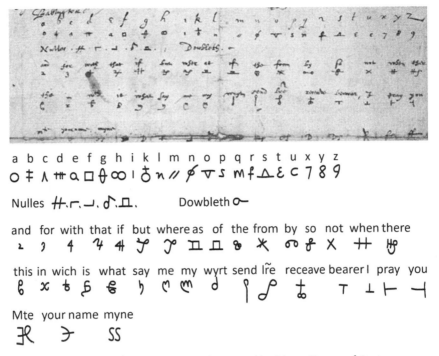

a b c d e f g h i k l m n o p q r s t u x y z
O ‡ ʌ ⧻ α ▢ ⑃ ∞ ⏊ ᛦ ᴨ // ⌀ ▽ ᛋ m f Δ ε c 7 8 9

Nulles ⧻. ⌐. ⌐. ♂. ⌂.   Dowbleth ⌐

and for with that if but where as of the from by so not when there
ᴌ ᛦ 4 ⅄ 4 ⅄ ⅃ ⊓ ⊔ ঌ ✕ ᴔ ⅃ ✕ ⧻ ᵸ

this in wich is what say me my wyrt send lr̃e receave bearer I pray you
ᛒ x ᛖ ᛢ ᛖ ᛗ ᙢ ᙢ d ৭ ⌀ ᵼ ⊤ ⊥ ⊢ ⊣

Mte your name myne
ℜ ᴣ SS

Figure 7-15: A sixteenth-century nomenclator used by Mary, Queen of Scots

With the encryption system broken, Walsingham could easily monitor the messages exchanged between Mary and the conspirators, which became more and more intense. Finally, Walsingham and Phelippes faked a message to Mary, asking her to provide a list of the conspirators—a plan that succeeded. Based on this evidence, Mary's conspirators were arrested, condemned to death, and executed in 1586. After a separate trial, Mary, Queen of Scots, was herself beheaded on February 8, 1587.

Twenty-first-century solution of a different Mary Stuart nomenclator

Another remarkable success story has to do with three people who are mentioned several times in our book: George Lasry, Norbert Biermann, and Satoshi Tomokiyo (see Figure 7-16). One of their hobbies for more than a decade has been checking archives around the world for any unknown encrypted messages so that they can document and crack them. Many large archives and private collections still have encrypted papers that can't be read and sometimes cannot even be attributed. Most of these papers are centuries old. The intrepid trio (and other colleagues of ours) have found that many encrypted documents like these can be found by searching the online catalogs for digitized documents that might be tagged with words such as *cipher*. Tomokiyo goes a step further, sometimes searching through documents one by one, to see if any parts of them are encrypted!

Figure 7-16: From left: George Lasry (Israel), Norbert Biermann (Germany), and Satoshi Tomokiyo (Japan) made a remarkable discovery while searching through the archives of the National Library of France.

In 2021, while combing the online collections of the Bibliothèque nationale de France (BnF) for enciphered documents, the team stumbled upon a large set of unlabeled papers, all in cipher, and all of which used the same set of graphical symbols (see Figure 7-17). According to the BnF catalog, the documents were supposed to be from the first half of the sixteenth century and related to Italian matters. In April 2021, the team first tried to crack this cipher with the assumption that the language was Italian, but they had no luck. In February 2022 they tried again, this time assuming the language might be French, and employing a hill-climbing program with a simulated annealing algorithm (see Chapter 16). This time they could obtain fragments of plausible text, such as "catholi" and "persecu."[39]

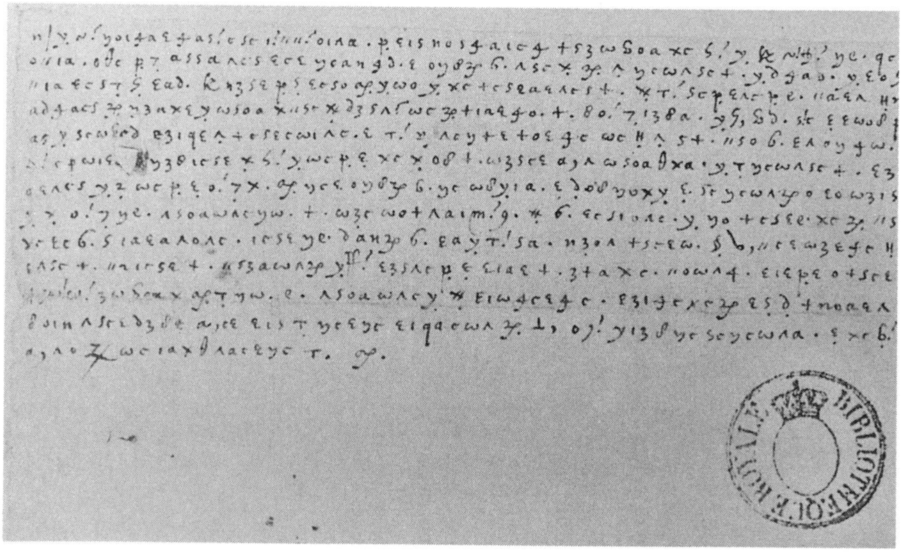

Figure 7-17: An encrypted letter from the sixteenth century, lost in the archives until it was discovered in 2021

They then followed up with manual codebreaking skills such as word guessing (see Chapter 4) to recover, bit by bit, the cipher key—in this case a nomenclator table combined with a homophonic cipher. This system was much more complex than the earlier one, as shown in Figure 7-15. In all, the team was able to identify 219 distinct symbols (see Figure 7-18), some of which stood for syllables or words. As they became able to read the documents, the team realized that the texts had been written by a prisoner, with mentions of captivity, phrases such as "my son," and the name Walsingham. That name was key, since in this time period, Sir Francis Walsingham was spymaster for Queen Elizabeth I, which aroused the suspicion that the letters might be from Mary, Queen of Scots, the imprisoned cousin of Queen Elizabeth. This hypothesis was confirmed after the team found copies of some corresponding plaintexts in British archives. The team then set out to transcribe and decipher an astonishing total of 57 encrypted letters by Mary.

Figure 7-18: Part of the Mary–Castelnau nomenclator table

The newly deciphered letters turned out to be part of a secret correspondence long considered by historians to have been lost. Most were written between 1578 and 1584 from Mary to Michel de Castelnau, the French ambassador in England. The letters constitute a voluminous body of new primary material on Mary Stuart—about 50,000 words in total. They highlight Anglo-French and Scottish politics, Mary's efforts to get herself released and reinstated as queen of Scotland, and a multitude of other topics. The find has opened a treasure trove for modern-day historians.

This sensational discovery, considered by expert historian John Guy from Cambridge to be "the most important new find on Mary Stuart, Queen of Scots, for 100 years,"[40] was announced on February 8, 2023 (coincidentally, the anniversary of Mary's beheading in 1587). It made international headlines and caused us, at the last minute, to add this new section to our book![41]

A good takeaway from this is that the work of crypto historians is not yet done. There are many such documents waiting to be found. At a HistoCrypt conference, it was estimated that there are hundreds, perhaps thousands of such nomenclator messages still to be located and deciphered, which can give us yet another window into the past.

Collinson's search expedition

Between 1850 and 1855, almost fifty encrypted advertisements were published at regular intervals in the London-based newspaper *The Times*, apparently in the same code. Here is an example, from October 1, 1851:

```
No. 16th.-S.lkqo. C. hgo & Tatty. F. kmn at npkl F. qgli lngk S
mhn F. olhi E qkpn. S. niql S mnhq, F. qgli. Austin S pgqn C. kioq
6th F. iqhl. born. 13th F. kipo a F khg. hmip. to E. mlhg by D oi.
S. pkqg C omgk B. hkq. qkng F. ioph. to hnio. S. ompi C. mkop F.
oiph to Mr. C. nhmg & F. mpkh. nmkq E. lhpq. J. de W.
```

A century later, in 1980, *The Times* published a competition to see whether anyone could solve a similar message from April 2, 1852. No one could, though it was pointed out that one message seemed to have something that looked like a latitude and longitude.

Several years passed before two experienced codebreakers independently succeeded in solving these messages. One of them, John Rabson, reported on his approach in 1992 in the scientific journal *Cryptologia*.[42] Rabson suspected the use of a code with additional letter-based encryption (superencryption). After some searching, he found that the *Universal Code of Signals* was a good candidate. Encryption had been used to convert the numbers in this code into sequences of letters. He decoded the message as follows:

```
No. 16th. your wife and family were all well when I left Bernard
& Tatty both at home Captain Penny arrived at from Baffin's Bay
early in September without success Captain Austin hourly expected
```

Margarets 6th son born 13th September a box went to Sandwich Isles by Antelope early in January Emily Sophia Thomason go to Wales early in October James goes to Mr. Hawk & lives in Gateshead. J. de W.

Now the context of the advertisement series was clear. The encrypted messages were likely published by a family member of British navigator Richard Collinson (1811–1883), who led an expedition to the North American Arctic from 1850 to 1855 to attempt a rescue of the lost polar explorer Lord John Franklin and his crew, who had not returned from their attempt to discover the Northwest Passage.

It is unlikely that these encrypted ads were meant for military or commercial secrets. More likely, they were simply encrypted for the matter of privacy. The ads were meant to tell Collinson about his family and friends during his five-year expedition. It seems that the creator of the messages hoped that *The Times*, which was the most important newspaper in the world at that time, could be obtained even in very remote places.

Even with a codebook, coming up with an exact translation can be tricky. For instance, here is another of the messages, from January 1, 1853:

```
S lmpi F. npi npil pil pink. C. klmh F. oimg ogq, khq lqkh ikpg
ogql, lqoi qoin oing lqkh. hmig C, omgk F, npi npil qmk. C hgo, F,
ploi omnl. qoip, C qkin. F oing ihlm, ik, lmhn, C nhgq F, iomn hkom
C. okiq F, mqho, olhi. C, iko. F olhi B, nlo, F. pgnq. kipo 17th
S lmpi. F mpoh C. ngil B opkg F npi npil qmk ikpg npkl. okgh. P.
F, pil. M. mhik lph hqpm oilg qolg. nmkq ikpg npkl C. nkq S lmpi C
kgql F, oing ihlm mlgi mkiq qnhi koil lgoq lgqo. olhi B. qnp.
```

The numbers of the key have been turned into letters:

0987654321
ghiklmnopq

As Elonka worked on this message, it became clear that decrypting it would require a great deal of guesswork, as well as an allowance for human error. For example, npil, translated directly with the cipher key, comes out to 4286, which in the codebook means **hook**. This didn't make sense in context, producing sentences like **At hook and elsewhere** and **All is well at hook**. The 4286 number appeared frequently, but then, sometimes in the same context, she would instead find npkl, or 4276, which means **home**. When she swapped out **hook** for **home** to get phrases like **All is well at home**, the message started to make a lot more sense!

Other places in the message were similarly vague, making it difficult to tell whether the decryption was wrong or if there was a typo. That turned things into a real puzzle. Another difficulty was that the publisher of the *Universal Code of Signals* reprinted it from time to time, and it was unclear exactly which version the author had used for these messages. Of course, it couldn't have been later than 1855. But Elonka was only able to find the 1864 version or later ones, which couldn't have been used for a message sent in 1853.

Her best guess for plaintext is this:

```
All are well at home and elsewhere. Margaret had another boy on
the evening of Christmas Day, going on well. Emily is home again.
Bernard is down for Christmas. Charlotte going too adding to
popularity. Harriet is staying with Fanny. Letters arrived from
Benjamin on the Royalist, all are well, liking Frederickshaven.
Stokesley at home again, home is full. P and M never better, 12
grandchildren in the home. Sarah & Jane, all are well. Laurence
Delaney is going to marry Miss Colridge. No news from Resolute.
```

In any case, after Collinson's expedition, his brother compiled his logs into a book called the *Journal of HMS Enterprise* (1889), after the name of the ship. According to this book, Collinson did receive at least four of the messages, when he reached "Bangu Wangie" (probably the town of Banyuwangi), in Indonesia (see Figure 7-19).[43]

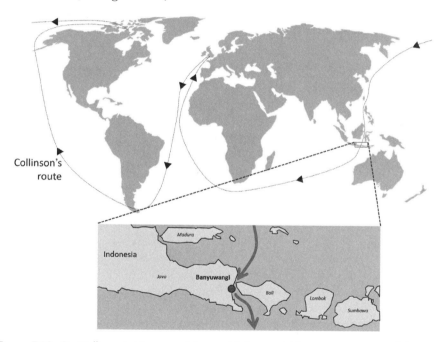

Figure 7-19: On Collinson's trip around the world, he was able to receive some of these encrypted messages when his ship put into port at Banyuwangi, Indonesia.

We might say that this was the first secure worldwide communications system!

The Japanese JN-25 code

In the World War II Pacific theater, the United States' armed forces encountered numerous Japanese encryption systems. US and British codebreakers were quite successful in deciphering these. Their two most famous accomplishments were breaking JN-25, the primary Japanese naval code, and PURPLE, a machine-based encryption system used for Japanese diplomatic messages.[44] The US Army SIS (Signals Intelligence Service), led by the legendary William Friedman, and his team, led by Frank Rowlett, even broke PURPLE without ever having seen a copy of the machine (see Chapter 15).

The other history-changing success was the breaking of JN-25. Besides encryption machines (such as PURPLE), the Japanese had been using a number of manual codes for encrypting their communications. The most important of these was JN-25, so named by American cryptologists because it was the twenty-fifth Japanese Navy encryption system they had identified.[45] JN-25 had been introduced in early 1939, just a few months before the German invasion of Poland and the beginning of the war. The encryption system was immediately brought under cryptanalytic scrutiny by groups in Britain and the United States.

Bletchley Park's John Tiltman made the first break into JN-25 by September 1939. Independently, in the United States, the comparable group in the US Navy's OP-20-G, led by "First Lady of Naval Cryptology" Agnes Meyer Driscoll, made a similar discovery in 1940.[46] Both had discovered that JN-25 was a superencrypted code that produced five-digit groups. The massively complicated system comprised up to 30,000 codegroups that were listed in a codebook and had hundreds of pages of other numbers, or additives, used for superencryption.

The codebreakers had learned that JN-25 contained an error-detection scheme they could exploit: all codegroups were numbers divisible by three.[47] But, even knowing this, they could decipher only about 10% to 20% of the Japanese messages. Progress was hampered somewhat simply because there was not much traffic for the Allied cryptanalysts to intercept and analyze.[48]

After the Japanese attack on Pearl Harbor on December 7, 1941, the United States entered the war and resources devoted to cryptology increased dramatically. The Americans first used punch card tabulating machines manufactured by IBM, then designed completely new codebreaking machines to assist with further cryptanalytic attacks. The Japanese changed codebooks and additives from time to time, so analysts had to break several systems in parallel, but within a few months after Pearl Harbor, they could read approximately 90% of JN-25 messages.[49]

This proved especially important in mid-1942, when the encrypted Japanese radio messages mentioned plans to attack a target codenamed AF. US Naval intelligence specialists knew that codenames starting with the letter A were generally used for islands near Hawaii (for example, Oahu was AH), but they were not sure of the location of AF. They guessed that it represented the tiny island of Midway.

To confirm this suspicion, cryptanalysts Jasper Holmes and Joseph Rochefort suggested that the US military base on Midway broadcast a "plain language" radio message stating that Midway's water purification system had broken down and that fresh water was urgently needed. The plan was approved by Commander Edwin T. Layton and Admiral Chester W. Nimitz and put into effect. The Japanese took the bait, and within twenty-four hours, the American codebreakers picked up a Japanese intelligence report encrypted with JN-25 saying, "AF is short on water." The suspicion that AF stood for Midway was confirmed.

This information allowed the Americans to correctly position their fleets to engage the Japanese Navy near Midway,[50] a battle that became a major turning point in the war. Crypto-historians often cite this as one of the cases where the deciphering of a single message could change an entire war.

Challenges

The Mount Everest telegram

The telegram depicted in Figure 7-20, sent to London in 1924 by a British expedition at the Mount Everest base camp, contains the following partially encrypted message:[51] MALLORY IRVINE NOVE REMAINDER ALCEDO. George Mallory (best known for having replied to the question, "Why did you want to climb Mount Everest?" with "Because it's there!") and Andrew Irvine were two of the expedition participants. The words NOVE and ALCEDO are codegroups. Can you find the codebook used? If so, you can certainly decipher this telegram.

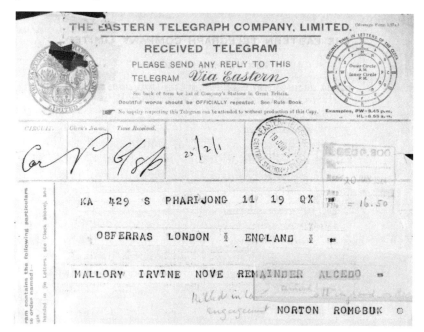

Figure 7-20: A telegram sent by a British expedition from Mount Everest in 1924

Unsolved cryptograms

The silk dress cryptogram

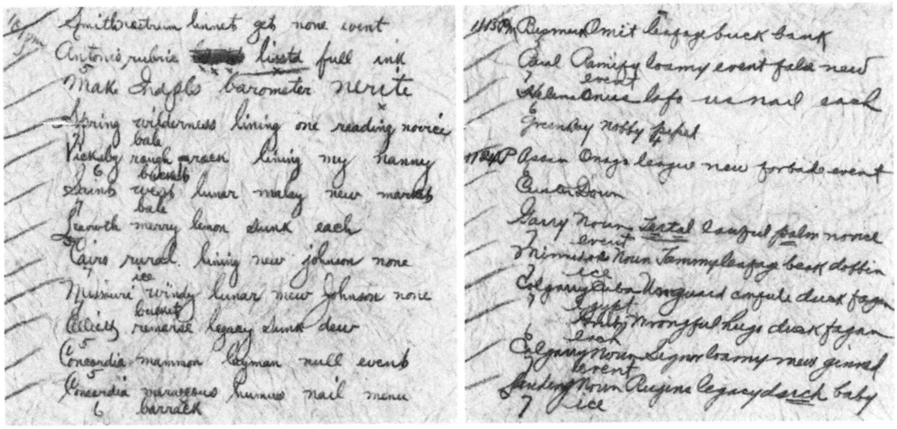

Figure 7-21: This message encrypted in a code was contained in a hidden pocket of a late nineteenth-century dress.

In 2013, antique-costume collector Sara Rivers-Cofield acquired what she described in her blog as a "mid-1880s two-piece bustle dress of bronze silk with striped rust velvet accents and lace cuffs."[52] When she turned the skirt inside out, she discovered a hidden pocket that contained two pieces of paper, both of which contained encrypted writing (Figure 7-21). Here's a transcript of sheet 1:

```
Smith nostrum linnets gets none event
101pm Antonio rubric lissdt full ink
Make Snapls barometer nerite
Spring wilderness lining one reading novice bale
Vicksbg rough rack lining my nanny bucket
Saints west lunar malay new markets bale
Seawoth merry lemon sunk each
Cairo rural lining new johnson none ice
Missouri windy lunar new Johnson none bucket
Cellictte memorise legacy Dunk dew
Concordia mammon layman null events
Concordia meraccons humus nail menu barrack
```

And here is sheet 2:

```
1113 PM Bismark Omit leafage buck bank
Paul Ramify loamy event false new event
Helena Onus lofo usual each
Greenbay nobby peped
1124 P Assin Onays league new forbade event
Cusin Down
```

```
Harry Noun Lertal laubul palm novice event
Mimedos Noun Jammyleafage beak dobbin ice
Calgary Duba Unguard confute duck tagan egypt
Knit wrongful hugs duck fagan each
Calgary Noun Signor loamy new ginnet event
Landing Noun Rugins legacy duch baby ice
```

It is not difficult to see that this message was created with a code. Rather than seemingly random text or numbers, the codegroups are meaningful words, like Cairo, Greenbay, Calgary, duck, and loamy. Such codes were not uncommon in the second half of the nineteenth century. The text was probably meant to be sent as a telegram, as below each line, the number of words contained in that line is noted. (These numbers are omitted in the transcript.) Note that just as our book was going to press, we heard that this might have been solved! See *https://codebreaking-guide.com/errata/*.

The train station robbery cryptogram

On June 27, 1916, a man robbed the ticket counter at the Western Ohio Railway in Lima, Ohio. The robber held up a ticket agent at gunpoint and forced him to hand over the contents of a safe. He escaped with $265 (equivalent to about $6,000 today). A few weeks later, the magazine *Enigma*, published by the National Puzzlers' League, wrote this:

> The police department of Lima, O., is greatly puzzled over a cryptic message received in connection with the robbery of a Western Ohio ticket agent. Here it is: WAS NVKVAFT BY AAKAT TXPXSCK UPBK TXPHN OHAY YBTX CPT MXHG WAE SXFP ZAVFZ ACK THERE FIRST TXLK WEEK WAYX ZA WITH THX.

This interesting story was discovered in 2013 by Zodiac Killer expert Dave Oranchak and popularized by British cipher mysteries blogger Nick Pelling.[53] Nick found two articles about this cryptogram in old issues of the *Lima Times-Democrat*. The version of the ciphertext printed there is slightly different from the one published by the National Puzzlers' League. As the *Enigma* author probably copied it from the newspaper, we should work with the *Lima Times-Democrat* version. Here it is:

> Was nvlvaft by aakat txpxsck upbk txphn ohay ybtx cpt mxhg wae sxfp zavfz ack there first txlk week wayx za with thx

To our regret, we don't know the full relationship of the cryptogram to the robbery. The most likely explanation is that this message is a codebook-encrypted telegram. The sender seems to have left a few of the less-important words (WAS, BY, FIRST, THX . . .) in cleartext and looked up the others in a (not-yet-discovered) codebook.

If the train station robbery cryptogram really is a telegram, it seems possible that the robber sent it immediately before or after the act. Perhaps the telegraph clerk became suspicious after the telegram was sent and informed the police that he might have dealt with a criminal.

The train station robbery cryptogram has never been deciphered.

A Pollaky newspaper advertisement

Ignatius Pollaky (1828–1918), a successful private detective in Victorian England, was one of the individuals who inspired Arthur Conan Doyle's Sherlock Holmes.[54] Pollaky frequently used newspaper advertisements to search for witnesses or communicate encrypted messages. He published the ad in Figure 7-22 in *The Times* (London) on February 20, 1871.[55, 56] This ciphertext looks very much like a message encrypted in a code. Perhaps some superencryption was used. There were many codebooks in use during the Victorian era, so Pollaky had many options to choose from.

So far, nobody has been able to decipher this message.

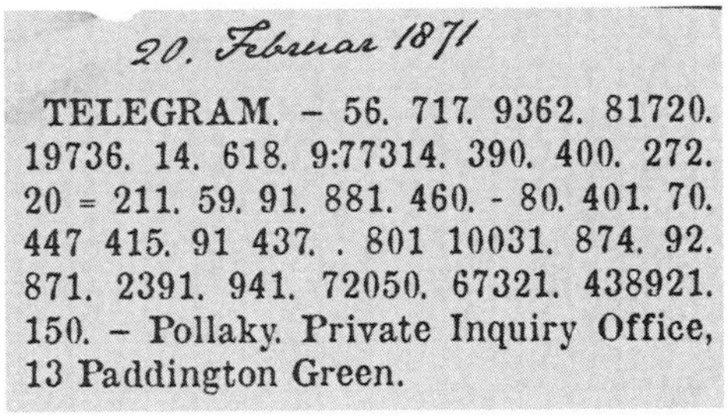

Figure 7-22: An encrypted newspaper ad published by private detective Ignatius Pollaky

Lord Manchester's letter

The letter depicted in Figure 7-23 was sent by George Mantagu, fourth duke of Manchester and British ambassador to France, in 1783.[57]

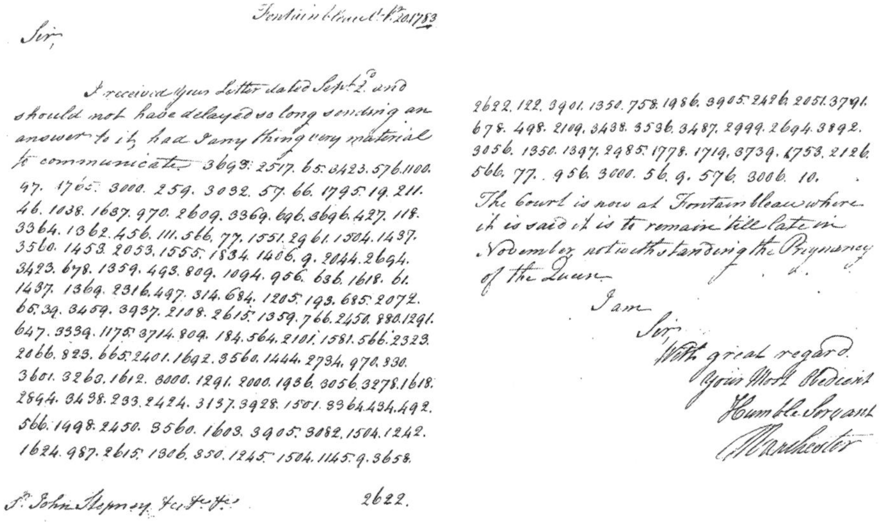

Figure 7-23: A page from a letter sent by the British ambassador to France in 1783

Here is a transcript:

```
Fontainbleau Sep 20, 1783

Sir,

I received your letter dated Sep 2nd and
should not have delayed so long sending an
answer to it, had I anything very material
to communicate. 3693.2517.65.3423.576.1100.
97.1765.3000.259.3032.57.66.1795.19.211.
46.1038.1637.970.2609.3369.696.3696.427.118.
3364.1362.456.111.566.77.1551.2961.1504.1437.
3560.1453.2053.1555.1834.1406.9.2044.2694.
3423.678.1359.493.809.1094.956.636.1618.61.
1437.1369.2316.497.314.684.1205.193.685.2072.
65.39.3459.3937.2108.2615.1359.766.2450.880.1291.
647.3339.1175.3714.809.184.564.2101.1581.566.2323.
2066.823.665.2401.1692.3560.1444.2784.970.830.
3601.3263.1612.3000.1291.2000.1936.3056.3287.1618.
2894.3498.233.2424.3137.3928.1501.3364.434.492.
566.1998.2450.3560.1603.3905.3082.1504.1242.
1624.987.2615.1306.350.1245.1504.1145.9.3658.
S John Stepney 2622.

2622.122.3901.1350.758.1986.3905.2426.2051.3791.
678.498.2109.3438.3536.3487.2999.2694.3892.
3056.1350.1397.2985.1778.1719.3739.1753.2126.
566.77.956.3000.56.9.576.3006.10.
The Court is now at Fontainebleau where
it is said it is to remain till late in
November notwithstanding the Pregnancy
of the Queen
I am
Sir
With great regard
Your most obedient
Humble Servant
Manchester
```

High-resolution scans of this letter, as well as a transcript, are available online at *https://codebreaking-guide.com*. The letter appears to have been encrypted with a code. Considering that this code probably contained several thousand codegroups and that there are only two pages of encrypted text for analysis, breaking this message with conventional codebreaking tools likely won't work. The only realistic chance of deciphering it is to find the codebook.

POLYALPHABETIC CIPHERS

The fourth inscription on *Kryptos*, the sculpture located at CIA headquarters in Langley, Virginia, is the most famous unsolved crypto mystery created in the last four decades. The other three ciphertexts on this artwork have been solved.

Kryptos and at least two other artworks by the sculptor Jim Sanborn involve a kind of encryption called a *polyalphabetic cipher*, meaning a cipher that switches between different substitution tables. An overview of *Kryptos* is given in Appendix A.

How a polyalphabetic cipher works

To introduce polyalphabetic ciphers, we start with a miniature sculpture (called a maquette) that Sanborn made in the late 1980s, before he created the actual sculpture (Figure 8-1). This shoebox-sized model looks similar to the original but bears a completely different message.

Figure 8-1: A shoebox-sized maquette of Kryptos with a simpler encryption. The cipher used is the most common polyalphabetic encryption method: the Vigenère cipher.

For decades, this maquette was unknown to the public; but in 2015, Ed Scheidt, Sanborn's crypto consultant, showed it to participants at a *Kryptos* meeting organized by Elonka.[1] Here's the encrypted part:

```
TIJVMSRSHVXOMCJVXOENA
KQUUCLWYXVHZTFGJMKJHG
DYRPMASMZZNAKCUEURRHJ
KLGEMVFMOKCUEURKSVVMZ
YYZIUTJJUJCZZITRFHVCT
XNNVBGIXKJNZFXKTBVYYX
NBZYIAKNVEKPYZIUTJYCA
```

Jew-Lee Lann-Briere and Bill Briere broke the cryptogram a few hours after the dinner was over, using only paper and pencil. After publication, Christoph Tenzer found the solution as well. It turned out that Sanborn had used the so-called Vigenère cipher to encrypt this message.

Vigenère cipher

The cipher today known as the Vigenère cipher was first described in the sixteenth century by Giovan Battista Bellaso (1505–?). Later, in the nineteenth century, its invention was misattributed to Bellaso's contemporary Blaise de Vigenère (1523–1596). We'll explain how this encryption method works using the plaintext of the cryptogram on the *Kryptos* maquette (which contains a few spelling errors; the last word resulted from a mistake Sanborn made):[2]

```
CODES MAY BE DIVIDED INTU TWO DIFFERENT CLASSES, NAMELY
SUBSTITUTIONAL AND TRANSPOSITIONAL TYPES, THE TRANSPOSITIONAL
BEING THE HARDEST TO DECHPHER WHTHOUT TPNQJHFCDZDHIU.
```

To encrypt this message using the Vigenère cipher, we repeatedly write some keyword on the line below our plaintext, assign each letter a number value (e.g., **A** = 0, **B** = 1, **C** = 2, etc.), and then add the letters of the plaintext and keyword column-wise. If the result is greater than twenty-five, we subtract twenty-six. Each number is then converted back into a letter.

Sanborn reportedly intended to use the keyword **GRU**. However, he started encrypting his plaintext with the second letter of his key, effectively changing it to **RUG**. For purposes of this demonstration, we'll consider the keyword to be **RUG**:

```
CODES MAY BE DIVIDED INTU TWO DIFFERENT CLASSES NAMELY SUBSTITUTIONAL . . .
RUGRU GRU GR UGRUGRU GRUG RUG RUGRUGRUG RUGRUGR UGRUGR UGRUGRUGRUGRUG . . .
--------------------------------------------------------------------
TIJVM SRS HV XOMCJVX OENA KQU UCLWYXVHZ TFGJMKJ HGDYRP MASMZZNAKCUEUR . . .
```

We get the exact ciphertext written on the miniature sculpture. To decrypt the ciphertext, we subtract the keyword from the ciphertext.

It is easy to see that a Vigenère cipher effectively consists of several Caesar ciphers (Figure 8-2). So, with a three-letter keyword (**RUG**), we derive the following:

- The first, fourth, seventh, and tenth letters of the plaintext are encrypted with a Caesar cipher and with the key **A** = R.
- For letters two, five, and eight, the Caesar substitution **A** = U is applied.
- The third Caesar cipher key is **A** = G.

Note that Sanborn defined the scheme **A** = 0, **B** = 1, **C** = 2, etc. This is the way the Vigenère cipher is usually used today, because computer-savvy people tend to start counting at zero. However, before the computer age, almost all Vigenère encipherers used the scheme **A** = 1, **B** = 2, **C** = 3, etc.

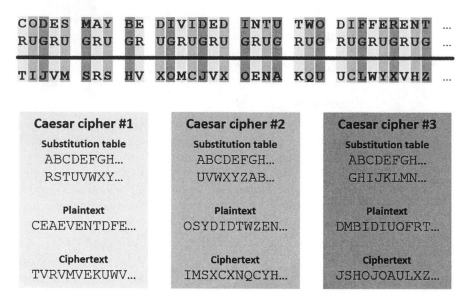

CODES MAY BE DIVIDED INTO TWO DIFFERENT ...
RUGRU GRU GR UGRUGRU GRUG RUG RUGRUGRUG ...

TIJVM SRS HV XOMCJVX OENA KQU UCLWYXVHZ ...

Caesar cipher #1

Substitution table
ABCDEFGH...
RSTUVWXY...

Plaintext
CEAEVENTDFE...

Ciphertext
TVRVMVEKUWV...

Caesar cipher #2

Substitution table
ABCDEFGH...
UVWXYZAB...

Plaintext
OSYDIDTWZEN...

Ciphertext
IMSXCXNQCYH...

Caesar cipher #3

Substitution table
ABCDEFGH...
GHIJKLMN...

Plaintext
DMBIDIUOFRT...

Ciphertext
JSHOJOAULXZ...

Figure 8-2: A Vigenère cipher with a three-letter keyword (here, RUG) can be regarded as consisting of three Caesar ciphers.

Today, numerous computer programs and commonly available utilities implement the Vigenère cipher.

Other polyalphabetic ciphers

The Vigenère cipher originated from the insight that a simple substitution cipher is easy to break with frequency analysis. An obvious way to prevent this is to use several substitution tables instead of one and to switch among them. If we have, say, five substitution tables, we can use the first one for the first letter of the plaintext, the second one for the second letter, and so on. When we have reached the sixth plaintext letter, we return to the first substitution table.

The second row of a substitution table is sometimes referred to as a *cipher alphabet*, or simply *alphabet*, in cryptology. Because a simple substitution cipher is based on only one substitution table, it is called *monoalphabetic*. A cipher that switches between different substitution tables is called *polyalphabetic*. The Vigenère cipher is a polyalphabetic cipher, because it uses as many substitution tables as there are letters in the keyword. For example, when it uses the keyword RUG (like on the *Kryptos* maquette), three tables are applied:

```
ABCDEFGHIJKLMNOPQRSTUVWXYZ
--------------------------
RSTUVWXYZABCDEFGHIJKLMNOPQ

ABCDEFGHIJKLMNOPQRSTUVWXYZ
--------------------------
UVWXYZABCDEFGHIJKLMNOPQRST
```

```
ABCDEFGHIJKLMNOPQRSTUVWXYZ
--------------------------
GHIJKLMNOPQRSTUVWXYZABCDEF
```

We can conveniently merge these three tables into one called a Vigenère table:

```
  ABCDEFGHIJKLMNOPQRSTUVWXYZ
  --------------------------
1 RSTUVWXYZABCDEFGHIJKLMNOPQ
2 UVWXYZABCDEFGHIJKLMNOPQRST
3 GHIJKLMNOPQRSTUVWXYZABCDEF
```

This merged table includes three alphabets, represented by the lines numbered 1, 2, and 3.

Apart from the Vigenère cipher, many other polyalphabetic ciphers are mentioned in cryptologic literature. For an overview, check out the website of the American Cryptogram Association, which has done a great job of classifying encryption methods.[3] In this book, we limit ourselves to those polyalphabetic ciphers we have encountered in practice. All of these can be regarded as variants of the Vigenère cipher.

One-time pad

The Vigenère cipher becomes more secure the longer the keyword is. For maximum security, we could even choose a key that is as long as the message! This can be done by using very long text, for instance, a poem or a paragraph from a novel.

It is, however, much more common to use a key that has a sequence of random letters of the same length as the plaintext, for example, the random string LAVBF HJHWQ UIELS KJFLS JFKSA JHFQI UDAJL KX. Now, the plaintext I TRAVEL OVER THE SEA AND RIDE THE ROLLING SKY (taken from the 1975 Fairport Convention song "Rising for the Moon") encrypts as follows:

```
Plaintext:   ITRA VELOVE RT HESEAAN DRIDE THER OLLINGS KY
Key:         LAVB FHJHWQ UI ELSKJFL SJFKS AJHF QIUDAJL KX
------------------------------------------------------------------
Ciphertext:  TTMB ALUVRU LB LPKOJFY VANNW TQLW ETFLNPD UV
```

We call this type of cipher a *one-time pad*. The name comes from early implementations of the cipher, when the random-letter sequence was distributed as a pad of paper that allowed the top sheet to be torn off and destroyed after use.

If used properly, meaning the key is random and only used once, then the one-time pad is an encryption method that cannot be broken. This is because, with this method, any plaintext can be encrypted to every possible ciphertext of the same length. Considered the other way, a single ciphertext could be decrypted to any possible plaintext of that length, with no way of distinguishing one possible plaintext from another.

Because of its security, the one-time pad used to be very popular. Militaries and diplomatic services heavily used it in the early Cold War era of the 1950s. Many spies communicated via one-time pad encryption with their case officers, who provided them with a long list of random letters or numbers to use as keys.

Cipher machines also applied the one-time pad. Most of these devices looked like typewriters, and virtually all of them used a binary version of the one-time pad scheme that was also known as the Vernam cipher, after Gilbert S. Vernam (1890–1960). This means that every character was encoded as a sequence of zeros and ones; the key, too, was a series of zeros and ones usually taken from a punched tape. Adding the plaintext to the ciphertext meant applying an *exclusive-or operation* (see Appendix C).

However, all users of the one-time pad faced a serious problem: they needed a huge amount of key material and, as a result, elaborate processes to distribute these keys to the users. This is because, by definition, each key can only be used once, and a one-time pad's key is always as long as the message to be encrypted. This laborious key handling is the reason the one-time pad began to lose its significance when electronics and computer technology emerged in the 1960s and a new generation of encryption methods became available.

How to detect a polyalphabetic cipher

To detect a Vigenère cipher, we need a frequency analysis and the index of coincidence of the ciphertext. Figure 8-3 shows the letter frequencies of the Vigenère-encrypted text on the *Kryptos* maquette and, for comparison, that of a typical English text. Note that the frequency of the most common letter is 7.48% in this Vigenère cryptogram, compared to around 11.89% in plain English. In general, the frequency distribution of a Vigenère cryptogram is flatter than that of a text encrypted in a simple substitution cipher: frequent letters are less frequent and rare letters are less rare.

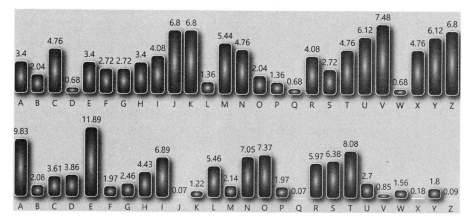

Figure 8-3: The letter frequency diagrams of a Vigenère ciphertext (top) and an English plaintext (bottom). As can be seen, the frequency distribution of a Vigenère cryptogram is flatter. (Note that the scales are slightly different between the two diagrams.)

Remember that the index of coincidence of an English text (i.e., the probability that two randomly drawn letters of the cryptogram are the same) is about 6.7%. This doesn't change if the text is encrypted in a simple substitution cipher. The index of coincidence of the *Kryptos* maquette text is about 4.3%, which is considerably lower. (We can compute this value with the Cipher Tools utilities at *https://rumkin.com/tools/cipher/* or the dCode website at *https://dcode.fr/en.*) Completely random text has an index of coincidence of around 3.8%. In general, the index of coincidence of a Vigenère cryptogram lies somewhere between the values of plain language and random text. A one-time pad cryptogram is indistinguishable from random text and therefore has an index of coincidence of about 3.8%.

It is important to note that polyalphabetic ciphers often resemble letter-pair substitutions. We will explain in Chapter 12 how to distinguish between these two techniques.

How to break a polyalphabetic cipher

For centuries, the Vigenère cipher and other polyalphabetic ciphers were widely considered unbreakable, deemed "le chiffre indéchiffrable." Of course, this designation was far from justified, since, as early as the seventeenth century, word guessing had been described as a method for solving systems of this kind.[4] In the nineteenth century, Kasiski's method (discussed later in this section) was developed. Today, there are many approaches to breaking polyalphabetic ciphers, most of which work well as long as one is not dealing with a one-time pad. Some of these codebreaking methods can be employed manually; others require computer support. Like many other encryption algorithms covered in this book, most polyalphabetic ciphers can be attacked with the computerized hill-climbing method (see Chapter 16).

In the following, we will focus on the Vigenère cipher and introduce a number of methods to solve it. Most of these can also be transferred to other polyalphabetic ciphers and, even if they can be applied manually, have long been implemented in computer programs. If you enter "Vigenère solver" in a search engine, you will find numerous websites that break Vigenère cryptograms with various methods (sometimes not even documenting the method used). In addition, you can, of course, use a utility such as CrypTool 2 or dCode for solving a Vigenère cipher with various methods.

Word guessing

In the 1990s, when Klaus was a computer science student at a German university, he was tasked with solving a cryptogram as homework—something he had never done before. He knew that the cipher was a Vigenère and that the text and keyword were in English. Also, the mapping between letters and numbers was performed according to the **A** = 0, **B** = 1, **C** = 2 scheme. Here's an excerpt of the ciphertext:

```
"VMFA CKT ZM, KK ZSSH,", YX QTER, "DCL VYG'P KNB PHS DJCB. MFN
ATJ'H QWV BL YNCSH FY RAA PZZCWMSAF NBUXDBJWYSCR." FX PFNSU MM
FWYJ VZL CRAG GZRSC YESWQVEW UQH YVVR HNOH BCLEBG'P RT WK.
```

```
TPMDIW ZRR GG PVJ ALW YGZ GVIVEAAAR FH YBK.

"B'I UFAV," AC LWWI, "KV'EJ LAS BVF KSLPG KWILR."
```

As can be seen, punctuation and spaces are visible. This made it possible, as with an Aristocrat cipher, to guess words. For instance, the letter sequences YX QTER are located between two passages in quotation marks, which probably indicate direct speech. Klaus thought that **HE SAID** was a good guess. To check this hypothesis, he subtracted the plaintext from the guessed plaintext:

```
YX QTER
HE SAID
-------
RT YTWO
```

For a computer science student, the rest of the keyword was not hard to guess: it's FORTYTWO, the answer to the ultimate question of life, the universe, and everything in Douglas Adams's bestselling 1979 novel *The Hitchhiker's Guide to the Galaxy* (see Figure 8-4). Decrypting the whole text with this keyword revealed that the plaintext had been taken from the novel, as well. Klaus had solved the challenge, igniting his lifelong interest in codebreaking.

Figure 8-4: A Vigenère-encrypted passage from Douglas Adams's famous 1979 novel was the first cryptogram ever broken by author Klaus Schmeh. The keyword was FORTYTWO.

Checking for repeating patterns (Kasiski's method)

If no punctuation or spaces are given, breaking a Vigenère cipher becomes a little more difficult. Nevertheless, a skilled codebreaker can solve a simple Vigenère cryptogram in under twenty minutes without computer support. Here is a larger encrypted excerpt from the previous example, with punctuation and spaces omitted:

```
KWWMC XJGJQ FGBLH OYSIA CPWGT IKHDM DSMCL LCTJR QMZGE BJTWC
EMMYW PNUPX JEKKG ICEBH VSWHY TRPWG FRMTL VEBLI GAGLC OWRVG
NTPVR FCIPH OGJFN TQTOH MSPLY RKBQM YNKTJ WSCKA CKSCW RJACP
WGFQR KZHJP FGVWJ BBSKC IFBXO QJBUX BYNCR OETNX ICWSJ ICVET
NQREJ RDSBO JYMKP MKOKT LWOVF PSRYG ZKTFB XBYKF YVVEM VWZHC    5
LGABH QZFZH SLHMJ BFNEA PVTIX AFXZW IBKDL HSWYV VPYLW ZXCRW
GKAQY ARECE EBJRV LAXJR FBKHD ZABLV ZLIAW BYVFN EAEBY SIOCG
EBLUV GCKWH NCELY GZFFQ ZTJFE LNBXA YWOCO IXZJX ZVNGX XLXOH
MOKAC AWRSC UBQVA FSWSE CFKBL CCHGW YVFFR VRXNW XHZVQ TJRYV
VHLEU JJGKB EXOZJ TKBLF NZUFF LQXNC KVZLK BCVYM RGAXO HWMNX    10
PXWDW CEHSG YSIGK HSMJS XGRUM NPHMS KNKTJ RFDIX BBHSH HZHLY
KFQWK MJXBI WVRMQ AAKFG SRLHI SFBJT EKAOY KRKPB KFNBW TAMDS
BOJTL XNJTI JPMKN WJRDT LMKRF MYXUT ODFFK BANHO WZPGC KRCZG
RGBPK FWWVW ZXYOZ GVLMF AHMWE ZFTZU TBVLC KECZG CRUKK BLKZM
FAEGO CSPFB YVBOJ MMLAS YVRMY KPVZF UXLMO VTIJX EHPQQ SRKCW    15
KIYCW MFXSO DPVYM KAHMS UTWPW GTIKV MFACK TZMKK ZSSHY XQTER
DCLVY GPKNB PHSDJ CBMFN ATJHQ WVBLY NCSHF YRAAP ZZCWM SAFNB
UXDBJ WYSCR FXPFN SUMMF WYJVZ LCRAG GZRSC YESWQ VEWUQ HYVVR
HNOHB CLEBG PRTWK TPMDI WZRRG GPVJA LWYGZ GVIVE AAARF HYBKB
IUFAV ACLWW IKVEJ LASBV FKSLP GKWIL RBIOK FRBBR KIWSX HGGCH    20
TVROC MKOHQ VIRBP GFWUF PINCX GVKEK EDUWE ZFBOT ZFYTR TJRWC
CEGGC WYFFN LWPVJ HFIMY DWXVV TBMDW XPPIY LOVFG XHRMK PJPLB
JMWBI WKLEH EBLHF UCUQW QHWBP LPWAS YXYKZ CKWKL YBZOW HYNPP
DMXWK ZMBJU YCSXZ NEZYA IIPHO GJFJA MHGVN GWBLZ AFFHY BKYKF
FPZMR AABXH FINXZ OSRGN RBPOB OPTET EBBVR MBHUC ZAVTL PDMXW    25
KZMMP CGSSN GEPVJ GRBBB PGFPP IYLOM TIMXE HPHTP LBJWX MUOJL
CLXMU OJLCL WFJRV OGVAG BVZVF THZTK JHKXL STDCX RHZFN JVYPH
IDTWE MYMKD TWEMZ OAFDT RLRPD WQGKH RAAFU SFIJX ZOXVW KMFLC
NBKUR HLCNB KTTXN MKOJM NXKDQ SCBTB JUFHG HGGPQ GSZGE TLCNB
KWGKA QYZPB LUAHB SVGYK ACKHV GEBRS SHFPM GZSWK YTRLO CLFVT    30
RTXCZ HGHGG POYVR MQHIO SMGXM IHSTT GHGGP PFFVL MDASS HFZCM
PVJFV TLWSV FHJLM ZNSFH RUMNP DTWEM ZMDOY GFFYG UDJCG ECHBD
TWEMY TNSXC BXCGP CLSKM FXNSY VVRMY PSSKZ LFMDO YDVHN EAKTI
CWHNO HTBTX YGZTT FREJP KFPCL MUAAF JHYXF XHZYV VRUTJ HJRKH
ZXIFU FFLQX NKFBK XBMKP JOKIM BJHID FBLMZ KFGEM YGUKM SIXGG    35
LOWHZ VSEWF NHNTQ CQGYO ERAHJ JJBZX LMLCN BKTTX NMQCE ZUTUT
WCDIM BJHXO STLWY VJKFN JWDOA SRGGV AZNHK ECVKH YOXXY MLCNB
KWUBP VFLVL MOAFY VVWMH NOSRJ ICGZO UZVTQ TJHFA FNLMK TYWDX
YMLCN BKXUA EQMKF NJWXS YVVGC TNSXH GNZMK DTWEM BAEGB WWXMY
YCZFJ XUTJH JRTEG FXWSU IHQXO PZHYX UTJHJ RRQCL DSIWU GRDJC    40
BKYRF XFIXH CBIXZ OCSJA CYHIX VVWFH PZDIE WCKPV JRVKG LEJJU
IBLLK TYVV
```

The trick is to first discover the length of the keyword. Once we know it, solving a Vigenère cipher means solving a few Caesar ciphers. A good way to guess the keyword length is to look for repeating patterns in a cryptogram, a technique referred to as *Kasiski's method*. For instance, in lines 22 and 26, we find the repeating pattern PPIYLO:

```
CEGGC WYFFN LWPVJ HFIMY DWXVV TBMDW XPPIY LOVFG XHRMK PJPLB
JMWBI WKLEH EBLHF UCUQW QHWBP LPWAS YXYKZ CKWKL YBZOW HYNPP
DMXWK ZMBJU YCSXZ NEZYA IIPHO GJFJA MHGVN GWBLZ AFFHY BKYKF
FPZMR AABXH FINXZ OSRGN RBPOB OPTET EBBVR MBHUC ZAVTL PDMXW
KZMMP CGSSN GEPVJ GRBBB PGFPP IYLOM TIMXE HPHTP LBJWX MUOJL
```

The distance between the beginnings of the first and the second appearance of the pattern is 192 letters.

In lines 28 and 33, we find another repeating pattern, DTWEMY:

```
IDTWE MYMKD TWEMZ OAFDT RLRPD WQGKH RAAFU SFIJX ZOXVW KMFLC
NBKUR HLCNB KTTXN MKOJM NXKDQ SCBTB JUFHG HGGPQ GSZGE TLCNB
KWGKA QYZPB LUAHB SVGYK ACKHV GEBRS SHFPM GZSWK YTRLO CLFVT
RTXCZ HGHGG POYVR MQHIO SMGXM IHSTT GHGGP PFFVL MDASS HFZCM
PVJFV TLWSV FHJLM ZNSFH RUMNP DTWEM ZMDOY GFFYG UDJCG ECHBD
TWEMY TNSXC BXCGP CLSKM FXNSY VVRMY PSSKZ LFMDO YDVHN EAKTI
```

This time, the number of letters before the repetition begins is 248.

In line 28, a third repetition can be found, DTWEM:

```
IDTWE MYMKD TWEMZ OAFDT RLRPD WQGKH RAAFU SFIJX ZOXVW KMFLC
```

Here, the distance is 8.

The distances we have found are 192, 248, and 8. The greatest common divisor of these three numbers is 8. This means that the key length is probably 8 or a divisor of 8. A keyword length of 8 means that we are dealing with eight Caesar ciphers. In the next step, we therefore perform eight frequency counts. We start by counting the letters at positions 1, 9, 17, 25, 33, 41, and so on. Here is what we get:

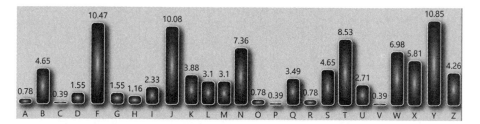

If we compare this with the frequencies of an ordinary English text (see Appendix B), we see that the Caesar cipher used here is a direct one-to-one correlation, with **A** = F, **B** = G, **C** = H . . . This means that the first letter of the keyword is probably F.

Now let's count the letters at positions 2, 10, 18, and so on:

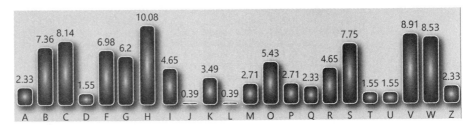

This time, we get **A** = O, **B** = P, **C** = Q . . . The second keyword letter therefore is very likely to be O.

If we repeat this procedure six more times, we get the letters F, O, R, T, Y, T, W, and O. This suggests that the keyword length really is eight. If we had received a keyword like FORTFORT, we would know that the four-letter FORT was the actual keyword. Using the keyword FORTYTWO, we can easily decrypt the ciphertext and retrieve the *Hitchhiker's Guide to the Galaxy* excerpt.

Using the index of coincidence

Kasiski's method is usually the best way to determine the Vigenère keyword length by hand. If a computer is available, there are better methods. Quite often, the index of coincidence can help us determine the number of letters in the keyword. A good way to use this value is to assume different keyword lengths (for instance, lengths between three and twenty-five) and compute the index of coincidence for each case. Assuming an English plaintext, the index of coincidence that is the closest to a normal English value of 6.7% is probably correct.

The dCode website (*https://dcode.fr/en*) provides us with a tool that performs such a test. Here are the results we get for *The Hitchhiker's Guide to the Galaxy* excerpt:

Length = 24: index of coincidence = 6.4%

Length = 8: index of coincidence = 6.3%

Length = 16: index of coincidence = 6.2%

Length = 4: index of coincidence = 4.9%

Length = 12: index of coincidence = 4.9%

Length = 20: index of coincidence = 4.8%

Length = 26: index of coincidence = 4.6%

Length = 14: index of coincidence = 4.6%

The keyword length of twenty-four renders the highest index of coincidence, which is closest to the English 6.7%. Twenty-four is wrong, but we can live with this, because it is a multiple of 8. When we solve twenty-four Caesar ciphers in the next step, we will get FORTYTWOFORTYTWOFORTYTWO as the keyword. The second guess (a keyword length of 8 letters) is the correct one.

Now that we know the keyword length, we can tell the dCode utility to solve the cryptogram. By solving a Caesar cipher for each letter of the keyword, dCode renders the correct solution. This is shown in Figure 8-5.

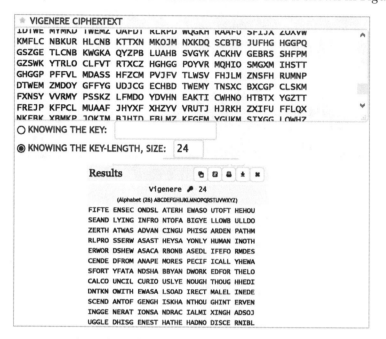

Figure 8-5: The website dCode (https://dcode.fr/en) provides tools to solve a Vigenère cipher step-by-step.

Let's now try the same with the text on the *Kryptos* maquette. Here is what dCode delivers us:

Length = 3: index of coincidence = 6.3%

Length = 6: index of coincidence = 6.2%

Length = 9: index of coincidence = 5.9%

Length = 13: index of coincidence = 5.2%

Length = 11: index of coincidence = 4.9%

Length = 12: index of coincidence = 5.5%

Length = 15: index of coincidence = 5.8%

Length = 18: index of coincidence = 5.9%

Length = 8: index of coincidence = 4.3%

Length = 1: index of coincidence = 4.3%

As can be seen, the keyword length of three provides the best result. This is correct, as the keyword is RUG.

William Friedman, who introduced the index of coincidence to codebreaking, developed a formula that uses it to compute an estimated keyword length from the ciphertext. This formula is known as the *Friedman test*. It requires fewer calculations than performing the index-of-coincidence comparisons we just walked through, but it is also less accurate, especially if the plaintext language is not known. For a detailed treatise on the index-of-coincidence method and the Friedman test, we recommend Craig Bauer's book *Secret History*.[5]

Dictionary attacks

Another way to break a Vigenère cipher is the so-called dictionary attack, which requires the use of a computer program. A dictionary attack requires a long list of words, called a *dictionary*, which is stored in a file. Dictionary files of all kinds are available on the internet in great numbers. For example, there are files containing the 20,000 most popular words of the English language. Similar collections have been created for many other languages, geographical expressions, names, abbreviations, and more. In addition, there are programs that create dozens of different versions of a given word (for instance, *CALIFORNIA, CALIFORNYA, CALIF, CA, AINROFILAC . . .*).

A program executing a dictionary attack on the Vigenère cipher takes one word after another from such a source, derives different versions of it, and uses each one as a possible key to decrypt the ciphertext. Then it checks whether the result looks like plain English (or whatever language is used). Methods to distinguish meaningful text from gibberish will be introduced in Chapter 16. When the test for meaningful language is positive, the deciphering has succeeded; otherwise, the next keyword candidate is tested.

While trying to break a Vigenère cipher with a dictionary attack is feasible,[6] it is not very common. This is probably because more powerful computer-based attacks on the Vigenère cipher are available, such as hill climbing, which is discussed in Chapter 16.

Tobias Schrödel's method

In 2008, our colleague, the German crypto expert Tobias Schrödel, published a hitherto unknown Vigenère cipher-breaking method in *Cryptologia*.[7] This attack is based on the elimination of rare letter combinations in both the plaintext and the keyword. It requires a computer program (and, in fact, is part of CrypTool 1, the forerunner of CrypTool 2). Tobias's method is particularly helpful in cases when the message is not much longer than the keyword (e.g., a fifteen-letter plaintext encrypted with a seven-letter keyword). However, the keyword must be a real word and not a random-letter sequence—otherwise, eliminating rare letter combinations is useless.

In his article, Tobias introduces the ciphertext IZRUOJVREFLFZKSWSE, which was encrypted with a Vigenère cipher. The traditional methods used to attack a Vigenère cipher don't work here. For instance, no words can be guessed, because the text contains no spaces. In addition, the cryptogram is short, and there are no repetitions that might reveal the keyword length. Even if we know or guess the length of the keyword, performing, say, six frequency analyses won't help, because there are too few letters.

However, Tobias's method can break this cryptogram. By eliminating rare letter combinations, it finds that the common trigraphs *BLA* and *HOR* generate IZR (the first three letters of the ciphertext) when one is encrypted with the other. Based on frequency considerations, the method next suggests *BLACK* and *HORSE* as extensions of the two trigraphs. It is not clear which word is the keyword and which is the plaintext, but further tests reveal that the keyword HORSE makes sense. When it is used to decrypt the cryptogram, the resulting plaintext is **BLACK CHAMBER IS OPEN**.

Other Vigenère breaking methods

In her 1939 book *Cryptanalysis*, Helen Fouché Gaines described a linguistic approach to solving a Vigenère cipher.[8] It requires luck and a lot of trial and error. Richard Hayes described a similar but more advanced technique, based on common trigraphs, in 1943.[9] Both methods are rarely used today, as more powerful alternatives have emerged since the advent of computer technology.

Another method we won't discuss in this book is Viterbi analysis, which is based on hidden Markov models. Interesting articles about this approach have been published in the scientific journal *Cryptologia*.[10, 11]

How to break a one-time pad

As we mentioned, it is impossible to break a one-time pad if the key is a random sequence without any regularities and is only used once. However, more often than not over the course of history, these requirements have been breached. One of the most common mistakes occurred when the same key was used several times.

In the following, we explain how a one-time pad can be broken if the same key is employed for two messages. To demonstrate this, let's first encrypt the plaintext **WASHINGTON** with the (random) key KDFYDVKHAP:

```
WASHINGTON
KDFYDVKHAP
----------
GDXFLIQAOC
```

Next, we encrypt the plaintext **CALIFORNIA** with the same key:

```
CALIFORNIA
KDFYDVKHAP
----------
MDQGIJBUIP
```

Now, we decrypt the first plaintext with the second one:

```
WASHINGTON
CALIFORNIA
----------
UAHZDZPGGN
```

If we decrypt the first ciphertext with the second one, we receive the same result:

```
GDXFLIQAOC
MDQGIJBUIP
----------
UAHZDZPGGN
```

This means that if a codebreaker knows both ciphertexts (GDXFLIQAOC and MDQGIJBUIP) and that one of the plaintexts is **WASHINGTON**, they can easily derive the second plaintext, **CALIFORNIA**. This also works the other way around: if **CALIFORNIA** is known, **WASHINGTON** can be derived.

We can easily generalize this approach to longer messages. If a cryptanalyst knows two one-time pad ciphertexts encrypted with the same key and has a crib in one of the two cryptograms, they can easily derive a part of the other plaintext. If the latter part is, say, **E UNITED S**, this can be extended to **THE UNITED STATES**, which means that **TH** and **TATES** become new cribs. With this method, it may be possible to completely derive both plaintexts.

Success stories

The Diana Dors message

English actress Diana Dors (1931–1984) was once considered the British counterpart to Marilyn Monroe. In dozens of films, she played a seductive blonde and lived a private life worthy of a film diva. Before dying of cancer at age fifty-two, she gave her son Mark Dawson an encrypted message, telling him that it described the whereabouts of a substantial sum that she had hidden away: £2 million.

The headline of the text was encrypted using a pigpen cipher:

After some research, Dawson deciphered this to **LOCATIONS AND NAMES**. It turned out that his mother had used the following substitution table:

```
A│B│C        M       N.│Q.│P
─┼─┼─    L ◇ J     ──┼──┼──
D│E│F        ˙       Q˙│˙R│˙S
─┼─┼─        K       ──┼──┼──
G│H│I                T│Ù│˙V
```

The main part of the cryptogram was written in ordinary letters:

```
EAWVL XEIMO RZTIC SELKM KMRUQ
QPYFC ZAOUA TNEYS QOHVQ YPLYS
OEOEW TCEFY ZZEPI NYAUD RZUGM
SSONV JDAER SZNVS QSHRK XPVCC
WUAEJ JTWGC WQRCC NRBKZ VIITF
RZLTS VOAIB NQZOK VANJJ TFAJO
GYUEB XZHRY UFSDM ZEBRK GIECJ
QZHFY QBYVU FNEGD EDIXF YZHOM
PMNLQ XFHFO UXAEB HZSNO EAUIL
JXIWD KTUDN MCCGC EURDG SRBCW
GMNKC RLHER HETVP GWOGC WANVJ
NGYTZ RALTM TAYTL UUSKM QIRZH
```

As Dawson couldn't decipher this ciphertext, he consulted a team of British cryptologists, including Andrew Clark, who succeeded in breaking the cryptogram. However, the message's meaning remained a mystery. A 2004 TV documentary later chronicled the team's work.[12]

To begin with, Clark and his colleagues performed a few statistical analyses of the cryptogram. The results proved consistent with a Vigenère cipher, and they had no trouble breaking it (probably by first determining the keyword length using one of the methods described earlier in this chapter). The keyword turned out to be DMARYFLUCK (likely derived from Dors's legal name, Diana Mary Fluck).

Here is how the first line is decrypted:

```
Ciphertext:   EAWVL XEIMO RZTIC SELKM KMRUQ . . .
Key:          DMARY FLUCK DMARY FLUCK DMARY . . .
Plaintext:    BOWEN STOKE ONTRE NTRIC HARDS . . .
```

The text consisted of a list of surnames, each followed by a city in England or Wales:

```
Bowen, Stoke-on-Trent
Richards, Leeds
Woodcock, Winchester
Wilson, York
Downey, Kingston Upon Hull
Grant, Nottingham
Sebastian, Leicester
Leigh, Ipswich
Morris, Cardiff
Mason, Slough
Edmundson, Portsmouth
Padwell, London
Pyewacket, Brighton
```

```
McManus, Sunderland

Coyle, Bournemouth

Humphries, Birmingham

Dante, Manchester

Bluestone, Liverpool

Cooper, Bristol
```

The meaning of this list is not known, and we have no idea whether these names refer to real people. Diana Dors's son never found the millions his mother had allegedly left behind, and it is doubtful that this estate really existed. Although Dors had done well during her early career, she declared bankruptcy in 1968 and from then on supported herself with minor engagements.

Kryptos 1 and 2

The two panels on the right side of the *Kryptos* sculpture located at CIA headquarters show a Vigenère-type table with an alphabet written in the following order. The letters of the word **KRYPTOS** are shifted to the beginning:

```
KRYPTOSABCDEFGHIJLMNQUVWXZ
```

The top-left panel contains the following ciphertext:

```
EMUFPHZLRFAXYUSDJKZLDKRNSHGNFIVJ
YQTQUXQBQVYUVLLTREVJYQTMKYRDMFD
VFPJUDEEHZWETZYVGWHKKQETGFQJNCE
GGWHKK?DQMCPFQZDQMMIAGPFXHQRLG
TIMVMZJANQLVKQEDAGDVFRPJUNGEUNA
QZGZLECGYUXUEENJTBJLBQCRTBJDFHRR
YIZETKZEMVDUFKSJHKFWHKUWQLSZFTI
HHDDDUVH?DWKBFUFPWNTDFIYCUQZERE
EVLDKFEZMOQQJLTTUGSYQPFEUNLAVIDX
FLGGTEZ?FKZBSFDQVGOGIPUFXHHDRKF
FHQNTGPUAECNUVPDJMQCLQUMUNEDFQ
ELZZVRRGKFFVOEEXBDMVPNFQXEZLGRE
DNQFMPNZGLFLPMRJQYALMGNUVPDXVKP
DQUMEBEDMHDAFMJGZNUPLGEWJLLAETG
```

As you can read about in Appendix A, this cryptogram was broken independently at least three times by codebreakers who were not aware of each other's achievements. In this section, we provide the approach used by CIA employee David Stein, who was the second one to solve it. His work is documented in a paper that is available online.[13]

Stein started by performing a frequency analysis. He realized that the encrypted message had the appearance of a Vigenère cryptogram. Using Friedman's method, based on the index of coincidence, Stein found out that the most likely keyword length was eight. This was confirmed by the repetition of the trigraph DQM after eight letters in the fourth line (Kasiski's method):

```
D Q M C P F Q Z D Q M
1 2 3 4 5 6 7 8
```

Stein's first guess was that the DQM trigraph stood for the most common trigraph in the English language, THE. In another attack on the ciphertext, he did an additional frequency analysis. Knowing that a Vigenère cipher with an eight-letter keyword is equivalent to eight Caesar encryptions, Stein counted the frequencies of every eighth letter. However, neither of these approaches led to a solution.

He then guessed that a Vigenère cipher with a permutated alphabet—one starting with KRYPTOS, as on the other side of the sculpture—had been used. Based on this assumption, he tried to solve the eight Caesar ciphers with frequency analysis once again. This time, he was on the right track. The Vigenère keyword he found was ABSCISSA, a word referring to the *x*-coordinate of a point on a graph. The DQM ciphertext came out to THE(Y) and THE.

However, only lines 3 through 13 of the encrypted message produced meaningful plaintext, while the first two decrypted to gibberish. Stein guessed that these two lines were encrypted with the same method but a different keyword. This conjecture proved correct, and Stein determined that the keyword for those lines was PALIMPSEST. (A *palimpsest* is a manuscript page whose text has been scraped or washed off so that it can be reused for another text, in such a way that bits of the older message can be seen through the new one.) Here's the Vigenère table used to encrypt lines 1 and 2 (note the keyword PALIMPSEST in the first column):

```
KRYPTOSABCDEFGHIJLMNQUVWXZ
--------------------------
PTOSABCDEFGHIJLMNQUVWXZKRY
ABCDEFGHIJLMNQUVWXZKRYPTOS
LMNQUVWXZKRYPTOSABCDEFGHIJ
IJLMNQUVWXZKRYPTOSABCDEFGH
MNQUVWXZKRYPTOSABCDEFGHIJL
PTOSABCDEFGHIJLMNQUVWXZKRY
SABCDEFGHIJLMNQUVWXZKRYPTO
EFGHIJLMNQUVWXZKRYPTOSABCD
SABCDEFGHIJLMNQUVWXZKRYPTO
TOSABCDEFGHIJLMNQUVWXZKRYP
```

The plaintext of the first two lines reads as follows. It includes a misspelled word:

```
BETWEEN SUBTLE SHADING AND THE ABSENCE OF LIGHT LIES THE
NUANCE OF IQLUSION
```

For lines 3 through 13, Sanborn used the following Vigenère table based on the keyword ABSCISSA:

```
KRYPTOSABCDEFGHIJLMNQUVWXZ
--------------------------
ABCDEFGHIJLMNQUVWXZKRYPTOS
BCDEFGHIJLMNQUVWXZKRYPTOSA
SABCDEFGHIJLMNQUVWXZKRYPTO
CDEFGHIJLMNQUVWXZKRYPTOSAB
IJLMNQUVWXZKRYPTOSABCDEFGH
SABCDEFGHIJLMNQUVWXZKRYPTO
SABCDEFGHIJLMNQUVWXZKRYPTO
ABCDEFGHIJLMNQUVWXZKRYPTOS
```

Here is the corresponding plaintext result (including another spelling error):

```
IT WAS TOTALLY INVISIBLE HOWS THAT POSSIBLE? THEY USED THE EARTHS
MAGNETIC FIELD X THE INFORMATION WAS GATHERED AND TRANSMITTED
UNDERGRUUND TO AN UNKNOWN LOCATION X DOES LANGLEY KNOW ABOUT THIS?
THEY SHOULD ITS BURIED OUT THERE SOMEWHERE X WHO KNOWS THE EXACT
LOCATION? ONLY WW THIS WAS HIS LAST MESSAGE X THIRTY EIGHT DEGREES
FIFTY SEVEN MINUTES SIX POINT FIVE SECONDS NORTH SEVENTY SEVEN
DEGREES EIGHT MINUTES FORTY FOUR SECONDS WEST ID BY ROWS
```

In 2006, several years after the solution was made publicly available, Sanborn, the creator of *Kryptos*, indicated that the last three words of the plaintext, **ID BY ROWS**, were wrong because of a missing S in the last line of the ciphertext. The intended ending of the plaintext was **X LAYER TWO**. None of the previous solvers had noticed this error, as by mere coincidence, the expression **ID BY ROWS** seemed to make sense.

The Cyrillic Projector

Sanborn is the creator not only of *Kryptos* but also of several other encrypted works. For example, in the 1990s, he created another sculpture bearing an encrypted message: the *Cyrillic Projector*. It was first displayed in his gallery shows, and then in 1997, it found its way to its current location on the campus of the University of North Carolina at Charlotte. The *Cyrillic Projector* consists of a large bronze cylinder over two meters high, with hundreds of letters carved into it. A bright light in the center of the sculpture shines through the letters, projecting their images around the courtyard.

Like in *Kryptos*, the letters on the *Cyrillic Projector* are carved into four panels that form the cylinder. The two panels located out of sight in Figure 8-6 display a Vigenère-type tableau in the Russian (Cyrillic) alphabet, transposed such that the letters of the word ТЕНЬ (Russian for *shadow*) occur at the beginning. It is important to note that the untransposed order of the letters in the Cyrillic alphabet varies depending on, among other things, the region where it is used. The letter order used for the *Cyrillic Projector* is not the most common one.

Figure 8-6 *The* Cyrillic Projector, *located on the campus of the University of North Carolina at Charlotte, is a sculpture bearing an encrypted inscription. The upper-right photograph shows Elonka serving as a screen for the projected word* MEDUSA *(the only portion not written in Cyrillic letters).*

The text on the two other panels (shown in the picture) is an encrypted message. It is written in Cyrillic script, too, except for the word MEDUSA in the fourteenth line. In Cyrillic, one would expect this to be spelled МЕДУЗА; the use of Latin letters instead gives a hint about one of the keys.

The ciphertext on the *Cyrillic Projector* is reproduced here:

```
ЛТФЕЮТФЯЙЯМПХЦФАЧНЩПВБГЖЧСКЬГГЛЗДЭЙП
ЪКХСЙРЭАФНФПЩВПЕЦРДФАШТКСХСЧУУХХЕЮ
КУМЛЕЧЛЫТОБНЕЯЖЖИЬНЭЗЩЦРЛЫБПНФОИИАБЬ
ПИКЛЕУРЫСМЪШЛЛБХМХЛЖШРАЩРЙЛПЕООЙЙВЦ
ИЪЛБХЦРЫЧСКАРСРВЯЭФКЮФРЮМОЯЗОЛОДЭШРЗУ
ДХМАЭХОЙГЙЮФМЩХХСВИИЗХАГЙЯЬПСИБРРШОМ
КТСУЯГХУЬЛЕУРЫСМЪШСППЯЯЦШУШАЦЧПИМШН
РБЧРЯЫМИУРАДФАИЮЙЫЦЯЛОНУФЖОФШХФЖСБ
ВЪЧДЦСФБМДЭШРЗУДХУРБШТОКЩЬМХПОТОХОЩЧ
ЖАЦДЩРАЮГОЙВРБГЮБЗГЕЖРЙЛПЕООЙЙВЦНЗПГФ
ЦЗАИВЯЮФЛЬЦХСЧШЬБЕОМЩЖТЭДЙОТТФХПР
ПЛОДЭЩРЗУДХКПГФОЦБЩЬММЭКЧЕРЛМКЬЦЦЗЩЛ
ФЦЧЪЩКВНФАЕСДПТДФПРЯЙКЮНХВЦБЮЕИСЧЯЧЦ
ХМЖЛСПРЧУЛЭШЖЫИИMEDUSAИНХЕЗЛЧЗРЗЙКЛ
ППЕВЛЧСХЦЫОЙВРБУДХСВЪГЖЧСКАРСРВЯЭФРЩФ
ЯЦЩПЪЗЫТФОЙЙУСДТЮТВСБРХСПБЩЛШКУВЙЙГЗ
ЙАЧЛЬРЙЭМДЧЧРЬСТНКЙЕКДОБЖБЛШИЫЙБЙИДРР
ЦХОЩЖВЪКБЧКЖНФПШЦЗУЙДЯГАЧЙКУЗФЕЦИЯИ
```

```
ЙФЭБЛСДТГЗШРЖЕДФЩЖЙЯНБООЬШФПЮКЗЦУДИ
НХЕОХПОЙАХДЭСБШЙЖЭШВЪОДЩВУСЛМЩГЖШУД
ИГЛЕШКПУУЕЧДЛСУЦЮТЮНХЪПБУПРЬГИУСБЙЙПЮ
ГАФФЕШБФБМЙПИМЬЮКЩХХТНФЩШПЕЯБЧККЩ
ВЙЩЗЛЮСВЮЙКУКФСЫТЫСВЛСЛЬЗУЦИКЩДРСУРЗ
ХРФЙРЭМРХФЛКФАЙЙКУАЛЩГМЙЖЪЙЬЩКФНФ
ИДЙРФГКУКАЯЙОУМАТЭТЦКВЕЖОЙИДЦДКГЩФЕЖ
БЮХЛЕССЭСНЩШХПОЬДЖЙЙЗГЕИТЙМАШЙЙУМФС
ЫТЫСВСИДСДРБФНУОРУШТБЗПЪДЗЯЫААЧКУМАЯХ
ТМЦРИЦЗЩЛЛЕУУПФЖТЭДУХРШЙОРБЭЦЙОПЙЛЪЙ
ТЧШЙАФНПШФЭМБЩЪЖТПДЛРШБШБЧРЖЫМНЧЗЫ
ТЙЖЪСМЬЧДХКЛНЦПЗХРФЙРЭМРХФМЫББЪЧБШЕФ
БЖТЩВВЪУБЧКЖАЦПЫГШАМИПРЙЪГОЦКЙГРЛЮБУ
СПБЮРРХФТЫХЖТГИЙКАФМТНКЙФФНЦЙЫСЧБШЕ
```

After Sanborn made the sculpture accessible to the public, several years passed before anyone seriously tried to break the encryption. In 2003, a group of seventy *Kryptos* enthusiasts led by Elonka finally took up the cause. Group member Randall Bollig captured multiple photos of the *Cyrillic Projector*. Through weeks of painstaking work, three other group members, Elonka, Bill Houck, and Brian Hill, each created an independent transcript. They later compared their transcripts to generate a fully accurate one. (Imagine the difficulty of transcribing Cyrillic letters read from backward images of a cylindrical sculpture!) Elonka then published the corrected transcript on her website.[14]

Soon after the transcript was published, two hobbyist codebreakers, Frank Corr and Mike Bales, independently broke the encryption. Neither announced a full English solution, as they didn't speak Russian, the language of the plaintext, and couldn't translate it. When Elonka learned of their potential success, she located a native speaker, Anatoly Kolker. He was a colleague of Elonka's father, Stanley Dunin, at the World Bank. Anatoly confirmed that the solution was written in Russian and provided the final English translation. The plaintext proved to be composed of two texts from the Cold War. It starts as follows:

```
ВЫСОЧАЙЪИМИСКУССТВОМВТАЙНОЙРАЗВ
ЕДКЕСПИТАЕ...
```

The cipher used turned out to be a Vigenère variant with the keyword МЕДУЗА (MEDUSA) and the alphabet reordered in the same way as on the tableau, with the letters Т, Е,Н, and Ь transposed to the beginning.[15] To create the Vigenère tableau necessary for encrypting the plaintext, we first need the following table:

```
АБВГДЕЖЗИЙКЛМНОПРСТУФХЦЧШЩЪЫЬЭЮЯ
--------------------------------
А  ТЕНЬАБВГДЖЗИЙКЛМОПРСУФХЩЦЧЩЪЫЭЮЯ
Б  ЕНЬАБВГДЖЗИЙКЛМОПРСУФХШЦЧЩЪЫЭЮЯТ
В  НЬАБВГДЖЗИЙКЛМОПРСУФХШЦЧЩЪЫЭЮЯТЕ
Г  ЬАБВГДЖЗИЙКЛМОПРСУФХШЦЧЩЪЫЭЮЯТЕН
```

```
Д АБВГДЖЗИЙКЛМОПРСУФХШЦЧЩЪЫЭЮЯТЕНЬ
Е БВГДЖЗИЙКЛМОПРСУФХШЦЧЩЪЫЭЮЯТЕНЬА
Ж ВГДЖЗИЙКЛМОПРСУФХШЦЧЩЪЫЭЮЯТЕНЬАБ
З ГДЖЗИЙКЛМОПРСУФХШЦЧЩЪЫЭЮЯТЕНЬАБВ
И ДЖЗИЙКЛМОПРСУФХШЦЧЩЪЫЭЮЯТЕНЬАБВГ
Й ЖЗИЙКЛМОПРСУФХШЦЧЩЪЫЭЮЯТЕНЬАБВГД
К ЗИЙКЛМОПРСУФХШЦЧЩЪЫЭЮЯТЕНЬАБВГДЖ
Л ИЙКЛМОПРСУФХШЦЧЩЪЫЭЮЯТЕНЬАБВГДЖЗ
М ЙКЛМОПРСУФХШЦЧЩЪЫЭЮЯТЕНЬАБВГДЖЗИ
Н КЛМОПРСУФХШЦЧЩЪЫЭЮЯТЕНЬАБВГДЖЗИЙ
О ЛМОПРСУФХШЦЧЩЪЫЭЮЯТЕНЬАБВГДЖЗИЙК
П МОПРСУФХШЦЧЩЪЫЭЮЯТЕНЬАБВГДЖЗИЙКЛ
Р ОПРСУФХШЦЧЩЪЫЭЮЯТЕНЬАБВГДЖЗИЙКЛМ
С ПРСУФХШЦЧЩЪЫЭЮЯТЕНЬАБВГДЖЗИЙКЛМО
Т РСУФХШЦЧЩЪЫЭЮЯТЕНЬАБВГДЖЗИЙКЛМОП
У СУФХШЦЧЩЪЫЭЮЯТЕНЬАБВГДЖЗИЙКЛМОПР
Ф УФХШЦЧЩЪЫЭЮЯТЕНЬАБВГДЖЗИЙКЛМОПРС
Х ФХШЦЧЩЪЫЭЮЯТЕНЬАБВГДЖЗИЙКЛМОПРСУ
Ц ХШЦЧЩЪЫЭЮЯТЕНЬАБВГДЖЗИЙКЛМОПРСУФ
Ч ШЦЧЩЪЫЭЮЯТЕНЬАБВГДЖЗИЙКЛМОПРСУФХ
Ш ЦЧЩЪЫЭЮЯТЕНЬАБВГДЖЗИЙКЛМОПРСУФХШ
Щ ЧЩЪЫЭЮЯТЕНЬАБВГДЖЗИЙКЛМОПРСУФХШЦ
Ъ ЩЪЫЭЮЯТЕНЬАБВГДЖЗИЙКЛМОПРСУФХШЦЧ
Ы ЪЫЭЮЯТЕНЬАБВГДЖЗИЙКЛМОПРСУФХШЦЧЩ
Ь ЫЭЮЯТЕНЬАБВГДЖЗИЙКЛМОПРСУФХШЦЧЩЪ
Э ЭЮЯТЕНЬАБВГДЖЗИЙКЛМОПРСУФХШЦЧЩЪЫ
Ю ЮЯТЕНЬАБВГДЖЗИЙКЛМОПРСУФХШЦЧЩЪЫЭ
Я ЯТЕНЬАБВГДЖЗИЙКЛМОПРСУФХШЦЧЩЪЫЭЮ
```

As can be seen, the Cyrillic alphabet (А,Б,В,Г . . .) is used to index the rows of the table. To encrypt this message, only the rows М,Е,Д,У,З, and А are relevant. We arrange them such that they form the word МЕДУЗА:

```
АБВГДЕЖЗИЙКЛМНОПРСТУФХЦЧШЩЪЫЬЭЮЯ
-------------------------------
М ЙКЛМОПРСУФХШЦЧЩЪЫЭЮЯТЕНЬАБВГДЖЗИ
Е БВГДЖЗИЙКЛМОПРСУФХШЦЧЩЪЫЭЮЯТЕНЬА
Д АБВГДЖЗИЙКЛМОПРСУФХШЦЧЩЪЫЭЮЯТЕНЬ
У СУФХШЦЧЩЪЫЭЮЯТЕНЬАБВГДЖЗИЙКЛМОПР
З ГДЖЗИЙКЛМОПРСУФХШЦЧЩЪЫЭЮЯТЕНЬАБВ
А ТЕНЬАБВГДЖЗИЙКЛМОПРСУФХШЦЧЩЪЫЭЮЯ
```

The following lines show how the plaintext is mapped to the ciphertext using the reduced table:

```
Plaintext:   ВЫСОЧАЙЪИМИ . . .
Ciphertext:  ЛТФЕЮТФЯЙЯМ . . .
```

We will leave the full solution as an exercise for those readers who wish to try, Cold War–style, to decipher a message in the Cyrillic alphabet!

Thouless's second cryptogram from the crypt

In 1948, British psychologist and parapsychologist Robert Thouless (1894–1984) started an unusual experiment.[16] He took a short text, encrypted it, and published the ciphertext, keeping the plaintext and key secret. His plan was to channel the key from the beyond after his death. If somebody received the correct key via this paranormal method, they would be able to decipher the cryptogram. This experiment, if successful, would prove that there is life after death and that the dead can communicate with the living—which would certainly be one of the greatest discoveries in the history of science.

As far as we know, Thouless's experiment did not prove successful—nobody ever came up with a correct solution received from the beyond. This is also true for a similar message created by Thouless's fellow parapsychologist T.E. Wood, whose cryptogram is covered later in this chapter.

To be on the safe side, Thouless even published a second ciphertext in 1948, encrypted in a different way. However, his plan was foiled, as just a few weeks later, an unknown codebreaker solved his first ciphertext. In response, Thouless created a third cryptogram. This means that altogether, he left behind three messages in 1948. The first and third are encrypted with variations of a Playfair cipher and are covered in Chapter 12.

The encryption method Thouless used for the second message is complicated but has some elements that are similar to the Vigenère cipher. It used a phrase or text passage as a key. Here's an example:

```
TO BE OR NOT TO BE THAT IS THE QUESTION
```

From this phrase, he eliminated words that had already appeared in the sequence (in this case, **TO** and **BE**), thus shortening the text:

```
TO BE OR NOT THAT IS THE QUESTION
```

Next, he converted each letter to a number (such that **A** = 1, **B** = 2, **C** = 3 . . .):

```
20.15 2.5 15.18 14.15.20 20.8.1.20 9.19 20.8.5 17.21.5.19.20.9.15.14
```

Lastly, he added the numbers in each word. For example, the word NOT yielded 14 + 15 + 20 = 49. If the result was larger than 26, he repeatedly subtracted 26 until he could derive a value between 1 and 26. In our example, we thus get the following number sequence to be used as the key:

```
9 7 7 23 23 2 7 16
```

To encrypt a message, he added each number to the respective letter of the plaintext. If the result was larger than 26, he reduced it by 26 once again. For the plaintext **NEBRASKA**, we get the ciphertext WLIOXURQ:

Plaintext:	N	E	B	R	A	S	K	A
Key:	9	7	7	23	23	2	7	16
Ciphertext:	W	L	I	O	X	U	R	Q

Using this method, Thouless produced the following ciphertext for his second message:

```
INXPH CJKGM JIRPR FBCVY WYWES NOECN SCVHE GYRJQ
TEBJM TGXAT TWPNH CNYBC FNXPF LFXRV QWQL
```

Thouless described the sentence he had used for the key as an "identifiable passage in a printed work." Because the cryptogram consists of seventy-four letters, this passage had at least seventy-four words (though it could have had more, as Thouless had removed any duplicate words).

Thouless died in 1984, leaving his second and third cryptograms still unsolved. The third was broken (through non-psychic means) a decade later (see Chapter 12), while his second cryptogram remained unsolved for decades. Then, in August 2019, Klaus received a notice from Richard Bean, a computer expert and codebreaker from Brisbane, Australia,[17] who claimed to have broken this challenge. Klaus and his readers checked Richard's solution, and it proved correct.

Richard believed that the only way to solve the second Thouless challenge was to find the text that had been used as the key. Hoping that Thouless had taken this text from a publicly available book, Richard decided to start a search at Project Gutenberg, which is the largest digital book collection available on the internet. Just about every book Thouless might have known about in 1948 is available today in the Gutenberg collection.

Richard downloaded 37,000 (!) books from Project Gutenberg. Then, using a computer program, he extracted all possible phrases consisting of seventy-four words, not counting repetitions, which resulted in a collection of hundreds of millions of key candidates. Next, he let his program decrypt Thouless's ciphertext with every one of the candidate phrases and had it check whether the result looked like English. For this test, he used hexagraph frequencies (see Chapter 16).

After several days of computation time, Richard's computer program deemed that the following plaintext had the closest resemblance to English text:

```
CEVHHZGMKLUCCESSFULEXPERIMENTSOFTNEKKIWTDXDAU
GIVESTRVMGEVIDENCEFOROXRVIVAL
```

This letter sequence didn't look completely correct, but it was clear that there were fragments of recognizable English text within it. When Richard spotted the fragments **UCCESSFULEXPERIMENTSOF** and **EVIDENCEFOR**, he realized that he was close to the solution. After a few adjustments, the following plaintext appeared:

```
A NUMBER OF SUCCESSFUL EXPERIMENTS OF THIS KIND WOULD GIVE STRONG
EVIDENCE FOR SURVIVAL
```

After seventy-one years, Thouless's second challenge was broken! Though, of course, not in the way he had intended.

As it turned out, the passage Thouless had used as his key came from Project Gutenberg book 41215, *Selected Poems of Francis Thompson* (1908).

The passage in question consisted of the first seventy-four words (not counting doubles) of a poem titled "The Hound of Heaven." This excerpt from the poem is reproduced here, with duplicates crossed out:

I FLED HIM, DOWN THE NIGHTS AND ~~DOWN THE~~ DAYS;
~~I FLED HIM, DOWN THE~~ ARCHES OF ~~THE~~ YEARS;
~~I FLED HIM, DOWN THE~~ LABYRINTHINE WAYS
~~OF~~ MY OWN MIND; ~~AND~~ IN ~~THE~~ MIST ~~OF~~ TEARS
I HID FROM ~~HIM, AND~~ UNDER RUNNING LAUGHTER
UP VISTAED HOPES I SPED;
~~AND~~ SHOT, PRECIPITATED,
ADOWN TITANIC GLOOMS ~~OF~~ CHASMÈD FEARS,
~~FROM~~ THOSE STRONG FEET THAT FOLLOWED, ~~FOLLOWED~~
AFTER.
BUT WITH UNHURRYING CHASE
~~AND~~ UNPERTURBÈD PACE
DELIBERATE SPEED, MAJESTIC INSTANCY,
THEY BEAT ~~—AND A~~ VOICE ~~BEAT~~
MORE INSTANT THAN ~~THE FEET—~~
'ALL THINGS BETRAY THEE, WHO BETRAYEST ME.'
I PLEADED, OUTLAW-WISE,
BY MANY ~~A~~ HEARTED CASEMENT, CURTAINED RED,
TRELLISED . . .

Richard had even known this poem. Its creator, Francis Thompson (1859–1907), was a well-known English poet of the Victorian era. "The Hound of Heaven" was his most famous work.

In 1995, Jim Gillogly and Larry Harnisch, who solved Thouless's third message (see Chapter 12), had started a very similar attack on Thouless's second challenge.[18] They tried several hundred books from Project Gutenberg, to no avail. As it turned out, their attempt on the second message had simply come too early. The book that contained the passage they were looking for, which would have helped them solve the second message, entered the Gutenberg collection just seventeen years later, in 2012.

The Smithy Code

In early 2006, authors Michael Baigent and Richard Leigh filed suit against Random House, the publisher of Dan Brown's bestselling 2003 novel *The Da Vinci Code*. They alleged that parts of this bestseller were plagiarized from their 1982 nonfiction book *Holy Blood, Holy Grail*. Judge Peter Smith, who presided over the trial, ruled against Baigent and Leigh, arguing that, as a novelist, Brown was free to use ideas from a nonfictional work in a fictional context.

Incredibly, Smith hid his own code in his written judgment! He italicized forty-one letters throughout the text, producing the following character sequence:

smithycodeJaeiextostgpsacgreamqwfkadpmqzv

After "smithy code," the rest of the characters represent an encrypted message:

Jaeiextostgpsacgreamqwfkadpmqzvs

The assumption that this line is a cryptogram is supported by the following sentence contained in Smith's text: "The key to solving the conundrum posed by this judgment is in reading HBHG and DVC." HBHG and DVC are abbreviations of the book titles involved in the trial, namely, *Holy Blood, Holy Grail* and *The Da Vinci Code*.

Many codebreakers all over the world tried to decipher the "Smithy Code" message, and Dan Tench, a British lawyer and journalist, was the first one to succeed (after a few hints from the judge).[19] Based on frequency analysis, Tench guessed that he was dealing with a Vigenère cipher or a similar polyalphabetic encryption system. The repetition of the digraph MQ after eight letters suggested that Smith had used an eight-letter keyword. (This reasoning is an application of Kasiski's method.)

Following Smith's hint that the solution to the challenge could be found in the two books involved in the lawsuit, Tench tried to use Fibonacci numbers as the key. The Fibonacci sequence is a famous pattern that starts with 1, 1 and continues with numbers that are the sum of the two preceding ones, like this: 1, 1, 2, 3, 5, 8, 13, 21, 34, 55, 89, and so forth. Fibonacci numbers play a role in both *Holy Blood, Holy Grail* and *The Da Vinci Code*, so it seemed plausible that Smith had used them as a key of some sort.

Assuming that Smith had applied an eight-character Vigenère keyword, Tench tried the first eight Fibonacci numbers: 1, 1, 2, 3, 5, 8, 13, and 21. After some trial and error, he saw that this keyword delivered meaningful words when added to the ciphertext (instead of the usual method of being subtracted from it). In addition, each number in the key had to be diminished by one. So, instead of 1, 1, 2, 3, 5, 8, 13, 21, it started with 0, 0, 1, 2, 4, 7, 12, 20, and then repeated. There was a further twist: the judge's key combined the fourth and fifth numbers of the modified Fibonacci sequence, which became 0, 0, 24, 2, 4, 7, 12, 20. Here's a description of the decryption process:

```
Ciphertext: J   a   e   i   x   t   o   s   t   g   p   s   a   c
Key:        0   0   24  2   4   7   12  20  0   0   24  2   4   7   12
Plaintext:  J   A   C   K   I   E   F   I   S   T   E   R   W   H   O

Ciphertext: g   r   e   a   m   q   w   f   k   a   d   p   m   q   z   v
Key:        20  0   0   24  2   4   7   12  20  0   0   24  2   4   7   12
Plaintext:  A   R   E   Y   O   U   D   R   E   A   D   N   O   U   G   H
```

This produced the following plaintext:

JACKIEFISTERWHOAREYOUDREADNOUGH

The text contains two mistakes: the **T** should be an **H**, and a **T** is missing at the end. Here's the correct plaintext:

JACKIE FISHER WHO ARE YOU DREADNOUGHT

These words refer to Admiral Jackie Fisher (1841–1920), an important figure in British naval history, and the battleship HMS *Dreadnought*, which Fisher commissioned and planned. Judge Smith was known to be a great admirer of Jackie Fisher, and the launch of the first dreadnought-class battleship, whose design was revolutionary and made all earlier battleships obsolete, had taken place one hundred years before the trial. This cryptogram was his way of commemorating the centennial.

Challenges

The Schooling challenge

In 1896, British statistician and journalist John Holt Schooling (1859–1927) published a challenge cipher.[20] It consists of a sequence of two-digit numbers. To make things a little easier, we will also reveal that each number represents a letter, as shown in the following table (note that **J** is missing):

```
  12345
  -----
1|ABCDE
2|FGHIK
3|LMNOP
4|QRSTU
5|VWXYZ
```

The substitution takes place as follows: **A** = 11, **B** = 12, **C** = 13 . . . **Y** = 54, **Z** = 55. We can then define a Vigenère cipher based on this number system. For instance, if we encrypt the plaintext **CODEBREAKING** (13 34 14 15 12 42 15 11 25 24 33 22) with the keyword ABC (11 12 13), we get:

```
13 34 14 15 12 42 15 11 25 24 33 22
11 12 13 11 12 13 11 12 13 11 12 13
-----------------------------------
24 46 27 26 24 55 26 23 38 35 45 35
```

Here's a ciphertext Schooling created with this method, using the keyword TYRANT:

```
76 69 57 55 65 59 68 87 77 22 75 68 87 88 75 43 67 77 58 65 96
```

Can you solve this challenge cipher?

A German radio message from the Second World War

In October 1941, a US Coast Guard unit intercepted the following radio message transmitted from Hamburg, Germany, to a recipient in Rio de Janeiro, Brazil:[21]

```
DDLUX CQSFV INNNW FRFZA GQBGI
WREKU ZPRIY HJXFS JRUJP TYXRH
SABWC GQFYD MIWYP VHJBE KMEHJ
```

```
WGQAI JYNPV USQLJ DHOIV HQXRN
HSJRU VJKTY NPPBI SEKKV OIVSC
GQBTS NUPXS FVHQU WBFFS PTXQT
FSXJQ FWJSW UWPTC JIWHH PJHQD
HUVFZ DPJBF XFAVH URBHQ TLDLU
XCQSD ESQXU
```

American codebreakers soon discovered that this message was encrypted with a Vigenère cipher. The plaintext is in German, and the key is not a word but is derived from a mathematical constant. Can you break this cryptogram?

Unsolved cryptograms

Wood's cryptogram from the crypt

Robert Thouless, whose unusual life-after-death experiments were discussed in a previous section of this chapter, encouraged others to perform similar attempts at communicating after their death. The more people who took encryption keys to their grave, he hoped, the higher the probability that somebody would be able to channel this information from the beyond. One person who answered this call to arms was solicitor T.E. Wood (1887–1972) from Bournemouth, United Kingdom. Wood used the same method as Thouless used for his second message for encryption, which means that his key is a passage from a text available to the public (such as a book chapter). However, he added a twist; his plaintext was written in multiple languages, and his key was taken from a non-English work. Wood's cryptogram is reproduced below.

```
FVAMI NTKFX XWATB OIZVV X
```

Wood's encrypted message is unsolved to date. Apparently, nobody has yet received the key from the beyond!

9

COMPLETE COLUMNAR TRANSPOSITION CIPHERS

In 1935, somebody sent the anonymous message shown in Figure 9-1 to President Franklin D. Roosevelt.[1,2] While the second line, **OR ELSE YOU DIE**, is readable, the first is obviously encrypted. We can recover the plaintext by writing the message in lines of two letters each:

ND
OI
MD
EY
LO
AU
EE
TV
IE
BR

Figure 9-1: An anonymous encrypted message sent to President Franklin D. Roosevelt in 1935

Notice that, from top to bottom, the second column reads, **DIDYOUEVER**. The first column, from the bottom up, reads, **BITEALEMON**. These produce the intended plaintext, **DID YOU EVER BITE A LEMON?**

Roosevelt suffered from polio (or a similar disease that, at the time, could not be distinguished from it). According to a since-refuted theory, lemon juice can cure polio. It seems the sender of this message wanted to recommend the lemon juice therapy to Roosevelt in this unconventional way.

One special thing about the encryption method used here is that no letter or word of the plaintext has been substituted. Instead, only the order of the letters has been changed. A cipher with this property is referred to as a *transposition cipher*.

How complete columnar transposition ciphers work

There are as many different transposition ciphers as there are ways to change the order of the letters in a message. The Roosevelt plaintext consists of twenty letters, which means that there are 2,432,902,008,176,640,000 (over two quintillion) ways to reorder it! In general, a message with n letters can be transposed in n-factorial ($n! = 1 \times 2 \times 3 \times 4 \times 5 \times \ldots \times n$) ways and not necessarily distinct. However, using a random transposition method for encryption is not practical. Instead, a convenient transposition rule needs to be defined.

The postcard in Figure 9-2 was written with a transposition rule that is certainly convenient, but not very secure.[3]

Figure 9-2: This encrypted postcard is not very hard to decipher.

As will become obvious after you look at it for a moment, the message on the postcard is written backward. Writing in this way is an especially simple variant of a transposition cipher. Another approach is to write every word of a plaintext backward. The author of the following newspaper ad, published in the *Morning Post* on April 4, 1888, used this method:[4]

```
Ma gniyrt ym tseb ot esaelp uoy.
```

It should be clear that, to be of practical value in terms of concealing a message from an unwanted recipient, a transposition rule needs to be more complex. In addition, it should be possible to vary the transposition based on a key. For instance, we could divide a message into blocks of five letters and rearrange each block according to a defined scheme. Using such a scheme, the plaintext **SWISS CHEESECAKE** can be encrypted as follows:

SWISS CHEES ECAKE
WISSS HESEC CAEKE

This explains how the sign in Figure 9-3, which we encountered at a party, was encrypted. It used the key **1** = 5, **2** = 1, **3** = 2, **4** = 4, **5** = 3, or simply 5, 1, 2, 4, 3.

Figure 9-3: The name of this cake is encrypted in a transposition cipher.

This method is equivalent to the following, which uses the keyword TABLE. First, we write the message in lines below the keyword:

```
TABLE
-----
SWISS
CHEES
ECAKE
```

Then, we sort the columns such that the letters of the keyword are in alphabetical order:

```
ABELT
-----
WISSS
HESEC
CAEKE
```

This produces the ciphertext WISSS HESEC CAEKE that we saw on the sign.

We could expand on this line-based transposition by transcribing the letters column-wise, which results in the following encrypted message: WHC IEA SSE SEK SCE. We could also transcribe the message from the bottom up, from right to left, or in some other way.

The strength of transposition ciphers was long underestimated. Many cipher designers thought that rearranging letters was less secure than replacing them. Only in the twentieth century did it become known that transposition ciphers can be quite secure.

In this chapter, we will limit ourselves to cases in which the plaintext is written in lines of equal length, transposed column-wise, and transcribed in an arbitrary direction. In addition, we will assume that the last line is filled completely, containing no blank spaces. Transpositions of this kind are called "complete columnar transpositions." The Roosevelt cryptogram shown earlier in this chapter is a complete columnar transposition, with a line length of two. So is the backward-written postcard (where the line length is equal to the message length). The newspaper ad that spells every word backward is definitely a transposition but not a complete columnar transposition, because it is not based on lines of constant length.

How to detect a complete columnar transposition cipher

From a codebreaker's perspective, the nice thing about a transposition cipher (of any kind) is that the message's letter frequencies do not change as a result of encryption. Therefore, frequency analysis helps us detect a cipher of this type. For instance, look at the following encrypted ad from the *Evening Standard* published on June 16, 1882:[5]

```
ECALAP Ardnaxela eht ta sekal elpirt eht no strecnoc ocserf la eh
tot og syadrutasdna syadsruht syadseut no.
```

If we perform a frequency analysis . . .

. . . we see that A, E, and T are especially frequent, while B, Q, J, M, V, W, and Z don't appear at all. This is consistent with a short text written in English (in a longer text, we would expect E to be more frequent than A). The only common kind of encryption algorithm that produces a ciphertext with these letter frequencies is a transposition cipher.

Just like the letter frequencies, the index of coincidence doesn't change when a transposition cipher is applied. Using CrypTool 2 or *http://dcode.fr/en*, we can compute the index of coincidence of the 1882 newspaper ad as 7.0%, which is very close to the index of coincidence of the English language, 6.7%.

How to break a complete columnar transposition cipher

There are multiple ways to decrypt line-based transpositions with constant line lengths (i.e., complete columnar transposition ciphers). In each technique, detecting the length of the lines plays a key role.

The arrange-and-read method

Let's take another look at the encrypted note sent to President Roosevelt: NDOIMDEYLOAUEETVIEBR. This message consists of twenty letters. Assuming that we are dealing with a complete columnar transposition, there are only a few possible line lengths, namely, the divisors of twenty: two, four, five, and ten.

As a first attempt, let's write the message in lines of ten characters:

```
NDOIMDEYLO
AUEETVIEBR
```

Now, let's try reading this two-line text in all four directions: from left to right, backward, from top to bottom, and bottom-up. However, no matter which way we read it, it makes no sense. So next, let's try five-letter lines:

```
NDOIM
DEYLO
AUEET
VIEBR
```

Still nothing. Here is the message written in four-letter lines:

```
NDOI
MDEY
LOAU
EETV
IEBR
```

Again, we read these lines in the four different ways; nothing stands out. Let's move on to two-letter lines:

```
ND
OI
MD
EY
LO
AU
EE
TV
IE
BR
```

Now the first column, read from the bottom-up, says **BITE A LEMON**. Or perhaps it's easier to first see the second column, read downward: **DID YOU EVER**. The cryptogram is solved. Sometimes, breaking a complete columnar transposition cipher is as simple as that!

Let's look at another example of this kind. The cryptogram in Figure 9-4 is a challenge ciphertext published by the British intelligence agency GCHQ in 2013.[6]

AWVLI QIQVT QOSQO ELGCV IIQWD LCUQE EOENN WWOAO

LTDNU QTGAW TSMDO QTLAO QSDCH PQQIQ DQQTQ OOTUD

BNIQH BHHTD UTEET FDUEA UMORE SQEQE MLTME TIREC

LICAI QATUN QRALT ENEIN RKG

Figure 9-4: A challenge cryptogram published by the British intelligence agency GCHQ

Frequency analysis reveals that the letter frequencies match the English language quite well, except for the many Qs. We can therefore assume that this ciphertext was created with a transposition cipher and that Q stands for the space character.

The cryptogram consists of 143 letters. There are only two factors of 143, both of which are prime numbers: 11 and 13. Assuming that we are dealing with a complete columnar transposition, we should check line lengths of eleven and thirteen. Let's start with eleven:

```
AWVLIQIQVTQ
OSQOELGCVII
QWDLCUQEEOE
NNWWOAOLTDN
UQTGAWTSMDO
QTLAOQSDCHP
QQIQDQQTQOO
TUDBNIQHBHH
TDUTEETFDUE
AUMORESQEQE
MLTMETIRECL
ICAIQATUNQR
ALTENEINRKG
```

No matter how we read this paragraph—left to right, backward, from top to bottom, or bottom-up—it does not look like real language. Next, let's check the thirteen-letter line variant:

```
AWVLIQIQVTQOS
QOELGCVIIQWDL
CUQEEOENNWWOA
OLTDNUQTGAWTS
MDOQTLAOQSDCH
PQQIQDQQTQOOT
```

```
UDBNIQHBHHTDU
TEETFDUEAUMOR
ESQEQEMLTMETI
RECLICAIQATUN
QRALTENEINRKG
```

If we read the first column from top to bottom, we get AQCOMPUTERQ. Remembering that Q stands for a blank space, this message makes sense. Reading it column-wise with the Qs replaced by spaces, the paragraph becomes this:

```
A COMPUTER WOULD DESERVE TO BE CALLED INTELLIGENT IF IT
COULD DECEIVE A HUMAN INTO BELIEVING THAT IT WAS HUMAN
WWW DOT METRO DOT CO DOT UK SLASH TURING
```

The plaintext is a summary of what is commonly known as the "Turing Test," named after the brilliant mathematician Alan Turing (1912–1954).

Vowel frequencies and multiple anagramming

The arrange-and-read method we just covered only works if the second step of the transposition, permutation of the columns, is omitted. If this is not the case, we need more sophisticated codebreaking methods. To proceed, it will be helpful to know that the ratio of vowels to consonants in the English language is roughly forty to sixty. More than three vowels or consonants occurring in a row are possible, but they are rarely seen in practice.

Let's look at the following cryptogram taken from *Military Cryptanalysis IV* by William Friedman (1959):[7]

```
ILHHD   TIEOE   UDHTS   ONSOO   EEEEI   OEFTR

RHNEA   TNNVU   TLBFA   EDFOY   CAPDT   RRIIA

RIVNL   RNRWE   TUTCU   VRAUO   OOFDA   ONAJI

UPOLR   SOMTN   FRANF   MNDMA   SAFAT   YECFX

RTGET   A
```

Frequency analysis reveals a distribution very similar to that of the English language, suggesting that this ciphertext was probably created with a transposition cipher. We start by assuming that it is a complete columnar transposition.

As the message consists of 126 letters, the possible line lengths are two, three, six, seven, nine, fourteen, eighteen, twenty-one, forty-two, and sixty-three. Lines of two, three, and six are insecure, because there is little to transpose; and twenty-one, forty-two, and sixty-three are impractical because the lines are too long. Therefore, these line lengths are rarely used. Thus, we start by examining the line lengths of seven, nine, fourteen, and eighteen.

If we write the ciphertext in lines of seven letters, we get the following table. (Since we assume that the ciphertext was read out column-wise, we are writing the text in columns instead of rows.)

```
1    IONTTUM
2    LONRCPA
3    HEVRUOS
4    HEUIVLA
5    DETIRRF
6    TELAASA
7    IIBRUOT
8    EOFIOMY
9    OEAVOTE
10   EFENONC
11   UTDLFFF
12   DRFRDRX
13   HRONAAR
14   THYRONT
15   SNCWNFG
16   OEAEAME
17   NAPTJNT
18   STDUIDA
```

Lines 12 and 15 consist of consonants only. As seven consonants in a row are almost impossible in an English text, we conclude that we are on the wrong track. Let's now try nine-letter lines, again written in columns from top to bottom:

```
1    ISTBRTATF
2    LORFIUONA
3    HNRAITNFT
4    HSHEACARY
5    DONDRUJAE
6    TOEFIVINC
7    IEAOVRUFF
8    EETYNAPMX
9    OENCLUONR
10   EENAROLDT
11   UIVPNORMG
12   DOUDROSAE
13   HETTWFOST
14   TFLREDMAA
```

This looks better. The number of vowels in each line is plausible. We'll keep the nine-letter variant in mind as a promising candidate.

The next candidate is the fourteen-letter version:

```
1    IFOFNETNTOUNMC
2    LUOTNDRLCFPFAF
3    HDERVFRRUDORSX
```

```
4    HHERUOINVALAAR
5    DTEHTYIRRORNFT
6    TSENLCAWANSFAG
7    IOIEBAREUAOMTE
8    ENOAFPITOJMNYT
9    OSETADVUOITDEA
```

The ten vowels in line 7, while not impossible, are pretty improbable. So, this guess is not a good first choice. Here's the last candidate, with eighteen letters per line:

```
1    IESETTBYRNTAAPTMFX
2    LOOERNFCILUUOONNAR
3    HENERNAAIRTONLFDTT
4    HUSIHVEPANCOARRMYO
5    DDOONUDDRRUOJSAAEE
6    THOEETFTIWVFIONSCT
7    OTEFALORVERDUMFAFA
```

This looks good, too.

We now have two good candidates (lines of nine and eighteen letters), one unlikely one (lines of fourteen letters), and one that is extremely unlikely (lines of seven letters). We will proceed with the two good candidates by applying a technique called *multiple anagramming*. This method consists of rearranging the columns of a block until a meaningful word appears in one of the lines. Then we check if the other rearranged lines look like they might have been taken from an English text, too. If this is the case, we are probably on the right track; if not, we'll try another word.

Let's first look for words that can be spelled by permuting the lines of the eighteen-letter-line candidates, checking for lines that may contain anagrammed words of interest. In line 4, we see the letters we need to spell ARMY—a likely word in a military message. Let's use it for our first multiple-anagramming try. As there are two As and two Rs in the fourth line, we can construct this word in four possible ways:

9	14	16	17		13	14	16	17		9	15	16	17		13	15	16	17
R	P	M	F		A	P	M	F		R	T	M	F		A	T	M	F
I	O	N	A		O	O	N	A		I	N	N	A		O	N	N	A
I	L	D	T		N	L	D	T		I	F	D	T		N	F	D	T
A	**R**	**M**	**Y**		**A**	**R**	**M**	**Y**		**A**	**R**	**M**	**Y**		**A**	**R**	**M**	**Y**
R	S	A	E		J	S	A	E		R	A	A	E		J	A	A	E
I	O	S	C		I	O	S	C		I	N	S	C		I	N	S	C
V	M	A	F		U	M	A	F		V	F	A	F		U	F	A	F

The first possibility is very unlikely, as the patterns RPMF in the first line and VMAF in the last line are not common English tetragraphs. The second block is not much better—look at APMF in the first line and JSAE in the fifth. For similar reasons, the third and the fourth combinations don't make sense either. We have reached a dead end.

Let's look for another word we can spell. We easily find a few, some of which can be formed in different ways. For instance, the letters T, T, T, T, 0, 0, and W in line 6 might spell **TWO** (numbers are common in military messages). The following are eight ways to assemble this word:

```
1 10 3     6 10 3     8 10 3     18 10 3
I  N  S    T  N  S    Y  N  S    X  N  S
L  L  O    N  L  O    C  L  O    R  L  O
H  R  N    N  R  N    A  R  N    T  R  N
H  N  S    V  N  S    P  N  S    O  N  S
D  R  O    U  R  O    D  R  O    E  R  O
T  W  O    T  W  O    T  W  O    T  W  O
I  E  E    L  E  E    R  E  E    A  E  E

1 10 14    6 10 14    8 10 14    18 10 14
I  N  P    T  N  P    Y  N  P    X  N  P
L  L  O    N  L  O    C  L  O    R  L  O
H  R  N    N  R  N    A  R  N    T  R  N
D  R  S    U  R  S    D  R  S    E  R  S
T  W  O    T  W  O    T  W  O    T  W  O
I  E  M    L  E  M    R  E  M    A  E  M
```

Each of these eight guesses leads to letter combinations in other lines that don't appear very often in English texts, such as HNR, VNR, and XNP. We seem to be on the wrong track again.

Next, we could try **AIR FORCE**, which might appear in line 2. As there are four 0s and two Rs in this row, there are eight ways to spell it. Other possibilities include **BY TRAIN** in line 1, **THOSE** in line 6, and **OVER** in line 7. However, all of these lead to implausible letter combinations in other lines.

Reluctantly, we conclude that the eighteen-character-long-line candidate is probably not correct, so we turn to the nine-letter-long block:

1	ISTBRTATF
2	LORFIUONA
3	HNRAITNFT
4	HSHEACARY
5	DONDRUJAE
6	TOEFIVINC
7	IEAOVRUFF
8	EETYNAPMX
9	OENCLUONR
10	EENAROLDT
11	UIVPNORMG
12	DOUDROSAE
13	HETTWFOST
14	TFLREDMAA

While looking for likely candidates, we find a few words related to numbers. The first line provides the letters we might need to form the word **FIRST**. Both lines 6 and 7 contain the letters of the word **FIVE**. Because **V** is a relatively uncommon letter, let's take **FIVE** in line 6 as our first guess. The line contains two **I**s, so there are two ways to spell the word:

```
4 5 6 3     4 7 6 3
B R T T     B A T T
F I U R     F O U R
A I T R     A N T R
E A C H     E A C H
D R U N     D J U N
F I V E     F I V E
O V R A     O U R A
Y N A T     Y P A T
C L U N     C O U N
A R O N     A L O N
P N O V     P R O V
D R O U     D S O U
T W F T     T O F T
R E D L     R M D L
```

It should be immediately clear that the second block looks very promising. In addition to FIVE, it produces the English words FOUR and EACH, along with promising word fragments such as BATT, OURA, COUN, ALON, and PROV. Only the last line, RMDL, doesn't look like English, but this might be due to an abbreviation. Let's assume that this guess is correct.

How can we proceed? Since we think we know columns 4, 7, 6, and 3, it's best to check which of the five remaining columns (1, 2, 5, 8, and 9) makes the most sense if put in front of the block we have chosen. There are five options:

```
1 4 7 6 3     2 4 7 6 3     5 4 7 6 3     8 4 7 6 3     9 4 7 6 3
I B A T T     S B A T T     R B A T T     T B A T T     F B A T T
L F O U R     O F O U R     I F O U R     N F O U R     A F O U R
H A N T R     N A N T R     I A N T R     F A N T R     T A N T R
H E A C H     S E A C H     A E A C H     R E A C H     Y E A C H
D D J U N     O D J U N     R D J U N     A D J U N     E D J U N
T F I V E     O F I V E     I F I V E     N F I V E     C F I V E
I O U R A     E O U R A     V O U R A     F O U R A     F O U R A
E Y P A T     E Y P A T     N Y P A T     M Y P A T     X Y P A T
O C O U N     E C O U N     L C O U N     N C O U N     R C O U N
E A L O N     E A L O N     R A L O N     D A L O N     T A L O N
U P R O V     I P R O V     N P R O V     M P R O V     G P R O V
D D S O U     O D S O U     R D S O U     A D S O U     E D S O U
H T O F T     E T O F T     W T O F T     S T O F T     T T O F T
T R M D L     F R M D L     E R M D L     A R M D L     A R M D L
```

The fourth option, 84763, produces the best results: REACH, NFOUR, and MYPAT. Most of the other five-letter groups can easily be imagined as having been taken from an English text. The remaining columns (1, 2, 5, and 9) can now easily be added in a similar way. We check the placement of each one before or after our existing block to see what makes the most sense. In the end, we get the following:

```
FIRSTBATT
ALIONFOUR
THINFANTR
YHASREACH
EDROADJUN
CTIONFIVE
FIVEFOURA
XENEMYPAT
ROLENCOUN
TEREDALON
GUNIMPROV
EDROADSOU
THWESTOFT
ATEFARMDL
```

This plaintext can be read line-wise. X is used as a period:

FIRST BATTALION FOURTH INFANTRY HAS REACHED ROAD JUNCTION FIVE FIVE FOUR A. ENEMY PATROL ENCOUNTERED ALONG UNIMPROVED ROAD SOUTHWEST OF TATE FARM DL

Half of that tetragraph of consonants we saw above, RMDL, is the end of the word FARM. We are not certain what the remaining letters, DL, might mean. Perhaps a signature or filler letters to reach a certain message length?

As should have become clear, multiple anagramming is a *nondeterministic* method, meaning that it is possible to come up with multiple solution candidates. Thus, it must be done with care, creativity, and trial and error. There are, however, some tricks that might simplify the codebreaking process:

1. The letter *Q* is very helpful for multiple anagramming, as it is usually followed by a *U*.
2. The letters *J*, *V*, and *Z* are almost always followed by a vowel.
3. The letters *A*, *O*, and *U* are usually followed by a consonant.
4. The letter *H* is usually preceded by a consonant and followed by a vowel.

If you want to learn more about multiple anagramming, we recommend Helen Fouché Gaines's classic 1939 book *Cryptanalysis*.[8]

Success stories

Donald Hill's diary

Donald Hill (ca. 1915–1995) was a British military pilot in World War II. Stationed in Hong Kong, he was captured by the Japanese and sent to a prisoner-of-war camp. After four years of incarceration, he was released. Even before his years in captivity, Hill had kept a diary. But because British soldiers were not allowed to keep private notes, he used numbers instead of letters and camouflaged the diary as a collection of multiplication tables, titling his booklet *Russel's Mathematical Tables*. This did not look suspicious, as multiplication tables were quite common before pocket calculators were invented. While in captivity, Hill continued to write his journal.

After his return to England, Hill married his fiancée and never again talked about his diary or its contents. Only after Hill's death in 1995 did his wife investigate the strange number sequences in the booklet he left behind. She asked mathematics professor Philip Aston from the University of Surrey to analyze them. He was able to deduce their meaning and published a paper about his deciphering of the diary.[9] The story of Donald Hill is also told in Andro Linklater's 2001 book *The Code of Love*.[10]

When Aston first examined Hill's alleged mathematical tables, he saw that most of the pages were filled with groups of four digits (see Figure 9-5). These numbers were purportedly multiplication results, but the results didn't fit with the multiplications. Aston concluded that the real purpose of these numbers was to encode a text.

Figure 9-5: Prisoner-of-war Donald Hill disguised his diary as a collection of mathematical tables. In addition, he used a transposition cipher.

The most obvious way to interpret the numbers was that each four-digit group encoded two letters. (In other words, each digit pair encoded a letter.) When Aston saw that almost all digit pairs represented numbers between ten and thirty-five, he determined that the most obvious encoding was **A** = 10, **B** = 11, **C** = 12, **D** = 13, etc. Aston performed a frequency analysis based on this encoding and saw that the letter frequencies almost exactly matched the ones of the English language. However, the letter sequences he received didn't make sense. So, he assumed that Hill had used a transposition cipher in addition to the substitution.

Taking a closer look at the numbers in the diary, Aston noticed that occasionally, a group consisting of four zeros (0000) appeared. This didn't fit with the encoding. Aston's guess was that these zero-blocks were separators. As it turned out, there were exactly 561 four-digit groups (1,122 letters) between each two separators. This made it likely that Hill had applied a transposition cipher on units of 1,122 letters.

One can arrange 1,122 letters in a rectangle very easily because the number 1,122 has many factors. This suggested that Hill had applied a complete columnar transposition cipher using a rectangle size such as 66×17, 11×102, or 33×34. Aston didn't have to search very long for the best guess, however, as on the first diary page were written a right-hand arrow next to the number 340 and a down arrow next to the number 330. Aston assumed that the zeros in these numbers were there to confuse the reader, and then he arranged one of the 1,122-letter units in a table containing thirty-three columns and thirty-four lines. Writing the text line-wise in such a table quickly produced meaningful words in the columns. To our regret, Aston's paper doesn't describe what exactly he saw, but the 33×34 table may have looked like this:

```
DMSTIINSKDSEATALDSGMTOOARNRRBUENDE
IBABLAWTBAARMRLEETHEOENPTIEESTAOOF
WEFLMMESYMBSEALTTWTIASEPWSTTANRTAT
AREAADDTTALCRTWEHEENSUPEEIAHMOAUNR
KSTZCIAHHGAOTEELEARDHPLANMREOCNNYE
EEYIHSSEEEZMCDVYBRSIETARTMYINAOSTP
TSANITHBFBEEAFEBLESALNNHYIRRGSMCHR
HCNGNUDOTOAONIGUATWNTSEEMNILSUIAIA
EODAEROMGTNVCRORZOOTEMIATENETANRNY
ORBNSBWBHHOELETNELORRONDNNGWTLORGI
TTYDAENETWTRIIWETDPOTKTIUTSIATUEEN
HEASROTREAHAPNHDSTDONEANTHUSEISDXG
EDMIEEOSRLEGPTIWTHOPTACGEEPGRERWCT
RBINBAFPSRRAEOCTOAWSHNTOSLTUUSOEEH
OYRKURLATUBIROHTOTNGEDWUOLONITAHPA
FOAFRLISHSANIUIHFWOETITRFTSTNOROTT
FVCINYGSEADBNRSTIENTRHAWCHAHSPOPTT
IELNTAHOBRLOTPPWEAUPEETAOEYEOEFEOH
CREAOSTVEEYMHLRORRSAXTTYNRTRNRPAME
ETNLUTSEEGDBEAERCEANCWETCEHEESLNAB
```

```
RHOLTHJRSOATANCEEANITOMHEGATAOADNO
SIOYIEUHTNMWFETDATDCTWPENOTSINNWOM
ORNTNCSEEEAGTSOHNWPKEATRTEWARNEEUB
VTEHCOTAWOGTEWUODAOYMLTERSAMCESTRS
EYIELLLDINERHRSTSRUAEROSAMRARLANDW
RFSYUONBTEDENGLHHWNNNUPNTYWDAENSEO
BIHMDNTUHBLDOTIEETADTSUOESTRFIDPFN
RGIATIITBEEOOVTATICRTATTDITUTGNEET
EHTKNAMTOEACNETVSHOUHROTAEHSLHICNE
ATAEGLEHMSVKBTLYCJNSEEUMTEJHETNTCX
KEFOTSTEBTISOHEBOACHYLTETPAFFCETEP
FRTFHEOFSENAMESOMPETFETTAAPOTIBHPL
ASEFECHIGIGABMOMPANNIFHOCNARBVOEOO
```

The first column, beginning from the top, contains the message **I WAKE THE OTHER OFFICERS**. The second column, MBERSESCORTEDBYOVE, does not appear to directly follow the first column but certainly looks like a fragment of English. It was clear that the order of the columns had to be changed. Had Donald Hill used a keyword for this transposition? Again, Aston didn't have to search very long for a solution. On the front page of the diary, he found the full names of Hill and his fiancée, consisting of thirty-four letters:

```
DONALD SAMUEL HILL PAMELA SEELY KIRRAGE
```

Sorted alphabetically, these thirty-four letters read as follows:

```
AAAAADDEEEEEGHIIKLLLLLLMMNOPRRSSUY
```

To decrypt the diary, Aston wrote these letters in the first line of the table:

```
AAAAADDEEEEEGHIIKLLLLLLMMNOPRRSSUY
----------------------------------
DMSTIINSKDSEATALDSGMTOOARNRRBUENDE
IBABLAWTBAARMRLEETHEOENPTIEESTAOOF
```
. . .

Then he rearranged the columns such that the keyword appeared again:

```
DONALDSAMUELHILLPAMELASEELYKIRRAGE
----------------------------------
IRNDSNEMADSGTAMTRSRKOTNDSOEDLBUIAE
AETITWABPOTHRLEOEATBEBOAANFEESTLMR
MTSWWEREPASTALIATFWYSLTMBEITTANMES
DATAEDARENTETWNSHEETUAUALPRHEMOARC
IRMKAANSAYHREEDHETNHPZNGALEELOCCIO
SYMERSOERTESDVIETYTEIISEZAPBYNAHCM
TRITEHMSHHBSFEALRAYFNNCBENRLBGSIAE
UINHTDICEIOWIGNTLNMISGAOAEAAUSUNNO
RNEEOONOANMOROTEEDIGMARTNIYZRTAECV
BGNOLWORDGBOETRRWBNHONRHONIENTLSLE
ESTTDNUTIEEPIWOIIYUTKDEWTTNIEHTAIR
```

```
DUHHTTSENXRDNHONSATEESDAHAGSDEIRPA
EPEBHORDGCSOTIPTGMERAIWLECTTWREEPG
ATLRAFOBOEPWOCSHUISSNNERRTHOIUSBEA
ROLOTLAYUPANOHGENROTDKHUBWAOTITURI
LSTFWIRORTSOUIEITAFHTFOSAETFHNORIN
YAHFEGOVWTSNRSTRHCCEHIPADATITSPNNB
AYETAHFEAOOUPPPEELOBENERLTHEWOETTO
STRCRTPRYMVSLRAXRENETAAEYTERONROHM
THEEESLTTAEAAENCENCEWLNGDEBCRESUEB
HAGRAJAHHNRNNCIIIOESOLDOAMOEEAOTAI
ETOSTUNIEOHDEICTSONTWYWNMPMADINIFN
CWEOWSERRUEPSOKEANTEATEEATBNHRNNTG
OASVATSTERAOWUYMMERWLHIOGTSDOCECET
LRMERIAYSDDUESAEAIAIRENNEOWSTRLLRH
OWYRWNNFNEBRGLNNDSTTUYSEDPOHHAEUNE
NISBITDIOFUAITDTRHEHSMPBLUNEEFIDOD
ITLRTINGTETCVTRTUIDBAAEEETTIATGIOO
AHEEHMIHINTOETUHSTAORKCEAOESVLHNNC
LJEAJENTMCHNTLSEHATMEETSVUXCYETGBK
SAPKATEHEEECEEHYFFTBLOTTITPOBFCTOS
EPAFPOBRTPFEESIFOTASEFHENTLMOTIHMA
CANAAHOSOOINMONTRECGFFEIGHOPMBVEBN
```

Now, the deciphering was complete. Read column-wise, here is the plaintext, a diary entry written on December 8, 1941:

```
I am disturbed early as the Colonial Secretary rings up to say
that war with Japan is imminent. Hell there goes my sleep and I
wake the other officers. Over breakfast we are told that we are at
war with Japan. We dash down to flights just in time to hear an
ominous roar of planes and nine bombers escorted by over thirty
fighters appear heading our way. There's no time to do anything
except to man our defense posts. The bombers pass overhead but
the fighters swoop down on us and pour a concentrated fire into
our planes. We give them all we've got which is precious little.
Some Indian troops get panicky and rush into a shelter, in their
excitement they fire their Lewis gun. There is a mad rush for
safety and by a miracle no one is hit. After twenty minutes of
concentrated attack by the fighters the Beeste with bombs goes up
in smoke and the two Walrus are left blazing and sink. Finally
they make off, not unscarred we hope, and we inspect the damage.
Both Walrus are gone, one Beeste is ablaze, another badly damaged,
leaving one plane intact. We attempt to put out the fire praying
that the bombs won't explode. The blaze is too fierce and she is
completely burned with two red hot heavy bombs amongst the ruins.
One aircraft left but no casualties to personnel. Eight civil
machines are burnt out including the American clipper. In the
afternoon, bombers come over again bombing the docks an . . .
```

The rest of the diary can be read in Aston's 1997 paper and in the 2001 book *The Code of Love* by Andro Linklater.

The Pablo Waberski spy case

In his 1931 book *The American Black Chamber*, which caused a scandal because of its discussion of America's secret cryptographic abilities, American codebreaker Herbert Yardley (1889–1958) describes a German transposition cipher.[11] According to Yardley, on February 10, 1918, during World War I, American agents arrested a man on the Mexican border who called himself Pablo Waberski. The investigators suspected that the detainee was actually a German secret agent named Lothar Witzke.[12, 13] Sewn into the left sleeve of the suspect's coat, they found the following encrypted note:[14]

```
SEOFNATUPK ASIHEIHBBN UERSDAUSNN
LRSEGGIESN NKLEZNSIMN EHNESHMPPB
ASUEASRIHT HTEURMVNSM EAINCOUASI
INSNRNVEGD ESNBTNNRCN DTDRZBEMUK
KOLSELZDNN AUEBFKBPSA TASECISDGT
IHUKTNAEIE TIEBAEUERA THNOIEAEEN
HSDAEAIAKN ETHNNNEECD CKDKONESDU
ESZADEHPEA BBILSESOOE ETNOUZKDML
NEUIIURMRN ZWHNEEGVCR EODHICSIAC
NIUSNRDNSO DRGSURRIEC EGRCSUASSP
EATGRSHEHO ETRUSEELCA UMTPAATLEE
CICXRNPRGA AWSUTEMAIR NASNUTEDEA
ERRREOHEIM EAHKTMUHDT COKDTGCEIO
EEFIGHIHRE LITFIUEUNL EELSERUNMA
ZNAI
```

Herbert Yardley was commissioned to crack this encryption. He and his team performed a frequency analysis and a few other statistical tests. These revealed that E was the most frequent letter, followed by N, while Q, X, and Y were completely absent. These features are typical of the German language (see Appendix B), suggesting the author had used a transposition cipher.

Yardley knew how to break such an encryption with the help of common digraphs (pairs of letters). In German, the letter C is particularly helpful, because it usually precedes H, occasionally precedes K, and is rarely found in front of any other letter. Yardley therefore tagged all Cs in the text and then looked for Hs. Then he determined the distances between each C and H. As it turned out, a distance of 108 letters appeared conspicuously often. When Yardley transcribed the message in lines of length 108, he received the following letter sequences:

```
SEOFNATUPK ASIHEIHBBN UERSDAUSNN LRSEGGIESN NKLEZNSIMN . . .
CNDTDRZBEM UKKOLSELZD NNAUEBFKBP SATASECISD GTIHUKTNAE . . .
HPEABBILSE SOOEETNOUZ KDMLNEUIIU RMRNZWHNEE GVCREODHIC . . .
AATLEECICX RNPRGAAWSU TEMAIRNASN UTEDEAERRR EOHEIMEAHK . . .
```

Read from top to bottom, virtually every column produced a four-letter sequence typical of the German language: column 1 is SCHA, column 10 is KMEX, and column 20 contains NDZU. Next, Yardley and his team organized the columns in a meaningful order, which turned out to be fairly straightforward. For instance, KMEX, followed by IKOP, produced the word **MEXIKO** (German for **MEXICO**). In the end, Yardley was able to read the following plaintext:

```
AN DIE KAISERLICHEN KONSULARBEHOERDEN IN DER REPUBLIK MEXIKO
PUNKT STRENG GEHEIM AUSRUFUNGSZEICHEN DER INHABER DIESES IST
EIN REICHSANGEHOERIGER DER UNTER DEM NAMEN PABLO WABERSKI ALS
RUSSE REIST PUNKT ER IST DEUTSCHER GEHEIMAGENT PUNKT ABSATZ ICH
BITTE IHM AUF ANSUCHEN SCHUTZ UND BEISTAND ZU GEWAEHREN KOMMA
IHM AUCH AUF VERLANGEN BIS ZU EINTAUSEND PESOS ORO NACIONAL
VORZUSCHIESSEN UND SEINE CODETELEGRAMME AN DIESE GESANDTSCHAFT ALS
KONSULARAMTLICHE DEPESCHEN ABZUSENDEN PUNKT
VON ECKHARDT
```

Here's a translation:

```
To the Imperial consular authorities in the Republic of Mexico.
Top secret! The owner of this [paper] is a member of the Reich,
who travels under the name Pablo Waberski as a Russian. He is a
German secret agent. I kindly ask you to grant him protection and
support on request, to pay him up to 1000 Pesos Oro National on
request, and to send his encrypted telegrams to this consulate as
diplomatic correspondence.
Von Eckhardt
```

This letter proved that the suspect, Pablo Waberski, was in fact a German spy. He was sentenced to death in 1918. After the war, when relations between Germany and the US improved, he was pardoned, and his charges were eventually dismissed in 1923.

Challenges

The Lampedusa message

The 1980 book *Love in Code* by Donald McCormick is a nice overview of the use of encryption by lovers.[15] It covers hundreds of years of encrypted love letters, diaries, newspaper advertisements, and other cryptograms created by romantic couples seeking to keep their communications private. In one of the chapters, titled "Love at War," McCormick reports on a woman who lived on the tiny Italian island of Lampedusa in the Mediterranean Sea when the US Army bombarded it in 1943.[16] This woman painted the following message in bold letters on a white cloth and put it on the beach for the intruders to see:

```
TSURT EM, SYOB. I NEEUQ FO ASUDEPMAL
```

It is a lot easier to decipher this cryptogram than to understand its meaning. The woman was never identified, and the purpose of this message is not known.

The Friedmans' love messages

William and Elizebeth Friedman (1891–1962 and 1892–1980, respectively) were a codebreaking dream team. Both had long careers as cryptanalysts working for the military, the police, and other institutions. In 2017, US author Jason Fagone wrote a fascinating book about Elizebeth Friedman that covers not only the couple's codebreaking work, but also their courtship and marriage.[17] (Many other biographical books about Elizebeth have appeared recently; see Chapter 17.[18, 19])

William and Elizebeth were allegedly so enthusiastic about crypto that they even used encryption in their private life. Figure 9-6 shows a love message William wrote to Elizebeth around 1917, as well as another one Elizebeth sent back to him. Both messages are encrypted in a simple transposition cipher. While William's plaintext is in English, Elizebeth's is in French. Can you solve these two cryptograms?

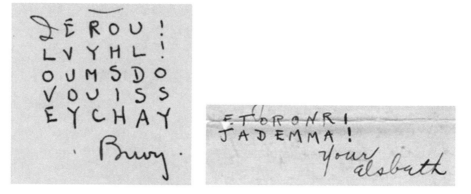

Figure 9-6: A message sent from William Friedman (signed "Biwy") to his wife Elizebeth around 1917 and another sent back to him (signed "Elsbeth"). Both are encrypted in a simple transposition.

An encrypted "agony" ad

We've already mentioned *The Agony Column Codes & Ciphers*, Jean Palmer's 2005 book that lists over a thousand encrypted newspaper ads. Some (but not very many) of these ads are encrypted in transposition ciphers. The following were published in the British *Evening Standard* in 1882:[20]

    CEM.-I e g c n e h d n h a o a s s b i s e r c g d h l i h u s a c
    c b k h e i e . Monday, July 31, 1882

    CEM.-Key 11. - L k e o i s v s t e s o e e m l d y o d b v e n s e
    d t p l i a a n a e g l m s l y h b r m n e b e m r s e a o u t f
    W e y r w o i h o a e u v n l e y e . Saturday, August 5, 1882

The first message is in German and the second is in English. Can you solve them?

Yardley's eleventh ciphergram

Chapter 11 of Herbert Yardley's 1932 book *Ciphergrams*[21] describes an encrypted message sent from a radio station in Mexico to a German spy in the United States during World War I. This story, including the message, is fictional, but breaking the encryption (a complete columnar transposition cipher) is still entertaining:

```
TSKGL AATYI LTLPA SAHLM DPLGI ENEAI WTUEN N
```

Hint: Count!

Edgar Allan Poe's first challenge

In 1841, Edgar Allan Poe published two cryptograms allegedly created by a W.B. Tyler. The second of these cryptograms, along with the background story, is covered in Chapter 6. The first message was broken in 1991 by Poe expert Terence Whalen of the University of Illinois at Chicago, though his dissertation was not published until 1994. In the meantime, it was also solved independently by John Hodgson in 1993.[22] The cipher turned out to be a simple substitution cipher without spaces, combined with a transposition.

Tyler's first cryptogram is depicted in Figure 9-7.

Figure 9-7: This reproduction of a cryptogram published by Edgar Allan Poe in 1841 was solved 150 years later.

As can be seen, Tyler used a nonstandard alphabet. Some cryptanalysts believed this to be a simple substitution cipher without spaces (a Patristocrat), but that assumption didn't lead anywhere. When Whalen studied the correspondence between Tyler and Poe, he found a hint stating that the letters of each word in the message were reversed. Further analysis showed that the trigraph ,†§ was especially frequent. Whalen guessed that it stood for EHT, the reversed version of **THE**, which is the most frequent trigraph in the English language.

Whalen's guess proved correct. Knowing three letters and the cipher method, he could decipher the message. Can you do it, too?

An IRA message

Courtesy of master codebreaker Jim Gillogly, here is a message sent by an IRA member in the 1920s and encrypted in a complete columnar transposition system:[23]

```
TTSEW UDSEE OOEHS BERTN TCEUG EHYNT CLCER TNMEF KCUFE HDPDE SIDRN
EESDT TREDM EIHUS WHRTB DLETI IEERE TAIRF FLABI FOPWV EEROI RTLAC
OWNOT ATLAE
```

Hint: Count the letters. Can you find any good factors?

10

INCOMPLETE COLUMNAR TRANSPOSITION CIPHERS

Having covered complete columnar transposition ciphers in the previous chapter, we now devote our attention to the more general case: columnar transposition with incompletely filled-in rectangles, also known as *incomplete columnar transposition*. This method works in almost the same way as the one introduced in Chapter 9, the only exception being that the line length is not a divisor of the message length.

How an incomplete columnar transposition cipher works

To explain how an incomplete columnar transposition cipher works, let's start with the following plaintext, which is an original message encrypted and sent by the Irish Republican Army, or IRA, in the 1920s (see Chapter 16 for background information):

ARGUMENTS FOR SUCH MATCHES HELPED BY FACT OF TOUR BEING PRIVATE
ENTERPRISE AND FOR PERSONAL GAIN OF PROMOTERS

To encrypt this note, we first conduct a transposition based on the keyword CMOPENSATION. The IRA really used this keyword, including the spelling error. Note that the last line of the rectangle is not completely filled:

```
CMOPENSATION
------------
ARGUMENTSFOR
SUCHMATCHESH
ELPEDBYFACTO
FTOURBEINGPR
IVATEENTERPR
ISEANDFORPER
SONALGAINOFP
ROMOTERS
```

Now we sort the columns, as we did in Chapter 9, such that the letters of the keyword are in alphabetical order:

```
ACEIMNNOOPST
------------
TAMFRERGOUNS
CSMEUAHCSHTH
FEDCLBOPTEYA
IFRGTBROPUEN
TIERVERAPTNE
OINPSDREEAFR
ISLOOGPNFAAN
SRT OE M OR
```

If we now read out the ciphertext column-wise, we get the following:

TCFITOIS ASEFIISR MMDRENLT FECGRPO RULTVSOO EABBEDGE RHORRRP
GCPOAENM OSTPPEF UHEUTAAO NTYENFAR SHANERN

This is the same encrypted message our colleague Jim Gillogly found in an IRA file from the 1920s:[1]

```
TCFIT OISAS EFIIS RHHDR ENETF ECGRP ORULT VSOOE
ABBED GERHO RRRPG CPOAE NMOST PPEPU HEUTA AONTY
ENFAR SHANE RN
```

Even with a legitimate decryption (by an intended recipient who knows the key), this type of cipher system requires more work to decrypt than a complete columnar transposition does. The recipient first needs to look at the length of the message (here, ninety-two letters) and the length of the keyword (here, twelve letters). Ninety-two divided by twelve equals seven, with a remainder of eight. The recipient therefore needs a table with twelve columns that contains seven complete rows and one incomplete row of eight columns, in addition to a header row that contains the keyword:

	C	M	O	P	E	N	S	A	T	I	O	N
1												
2												
3												
4												
5												
6												
7												
8												

Next, the recipient writes the ciphertext column-wise into the table, starting with the A column, as A is the first letter of the alphabet that appears in the keyword:

	C	M	O	P	E	N	S	A	T	I	O	N
1								T				
2								C				
3								F				
4								I				
5								T				
6								O				
7								I				
8								S				

The next keyword letters, in alphabetical order, are C, E, and I, so the recipient proceeds with these (note that the I column has only seven cells):

	C	M	O	P	E	N	S	A	T	I	O	N
1	A				M			T		F		
2	S				M			C		E		
3	E				D			F		C		
4	F				R			I		G		
5	I				E			T		R		
6	I				N			O		P		
7	S				L			I		O		
8	R				T			S	■	■	■	■

Then, the recipient fills in the columns below the letters M, N, N, O, O, P, S, and T:

	C	M	O	P	E	N	S	A	T	I	O	N
1	A	R	G	U	M	E	N	T	S	F	O	R
2	S	U	C	H	M	A	T	C	H	E	S	H
3	E	L	P	E	D	B	Y	F	A	C	T	O
4	F	T	O	U	R	B	E	I	N	G	P	R
5	I	V	A	T	E	E	N	T	E	R	P	R
6	I	S	E	A	N	D	F	O	R	P	E	R
7	S	O	N	A	L	G	A	I	N	O	F	P
8	R	O	M	O	T	E	R	S	■	■	■	■

The recipient can now read the plaintext (**ARGUMENTS FOR SUCH MATCHES** . . .) line-wise.

It is also possible to perform two successive incomplete columnar transpositions, in which the result of the first transposition is transposed again. This method, called *double columnar transposition*, was frequently used during World War II and then in the ensuing Cold War into the 1980s. Considered one of the best manual encryption methods, it was especially popular among intelligence operatives in the field. It goes without saying that a double columnar transposition should be used with two different keywords (preferably with different lengths). Despite the recommendation, of course, this best practice was not always followed.

How to detect an incomplete columnar transposition cipher

As explained in Chapter 9, a transposition cipher is usually straightforward to detect. When letters of a message are transposed, neither the language's index of coincidence nor its properties of frequency analysis change. So, if these values for a ciphertext resemble a known language—in this case, English—a transposition is by far the most likely candidate.

From there, how do we determine what kind of transposition cipher was used? To keep things reasonably simple, let's assume that we have ruled out other transposition ciphers (discussed in Chapter 11) and that the only options are complete or incomplete columnar transposition. At this point, we should check the length of a message. For instance, look at the following IRA message, which was sent in the 1920s (see Chapter 16 for details):

```
3.    119.  KSOAA. TNINA. CECTW. UIAAT. OAOAE. BOGTE. TELND.
INETU. SSDEO. DLDHC. PUTNF. UNNWS. TNNOO. MGEEN. ICTBB. OAMDO.
ERUIS. SONDS. RRBDR. TEAIS. TTNDN. EYIAC.  IAEJO. ARTS.
```

It consists of 119 letters. As 119 is a prime number, this message could not have been encrypted with a completely filled-in rectangle (unless the rectangle consisted of only one line with a length of 119, which is unlikely). Likewise, the following IRA message from the same time period . . .

```
5.    46.  OHOEE. WHDTT. EETWE. AHELI. WTCDO. EHINN. ESFOT.
TOOIE. NCNMT. L.
```

. . . has forty-six letters. The sender might have used a 23 × 2 rectangle, but experience has shown that the IRA rarely chose twenty-three-letter keywords. In both cases, we are probably dealing with an incomplete columnar transposition.

The situation changes when we encounter a message consisting of, say, eighty letters. In this case, a complete columnar transposition is possible but not guaranteed. To our regret, we are not aware of any simple method of distinguishing between complete and incomplete columnar transpositions if the message length allows for both options. All we can do is check whether solutions for a complete columnar transposition case work (as we described in Chapter 9). If not, we may be dealing with an incomplete columnar transposition or something else.

How to break an incomplete columnar transposition cipher

A transposition cipher with an incompletely filled-in rectangle is much more difficult to break than one whose rectangle is complete. This is for two reasons:

1. It is much more difficult to guess the line length because it is, by definition, not a divisor of the message length.

2. The technique of multiple anagramming doesn't work very well here because the lengths of the columns vary and are unknown to the codebreaker.

Therefore, the best way to attack these transpositions is with computer-assisted hill climbing (see Chapter 16).

If you want to solve an incomplete columnar transposition without computer support, there are still ways to do so. For example, we could test different line lengths and various blank positions in the short line in order to perform multiple anagramming, but this would be extremely laborious. However, we do describe a success story involving such a technique for the *Kryptos* K3 message later in this chapter.

A more promising method is to guess words or expressions that appear in the plaintext. This strategy requires knowledge of the plaintext and some luck, but often, there is no alternative.

As an example, we look at another IRA cryptogram from the 1920s, provided to us by Tom Mahon and Jim Gillogly (see Chapter 16):

I. II3: UHTAO, EUESI, YSOIO, OMTOG, OSMNY, DMHRS, OSRAS, NOEEO, MRYUR, TRRRF, CNTYR, NIRIH, IUSNR, TNENF, UMYOA, SRREO, TOIME, IPEFR, TIAOT, TRHDT, AOTNP, TOCOA, NMB.

Here's a transcript, omitting the numbers at the beginning:

```
UHTAO EUESI YSOIO OMTOG OSMNY DMHRS OSRAS NOEEO
MRYUR TRRRF CNTYR NIRIH IUSNR TNENF UMYOA SRREO TOIME
IPEFR TIAOT TRHDT AOTNP TOCOA NMB
```

Frequency analysis confirms that we are probably dealing with a transposition cipher. This comes as no surprise, as the majority of the IRA messages that our colleague Gillogly broke were of this kind. The message contains 113 letters. As 113 is a prime number, it cannot be a cryptogram of the completely filled-in rectangle type. We therefore assume that we are dealing with an incomplete columnar transposition.

To make things easier, let's say that we have a crib: the plaintext contains the phrase **DESTROY ANY AMMUNITION** (twenty letters). Of course, having knowledge of three consecutive plaintext words is a rare case in practice, but without such a crib, it would be extremely difficult to break the encryption manually.

Assuming that the keyword has fewer than twenty letters, the phrase spreads to at least two lines. If the keyword has, say, fifteen letters, it might look like this:

```
......DESTROYAN
YAMMUNITION....
```

In this example, the letter pairs D and I, E and T, S and I, T and O, and R and N align from different rows. This means that, if our guess is correct, the digraphs DI, ET, SI, TO, and RN must appear in the ciphertext. As we don't see all of them in practice, we can conclude that our assumed keyword length is wrong.

Let's now look for other possibilities in a systematic way. The following table lists the letter pairs in the ciphertext that start with one of the first four letters of our crib:

Letter	Ciphertext digraph starting with this letter	Distance of digraph letters in the phrase
D	DM	11, 12
	DT	3
E	EE	—
	EI	14, 16
	EF	—
	EN	7, 13, 18
	EO	4
	ES	1
	EU	12
S	SI	14, 16
	SM	9, 10
	SN	6, 12, 17
	SO	16
	SR	2
T	TA	4, 7
	TI	1, 12, 14
	TN	3, 5, 11, 16
	TO	2, 15
	TR	1
	TT	13
	TY	3, 6

As can be seen, a distance of twelve appears for every letter at least once. We can therefore conclude that the keyword we are looking for has twelve letters, and we can set up the following (empty) twelve-column transposition table:

	?	?	?	?	?	?	?	?	?	?	?	?
1												
2												
3												
4												

	?	?	?	?	?	?	?	?	?	?	?	?
5												
6												
7												
8												
9												
10						■	■	■	■	■	■	■

The letter pairs with a distance of twelve are DM, EU, SN, and TI. We get a match if we write the crib into the table as follows:

?		D	E	S	T	R	O	Y	A	N	Y	A
?	M	M	U	N	I	T	I	O	N			

The letter pair DM appears only once in the ciphertext and is followed by an H. The same is true for EU (followed by an E), SN (followed by an R), TI (followed by an A), YO (followed by an A), and AN (followed by an M). The letter pairs RT and OI appear several times. We can now add a third line to our table excerpt:

?		D	E	S	T	R	O	Y	A	N	Y	A
?	M	M	U	N	I	T	I	O	N			
?		H	E	R	A	I/N/R	O/M	A	M			

Now, we try to add further rows to the table, above and below the three lines we already have. Of course, we can never be sure that these lines really exist; we might have reached the bottom or the top of the table. Let's try to put a line on top of our table fragment:

?		Y	O	U	R	F/N/U	S/T	M	O			
?		D	E	S	T	R	O	Y	A	N	Y	A
?	M	M	U	N	I	T	I	O	N			
?		H	E	R	A	I/N/R	O/M	A	M			

The new line contains the word **YOUR**. This makes sense, so we can assume that the line really exists. Next, take a look at the first and last lines of the sixth and seventh columns. Which of the choices (F/N/U, S/T, I/N/R, or O/M) is correct? YOURFSMO in the first line wouldn't make sense. Because S and T are consonants, it is very likely that U (the only vowel among the three options) is correct.

This gives us the choice between the combinations YOURUSMO (line 1) / HERAROAM (line 4) and YOURUTMO (line 1) / HERARMAM (line 4). The latter option is more likely, as the words **UTMOST** and **ARMAMENT** can be derived from it. Here's the new version of our table:

?		Y	O	U	R	U	T	M	O			
?		D	E	S	T	R	O	Y	A	N	Y	A
?	M	M	U	N	I	T	I	O	N			
?		H	E	R	A	R	M	A	M			

Now, we add further lines in a similar manner:

?		O	U	R	I	O	R	E	P			
?		S	H	I	P	M	E	N	T			
?		M	T	H	E	R	E	F	O			
?		N	A	I	F	Y	O	U				
?		Y	O	U	R	U	T	M	O			
?		D	E	S	T	R	O	Y	A	N	Y	A
?	M	M	U	N	I	T	I	O	N			
?		H	E	R	A	R	M	A	M			

As the string UHTAO (in the third column) appears at the beginning of the cipher message, we know that there can't be a row above OURIO . . . Now that we have reached the top of the table, the rest of it can be derived easily:

	?	?	?	?	?	?	?	?	?	?	?	?
1	Y	O	U	R	I	O	R	E	P	O	R	T
2	S	S	H	I	P	M	E	N	T	S	F	R
3	O	M	T	H	E	R	E	F	O	R	C	H
4	I	N	A	I	F	Y	O	U	C	A	N	D
5	O	Y	O	U	R	U	T	M	O	S	T	T
6	O	D	E	S	T	R	O	Y	A	N	Y	A
7	M	M	U	N	I	T	I	O	N	O	R	O
8	T	H	E	R	A	R	M	A	M	E	N	T
9	O	R	S	T	O	R	E	S	B	E	I	N
10	G	S	I	N	T							

Here's the plaintext:

```
YOURIOREPORT
SSHIPMENTSFR
OMTHEREFORCH
INAIFYOUCAND
OYOURUTMOSTT
ODESTROYANYA
MMUNITIONORO
THERARMAMENT
ORSTORESBEIN
GSINT
```

As you may have noticed, we have broken this encryption without reconstructing the keyword. (The table's header row contains only question marks.) Usually, a codebreaker is not really interested in obtaining the keyword, so long as they can discover the plaintext.

In this case, it is not even possible to recover the keyword with certainty. All we know is that the keyword has twelve letters and that, if we sort these letters alphabetically, we get a certain transposition. Using a computer program, Gillogly searched for English words that have the desired property. The only plausible candidate he found was **CHAMPIONSHIP**. It is very likely that this is the keyword the IRA used. This provides us with the complete transposition table:

	C	H	A	M	P	I	O	N	S	H	I	P
1	Y	O	U	R	I	O	R	E	P	O	R	T
2	S	S	H	I	P	M	E	N	T	S	F	R
3	O	M	T	H	E	R	E	F	O	R	C	H
4	I	N	A	I	F	Y	O	U	C	A	N	D
5	O	Y	O	U	R	U	T	M	O	S	T	T
6	O	D	E	S	T	R	O	Y	A	N	Y	A
7	M	M	U	N	I	T	I	O	N	O	R	O
8	T	H	E	R	A	R	M	A	M	E	N	T
9	O	R	S	T	O	R	E	S	B	E	I	N
10	G	S	I	N	T							

Success stories

Kryptos K3

Earlier chapters discussed portions of the *Kryptos* sculpture (see Appendix A). In this section, we focus on the third part of the *Kryptos* message, known to its aficionados as K3. This 336-letter cryptogram was solved by, among others, CIA employee David Stein in 1998.[2] Stein did not use a computer for his codebreaking work, instead relying only on pencil-and-paper methods.

The full ciphertext on *Kryptos* consists of 869 characters, which are all letters and a few question marks. Not realizing that *Kryptos* contained more than one encrypted message, Stein started, like most codebreakers do, with a frequency count. His first successes were to solve K1 and K2 on the upper ciphertext plate (see Chapter 8).

When he set his sights on the section in the lower plate, he noticed a substantial difference between it and the ciphertext on the upper plate. Among other things, the frequencies of the letters preceding the only question mark on that lower plate differed from the frequencies of the letters that followed it. (This question mark can be seen in the transcript of the entire *Kryptos* text in Appendix A.) The section of text starting at the beginning of the lower plate and ending at that question mark are what eventually became known as K3. It reads as follows:

```
ENDYAHROHNLSRHEOCPTEOIBIDYSHNAIA
CHTNREYULDSLLSLLNOHSNOSMRWXMNE
TPRNGATIHNRARPESLNNELEBLPIIACAE
WMTWNDITEENRAHCTENEUDRETNHAEOE
TFOLSEDTIWENHAEIOYTEYQHEENCTAYCR
EIFTBRSPAMHHEWENATAMATEGYEERLB
TEEFOASFIOTUETUAEOTOARMAEERTNRTI
BSEDDNIAAHTTMSTEWPIEROAGRIEWFEB
AECTDDHILCEIHSITEGOEAOSDDRYDLORIT
RKLMLEHAGTDHARDPNEOHMGFMFEUHE
ECDMRIPFEIMEHNLSSTTRTVDOHW
```

Stein determined the following frequencies for K3:

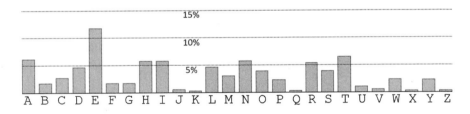

The letters had frequencies similar to normal English, so he assumed that a transposition cipher had been used. His first guess was that he was dealing with a complete columnar transposition. For instance, a table consisting of sixteen columns and twenty-one rows seemed possible, as did six columns and fifty-six rows. However, his further examinations did not confirm this hypothesis.

Stein next considered an incomplete columnar transposition consisting of, for example, a 17 × 20 table with only thirteen letters in the bottom row. As mentioned earlier in this chapter, breaking an incomplete columnar transposition by hand without a crib is very difficult—and Stein didn't have a crib. So, he decided to do it the hard way and check every table size that seemed plausible. Because the cryptogram consisted of 336 letters, there were, in theory, no fewer than 336 different line lengths to test. Even after removing especially short and long lines, at least 200 options remained.

To make things easier, Stein assumed that the transposition table had four lines. This was just a guess, but he had to start somewhere. This limited the number of table variants to twenty-eight. For each variant, Stein had to check many potential positions of the shorter three-letter (as opposed to four-letter) columns. Here is one example, with a line length of eighty-eight:

```
EAHRCODHITYSSOORNRANPNLPAWNEAEUTETSIHOYEAETPHNMGETOIEEAAENBDATEEGEBTIHIOSYRKEGANMMHDPMLTD
NHNHPIYNANULLHSWENTRENEICMDEHNDNOFEWAYQNYIBAEAAYREAOTORERSDAMWRRWADLITEDDILHTREGFEMFESRO
DRLETBSACRLLLSMXTGIASEBIATINCERHEODEETHCCFRMWTTELESTUTMRTENHSPOIFEDCSEADLTMADDOFEEREHSTH
YOSOEI  HED NN MP HRL L EWTRT EA LTNIEETR SHEAE BFFUAOATI ITTIA ECHE GORORL HPH UCIINTVW
```

To check whether a certain line length and the positions of the three-letter columns were correct, Stein tried to reorder the columns until common letter combinations such as EN, AS, LLY, and THE appeared. In other words, he used multiple anagramming based on columns. In the example above, it seems possible that the first two columns belong together, as EA, NH, DR, and YO are all common English digraphs. On the other hand, the last two columns don't fit, as the letter pair VW is rarely encountered in an English text, whether in a single word or connecting two words (comprising the end of one and the beginning of another). It could be an abbreviation for "Volkswagen," but that term appearing in *Kryptos* seems highly unlikely!

As you can see, Stein's method was quite laborious. Not only was it difficult to check the plausibility of two columns appearing next to each other based on only three or four digraphs, but the columns also changed considerably as soon as only a few of the three-letter columns were moved. Nevertheless, Stein could rule out the line lengths of eighty-four and eighty-five (the two shortest possible, if there are four lines).

Next, he tested a line length of eighty-six. This left seventy-eight letters in the last line. Here's one of the many setups he likely tried:

```
EYOSOEIHANULLHSXTGHRLLPCANEAEDNOODEEIQNYIRMWTTEBFOTUTMRTEITTIEIECHEIOSYRKLGANMFEMFESRO
NAHRCODNCRLSLSMMPANPNEIEMDEHNRHELTNOTHCCFSHEAEETAFUAOATIDATERAEBTIITEDDIMETREGEEREHSTH
DHNHPIYAHEDLNNRNRTRENBIWTINCEEATSIHYEETRTPHNMGRESIEEAENBDAMWOGWADLHEADLTLHDDOFUCIINTVW
RLETBSITYS OOWENIASELA WTRTUTEFEWA YEAEBAEAAYLE OTORERSNHSP RFEDCSGOROR AHPHMHDPMLTD
```

When working through this and numerous other combinations containing eighty-six letters in the first three lines and seventy-eight in the last, Stein realized that this time, multiple anagramming delivered more promising results. The digraphs seemed plausible; however, he couldn't determine the correct positions of the three-letter columns.

After some additional examination, Stein concluded that the empty fields of the three-letter columns belonged in the top row, not in the lowest one, meaning that the first rather than the last line was incomplete. Then, after countless hours of manual multiple anagramming (all done on his own time, not as an employee), Stein finally found out that the following combination . . .

YOSOEIHANU LHSXTGHRLLP ANEAEDNOODE IQNYIRMWTTEB OTUTMRTEITT EIECHEIOSYR LGANMFEMFESR
EAHRCODNCRLLLSMMPANPNEICMDEHNRHELTNETHCCFSHEAEETFFUAOATIDATEIAEBTIITEDDIKETREGEEREHSTO
NHNHPIYAHEDSNNRNRTRENBIETINCEEATSIHOEETRTPHNMGREAIEEAENBDAMWRGWADLHEADLTMHDDOFUCIINTVH
DRLETBSITYSLOOWENIASELAWWTRTUTEFEWAYYEAEBAEAAYLESOTORERSNHSPORFEDCSGORORLAHPHMHDPMLTDW

. . . could be reordered to this meaningful text:

FLICKERBUTPRESENTLYDETAILSOFTHEROOMWITHINEMERGEDFROMTHEMISTXCANYOUSEEANYTHINGQ
OLEALITTLEIINSERTEDTHECANDLEANDPEEREDINTHEHOTAIRESCAPINGFROMTHECHAMBERCAUSEDTHEFLAMETO
ASREMOVEDWITHTREMBLINGHANDSIMADEATINYBREACHINTHEUPPERLEFTHANDCORNERANDTHENWIDENINGTHEH
SLOWLYDESPARATLYSLOWLYTHEREMAINSOFPASSAGEDEBRISTHATENCUMBEREDTHELOWERPARTOFTHEDOORWAYW

In finding the correct arrangement of the columns, Stein was aided by the fact that they had been reordered in a regular way. As shown in the following diagram, the first column (END) was moved to position 79, the second one (YAHR) to 72, the third one (OHNL) to 65, the fourth one (SRHE) to 58, the fifth one (OCPT) to 51, and so on. With each step, the number was lowered by seven:

YOSO ...		... DFROMTHEMISTXCANYOUSEEANYTHINGQ
EAHRC ...	→	... RESCAPINGFROMTHECHAMBERCAUSEDTHEFLAMETO
NHNHP ...		... EUPPERLEFTHANDCORNERANDTHENWIDENINGTHEH
DRLET ...		... THATENCUMBEREDTHELOWERPARTOFTHEDOORWAYW

The last deciphering step was to read the four lines in reverse order:

SLOWLY DESPARATLY SLOWLY THE REMAINS OF PASSAGE DEBRIS THAT
ENCUMBERED THE LOWER PART OF THE DOORWAY WAS REMOVED WITH
TREMBLING HANDS I MADE A TINY BREACH IN THE UPPER LEFT HAND CORNER
AND THEN WIDENING THE HOLE A LITTLE I INSERTED THE CANDLE AND
PEERED IN THE HOT AIR ESCAPING FROM THE CHAMBER CAUSED THE FLAME
TO FLICKER BUT PRESENTLY DETAILS OF THE ROOM WITHIN EMERGED FROM
THE MIST X CAN YOU SEE ANYTHING Q

This text is a paraphrased excerpt from the diary of Howard Carter, the archaeologist who discovered the tomb of the Egyptian pharaoh Tutankhamun on November 26, 1922.

Stein spent hundreds of hours breaking this ciphertext, but his solution still required luck, as is the case with the successes of many codebreakers. For example, one sequence that he guessed represented the word **THE** turned out to be **THEY**. Also, his (quite speculative) assumption that there were four lines in the table proved correct. Lastly, the third of twenty-eight possible line lengths he checked turned out to be the right one. Sometimes, luck is the companion of the diligent.

Antonio Marzi's radio messages

Antonio Marzi (1924–2007) was a spy and partisan working against the German occupying force in Udine, in northern Italy, during World War II.[3, 4]

Every day, Marzi radioed an encrypted report about the current situation in the city to an outside contact, probably a British intelligence officer. Contrary to usual precautions, he didn't destroy his messages after sending them—a dangerous practice, but one that left behind a treasure trove for crypto-historians! His collection of reports has been preserved as a 200-page encrypted war journal with scores of encrypted entries created between 1944 and 1945 (Figure 10-1).

Decades later, when historians became interested in Marzi's report, Marzi himself could no longer decrypt it. He remembered that he had used a double columnar transposition and that he had chosen the keywords from the poem "Un giovinetto pallido e bello" by Italian poet Aleardo Aleardi (1812–1878). But whenever he tried to decrypt a message in this way, no meaningful text emerged. In 2003, Marzi finally asked Italian encryption expert Filippo Sinagra for help. Sinagra could not decipher the messages either, so he shared them with other experts.

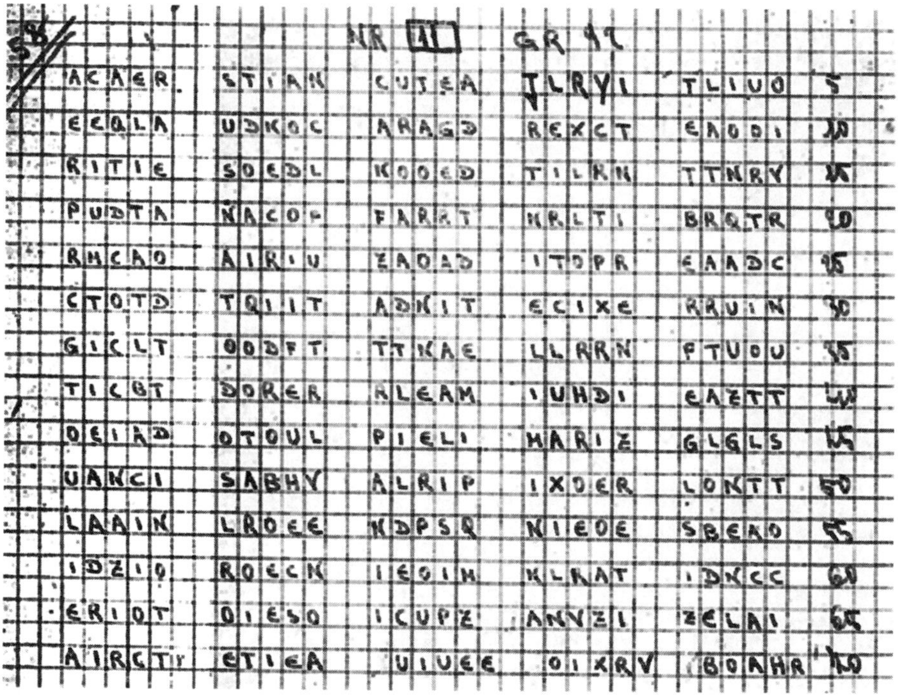

Figure 10-1: During World War II, Italian spy Antonio Marzi sent encrypted reports from the city of Udine to an outside contact. Seventy years later, these cryptograms were broken by German cryptanalyst Armin Krauß.

In 2011, the crypto puzzle website MysteryTwister published Antonio Marzi's radio messages as an unsolved challenge. For two years, none of this portal's many users came up with a solution. Then, our colleague Armin Krauß (Krauss), the top-scoring participant at that time, examined this mystery. He started by writing a computer program that attempted decipherment with a double columnar transposition. Examining many configuration possibilities, he tried words that appeared in Aleardi's poem as keywords for decipherment, checking all combinations of one to five words; however, even after 2.6 million attempts, the program delivered nothing but gibberish.

The breakthrough came when Armin guessed that the first and last five-letter group of each entry might not belong to the encrypted message but instead provided some metainformation (also known as an *indicator*). When Armin omitted these two groups, the decryption program suddenly began delivering meaningful words. The first phrase he recognized was **SITUAZIONE LOCALE TRANQUILLA (LOCAL SITUATION QUIET)**.

At that point, Armin could decrypt all the radio messages, although he kept encountering a surprising number of spelling mistakes. After some further investigation, he found the reason for this: the metainformation was contained in the fourth group instead of the first group. When Armin adjusted his program accordingly to omit the fourth and last groups of each message, most of the spelling errors vanished.

Finally, Armin wanted to know what the metainformation given in the fourth and the last group of every message meant. The most obvious explanation was that these groups hid the keywords Marzi had chosen from the poem. This guess proved correct; we will explain the details of this system later in this section.

Let's encrypt an excerpt of the diary as an example. On April 28, 1945, Marzi wrote the message reproduced below. The letters ZC at the beginning of the message and SL at the end are meaningless nulls. Roman numerals are used to encode numbers; the word ALT serves as a period:

```
ZC NR LXXXIV DEL XXVIII ORE DICIOTTO
ALT
QUESTA NOTTE FORZE PARTIGIANE DELLA GARIBALDI ET OSOPPO FRIULI CHE
HANNO REALIZZATO ACCORDO COMANDO UNICO TENTERANNO OCCUPAZIONE UDINE
ALT
PREFETTO MEDIAZIONE RESA COMANDO PIAZZA TEDESCO ANCORA ESITANTE
ACCETTAZIONE
ALT
OGGI PATRIOTI TENTATO INVANO PRESA CIVIDALE
ALT
TARCENTO ET CISTERNA GIA POSSESSO PATRIOTI
ALT
TEDESCHI AVVIANO NORD QUANTI AUTOMEZZI POSSIBILE MA PARE ORMAI
SICUR O BLOCCAGGIO PATRIOTI
ALT
TEDESCHI ORDINATO COPRIFUOCO ORE VENTI PERQUISIZIONI STRADE
FINE
SL
```

Here's a translation:

```
Number 84 from 28th, 6pm
Tonight, partisan forces of the Garibaldi and the Osoppo Friuli who
have implemented single command agreement will try to occupy Udine.
```

Prefect is mediating surrender. The German place command still hesitating to accept. Today patriots attempted to capture Cividale, but to no avail. Tarcento and Cisterna are already owned by the patriots. Germans start north with as many vehicles as possible, but situation still seems safe because of the blocking patriots. Germans ordered curfew with street patrols after 8pm. End.

Marzi always took his keywords from the following excerpt of the poem. Each word is marked with a letter of the alphabet, and the letters R, E, N, A, T, and O are skipped. *Renato* is a common name in Italian; it means "Reborn."

$_B$UN $_C$GIOVINETTO $_D$PALLIDO $_F$BELLO $_G$COLLA $_H$CHIOMA $_I$DORO $_J$COL $_K$VISO $_L$GENTIL $_M$DA $_P$SVENTURATO $_Q$TOCCO $_S$SPONDA $_U$DOPO $_V$LUNGO $_W$MESTO $_X$REMIGAR $_Y$DELLA $_Z$FUGA

The English translation is as follows: "A pale beautiful boy with golden hair and the friendly face of the unfortunate man, touched the shore after a long and sad rowing of his escape."

Marzi chose the second and twelfth words of the poem to be his keys for that day: **GIOVINETTO** and **SVENTURATO**, producing the keyword **GIOVINETTOSVENTURATO**. The two letters identifying this keyword in the poem are C and P, which will become important later. Here's the plaintext written below the keyword:

```
GIOVINETTOSVENTURATO
--------------------
ZCNRLXXXIVDELXXVIIIO
REDICIOTTOALTQUESTAN
OTTEFORZEPARTIGIANED
ELLAGARIBALDIETOSOPP
OFRIULICHEHANNOREALI
ZZATOACCORDOCOMANDOU
NICOTENTERANNOOCCUPA
ZIONEUDINEALTPREFETT
OMEDIAZIONERESACOMAN
DOPIAZZATEDESCOANCOR
AESITANTEACCETTAZION
EALTOGGIPATRIOTITENT
ATOINVANOPRESACIVIDA
LEALTTARCENTOETCISTE
RNAGIAPOSSESSOPATRIO
TIALTTEDESCHIAVVIANO
NORDQUANTIAUTOMEZZIP
OSSIBILEMAPAREORMAIS
ICUROBLOCCAGGIOPATRI
OTIALTTEDESCHIORDINA
TOCOPRIFUOCOOREVENTI
PERQUISIZIONISTRADEF
INESL
```

Next, the columns were sorted such that the letters in the top row were in alphabetical order:

```
AEEGIINNOOORSTTTTUVV
--------------------
IXLZCLXXNVOIDXIXIVRE
TOTRECIQDONSATTUAEIL
NRTOTFOITPDAAZEGEIER
ORIELGAELAPSLIBTPOAD
AINOFULNREIEHCHOLRIA
DCCZZOAOARUNDCOMOATO
UNNNITEOCRACATEOPCON
EDTZIEUPOETFAINRTENL
MZEOMIASENNOEIOAACDR
CZSDOAZCPERNDATOOAIE
INEAETATSANZCTETOAIC
EGIEAOGOLATTTIPTNITR
IASATNVAOPAVRNOCDIIE
SAOLETTEAEEINRCTTCLT
RPSRNIAOASOTEOSPIAGS
AEITITTAASOICDEVNVLH
ZATNOQUORIPZANTMIEDU
ALROSBIESASMPEMOIRIA
TLGICOBIUCIAAOCORPRG
ITHOTLTIIEADSEDONRAC
NIOTOPRRCOIECFUETVOO
DSIPEUISRIFAOIZTERQN
   INL  E        S
```

Transcribing the message column-wise, Marzi derived the following intermediate message:

```
ITNOADUEMCIEISRAZATINDXORRICNDZZNGAAPEALLTISLTTINCNTESEISOSITRGHOI
ZROEOZNZODAEALRTNOIOTPICETLFZIIMOEATENIOSCTOENLCFGUOTEIATONTITQBOL
PULXIOALAEUAZAGVTATUIBTRIXQIENOOPSCTOAEOAOEIIRSNDTLRACOEPSLOAAARSU
ICREVOPAERRENEAAPESSIACEOIONDPIUATNRNTAEOOPSIAIFISASENCFONZTVITIZM
ADEADAALHDAAEDCTRNECAPASCOXTZICCTIIATINRODNEOEFIITEBHOENOTEPOCSETM
CDUZXUGTOMORAOTTCTPVMOOOETIAEPLOPTAOONDTINIIRNTEVEIORACECAAIICAVER
PRVRRIEAITONDIITILGLDIRAOQSELRDAONLRECRETSHUAGCON
```

In order to get a double columnar transposition, Marzi now had to repeat the previous procedure. Of course, it would have been a good idea to use a different keyword at this point, but, perhaps unwisely, Marzi always chose the same expression he had used for the first transposition (in this case, **GIOVINETTOSVENTURATO**).

Here's the intermediate message written below the keyword:

```
GIOVINETTOSVENTURATO
--------------------
ITNOADUEMCIEISRAZATI
NDXORRICNDZZNGAAPEAL
```

```
LTISLTTINCNTESEISOSI
TRGHOIZROEOZNZODAEAL
RTNOIOTPICETLFZIIMOE
ATENIOSCTOENLCFGUOTE
IATONTITQBOLPULXIOAL
AEUAZAGVTATUIBTRIXQI
ENOOPSCTOAEOAOEIIRSN
DTLRACOEPSLOAAARSUIC
REVOPAERRENEAAPESSIA
CEOIONDPIUATNRNTAEOO
PSIAIFISASENCFONZTVI
TIZMADEADAALHDAAEDCT
RNECAPASCOXTZICCTIIA
TINRODNEOEFIITEBHOEN
OTEPOCSETMCDUZXUGTOM
ORAOTTCTPVMOOOETIAEP
LOPTAOONDTINIIRNTEVE
IORACECAAIICAVERPRVR
RIEAITONDIITILGLDIRA
OQSELRDAONLRECRETSHU
AGCON
```

After sorting the columns alphabetically, the table looked like this:

```
AEEGIINNOOORSTTTTUVV
--------------------
AUIITADSNCEIZIEIMRTA
EINNDRRGXDLPZCNAAAOZ
OTELTLTSICISNINESIST
EZNTROIZGELAOROOADHZ
MTLRTIOFNCEIEPIZOIOT
OSLATIOCEOECECTFTGNN
OIPIANTUTBLIOTQLAXOL
XGIAEZABUAIITVTTQRAU
RCAENPSOOANIETOESIOO
UOADTACALSCILEPAIRRO
SEAREPAAVEASNRRPIEOE
EDNCEONROUOAAPINOTIT
TICPSIFFISIZESAOVNAN
DEHTIADDZATEAADACAML
IAZRNAPIEOATXSCCICCT
ONITIODTNENHFEOEEBRI
TSUOTOCZEMMGCETXOUPD
ACOORTTOAVPIMTPEETOO
EOILOAOIPTETINDRVNTN
RCAIOCEVRIRPIAAEVRAC
IOIRIITLEIADINDGRLAT
SDEOQLRCSNUTLAORHEER
    AGN  C        O
```

Transcribing this new version column-wise, Marzi next derived the following ciphertext:

```
AEOEMOOXRUSETDIOTAERISUITZTSIGCOEDIEANSCOCODINENLLPIAAANCHZIUOIAIE
INLTRAIAEDRCPTRTOOLIROATDTRTTAENTEESINITROOIQGARLOIINZPAPOIAAOOTAC
ILNDRTIOOTASCANFDPDCTOETRSGSZFCUBOAARFDITZOIVLCNXIGNETUOLVOIZENEAP
RESCCDCECOBAASEUSAOEMVTIINILILEELINCAOITANMPERAUZPSAIUIIISSAZETHGI
TPDTIZNOEEOTELNAEAXFCMIIILECIRPCTVTERPSASEETNANAMNNOITQTOPRIADCOTP
DADORAEOZFLTEAPNOACEXEREGRTASAOTAQSIIOVCIEOEVVRHAAIDIGXRIRETNACBUT
NRLEOOSHONOAOROIAMCRPOTAAEOEZTZTNLUOOETNLTIDONCTR
```

In the last step, Marzi needed to include identifiers of the keywords he had used. As mentioned, **GIOVINETTO** and **SVENTURATO** were identified by the letters C and P. Marzi extended these two characters to the five-letter group CRPEN, adding the null characters R, E, and N. (Remember that the letters R, E, N, A, T, and O didn't stand for words in the poem and therefore could be used as meaningless filler material.) Then, he converted this filler to numbers and added 44,739 to this expression. This number was the same for all messages. To perform the number-to-letter conversion, he used an alphabet written in the following order: B, C, D, F, G, H, I, J, K, L, M, P, Q, S, U, V, W, X, Y, Z, R, E, N, A, T, O. The complete operation looked like this:

```
CRPEN
44739
-----
HTYTH
```

Next, Marzi repeated the procedure, extending CP with the null characters A, T, and O to build the five-letter block ATOCP and then adding 44739:

```
ATOCP
44739
-----
CDIGR
```

Finally, Marzi recorded the message in groups of five, adding the block indicating the first keyword (**HTYTH**) at the fourth position and the block indicating the second keyword (**CDIGR**) at the end:

```
AEOEM OOXRU SETDI HTYTH OTAER ISUIT ZTSIG COEDI EANSC OCODI NENLL
PIAAA NCHZI UOIAI EINLT RAIAE DRCPT RTOOL IROAT DTRTT AENTE ESINI
TROOI QGARL OIINZ PAPOI AAOOT ACILN DRTIO OTASC ANFDP DCTOE TRSGS
ZFCUB OAARF DITZO IVLCN XIGNE TUOLV OIZEN EAPRE SCCDC ECOBA ASEUS
AOEMV TIINI LILEE LINCA OITAN MPERA UZPSA IUIII SSAZE THGIT PDTIZ
NOEEO TELNA EAXFC MIIIL ECIRP CTVTE RPSAS EETNA NAMNN OITQT OPRIA
DCOTP DADOR AEOZF LTEAP NOACE XEREG RTASA OTAQS IIOVC IEOEV VRHAA
IDIGX RIRET NACBU TNRLE OOSHO NOAOR OIAMC RPOTA AEOEZ TZTNL UOOET
NLTID ONCTR CDIGR
```

This is exactly the ciphertext radio message Marzi transmitted on April 28, 1945.

Challenges

Yet another IRA message

Figure 10-2 shows a message encrypted using an incomplete columnar transposition and sent by the IRA in the 1920s.[5]

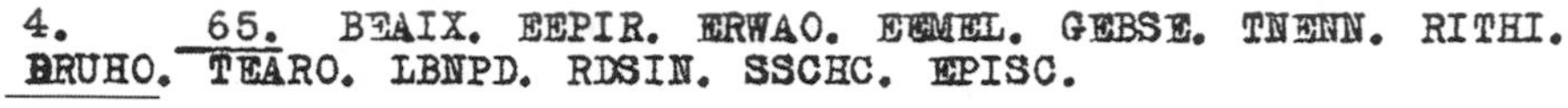

```
4.      65.   BEAIX.  EEPIR.  ERWAO.  EEMEL.  GEBSE.  TNENN.  RITHI.
BRUHO.  TEARO.  LBNPD.  RDSIN.  SSCHC.  EPISC.
```

Figure 10-2: An IRA message encrypted with an incomplete columnar transposition

You can try to solve it yourself.

The Double Columnar Transposition Reloaded challenge

We mentioned that double columnar transposition (DCT) is one of the best manual ciphers known. In Chapter 16, we will introduce a quite difficult DCT challenge that our colleague, the Israeli codebreaker George Lasry, solved in 2013 with a hill-climbing algorithm. After this success, Arno Wacker, Bernhard Esslinger, and Klaus decided to create a new and even more difficult puzzle.

In fact, they created three new challenges, calling them DCT Reloaded 1, 2, and 3. The first puzzle is the easiest and the last is the most difficult. Details of these and other DCT challenges are available on the crypto puzzle website MysteryTwister (*https://mysterytwister.org*).

Here, for example, is DCT Reloaded 2. Both keywords used in this transposition are randomly chosen letter strings with a length of twenty to twenty-seven characters each:

```
NWTDSSHAUIASOOTLDEDNLTHOBENHETCWTHERTPSNTMCTIAYEINNIUIYOPLEIRGHMNU
TARFONYMLDSERSAELANNLOSAWALTODOCAHUOTOPAREAEEESPDEYATUENINNCNBDPCO
FORETSYHAHANTEDERPERCRSGEANNIHYTTEDNGICOIOLABSRONNWLNTALWLVRIBHKTE
TECNPSFHACMIGTYODEONMTOIVUAIAEESKKLAROMBAYKOSRNEEHTHSIMSEOUAWLYAWH
SWWSSWLCIYCEONUPNEESURSBETDALHDAHLIOAAETONNDOELTHHNHHDCOTUIITEAYTE
RRHOENKEUCTIRANECYQNACTMBWAPDIAEXEUTIATAJLITEALFISIEATATAEOTNEESME
UDDADOROEGORPELGPVMETHHSDDRMSNDERMSLEOANENHTCHPHSSEASSEDBHVESNUGON
IOLELSUCASELSTEIESYATREEELADIEYOEOKAREEELETCOSDHCSAETSTSFRTSELEITD
NHBRINSERHRTLNAXYONAMECAIESATAEERIAOTCEENETFARMRTSREAPAYNIRTNITSRA
THIWRIPRTDIIRECSWADSOATUTENMVVOAISISONGGWTH
```

There is no doubt that this challenge is an extremely difficult one!

Unsolved cryptograms

The Catokwacopa ad series

One of the most puzzling encrypted newspaper ad series we are aware of was published in the London *Evening Standard* in 1875. Like most of the other newspaper ads covered in this book, we found these in Jean Palmer's 2005 book *The Agony Column Codes & Ciphers.*[6] This particular series consists of two ads. The first was printed in the May 8, 1875, issue:

W. Str 53. Catokwacopa. Olcabrokorlested. Coomemega. Sesipyyocashostikr. Rep.—Itedconlec mistrl. —Hfsclam 54, 3 caselcluchozamot. 1. 6. 9. Moprediso. Contoladsemot. Iadfilisat. Qft. Cagap. Balmnopsemsov. Ap. 139.—Hodsam 55, 6. Iopotonrogfimsecharsenr. Tolshr. Itedjolec. Mistrl.—Ding Declon. Ereflodbr.

Twelve days later, on May 20, a similar ad was published in the same newspaper:

W.—Umem 18. Poayatlgerty. Dpeatcnrftin. Nvtinrdn. Dmlurpinrtrcamur. Etd.—Atndngtnsurs. Otenpu.—Eftdorshpxn. 18. Ndtsfindseseo. Cotegr Tavlysdinlge. Ngtndusdcndo. Edrstneirs. Ui, Ndted. Iolapstedtioc. A. P. 138.—Yxn. 18. 18. Wtubrfftrstendinhofsvmnr. Dily.—Atdwtsurs. Oatvpu.—Y Arati. Rileohmae.—This will be intelligible if read in connection with my communication published in this column on the 8th inst.

Note that the last sentence of the second ad is unencrypted. If it is correct, the first ad could be the key for decrypting the second (or vice versa). The letter frequencies are consistent with those of an ordinary English text. This makes it likely that we are dealing with a transposition cipher. Our guess is that the two ciphertexts need to be mixed somehow (e.g., letter 1 from ad 1, letter 1 from ad 2, letter 2 from ad 1, letter 2 from ad 2 . . .). However, so far, nobody has found a mixing rule that makes sense. Can a reader do better?

11

TURNING GRILLE
TRANSPOSITION CIPHERS

It should come as no surprise that there are types of transposition ciphers other than the two systems, complete and incomplete columnar transposition, covered in the previous chapters. Here are a few examples:

A. *Rubik's Cube encryption*: Douglas W. Mitchell proposed a transposition cipher that uses a Rubik's Cube.[1] The plaintext is written on the fields of the cube. A sequence of moves forms the key. Subsequently, one reads the ciphertext from the cube. When used properly, this kind of encryption is difficult, yet not impossible, to break.[2]

B. *Crossword encryption*: In World War II, German spies sometimes used crossword puzzles as keys for transposition ciphers.[3] The sender wrote their message in the empty fields while the black fields remained empty. Afterward, the letters were read out column-wise. The receiver had to follow the same procedure with the same crossword puzzle in reverse order. Though this system is clever, we know today that enemy cryptanalysts of the era broke it.

C. *Rasterschlüssel 44*: The German army also used this kind of transposition cipher during World War II. It is based on rectangular forms that look similar to crossword puzzles.[4] This system was mainly applied to less-important messages and as an Enigma substitute. The British could break this kind of encryption, but deciphering it was laborious and often took several days. As the intelligence gained from these decipherments was usually not vital, they finally gave up trying to break Rasterschlüssel 44 messages, deciding it was not worth the effort.

Figure 11-1 illustrates these three transposition types.

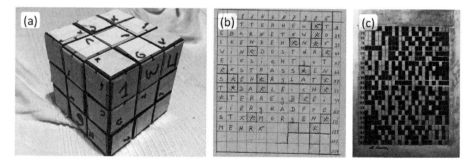

Figure 11-1: Examples of various transposition types: (a) a Rubik's Cube being used as a cipher device; (b) an encryption method based on a crossword puzzle (used by a secret agent in World War II); and (c) a form used for the German World War II cipher Rasterschlüssel 44

There are many other types of transposition ciphers commonly mentioned in cryptography books; however, we have not included them here because they tend not to be used in practice, only as puzzle challenges for crypto-enthusiasts. For example, competitions of the American Cryptogram Association routinely include systems such as the rail fence cipher and route transposition.[5]

Apart from these, there is one transposition method encountered so often that it merits its own chapter: the turning grille encryption.

How turning grille encryption works

The sample Christmas card in Figure 11-2, which could have been sent in 2009 from one crypto-enthusiast to another, bears an encrypted inscription consisting of thirty-six letters: TDHOAA PYHPEH UNFYAS MFNROH OLTIII NLMGYT.

Figure 11-2: A Christmas card encrypted with a turning grille

The plaintext of this inscription is **HAPPY HOLIDAYS FROM THE HUNTINGTON FAMILY**. It was encrypted with a so-called turning grille, also known as a Fleissner grille after nineteenth-century crypto book author Edouard Fleissner von Wostrowitz (1825–1888).

A *turning grille* is usually a square stencil with holes that is used in four steps. In each step, a quarter of the plaintext is written into the holes from left to right and top to bottom. Each step is followed by a ninety-degree clockwise turn of the grille. For example, here are the steps for encrypting the aforementioned **HAPPY HOLIDAYS . . .** message with a 6 × 6 grille:

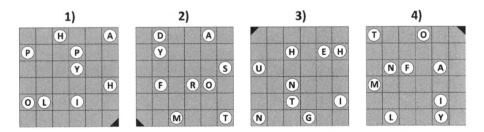

When we remove the stencil after the fourth step, we get the message on the Christmas card:

```
T D H O A A
P Y H P E H
U N F Y A S
M F N R O H
O L T I I I
N L M G Y T
```

The turning grille encryption method is a transposition cipher. The grille can be of any size but must be square. Most turning grilles we have encountered have an even number of rows and columns, because if the stencil uses an odd number of rows, there will be a "center" to the square, which usually remains empty.

The larger a turning grille, the more secure it is.

To construct a turning grille, one can proceed, as shown in Figure 11-3, by following these steps:

1. Begin with a rectangular matrix that is one-quarter the size of the final grille. For example, if your final grille is 6 × 6, meaning that it has four quarters, each of which is 3 × 3, start with one of those 3 × 3 sections. In this smaller section, which has nine possible positions, write the numbers 1 through 4 in random locations, filling in all nine locations. (No matter the size of your grille, you will always use the numbers 1 through 4, as these represent the four directions in which the grille will be turned.)

2. Place the smaller matrix on top of the larger grille's top-left corner and copy the 1 sections to the larger grille. Next, move the smaller matrix to the top right of the grille, rotate it ninety degrees clockwise, and then mark the 2s in the larger grille. Move the smaller matrix to the bottom right of the grille, again rotating it ninety degrees clockwise, and then mark the 3s. Finally, move the smaller matrix to the bottom left of the grille, rotating it again by ninety degrees, and mark the 4s.

3. Punch or cut holes in the larger matrix wherever there is a number.

The grille constructed in Figure 11-3 is the one that was used to encrypt the Christmas card.

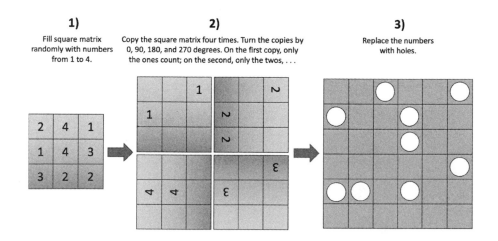

Figure 11-3: A turning grille can be constructed with a square matrix that is filled with numbers from 1 to 4 at random. The resulting grille is four times as big.

A message encrypted with this stencil must have exactly thirty-six letters. If it has fewer, we'll need to add a few nulls.

How to detect a turning grille encryption

Turning grille cryptograms are usually easy to detect. If a message is written in a square form and if frequency analysis indicates that it is a transposition cipher, chances are that you are dealing with a turning grille ciphertext. Of course, it is easy to arrange a message of this kind in a form other than a square, but experience shows that many turning grille users waive this simple security measure. The message in Figure 11-4, which was published by Dutch cryptologist Auguste Kerckhoffs (1835–1903) in his 1883 book *La Cryptographie Militaire*, is a typical example.[6]

Figure 11-4: A turning grille cryptogram created by Auguste Kerckhoffs in the nineteenth century

If a message is not written in square form, the message length is a possible indicator that you are dealing with a turning grille. A turning grille with an even line length produces messages that have the length of a squared even number (for instance, 16, 36, 64, or 100). If the line length is odd and the square in the middle is left empty, the message length is a squared odd number minus one (for instance, 24 or 48). Of course, this length, too, can be changed, for instance, by adding a few nulls. But again, in our experience, most turning grille users do not take this extra step to make their system more secure.

How to break a turning grille encryption

Breaking a turning grille cryptogram works very well with hill climbing cryptanalysis, which is an iterative computer technique we will introduce in Chapter 16. Still, it is possible to break a turning grille cryptogram by hand, though you usually need a crib or at least a few letters from the plaintext that can be guessed. We will demonstrate this strategy with the cipher message on the simulated birthday card in Figure 11-5.

Figure 11-5: The message on this birthday card (created by the authors for this book) is encrypted using a turning grille cipher.

Here's a transcript of the message:

```
H L H O D V
T A I A E P
Y B P E T T
I Y L O H T
Y B O L W Y
I E R U T N
```

This cryptogram consists of thirty-six letters written in a square. Analysis reveals letter frequencies that are similar to that of the English language. We therefore assume that we are dealing with a turning grille encryption.

Can we guess a plaintext word? Considering that this message is a birthday greeting, BIRTHDAY is a promising candidate. This guess is confirmed by the fact that the letters B, I, R, T, H, D, A, and Y all appear in the cryptogram.

One of the inherent properties of every turning grille message is that the average distance between two letters that are neighbors in the plaintext is four (i.e., there are three letters in between them), no matter the size of the grid. This is because the grille always has exactly four different positions.

So, our first step is to find the letters of the crib, bearing in mind this average letter interval. If we look for BIRTHDAY, finding the word's start is easy, as there is only one B in the message. Continuing on to the right, we encounter an I five cells later. There are also an R and a T in the following line:

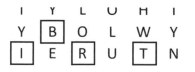

Assuming that we have discovered the letters BIRT from BIRTHDAY, we now turn the grille 180 degrees and place it along the top of the grid to see which letters are "seen through the holes":

H [L] H [O] D [V]
T [A] I A [E] P
Y R P F T T

The four squares we have identified show the letters LOVE—a word that makes sense on a birthday card. Let's now look for the letters HDAY, which we expect to follow BIRT. As the T of BIRT stands close to the end of the cryptogram, we need to look for HDAY at its beginning. There are four different possibilities (indicated by squares with solid lines; the dotted squares indicate the letter sequences we get when we turn this proposed grille fragment by 180 degrees):

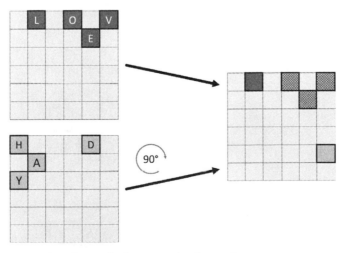

The potential four-letter sequences we get when turning the grille are TWEN, HLIR, TOEN, and TOEU. All of these might appear in an English text. However, as we are dealing with a birthday card, TWEN makes the most sense, because TWENTY or TWENTIETH might refer to the age of the receiver. This means that the first of the four options is the most likely one. Now, we have identified two four-hole fragments of the grille. They can be connected to one five-hole fragment, as shown in Figure 11-6.

Figure 11-6: Two grille fragments that fit together

The N of TWEN is the last letter in the last line. If we assume that the next letter is T (as in TWENTY or TWENTIETH), we need to look at the top of the grid for the continuation. As an aid, we turn the five-hole grille fragment by ninety degrees.

In fact, the grille fragment now indicates a T at a position that makes sense. What letters might be between the T and BIRT? The sequence IETH would make sense, as it renders TWENTIETH BIRTHDAY. The positions of the I and the H of IETH are clear. (Note that the I at the beginning of the fourth line can't be the right one, as there is no ETH after it.) There are two Es, but the first one is already used. It is unclear, though, which of the two Ts is the right one:

To determine which T is correct, we again turn the grille fragment by 180 degrees:

It should be apparent that the letter sequence BILLY is more likely than BYLLY. This means that the second T is the right one.

We have now found the position of eight of the nine holes in the grille. For the remaining one, there are four choices: I, T, Y, and L:

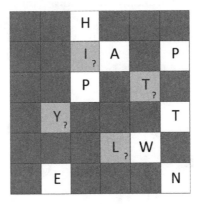

Only Y makes sense here, as it renders us HAPPYTWEN for the first nine letters of the plaintext. We are done. Figure 11-7 shows the grille we have derived.

Figure 11-7: The grille used to encrypt the birthday card

The plaintext is **HAPPY TWENTIETH BIRTHDAY TO YOU LOVE BILLY**.

Success stories

Paolo Bonavoglia's turning grille solution

Our colleague Paolo Bonavoglia, a prolific modern author of articles about Italian cryptologic history, is also the grandson of Luigi Sacco (1883–1970). Sacco was a notable Italian cryptologist who, among other achievements, set up a cipher office for the Italian army during World War I to break messages from the Austrian and German armies.

In a notebook that his grandfather left behind, Paolo found numerous German ciphertexts, including the one depicted in Figure 11-8.[7] He set out to solve this apparently unsolved message. The letter Ö, which appears in the first line, confirmed to Paolo that the message was in German. His eye was also immediately drawn to the presence of the letters X and Y in the lower-left corner, as both letters are quite rare in German texts. Paolo therefore suspected that the two letters had been used as nulls to complete the grille.

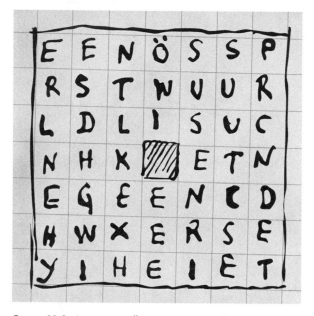

Figure 11-8: A turning grille cryptogram Paolo Bonavoglia found in a notebook belonging to his grandfather, Luigi Sacco

In addition, Paolo guessed that the cryptogram contained the word SUCHE (SEARCH) or SUCHEN (TO SEARCH), starting on the right-hand side. Any of the text's four Ss, three Us, four Es, and two Ns could form one of these words. Paolo had to check dozens of combinations, but after many attempts, he found the following solution:

ES WURDEN DREI PUNKTE GESEHEN ÖTLLICH WEITESRSSUCHEN XY

The word ÖTLLICH is misspelled; it should be ÖSTLICH (EAST OF). This message translates to: THREE POINTS HAVE BEEN SEEN. KEEP ON SEARCHING IN THE EAST XY.

Paolo published his solution in 2017, and shortly afterward, New Zealand–based crypto expert Bart Wenmeckers broke the same cryptogram with a computer-based hill-climbing method (see Chapter 16).

As an interesting side note, while we were writing our book and asking these brilliant codebreakers to assist with reviewing our work, when Tobias Schrödel proofread this chapter in 2020, he discovered something previously unknown! Double-checking Sacco's notebook page containing the turning grille cryptogram, he noticed a sequence of forty-eight numbers, starting with 1, 37, 25, 26, 38, and 2. He realized that this was the solution of the ciphertext: letter 1 in the ciphertext (E) is at position 1 in the plaintext, letter 2 in the ciphertext (E) is at position 37 in the plaintext, letter 3 in the ciphertext (N) is at position 25 in the plaintext, and so on.

Tobias sent this information to Paolo, who had not made the connection; this meant that his grandfather had solved this ciphertext and left an encrypted clue behind!

André Langie's turning grille solution

In his marvelous 1922 book *Cryptography*, Swiss cryptologist André Langie (1871–1961) tells the story of a gentleman who received an encrypted message while staying in a hotel called the North Pole.[8] The sender was a person this gentleman knew, and the two had agreed that the cipher would be a turning grille. However, the man in the hotel had lost the notes that contained a description of the grille, so he could not decrypt the message. Thus, he contacted Langie.

Here is the sixty-four-character English version of the message. Different versions were provided in each translation of the book:

> AITEGFLYTBOEEHREAUWNANOARRDRTEETHOSHFPETAPO
> TOYHLRETIHENEMGAOARNT

To decrypt the message, Langie wrote it down in a grid format and numbered the sixty-four squares for easy identification (see Figure 11-9). Langie's attention was immediately drawn to the letters A and T (squares 1 and 3), as AT is a common word in English and one that might easily form the beginning of a message. Accordingly, he marked the position of these two letters on tracing paper and turned his grille by 180 degrees.

I II

1 A	2 I	3 T	4 E	5 G	6 F	7 L	8 Y
9 T	10 B	11 O	12 E	13 E	14 H	15 R	16 E
17 A	18 U	19 W	20 N	21 A	22 N	23 O	24 A
25 R	26 R	27 D	28 R	29 T	30 E	31 E	32 T
33 H	34 O	35 S	36 H	37 F	38 P	39 E	40 T
41 A	42 P	43 O	44 T	45 O	46 Y	47 H	48 L
49 R	50 E	51 T	52 I	53 H	54 E	55 N	56 E
57 M	58 G	59 A	60 O	61 A	62 R	63 N	64 T

IV III

Figure 11-9: A turning grille cryptogram solved by André Langie in the early twentieth century

The marks on the tracing paper coincided with the letters R and T (squares 62 and 64). RT is a common word ending, and it is evident that, from the last two lines, one could easily extract the word HEART in squares 53, 54 (or 56), 59 (or 61), 62, and 64. Marking these and again reversing the tracing paper, Langie found, in the corresponding squares—1, 3, 4 (or 6), 9 (or 11), and 12—the letters ATE (or F), T (or O), and E. As this was not very satisfactory, he abandoned the combination and tried another.

Next, Langie turned his attention to the second line and decided to mark THE (squares 9, 14, and 16), the most common trigraph in English. Reversing the tracing paper brought the marks to the corresponding squares 49, 51, and 56 in the sixth line, indicating the letters RTE—a promising combination. Looking for the vowel that preceded it, Langie first noticed the O (in square 45). Three squares earlier (at 42) was a P. He now had the group PORTE, which seemed to call for the final R, which occurred in the last line, at square 62.

Langie again turned the paper by 180 degrees, which brought to light T (square 3) and NO (20 and 23), producing the sequence TTHENO. The first of these letters was doubtlessly the final one of some other word, and the last two were the beginning of a new word.

The next step was, tentatively, to begin the construction of the grille, which Langie did by drawing squares around the letters PORTER (42, 45, 49, 51, 56, and 62). He then made a small mark on each of these six letters. Next, he turned the tracing paper, this time by only ninety degrees. His six marked squares now covered the letters IOUSAG (2, 11, 18, 35, 41, and 58). These he labeled with a different mark.

A further turn brought him to the group TTHENO (squares 3, 9, 14, 16, 20, and 23), which he marked, too:

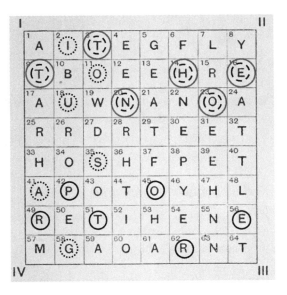

A final turn produced LAEHEN (squares 7, 24, 30, 47, 54, and 63), which he indicated in another way:

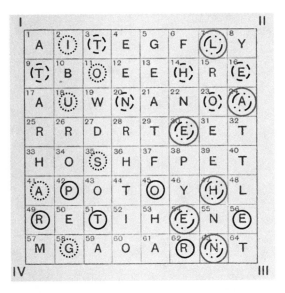

Langie had now neutralized twenty-four out of the sixty-four squares, thereby considerably narrowing his field of research. Coming back to his original group, **PORTER**, he looked for a word likely to precede it and was favorably inclined toward **THE** (32, 36, and 39). There were two Hs between the T and E, and he adopted the second experimentally.

Marking these and reversing the tracing paper, Langie found the three corresponding letters to be RTH (26, 29, and 33). This enlarged the group TTHENO to T **THE NORTH**—a result that proved he was on the right track. Accordingly, he marked in four colors the corresponding letters in the four positions, bringing the total number of neutralized squares to thirty-six.

Progress subsequently was by leaps and bounds. For instance, upon scrutinizing the words THE NORTH and the unmarked letters following them, Langie discerned a P and an O and thought of POLE. These letters were duly found in squares 38, 43, 48, and 50. Having marked these and the corresponding letters in the other positions, he found that only twelve squares remained to be accounted for. With some additional guessing, he deduced the following plaintext:

IF YOU ARE STAYING AT THE NORTH POLE HOTEL BEWARE OF THE MANAGER AND THE PORTER

Karl de Leeuw's turning grille solution

In 1993, crypto expert Karl de Leeuw, who is a colleague of ours, and crypto expert Hans van der Meer found in an Amsterdam archive an encrypted message (Figure 11-10) left behind by Dutch governor and Prince of Orange William V (1748–1806).[9] The cryptogram's shape suggested that the writer had used a 16 × 16 turning grille. As the message was too long for the grille's 256 fields, some fields contained two letters.

The letter frequencies indicated that the plaintext language was German. The letter Ü in the second-to-last position of the third line, with its distinctive dots, confirmed this suspicion.

Figure 11-10: Eighteenth-century turning grille cryptogram solved by Karl de Leeuw and Hans van der Meer in the twentieth century

In 1993, the technique of breaking turning grille ciphers with computer support (such as with hill climbing) was still in its infancy. Karl and Hans therefore tried their luck with manual methods, which is usually quite difficult when the stencil is as large as the one used here. Nevertheless, the two found a surprisingly simple way to decipher the cryptogram. They took advantage of the fact that the writer had been sloppy when placing letters into the holes. This can be seen most clearly in line 6, where the letters E (at position 8), I (at position 10), and N (at position 16) are written slightly lower than the others, which implies that they were all written with the stencil in a certain position.

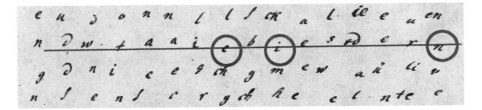

In line 7, the same applies to G, E, G, and A:

In the eighth line, though not quite so clear, N, G, E, and N are a little lower than the other letters, too. Together, these letters form EINGEGANGEN, which is a German word meaning GONE IN.

Reversing the stencil resulted in BIERWELCHESI, which also makes sense in German (BIER means BEER and WELCHES means WHICH). Based on these observations, Karl and Hans were able to reconstruct the positions of eleven holes, which gave them a total of forty-four letters. Then, with the technique described earlier in this chapter, they could solve the rest of the message. The grille they derived can be seen in Figure 11-11. Here's the plaintext:

> die franszosen sind laut eingegangener erkundigung und nach richt von camberg abmarchiret es sollen aber dem verlaut nach andere an deren stelle einrucken vielleicht fürchten sie das en gelische bier welches ihnen wohl übel bekommen durfte wan es recht getruncken wird ich wünschet dass sie die rechte maass be kommen mögten [separation mark] koenig

It translates to the following:

> According to an inquiry that has arrived and a message, the French have left Camberg. However, according to rumors, others will replace

them soon. Perhaps they fear the English beer, which will make them sick when it is drunk. I hope they will get the right amount of it. Koenig

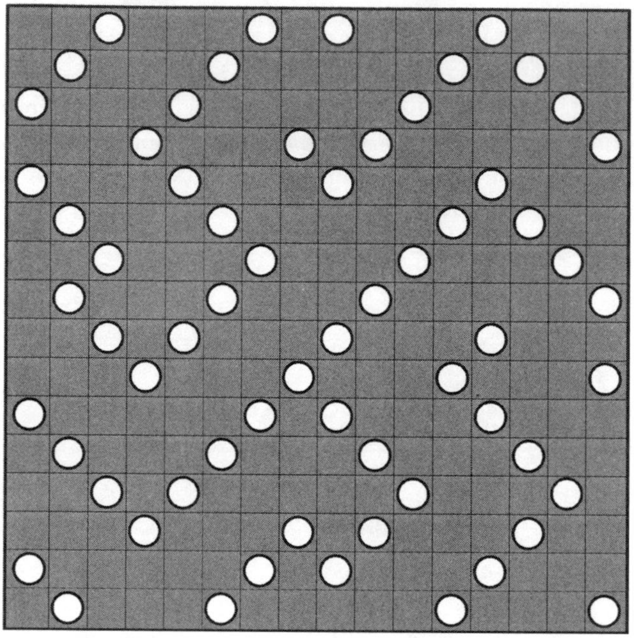

Figure 11-11: The turning grille Karl de Leeuw and Hans van der Meer derived when they solved the message left behind by Dutch governor William V. This message was written in a somewhat sloppy way, which allowed it to be solved more easily. In addition, the regular pattern of the holes is helpful for a codebreaker.

Apparently, the author of this note was joking about English beer—certainly an interesting find, especially because they took the time to encrypt the joke!

The Mathias Sandorf cryptogram

In his famous 1885 novel *Mathias Sandorf,* French author Jules Verne (1828–1905) describes two petty criminals who find an encrypted message attached to the leg of a carrier pigeon and later find a turning grille that they use to decrypt the cryptogram (Figure 11-12). The message reads as follows:

```
IHNALZ ARNURO ODXHNP AEEEIL SPESDR EEDGNC
ZAEMEN TRVREE ESTLEV ENNIOS ERSSUR TOEEDT
RUIOPN MTQSSL EEUART NOUPVG OUITSE ERTUEE
```

In 2000, German cryptology professor Klaus Pommerening published a paper that explains how a codebreaker could have solved the message without knowing the grille.[10] The codebreaking process Pommerening describes is too lengthy to be covered in full in our book, so we will use a few shortcuts.

Let's start with Pommerening's assumptions that the plaintext is in French, that each line of thirty-six letters is encrypted separately with a 6 × 6 turning grille, and that the same grille was used for each line.

For cryptanalysts, one of the nice things about the French language is that the letter Q is relatively frequent in short words, such as QUE, QUOI, and QUEL, and that, as in many other languages, Q is usually followed by a U. (The word CINQ, which means FIVE, is the only common exception.) This means that, when working with a French plaintext, looking for a Q is a good start. As we can see, the third row contains a Q in position 9. Unfortunately, in the same line are five Us, which makes things a little more complex.

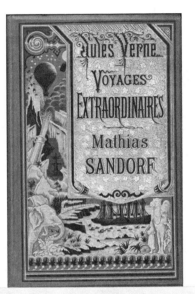

IHNALZ ARNURO ODXHNP AEEEIL SPESDR EEDGNC
ZAEMEN TRVREE ESTLEV ENNIOS ERSSUR TOEEDT
RUIOPN MTQSSL EEUART NOUPVG OUITSE ERTUEE

Figure 11-12: The 1885 novel Mathias Sandorf by Jules Verne contains a message encrypted with a turning grille.

Pommerening knew that the same grille had been used for all three lines, so he could apply the technique of multiple anagramming (see Chapter 9) to check the most plausible combination. With this method, the five Us after the Q in the third line lead to the following five options in the first and second lines:

```
NH NX NE NP NG
VA VT VN VR VE
QU QU QU QU QU
```

While the letter pairs NH, NX, VT, and VN are rare in French, NG and VE are quite common. For this reason, the last option looks best, so

Pommerening assumed that it was correct. As QU is usually followed by E or I in French, he had eight plausible possibilities to proceed:

```
NGN NGO NGD NGE NGR NGE NGN NGC
VEE VEE VES VES VER VET VED VET
QUI QUE QUE QUI QUE QUE QUE QUE
```

Possibilities 4, 5, and 6 look promising. Typically, a codebreaker would have to check all three options, but to make things easier, let's select the fifth block (the correct one, as will become clear). As another shortcut, we assume, based on the content of the novel, that NGR is a part of the word HONGRIE, which is French for HUNGARY. This assumption is supported by the fact that the first row of the cryptogram also contains the letters H and O (even two of each), providing Pommerening with four possible arrangements:

```
HONGR HONGR HONGR HONGR
AEVER AEVER LEVER LEVER
ULQUE UEQUE ALQUE AEQUE
```

Pommerening now chose block 3, as the letter sequences LEVER and ALQUE make sense in French, while the letter combination AE is quite rare. He continued by appending an I to HONGR (remember that we want to construct the word HONGRIE), which produced two possibilities:

```
HONGRI HONGRI
LEVERZ LEVERO
ALQUER ALQUEV
```

The second possibility seemed more plausible, as ERZ is not a common trigraph in French. Pommerening now needed an E after HONGRI, resulting in six variants:

```
HONGRIE HONGRIE HONGRIE HONGRIE HONGRIE HONGRIE
LEVERON LEVERON LEVEROI LEVEROS LEVEROT LEVEROO
ALQUEVO ALQUEVU ALQUEVP ALQUEVI ALQUEVA ALQUEVR
```

He recognized here the word LEVERONT ("will stand up"), with the last letter missing. This meant that the initial two options were the most likely ones. The first appeared to be the correct one, as VO in the last line could be extended to VOUS ("you"). To produce this word, Pommerening added a U (omitting the S, as there were several choices for it):

```
HONGRIEX
LEVERONT
ALQUEVOU
```

The X didn't fit especially well, but it could be padding. As the word LEVERONT is reflexive (the complete expression is SE LEVERONT), Pommerening now needed an E in the second line, before LEVERONT.

Two of the ten Es in the second row were already absorbed, but there were still eight choices:

```
NHONGRIEX  LHONGRIEX  RHONGRIEX  OHONGRIEX
ELEVERONT  ELEVERONT  ELEVERONT  ELEVERONT
IALQUEVOU  PALQUEVOU  SALQUEVOU  EALQUEVOU

NHONGRIEX  AHONGRIEX  SHONGRIEX  DHONGRIEX
ELEVERONT  ELEVERONT  ELEVERONT  ELEVERONT
RALQUEVOU  NALQUEVOU  OALQUEVOU  TALQUEVOU
```

Options 1, 3, 5, and 6 looked the most promising. In a real codebreaking process, one would have to follow all four paths to find out the right one. However, this is only a summary, so we will only cover option 6, which is the correct one. In order to get SE LEVERONT, Pommerening needed an S at the beginning of the second line. There were four to choose from:

```
DAHONGRIEX  LAHONGRIEX  EAHONGRIEX  SAHONGRIEX
SELEVERONT  SELEVERONT  SELEVERONT  SELEVERONT
ENALQUEVOU  GNALQUEVOU  INALQUEVOU  TNALQUEVOU
```

The second option renders LA HONGRIE ("the Hungary") in the first line, which looks good, as the French usually refer to nations with a definite article. Pommerening now searched the third row for extensions. He found SIGNAL QUE VOUS ("signal that you" or "signal which you"). Adding an I on the left side of the third line yielded two possibilities:

```
NLAHONGRIEX  ELAHONGRIEX
ESELEVERONT  SSELEVERONT
IGNALQUEVOU  IGNALQUEVOU
```

The first option led to nothing, so Pommerening took the second and added an S on the left side of the third line:

```
UELAHONGRIEX  RELAHONGRIEX  DELAHONGRIEX
RSSELEVERONT  ESSELEVERONT  USSELEVERONT
SIGNALQUEVOU  SIGNALQUEVOU  SIGNALQUEVOU
```

The third variant stood out because of the sequence DE LA HONGRIE ("from Hungary") in the first line.

For space reasons, we'll skip the rest of the multiple-anagramming process. Pommerening proceeded to solve the rest of the cryptogram, resulting in the following plaintext:

```
SSEPOURLI  NDEPENDAN  CEDELAHON  GRIEXRZAH
SENVERREZ  DETRIESTE  TOUSSELEV  ERONTENMA
TOUTESTPR  ETAUPREMI  ERSIGNALQ  UEVOUSNOU
```

However, this message only makes sense if one reads the third line first, then the second, and then the first:

```
TOUTESTPR  ETAUPREMI  ERSIGNALQ  UEVOUSNOU
SENVERREZ  DETRIESTE  TOUSSELEV  ERONTENMA
SSEPOURLI  NDEPENDAN  CEDELAHON  GRIEXRZAH
```

With punctuation, the plaintext reads as follows:

TOUT EST PRÊT. AU PREMIER SIGNAL QUE VOUS NOUS ENVERREZ DE TRIESTE, TOUS SE LÈVERONT EN MASSE POUR L'INDÉPENDANCE DE LA HONGRIE. XRZAH.

It translates to this:

All is ready. At the first signal you send us from Trieste, all will stand up en masse for the independence of Hungary. Xrzah

XRZAH is the sender's codename.

The French plaintext (TOUT EST PRÊT . . .) is exactly the message contained in Jules Verne's French original edition of *Mathias Sandorf*. In the English translation of this novel (at least, the one we found online), the message was not translated.

Note that Pommerening didn't use any special information about turning grilles in his codebreaking process. He used only multiple anagramming to determine the order of the thirty-six letters in each line.

Identifying the kind of grille used is usually trivial if one knows both the plaintext and the ciphertext. However, in this case, no turning grille can produce the given ciphertext from the given plaintext, at least with typical methods. However, if we write each line backward, we can find a grille that fits. The turning grille used for this transformation can be seen in Figure 11-13.

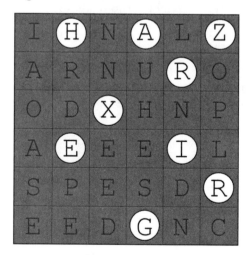

Figure 11-13: The turning grille used for the cipher message in Jules Verne's 1885 novel Mathias Sandorf. The letters seen through the holes read (from the bottom) (HON)GRIE XRZAH (Hungary XRZAH), the final part of the plaintext.

As has been shown, the third line of the plaintext needs to be read before the second and the first one. In addition, each line must be read backward. These observations can be explained in a simple way: the encipherer wrote the whole message backward before encrypting it in chunks of thirty-six letters, each with a 6 × 6 turning grille.

Challenges

The Friedmans' Christmas card

The Christmas card in Figure 11-14 was created by world-renowned code-breakers William and Elizabeth Friedman in 1928.[11]

Figure 11-14: An encrypted Christmas card sent by William and Elizabeth Friedman in 1928

Here's a transcript. Note that, in the original, the number 28 at the end is treated as one character:

```
ABFWORREC
U SRIYEPN G
CT HARSI OS
YMO UTE AWN
ETLM   AESP
OSRQ   DUOI
GHRO   TEOE
```

```
FTX MTE UAP
GI RTASM NH
O DGCSAIH E
   NEETRREE28
```

This cryptogram is straightforward to solve, possibly to make it easier for the Friedmans' non-cryptanalyst friends! Just use the turning grille depicted on the left side of the card. If you want a harder challenge, try to decipher this encrypted message without using the grille.

Jew-Lee and Bill's Cryptocablegram

The "Cryptocablegram" in Figure 11-15 was created by modern codebreaking enthusiasts Jew-Lee Lann-Briere and Bill Briere for their talk about William and Elizebeth Friedman at the NSA Symposium on Cryptologic History in 2017.

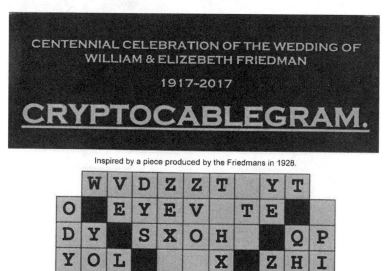

Figure 11-15: A challenge cipher created by Jew-Lee Lann-Briere and Bill Briere

Jew-Lee and Bill applied two encryption steps to the plaintext. First, they encrypted it with a simple substitution cipher. Then, they used a turning grille. Here's the table that inverts the substitution:

```
ABCDEFGHIJKLMNOPQRSTUVWXYZ
HJKLOPQSTUVWXYZFRIEDMANBCG
```

There is an easy way to solve this cryptogram—and a hard one. Without any further hints, can you decipher this turning grille encryption?

A MysteryTwister challenge

MysteryTwister (*https://mysterytwister.org*) is a large crypto puzzle website with hundreds of challenges, ranging from easy to difficult, and a community of thousands of members trying to solve them to gain points. One of its many difficult cryptograms involves a turning grille (Figure 11-16).[12]

Figure 11-16: A 2011 turning grille challenge available on the MysteryTwister website

The solution is an English sentence. If you want a hint, check out *https://codebreaking-guide.com/challenges/*.

A Kerckhoffs cryptogram

Earlier in this chapter, we introduced a turning grille cryptogram published in 1883 by Auguste Kerckhoffs (Figure 11-4). The plaintext is French. Can you solve it?

12

DIGRAPH SUBSTITUTION

In his 1563 book *De Furtivis Literarum Notis*, Italian polymath and cryptologist Giambattista della Porta (1535–1615) proposed an interesting encryption method. Instead of replacing single letters, his system substituted letter pairs (also known as digraphs). In the centuries that followed, different variants of this digraph substitution were developed—including the so-called Playfair cipher. In this chapter, we will cover both methods: Playfair and Porta's original system.

How general digraph substitution works

The method Giambattista della Porta suggested is based on a digraph substitution table with 400 unique entries. It provides a different symbol for each possible letter pair, as shown in Figure 12-1.[1] (The alphabet he used had twenty letters.)

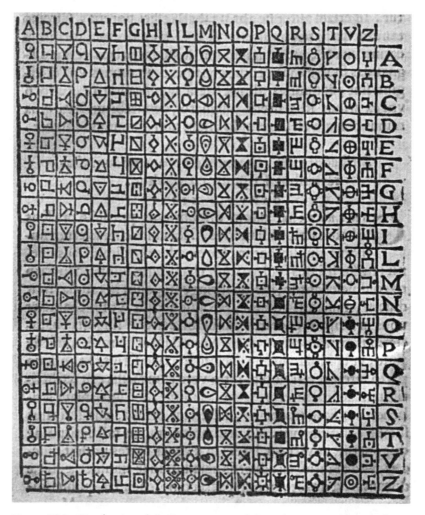

Figure 12-1: Giambattista della Porta suggested this substitution table, which provides a different symbol for every digraph.

For example, if we wanted to encrypt the word **STREET** using this table, we would first need to think of it as a sequence of three digraphs: **ST**, **RE**, and **ET**. If we look up each pair in the table (using the first letter along the top of the table and the second letter along the right-hand side), we get this:

However, Porta's table was probably never used in practice, as dealing with 400 different symbols is quite cumbersome. Other cipher designers preferred replacing digraphs with three-digit substitutes (we will provide an example of this in Chapter 16), but in the end, it turned out that the most convenient way to replace a digraph is with another digraph. Here's an excerpt, from the top left-hand corner of a table with 26 × 26, or 676, entries, that substitutes a new digraph for every existing one:

```
  A   B   C   D   E   F   G   H   I  . . .
A KF  SW  JL  OO  QA  CP  DA  BN  CX . . .
B LH  WS  WM  CO  XE  YP  WW  NV  CH . . .
C JX  KV  AS  PI  CS  PX  NU  SR  LS . . .
D TR  AL  FG  AD  WU  QM  GH  PG  JC . . .
E ND  SG  RE  AT  NA  TU  RX  SS  OD . . .
. . .
```

Using this table, the word **BEAD** encrypts to SGTR (again, assuming that the first letter of each digraph is taken from the top row). The alphabets at the top and on the left can also be written in a keyword-dependent way. The following table, for instance, was created with the keywords **AMERICA** and **BALL**:

```
  A   M   E   R   I   C   B   D   F  . . .
B KF  SW  JL  OO  QA  CP  DA  BN  CX . . .
A LH  WS  WM  CO  XE  YP  WW  NV  CH . . .
L JX  KV  AS  PI  CS  PX  NU  SR  LS . . .
C TR  AL  FG  AD  WU  QM  GH  PG  JC . . .
D ND  SG  RE  AT  NA  TU  RX  SS  OD . . .
. . .
```

When using such a table, one usually keeps the digraphs in the matrix constant while changing the two keywords frequently.

How the Playfair cipher works

Even a table with 26 × 26 (or 676) entries is quite tedious to build and use. For this reason, digraph substitution with an exhaustive table, though reasonably secure, never played much of a role in the history of cryptography. Instead of using a large table, practitioners tended to prefer a set of rules more desirable for substituting digraphs. While they could have constructed such a rules set in numerous ways, only one method (with many variants) was frequently used in practice: the Playfair cipher. It was invented by Charles Wheatstone (1802–1875) in 1854 and later recommended to the British military by Lord Lyon Playfair (1818–1898), hence the name.[2]

British psychologist and parapsychologist Robert Thouless (1894–1984), who appears several times in our book, created two famous cryptograms of this type. Remember from Chapter 8 that, in 1948, Thouless started an interesting experiment: in order to check whether it was possible to send a message from the realm of the dead to the living, he published an encrypted text, keeping the plaintext and the keyword secret. His plan was to channel the keyword from the beyond after his death. Before his death in 1984, Thouless published three trials of his parapsychological experiment: two with Playfair and one with a polyalphabetic system. His two Playfair attempts are covered in this chapter.

In his first trial, Thouless encrypted a Shakespearean quote using the Playfair system. The plaintext was this:

BALM OF HURT MINDS GREAT NATURE'S SECOND COURSE CHIEF NOURISHER IN LIFE'S FEAST

Written in digraphs, this reads:

BA LM OF HU RT MI ND SG RE AT NA TU RE SS EC ON DC OU RS EC HI EF NO UR IS HE RI NL IF ES FE AS T

Typically, the Playfair cipher requires that no pair consist of two equal letters, because the standard set of rules has no method for encrypting an identical pair, as we will explain shortly. Therefore, as is often done in these cases, Thouless added an X between the two Ss:

BA LM OF HU RT MI ND SG RE AT NA TU RE SX SE CO ND CO UR SE CH IE FN OU RI SH ER IN LI FE SF EA ST

If the number of letters in this plaintext were odd, he would have had to add another X in the last position so that each letter belonged to a pair, but this is not necessary here. Thouless chose, as his keyword, **SURPRISE**. Based on this word, he used the following transposed alphabet. It starts with the keyword, omits repeating letters, and considers I and J to be equivalent in order to produce an alphabet of twenty-five letters: SURPIEABCDFGHKLMNOQTVWXYZ. Next, Thouless wrote this alphabet out in a 5 × 5 grid (also known as a Playfair matrix):

```
S U R P I
E A B C D
F G H K L
M N O Q T
V W X Y Z
```

From here, Thouless replaced the plaintext digraphs (**BA**, **LM**, **OF**, **HU** . . .) according to the following most common three Playfair rules, which are visualized in Figure 12-2:

Rule 1 If the two letters are neither in the same column nor in the same row (which is the most frequent case), find a rectangle formed by the two letters when they are at opposite corners and replace the two letters with the other two corner letters (replacing the upper plaintext letter with the other upper letter in the rectangle and the lower plaintext letter with the other lower letter). In this example, **LM** becomes FT.

Rule 2 If the two letters are in the same row, replace each one with its neighbor to the right. Here, **BA** becomes CB.

Rule 3 If the two letters are in the same column, replace each one with its lower neighbor. In our example, **AN** becomes GW.

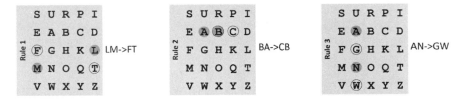

Figure 12-2: The Playfair cipher replaces letter pairs based on three rules.

When we apply the Playfair rules to the 5 × 5 grid shown above, the Shakespeare quote encrypts to the following:

CB FT MH GR IO TS TA UF SB DN WG NI SB RV EF BQ TA BQ RP EF BK SD
GM NR PS RF BS UT TD MF EM AB IM

This is the cryptogram Robert Thouless published in 1948. He wrote it in five-letter groups, except for the last six letters:

CBFTM HGRIO TSTAU FSBDN WGNIS BRVEF BQTAB
QRPEF BKSDG MNRPS RFBSU TTDMF EMA BIM

To learn more about the follow-up to this experiment, see Chapter 8.

Of course, the Playfair method we described can be modified in many ways. For instance, we can use a 4 × 6 or a 5 × 6 Playfair matrix, instead of the 5 × 5 version. The 5 × 6 matrix provides room for a few more characters, such as a space, a period, or meaningless letters (nulls). The replacement rules can be changed in many ways, as well. For instance, one can add a rule for substituting double letters or for shifting letters to the left instead of to the right.

In World War II, the German army implemented a Playfair version that used two 5 × 5 matrices instead of one, constructing each grid with a different keyword. This system was known as the Doppelkasten ("Double Box") method.[3] Examples can be found in back issues of the academic journal *Cryptologia*.

How to detect a general digraph substitution

Klaus created the following ciphertext with a general digraph substitution, not a Playfair cipher. He published it as a challenge for his blog readers, to test whether a digraph substitution cryptogram of this length could be solved. We will come back to this story in the "Challenges" section of this chapter.[4]

```
UNGOZIHIJGSLGVWPIVGJSOKEFMAHSDBDGLUBUNZIWPIEBIUNKFVOUNB
DSLPPHELVAQBAHEBIFJMHKVFLHXQQEFSLQQBDAQRIBVBIBYGJMOSOZB
SDUXZINXUNEQVKUGYHUNVOWPSGSMGEFLFKRUHELFPHGVUXFGHRJYFUH
IPBMHUNVOWPSGHXVKRSSGPHPWQXPLKCXGUNFGBICJFGJGCLLCFPNXUN
TUUKKIZBKFABEQNHRFWLKCYHDJHJOPBZRLAHQVFTHETGRQRJTDAYDTX
TVDBDKFEFZKSDHETUFVIQBIYABDEXZIKCHXRUKQRLGECJAQAOBKZIOB
TEFMFRZNZACLWDWAUNEBBISLMREQKWRJRCUGHERGJMXONWGJHIPBEYG
DZOHXIXKFOXFLKVRUDWAOBIDLSRRICSICJGKFZBBUMRFMGQKFYBXOHE
TGHEOAMUEMWLAYRJWPKIGXUOSKZIHIJGSLHIGIBLFUXXUKUQPHGEGWH
IOPZIBDLVBUKQRJSMUGFPWLWPSGPHFIKVYXCJLVULKVQSZIBDLVBUUI
SRRUGJAIYXXGLKQXFRPBUOJIBTGHGDTGRCICUNVOWPSGDTLIEMTAVOU
NVUQQKCRTLHBDAIUXFGOAKPBTKVFLAHVWRHWAUGKCXGUNFGBIXAGJHE
HXGLBIRNGDOEBPUQSGBDIKACVORUBLKVVLZIHIJGSLWPIEUNCEPHFOM
KFVMHUGNOPKBGLKCGCLHEXFAYUOMKTAGDZOHEKFLVBWKVPLGXBPHEGI
XOTJWURUUNCLSOFMKVWGFMFPIKGJLLJYOGDWFRGLFQQEYDFVCAHYZPJ
GKFBIRQHEBAHELFHEFSVUCLWDBWIGJGDRAYVKFPWLZNLQFGGJQAKFBL
FUWQPWGJOBSLRIVVBXBDVUMHYIZYBZKFGQLWROZIOBMACTPHSMGECLF
GVOSGUNTUJYOGBIHECERCUGWDEMFGKPAYSQKCBWONQVGEKVDHBIDWPH
EMGEAQAONOEXZIOBMAUNTUPHFYNXXGUNFGBIFNFMMFOXJBBDCLBIBIF
JMHKVFLFJMHXNHXVKUNKFZBTFFMHMFVLVWLYHHEMFOFICOJVUYXMFZN
WLLWICLVSDZIFSEBUNNXVUFIHARCXOZKMMFPKVRUUNVOWPSGLCQWUGC
ECJTGHIVKWAFLPHAQVKPHHJSGMFHMRLDDHJZUBPTDBOFGVOSGUNTUJY
OGXGUNFGBIXAFMWAAQFPAIEQQQKCFIHAQWFIBPGLUBZNNNSOWDXMXGU
NFGBIEAHAKCAHAQSGRLMSKFWDBAHEFVMHWGPHFYBIUNTUJYOGAIYXWA
ZIFLYNKCRUSOKVLKBOWARIBIHJ
```

It is fairly easy to distinguish a digraph substitution from a simple substitution cipher by using frequency analysis. Look at the two diagrams in Figure 12-3. The top part shows the frequency of letters in our ciphertext, and the lower part shows the frequency of letters in a simple-substitution-cipher encryption of the same plaintext. As can be seen, the frequency distribution of the upper chart, with digraph substitution, is a lot flatter (i.e., the frequent letters are less frequent, and the rare letters are less rare).

The index of coincidence is different, too. While an English text encrypted in a simple substitution cipher (as well as plain English) has an index of coincidence of 6.7%, our letter pair cryptogram has an index of coincidence of only 4.3%.

But what about other ciphers that are not simple substitutions? Do they have a similar frequency distribution?

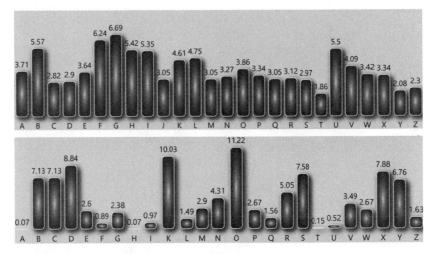

Figure 12-3: The letter frequency distributions of a digraph substitution (top) and a simple substitution cipher (bottom)

We can conduct a frequency count of the digraphs to help determine whether the algorithm is Playfair, another digraph system, transposition, polyalphabetic, or something else. However, the digraph frequency count we need to use here is different from the one we applied in Chapter 4, where we included overlapping pairs. For instance, the string ABCDEF consists of five overlapping digraphs (AB, BC, CD, DE, and EF). In the context of a digraph substitution, we should consider nonoverlapping pairs only. ABCDEF consists of three of these: AB, CD, and EF. Mathematically speaking, if there is an even number of n letters in a text, there are $n - 1$ overlapping digraphs and $n/2$ nonoverlapping ones.

Figure 12-4 shows a (nonoverlapping) digraph frequency analysis of our cryptogram, followed by a digraph frequency analysis of the same plaintext encrypted in a Vigenère cipher. We used *https://dcode.fr/en* to count the letter pairs and Excel to plot the diagrams. Note that there are only about 220 different pairs in the digraph cryptogram, while there are some 380 in the Vigenère cryptogram.

The lower part of the diagram also shows that only a few letter pairs in the Vigenère cryptogram have a frequency of over 1%, while in the upper part, we see some twenty-five of these in the digraph substitution cryptogram, with the most frequent one almost reaching 4%.

It is worth noting that, even in longer English texts, the plaintexts will show properties of only having about three hundred different digraphs, regardless of whether we count overlapping digraphs or not. All other possible digraphs (of the 676 total) would probably have a frequency of zero. This is because, in English, many letter pairs such as *QZ*, *VH*, *II*, and *JN* are extremely rare.

All in all, the risk of confusing a digraph substitution with another cipher is not very high if one compares the frequency counts of nonoverlapping digraphs.

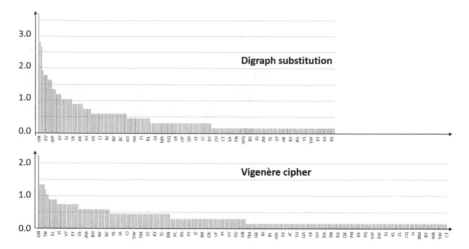

Figure 12-4: Two frequency distribution charts using nonoverlapping digraphs. The pattern for our digraph substitution cryptogram (top) looks different from that of a Vigenère ciphertext (bottom) because fewer digraphs appear, while the frequencies of the most common digraphs are much higher (above 3.0).

How to detect a Playfair cipher

How can we check whether a certain cryptogram has been created with a Playfair cipher? As an example, consider a message sent in World War II. During the war, the US Navy and the United States' allies used the Playfair cipher frequently for tactical communication in the Pacific. One story involves *PT-109*, a patrol torpedo boat commanded by the young naval officer and later president, John F. Kennedy.[5] After the much larger Japanese destroyer *Amagiri* crashed into *PT-109*, slicing it in half and sinking it, the American crew swam for miles and finally washed up on the beach of nearby Plum Pudding Island.

Australian coastwatcher Sublieutenant Arthur Reginald Evans, who observed the crash, received and decrypted multiple messages in Playfair and coordinated a rescue effort involving dispatching one of his teams of Solomon Islanders to try to find the crew.[6] At the suggestion of one of his team members, Biuku Gasa, Kennedy sent a note (in English) carved into a coconut with his pocketknife. We will come back to this story in Chapter 15. For now, we are only interested in one of the Playfair messages (Figure 12-5) sent to Evans, which reported the loss of *PT-109*.

The plaintext of this Playfair cryptogram, received at 9:20 AM on August 7, 1943, five days after the crash, is noted on the upper half of the sheet and reproduced here:

```
ELEVEN SURVIVORS PT BOAT ON GROSS IS X HAVE SENT FOOD AND LETTER
ADVISING SENIOR COME HERE WITHOUT DELAY X WARN AVIATION OF CANOES
CROSSING FERGUSON RE
```

As you can see, this message has 125 letters. The **RE** at the end stands for Reginald Evans, while **GROSS IS** means Gross Island (also known as Cross Island or Nauru). The **X** represents a period.

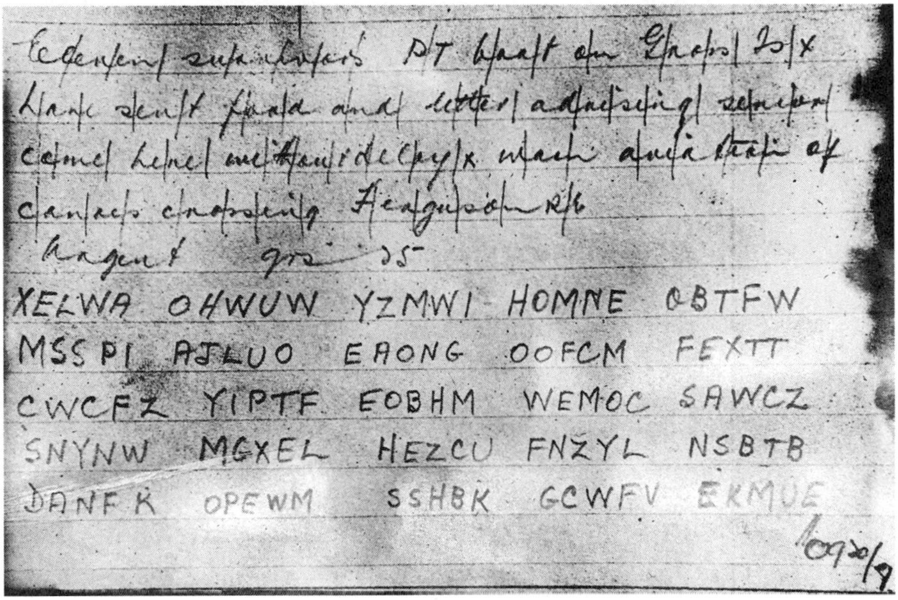
XELWA OHWUW YZMWI HOMNE OBTFW
MSSPI AJLUO EAONG OOFCM FEXTT
CWCFZ YIPTF EOBHM WEMOC SAWCZ
SNYNW MGXEL HEZCU FNZYL NSBTB
DANFK OPEWM SSHBK GCWFV EKMUE

Figure 12-5: The Playfair-encrypted message received by the Australian coastwatcher Sub-lieutenant Arthur ("Reg") Reginald Evans, which reported the loss of PT-109 *in World War II*

This message used the key **PHYSICAL EXAMINATION** and an encryption method that is almost identical to the standard Playfair technique we saw earlier in this chapter, with three minor exceptions. First, pairs of equal letters are not avoided by adding an additional letter; instead, they are simply left unchanged. For instance, the **TT** in **LETTER** encrypts to a ciphertext TT. Second, J is used as an equivalent of I in the ciphertext. Third, the last letter of the message, **E**, for "Evans," being unpaired because of the odd number of letters in the text, is left unchanged, without being paired with a padding letter.

Detecting a Playfair cipher can be quite easy, as it produces messages that have a number of very special and easy-to-see properties:

- The number of letters in the ciphertext is even.
- The letter J does not appear because it is represented by I.
- No digraph consists of two letters of the same kind.

However, all these properties can be hidden easily, as the World War II Playfair ciphertext above shows. This message has an uneven number of letters because the last one is left unencrypted; it includes a J, which is used as an equivalent of I; and it has identical digraphs, which are double letters left unchanged instead of avoided by the insertion of an X. However, in most cases we have encountered in practice, the encipherer of a Playfair cryptogram does not take these precautions.

If these criteria are not sufficient to identify the use of a Playfair cipher, we can turn to statistics to learn more. While counting nonoverlapping digraphs helps to distinguish digraph substitution from many other ciphers, it doesn't differentiate a Playfair cipher from a general digraph substitution based on a 26 × 26 chart. To do that, we can perform an ordinary frequency count of the individual letters. The frequency distribution of a Playfair cryptogram is flatter—meaning that the frequent letters are less frequent, while the rare ones are less rare—than that of a simple substitution cipher, but less flat than that of a general digraph substitution (see Figure 12-6).

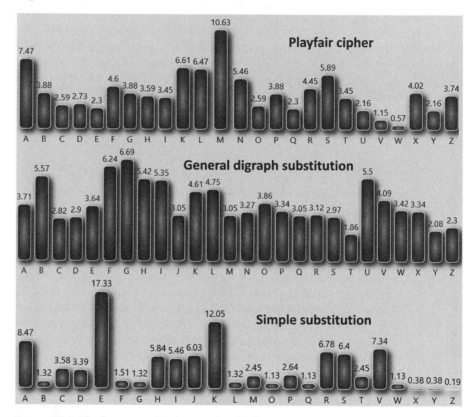

Figure 12-6: The frequency distribution of a Playfair cryptogram (top) is flatter than the distribution of a simple substitution cipher (bottom), but it is not as flat as the distribution of a general digraph substitution (middle).

How to break a digraph substitution

We can break the Playfair cipher, as well as digraph substitution in general, quite effectively and without a crib, using a computer program that implements hill climbing (see Chapter 16). In the following sections, we introduce a couple of other methods and then focus on one that can be used manually. As will become clear, a general digraph substitution is harder to break, requiring more ciphertext than a Playfair cipher.

Frequency analysis

One way to attack a digraph substitution is to perform digraph frequency analysis of the nonoverlapping variant. The most frequent digraphs in the English language are *TH*, *HE*, *IN*, and *ER*. A more comprehensive list is available in Appendix B. However, this method only works for long cryptograms. You'll need about 2,000 letters to get a meaningful digraph frequency chart. Unfortunately, digraph substitution cryptograms are rarely this long in practice, so we rarely use frequency analysis alone to attack a digraph substitution.

Dictionary attacks

If a cryptogram has been created with a Playfair cipher based on a keyword (as shown above), we can try a dictionary attack by using a computer program that decrypts the cryptogram with one keyword candidate after another until the resulting plaintext candidate looks like a meaningful text. To check whether a letter sequence looks meaningful, the program can employ a fitness function, as described in Chapter 16. The keyword candidates can be taken from a dictionary file (i.e., a file that lists all common words of a certain language). There are plenty of dictionary files, containing millions of words from many languages, available online. We describe an example of a dictionary attack on a Playfair cryptogram in the "Success stories" section of this chapter.

Manual attacks

It is definitely possible to break the Playfair cipher without computer support. However, it is considerably more difficult than solving a simple substitution cipher or a complete columnar transposition cipher—especially if we are dealing with a ciphertext that is no longer than, say, 200 letters. Most Playfair messages we have encountered are of this kind.

Solving a Playfair cryptogram manually usually requires knowing or guessing the plaintext equivalents of a few ciphertext digraphs and deriving others from those, following a few rules we will introduce here. In doing so, we will reconstruct the Playfair matrix used. Of course, this method becomes easier if we have a crib. Our success therefore depends on the crib available, the quality of our guesses, the length of the ciphertext, and chance.

It is important to note that different Playfair matrices may implement the same cipher. Generally speaking, a Playfair matrix can be circularly shifted column-wise and row-wise without changing the encryption method it defines. For example, the following three matrices are equivalent:

```
S U R P I     U R P I S     V W X Y Z
E A B C D     A B C D E     S U R P I
F G H K L     G H K L F     E A B C D
M N O Q T     N O Q T M     F G H K L
V W X Y Z     W X Y Z V     M N O Q T
```

It is therefore possible that the matrix we reconstruct while deciphering a message is a column-wise and row-wise circularly shifted version of the one the message creator used. Once we've found a matrix, we can discover the likely original orientation by seeing which shift produces a plausible keyword.

To break a Playfair cipher (in English), we can use a number of rules that are derived from weaknesses of this system:

1. We mentioned that digraph frequencies are hard to exploit unless a cryptogram has thousands of letters. Nevertheless, we might be able to use the fact that in English texts, some letter pairs, such as *TH*, *HE*, *IN*, and *ER*, are especially frequent, while others, including *QG* and *JN*, are almost nonexistent.

2. The most frequent tetragraphs (i.e., groups of four letters) in the English language are *THER*, *TION*, *ATIO*, and *THAT*. This means that two of the most frequent digraphs (*TH* and *ER*) form *THER*, one of the most frequent tetragraphs.

3. If *<letter1><letter2>* encrypts to *<letter3><letter4>*, then *<letter2><letter1>* will encrypt to *<letter4><letter3>*. For instance, if **AB** encrypts to XY, then **BA** will encrypt to YX.

4. The most frequent pair of digraphs that is routinely mirrored is *ER/RE*, followed by *ES/SE*.

5. No letter will ever be encrypted to itself. For instance, **AB** won't become AY or YB.

6. If *<letter1><letter2>* is replaced with *<letter2><letter3>*, the letters *<letter1> <letter2><letter3>* will appear in a row or column together in exactly that order. The same is true if *<letter1><letter2>* is replaced by *<letter3><letter1>*. For instance, if **XY** is replaced with YZ, you'll find the letters XYZ in a row or column rather than as part of a rectangle. Similarly, if **XY** is replaced with ZX, the letters XZY will be in a row or column in that order.

7. If *<letter1>* and *<letter2>* form a rectangle in the Playfair matrix (which happens in sixteen of twenty-four cases), the following rule holds: if *<letter1><letter2>* encrypts to *<letter3><letter4>*, then *<letter3><letter4>* encrypts to *<letter1><letter2>*. For instance, if A and B form a rectangle, then if **AB** encrypts to XY, **XY** encrypts to AB.

8. Each letter can only be encrypted to five specific ciphertext letters in any Playfair tableau.

9. Letters that appear in a row or column with frequent letters (especially E and T) are more frequent in the ciphertext than others.

10. If the Playfair cipher uses a keyword in the way shown above, it is likely that the more frequent letters will appear at the top of the square. In many cases, the letters VWXYZ form the last line because these letters have a low frequency (and thus have a low likelihood of occurring in the keyword). The line UVWXZ is also encountered quite often at the bottom of a matrix, because Y is more frequent than its neighbors.

To apply these rules, we'll now break a Playfair message described in Chapter 26 of Dorothy L. Sayers's 1932 crime novel *Have His Carcase* (Figure 12-7).

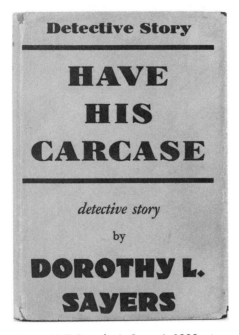

Figure 12-7: Dorothy L. Sayers's 1932 crime novel Have His Carcase *contains a Playfair cryptogram.*

Here is the encrypted message:

```
XNATNX
RBEXMG

PRBFX ALI MKMG BFFY, MGTSQ IMRRY. ZBZE
FLOX P.M. MSIU FKX FLDYPC FKAP RPD KL DONA
FMKPC FM NOR ANXP.

SOLFA TGMZ DXL LKKZM VXI BWHNZ MBFFY

MG. TSQ A NVPD NMM VFYQ. CIU ROGA K.C. RAC
RRMTN S.B. IF H.P. HNZ ME? SSPXLZ DFAX LRAEL
TLMK. XATL RPX BM AEBF HS MPIKATL TO
HOKCCI HNRY. TYM VDSM SUSSX GAMKR. BG AIL
AXH NZMLF HVUL KNN RAGY QWMCK. MNQS
TOIL AXFA AN IHMZS RPT HO KFLTIM. IF MTGNLU
H.M. CLM KLZM AHPE ALF AKMSM, ZULPR FHQ --
CMZT SXS RSMKRS GNKS FVMP RACY OSS QESBH
NAE UZCK CON MGBNRY RMAL RSH NZM, BKTQAP
```

MSH NZM TO ILG MELMS NAGMIU KC KC.

TQKFX BQZ NMEZLI BM ZLFA AYZ MARS UP QOS
KMXBP SUE UMIL PRKBG MSK QD.

NAP DZMTB N.B. OBE XMG SREFZ DBS AM IMHY
GAKY R. MULBY M.S. SZLKO GKG LKL GAW
XNTED BHMB XZD NRKZH PSMSKMN A.M. MHIZP
DK MIM, XNKSAK C KOK MNRL CFL INXF HDA
GAIQ.

GATLM Z DLFA A QPHND MV AK MV MAG C.P.R.
XNATNX PD GUN MBKL I OLKA GLDAGA KQB
FTQO SKMX GPDH NW LX SULMY ILLE MKH
BEALF MRSK UFHA AKTS.

Here is the same text broken into digraphs:

XN AT NX RB EX MG PR BF XA LI
MK MG BF FY MG TS QI MR RY ZB
ZE FL OX PM MS IU FK XF LD YP
CF KA PR PD KL DO NA FM KP CF
MN OR AN XP SO LF AT GM ZD XL
LK KZ MV XI BW HN ZM BF FY MG
TS QA NV PD NM MV FY QC IU RO
GA KC RA CR RM TN SB IF HP HN
ZM ES SP XL ZD FA XL RA EL TL
MK XA TL RP XB MA EB FH SM PI
KA TL TO HO KC CI HN RY TY MV
DS MS US SX GA MK RB GA IL AX
HN ZM LF HV UL KN NR AG YQ WM
CK MN QS TO IL AX FA AN IH MZ
SR PT HO KF LT IM IF MT GN LU
HM CL MK LZ MA HP EA LF AK MS
MZ UL PR FH QC MZ TS XS RS MK
RS GN KS FV MP RA CY OS SQ ES
BH NA EU ZC KC ON MG BN RY RM
AL RS HN ZM BK TQ AP MS HN ZM
TO IL GM EL MS NA GM IU KC KC
TQ KF XB QZ NM EZ LI BM ZL FA
AY ZM AR SU PQ OS KM XB PS UE
UM IL PR KB GM SK QD NA PD ZM
TB NB OB EX MG SR EF ZD BS AM
IM HY GA KY RM UL BY MS SZ LK
OG KG LK LG AW XN TE DB HM BX
ZD NR KZ HP SM SK MN AM MH IZ
PD KM IM XN KS AK CK OK MN RL
CF LI NX FH DA GA IQ GA TL MZ
DL FA AQ PH ND MV AK MV MA GC

```
PR XN AT NX PD GU NM BK LI OL
KA GL DA GA KQ BF TQ OS KM XG
PD HN WL XS UL MY IL LE MK HB
EA LF MR SK UF HA AK TS
```

Before we start deciphering, we have to do some statistical analysis. The ciphertext has 696 letters. Figure 12-8 shows the letter and nonoverlapping digraph frequencies. M is the most frequent character in the cryptogram. This suggests that it is in a line or column with E, the most frequent letter of the English language.

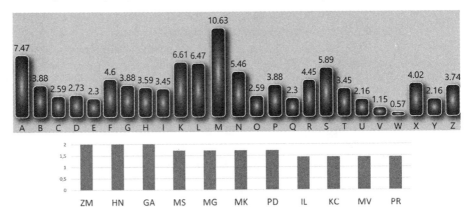

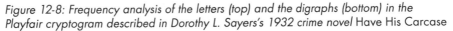

Figure 12-8: Frequency analysis of the letters (top) and the digraphs (bottom) in the Playfair cryptogram described in Dorothy L. Sayers's 1932 crime novel Have His Carcase

The most frequent reversible letter pairs appearing in the ciphertext are the following:

ZM/MZ appears seven and four times, respectively.

MK/KM appears six and three times, respectively.

IL/LI appears five and four times, respectively.

It is possible to solve a Playfair cryptogram by applying only the rules mentioned so far. However, doing so requires a lot of trial and error—a procedure that is too lengthy and complex to document in this book. To make things a little easier, we'll assume that we have some information about the contents of the text. Researching the context in which a cipher message was created can be a powerful tool. In this example, we learn the following:

• This message was sent from Warsaw, Poland.

• A treaty concluded with Poland might be mentioned.

• The recipient of the message is usually addressed as "His Serene Highness."

This information delivers us a few cribs. For instance, the first line of the cryptogram consists of only six letters: XN AT NX. Note that the third letter pair is the reverse of the first one, which means that its plaintext representation is a reversed version of the other, too. Because the letter was sent from Warsaw, it appears that **WARSAW** is a potential match. So, let's use **WARSAW** as a first crib. If our guess is correct, we can conclude the following:

WA = XN
RS = AT
AW = NX

Moreover, by reversing the letter pair of the second statement, we get this:

SR = TA

The digraphs XN AT NX (**WARSAW**) appear again on line 32 of the ciphertext. Before it, we find the letter pair PR. With five appearances, PR is one of the twelve most frequent digraphs in the ciphertext. What does it stand for? Possibilities like **THWARSAW**, **ENWARSAW**, **ERWARSAW**, and **ONWARSAW**, as well as a few other guesses based on letter pair frequencies, are unlikely. The most plausible option is **TOWARSAW**, which gives us the following:

TO = PR

Again, we gain another mapping by reversing the letters:

OT = RP

Based on rule 7 for breaking Playfair messages, listed earlier in this chapter, we can assume that the following six statement pairs are most likely correct. These mappings result from switching the plaintext and ciphertext in the statements we already know, and each has a probability of sixteen in twenty-four (or 66.6%) of being correct:

XN = WA
NX = AW
AT = RS
TA = SR
PR = TO
RP = OT

To check if these mappings are plausible, we can look at their frequencies. WA doesn't appear in the ciphertext, so we don't have to worry about it. AW appears once; at the moment, we can't say whether it really stands for **NX**, but **NX** is a plausible digraph, provided that the letter **X** was used to separate pairs of equal letters. Furthermore, **AT** = RS and **TA** = SR are plausible because RS appears three times in the ciphertext, as expected for the ciphertext equivalent of the common letter pair **AT**. It is hard to say whether **PR** = TO and **RP** = OT make sense, but to keep things simple, we take it as given that they do. (In real life, further analysis would be necessary to confirm this.)

In conclusion, we assume that all of these mappings are correct. Now, we fill in the letter pairs we have guessed so far:

```
XN AT NX RB EX MG PR BF XA LI
WA RS AW          TO
```

MK MG BF FY MG TS QI MR RY ZB

ZE FL OX PM MS IU FK XF LD YP

CF KA PR PD KL DO NA FM KP CF
         TO

MN OR AN XP SO LF AT GM ZD XL
RS

LK KZ MV XI BW HN ZM BF FY MG

TS QA NV PD NM MV FY QC IU RO

GA KC RA CR RM TN SB IF HP HN

ZM ES SP XL ZD FA XL RA EL TL

MK XA TL RP XB MA EB FH SM PI
         OT

KA TL TO HO KC CI HN RY TY MV
         PR

DS MS US SX GA MK RB GA IL AX

HN ZM LF HV UL KN NR AG YQ WM

CK MN QS TO IL AX FA AN IH MZ
         PR

SR PT HO KF LT IM IF MT GN LU
TA

HM CL MK LZ MA HP EA LF AK MS

MZ UL PR FH QC MZ TS XS RS MK
         TO   **AT**

RS GN KS FV MP RA CY OS SQ ES
AT

BH NA EU ZC KC ON MG BN RY RM

AL RS HN ZM BK TQ AP MS HN ZM
         AT

```
TO IL GM EL MS NA GM IU KC KC
PR

TQ KF XB QZ NM EZ LI BM ZL FA

AY ZM AR SU PQ OS KM XB PS UE

UM IL PR KB GM SK QD NA PD ZM
        TO

TB NB OB EX MG SR EF ZD BS AM
                TA

IM HY GA KY RM UL BY MS SZ LK

OG KG LK LG AW XN TE DB HM BX
                NX WA

ZD NR KZ HP SM SK MN AM MH IZ

PD KM IM XN KS AK CK OK MN RL
        WA

CF LI NX FH DA GA IQ GA TL MZ
        AW

DL FA AQ PH ND MV AK MV MA GC

PR XN AT NX PD GU NM BK LI OL
TO WA RS AW

KA GL DA GA KQ BF TQ OS KM XG

PD HN WL XS UL MY IL LE MK HB

EA LF MR SK UF HA AK TS
```

These known letter pairs are not sufficient to reconstruct complete words. Additional guesses are necessary, and admittedly, this is not an easy task. The following sequence (starting on line 17 of the cryptogram) might be helpful: RS MK RS, which decrypts to AT**AT. Remember that MK is an especially frequent reversible letter pair in our ciphertext. Does it stand for **RE**, the most common reversible letter pair in the English language? If so, we get **ATREAT**, which might stand for a **TREATY**. Remember that **TREATY** is a word we expect to appear in the plaintext. The new guess gives us this:

RE = MK and **ER** = KM

Assuming that we have identified the word **TREATY**, we could plausibly guess that the phrase **WITH POLAND** follows it. Remember that we know that the plaintext might mention a treaty with Poland. This means that RS MK RS GN KS FV MP RA could stand for **AT RE AT YW IT HP OL AN**, giving us the following pairings (including their reversed versions):

YW = GN and **WY** = NG
IT = KS and **TI** = SK
HP = FV and **PH** = VF
OL = MP and **LO** = PM
AN = RA and **NA** = AR

The last substitution pair (**AN** = RA and **NA** =AR) also indicates that one line or column of the substitution table contains the letters NAR, in that order (according to rule 6). Here's our next look at the ciphertext and the plaintext parts we already know:

```
XN AT NX RB EX MG PR BF XA LI
WA RS AW          TO

MK MG BF FY MG TS QI MR RY ZB
RE

ZE FL OX PM MS IU FK XF LD YP
         LO

CF KA PR PD KL DO NA FM KP CF
   TO             ON

MN OR AN XP SO LF AT GM ZD XL
      NO    PA    RS

LK KZ MV XI BW HN ZM BF FY MG

TS QA NV PD NM MV FY QC IU RO

GA KC RA CR RM TN SB IF HP HN
   ED AN

ZM ES SP XL ZD FA XL RA EL TL
   IL                AN

MK XA TL RP XB MA EB FH SM PI
RE       OT

KA TL TO HO KC CI HN RY TY MV
      PR    ED
```

DS MS US SX GA MK RB GA IL AX
                RE

HN ZM LF HV UL KN NR AG YQ WM

CK MN QS TO IL AX FA AN IH MZ

SR PT HO KF LT IM IF MT GN LU
TA   **YW**

HM CL MK LZ MA HP EA LF AK MS
        RE

MZ UL PR FH QC MZ TS XS RS MK
        TO   **AT RE**

RS GN KS FV MP RA CY OS SQ ES
AT YW IT HP OL AN

BH NA EU ZC KC ON MG BN RY RM

AL RS HN ZM BK TQ AP MS HN ZM
    AT

TO IL GM EL MS NA GM IU KC KC
PR

TQ KF XB QZ NM EZ LI BM ZL FA

AY ZM AR SU PQ OS KM XB PS UE
            NA   **ER**

UM IL PR KB GM SK QD NA PD ZM
        TO   **TI**   **ON**

TB NB OB EX MG SR EF ZD BS AM
                TA

IM HY GA KY RM UL BY MS SZ LK

OG KG LK LG AW XN TE DB HM BX
                NX WA

ZD NR KZ HP SM SK MN AM MH IZ
                TI

PD KM IM XN KS AK CK OK MN RL
    ER   **WA IT**

```
CF LI NX FH DA GA IQ GA TL MZ
        AW

DL FA AQ PH ND MV AK MV MA GC

PR XN AT NX PD GU NM BK LI OL
TO WA RS AW

KA GL DA GA KQ BF TQ OS KM XG
                        AP ER

PD HN WL XS UL MY IL LE MK HB
                        RE

EA LF MR SK UF HA AK TS
        TI
```

Now, we extend **APER** to **PAPER**, a plausible word in a diplomatic message. But which letter comes before **P**? In other words, what is the * in *P = TQ? Because TQ appears three times in the cryptogram, we can almost be sure that the missing letter is **S**, producing **SP** = TQ, as **SP** is the most frequent letter pair ending with a **P** in English. Including the reverse pairing, we get this:

SP = TQ and **PS** = QT

What might come before **SPAPERS**? The best option looks to be **HIS PAPERS**, giving us **HI** = BF and the reverse, **IH** = FB. The expression **PA**S in the fifth line of the ciphertext might also stand for **PAPERS**, which gives us the statements **PE** = LF and **EP** = FL.

Now, recall our third crib. Say we know that the expression **HIS SERENE HIGHNESS** usually appears early in the letter. In this case, it probably follows the word **TO** in the first line. Including the reversed versions, this crib reveals the statements **SX** = XA, **XS** = AX, **SE** = LI, **ES** = IL, **NE** = MG, **EN** = GM, **GH** = FY, and **HG** = YF.

According to rule 6, the statement **SX** = XA indicates that the letters SXA are found in a row or line of the Playfair matrix, in this order, and without any other letter in between. Remember that we also identified the letter sequence NAR as belonging to a line or row. Because both triples contain an A, we can reconstruct the following part of the matrix:

```
S
X
NAR
```

Combining this with the statements **WA** = XN and **RS** = AT, which we already know, we get the following:

```
 ST
WX
NAR
```

Let's now apply our newly detected statements to the ciphertext:

XN AT NX RB EX MG PR BF XA LI
WA RS AW   **NE TO HI SX SE**

MK MG BF FY MG TS QI MR RY ZB
RE NE HI GH NE

ZE FL OX PM MS IU FK XF LD YP
    EP   **LO**

CF KA PR PD KL DO NA FM KP CF
      TO   **ON**

MN OR AN XP SO LF AT GM ZD XL
      NO   **PA PE RS EN**

LK KZ MV XI BW HN ZM BF FY MG
                    HI GH NE

TS QA NV PD NM MV FY QC IU RO
                GH

GA KC RA CR RM TN SB IF HP HN
ED AN

ZM ES SP XL ZD FA XL RA EL TL
                  AN

MK XA TL RP XB MA EB FH SM PI
RE SX   **OT**

KA TL TO HO KC CI HN RY TY MV
      PR   **ED**

DS MS US SX GA MK RB GA IL AX
              RE   **ES SX**

HN ZM LF HV UL KN NR AG YQ WM
      PE

CK MN QS TO IL AX FA AN IH MZ
              ES SX

SR PT HO KF LT IM IF MT GN LU
TA   **YW**

HM CL MK LZ MA HP EA LF AK MS
      RE   **PE**

MZ UL PR FH QC MZ TS XS RS MK
     TO   **AT RE**

RS GN KS FV MP RA CY OS SQ ES
AT YW IT HP OL AN

BH NA EU ZC KC ON MG BN RY RM
     ON   **NE**

AL RS HN ZM BK TQ AP MS HN ZM
     AT   **SP**

TO IL GM EL MS NA GM IU KC KC
PR ES EN   **ON EN**

TQ KF XB QZ NM EZ LI BM ZL FA
SP   **SE**

AY ZM AR SU PQ OS KM XB PS UE
       NA   **ER**

UM IL PR KB GM SK QD NA PD ZM
ES TO   **EN TI**   **ON**

TB NB OB EX MG SR EF ZD BS AM
           EN TA

IM HY GA KY RM UL BY MS SZ LK

OG KG LK LG AW XN TE DB HM BX
           NX WA

ZD NR KZ HP SM SK MN AM MH IZ
               TI

PD KM IM XN KS AK CK OK MN RL
     ER   **WA IT**

CF LI NX FH DA GA IQ GA TL MZ
     SE AW

DL FA AQ PH ND MV AK MV MA GC

PR XN AT NX PD GU NM BK LI OL
TO WA RS AW   **SE**

KA GL DA GA KQ BF TQ OS KM XG
               HI SP AP ER

```
PD HN WL XS UL MY IL LE MK HB
         ES    RE


EA LF MR SK UF HA AK TS
   PE    TI
```

For brevity's sake, we'll skip the rest of the codebreaking process. In the end, we receive the following plaintext:

```
WARSAW AD IUNE TO HIS X SERENE HIGHNESQS GRANDX DUKE PAVLO
ALEXEIVITCHQ HEIR TO THE THRONE OF THE ROMANOVS PAPERS ENTRUSTED
TO US BYX YOUR HIGHNESQS NOW THOROUGHLY EXAMINED AND MARQRIAGE OF
YOUR ILQLUSTRIOUS ANCESTRESXS TO TSAR NICHOLAS FIRST PROVED BEYONDQ
DOUBT ALXL IS IN READINESXS YOUR PEOPLE GROANING UNDER OPQPRESXSION
OF BRUTAL SOVIETS EAGERLY WELCOME RETURN OF IMPERIAL RULE TO HOLY
RUSQSIA TREATY WITH POLAND HAPQPILY CONCLUDED MONEY AND ARMS AT
YOUR DISPOSAL YOUR PRESENCE ALONE NEXEDED SPIES AT WORK USE CAUTION
BURN ALXL PAPERS ALQL CLUES TO IDENTITY ON THURSDAY AH IUNE TAKE
TRAIN REACHING DARLEY HALT X TEN FIFTEQEN X WALK BY COASTROAD
TO FLATIRON ROCK X THERE AWAIT RIDER FROM THESE A WHO BRINGS
INSTRUCTIONS FOR YOUR IOURNEY TO WARSAW THE WORD IS EMPIRE Q BRING
THIS PAPER WITH YOU QSILENCE SECRECY IMPERATIVE BORISQ
```

Here's the complete Playfair matrix, which is based on the keyword **MONARCHY**. We can circularly shift rows and columns with respect to the matrix to reproduce a meaningful keyword:

```
M O N A R
C H Y B D
E F G I K
L P Q S T
U V W X Z
```

We might now find it interesting to take a second look at the text statistics generated at the start of our analysis. M, which is the most frequent letter in the cryptogram, appears in the same column as E—just as we expected. The most frequent digraphs, ZM, HN, and GA, decrypt to UR, YO, and IN. The digraph UR is not typically this common in an English text; here, its frequent appearance is caused by the example's frequent use of the word **YOUR**. The plaintext equivalents of the frequent reversible digraphs, ZM/MZ, MK/KM, and IL/LI, are UR/RU, RE/ER, and ES/SE. Again, UR/RU appears more commonly than one would expect, but things like this happen in the life of a codebreaker. All in all, text statistics were not particularly helpful in breaking this Playfair cryptogram, though they may be in other cases.

It should now be clear that manually breaking a Playfair cryptogram is a difficult task. Although we had several cribs (which we cannot, of course, always expect in practice), we had to make a few quite optimistic guesses. We also cheated by only following the guesses we knew were correct. A real codebreaking process would require a lot more trial and error. Still, in the pre-computer age, people really did solve Playfair encryptions with the method described here. We can't help but tip our hats to them.

If you are looking for resources that explain the techniques introduced in this chapter in more detail, check out the cited chapters in *Cryptanalysis* by Helen Fouché Gaines,[7] *Manual for the Solution of Military Ciphers* by Parker Hitt,[8] or *Cryptography* by André Langie.[9] In *Solution of a Playfair Cipher*, Alf Monge also walks through the breaking of a Playfair cryptogram consisting of only thirty letters.[10]

Success stories

Thouless's first message

As mentioned earlier in this chapter, British parapsychologist Robert Thouless (1894–1984) published a Playfair message in 1948, intending to psychically transmit its key after his death (see Chapter 8 for details).[11] This message is reproduced here and in Figure 12-9:

```
CBFTM HGRIO TSTAU FSBDN WGNIS BRVEF BQTAB
QRPEF BKSDG MNRPS RFBSU TTDMF EMA BIM
```

A codebreaker, who wanted to stay anonymous, deciphered this message only a few weeks after its publication, causing Thouless's first attempt at his experiment to fail. We do not know how this individual deciphered this cryptogram—the codebreaker is referenced only briefly in Thouless's next paper—but we can make a few educated guesses.

The passage I have prepared is the following: CBFTM HGRIO TSTAU FSBDN WGNIS BRVEF BQTAB QRPEF BKSDG MNRPS RFBSU TTDMF EMA BIM. It uses one of the well-known methods of encipherment with a key-word which I hope to be able to remember

253

254   *Robert H. Thouless*   [PART

in the after life. I have not communicated and shall not communicate this key-word to any other person while I am still in this world, and I destroyed all papers used in enciphering as soon as I had finished.

Figure 12-9: Robert Thouless (pictured) wanted to channel the solution to this Playfair-encrypted message after his death in order to prove that the dead can communicate with the living. However, long before Thouless died, a codebreaker solved the cryptogram—without psychic powers.

As Thouless did not reveal the encryption system he had used, the first hurdle involved finding out his method. Frequency analysis clearly shows that Thouless had not used a simple substitution cipher. The unknown codebreaker probably saw that the message didn't contain a J and had an even number of letters, as is typical of a Playfair cipher. The fact that no digraph in the ciphertext consists of two identical letters is consistent with Playfair, too. Considering all this evidence, the codebreaker had enough reason to conclude that they were dealing with a Playfair cryptogram.

But, once they had identified the system as Playfair, how did they solve it? In his 2017 book *Unsolved!*, our colleague Craig Bauer points to a few promising starting points.[12] We mentioned earlier in this chapter that the last line of a Playfair matrix derived from a keyword is often VWXYZ, because these five letters are unlikely to be included in a keyword in English. In this case, this assumption turns out to be correct. In addition, Craig writes:

> We see that some digraphs (BQ, EF, SB, and TA) appear twice. These are likely to represent high-frequency digraphs in normal English. A lot of trial and error may be involved in matching these up correctly, but cryptanalysts are patient.

It might also have helped that Thouless's message contains BS and SB, a reversing digraph. The most frequent reversing digraph in English texts is *ER/RE*. So, does BS stand for **ER** and SB for **RE**, or vice versa? It turns out that the mappings BS = **ER** and SB = **RE** are correct.

The unknown codebreaker might also have taken a completely different approach. While Thouless did not reveal the cipher he used, he mentioned that the plaintext was a Shakespearean quote. Perhaps the codebreaker worked through a list of famous Shakespeare quotes, looking for one that contains the same digraph repetitions as the ciphertext. The pattern BQTABQ, consisting of two identical digraphs with a different one in between, might have been helpful for this purpose. It is certainly possible to identify the correct plaintext in this way.

Whichever method the codebreaker used, they finally came up with the following Playfair matrix (based on the keyword **SURPRISE**):

```
S U R P I
E A B C D
F G H K L
M N O Q T
V W X Y Z
```

From this matrix, they derived the following plaintext, which is from Shakespeare's *Macbeth*, Act 2, Scene 2, and proved correct: **BALM OF HURT MINDS GREAT NATURE'S SECOND COURSE CHIEF NOURISHER IN LIFE'S FEAST.**

Thouless's third message

Robert Thouless's third cryptogram is also encrypted with the Playfair cipher (see Chapter 8 for the background story). However, this time, Thouless double-encrypted the message, using Playfair twice with two different keywords, in order to increase its security. Between the two encryptions, he added the same letter to the start and end of the result, to make decryption a bit more difficult. Here's the cryptogram he published:

```
BTYRR OOFLH KCDXK FWPCZ KTADR GFHKA
HTYXO ALZUP PYPVF AYMMF SDLR UVUB
```

This time, Thouless revealed the cipher he had used but kept the two keywords secret.

When he died in 1984, the solution remained unknown, and the interesting part of his experiment began. The Survival Research Foundation, an organization that studied after-death communications, offered a $1,000 reward for the correct solution to the second or third message, so long as it was provided by 1987.[13]

To our knowledge, nobody ever received the two keywords from the realm of the dead, and the reward was never paid. So, Thouless's messages did not prove that the dead could communicate with the living. Or perhaps the dead simply can't remember keywords!

In 1995, renowned codebreaker Jim Gillogly and his partner Larry Harnisch started a project that aimed to solve Thouless's second and third messages. They never solved the second but did succeed in breaking the third. It should come as no surprise that, rather than using psychic powers, the partners applied codebreaking methods and a computer.

As a first step, their computer program attempted to decrypt the message using each entry in a file of 64,000 keyword candidates (a dictionary attack). But, of course, this trial-and-error decryption could do only half of the job, as Thouless had used two Playfairs in a row. A question remained: How could they determine whether one keyword was correct without knowing the other one?

Gillogly and Harnisch found two simple ways to check this. First, they used the fact that Thouless had added the same letter to the start and the end of his intermediate result. Second, they knew that the decryption they performed needed to result in another Playfair cryptogram. As mentioned, Playfair cryptograms have certain predictable properties, such as a lack of double letters. A computer program could easily check both conditions.

Of the 64,000 keyword candidates Gillogly and Harnisch checked, 1,385 produced a result that fulfilled both criteria (they had the same first and last letters and no identical digraphs). For each of these candidates, they applied a second Playfair decryption, testing all 64,000 keywords, which resulted in about 88 million combinations. Next, for each combination, their program checked whether the plaintext candidate looked like an English text by analyzing its trigraph frequencies.

After 8.5 hours of calculations, the computer program returned a potential solution. Using **BLACK** as the first keyword and **BEAUTY** as the second one, the program produced a readable English sentence. The choice of keywords sounded plausible, as Robert Thouless certainly knew Anna Sewell's famous 1877 novel *Black Beauty*. The problem was solved:

```
THIS IS A CIPHER WHICH WILL NOT BE READ UNLESS I GIVE THE KEY
WORDS X
```

Gillogly and Harnisch presented their solution in the scientific journal *Cryptologia*, in a 1996 paper titled "Cryptograms from the Crypt."[14] Unfortunately, this was too late to earn the $1,000 prize. So, Gillogly and Harnisch ended their article with this lament: "Our successful computational séance must be its own reward."

Challenges

The cryptogram in National Treasure: Book of Secrets

Let's try an easy challenge. In the 2007 movie *National Treasure: Book of Secrets*, the following Playfair cryptogram appears:

ME IK QO TX CQ TE ZX CO MW QC TE HN FB IK ME HA KR QC UN GI KM AV

The keyword is **DEATH**. Can you decrypt it?

Unsolved cryptograms

The world record digraph challenge

The shortest message created with a general digraph substitution that was ever broken has a length of 750 letters.[15] We'll cover this record in Chapter 16, when we discuss the hill-climbing method.

Klaus created the following shorter ciphertext, encrypted in the same way, in March 2020, to encourage his blog readers to improve the record:

```
UGBZAEHINYQLBPZLNFTLUEBMULTLSLZPBZPZKPOVUGYSQPNYHL
RYFHATQKRHTZEHPDQUUGYSUJOVYTUGYVRHAJNFTLUEXFRUEOOJ
TZOSLUPZEICVADYMYLCRBZXOUGSVDJOIDYRHTZOSWZROYNKJRM
EIXOREOVNFTLUESAMNDJHIIWJGKRYFUBTIQPULBPRMJORECJCY
WZZPQRXXVNOSZLBLNYJMPLYNOVLCLKIOGUKUKFSAKAQRSVQXUJ
IOANYSWZSDKUKFLNRMEIRJYVEOLXLKMEYKERHXZPBZXOZXQPCR
KSYOSVHNTLIXKRYFUBTIMGWIZLOSONRMIDKYNYLCFFOMTTLLJH
WTADHLYNRHMZADOGMUKBWZZPPQBZBZNOCRHINYNFTLUEYNOVBZ
NOQPGCQMRHTZIDKYNYCRBZXOUGSVTTQPOSDYXOMQKKVNEALUYV
RMUFPYNXZAVLRHTZNYQXMFYVUCMZSAJMBZZPXPBZMNVFUCJTNY
QXGHEITPPYFWKUZFPZQUDEVLDBOMGRUEKFSCYTVNANLDRMNBYV
UTFNUJMUMMEOIXIISDVNZPMNRYRCTFUGZPDNUTLXJNSSVNCRJC
```

Also known as the Bigram 600 challenge, this message consists of 600 letters and has (as of this writing) withstood all attempts to break it.

The world record Playfair challenge

While general digraph substitution appears to protect a 600-letter plaintext quite well, as evidenced by the ciphertext in the previous section, the Playfair cipher has proven much easier to attack. As of this writing, the shortest Playfair cryptogram created with a random Playfair matrix (i.e., without a keyword) ever to have been solved consists of just twenty-six letters. We will cover this record in Chapter 16, when we address hill climbing. The thirty-letter Playfair ciphertext broken in 1936 by Alf Monge, which we mentioned earlier in this chapter, was based on a keyword and therefore doesn't count in this category.

In January 2020, Klaus, always seeking to challenge his blog readers, published an even shorter Playfair cryptogram containing only twenty-four letters:[16]

VYRSTKSVSDQLARMWTLRZNVUC

Can you decipher this message? If so, you may set a new record!

13

ABBREVIATION CIPHERS

The message depicted in Figure 13-1 is an example presented in the 1931 book *The Masonic Conservators* by Ray V. Denslow.[1] Each letter in the square is the starting letter of a word, and the resulting message should be read column-wise. For example, the first column stands for the following sentence: THE DEGREE OF ENTERED APPRENTICE IS DIVIDED INTO THREE SECTIONS.

```
T   r   h   j   b   f   r   t   d   f
d   d   v   s   w   y   i   o   k   j
o   c   s   r   n   m   i   o   l   g
e   a   s   r   t   y   u   n   b   f
a   v   f   r   d   s   e   r   r   t
i   m   h   j   i   u   i   m   k   l
d   q   a   s   e   r   t   v   d   r
i   l   o   u   y   g   t   r   e   f
t   n   b   f   d   r   e   s   b   v
s   o   p   i   o   i   p   o   i   p
```

Figure 13-1: When read column-wise, each letter of this message stands for the first letter of a word.

Any system that encodes a text in such a way is referred to as an *abbreviation cipher*. In this particular case, the reader was supposed to cross-reference the position of each letter against numbers in another table. These numbers then could be used in a separate book: *The Spelling Book*, which had columns of words to identify which initial stood for which word. However, most abbreviation ciphers rely only on oral tradition or memory to convey their meaning.

How abbreviation ciphers work

In general, an abbreviation cipher is not an encryption method in the narrow sense, as there is often no unambiguous way to reconstruct the plaintext from the ciphertext. The cryptology community disagrees about whether these are really ciphers, and most other cryptanalysis books therefore don't mention them at all. Nevertheless, we decided to include them here, for the main reason that they are quite common. The Freemasons (a worldwide organization that has existed for centuries) have extensively used this technique for their ritual books, because Freemasons are generally forbidden from recording their rituals in written form. Yet, humans being humans, they still want a way to remember things.

A Freemason book with abbreviated text is sometimes called a "Cypher." This is a misleading expression, as the term "cypher" or "cipher" has a different meaning in cryptology. As mentioned in Chapter 1, a *cipher* is defined as an encryption method that works on the level of letters. To avoid confusion, we do not use the term "Cypher" for these kinds of documents, calling them "mnemonic books" instead. The purpose of a *mnemonic book* is to assist the reader in memorizing a text, typically a ritual description. The truncation of words is used to conceal the content of the book, as secrecy traditionally plays an important role in the Freemason community. It is therefore justified to call it encryption in this context.

Of course, not only Freemasons have used abbreviation ciphers. We will introduce a few other applications of this method in the course of this chapter.

How to detect an abbreviation cipher

As mentioned, the majority of abbreviation cipher cryptograms one encounters today are contained in mnemonic books published by the Freemasons (or some other secret order). Mnemonic books look pretty mysterious to those who are not familiar with this kind of document. Virtually every crypto history expert has received inquiries from people who have come across such a book and could not make sense of it. To sustain secrecy, some mnemonic book editions don't contain information about the author or the publisher, which makes it even more difficult to understand what they are about.

On the other hand, recognizing a mnemonic book can be quite easy if one knows what to look for. Usually, it presents as an inconspicuous booklet in a format small enough to fit into a pocket. Most have no more than a few dozen pages. Figure 13-2 shows a few examples.

Figure 13-2: Most mnemonic books are inconspicuous booklets in a format small enough to fit into a pocket.

By definition, a mnemonic book contains truncated or otherwise abbreviated text. Figure 13-3 shows a text of this kind.[2] Most mnemonic books we have encountered were created between 1850 and 1940. Newer editions exist but usually are not revealed to non-Freemasons.

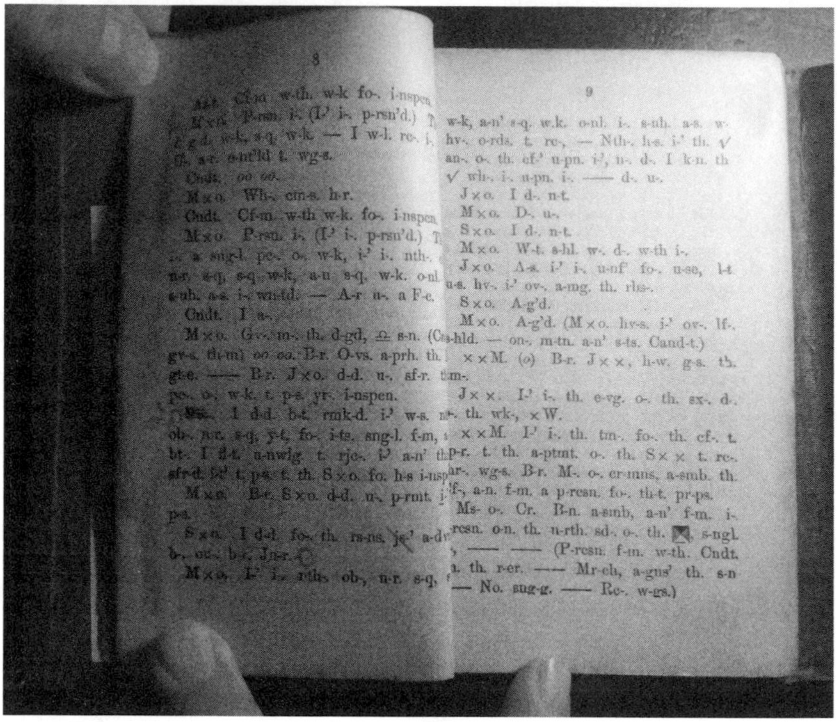

Figure 13-3: A view into a typical mnemonic book of the Freemasons

Lastly, most mnemonic books we have seen are printed, but there are also handwritten ones, like the one in Figure 13-4.[3]

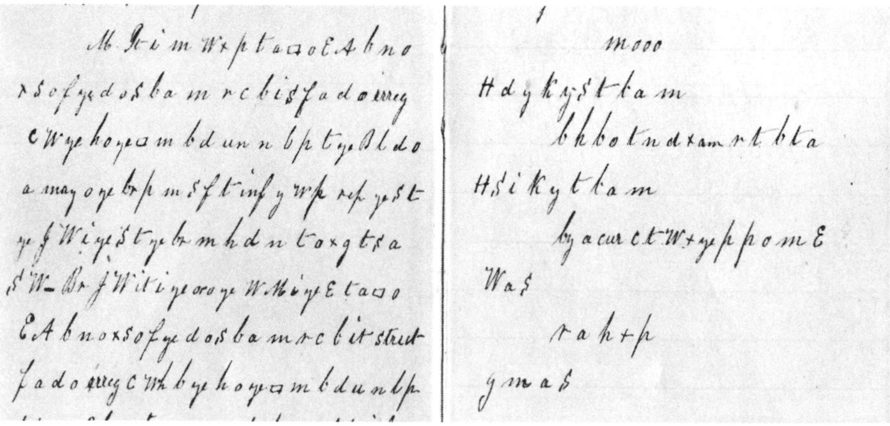

Figure 13-4: A handwritten Freemason's mnemonic book from the late nineteenth century, provided to us by Walter C. Newman

Abbreviation ciphers are not very well suited for transmitting a message from a sender to a receiver, because a nonambiguous decryption is usually not possible. For this reason, abbreviation ciphers are rarely encountered in letters, telegrams, or postcards. Writing a diary in this way doesn't work very well, either. Instead, an abbreviation cipher makes sense as a memorization aid for somebody who already knows the plaintext. Many people have encrypted poems or prayers in abbreviation ciphers, often as a means of learning them by heart. Cheat sheets, checklists, shopping lists, and similar documents sometimes consist of word initials or other abbreviations, too.

If the criteria mentioned in the previous paragraphs aren't sufficient to tell whether a certain cryptogram was created with an abbreviation cipher, text statistics are helpful. Frequencies of word initials are significantly different from overall letter frequencies. The letter *E*, which is rarely the first letter of a word, is otherwise the most frequent letter in the English language. If one is dealing with complete sentences, expressions such as *the*, *this*, and *than* are very popular and make *T* the most frequent initial letter. But in dictionaries, indexes, word lists, and telegram-style messages, words starting with a *T* are much rarer, and *S* occupies the first position in a word-initial frequency count (see Figure 13-5).

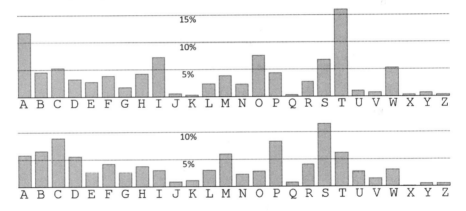

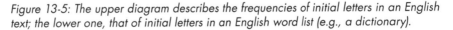

Figure 13-5: The upper diagram describes the frequencies of initial letters in an English text; the lower one, that of initial letters in an English word list (e.g., a dictionary).

If you don't want to bother with language statistics, there is an even simpler method for checking whether a cryptogram is consistent with an abbreviation cipher: try to find a sentence that fits it, regardless of whether the sentence is the one intended by the creator. The easier this exercise is, the more likely it is that you are dealing with word initials. For instance, take the first column of the message in Figure 13-1: TDOEAIDITS. You can probably easily find a nonsense phrase matching these word initials, like the following: "The dirty old enthusiasts are including dust in their shoes."

What is true of English is also true of virtually every other language: general letter frequencies differ substantially from word-initial frequencies. This is especially the case with languages that have articles, as English does. The French *la* and *le* influence text statistics, as do the Spanish *el* and *la* and the Italian *il* and *la*. In German, there are not only the articles *der*, *die*, and *das*, but also the demonstrative pronouns *dieser*, *diese*, and *dieses*, as well as the conjunction *dass*, which raises *D* from its 4% frequency in nonabbreviated German to 14% in a word-initial sequence.

How to break an abbreviation cipher

It should be clear that solving an abbreviation cipher with conventional codebreaking techniques is difficult, if not impossible. This is because there is no way to reliably reconstruct a word if only an abbreviation of it is known. Only in some cases are abbreviations constructed in such a way that it is possible to recognize the words. Figure 13-6 shows an example from a mnemonic book where the abbreviations are often created by omitting certain vowels.[4, 5] As can be seen, at least some of the words can be guessed (e.g., **THEIR**, **DUTIES**, and **WITH** in the first line).

```
                    113

t' thei dties wr invs. wth. ctn. mstc. sns.,
gps. an' wds., t' enab. thm. t' gn. adms. int.
th. M. Chm. o' K. S's. T. on th sm. d'y., an'
hr. K. S., acmpnd. b' hs cnfdntl. ofcs.,
cnstng. o' hs Sc., S. an' Jw's., reprd. t' th. M.
Chm. t' mt. thm.  Th. Sc. h' plcd. nr. h's.
psn., th. Sw. a' th. inr dr., and th. Jw. a'
th. outr dr., wth strc. injncns. t' sufr. nn.
t' ent. xcp sch. as wr invs. wth. ctn. mstc sns.,
gps., an' wds. prevsl estblshd., so tht. whn.
any dd. ent. h' knw th'y wre fthfl. wkm.
an' hd nthg t' d' bt. enrll. thei' nms as
suh, an' p'y. thr wgs. wh. thy. rcd i cn.,
wn., an' oi., mblmatcl. o' nrshmt., rfshmt.,
and j'y, an' aft admnshng thm o' th rvernc
d'e th grea an' sacrd nm o' Dei, sufrd
thm t' dprt i pce untl th tme shd arri
fo' cmneg. anthr. wks. wk.  Ths. u. wl.
prev ws al acmplshd on th evng o' th
sxth d'y, i ordr tht no unnesary labr shd
b perfrmd on th sevnth, thrby gving thm
freqnt oprtnits to obs th gloris wrks o' natr
an' t' ador th Grea Creatr.
   M' Br., w'e a'e nw. abt. endvrg. t' wk.
ou' w'y. int. a plc. rprsntg. th. M. Chm.
```

Figure 13-6: Some words in this mnemonic book can be reconstructed.

If simple word guessing does not work, there is usually only one method for deciphering an abbreviation cryptogram: finding the plaintext. Figure 13-7 shows a cryptogram for which this is possible. This text belonged to a very religious woman who died in 1996. It was published on the web portal Ask Metafilter.[6]

Figure 13-7: This abbreviation cryptogram can be solved by guessing the plaintext. It's the classic Christian text the Lord's Prayer.

The letter frequencies suggest that the characters in this cryptogram are the starting letters of words from an English text. Usually, it would be difficult to guess what the woman had in mind when she wrote these lines. However, some of the readers soon recognized the text. It's the Lord's Prayer: **Our Father, who art in heaven, hallowed be thy name . . .** We will introduce more abbreviation cryptograms whose plaintext was discovered in the "Success stories" section.

Success stories

Emil Snyder's booklet

In October 1978, the scientific journal *Cryptologia* published an article titled "'Action Line' Challenge."[7] The text of this article consisted of only one paragraph:

> We received a phone call from Bill Laitner of the *Detroit Free Press*, "Action Line". It seems that someone came to him with a 3½" by 4½" leatherbound, printed 9-page book given to him by his father. The man who passed on the book to his son was Emil Snyder, prominent Detroit attorney and trucking executive. He was killed in 1926. Other than that, we have not much to go on. But we put forward the nine pages of text. If anyone can "solve" it, please let us know.

Figure 13-8 shows two of the nine pages mentioned in the article. If you have read this chapter up to this point, you will probably immediately guess that the "leatherbound, printed 9-page book" is a mnemonic book created by the Freemasons or some similar organization.

Finding the solution was a team effort launched by Klaus. In 2013, after reading about the story in the *Cryptologia* article, Klaus (who had not yet learned of abbreviation ciphers) introduced this story on his *Cipherbrain* blog.[8] Blog reader "Flohansen" suggested that the cipher used was an abbreviation cipher. Other readers, Armin Krauß and Bernhard Gruber, pointed out that the Freemasons used books of this kind for their ritual descriptions.

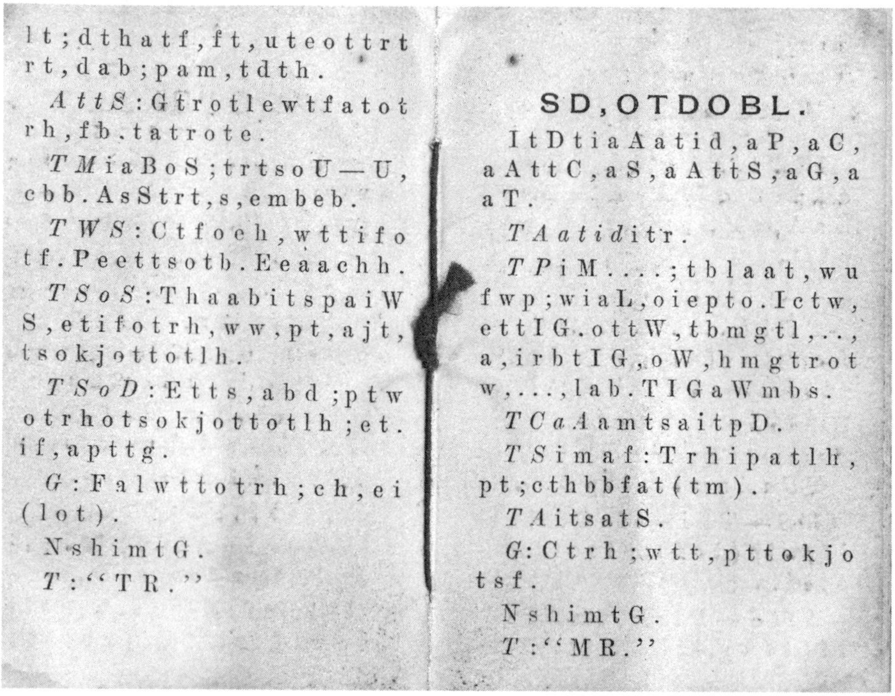

lt;dthatf,ft,uteottrt
rt,dab;pam,tdth.

AttS:Gtrotlewtfatot
rh,fb.tatrote.

TMiaBoS;trtsoU—U,
cbb.AsStrt,s,embeb.

TWS:Ctfoeh,wttifo
tf.Peettsotb.Eeaachh.

TSoS:ThaabitspaiW
S,etifotrh,ww.pt,ajt,
tsokjottotlh.

TSoD:Etts,abd;ptw
otrhotsokjottotlh;et.
if,apttg.

G:Falwttotrh;ch,ei
(lot).

NshimtG.

T:"TR."

SD,OTDOBL.

ItDtiaAatid,aP,aC,
aAttC,aS,aAttS,aG,a
aT.

TAatiditr.

TPiM....;tblaat,wu
fwp;wiaL,oiepto.Ictw,
ettIG.ottW,tbmgtl,..,
a,irbtIG,.oW,hmgtrot
w....,lab.TIGaWmbs.

TCaAamtsaitpD.

TSimaf:Trhipatlh,
pt;cthbbfat(tm).

TAitsatS.

G:Ctrh;wtt,pttokjo
tsf.

NshimtG.

T:"MR."

Figure 13-8: Two pages from an Oddfellows booklet left behind by attorney Emil Snyder in 1926

Another blog reader, Gordian Knauß (Knauss), suspected that Snyder's 9-page document was a booklet created by the Oddfellows, an organization similar to the Freemasons. Consequently, Klaus sent several enquiries to Oddfellows representatives in the United States and Europe, but none of them could make sense of the book.

Then, British crypto blogger Nick Pelling, one of our favorite colleagues, discovered that other copies of the booklet existed. (Until then, only the scans from the *Cryptologia* article had been available.) In 2014, Nick also discovered an 1899 Oddfellows book titled *Esoteric* from a Pennsylvanian bookseller.[9] The book's starting letters exactly corresponded with the letters in Snyder's booklet. The mystery of this abbreviation cryptogram was solved by finding the plaintext that belonged to it.

Esoteric is a book that describes the Oddfellows' rituals (see Figure 13-9). Evidently, Snyder was a member of this organization but didn't tell his son about it. (Such a practice is quite common among the Freemasons and similar organizations.)

Probably, Snyder used this booklet to learn ritual descriptions by heart. After Snyder's unexpected death, his son discovered the booklet but didn't know what it was about. Over eighty years passed before the mystery was solved.

Figure 13-9: The booklet left behind by Emil Snyder turned out to be an
abbreviated version of an Oddfellows book titled Esoteric.

Challenges

A birthday card

The unnumbered letters in Figure 13-10 form an abbreviation cryptogram.
Do you recognize the original text? P = **PETER**.

Figure 13-10: A birthday card with an abbreviation cipher

Unsolved cryptograms

The Tamám Shud mystery

In November 1948, several witnesses noticed an unknown man sitting alone, fully clothed, at Somerton Beach in Adelaide, Australia.[10] The next morning, he was found dead in the same place. The "Somerton Man," as he is called today, was around forty to forty-five years old at the time of his death. He was in good physical condition (aside, of course, from being dead), wore a nice suit, and had a well-groomed appearance.

Adelaide police were unable to identify the Somerton Man. He didn't carry any identification documents. All labels were removed from his clothes, and nobody had reported him missing. In addition, the cause of death has never been determined. The Somerton Man may have died of poisoning, but no particular poison could be detected using the methods available at the time. It is unclear if the man was murdered, killed himself, accidentally poisoned himself, or died of a different cause.

The mystery caused a sensation in Australia, with many media reports and a great deal of public interest. A few months after the Somerton Man's death, a police investigator found a folded note, carefully torn from a book, in a hidden pocket of the man's suit. The note bore the printed text "Tamám Shud," which means "end" in the Persian language (Farsi). This tiny note had been torn from a copy of the then quite popular 1859 book *The Rubáiyát of Omar Khayyám*, translated by Edward FitzGerald. Later, a man found the corresponding book copy from which the note had been torn in the back seat of his car, which had been parked near Somerton Beach.

On the inside of the book's back cover, the police found indentations showing what had been a handwritten inscription consisting of five lines (see Figure 13-11).

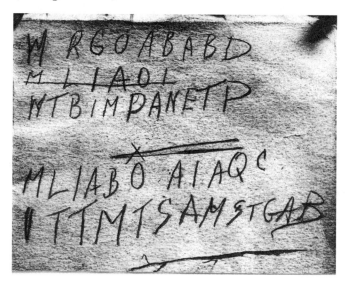

Figure 13-11: The message the Somerton Man left behind may be an abbreviation cryptogram.

This "Tamám Shud cryptogram," as it is called today, is usually transcribed as follows (some letters are ambiguous):

```
MRGOABABD
MLIAOI
MTBIMPANETP
MLIABOAIAQC
ITTMTSAMSTGAB
```

Numerous codebreaking experts and hobby cryptanalysts have tried to solve the Tamám Shud cryptogram, to no avail. The letter frequencies indicate that the author probably used an abbreviation cipher. If this assumption is correct, it will probably never be possible to solve this mystery unless somebody finds the original text.

In May 2021, the unknown man's body was exhumed in Australia, over seventy years after his death. Researchers hoped to discover new information, such as DNA evidence, to clarify the man's identity or determine if he had any living relatives.[11] In July 2022, an Adelaide University professor, Derek Abbott, announced that he had matched the Somerton Man's DNA to an engineer from Melbourne, Carl "Charles" Webb. As of this book's publication in 2023, this has not yet been confirmed.[12]

Two unsolved postcards

The two postcards in Figure 13-12, sent to Bromley, UK, in 1911, are apparently written in an abbreviation cipher.[13] The plaintext is unknown and will probably be difficult to find.

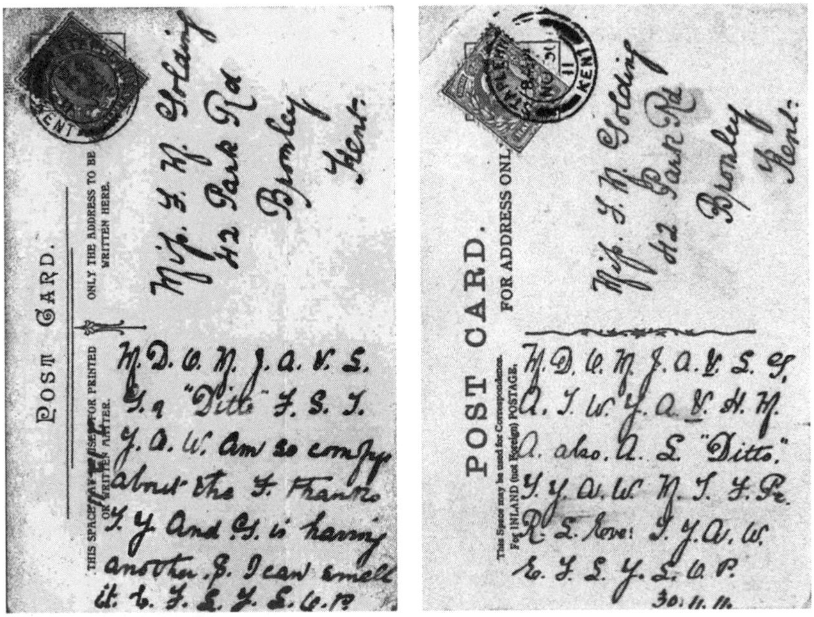

Figure 13-12: These two postcards are probably written in an abbreviation cipher.

14

DICTIONARY CODES
AND BOOK CIPHERS

In 1918, toward the end of World War I, a German radio station sent the following message to a recipient in Mexico:[1]

```
49138  27141  51336  02062  49140  41345
42635  02306  12201  15726  27918  30348
53825  46020  40429  37112  48001  38219
50015  43827  50015  04628  01315  55331
20514  37803  19707  33104  33951  29240
02062  42749  33951  40252  38608  14913
33446  16329  55936  24909  27143  01158
42635  04306  09501  49713  55927  50112
13747  24255  27143  02803  24909  15742
49513  22810  16733  41362  24909  17256
19707  49419  39408  19801  34011  06336
15726  47239  29901  37013  42635  19707
42022  30334  06733  04156  39501  03237
14521  37320  13503  42635  33951  29901
49117  46633  02062  16636  19707  01426
11511  42635  11239  04156  02914  12201
23145  55331  49423  03455  12201  30205
33951  30219  50015  04156  43827  06420
23309  19707  33104  42635  00308  29240
05732  54628  01355  39338  02914  12201
06420  11511  24909  27142  33951  49223
49618  42022  42635  17212  55320  15726
12201  06420  38219  21060  46633  37406
43644  33558  22527
```

A US listening post recorded the message and forwarded it to MI-8, the US wartime codebreaking unit, for analysis. Herbert Yardley, MI-8's famous lead, soon guessed that this cryptogram had been created with a so-called dictionary code.

We will use the analysis of this message as an example in this chapter.

How dictionary codes and book ciphers work

A *dictionary code*, which typically uses a commercially available dictionary, records the page and position of a word in the book as its ciphertext representation. This chapter's first example used the English-French half of *Clifton's Nouveau Dictionnaire Français*, according to Yardley's report. The five-digit group 43827, for instance, stood for the twenty-seventh word listed on page 438 of this dictionary. (As we discussed in Chapter 7, a dictionary code is not a cipher because it encrypts words, not letters.)

The following list explains the five-letter groups in the cryptogram's first line:

49138 (p. 491, 38th word): **TELEGRAM**

27141 (p. 271, 41st word): **JANUARY**

51336 (p. 513, 36th word): **TWO**

02062 (p. 20, 62nd word): **AND**

49140 (p. 491, 40th word): **TELEGRAPHIC**

41345 (p. 413, 45th word): **REPORT**

Thus, the plaintext starts as follows: **TELEGRAM [FROM] JANUARY TWO AND TELEGRAPHIC REPORT [FROM] S. ANTHONY DELMAR VIA SPAIN RECEIVED.**

A similar encryption scheme can be defined with any other book, such as a novel. We call these *book ciphers*. As it is usually quite difficult to find a particular word in a novel (unless it is a common expression like **THE**, **AND**, or **IF**), a book cipher usually references single letters instead of whole words, which is why it is a cipher, not a code.

A prominent user of a book cipher was Nicholas Trist (1800–1874), a US diplomat sent to Mexico by President James K. Polk in 1848, toward the end of the Mexican-American War. Trist negotiated a treaty with the Mexican government, which resulted in the annexation of a great deal of territory that became all or part of ten modern states.[2]

In order to protect letters sent to and from Washington, Trist needed an encryption system. He devised two of them, both book ciphers. See the "Success stories" section of this chapter for the sleuthing that was needed to find the correct book.

The following text is (partially) encrypted in his first cipher:

```
Sir,
In my last I said, "I consider the probabilities of an early peace
very strong." The enclosed will be found to corroborate this belief.
1,2,3,10–15,13,4,1–39,26,11,31–44,75,121,31–/47,1,6,16/7,3,15,20,
24,27,28,29/,,8,1,9/,,9,1/,,2,5/,,1,1/,,1,16,29/69,2,1/,, 6,7/,,2,
3,2/,,6,4,6,10,8/ under date July 29: 5,33,25,4–30,105,44,45,58–
from a foreign merchant to this correspondent here . . .
```

The book Trist used was an 1827 textbook for learning Spanish: *True Principles of the Spanish Language* by José Borras. Trist probably thought that a book of this kind in the possession of an American traveler in Mexico would not raise suspicion.

Each number group in Trist's first cipher, separated by commas, represents one or more letters taken from *True Principles of the Spanish Language* in the following way: page, line, letter, letter . . . This means that the group 1,2,3,10 encodes two letters, while the group 7,3,15,20,24,27,28,29 encodes six.

Likewise, 47,1,6,16 encodes two letters. If we know that the first line on page 47 is . . .

TABLE TWENTY-FIFTH - The fly and the bull

. . . then we can conclude that the numbers 47,1,6,16 stand for the letters **T** and **H** (the spaces and the dash are not counted). If a number group starts with two missing numbers (as in ,,2,3,2), then the page and line number from the previous group are used.

Many other book ciphers have existed in the course of history. We even mentioned one in Chapter 6: the system used to encrypt the second Beale cryptogram, where the "book" was the Declaration of Independence. Instead of identifying each letter with three numbers (page, line, and position), Beale's cipher recorded only the position of words. This means that the first word in the Declaration of Independence is number 1, the second word is number 2, and so on. To encode the plaintext, only the first letter of the word is used.

Nicholas Trist devised a second cipher based on the same concept as Beale's and using the same book as his other cipher. In a letter, he mentioned "**a short note [sent] to** 121,13,1,2,17,5,9,20." We can decrypt these eight letters, encrypted in his second cipher, by looking at the first page of the book (Figure 14-1). If you attempt this, you'll see that the expression 121,13,1,2,17,5,9,20 decrypts to **MR THNTON**. This probably refers to a Mr. Thornton. (Trist seems to have omitted two letters of the name.)

THE study of foreign languages, after the acquisition of our own, is undoubtedly one of the most interesting and agreeable, which can occupy the time of literary persons, or engage the attention of those who are desirous of presenting themselves in society, as objects of a polite and accomplished education.

The Spanish Language, which yields to none in elegance, expression, or strength, has now become, by reason of commercial treaties recently established with South America, as necessary and important to the British youth, as it is instructive and entertaining to the learned, by reason of the infinite number of works, which in all times, and on all subjects, have been written (notwithstanding the trammels of the Inquisition) by men of genius, in that once eminent, but now unfortunate country.

Figure 14-1: The first page of the book Nicholas Trist used for his book ciphers, True Principles of the Spanish Language

Dictionary codes and book ciphers were quite popular in the early years of the United States. During the American Revolution, Benedict Arnold, a traitor, encrypted a number of letters in a book cipher using Sir William Blackstone's *Commentaries on the Laws of England*.[3] As the book cipher proved cumbersome, he soon switched to a dictionary code based on *Nathan Bailey's Dictionary*.

Alexander Hamilton, one of the Founders of the United States and the hero of the eponymous Broadway musical by Lin-Manuel Miranda, was given a description of a dictionary code by his father-in-law, Philip Schuyler, whose system was based on the 1777 edition of *Entick's Spelling Dictionary*.[4] History has not recorded whether Hamilton ever used this code, but we do know that both the English and the US militaries employed this dictionary for the purposes of encryption. British generals Charles Cornwallis and Henry Clinton used it during the Revolutionary War, and a record suggests that US Vice President Aaron Burr, who killed Hamilton for unrelated reasons in a famous duel in 1804, used the 1805 version of that same dictionary in his own correspondence.[5]

How to detect a dictionary code or book cipher

Detecting a dictionary code can be quite simple. For instance, look at the World War II–era message shown in Figure 14-2.[6] This is an English translation of a German telegram.[7]

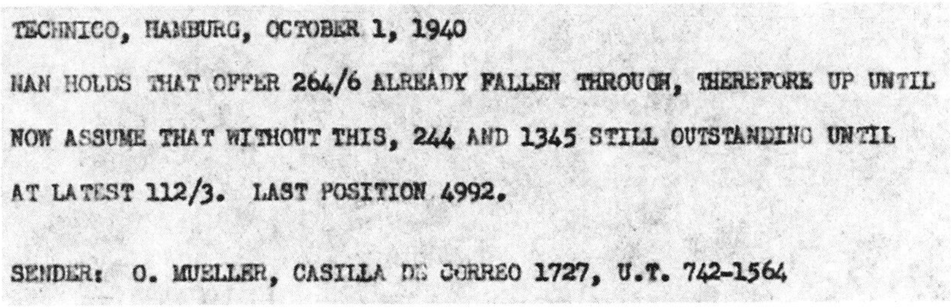

TECHNICO, HAMBURG, OCTOBER 1, 1940

MAN HOLDS THAT OFFER 264/6 ALREADY FALLEN THROUGH, THEREFORE UP UNTIL

NOW ASSUME THAT WITHOUT THIS, 244 AND 1345 STILL OUTSTANDING UNTIL

AT LATEST 112/3. LAST POSITION 4992.

SENDER: O. MUELLER, CASILLA DE CORREO 1727, U.T. 742-1564

Figure 14-2: This (translated) telegram from World War II includes two dictionary code expressions.

The numbers 244, 1345, and 4992 are probably codegroups from an unidentified codebook and are not relevant here.

Of note, this cryptogram contains the expressions 264/6 and 112/3. The most popular encryption methods that produce expressions using this slash format are dictionary codes and book ciphers. If this suspicion is correct, 264 in 264/6 probably stands for the page, while 6 represents the position of a word or letter. In fact, the two expressions were taken from the *Langenscheidt's Lilliput Dictionary English–German*; 264/6 stands for **PIER** and 112/3 for **DECEMBER**.

If there is no visible separation between the page number and the word position, detecting a dictionary code or a book cipher is a little more difficult. Such a system can, for instance, easily be confused with a code or nomenclator (see Chapter 7). In those cases, here is some helpful information: typically, there are fewer than one hundred words on a dictionary page and usually even fewer than fifty. So, if a cryptogram contains digit groups in the form XXXYY, one should check whether YY is smaller than fifty in every instance.

Of course, the code may be a reversed system such as YY–XXX or some other scrambled method. Also, if the number is greater than fifty, a book cipher, where larger numbers of words fit on one page, might have been used. For example, the Beale system counted the hundreds of words in the Declaration of Independence from beginning to end.

How to break a dictionary code or book cipher

Breaking a dictionary code or book cipher can be very difficult. If the code is used properly, and if the cryptanalyst does not know the book, it may even be impossible. However, the book can sometimes be found. Also, as is always the case in cryptography, the codebreaker can profit from mistakes the encipherer has made.

Identifying the book or dictionary

The most obvious way to break a dictionary code or a book cipher is to find the book it is based on. We have already seen an example (probably fictional) in Chapter 6: according to the Beale pamphlet, a man deciphered the second Beale cryptogram after identifying that it had used the Declaration of Independence for encryption.

Another (definitely fictitious) case occurs in the 1915 Sherlock Holmes novel *The Valley of Fear* by Arthur Conan Doyle. In this novel, Holmes receives an encrypted message from a certain Fred Porlock and suspects that he is dealing with a book-cipher cryptogram. He concludes that the book used is widely available, large (with at least 534 pages), and printed in two columns per page. Most almanacs meet these conditions exactly.

Holmes first tries the latest edition of *Whitaker's Almanack*, which he had received only a few days earlier, to no avail. He then tries the previous edition of the same book—and it works. With this almanac, Holmes is able to decipher the message and uncover a warning that "some devilry" is intended. Of course, in the end, he solves the case.

Reconstructing the dictionary

In his 1922 book *Cryptography*, Swiss cryptologist André Langie reports on the following cryptogram he was asked to solve:[8]

```
5761 3922 7642 0001 9219 6448 6016 4570 4368 7159
8686 8576 1378 2799 6018 4212 3940 0644 7262 8686
7670 4049 3261 4176 6638 4833 4827 0001 3696 6062
8686 2137 4049 2485 7948 0300 9712 0300 4212 9576
2475 8576 8337 0702 9185
```

As can be seen, the message consists of forty-five four-digit numbers. At first glance, it doesn't look like a dictionary code, as separating the four-digit numbers into "page" numbers and "word" numbers doesn't make sense unless the dictionary used has about a hundred pages with about a hundred entries per page, which is not very likely.

But what if the sender of the message numbered the entries of a dictionary from beginning to end, without including the page number? This option becomes much more likely when we consider that the number 0001 appears twice in this text. The first entry in an English dictionary is usually the article *A*. As *A* is a common word, it is plausible that it appears twice in a text of this length.

Let's assume that we may be dealing with a dictionary cipher of this kind. Here is a sorted list of the four-digit numbers appearing in the text:

0001, 0001, 0300, 0300, 0644, 0702, 1378, 2137, 2475, 2485, 2799, 3261, 3696, 3922, 3940, 4049, 4049, 4176, 4212, 4212, 4368, 4570, 4827, 4833, 5761, 6016, 6018, 6062, 6448, 6638, 7159, 7262, 7642, 7670, 7948, 8337, 8576, 8576, 8686, 8686, 8686, 9185, 9219, 9576, 9712

Along with 0001, we see that other groupings are repeated as well: 0300, 4049, 4212, 8576, and 8686.

The following table might be helpful. It shows how words with starting letters *A* through *Z* are distributed in a dictionary containing the 10,000 most frequent English words.[9] Along with the words' starting positions, this table shows how, for some letters, there are significantly fewer pages of entries than for others.

A	0001 – 0643
B	0644 – 1178
C	1179 – 2160
D	2161 – 2755
E	2756 – 3177
F	3178 – 3599
G	3600 – 3926
H	3927 – 4295
I	4296 – 4717
J	4718 – 4800
K	4801 – 4877
L	4878 – 5216
M	5217 – 5710
N	5711 – 5871
O	5872 – 6109
P	6110 – 6960
Q	6961 – 7019
R	7020 – 7513
S	7514 – 8715
T	8716 – 9298
U	9299 – 9453
V	9454 – 9637
W	9638 – 9929
X	9930 – 9941
Y	9442 – 9971
Z	9972 – 10000

Now look at group 0300, which appears twice in the cryptogram. If we are correct about the encryption system used, it is very likely that this word starts with an **A** and that the second letter is located somewhere in the middle of the alphabet. **AND** is a good candidate.

The number 8686 appears three times in the cryptogram, which makes it the most frequent digit group in this ciphertext. Close to it is 8576, which appears twice. According to the table we created, the words at these locations should start with **S**. But are there two common English words starting with **S** so close to each other in the alphabet? **STILL** and **SUCH** might be candidates, but further inspection shows that these are not good matches.

Instead, let's assume that the letter distribution in the dictionary used by the message's author differs a little from the one in our table. Perhaps looking at words starting with **T** will work. In fact, there are two words that seem to fit: **THE** and **TO**. This guess is confirmed by the fact that the sequence 8686 8576 appears in the ciphertext, and **TO THE** is a common word pair.

Based on our guesses, we can sketch the following:

```
5761 3922 7642 0001 9219 6448 6016 4570 4368 7159
               A

8686 8576 1378 2799 6018 4212 3940 0644 7262 8686
TO   THE                                      TO

7670 4049 3261 4176 6638 4833 4827 0001 3696 6062
                                    A

8686 2137 4049 2485 7948 0300 9712 0300 4212 9576
TO                       AND       AND

2475 8576 8337 0702 9185
     THE
```

The next step is to try to guess all other starting letters based on the distribution table:

```
5761 3922 7642 0001 9219 6448 6016 4570 4368 7159
N    G    S    A    T    P    O    I    I    R

8686 8576 1378 2799 6018 4212 3940 0644 7262 8686
TO   THE  C    E    O    H    H    B    R    TO

7670 4049 3261 4176 6638 4833 4827 0001 3696 6062
S    H    F    H    P    K    K    A    G    O

8686 2137 4049 2485 7948 0300 9712 0300 4212 9576
TO   C    H    D    S    AND  W    AND  H    Y

2475 8576 8337 0702 9185
D    THE  S    B    T
```

Admittedly, it gets difficult from here. We need to guess more words, but we only know the (probable) initial letter of each one.

To make things a little easier, let's assume that we know a small part of the plaintext (i.e., a crib). Say that we have been told that this message is military in nature and that it contains information about an enemy offensive. In fact, the numbers 2799 and 6018 in the second line might stand for **ENEMY OFFENSIVE**. If this is the case, 1378, which stands between **TO THE** and **ENEMY OFFENSIVE**, might be **COMING**. The number 6016 in the first line is pretty close to 6018 (**OFFENSIVE**). The most likely decryption is **OF**.

The second-highest number, 9576, is probably a **W** word, perhaps **WERE** or **WILL**. It is followed by 2475, a D word, which is itself followed by **THE**. What can it be? Alphabetically, it occurs somewhere between **COMING** (1378) and **ENEMY** (2799). The interval between these two is 1421, and the difference between 1378 and 2475 is 1097, roughly three-fourths of the interval. This leads us to the *Dis* and *Dos*. There is another number in the text occupying about the same dictionary position: 2485. Either 2475 or 2485 might be **DO**. Suppose we assign **DO** to 2485 and look for a word closely preceding it that suits our context. A dictionary file shows us **DIVULGE** and **DIVIDE**. The numbers 0300 through 8576 may therefore stand for **AND YOU AND I WILL DIVIDE THE**.

To solve the rest of the cryptogram, we can use similar guesses. We will certainly make a false step occasionally, but every word established strengthens our foothold. The more words we guess, the easier it will be to find further ones. Here's the plaintext we finally receive. (The first word is not known but is probably a name starting with **M**.)

    ???? HAS SECURED A VALUABLE PIECE OF INFORMATION IN REGARD TO THE
    COMING ENEMY OFFENSIVE. I HAVE BEEN REQUESTED TO SEND HIM FIVE
    HUNDRED POUNDS. IT IS A GOOD OPPORTUNITY TO DENOUNCE HIM. DO SO,
    AND YOU AND I WILL DIVIDE THE SUM BETWEEN US.

Breaking a dictionary code in this way is certainly not easy. However, as will be shown in the "Success stories" section of this chapter, it is possible.

Treating a book cipher like a simple substitution cipher

Depending on its construction, a book cipher can also be regarded as a simple substitution cipher, homophonic cipher, or nomenclator. This means that we can solve certain book cipher cryptograms using the techniques for breaking encryptions of each of those types. As an example, look at the handwritten dedication we found in a used copy of the esteemed Martin Gardner's 1972 book *Codes, Ciphers and Secret Writing*, which is a very basic introduction to cryptology (see Figure 14-3).[10]

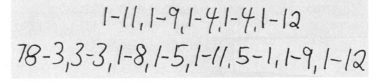

Figure 14-3: A dedication encrypted using a book cipher

Here's a transcript:

```
1-11,1-9,1-4,1-4,1-12 78-3,3-3,1-8,1-5,1-11,5-1,1-9,1-12
```

There are multiple ways to solve this cryptogram, but if we look at it as nothing more than a simple substitution cipher, we could use the following strategy. First, let's replace each hyphenated two-number group with a letter, going from left to right and introducing a new letter each time we encounter a new number pair. That would transcribe this cryptogram as follows:

```
ABCCD EFGHAIBD
```

Among the many words that match the pattern ABCCD is **HAPPY**. (A quick way to find such word-pattern matches is with a program such as CrypTool 2.) If we then replace the letters accordingly, it gives us the following second word: ****H*AY. It's not very hard from there to guess that the plaintext is **HAPPY BIRTHDAY**.

As another way of solving it (perhaps the method originally intended), if we look at the first paragraph of Gardner's *Codes, Ciphers and Secret Writing*...

```
Cryptography, the writing and deciphering of messages . . .
```

. . . we see that we are dealing with a book cipher. Here, 1-11 stands for the eleventh letter of the first word, **H**; 1-9 for the ninth letter of the first word, **A**; and so on.

Success stories

The FIDES ads

Between 1862 and 1866, a series of twenty-three advertisements was published in the London paper *The Times*. Each ad started with the word **FIDES**, and most were at least partially encrypted.[11] Here are a few examples:

```
1862-10-31
FIDES (Thought).—No myth, but a neighbouring town, where I shall
be detained a little time. I shall be in for a few hours on
Monday, and must take my chance of meeting you between 2 and
3 o'clock. Perhaps I may hear from you meantime. Direct to P.O.
```

```
1864-06-22
FIDES.—DOCUMENTS will AWAIT your ARRIVAL at No. 3. on and after
Tuesday next. Both of your letters to hand. (58.62) (171.53)
(248.74) (152.79) (223.84) (25.21) (222.64) (132.74). James gone
to Egypt instead.
```

1864-07-21

FIDES.–(218.57) (106.11) (8.93) (17.61) (223.64) (146.7)
(244.53) (224.21) (20) (192.5) (160.19) (99.39) (No. 8) (251.70)
(1) (223.64) (58.89) (151.79) (226.69) (8.93) (40.12) (149.9)
(248.101) (167.12) (252.35) (12.31) (135.100) (149.9) (145.76)
(225.53) (212.25) (20) (241.6) (222.22) (78.45) (12.31) (66.28)
(252.33) (158.33) (6.65) (20) (2) (11.50) (142.37) (223.87)
(12.31) (142.37) (105.33) (142.37) (157.20) (58.62) (133.89)
(250.86).

Our source for the FIDES cryptograms is, of course, the wonderful 2005 book *The Agony Column Codes & Ciphers* by Jean Palmer (a pen name of Tony Gaffney), which we have referenced many times in previous chapters.[12] Gaffney solved most of the encrypted ads listed in his book himself; however, he hadn't yet found a solution to the FIDES cryptograms when his book was published in 2005.

A few years later, Gaffney once again tried to solve the FIDES cryptograms, this time assuming that he was dealing with a dictionary code, in which case, an expression like 146.7 stood for the seventh word on page 146. Based on frequency analysis and cribs provided by the cleartext part of the advertisements, Gaffney was able to make some guesses. However, in order to completely solve the mystery, he needed to find the dictionary used. After many hours of searching the British Library, he had looked through no fewer than forty-eight English dictionaries from the nineteenth century. The forty-ninth proved to be the one that fit: *Johnson's Pocket Dictionary of the English Language*, published in 1862.

From there, it became clear exactly how the code worked. The first number of each pair turned out to be the page number plus one. The second number was the word number counted from the bottom of the page, starting from the right-hand column and then continuing down the left-hand one. In addition, 1 represented **I** and 2 represented **YOU**; 20 stood for a comma or a period.

The advertisement dated "1864-06-22" decrypts to **DARLING PRECIOUS WEARY OAF THOU BETTER THAN LIFE**. Some of these words might have made sense only to the people involved! The complete decryptions are available in Klaus's 2014 blog post.[13]

Nicholas Trist's key book

Earlier in this chapter, we mentioned that US diplomat Nicholas Trist used two book ciphers to communicate with the US government during his stay in Mexico.[14] Crypto-historian Ralph E. Weber described these ciphers in his 1979 book *United States Diplomatic Codes and Ciphers*, but he couldn't decipher all of Trist's messages, as he didn't know the book Trist had used.[15] All he knew was that both of Trist's ciphers were based on the same book.

A few years later, when cryptologist Stephen M. Matyas read Weber's book, he decided to try to solve the mystery.[16] Matyas observed that Trist mentioned a few facts about his key book in a letter, describing it as a small volume containing the dedication "To the British Nation." He also mentioned that it was divided into at least two parts and was written by a person in Washington who had been sent to Spain as consul. In addition, Weber found out that the book's text began with the words, "The study of foreign languages . . ."

To identify the author of Trist's key book, Matyas compiled a list of all people who had been sent from Washington to Spain or a Spanish colony as a consul. The final list contained approximately fifty people, many of whom, surprisingly, had published books. After some research, Matyas identified a man named José Borras as the most promising candidate. Borras, a US consul in Barcelona, had published a book titled *True Principles of the Spanish Language* in 1827. This book fit with the description, especially because it dealt with a foreign language.

Matyas managed to locate a copy of the book in the Newberry Library in Chicago, and it did indeed contain the dedication and starting words he was looking for. With a bit more work, the mystery was solved, and Nicholas Trist's correspondence could be deciphered. For examples, see the beginning of this chapter.

How William Friedman broke a Hindu conspiracy encryption

During World War I, Hindu groups in India began a rebellion against their British colonizers, and certain members of these groups operated from the United States to deliver arms and logistical support. The US authorities treated the Hindu conspirators as criminals violating weapons laws and planning a revolution against the British, who were considered friendly.

In 1917, a Scotland Yard representative in the United States forwarded to William Friedman a stack of encrypted correspondence that had been intercepted from Hindu conspirators. At the time, Friedman's codebreaking career had just begun.

Along with the letters, the representative provided Friedman with a list of suspects, the names of whom he could use as cribs. Unfortunately, neither the correspondence nor the suspects' names have ever been published. The only available information about this story (as far as we know) comes from a 1920 report by Friedman himself[17] and a short treatise contained in the 1996 edition of David Kahn's book *The Codebreakers*.[18] Neither of these provides much information about the content of the encrypted messages.

According to Friedman's report, the encrypted letters consisted of a series of numbers in groups of three, such as 7-11-3, 8-5-6, and 3-9-15. After preliminary study, Friedman concluded that he was dealing with a book cipher. Each figure group seemed to refer to a page, line, and letter position in a certain book. For instance, 7-11-3 represented the third letter in line 11 on page 7.

Friedman had no idea which book the conspirators might have used. However, he realized that they had not applied their encryption method properly, as only the more important parts of the messages were encrypted. The parts left in cleartext provided Friedman with helpful hints regarding what the message was about. The ciphertext was also presented with word breaks, revealing the lengths of the words, and the senders chose the same number groupings to represent certain letters again and again, although it would have been more secure to refer to different pages, lines, and positions to encode the same character.

Another poor technique used by the conspirators was consecutive sequences, such as 7–11–3, 7–11–4, 7–11–5, and 7–11–6, which revealed that a certain word or word part appeared in both the plaintext and the book. For example, the conspirators might have encrypted the plaintext word **APPLE** using the word **APPLE** in the key book, meaning the ciphertext numbers would have all been consecutive. Moreover, the senders often preferred the first appearance of a letter in a line, so frequent letters typically received low numbers while the rare ones were represented by higher numbers.

After considerable study, Friedman finally found a passage in one of the encrypted messages that appeared to represent the name of one of the suspects. We don't know what this name was, but in his description of the incident, Kahn provides another example of a text fragment that Friedman could have guessed. Look at the following two encrypted words (each on a different line):

83–1–2 83–1–11 83–1–25 83–1–1 83–1–8 83–1–13 83–1–18 83–1–3 83–1–1 83–1–6
83–1–3 83–1–6

If we number each letter based on its order of appearance, then the letters in these two words form the pattern 1234567849 89. Note that the characters 4, 8, and 9 are repeated; with modern cryptanalytic tools, this pattern could be solved quite quickly. Friedman noticed that the third character in the sequence, which appears in the ciphertext as 83–1–25, has a higher number than the other characters, indicating that it was probably the twenty-fifth letter of a line in the book. Friedman suspected that this was a rare letter; otherwise, the position number would have been lower. Through a mixture of persistence, intuition, and luck, he was able to determine that the letter was **V** and that these two words were **REVOLUTION IN**.

Friedman later wrote:

> From this, fragment by fragment, the plaintext of the messages was constructed, and not only the plaintext of the message, but we could state with reasonable certainty that on page so-and-so of the unknown book used, line so-and-so of that page, appeared the word "Germany." In another page and line, "government," and elsewhere, "constitution" and the like. From such evidence as that, we deduced that the subject matter of this unknown book was political economy.

As the trial of the conspirators grew near, the Department of Justice told Friedman that they would find it helpful to know the title of the key book in order to convince the jury that the messages had been correctly decrypted. Friedman and his team consulted book dealers throughout the United States and England, asking for a book about political economy that contained certain words at certain positions. When the trial opened, however, the book had not been identified.

Friedman prepared to explain the cipher in court without referencing the book used—and then, while staying in a Chicago hotel, waiting for his testimony to be scheduled, he happened to walk past McClurg's, Chicago's biggest bookstore. Rummaging through the political economy section, he found himself holding the book he'd been searching for: *Germany and the Germans*, by Price Collier (1913). The mystery was solved just in time.

When Friedman double-checked his work against the book, he found out that over 95% of his results were correct. Our sources don't mention how Friedman's testimony was received, but we know that quite a few of the Hindu conspirators were found guilty. This was the first major codebreaking success of Friedman's career. Many others would follow.

A dictionary code message sent to Robert E. Lee

Figure 14-4 shows an encrypted note sent to Civil War general Robert E. Lee in 1862.[19] (We found it on the Civil War Day by Day website created by the Louis Round Wilson Special Collections Library at the University of North Carolina, Chapel Hill,[20] and on Satoshi Tomokiyo's Cryptiana website.[21])The encrypted part of this message consists of units, each of which is composed of a number, a letter (`L`, `M`, or `R`), and another number.

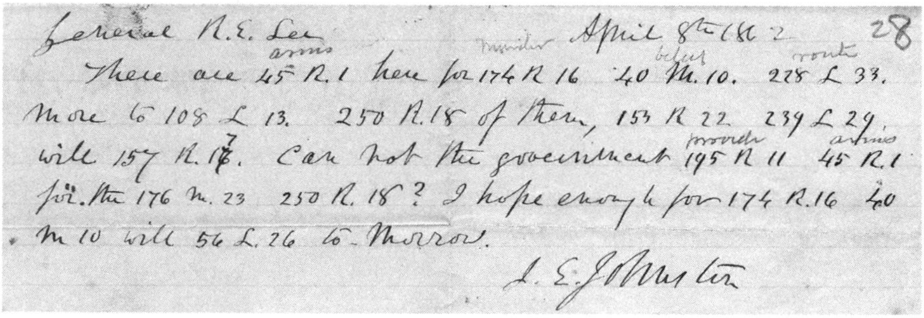
General R.E. Lee April 8th 1862 28
There are 45 R.1 here for 174 R 16 40 M.10. 228 L 33.
More to 108 L 13. 250 R.18 of them, 153 R 22 239 L 29.
will 157 R.17. Can not the government 195 R 11 45 R.1
for the 176 M. 23 250 R. 18? I hope enough for 174 R.16 40
M 10 will 56 L.26 to-Morrow.
J. E. Johnston

Figure 14-4: This message sent to Robert E. Lee is encrypted with a dictionary code.

Here's a transcript of the encrypted note provided by crypto-hobbyists David Allen Wilson and Thomas Bosbach:

```
31. August 2017
General R.E. Lee April 8th 1862
There are 45 R 1 here for 174 R 16 40 M 10. 228 L 33. More to 108
L 13. 250 R 18 of them, 153 R 22 239 L 29. Will 157 R 17. Can not
the government 195 R 11 45 R 1 for the 176 M 23 250 R 18? I hope
enough for 174 R 16 40 M 10 will 56 L 26 to-Morrow.
J.E. Johnston
```

The most likely explanation for this pattern is that the ciphertext passages are encrypted using a dictionary code, with the first number of each unit standing for the page, the letter for the column (left, middle, or right), and the second number for the line. The book, maybe an English dictionary, has at least 250 pages and thirty-three lines per page.

Above some of the units, somebody has already written what appears to be proposed plaintext representations. For instance, `45 R 1` is decrypted to **ARMS**, while `228 L 33` allegedly stands for **ROUTE**. Are these decryptions correct? If so, why did the author only decrypt some of the words? Does that second sentence, starting with **ROUTE MORE TO**, even make sense? And is it plausible that the word **ARMS** is listed on page 45 of a 250-page dictionary, which might only have a few pages of words starting with the letter *A*? It is possible that the cipher involves additional tricks, like adding a number to the page number, but the encryption systems popular during the Civil War are generally not known to be so sophisticated.

Klaus didn't know the answers to these questions when he introduced this encrypted message on his *Cipherbrain* blog in 2017. Several readers searched for a dictionary that could make sense of the ciphertext sections. This search was simplified by the requirements, as there weren't too many English dictionaries published around the 1860s with three columns per page and about 250 pages. Finally, a reader nicknamed Davidsch found it: the *Noah Webster, William Greenleaf Webster Dictionary* from 1857. It immediately became clear that the alleged plaintext representations noted above some of the ciphertext units were wrong.

Using the dictionary, blog reader Thomas Bosbach soon provided the following decryption of the message (the plaintext decryptions are in parentheses):

```
There are 45R1 (cars) here for 174R16 (one) 40M10 (brigade).
228L33 (six) more to 108L13 (follow). 250R18 (three) of them,
153R22 (long-) 239L29 (street) will 157R17 (march). Can not the
government 195R11 (procure) 45R1 (cars) for the 176M23 (other)
250R18 (three)? I hope enough for 174R14 (one) 40M10 (brigade)
will 56L26 (come) to-morrow.
```

Challenges

Dan Brown's book cipher challenge

In the lower-right corner of the back cover of Dan Brown's bestselling 2003 novel *The Da Vinci Code*, a darkly printed circular pattern can be seen:

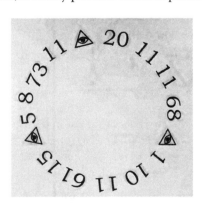

Here's a transcript:

20 11 11 68 • 1 10 11 61 15 • 5 8 73 11 •

Each number refers to the first letter in the respective chapter of the novel. (For those readers who do not have the book, we provide this information at *https://codebreaking-guide.com/challenges/*.) When rearranged correctly, the letters spell out a Latin sentence representing a motto of the United States.

A dictionary code challenge

In 2018, Klaus introduced a dictionary code challenge on his blog.[22] To create his dictionary, he first looked for a text file containing the 10,000 most popular words, acronyms, and initialisms of the English language, and then he made a few changes (adding words such as "ZZTOP," deleting a few others, and so on) in order to foil any codebreaker trying to guess which file he had used. Next, he sorted the words alphabetically in a spreadsheet. The resulting list became his codebook, with each word referenced by its position in the list. Here are the start and the end of the list:

```
0001: A
0002: AAA
0003: AAAA
0004: AACHEN
0005: AARON
0006: AATEAM
0007: AB
0008: ABANDONED
0009: ABC
0010: ABERDEEN
 . . .
9992: ZONING
9993: ZOO
9994: ZOOM
9995: ZOOPHILIA
9996: ZOPE
9997: ZSHOP
9998: ZSHOPS
9999: ZUT
10000: ZZTOP
```

The word list contains not only full words and abbreviations but also the twenty-six letters of the alphabet. These are treated as ordinary words, which means, for instance, that **E** comes between **DYNAMICS** and **EACH**. If a word one wants to encrypt does not appear on the dictionary list, it can be encoded letter by letter. Using this codebook, Klaus encrypted a plaintext consisting of about seventy words, which resulted in the following ciphertext:

```
8456 0619 8928 6116 9216 5992 9061 1263 0001 5326 2272 2827 5884
1142 8993 4906 8322 6163 8928 6841 6694 3564 8928 7658 6323 8928
1142 0212 0016 6207 4906 8785 0001 5069 0371 9647 0307 8928 9652
```

```
0212 8192 4316 5602 9967 9804 7254 0001 5385 4424 8928 1449 6163
4714 8949 4692 0001 8515 2212 6205 8928 7278 8131 6163 4714 9967
9804 3458 0001 9861 1390 2012 0001 2546 8926 9804 4139 9967 9061
2365 8928 5992 5589
```

Blog reader Norbert Biermann solved this challenge on the same day. Can you do it, too?

Unsolved cryptograms

Two encrypted newspaper advertisements from 1873

In 1873, two encrypted newspaper ads were published in London's *Daily Telegraph*.[23, 24] They are reproduced here. (Note that **TOUJOURS BLEU** is French for **ALWAYS BLUE**.)

```
1873-02-07
TOUJOURS BLEU.-7.64. 13,141. 24.24. 18,299. 1,317 8,481X-1,274.
32,561 29,375 13,127 28,801. 32,561. 21,8 21,221X 28,59. 39,629.
28,59 39,629 29,544 25,138 29,219 7,64X-29,219 17,77 6,582 1,384
16,243 29,219 19,367 8,226 18,176 33,383X-36,547. 8,39 2,379
2,4 27,609 32,561 9,324 21,367 9,629 28,59 12,361 32,104 6,381
1,268 38,498 25,411 32,561 2,140X-1,268 14,527 33,212 38,616
8,335X-2,495 3,379 20,320 32,561 29,422 1,257 24,24 24,485 40,618
1,268 40,338 15,198. 21,367X-19,420 2,407X-25,618 11,390 40,629
32,252 27,538X-18,411 10,422 2,185X-27,254 2,221X-40,204 8,347
20,388 8,347 40,325 8,347 36,621 8,347 25,239 32,24 1,268 8,306
1,268 8,306 1,268 5,58 40,629 5,19 5,19 4,386X 22,451 29,329
22,451X-12,262X 15,50 10,66X 13,572 32,561 1,384 12,579 12,194
40,325X 8,347 7,518 12,629 29,219 26,106 1,624 21,556X 40,238
16,438 2,555X.

1873-02-27
ANTETYPE.-8.347, 20.388X 1.317, 12.269, 20.28, 10.622, 15.50,
2.495 8.481. 32.561. 8.501X 1.268, 32,252, 12.455, 1.317, 8.226,
6.630 9.266, 2.4, 7.73X 24.627, 32.561, 27.556, 31.302. 28.185,
19.31X 25.264, 1.268, 32.252, 12.629, 29.219, 2.555X 21.367, 9.629,
12.361, 15.50, 25.138X 1.268, 13.572, 35.562, 2.555X 1.268, 8.306,
39.558, 11.606, 7.518X 40.204
```

Both ads mainly consist of number groups divided into two parts by a period or comma. The numbers before the period/comma are smaller than the ones after it, a pattern consistent with a book cipher. An expression such as 12.269 might stand for the 269th letter on page twelve of a certain book. The X at the end of some groups might mean that, instead of one letter, the group represents a whole word. Not much more is known about these two cryptograms.

15

ADDITIONAL ENCRYPTION METHODS

The techniques we have described in this book so far comprise many of the encryption algorithms used before cipher machines and computers were invented. If you encounter a cryptogram created prior to 1900, chances are very high that the encryption method used is covered in this book. The same is true if you are dealing with an encrypted letter, postcard, or diary, no matter when it was written. Many encrypted documents from the twentieth century are encrypted using one of the systems mentioned in this book, as well—especially those that have no military or intelligence connection.

Nevertheless, there are many encryption methods we have not covered in detail in this book so far. In the following sections, we will briefly introduce a few of these.[1]

Cipher tools

As mentioned in Chapter 2, cipher disks or slides can be used to apply simple substitution ciphers or polyalphabetic ciphers. Over the course of crypto history, people have developed many types of cipher disks and slides, along with many other tools. For instance, there are cipher disks with more than one letter ring, cipher cylinders, and strip ciphers (see Figure 15-1), just to name a few. While most of these tools implement a substitution cipher, the so-called *scytale* (pronounced "ski-ta-li"), which is a strip wound around a stick, can be used to realize a simple transposition.[2]

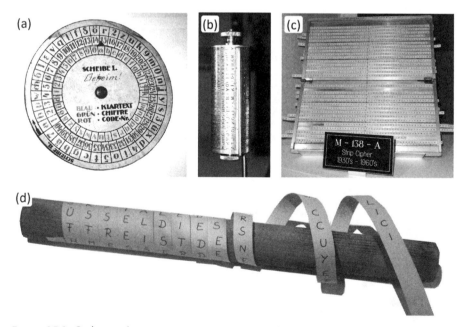

Figure 15-1: Cipher tools exist in many variations. Cipher disks (a), cipher cylinders (b), strip ciphers (c), and the scytale (d) have been used extensively throughout history.

If you are looking for an interesting success story related to cipher tools, we recommend Luis Alberto Benthin Sanguino's 2014 master's thesis "Analyzing Spanish Civil War Ciphers by Combining Combinatorial and Statistical Methods."[3] If you are interested in a cipher-tool challenge, check out the M-138 problems on MysteryTwister.[4]

Voice encryption

Telephony came into wide use in the late nineteenth century, followed by voice radio a few decades later. Unwanted parties can eavesdrop on communications in both technologies. Radio communication is especially threatened, as a listener needs only an antenna and a radio device to do so, which is why *voice encryption*—also known as "ciphony"—inevitably became an important issue. Especially in the military, which adopted telephony and voice radio early, there was a demand for secure and convenient voice encryption devices.

Voice encryption requires completely different, and far more sophisticated, technology than text encryption. When engineers started to work on voice encryption systems in the early twentieth century, they faced a number of severe challenges. Voice transmission was analog at that time, and even today, it is difficult to encrypt analog signals in a secure way. It therefore comes as no surprise that virtually all voice encryption machines of the first generation used algorithms that could be broken without much effort.

During World War II, none of the war's leading nations ever managed to design a voice encryption device that was secure and could also be built at a reasonable price. The most famous voice encryption machine of the war was the SIGSALY, an apparatus constructed by the Americans. It was extremely complex and filled a whole room. The SIGSALY encrypted digitized voice data with a one-time pad scheme, the keys of which were provided on vinyl records. The SIGSALY was probably the only secure means of voice encryption in World War II. However, the technology was expensive, which resulted in only a few copies being built. These devices were used only at the highest levels of the military.[5]

Early in the Cold War, voice communication increasingly replaced Morse code radio transmissions. Concurrently, voice encryption technology became more important and made considerable progress. The devices became smaller, easier to operate, and less expensive, while new digitization methods, combined with new ciphers, provided a higher level of security. Dozens, if not hundreds, of encrypting telephones and radio devices were developed during this period, mainly for military and diplomatic uses. However, little is known about the encryption methods these Cold War devices used, as most of this information is still classified.

With the advent of the computer, it became possible to treat digitized voice as binary code, represented by sequences of zeros and ones, and to encrypt these with the same algorithms that were used to encrypt text and images. When digital cell phones came into popular use in the 1990s, many were already equipped with encryption modules. Today, all mobile phone standards, including GSM, UMTS, and LTE, have encryption included—though only the wireless connection between the phone and the base station is protected by default.

Encrypting voice communication from one speaker to the other speaker (called *end-to-end encryption*) remains the domain of the military and diplomacy. The devices used for this purpose are usually expensive and rely on encryption algorithms that are not publicly known. Among ordinary users, end-to-end voice encryption is still rarely used, although some smartphone apps supporting encrypted communication are gradually gaining popularity.

As far as we know, there is no comprehensive book about the history of voice encryption on the market—though such a work could be highly interesting. However, a marvelous 2011 book, *How to Wreck a Nice Beach* by Dave Tompkins, covers the history of voice digitalization. It contains a lot of fascinating information about voice encryption, including the SIGSALY.[6] In addition, *How to Wreck a Nice Beach* covers the use of voice digitizers (commonly known as vocoders) in music and other areas.[7]

As voice encryption is completely different from the text encryption methods this book focuses on, breaking voice encryption requires techniques distinct from the codebreaking methods we have introduced. In the early days of voice encryption, cryptanalysis mainly consisted of unscrambling analog signals, which was often not very difficult. With the advent of voice digitization early in the Cold War, the job for the codebreakers became increasingly challenging. Today, voice encryption cryptanalysis is no longer its own topic, since the algorithms used for this purpose are not very different from other computer-based encryption methods.

Code talking

Rather than using a machine for voice encryption, a human can do the job by translating the message into a little-known language. This method is referred to as *code talking*. Most readers will probably know that the United States successfully applied this technique using Navajo (Diné) code talkers in World War II.[8] The 2002 Hollywood movie *Windtalkers*, starring Nicolas Cage, is about this practice.

However, the Navajo code talkers were not the only ones, or even the first, to use this technique. In World War I, the US Army engaged Cherokee, Choctaw, and other Native American people as code talkers, even though voice radio technology was not yet widespread. The British also employed Cherokees, and Canada used Native American code talkers as well.

These efforts only grew in scale. Three decades later, during World War II, telephone and voice radio played a more important role. Code talking was practiced on a larger scale and in a more systematic way. In several projects, the US armed forces recruited code talkers from over thirty Native American tribes. Most famously, the Navajos worked in the Pacific Theater and had an elaborate code with several hundred terms. The second-largest group was the Comanche code talkers, who joined the war effort in Europe.[9]

The work of code talkers in World War II did not just consist of translating messages into their native language. They also applied a code based on their language, which usually included a spelling alphabet that enabled the code talkers to transmit names, geographical expressions, and other words they could not translate. In addition, code words for military terms that did not exist in the code talkers' language were introduced. In many cases, TURTLE stood for TANK, while bird names denoted different kinds of airplanes. Before being sent into service, each code talker was trained in the code and became familiar with the radio technology he would use.

The US code talkers of World War II were quite successful. None of the language codes applied are known to have been broken, and the code talking itself proved quite efficient. Encrypting, transmitting, and decrypting a voice message via code talkers was considerably faster and less error-prone than sending it via encrypted Morse code.

After the war, code talking fell out of use. It had become less secure because of the ease of recording voice messages along with the development by linguists of better methods of analyzing spoken language. Also, during the Cold War, novel types of efficient voice encryption technology emerged that were more secure and easier to use.

Today, specialists could probably break virtually every kind of code talking with the help of linguistic computer programs. Breaking such a message, of course, requires completely different methods than the ones described in this book. It is more a matter of linguistics than of cryptography, and the best strategies for it are documented in wartime code books. These are currently available on the web.[10]

Shorthand (stenography)

The message on the postcard depicted in Figure 15-2, which was sent around 1910, is written in a so-called shorthand.[11] *Shorthand* is a writing method that increases the speed and brevity of writing, typically allowing someone trained in the technique to record spoken language in real time. Some people also used shorthand for low-level encryption (e.g., for postcards).

Figure 15-2: A postcard written in Pitman shorthand, provided by Dale Speirs

The craft of writing in shorthand is referred to as *stenography*—not to be confused with steganography, a technique we will explain in a later section. Stenography was in wide use before recording and dictation machines were invented. Secretaries, journalists, policemen, and many others were trained in shorthand writing and used this technique in their professions.

Over centuries, many shorthand scripts were developed. Most of these were created (and therefore optimized) for a certain language, so different shorthand systems became popular in different countries. In the English-speaking world, one usually encounters Pitman shorthand, which is most popular in the UK and was developed by Sir Isaac Pitman in the 1830s; or Gregg shorthand, which is most popular in the United States and was developed by John Robert Gregg in the 1880s.[12] Many others never became popular.

Virtually everybody interested in historical codebreaking occasionally encounters shorthand texts. Professional codebreakers of the pre-computer era had to deal with this stenography, too, because their customers usually couldn't tell the difference between shorthand and an encryption method—or didn't care.

It is usually not very difficult to detect a shorthand message, even if one doesn't know much about stenography. Most shorthand scripts look similar; this excerpt from Charles Dickens's *A Christmas Carol*, written in the Gregg system (see Figure 15-3), is a typical example.[13]

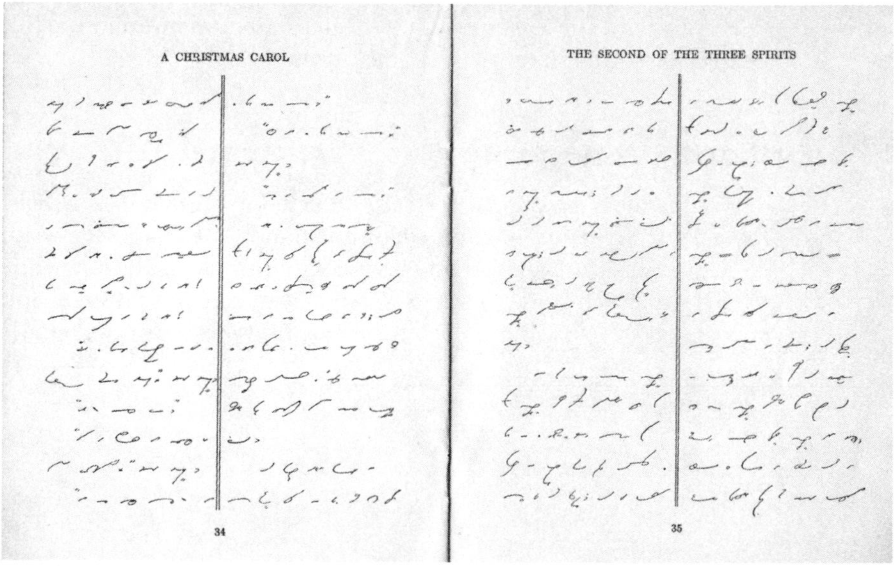

Figure 15-3: Two pages from Charles Dickens's 1843 A Christmas Carol in Gregg shorthand

Almost all shorthand scripts are based on simple symbols and especially short line characters. The reason for this is that these simple symbols can be assembled into words and sentences in a fluid way. If you encounter a script whose symbols are more complex, it probably isn't a shorthand.

Some glyphs represent letters; others stand for common letter combinations, words, or phrases. Here are a few common words in Gregg shorthand:

An experienced user might also combine words rather than writing them separately.

The postcard shown at the beginning of this section is encoded in Pitman shorthand. The message reads as follows:

```
I was very disappointed and
annoyed to find on my arrival at the
station at 5.5, that the train which I thought
always left at 5.15
had left very much earlier
```

Decoding a shorthand message is usually not considered an act of codebreaking. In most cases, it is sufficient to identify the shorthand method used and to ask somebody who knows it to reveal the meaning of the symbols (or use a description of the shorthand to decode it yourself). There are also now web utilities that accept a plaintext and convert it into Gregg or Pitman shorthand. Only on rare occasions, if one is dealing with an especially exotic shorthand, is cryptanalysis necessary. In such a case, a shorthand message should be treated like a nomenclator, as it will probably include both a cipher system for individual letters and symbols for entire words.

Hidden messages (steganography)

The seventeenth-century drawing depicted in Figure 15-4 (and provided to us by Gerhard Strasser) shows an apple tree.[14, 15, 16] Nothing appears suspicious about this picture at first glance. However, using the marks along the lower edge of the picture (which we have added to the original), we can divide the drawing into seventeen columns, each of which contains one apple. The uppermost apple is in the I column, the second in the N column, the third in the D column, and so on. If we read the entire drawing from top to bottom, the apples spell out the following Latin sentence: INDE HIC LONGAT IBI SINT TEMPORA PROSPERA FIAT (MAY YOU LIVE A LONG AND HAPPY LIFE HERE).

The message hidden in this unassuming drawing is an example of *steganography*, which is the practice of concealing messages in pictures, texts, and other objects. It is sometimes referred to as the sister of cryptography. While cryptography disguises information, steganography conceals its existence. The term is taken from the root words *steganos*, meaning "covered" or "roof," and *graphein*, meaning "writing."

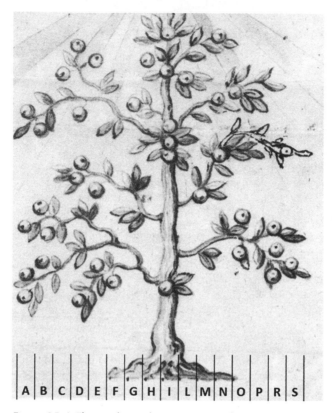

Figure 15-4: The apples in this picture encode a message.

Steganography has a history spanning thousands of years. The Greek historian Herodotus, for example, described the steganography technique of tattooing a message on a slave's head. Other stories included writing on a wooden tablet that was then covered with wax or hiding a message in the pattern of a woman's jewelry. Many other examples of steganography exist. The following list names just a small number of steganography techniques. If you want to know more about steganography and can read German, we also recommend Klaus's 2017 book *Versteckte Botschaften*.[17]

- The ancient Greeks knew about what is today called *sympathetic ink*, a colorless fluid used to write invisible messages on paper. If the paper is heated (or treated in some other way), the writing becomes visible. This technique has been used by countless schoolchildren, who often hide secret messages by writing them in lemon juice, but hundreds of other fluids can be used as sympathetic inks. For instance, fruit juice, sugar water, urine, and many other organic fluids are well suited, as all become visible when heated. More sophisticated sympathetic inks require treatment with certain chemicals in order to become visible. For centuries, the use of sympathetic inks was the most practical way for spies to communicate with their case officers, and during the Cold War, chemists developed high-tech sympathetic inks that were extremely difficult for mail censors to detect. If you want to know more about sympathetic inks, read the 2014 book *Prisoners, Lovers, and Spies* by Kristie Macrakis.[18]

- There are numerous ways to hide a message in a text. For instance, a text can be written such that the starting letters of each line spell out a message (a technique known as *acrostic writing*). Other methods include marking certain letters or writing a text in such a way that, say, every tenth letter spells out a secret message. Techniques of this kind have been used by, among others, prisoners, soldiers, and hostages in order to beat censorship. Other popular techniques include selecting certain letters or words from a text with a stencil (a so-called *Cardan grille*). A well-known example of this is the "hourglass cipher" used by British general Henry Clinton in 1777, during the American Revolutionary War (see Figure 15-5).[19]

Figure 15-5: In 1777, British general Henry Clinton wrote what seemed like an inconspicuous letter to his superior William Howe. The true message can be seen if an hourglass-shaped stencil is placed over the text.

- One of the most prominent users of steganography in the twentieth century was a young American naval officer who later became president: John F. Kennedy.[20] As we previously discussed in Chapter 12, after Kennedy and his crew escaped the sinking of the torpedo boat *PT-109*,[21] Australian coastwatcher Sublieutenant Reginald Evans dispatched one of his five teams of Solomon Islanders to find them. After a few days' search, one of the teams found Kennedy and his men. Because the rescuers, Biuku Gasa and Eroni Kumana, did not speak English, Gasa communicated that Kennedy should carve an English message into a coconut with his pocketknife. That way, they could carry it in something that would not raise suspicion from the Japanese. The text read: **NAURO ISL COMMANDER . . . NATIVE KNOWS POS'IT . . . HE CAN PILOT . . . 11 ALIVE NEED SMALL BOAT . . . KENNEDY**. The hidden message reached Evans, who then coordinated a way to bring the stranded men through Japanese lines and back to an Allied base. Later, John F. Kennedy used the coconut shell as a paperweight in the Oval Office (see Figure 15-6).

Figure 15-6: The message written on this coconut shell facilitated John F. Kennedy's rescue in World War II. During his presidency, he used it as a paperweight.

- Today, steganography can be performed with a computer. There are numerous programs that hide messages in digital images, videos, and other data.

- Lastly, there is a steganographic message hidden in this very book! For a hint on where to start looking, the cartoons may merit closer examination . . .

Finding a hidden steganographic message is known as *steganalysis*, which is similar to cryptanalysis (i.e., codebreaking) but much more difficult to practice in a systematic way. As far as we know, no book or comprehensive research paper about steganalysis (as opposed to steganography) has yet been published.

Success story: How Elonka found a hidden message on a tombstone

Arlington National Cemetery in Washington, DC, is the most famous cemetery in the United States. This national shrine has over 400,000 graves and a history that goes back to the 1800s. Primarily a military cemetery, it holds the graves of many notable people, two of whom are the famous cryptologists William and Elizebeth Friedman. Elizebeth Smith Friedman (1892–1980), one of the great cryptanalysts in American history, worked for the US Navy, the Coast Guard, and numerous related agencies. While working for the Coast Guard during the Prohibition era in the 1920s, she solved many rumrunner encryption systems.[22]

Elizebeth's husband William (1891–1969), whom she taught about codes during their courtship at Riverbank Laboratories, transitioned from his original career as a geneticist to become the most famous cryptologist in American history. During his long career in the US Army, he broke thousands of ciphers, led many renowned codebreaking teams, and wrote several groundbreaking works on cryptography, even coining the terms "cryptanalysis" and "index of coincidence."

The Friedmans not only had a professional interest in cryptography, but they also enjoyed crypto puzzles and mysteries. It therefore comes as no surprise that on their tombstone in Arlington National Cemetery, a steganographic message is hidden (see Figure 15-7). The tombstone was commissioned by Elizebeth after her husband died in 1969. The existence of this message was unknown until Elonka discovered it in 2017.[23]

When Elonka moved to Washington, DC, in 2017, one of her first explorations of the area was a visit to Arlington National Cemetery to see the Friedmans' grave, as Elonka was such a fan of their work. She was entirely expecting to find some kind of hidden message on their tombstone and was surprised when it looked quite ordinary. Still, she took many pictures, and later that evening, she posted a message on Twitter about her visit.

A colleague, journalist Jason Fagone, mentioned to her that he was conducting research for a new book about Elizebeth. He forwarded some pictures he had taken of Elizebeth's sketch of the tombstone, which he found in the George C. Marshall Library and Museum in Lexington, Virginia. Jason had been spending a great deal of time in the Marshall archives researching his excellent biography of Elizebeth, *The Woman Who Smashed Codes*, to be published later that year.[24]

One of the pictures showed a handwritten note, created by Elizebeth in 1969, with a sketch of the inscription that was to be put on William's tombstone after his death. The sketch included William's name and life data, a blank space where Elizebeth's information would be added after her own death, and, at the bottom of the tombstone, the words KNOWLEDGE IS POWER, a phrase that was a recurring theme throughout William's and Elizebeth's lives. When Elizebeth died in 1980, details of her own life were added to the tombstone.

While examining Elizebeth's sketch, Elonka noticed a potential steganographic message, hidden by the way that the letters were written in slightly different fonts. This message, concealed in the engraving KNOWLEDGE IS POWER, turned out to use the Baconian cipher, a cryptographic system well known to the Friedmans. They had used this steganographic technique before.

The *Baconian cipher*, which was invented by philosopher Francis Bacon in the early seventeenth century, can be used to hide a message in any text or picture ("anything can be made to signify anything").[25] In order to use it with a text, we need two different fonts, A and B. In the following example, we use ordinary letters as font A and bold-italic letters as font B. Using these two styles, we can encode all letters of the alphabet (Bacon used a twenty-four-letter alphabet) by changing the position of the bold-italic letters, as shown here in the word *HOUSE*:

A: HOUSE	B: HOUS*E*	C: HOU*S*E	D: HOU*SE*
E: HO*U*SE	F: HO*U*S*E*	G: HO*US*E	H: HO*USE*
I: H*O*USE	K: H*O*US*E*	L: H*O*U*S*E	M: H*O*U*SE*
N: H*OU*SE	O: H*OU*S*E*	P: H*OU*S*E	Q: H*OUSE*
R: *H*OUSE	S: *H*OUS*E*	T: *H*OU*S*E	U: *H*OU*SE*
W: *HO*USE	X: *HO*US*E*	Y: *HO*U*S*E	Z: *HO*U*SE*

Using this system, hiding the word **WILLY** in the text THIS IS AN ORDINARY SHORT TEXT would look like the following:

*TH*ISI SANOR D*I*NAR Y*S*HOR *TTEX*T

Or, written in a way that preserves the natural word boundaries:

*TH*IS IS *A*N ORD*I*NARY *S*HORT *TEX*T

Figure 15-7: The tombstone of William and Elizebeth Friedman bears a short hidden message in the words KNOWLEDGE IS POWER.

The Baconian cipher is one of the earliest known binary codes in history, predating Morse code by over 200 years and ASCII code by over 300. When Elonka took a closer look at the Friedmans' tombstone, she actually found a Baconian message in the words KNOWLEDGE IS POWER. Some of the letters spelling out this sentence have serifs (font A) and some do not (font B). This difference can be seen best in the Es; notice that the Es in the word KNOWLEDGE are slightly different from the one in POWER. Separating the letters with serifs from those without and transcribing them using our system of ordinary and bold-italic letters, we get the following:

KN*OW*LEDGE *IS* P*OW*ER

Written in groups of five, the Baconian cipher can be easily decrypted:

KN*OW*L EDGE*I* SP*OW*E R

The three groups encode the letters **WFF**. These are the initials of William Frederick Friedman. A brief message, to be sure, but very typical of the Friedmans.

Success story: Deciphering Steganographia

In the year 1500, German abbot and humanist Johannes Trithemius (1462–1516) finished the most remarkable of his over ninety works, a three-book set titled *Steganographia*. The first two books describe over fifty variants of a communication method that we doubt ever worked. This method requires the sender to cast a certain magic spell, causing a ghost to appear. This ghost subsequently transmits the message with the help of a number of supporting ghosts. The receiver then needs to cast another magic spell in order to access the message. For every variant of this process, Trithemius provides long lists of parameters, such as the number and names of supporting ghosts.

Steganographia gained instant notoriety, as it soon became known that the magic communication techniques described in the first two books were mere hoaxes. Their true purpose was to encode messages in the parameters listed: Trithemius disguised messages as descriptions of magic processes, a form of steganography. In fact, the title *Steganographia* even gave the science of steganography its name. The word "steganography" was, for centuries, used synonymously with "cryptography," until David Kahn popularized the definition given at the beginning of this chapter in his 1967 book *The Codebreakers*.[26]

We introduce here an example of a *Steganographia* communication method, using the description Jürgen Hermes provided in his 2012 PhD thesis.[27] This method lists the following supporting "ghosts":

Maseriel. **Bula**n. Lamodyn. **Charn**oty. Carmephin. **Iabru**n. Care. **Sath**royn. Asulroy. **Beu**esy. Cadumyn. **Turi**el. Busan. **Seue**ar. Almos. **Ly**. Cadusel. **Erno**ty. Panier. **Ieth**ar. Care. **Pheo**ry. Bulan. **Thort**y. Paron. **Vem**o. Fabelrenthusy.

If one only reads every second letter of every other word (which we have bolded for clarification), one gets the following Latin phrase (note that we've distinguished U and V, as well as I and Y, which were used interchangeably):

VACANTIBUS TRIBUS TRES VALENT ITA PER TOTUM

This phrase, which translates to **AFTER THREE EMPTY ONES, THREE ARE VALID, THUS THROUGHOUT**, is an instruction for decrypting another text contained in the same chapter of *Steganographia*. According to these instructions, reading the message requires one to skip the first three words, take the initial letters of the next three, skip the following three, and so on. We obtained the following result (the valid initial letters are bolded for clarification):

Omnipotens sempiterne Deus **b**onorum **r**emunerator æquissime, qui filium tuum **n**ostri **g**eneris **e**sse participem voluisti, ut **r**edimeret, **d**iabolica **i**nuidia nos miserrimos: qui **s**ola **b**enignitate **r**edundans, formam nostri suscepit **i**ncorruptam **ex f**lore virginalis uteri, archangelo **s**ancto **G**abriele **i**nsinuante, quod Virgo conceptura, **b**eatissimo **t**uo **S**piritui perpetua virgo permaneret, **i**mmaculata **c**larior **h**ominib. angelicisque spiritibus praeeminentior. **G**enuit **r**egem **o**mnipotentem, Deum et hominem, **s**antissima **e**t **r**euerendissima Virgo Maria, virilis **c**onsortii **o**mnino **n**escia, sine dolore pariens, **s**ine **t**ristitia **v**agientem Deum hominemque suscipiens, semper . . .

The bolded letters spell out the following German message:

BRÆNGER DIS BRIEFS GIBT SICH GROSER CONST US

This means: **THE CARRIER OF THIS LETTER CONSIDERS HIMSELF VERY SKILLED**. As with all the messages in *Steganographia*, the content of this message was not as important as its steganographic delivery, which Trithemius was illustrating by example.

While the true purpose of the first two *Steganographia* books soon became common knowledge, the function of the *liber tertius*, or the third book, remained a mystery. On the surface, it describes magical communication methods, too, but these look quite different from the ones in the first two books. Here, the main parameters allegedly required to transmit a message with the help of planetary angels are three-digit numbers that are supposedly needed to calculate the movements of planets and their rulers. Long lists of these numbers are provided (see Figure 15-8).

For centuries, highly regarded scholars tried to figure out what the third book of *Steganographia* was about. Did it encode messages, too, or was it meant to represent real magic? In the 1990s, almost 500 years after the creation of *Steganographia*, mathematician Jim Reeds, who worked for AT&T, took a closer look at the third book. When he analyzed the table depicted in Figure 15-8, he noticed that, in the first column, all numbers listed were between 626 and 650. So were the first ten numbers in the second column (those that appeared above the only written word in that column). This resulted in the following block of forty numbers between 626 and 650:

```
644, 650, 629, 650, 645, 635, 646, 636, 632, 646, 639 634, 641, 642,
649, 642, 648, 638, 634, 647, 632, 630, 642, 633, 648, 650, 655,
626, 650, 644, 638, 633, 635, 642, 632, 640, 637, 643, 638, 634
```

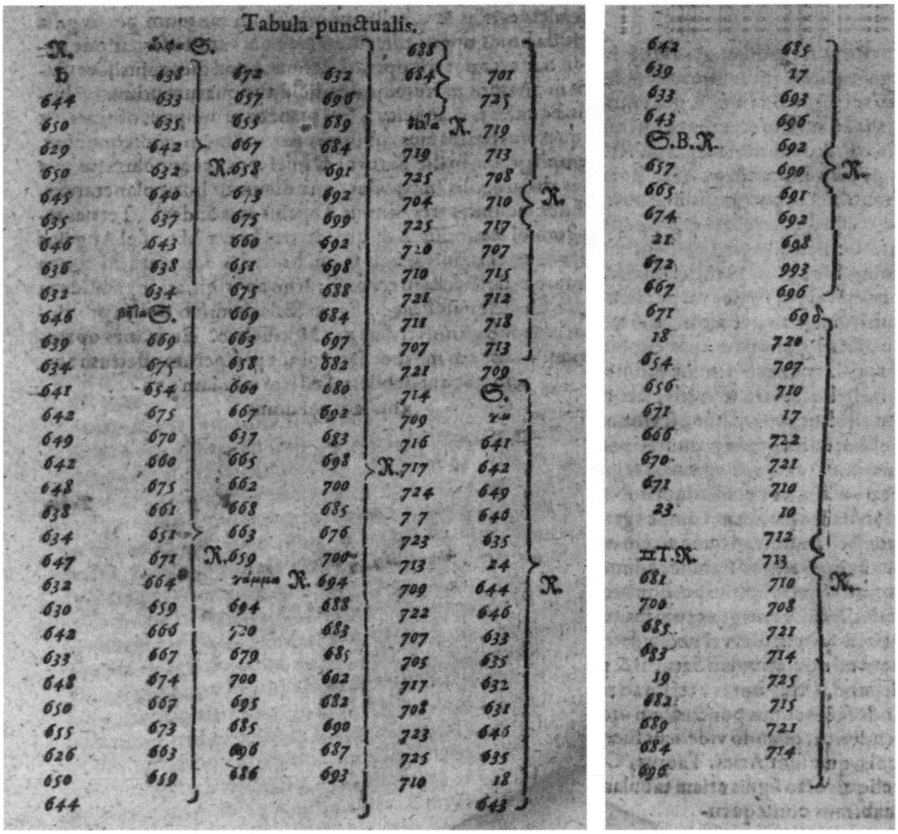

Figure 15-8: These numbers from the 1500 work Steganographia *are allegedly astrological parameters. In reality, they encode a message.*

This block is followed by numbers that are all greater than 650. Reeds suspected that these forty numbers represented an encrypted message. Frequency analysis revealed that the number 650 was not only the highest but also the most frequent one. Did this number stand for the letter **A**, which has the highest frequency in the Latin language? If so, the following substitution rule appeared likely: 650 = **A**, 649 = **B**, 648 = **C**, 647 = **D**, 646 = **E**, etc. A short test revealed that this substitution resulted in Latin word fragments. After some experimentation, Reeds came up with the following table:

650 = **A**, 649 = **B**, 648 = **C**, 647 = **D**, 646 = **E**, 645 = **F**, 644 = **G**, 643 = **H**, 642 = **I**, 641 = **L**, 640 = **M**, 639 = **N**, 638 = **O**, 637 = **P**, 636 = **Q**, 635 = **R**, 634 = **S**, 633 = **T**, 632 = **U**, 631 = **X**, 630 = **Y**, 629 = **Z**, 628 = **TZ**, 627 = **SCH**, 626 = **TH**

The alphabet used here lacked **J** (which is identified with **I** in Latin), **K** (which is rarely used in Latin), **V** (which is identified with **U** in Latin), and **W** (which does not exist in Latin). All this seemed to show that Reeds was on the right track and that the aforementioned forty-letter block decrypted as follows:

GAZA FREQUENS LIBICOS DUXIT CARTHAGO TRIUMPHOS

With this Latin phrase, which translates to **FREQUENTLY, CARTHAGE RECEIVED RICH BOOTY FROM THE DEFEATED LIBYANS**, the true meaning of the *Steganographia*'s third book was finally revealed—500 years after its creation. Reeds easily deciphered the remaining six tables with similar methods. The substitution tables he produced looked very similar to the one above, except that twenty-five, fifty, or seventy-five had to be added to or subtracted from the three-digit numbers. In other words: the relevant part was the remainder after division by twenty-five. Here are the plaintexts Reeds discovered:

```
GAZA FREQUENS LIBICOS DUXIT CARTHAGO TRIUMPHOS [repeated four times]
LIBER GETRUWER HINTUMB DIE ZWELFE WART UNSER
HEIMLICHE EFUR DER PORTEN AMEN
NIT LAIS DUHER ZU MIR NOIT GCH ANDEL US ZUDAS ICH LDEN BRENGE AIL
WEIS SOCH BEHALT
COMMEST NOCH HINTWAN IS DUET HABE EIN GROSEN RICHTEN MIT DIR DIR
HAB MIT DIR UND SEHD DIS ALLES GEBEN ZUALS DUNUST UQREBI DIR SERE
HAHW
BRENGER DIS BRIEFFS IST EIN BOSER SCHALG UND EIN DIEB HUET DICH
FUR EME ER WIRT DICH AN
MISERERE MEI DEUS SECUNDU MAGNUM DONUM TUUM AMEN ATH
GAZA FREQUENS LIBICOS DUXIT CARTHAGO TRIUMPHOS WTZSCH
GAZA FREQUENS LIBICOS DU RTHAGO XIT CA TRIUMPHOS SCH
```

Again, the content of these messages was not particularly important. Trithemius probably chose the phrase **GAZA FREQUENS LIBICOS DUXIT CARTHAGO TRIUMPHOS** because it includes all of the letters of the Latin language using only a few words—which makes breaking a message with frequency analysis more difficult. This sentence can be regarded as a Latin equivalent of "The quick brown fox jumps over the lazy dog," which is often used today to test fonts, printers, and keyboards.

The message beginning with **BRENGER DIS BRIEFFS** is German for "The carrier of this letter is a bad rogue and thief; be careful, he will betray you." The text beginning with **MISERERE MEI** stems from the Bible (Psalm 51).

In 1998, Jim Reeds published his findings in the scientific journal *Cryptologia*.[28] While working on his article, however, he came across an astonishing research paper from 1996, published in the literature journal *Daphnis* by our colleague, the Germanist Thomas Ernst.[29] As Reeds looked through the 200-page tome, he could hardly believe what he saw: apparently, Ernst had also solved the third book of the *Steganographia* just two years earlier!

This means that 500 years after the creation of *Steganographia*, two researchers—a mathematician and a Germanist—solved the mystery of the third book at almost the same time and independently of each other. This sounds like a Dan Brown story, but it is real.

Ernst broke Trithemius's steganographic cipher with the same initial table used by Reeds a few years later (see Figure 15-8). The table was sectionalized by the Greek symbols, some of which spelled out Greek letters such as alpha ($\alpha\lambda\phi\alpha$), beta ($\beta\eta\tau\alpha$), gamma ($\gamma\alpha\mu\mu\alpha$), and delta ($\delta\epsilon\lambda\tau\alpha$) in addition to the numbers. Transcription was difficult, and there are likely to be small errors here and there. Ernst assumed the Greek symbols to be separators. A simplified transcript, from a 1608 version of *Steganographia*, is here:

♄	αλφα						
644	638	672	632	688	701	642	685
650	633	657	696	684	725	639	17
629	635	655	689	δελτα	719	633	693
650	642	667	684	719	713	643	696
645	632	658	691	725	708		692
635	640	673	692	704	710	657	690
646	637	675	699	725	717	665	691
636	643	660	692	720	707	674	692
632	638	651	698	710	715	21	698
646	634	675	688	721	712	672	693
639	βητα	669	684	711	718	667	696
634	669	663	697	707	713	671	♋ δ
641	675	658	682	721	709	18	720
642	654	660	680	714	♈ α	654	707
649	675	667	692	709	641	656	710
642	670	657	683	716	642	671	17
648	660	665	698	717	649	666	722
638	671	662	700	724	646	670	721
634	661	668	685	717	635	671	710
647	657	663	676	723	24	23	10
632	671	659	700	713	644	♊ T	712
630	664	γαμμα	694	709	646	681	713
642	659	694	688	722	633	700	710
633	666	700	683	707	635	685	708
648	667	679	685	705	632	683	721
650	674	700	692	717	631	19	714
635	667	695	682	708	646	682	725
626	673	685	690	723	635	689	715
650	663	696	687	725	18	684	721
644	659	686	693	710	643	696	714

The four groups headlined "alpha (α)," "beta (β)," "gamma (γ)," and "delta (δ)" contained forty numbers each, and Ernst thus assumed that these four columns represented the same text. The first number of each group differed from the others by exactly twenty-five (they are 644, 669, 694, and 719). The same was true for the second, third, fourth, and all subsequent numbers of each group. Because every number in each group was removed from those of the other groups by a factor of twenty-five, the four groups were identical.

The number 650, which appears twice among the first four letters of the alpha group, delivered the breakthrough. Ernst guessed that 650 stood for either the first or the last letter of the Latin alphabet and that Trithemius had used either the substitution table **A** = 650, **B** = 651, **C** = 652, etc. or **Z** = 650, **Y** = 651, **X** = 652, etc. When he checked the first hypothesis, he didn't get a meaningful result, but the second one appeared to work. The first word he derived was **GAZA**, and his decryption of the rest of the text quickly fell into place.

Having found the solution, Ernst started to write his detailed research paper (in German) about his decryption, to be published in 1996. His research was comprehensive, leading him to another related unsolved cipher: Heidel's cryptogram.

In 1676, Wolfgang Ernst Heidel had also claimed to have solved Trithemius's third book, but he had only published an encrypted version of his solution, using a polyalphabetic cipher. Heidel's ciphertext was known in cryptological circles, but for the next three centuries, no one was able to crack it. Ernst thus accomplished another first, deciphering Heidel's cryptogram and proving that the solution of Trithemius's third book had already been found in the seventeenth century. Tom's original paper about his own solution continued to expand, incorporating the information about Heidel's cryptogram and a great deal more of the historical background. It eventually reached the substantial size of 200 pages, the length of a book. After three years, Tom's work was published in *Daphnis*.

Two years later, Reeds came across Tom's publication while working on his own *Cryptologia* article. After Reeds informed the *Cryptologia* editors about Tom's work, they asked Ernst to provide a shortened version of his paper.[30] So, in the October 1998 edition of *Cryptologia*, two articles about the decipherment of the third *Steganographia* book were published—written by two authors who hadn't known about each other.

There's no doubt that the double decipherment of the third book of *Steganographia* is a highlight in the history of codebreaking. To learn more about this fascinating story, see the 1998 article "A Mystery Unraveled, Twice" in the *New York Times*.[31] Twenty years later, the story again came to public awareness via a few German-language publications in Thomas Ernst's home country, including a comprehensive blog post by Jürgen Hermes[32] and two treatises written by Klaus.[33, 34]

Success story: Mysterious Stranger message

The image of stylized creatures in Figure 15-9 is one of many such pictures in the margins of magician David Blaine's 2002 book *Mysterious Stranger*. A message is hidden in the images, and when combined, they pointed to the location of a hidden $100,000 treasure (which has since been found). The puzzles were created by award-winning game developer Cliff Johnson.

Figure 15-9: A portion of a steganographic puzzle in the 2002 book
Mysterious Stranger

This particular image was one of several in the book that decrypted to two different sentences. One sentence was encoded by counting the scales on each serpent in a set of pages, and another was encoded with the numbers on their tails. The cipher key was in the form of a 5 × 5 lookup table. The numbers of either the tails or scales were used in pairs to represent the row and column of a letter in the table. The treasure was found in 2004, sixteen months after the book was published. There is a detailed explanation of the puzzles by Jeff Briden at Cliff Johnson's website.[35]

Challenge: Another steganographic message by the Friedmans

A Baconian cipher can be found not only on William and Elizebeth Friedman's tombstone but also in a book they wrote. Their 1957 work titled *The Shakespearean Ciphers Examined* evaluates a number of theories alleging that Francis Bacon (1561–1626) was the real author of the works usually attributed to William Shakespeare (1564–1616), and that Bacon included hidden messages in these writings that confirmed his authorship.[36] The story is of personal interest to the Friedmans, as it was through this research that they met. In the early 1900s, Elizebeth (née Smith) had been hired by the eccentric millionaire George Fabyan to search for hidden messages in Shakespeare's works. While working at Fabyan's think tank in Riverbank Laboratories near Chicago, she met a researcher in a different part of the lab, the young geneticist William Friedman. As a photographer, he helped with her research. She taught him about codes, they fell in love, and the rest is history. In their 1957 book, the Friedmans took time to closely examine the Shakespeare-Bacon controversy and definitively show that all the Bacon code theories were nonsense.

In their typical tongue-in-cheek style, within their book about why there weren't Baconian messages in the works of Shakespeare, the Friedmans hid a message in a Baconian cipher! On page 257 of the book, the following lines can be read:

progressively and judiciously, *the letters and the words already deter-mined permitting the limitation of the number of trials that remain for suggesting letters and words likely to follow* [our italics]. Erroneous

Can you find the hidden message? If it's not clear, check out our website at *https://codebreaking-guide.com/challenges/* for a larger version of this image and for hints.

Cipher machines

Encryption played an important role in World War I, especially for protecting radio messages. Virtually all systems used were either manual or based on simple tools, such as cipher disks and cipher slides. Unfortunately, most of these methods were broken by enemy forces quite quickly. They also suffered a further weakness in that they were complicated to use, especially in wartime conditions. Soldiers who had to encrypt or decrypt text while taking cover in a trench, suffering from bad weather, and being distracted by gunshots and bomb explosions nearby were already overtaxed. Inevitably, many errors occurred. Often, a recipient could not even decrypt an encrypted message due to a faulty encipherment.

Based on these experiences, many new encryption techniques were developed in the years following World War I. Because it had become obvious that manual encryption was not suited for high-security and high-volume radio traffic at any time, let alone under wartime conditions, new encryption machines were designed to be more secure and user-friendly than manual ciphers (see Figure 15-10). The concept of cipher machines was not necessarily new, as some designs had already been in existence for decades. But after the failure of cryptography in World War I, the pressure was high enough to finally put these ideas into practice.

Figure 15-10: Mechanical and electrical encryption machines reached their peak of usage from approximately 1920 to 1970. The picture shows a Siemens & Halske T52 (a), a Kryha Standard (b), a KL-7 (c), and a Hagelin C-35 (d). For more information about these and other machines, see https://cryptomuseum.com.

The most popular type of encryption apparatus was the so-called rotor cipher machine. This kind of device comprises a typewriter-like keyboard, an output unit (some designs used a set of lamps, with every lamp indicating a letter of the alphabet), a source of current, and a set of rotors. The diagram in Figure 15-11 shows a simplified three-rotor design with an alphabet of six letters. Real machines, of course, worked with an alphabet of twenty-six or more letters.

To encrypt a letter, the operator presses a key. This completes an electrical connection, which makes a lamp representing a ciphertext letter light up. After each letter is entered, the rightmost rotor turns by one unit. After a complete turn of this rotor, the next one turns by one unit, too, and once this one has revolved, the last one moves by one unit, like an odometer counter. Decryption on these machines works in a similar way: they need to be switched to a different mode, which causes the current to flow in the opposite direction through the rotors. The operator enters the ciphertext letter by pressing a key, after which the plaintext letter is indicated by a lamp.

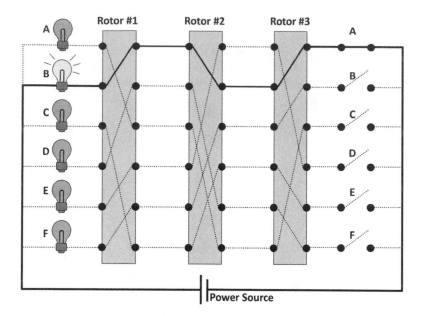

Figure 15-11: A rotor encryption machine uses a number of wired rotors. Pressing a key (plaintext) completes an electrical connection and causes a letter lamp (ciphertext) to light up.

The most famous rotor machine (as well as the most famous encryption machine ever) is the Enigma (see Figure 15-12), which was developed in the 1920s. The Germans used about 30,000 copies of the Enigma in World War II.

Figure 15-12: The Enigma, used by the Germans in World War II, is the most famous encryption machine in history.

In its most common configuration, the Enigma had three rotors, a plugboard to add a further level of complexity to the process, and an additional part called a *reflector* (see Figure 15-13). From 1942 on, German U-boats used a four-rotor version of the Enigma, also with a reflector. Concentration camps and police also made use of the Enigma.

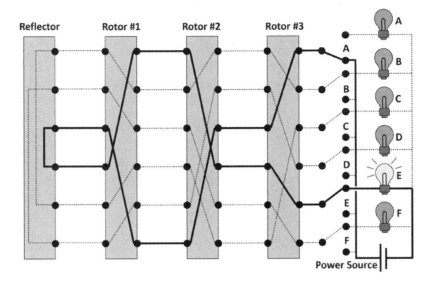

Figure 15-13: The Enigma is a rotor machine. Contrary to most designs of this kind, it included an additional element, referred to as a reflector.

The reflector caused the current to run twice through the rotors: once forward to the reflector, and then back to the rotors again. Due to this reflection, encryption and decryption worked exactly the same way; no decryption mode was necessary. This made the operation of the Enigma easier, but it also turned out to be a design weakness that helped the Allies to break the Enigma's encryption system.

As early as the 1930s, three young Polish mathematicians from the University of Poznań, Marian Rejewski and his associates Henryk Zygalski and Jerzy Różycki, found some of the weaknesses in the Enigma encryption algorithm, which allowed them to break messages regularly.

They created a device, a "bomba kryptologiczna" (cryptologic bomb), which assisted with their efforts. According to their contemporary at Bletchley Park, Gordon Welchman, Różycki proposed the "bomba" code-name for the machine based on a type of ice cream that was popular at the time; they were eating this dessert when Rejewski came up with the idea for the machine.[37, 38] Other reports claim that the name was chosen spontaneously or perhaps because of the sounds the machine made.[39]

After Poland was invaded by the Germans, Rejewski and his team escaped and provided their methodology and a Polish copy of the Enigma to aid in the Allies' work at Bletchley Park, a country estate outside London, where thousands of workers broke Enigma messages in a factory-like facility. British codebreakers, among them renowned mathematician Alan Turing, developed their own machine to help with their efforts. The design was partially based on the work of the Polish cryptanalysts, especially their deduction of the wiring of the Enigma rotors, but was otherwise substantially different. The British called their own machine a Bombe, and hundreds were built by the British Tabulating Machine Company for the war effort.

Other analysts around the world were also attacking the Enigma ciphers. The British codebreaker Dillwyn "Dilly" Knox broke Enigma messages in the 1930s as well. Also, informed by the British, the Americans started their own Enigma-breaking efforts, building an improved version of the Bombe targeted at the four-rotor version of the Enigma that was used by German U-boats. This initiative was spearheaded by Joseph Desch in Dayton, Ohio. Today, Joseph's daughter, Deb (Desch) Anderson, is an excellent resource for anything related to the Dayton Codebreakers.

Independently of all of the above, Elizabeth Friedman had her own pencil-and-paper way of cracking Enigma messages, as she was systematically attacking Nazi ciphers in South America.

Today, there are museums in both Poznań and Bletchley Park that tell the story of some of the Enigma cryptanalysis in a fascinating way. There is also a tremendous amount of literature on this topic; we especially recommend David Kahn's *Seizing the Enigma* (1991)[40] and Tom and Dan Perera's *Inside Enigma* (2019), which are available on the EnigmaMuseum.com website.[41] *Demystifying the Bombe* (2014) by Dermot Turing (the nephew of Alan Turing) may be interesting for codebreakers, as it explains the Bombe in an easy-to-understand way.[42] Then there are the movies *Enigma* (2001), with Kate Winslet; and *The Imitation Game* (2014), with Benedict Cumberbatch. We also recommend the documentary *Dayton Codebreakers* (2005).

Apart from rotor machines, numerous other types of electrical or mechanical encryption machines were created during a "golden age" that spanned World War II and the early Cold War. For instance, in World War II, Japanese diplomats used a cipher device that their US war opponents named PURPLE.[43, 44] The full Japanese name was "System 97 Typewriter for European Characters" (九七式欧文印字機, or 97-shiki ōbun injiki). The cipher was broken by one of William Friedman's teams in the US Army Signal Intelligence Service, led by Frank Rowlett. They did so by looking for helpful phrases that the Japanese used frequently at the beginning of their radio messages, such as "I have the honor to inform your excellency," which often provided a crib with which to start.

Two side notes about terminology:

- There is debate as to the origin of the name PURPLE. According to Stephen Budiansky in his 2000 book *Battle of Wits*,[45] American codebreakers named two of the earlier Japanese naval encryption systems, which were codes and not ciphers, "Red" and "Blue" because of the colors of the binders in which they kept the intercepted messages. They named other Japanese encryption systems other colors, such as JADE and CORAL, though it is not clear whether these names were also related to the color of their containers.

- There were two completely different Japanese encryption systems both code-named "Red." One of these, mentioned above, was a true code that used a codebook; the other was an unrelated cipher system whose messages were encrypted and decrypted with a machine. To distinguish the two, the codebook version was typically spelled normally, such as "Red" or perhaps "Red Book," while all machine cipher systems were generally referred to in all caps: RED, PURPLE, etc. But, to make things even more confusing, the cipher systems were sometimes (incorrectly) referred to as codes, as in the "Purple Code" system, which was really a cipher. Also, sometimes the code systems, not the cipher versions, were referred to in all caps! See Chapter 7 for more information about the terminology confusion between codes and ciphers.

Another important World War II–era German encryption machine, whose existence was only declassified in the last twenty years, was the Lorenz SZ40/42, also known by the British as "Tunny," meaning "tuna fish." It was introduced in 1940 as a cipher attachment that could be added in-line to large teleprinter machines, so it was not portable like the Enigma. It was used only at the highest military levels, such as for Hitler's direct communications with his generals. The Lorenz had twelve notched wheels and over five hundred pins, and it would encrypt the outgoing text and decrypt the incoming text of a teletype.

The device could accept input via Baudot on five-bit punched paper tape or manually. Then it would rapidly translate the plaintext into an encrypted version of Baudot code and send it to the receiver via radio or landline. At the receiving end, another in-line Lorenz attachment would decrypt the message and send it on to the receiver teleprinter so that a plaintext message could be printed out. All of this was considerably faster than the laborious letter-by-letter process required by the Enigma.[46]

Any mention of the Lorenz was kept classified for decades after World War II. Information about it only began to emerge in 1995, after the publication of a paper by Donald Davies in *Cryptologia*.[47] Following this publication, the US and UK governments gradually began declassifying various related documents over the next several years.[48] Now that a more complete picture of the Lorenz system has emerged, we know that it was another of the encryption methods cracked at Bletchley Park—this time in 1942 by a team including John Tiltman and William T. "Bill" Tutte. This was an impressive accomplishment, considering they had never even seen the machine.[49] Another team of fifty people, put together and led by Thomas H. Flowers, designed a different kind of decryption machine, distinct from the Bombe, to assist with efforts to decrypt the Tunny messages. It was called the Colossus, and it was a massive, room-sized apparatus that could be reconfigured from day to day. A Post Office factory in Birmingham was commandeered to build the necessary parts, and as the war went on, ten different Colossi were constructed.

After the Tunny's system was broken, the strategic intelligence gathered from it provided substantial information, both about the movements of the German army and about the German leadership's understanding (or misunderstanding) of Allied plans. According to Colossus engineer Thomas

Flowers, on June 5, 1944, a decrypted message was provided to US General Dwight D. Eisenhower showing that, though the Germans knew there was a planned invasion of Normandy, they didn't believe it was real. They thought, instead, that it was just a feint to draw German troops away from the ports.[50] This intelligence was thus a key factor in the Allied decision to launch the full "Operation Overlord" invasion of France on D-Day (June 6), which turned the tide of the war for the Allies in Europe.[51] Historians looking back on this era estimate that the intel from Bletchley, including the Tunny decrypts, shortened the war in Europe by several months. In 1954, Eisenhower described it as being of priceless value and that it had saved thousands of British and American lives.[52]

While early cipher machine designs, including the German Enigma and the Japanese PURPLE, could be broken, the more advanced ones, especially those of the Cold War, are still considered secure today. With the advent of inexpensive electronics and computers around 1970, electrical and mechanical encryption machines gradually became obsolete over the next decades, though they remained in use to some extent in less-developed countries.[53] Today, while this technology has a fascinating history, it no longer plays a role in modern communication security.

Breaking the ciphers of vintage encryption machines with modern means (i.e., with computer support) is an active field of research. In Chapter 16, we will address Enigma breaking with hill climbing. If you want to know more, read Craig Bauer's 2013 book *Secret History* (or the second edition published in 2021), which presents a great deal of mathematical background on cipher machines and introduces methods to break their encryption.[54]

16

SOLVING CIPHERS
WITH HILL CLIMBING

Many of the encryption methods introduced in this book can be broken with a strategy called *hill climbing*. Computer scientists developed this technique to solve certain kinds of optimization problems, most of which are not crypto related. It is well suited, for instance, to finding the shortest route that includes certain cities or determining the most efficient configuration of a production facility. The method is named "hill climbing" because it aims to improve a given configuration iteratively, until the "top of the mountain" is reached and no further improvement is possible, as represented in Figure 16-1.

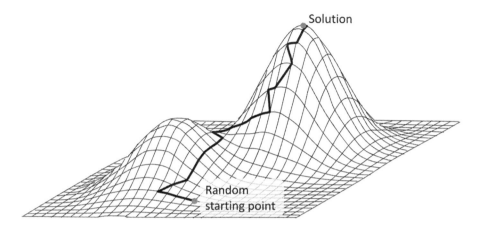

Figure 16-1: A hill-climbing algorithm takes a random key and checks whether the plaintext obtained with it looks like real language. By making small changes to the key, it tries to improve the result until no better one can be found. The last candidate often is the correct one.

Hill climbing is especially suited for problems that have too many potential solutions for the cryptanalyst to check every single one. It requires that the problem be "smooth," which means that a small change in the input may cause only a small change in the output. Most codebreaking tasks used on classical ciphers fulfill both requirements. For these deciphering methods, the number of potential solutions (i.e., the number of keys) is extremely large. For example, there are 403,291,461,126,605,635,584,000,000 (about 400 trillion trillion, or 4×10^{26}) ways to create a simple substitution table with twenty-six letters—way too many to check every one, even with the best computer. In addition, small changes in the key of many classical encryption methods cause only small changes in the ciphertext. For instance, if we switch two ciphertext symbols in a simple substitution table, the changes in the decryption result are only minor.

Hill climbing is only feasible when implemented as a computer program. Codebreakers have successfully used this method to break a wide range of encryption algorithms, including difficult machine ciphers such as the one used by the Enigma. Today, quite a few computer programs (for instance, CrypTool 2) support hill-climbing algorithms for codebreaking. However, codebreakers must still customize hill climbing for the system they are attacking. For this reason, a variety of hill-climbing implementations are available.

It is important to note that, while hill climbing is a powerful tool for breaking historically important ciphers, it is not suited at all to attacking modern encryption algorithms such as AES or DES. This is because modern encryption algorithms are not smooth, and a small change in their key or plaintext should cause a major change in the ciphertext.

Solving simple substitution ciphers with hill climbing

In this section, we explain the technique of hill climbing by applying it to a simple substitution ciphertext. As you will see later in this chapter, we can apply the same technique to other ciphers. Take a look at the following cryptogram, a challenge published in Sabine Baring-Gould's 1896 book *Curiosities of Olden Times:*[1, 2]

$$§ †431 \ 45 \ 2+9 \ +§51 \ 4=$$
$$8732+ \ 287 \ 45 \ 2+9 \ †¶=+$$

Let's first translate this cryptogram into a version that is easier for a computer program to process. We replace the symbol that appears first with A, the next one with B, the third one with C, and so on, keeping the word breaks:

```
A BCDE CF GHI HAFE CJ KLDGH GKL CF GHI BMJH
```

Step 1

We start by creating a random substitution table:

```
Plaintext:  ABCDEFGHIJKLMNOPQRSTUVWXYZ
Ciphertext: SNOIJRGYZLMBPDQWUVHFCTAXEK
```

Step 2

Then, we use the substitution table to decrypt the cryptogram, which gives us the following plaintext candidate:

```
S NOIJ OR GYZ YSRJ OL MBIGY GMB OR GYZ NPLY
```

Step 3

Now, we rate the correctness of the plaintext candidate with a so-called *fitness function*. Using a fitness function is the most sophisticated and critical part of a hill-climbing attack. There are many ways to check whether a certain text is more or less correct (i.e., whether it looks like real language). In our case, we take a simple approach based on letter frequencies. Advanced codebreakers will easily find better methods.

For each letter, we determine its frequency in the plaintext candidate and compare it with the distance from that frequency in an average English text of the same length. In our case, the ciphertext has thirty-three characters. Based on the fact that, in the English language, the letter *A* has a frequency of 8%, *B* of 1%, and *C* of 3%, we set the expected frequency of these letters in the plaintext candidate to three, zero, and one. The expected frequencies of the remaining letters are derived in a similar way.

Next, we compare the frequencies in the plaintext candidate with the expected frequencies and determine the distance:

Letter	Frequency in the plaintext candidate	Expected frequency	Distance
A	0	3	3
B	2	0	2
C	0	1	1
D	0	1	1
E	0	4	4
F	0	1	1
G	4	1	3
H	0	2	2
I	2	2	0
J	2	0	2
K	0	0	0
L	2	1	1
M	2	1	1
N	2	2	0
O	4	3	1
P	1	1	0
Q	0	0	0
R	3	2	1
S	2	2	0
T	0	3	3
U	0	1	1
V	0	0	0
W	0	1	1
X	0	0	0
Y	5	1	4
Z	2	0	2
			Sum: 34

The sum of the distances (here, thirty-four) is the result of the fitness function. The lower the result, the better the fit.

Step 4

Next, we slightly randomize the substitution table. In the following, the second line is the old substitution alphabet, while the third line is the new one:

```
Plaintext:       ABCDEFGHIJKLMNOPQRSTUVWXYZ
Old ciphertext:  SNOIJRGYZLMBPDQWUVHFCTAXEK
New ciphertext:  SNOIJFGYZLMBPDQWUVHRCTAXEK
```

As you can see, we have made only a small change, exchanging the positions of F and R.

Step 5

In the next step, we decrypt the ciphertext with the new substitution table and get a new plaintext candidate (the old plaintext is listed for comparison):

```
Old plaintext: S NOIJ OR GYZ YSRJ OL MBIGY GMB OR GYZ NPLY
New plaintext: S NOIJ OF GYZ YSFJ OL MBIGY GMB OF GYZ NPLY
```

Step 6

Again, we rate the correctness of the plaintext candidate with our fitness function:

Letter	Frequency in the plaintext candidate	Expected frequency	Distance
A	0	3	3
B	2	0	2
C	0	1	1
D	0	1	1
E	0	4	4
F	3	1	2
G	4	1	3
H	0	2	2
I	2	2	0
J	2	0	2
K	0	0	0
L	2	1	1
M	2	1	1

(continued)

Letter	Frequency in the plaintext candidate	Expected frequency	Distance
N	2	2	0
O	4	3	1
P	1	1	0
Q	0	0	0
R	0	2	2
S	2	2	0
T	0	3	3
U	0	1	1
V	0	0	0
W	0	1	1
X	0	0	0
Y	5	1	4
Z	2	0	2
			Sum: 36

The overall distance between the expected and real letter frequencies has become larger, which means that the correctness of the plaintext candidate has decreased. For this reason, we go back to the previous substitution alphabet. If there had been an improvement, we would have kept the current table.

Again, we change the substitution table slightly. Here, we have exchanged the positions of T and J:

```
Plaintext:       ABCDEFGHIJKLMNOPQRSTUVWXYZ
Old ciphertext:  SNOIJRGYZLMBPDQWUVHFCTAXEK
New ciphertext:  SNOITRGYZLMBPDQWUVHFCJAXEK
```

Step 5 (again)

We decrypt the ciphertext with the changed substitution table and get a new plaintext candidate:

```
Old plaintext: S NOIJ OR GYZ YSRJ OL MBIGY GMB OR GYZ NPLY
New plaintext: S NOIT OR GYZ YSRT OL MBIGY GMB OR GYZ NPLY
```

Step 6 (again)

Then, we rate the correctness of the plaintext candidate with our fitness function:

Letter	Frequency in the plaintext candidate	Expected frequency	Distance
A	0	3	3
B	2	0	2
C	0	1	1
D	0	1	1
E	0	4	4
F	0	1	1
G	4	1	3
H	0	2	2
I	2	2	0
J	0	0	0
K	0	0	0
L	2	1	1
M	2	1	1
N	2	2	0
O	4	3	1
P	1	1	0
Q	0	0	0
R	3	2	1
S	2	2	0
T	2	3	1
U	0	1	1
V	0	0	0
W	0	1	1
X	0	0	0
Y	5	1	4
Z	2	0	2
			Sum: 30

The result of the fitness function has now decreased, which means that the plaintext candidate looks more like a text in the English language. We therefore keep the table.

We repeat the procedure described in the previous paragraphs many times. If the new substitution table leads to a lower result from the fitness function, we keep it. Otherwise, we restore the previous table. We keep doing this until the result of the fitness function doesn't improve any further for, say, ten steps.

Usually, the last plaintext candidate is correct. However, there is no guarantee of this, as it is possible for a wrong plaintext candidate to deliver a better fitness function result than all of its tested neighbors, at which point, we call it a *local maximum*. In such a case, we simply restart the algorithm with a new randomly generated key. If several hill-climbing trials fail to produce a plaintext that makes sense, our assumption that we are dealing with a simple-substitution cryptogram might be wrong.

In the case of the Baring-Gould cryptogram, the correct plaintext is **A BIRD IN THE HAND IS WORTH TWO IN THE BUSH**. Here's the substitution table:

```
Plaintext:  ABIRDNTHESWOU
Ciphertext: ABCDEFGHIJKLM
```

Note that the plaintext contains only thirteen different letters.

Simulated annealing

To avoid getting stuck at local maxima, some codebreakers use a variation on hill climbing known as *simulated annealing*. Unlike regular hill climbing, a simulated-annealing algorithm moves to a new key candidate not only if the fitness function result improves but also, in some cases, when it decreases. In other words, the path from one key candidate to another can also go downhill. These downhill steps are, however, exceptions, which ensures that the general direction of our path is uphill, as shown in Figure 16-2.

The decision to take a downhill step depends on a random number and some configurable details. We can vary the probability of a downhill step during the process, based on a control parameter known as the *temperature*. A higher temperature means that downhill steps are more likely, and a lower temperature decreases their probability.

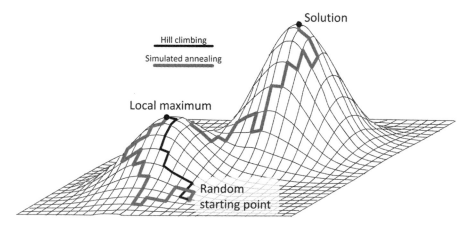

Figure 16-2: Simulated annealing is a variation on hill climbing. While the latter moves to a new key only if the fitness function result increases, simulated annealing allows for downhill steps.

Because simulated annealing allows for downhill steps, the algorithm can find a path leading away from a local maximum. However, simulated annealing is often slower than hill climbing, as the downhill steps cause the algorithm to take longer.

The term *simulated annealing* comes from the process of annealing in metallurgy, which is a method involving the heating and controlled cooling of a material to increase the size of its crystals and reduce their defects.

Success story: Bart Wenmeckers's solution to the Baring-Gould cryptogram

While CrypTool 2 supports hill climbing, some experienced codebreakers have written their own hill-climbing code, which allows them to adapt the fitness function and other parameters easily. This section considers the output of a program written by one of our colleagues, New Zealand-based crypto expert Bart Wenmeckers.[3]

Bart's program uses a much more sophisticated fitness function than the one above. It delivers a higher value each time a plaintext candidate looks more like real language. This is the opposite of what is done above. The program prints two lines when a substitution table delivers a better result than its predecessor. Here's an example:

```
AYISLNTHEPFRBDJXMWCQOKZGVU,313
A YISL IN THE HANL IP FRSTH TFR IN THE YDPH
```

This output indicates that the current substitution table is the following . . .

```
Plaintext:   ABCDEFGHIJKLMNOPQRSTUVWXYZ
Ciphertext:  AYISLNTHEPFRBDJXMWCQOKZGVU
```

. . . and that the result of the fitness function is 313. The output's second line is the plaintext candidate (see below). When Bart tried his program with the cryptogram from Sabine Baring-Gould's book, he received the following sequential results:

```
AYISLNTHEMBUQDVWCGPJZRXKOF,323
A YISL IN THE HANL IM BUSTH TBU IN THE YDMH

ARISDNTHEMBOUFQWKXCZGPVLYJ,327
A RISD IN THE HAND IM BOSTH TBO IN THE RFMH

ARISDNTHEMOBUFQWKXCZGPVLYJ,331
A RISD IN THE HAND IM OBSTH TOB IN THE RFMH

ARISDNTHEMOPUFQWKXCZGBVLYJ,333
A RISD IN THE HAND IM OPSTH TOP IN THE RFMH

ARISDNTHEGOPZFQWUXVJMBCLYK,334
A RISD IN THE HAND IG OPSTH TOP IN THE RFGH
```

```
ARISDNTHEGOFZPQWUXVJMBCLYK,343
A RISD IN THE HAND IG OFSTH TOF IN THE RPGH

ARISDNTHEMOFZPQWUXVJGBCLYK,347
A RISD IN THE HAND IM OFSTH TOF IN THE RPMH

ARISDNTHEMOFCYBKWXZJVLUGQP,348
A RISD IN THE HAND IM OFSTH TOF IN THE RYMH

ARISDNTHELOFZUJMBXCKGVQPYW,349
A RISD IN THE HAND IL OFSTH TOF IN THE RULH

ARILDNTHESOFJMXVUWGQCPBKZY,354
A RILD IN THE HAND IS OFLTH TOF IN THE RMSH

ARILDNTHESOFVUKMXGPYZJWCBQ,355
A RILD IN THE HAND IS OFLTH TOF IN THE RUSH

AMILDNTHESOFVUJQXGPYZKWCBR,357
A MILD IN THE HAND IS OFLTH TOF IN THE MUSH

AMIRDNTHESCOYUBQVXLPWZGJFK,358
A MIRD IN THE HAND IS CORTH TCO IN THE MUSH

ABIRDNTHESWOYUMXVQCZJLKGPF,365
A BIRD IN THE HAND IS WORTH TWO IN THE BUSH

ABIRDNTHESPOGUJMQXZYKCWLFV,366
A BIRD IN THE HAND IS PORTH TPO IN THE BUSH
```

As can be seen, Bart's program found the correct solution, rated 365, but didn't stop there. It rated **A BIRD IN THE HAND IS PORTH TPO IN THE BUSH** as an even better solution, with 366 points. Things like this can happen. Of course, a human watching the computer do its work would probably have guessed the correct solution much earlier than the computer, by operating as if they were on *Wheel of Fortune*.

Success story: The Florida murder case cryptogram

Some ciphers and cryptograms are associated with horrific crimes. In 2004, eleven-year-old Carlie Brucia was kidnapped from a car wash in Sarasota, Florida, and later killed. Based on a surveillance video, police identified car mechanic Joseph P. Smith as the murderer. In 2005, while in jail and awaiting his trial, he tried to send an encrypted message (Figure 16-3) to his brother.

The Cryptanalysis and Racketeering Records Unit (CRRU), the FBI's codebreaking unit, soon broke this cryptogram but did not publicly release any details.[4] In 2014, when Klaus read about the story in a 2005 FBI report,[5] he posted the encrypted message on his blog, after which, German crypto expert and CrypTool 2 developer Nils Kopal quickly solved it via hill climbing.[6]

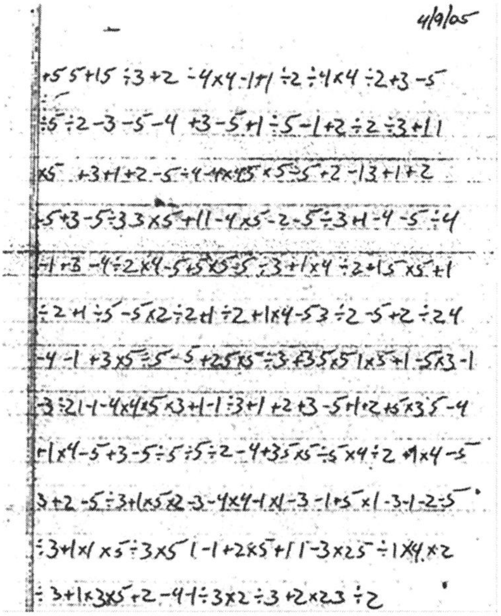

Figure 16-3: The murderer of Carlie Brucia tried to send this encrypted message from prison to his brother.

To start, Nils created the following transcript:

```
+5 5 +1 5 %3 +2 -4 x4 -1 +1 %2 %4 x4 %2 +3 -5
%5 %2 -3 -5 -4 +3 -5 +1 %5 -1 +2 %2 %3 +1 1
x5 +3 +1 +2 -5 %4 -4 x4 5 x5 -5 +2 -1 3 +1 +2
-5 +3 -5 %3 3 x5 +1 1 -4 x5 -2 -5 %3 +1 -4 -5 %4
-1 +3 -4 %2 x4 -5 +5 x5 -5 %3 +1 x4 %2 -1 5 x5 +1
%2 +1 %5 -5 x2 %2 +1 %2 +1 x4 -5 3 %2 -5 +2 %2 4
-4 -1 +3 x5 %5 -5 +2 5 x5 %3 +3 5 x5 1 x5 +1 -5 x3 -1
-3 %2 1 -1 -4 x4 x5 x3 +1 -1 %3 +1 +2 +3 -5 +1 +2 +5 x3 5 -4
+1 x4 -5 +3 -5 %5 %5 %2 -4 +3 5 x5 %5 x4 %2 +1 x4 -5
3 +2 -5 %3 +1 x5 x2 -3 -4 x4 -1 x1 -3 -1 +5 x1 -3 -1 -2 -5
%3 +1 x1 x5 %3 x5 1 -1 +2 x5 +1 1 -3 x2 5 %1 x4 x2
%3 +1 x3 x5 +2 -4 -1 %3 x2 %3 +2 x2 3 %2
```

Nils performed some statistical analyses involving letter frequency, the index of coincidence, and other tests. He realized that the cryptogram looked like a simple substitution cipher, but all his attempts to break it failed. So, he made some educated guesses, such as checking whether the text might have been written backward.

When he applied the simple-substitution hill climber in CrypTool 2 on the backward-written cryptogram, he succeeded immediately, deriving the following gruesome plaintext (which contains a number of spelling errors):

```
I WLSH L HAD SOMTHLN JULCY TO SAY OH OK THE BACKPACK AND CLOTHES
WENT IN FOUR DIFFERENT DUMPSTERS THAT MONDAY I CAME TO YOUR HOUSE
FOR ADVISE I WENT IT I LEFT IT OUT IN THE OPEN I DRAGED THE BODY
TO WHERE ST WAS FOUND DESTROY THIS AFTER DECIFERING IT AND SHUT UP
```

This leads to the following substitution table:

A	B	C	D	E	F	G	H	I	J	K	L	M	N	O	P	Q	R	S	T	U	V	W	X	Y	Z
-1	-2	-3	-4	-5	%5	%4	%3	%2	%1	x1	x2	x3	x4	x5	+5	+4	+3	+2	+1	5	4	3	2	1	

The letters **Q**, **X**, and **Z** don't appear in the plaintext. While the cipher-text equivalents of **Q** and **X** can be easily guessed (**Q**, for instance, lies between +5 and +3), the character for **Z** remains unknown.

In court, a CRRU specialist had presented the same result. Along with other evidence, it led to Smith being sentenced to death.

Solving a homophonic cipher with simulated annealing

When it comes to solving a homophonic cipher, hill climbing and simulated annealing are obvious methods to use. After all, a small change in the cipher's substitution table causes only small changes in the ciphertext. Moreover, because a homophonic cipher has far more potential keys than we can exhaustively check one by one, hill climbing, as well as simulated annealing, provides much more efficient methods than brute force. Since most implementations that we know of use simulated annealing for this purpose, we will focus on only simulated annealing for the following.

Solving a homophonic cipher with simulated annealing is a relatively new field of research, with only a few papers published on the topic to date. One frequently cited article, written by Nils Kopal in 2019, offers an introduction to the subject.[7] However, various researchers around the world are studying this area and may publish the results of their homophonic-simulated-annealing projects in the years ahead.

The best software for homophonic simulated annealing we have found, AZDecrypt, was written by Belgian codebreaking expert Jarl Van Eycke (who released version 1.21 in 2023). AZDecrypt comes with an impressive number of configuration options and implements a strong fitness function. It is available for free at *http://www.zodiackillerciphers.com*.

Success story: Dhavare, Low, and Stamp's Zodiac Killer solutions

One of the few research papers about hill-climbing attacks on homophonic ciphers that we know of is "Efficient Cryptanalysis of Homophonic Substitution Ciphers," published by Amrapali Dhavare, Richard M. Low, and Mark Stamp in 2013.[8] The authors describe a method that involves two hill-climbing steps: the first, called *outer hill climbing*, determines the number of homophones each plaintext letter maps to; while the second, *inner hill climbing*, reconstructs the substitution table.

Dhavare, Low, and Stamp initially tested their method on Z408, the first message written by the Zodiac Killer (see Chapter 6). Z408 was solved back in 1969, and the researchers wanted to see whether their algorithm could repeat this deciphering success. In fact, it could, quite easily (see Figure 16-4).

The authors next applied their technique to a homophonic cipher challenge, titled Zodiac Cipher, which was available on the crypto-puzzle platform MysteryTwister.[9] This challenge mimics Z340, the second Zodiac Killer message, which, unlike Z408, hadn't yet been solved. Again, the hill-climbing program had no trouble solving the cryptogram.

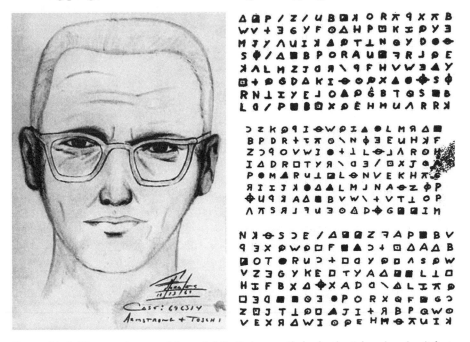

Figure 16-4: Dhavare, Low, and Stamp's hill climber easily broke the (already-solved) first Zodiac Killer message.

Finally, Dhavare, Low, and Stamp used their method to attack Z340 itself, which was one of the most famous unsolved mysteries in the world. Unfortunately, this time, they did not succeed. The details of their efforts can be seen in their article. For the trio of solvers that did manage to crack Z340 in 2020, see Chapter 6.

Solving a Vigenère cipher with hill climbing

As pointed out in Chapter 8, there are many ways to break a Vigenère cipher: some that require a computer and others that can be carried out by hand. One of the computer-based Vigenère-breaking methods is hill climbing. However, hill-climbing attacks on the Vigenère cipher seem to be less popular than on other ciphers, probably because there are efficient alternatives. We are not aware of a research paper that comprehensively covers Vigenère-cipher hill climbing, but at least a few implementations exist, including in CryptTool 2.

Hill-climbing software can either discover the keyword length as part of the hill climbing or determine the information in a different way. Most tools use the latter approach. The program either guesses the length of the keyword with Friedman's method before it starts the hill-climbing procedure, or it conducts a separate hill-climbing attack for every keyword length between, say, three and twenty-five.

These implementations can use the same fitness function as for a simple substitution cipher.

Success story: Jim Gillogly's solution to IRA Vigenère cryptograms

In 2001, historian Tom Mahon found around 300 documents containing encrypted messages in a Dublin archive. These documents originated from the estate of activist Moss Twomey (1897–1978), who was the leader of the IRA from 1926 to 1936. Most of the encrypted texts Mahon found were dispatches exchanged between the IRA headquarters in Dublin and IRA activists in the British Isles or the United States. In all, the corpus comprised about 1,300 individual cryptograms.

As Mahon lacked the expertise to decipher these messages, he asked the American Cryptogram Association for support. Our colleague, ACA member Jim Gillogly, became interested, initiating a fruitful partnership between the two researchers. Over the next months, Jim managed to decipher almost all the cryptograms Twomey had left behind, providing insights into the work and structure of the IRA in the 1920s. In 2008, Jim and Mahon published their results in a book titled *Decoding the IRA*.[10] The book is an interesting read about Irish history, and the first chapter, in which Jim explains his decryptions, is a fascinating resource for anyone interested in codebreaking.

As it turned out, most of the IRA ciphertexts were encrypted using a column-based transposition, which is covered in the next section of this chapter. A smaller share consisted of short ciphertext passages, which contained strikingly many ampersand characters, embedded in cleartext sentences. The following message (dated May 4, 1923) is a typical example:

1.   Have you yet got X&OYC&UIJO&MN? Did you look up that man
FX&WA HKGKH/ whom I spoke to you about. I am most anxious that
this case be followed up.   I would suggest that if nesessary you put
your Staff Officer entirely on it until it is carried through.

Here's a transcript of the first two sentences:

Have you yet got X&OYC&UIJO&MN? Did you look up that man FX&WA
HKGKH/ whom I spoke to you about.

The letter frequencies and some other statistics suggested that its author had applied a Vigenère cipher. Hoping that the author had used the same key for each of these ciphertexts, Jim selected the first six letters of each one. As he didn't know what to do with the ampersand, he ignored all six-letter blocks that contained this character. The following twenty-two remained:

SDRDPX VVQDTY WXGKTX SJMCEK LPMOCG MVLLWK HMNMLJ VDBDFX UMDMWO
GGCOCS MMNEYJ KHAKCQ LPQXLI HMHQLT IJMPWG DDMCEX HVQDSU OISOCX
DXNXEO IJLWPS IJNBOO OIREAK

Jim fed this block series into a hill-climbing program of his own design, starting with a keyword length of six. Although the twenty-two blocks came from different ciphertexts, characteristics reflected by the fitness function remained valid. In fact, the hill climber found a six-letter keyword candidate that produced promising results right away:

```
MISTER PARTIS QCHAIR MONSTE FUNERA FAMBLE BROCAD PICTUR ORECLI
ALDERM GROUND EMBARK FURNAC BRIGAN CONFLA XINSTR BARTHO INTERR
XCONTI COMMEM COORDI INSUPE
```

As every six-letter block represented a plausible English letter sequence, Jim knew that he was on the right track.

The hill climber had delivered the keyword GVZKLG. Jim used it to decrypt all the Vigenère messages and learned that the ampersand served as a replacement for the letter **Z**, which is why no **Z** appears in the ciphertexts. The message shown above decrypted to the following plaintext (the **Z** and **X** in **Z XCAMPBELLZ** were used for padding):

```
Have you yet got REPORT ON KEOGH? Did you look up that man
ZCAMPBELLX whom I spoke to you about.
```

Why did the IRA use the keyword GVZKLG? After some experimentation, Jim found that it was the word **TEAPOT** encrypted with a simple substitution cipher, based on the following substitution table:

```
Plaintext:  ABCDEFGHIJKLMNOPQRSTUVWXYZ
Ciphertext: ZYXWVUTSRQPONMLKJIHGFEDCBA
```

As you can see, the substitution used an easy-to-remember backward alphabet.

Solving a columnar transposition with hill climbing

We can use hill climbing to solve both complete and incomplete columnar transposition ciphers, which are described in Chapters 9 and 10. However, the fitness function employed to break a simple substitution cipher doesn't work here. In general, we can't break a transposition with any fitness function that is based on the frequency of letters, because transposing letters doesn't change their frequencies.

Instead, we can rely on the frequency of letter groups to rate the correctness of a plaintext candidate. We have encountered anything from letter pairs (digraphs) to groups of eight letters (octagraphs) used in this context.

Next, we need a way to change the transposition cipher's key slightly. If we are dealing with a columnar transposition of, say, ten columns, we can write the key like this:

```
8,4,5,2,9,7,1,10,3,6.
```

To make a small change in the key, we might switch two randomly chosen numbers in this sequence. For instance, 8,4,5,2,9,7,1,10,3,6 might become 8,4,1,2,9,7,5,10,3,6.

Note that the keyword used to encrypt a columnar transposition ciphertext doesn't play a role in this process. Hill climbing works even if the keyword is a random string, like VKWJIDPQFH, and delivers the plaintext without re-creating the original keyword. In fact, determining the keyword is often impossible, as there might be several equivalent ones.

Breaking an incomplete columnar transposition is, of course, more complex than solving a complete one. Still, we can think of the process as merely a special case of solving complete columnar transpositions. Because a computer usually does this task using a hill-climbing program, the complexity is generally not a problem, but the task may take longer.

If we do not know the length of the keyword (as is usually the case in practice), we have two possible approaches. First, we can make the keyword length a part of the key and change it slightly between hill-climbing rounds; however, this adds to the complexity of the program. The better approach is usually to perform several hill-climbing attacks for different keyword lengths. If we assume that the keyword has a length of between five and twenty letters, then we need sixteen tries—not much of a problem for today's computers.

The software CrypTool 2 includes a powerful transposition hill climber. Bernhard Esslinger, the head of the CrypTool project, has demonstrated that this hill climber (even running on a PC) can easily break some of the IRA transposition cryptograms introduced in Chapter 10 within two minutes.

Success story: Jim Gillogly's solution to IRA transposition cryptograms

Let's return to that 2008 book *Decoding the IRA* by Jim Gillogly and Tom Mahon. The following IRA cryptogram is one of six messages that Mahon, the historian, initially sent to the American Cryptogram Association in 2005. It was subsequently shared on the association's mailing list and then solved by Jim:

```
AEOOA IIIEO AEAEW LFRRD ELBAP RAEEA EIIIE AAAHO IFMFN COUMA
FSOSG NEGHS YPITT WUSYA ORDOO ERHNQ EEEVR TTRDI SOSDR ISIEE ISUTI
ERRAS TTKAH LFSUG RDLKP UEYDM ERNEO RULDC ERWTE ICNIA T
```

This cryptogram consists of 151 letters. When analyzing the ciphertext, Jim saw that E was by far the most common letter, with twenty-three appearances, followed by A, R, and I. The letters Q, B, and V turned out to be very rare. These frequencies are consistent with the English language, although the ratio of vowels (47%) seemed a little high (40% is typical). Jim assumed that he was dealing with a transposition cipher. As 151 is a prime number, it could not be a complete columnar transposition, but an incomplete one seemed possible.

In his forty years as a codebreaker, Jim had written a considerable amount of cryptanalysis software for his personal use. Among other things, he was one of the first to use hill climbing for cryptanalysis. To solve this particular encryption, he used a hill-climbing program tailored to breaking an incomplete columnar transposition, assuming a line length of between eight and fifteen and starting separate runs for each length. When he tried a length of twelve, he received the following plaintext candidate:

```
THEAADDARESSTOWHECIEHYOUWILLOESENDSTUFFFOR . . .
```

This string, as you can tell, contains many words that make sense. It is even possible to read a meaningful sentence from it (**THE ADDRESS TO WHICH YOU WILL SEND STUFF . . .**). However, quite a few letters seem unnecessary.

Jim restarted his hill-climbing program about a hundred times, with a different initial keyword candidate on each occasion, but he didn't get a better result. His software had determined that the keyword was FDBJALHCGKEI—certainly not the original one used by the IRA, but equivalent. For further analysis, he looked at the transposition table his program had created:

```
FDBJALHCGKEI
------------
THEAADDARESS
TOWHECIEHYOU
WILLOESENDST
UFFFOROAQMGI
SMRSAWSEEENE
YFRUITDIERER
ANDGIERIENGR
OCERIIFIVEHA
ROLDECSEROSS
DUBLONIATRYT
OMAKAIEATUET
OAPPEAEARLLK
EFRHATI
```

Jim immediately recognized why his software had delivered strange results. The encipherer had inserted two columns (the fifth and eighth) of meaningless vowels into the table. In addition, his hill-climbing program had switched the L and H columns. Here is the correct table (with the extra vowels omitted):

```
FDBJAHLCGKEI
------------
THEA DD RESS
TOWH IC HYOU
WILL SE NDST
UFFF OR QMGI
SMRS SW EENE
YFRU DT ERER
ANDG RE ENGR
OCER FI VEHA
ROLD SC ROSS
DUBL IN TRYT
OMAK EI TUET
OAPP EA RLLK
EFRH IT
```

The correct plaintext reads as follows:

THE ADDRESS TO WHICH YOU WILL SEND STUFF FOR QMG IS MRS SWEENEY
FRUDTERER AND GREENGROCER FIVE HAROLD'S CROSS DUBLIN TRY TO MAKE
IT UP TO APPEAR LIKE FRUIT.

The actual keyword used by the IRA has never been determined.

Success story: Richard Bean's solution to the last unsolved IRA cryptogram

As described in the previous section, Jim Gillogly solved hundreds of transposition cryptograms left behind by IRA activist Moss Twomey, but there was one he couldn't break:

GTHOO RCSNM EOTDE TAEDI NRAHE EBFNS INSGD AILLA YTTSE AOITDE

In the Twomey files, every encrypted message has a header that indicates its length. In this case, the number of letters is specified to be fifty-two, though the ciphertext consists of only fifty-one characters. It was clear that something had gone wrong; perhaps this was the reason Jim had not succeeded in breaking the message.

In 2018, our colleague Richard Bean, a mathematician from Brisbane, Australia, specializing in combinatorics and statistics, became interested in this cryptogram after reading Jim Gillogly and Tom Mahon's book.[11] He tried to solve it with hill climbing, checking different keyword lengths and iteratively improving his fitness function. Drawing from George Lasry's PhD thesis,[12] he realized that hexagraph frequencies would prove especially helpful for distinguishing meaningful text from gibberish. He also noticed that a keyword length of eleven produced the best hill-climbing scores. When adding letters to all different parts of the ciphertext, he received the most meaningful results by inserting a character between the two Es (letters twenty-five and twenty-six).

Richard also observed that, in some of the best-scoring ciphertext candidates, the string **LIGNIT** appeared. As the IRA used gelignite (an explosive) in the 1920s, this discovery provided a potential crib. When Richard forced the string **GELIGNIT** into the hill-climbing output, many other meaningful words became visible, such as **THEYRAID** and **ANDOBTAINED**. The additional letter ended up in the string **SCOT*AND**, so he could easily identify it as an **L**. Finally, Richard detected the following plaintext:

REGELIGNITSCOTLANDSTAESTHEYRAIDEANDOBTAINEDOMEOFTHLS

Here is the message in a more readable form: **RE GELIGNIT[E] SCOTLAND STA[T]ES THEY RAIDE[D] AND OBTAINED [S]OME OF THLS**.

Note that four letters in the plaintext (**E**, **T**, **D**, and **S**) are missing and that there's a typo in the last word. Along with the missing ciphertext letter **L**, these mistakes made it extremely difficult to break the message. After some more analysis, Richard found that he could obtain a better result if he assumed a twelve-letter keyword and an additional column in the transposition table containing the letters **E**, **T**, **D**, and **S** (four of the missing plaintext letters). Because the original location of this additional column isn't known, it is very difficult to determine the keyword used. As we will show, **BCAFIEHGKDLJ** works, though this is certainly not the keyword used by the IRA.

Based on this information, we can reconstruct the process by which the message was encrypted. We start with the plaintext, including the letters **E**, **T**, **D**, **S**, and **L** (which were lost at a later point in time) and keeping the typo in the last word:

```
RE GELIGNITE SCOTLAND STATES THEY RAIDED AND OBTAINED SOME OF THLS
```

Next, we write this text below the keyword. (Note that the letters **E**, **T**, **D**, and **S** appear in the next-to-last column.)

```
BCAFIEHGKDLJ
------------
REGELIGNITES
COTLANDSTATE
STHEYRAIDEDA
NDOBTAINEDSO
MEOFTHLS
```

Now, we transpose the columns such that the keyword letters are in alphabetical order:

```
ABCDEFGHIJKL
------------
GRETIENGLSIE
TCOANLSDAETT
HSTEREIAYADD
ONDDABNITOES
OME HFSLT
```

Reading out the text column-wise, we receive:

```
GTHOO RCSNM EOTDE TAEDI NRAHE LEBFN SINSG DAILL AYTTS EAOIT DEETDS
```

This message consists of fifty-six letters. Somehow, the final five characters were later lost (the ETDS at the end and the L in LEBEN):

```
GTHOO RCSNM EOTDE TAEDI NRAHE L̶EBFN SINSG DAILL AYTTS EAOIT DEE̶T̶D̶S̶
```

In August 2019, Richard Bean informed Klaus and Jim of this solution he had found. Jim was able to verify it, confirming that it was correct. Over a decade after his initial success, the last of Twomey's messages had finally been deciphered.

Success story: George Lasry's solution of the double columnar transposition challenge

In 1999, Otto Leiberich, the former president of the German crypto authority *Zentralstelle für das Chiffrierwesen (ZfCh)*, or the Central Authority for Cipher Affairs, published an article in the German science journal *Spektrum der Wissenschaft*.[13] In this article, Leiberich discussed double columnar transposition (see Chapter 10), which East German agents had used during the Cold War.

Double columnar transposition is one of the best manual ciphers known. Leiberich and his team worked intensively on the cryptanalysis of this method, and in 1974, one of their results led to the unmasking of a top spy: Günter Guillaume, the personal secretary of the West German Chancellor, Willy Brandt. Guillaume had been feeding information to the East Germans. He was arrested, tried, and sentenced to prison but freed in 1981 as part of a prisoner exchange.

In his 1999 article, published long after the end of the Cold War, Leiberich encouraged researchers to study double columnar transposition further, for the technique's historical value. He also suggested that a challenge cryptogram be created with this cipher. His recommendations for this challenge included the following items:

- Both keywords should have twenty to twenty-five characters.
- The lengths of the two keywords should have no common divisor except one.
- The length of the ciphertext should not be a multiple of the length of either keyword.
- The ciphertext should have approximately five hundred characters (roughly the product of the lengths of the two keywords).

Leiberich never published a challenge of this kind himself, so Klaus decided to do so because he was always interested in challenging his readers. He chose a few paragraphs from the 1910 novel *Mistress Wilding* by Rafael Sabatini and encrypted them using two keywords consisting of English phrases with twenty to twenty-five letters.[14] The length of the plaintext was 599. Klaus published this challenge ciphertext in 2007 in an online article:[15]

```
VESINTNVONMWSFEWNOEALWRNRNCFITEEICRHCODEE
AHEACAEOHMYTONTDFIFMDANGTDRVAONRRTORMTDHE
OUALTHNFHHWHLESLIIAOETOUTOSCDNRITYEELSOAN
GPVSHLRMUGTNUITASETNENASNNANRTTRHGUODAAAR
AOEGHEESAODWIDEHUNNTFMUSISCDLEDTRNARTMOOI
REEYEIMINFELORWETDANEUTHEEEENENTHEOOEAUEA
EAHUHICNCGDTUROUTNAEYLOEINRDHEENMEIAHREED
OLNNIRARPNVEAHEOAATGEFITWMYSOTHTHAANIUPTA
DLRSRSDNOTGEOSRLAAAURPEETARMFEHIREAQEEOIL
SEHERAHAOTNTRDEDRSDOOEGAEFPUOBENADRNLEIAF
```

```
RHSASHSNAMRLTUNNTPHIOERNESRHAMHIGTAETOHSE
NGFTRUANIPARTAORSIHOOAEUTRMERETIDALSDIRUA
IEFHRHADRESEDNDOIONITDRSTIEIRHARARRSETOIH
OKETHRSRUAODTSCTTAFSTHCAHTSYAOLONDNDWORIW
HLENTHHMHTLCVROSTXVDRESDR
```

Neither Klaus nor Leiberich expected that this cryptogram could be broken; however, six years later, in 2013, Klaus received an email from our colleague, the then-unknown Israeli George Lasry, who claimed to have solved the double columnar transposition challenge. His solution proved correct:

```
THEGIRLHADARRIVEDATLUPTONHOUSEAHALFHOURAH
EADOFMISSWESTMACOTTANDUPONHERARRIVALSHEHA
DEXPRESSEDSURPRISEEITHERFEIGNEDORREALATFI
NDINGRUTHSTILLABSENTDETECTINGTHEALARMTHAT
DIANAWASCAREFULTOTHROWINTOHERVOICEANDMANN
ERHERMOTHERQUESTIONEDHERANDELICITEDTHESTO
RYOFHERFAINTNESSANDOFRUTHSHAVINGRIDDENONA
LONETOMRWILDINGSSOOUTRAGEDWASLADYHORTONTH
ATFORONCEINAWAYTHISWOMANUSUALLYSOMEEKANDE
ASELOVINGWASROUSEDTOANENERGYANDANGERWITHH
ERDAUGHTERANDHERNIECETHATTHREATENEDTOREMO
VEDIANAATONCEFROMTHEPERNICIOUSATMOSPHEREO
FLUPTONHOUSEANDCARRYHERHOMETOTAUNTONRUTHF
OUNDHERSTILLATHERREMONSTRANCESARRIVEDINDE
EDINTIMEFORHERSHAREOFTHEM
```

Interestingly, George had found two different methods for breaking the challenge. In the first, a dictionary attack, his computer program had guessed the two keywords: **PREPONDERANCEOFEVIDENCE** and **TOSTAYYOUFROMELECTION**. His second method was based on hill climbing. Later, Jim came up with a third method: using a computer program, he checked all nineteenth-century texts available online and identified the one Klaus had chosen.

Readers interested in this ingenious act of cryptanalysis are advised to read George's 2014 publication in *Cryptologia* (co-written with Arno Wacker and Nils Kopal).[16] If you are interested in an even more difficult cryptogram of this type, see the "Double Columnar Transposition Reloaded Challenge" in the "Challenges" section of Chapter 10.

Solving a turning grille cipher with hill climbing

Hill climbing has proven to be a very powerful method of breaking turning grille cryptograms. As we will show, we can solve even large turning grilles, consisting of 20×20 squares or more, with this technique. This is because we can easily construct a turning grille of size $2n \times 2n$ with an $n \times n$ matrix, as described in Chapter 11. As an example, the following diagram shows how a 3 × 3 matrix can become a 6 × 6 grille:

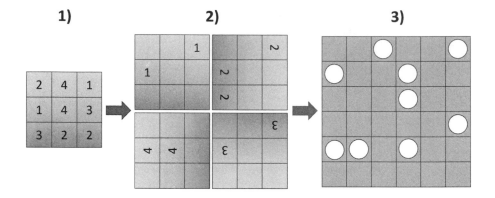

In a computer program, the number sequence in the 3 × 3 matrix (2,4,1,1,4,3,3,2,2) can represent the grille, which serves as this encryption method's key. Next, we need a way to change the grille slightly. We can do this, for instance, by adding 2 to one of the numbers representing the grille, as in the following example. If the result were greater than 4, we would subtract 4 from it:

```
Old key: 2,4,1,1,4,3,3,2,2
New key: 2,4,3,1,4,3,3,2,2
```

For a turning grille hill climber, we also need to modify the kind of fitness function that we employ to rate the correctness of a plaintext candidate. We can't base it on the frequency of letters, as this kind of encryption doesn't change a plaintext's letter frequencies. (No transposition cipher does.) Instead, we might create a fitness function based on the frequencies of digraphs, trigraphs, or other *n*-graphs.

The computer program JCrypTool offers a turning grille solver based on hill climbing.

Success story: Bart Wenmeckers's solution to a turning grille cryptogram

In Chapter 11, we mentioned that the Italian crypto-history expert Paolo Bonavoglia recently found a turning grille cryptogram in a notebook belonging to his famous grandfather, Luigi Sacco (1883–1970).[17] After solving the cryptogram himself, Paolo also published it as a challenge in the "Cryptograms & Classical Ciphers" Facebook group. Our colleague Bart Wenmeckers, the host of the group, took up the challenge.[18]

Like many other specialists in breaking classical ciphers, Bart makes frequent use of hill climbing, employing a modified program that he wrote himself. The program returns the grille written in a line, with the letter C representing a hole and D representing no hole. It also returns the result of its fitness function (the higher, the better) and the plaintext candidate produced each time that result increases. Here's the final part of the log of Bart's hill-climbing attack on Sacco's turning grille cryptogram:

```
DDCCCDCDDDDDDDDCDDCDDDDDDCDDDDDDDDDCDDCCCCDDDDDDD, 323
NOSPDSEHERSEEUCHNGENDWITRSTWRKECYHEIESULLIUNTEXE

DDCCCDCDDDDDDDDCDDCDDDDDDCDDDDDDDDDCCDCCDCDDDDDDD, 329
NOSPDSEHWEREESUCHNGENDITRTWURKECYHEIESLLIUNTEXSE

DDCCCDCDDDDDDDDDDCDDDDDDCDDDDDDDCDCCDCCDCDDDDDDD, 334
NOSPSECHWEREESCHNGENDXITRTWURDKEYHEIESULLIUNTESE

DDCCCDDDDDDDDDDDDCDDDDDDCDDDDDDDCDCCDCCDCCDDDDDD, 344
NOSSECHWEREYEESCHNGENDXIPRTWURDKEHEISULLIUNTESET

CDCCCDDDDDDDDDDDDCDDDDDDCDDDDDDDCDCCDCCDCDDDDDDD, 362
ENOSSECHWEREEPSCHNGENDXIRTWURDKEHEITSULLIUNTESYE

CDCCCDDDDDDDDDDDDCCDDDDDDDDDDDDDCDCCDCCDCDDDDDDD, 385
ENOSISCHWEREEPSCHENGNDXIRTWURDEEHEITSULLUNKTESYE

DDCCCDDDDDDDDDDDDCCDDDDDDDDDDDDDDDCDCCDCCDCDDDDDDC, 402
NOSISCHWERETESCHENGNDXYIERTWURDEEHEISPULLUNKTESE

DDCCDDDDDDDDDDCDCCDDDDDDDDDDDDDDDDCDCCDCCDCDDDDDDC, 410
NOLLICHWERETESSSCHENGXYIERTWURDENDEISPUUNKTEESHE

DDDDDCDDDCCDCCDCDDDDDDDDDDDDDDDDDCCDCDDDDDDDDDDCCDC, 416
STWURDENDEITUUNKTEESEYHEENOLLICHWERIESPRSSCHENGX

CDDDDCDDDCCDCCDCDDDDDDDDDDDDDDDDDCCDCDDDDDDDDDDCCDD, 424
ESTWURDENDEIPUUNKTEESEHENOLLICHWERITESRSSCHENGXY

CDDDDCDDDCCDCCDCDDDDDDDDDDDDDDDDDCCDDDDDDDDDDDCCCDD, 425
ESTWURDENHEIPULUNKTEESEENOSLICHWERITERSSCHENGDXY

CDDDDCDDDCCDCCDCDDDDDDDDDDDDDDDDDCCDDDDDDDDDDDCCCDD, 428
ESTWURDEEHEIPULLUNKTESEENOSISCHWERITERSCHENGNDXY

CDDDDCDDDDCDCCDCDDDDDDDDDDDDDDDDDCCDCDDDDCDDDDDCCDD, 442
ESWURDENDREIPUNKTEGESEHENOTLLICHWEITESRSSUCHENXY
```

If you know German (the language of the original message), you'll see words show up immediately. Here's the plaintext (the mistakes were present in the original): **ES WURDEN DREI PUNKTE GESEHEN OTLLICH WEITESRSSUCHEN XY**.

It translates to **THREE POINTS HAVE BEEN SEEN. KEEP ON SEARCHING IN THE EAST XY.** The **X** and **Y** at the end of the message are almost certainly padding that was added to ensure a plaintext of exactly forty-eight letters.

Success story: Armin Krauss's solution to a turning grille challenge

Can a 20×20 turning grille cryptogram be broken with hill climbing? Because Klaus had never found an answer to this question in the literature, he decided to create a challenge for his blog readers that tested the idea. He took an English text consisting of 400 letters, encrypted it with a 20×20 turning grille, and published the ciphertext on his blog in 2017:[19]

```
ENPAIGEZLANEDMTHSENF
EIORDEMATANNATMOOFSL
AEPLMHOIERITOECDMVNE
OXNPBROEDOIETRANEEIU
XPNPONRNTAREOMMYDWIT
IANHTNEIOODNSOUOTETD
MOOVEARPHRIOLAEGNALN
INATTFINOREATDNGWDDA
UHSIEURININGTTEDASTN
ATGHPEESAOMEISEADRMM
YANTSOEJOESYTERTHACH
BNINCALURDCHLEALLHLA
OIFWESTEHENGREERRTHE
SAAMSIBEIOVNSAINARLI
DTESGIIETTUCNARILYLO
ESENRUUISINEADSRANLA
COUWNEAUETCPOHRNSDTW
BYEOFNINGHERHIVNTOTE
MNTBERAEHEUNSPNSUTIX
NPOITYPFIKSAVULEATRA
```

Three days after Klaus's publication, our colleague Armin Krauss posted the solution:[20]

```
PLANS FOR MANNED MOON EXPEDITIONS ORIGINATED DURING THE EISENHOWER
ERA IN AN ARTICLE SERIES WERNHER VON BRAUN POPULARIZED THE IDEA
OF A MOON EXPEDITION A MANNED MOON LANDING POSED MANY TECHNICAL
CHALLENGES BESIDES GUIDANCE AND WEIGHT MANAGEMENT ATMOSPHERIC
REENTRY WITHOUT OVERHEATING WAS A MAJOR HURDLE AFTER THE SOVIET
UNIONS LAUNCH OF THE SPUTNIK SATELLITE VON BRAUN PROMOTED A PLAN
FOR THE UNITED STATES ARMY TO ESTABLISH A MILITARY LUNAR OUTPOST
BY NINETEEN SIXTY FIVE
```

Armin had used a hill-climbing and simulated-annealing program of his own design to break this cryptogram. The fitness function he applied was based on trigraph frequencies. In addition, Armin used a sequence of numbers between one and four to represent a grille, as explained in the introduction to this section. In each round, he changed one of the numbers at random.

Because the original ciphertext contained a mistake, Armin had to perform some additional manual codebreaking. After he learned via Google that Klaus's plaintext was derived from a Wikipedia article, he managed to solve the challenge in spite of the error.

Solving a general digraph substitution with hill climbing

Hill climbing is a perfect approach to solving general digraph substitutions. This technique resembles the breaking of simple substitution ciphers; we can even use a comparable fitness function, based on letter or n-graph frequencies, to check whether a plaintext candidate looks like real language. However, we need a larger substitution table (one with 676 columns, in the case of a twenty-six-letter alphabet) and a larger ciphertext.

Success story: Some digraph challenges

Because researchers have published little in the field of general digraph substitution, Klaus decided to challenge his blog readers with digraph cryptograms. This led to a series of notable codebreaking records:

- In February 2017, on his blog, Klaus published two digraph challenges: "Bigram 5000" and "Bigram 2500."[21] *Bigram* is another word for *digraph*, while 2,500 and 5,000 were the number of letters contained in the challenge ciphertexts. Within three days, German codebreaker Norbert Biermann, supported by Armin Krauß, found both plaintexts with a hill-climbing program of Norbert's own design.

- Two years later, in July 2019, Klaus created a new and even shorter challenge. This time, the ciphertext consisted of only 1,346 letters: the "Bigram 1346."[22] Four weeks later, Biermann once again broke this challenge, setting a new record.[23]

- A few months later, in October 2019, Klaus challenged his readers yet again with an even shorter ciphertext of the same kind, consisting of exactly 1,000 letters.[24] Again, the cryptogram was broken quickly, setting another record. This time, the solution came from two blog readers: Jarl Van Eycke of Belgium and Louie Helm of Switzerland, who worked together.[25] They solved the challenge with a highly sophisticated hill-climbing program that included a fitness function based on octagraph frequencies. Given that a twenty-six-letter alphabet can generate approximately 200 billion eight-letter blocks, the codebreakers needed huge amounts of text to generate useful reference statistics. They used about two terabytes of English text taken from a database they created from millions of books, all of Wikipedia, seven billion words extracted from Usenet posts, and more.

- Two months later, in December 2019, Klaus published an even shorter challenge, consisting of only 750 letters: "Bigram 750."[26] Again, Van Eycke and Helm solved it within two days.[27]

- After Van Eycke and Helm's success, Klaus published the "Bigram 600" challenge in March 2020 (see Chapter 12).

As of this writing, the "Bigram 750" ciphertext remains the shortest general digraph cryptogram ever solved.

Solving a Playfair cipher with hill climbing

Hill climbing has proven very efficient for breaking Playfair cryptograms. It works much better than the manual codebreaking technique we introduced in Chapter 12. It is also superior to a dictionary attack, as it doesn't require the codebreaker to derive the Playfair matrix from a guessable keyword.

To introduce a small change in the Playfair matrix, all we need to do is switch the positions of two letters. Defining a fitness function is also straightforward, because we can rely on letter frequencies to judge whether a plaintext candidate looks like real language. Using the frequencies of other *n*-graphs (ranging from digraphs to octagraphs) can be even more helpful for deducing the final plaintext.

How quickly could a computer handle this task? The software CrypTool 2 features a powerful Playfair hill climber, named Playfair Analyzer, which includes a fitness function based on hexagraph frequencies. Esslinger, the head of the CrypTool project, showed us how this component performed on a Playfair cryptogram from Dorothy L. Sayers's 1932 novel *Have His Carcase*. In Chapter 12, we dedicated multiple pages to describing how difficult this same cryptogram is to break without computer support. Figure 16-5 shows how Playfair Analyzer works.

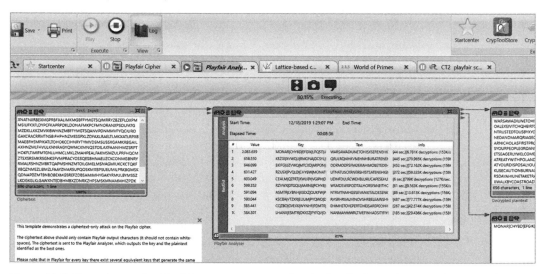

Figure 16-5: The software CrypTool 2, running on a PC, breaks the Playfair cryptogram from Dorothy L. Sayers's novel Have His Carcase *within a minute.*

After the user has copied the ciphertext into the left window and started the hill climber, the software displays every climbing step in the middle window. CrypTool 2 needs about a minute to produce both the cryptogram's key and the plaintext. Even an experienced codebreaker would require hours to perform this task without computer support.

The software displays the following correct Playfair matrix, written on one line, in the lower-right window. It uses the keyword **MONARCHY**:

MONAR|CHYBD|EFGIK|LPQST|UVWXZ

You can see the plaintext in the upper-right window or reproduced in Chapter 12.

Success story: Dan Girard's solution to the Cheltenham Letter Stone

In 2005, British artist Gordon Young created the *Listening Stones* in Cheltenham, United Kingdom (see Chapter 4). Two of these ten-foot-tall stones, called the Number Stone and the Letter Stone, bear encrypted inscriptions. Here is the message on the Letter Stone, as provided to us by the sculptor:

```
EC KH LO PT OA DL LU AB KW LO YS NA EC BF MZ FA LC NQ XR UT DK
SQ KH EC ZK NL CK SQ CB SA SA QU LF MZ IV FA LC OA VB OK CK AV
DY SY LO WL KL NI BH BX LO MY VA EK AP LB CW PY OA OK MO AV BL
VM PK LC UP BY KQ MK BN AN BF GA YM LO AK NI BP PI HT TI NT CV
EC FI LW CQ GL TI KL NI BH RP GZ SU LQ AS YT GA VB FW NM XC UP
EB NA WL ID PM ZK LM WL RO VI AO LC IC VI KQ FW OA PA XC UP EQ
SO PM QU MB PU CL VA KI OM NE LM BF UP IG BC FR LO CV KI OM VT
BF YF IP EQ CQ SX NK MZ CQ YS GZ BF UI XD SQ QK AG KL SQ YF PM
RF TV KE CW LW ME VA KN UP FA UI FI KM NQ XR AV TR LO CV EL NL
LQ FY UP PN NK IG NO BN EC NP BF GA NE HM IV FY DQ LM YF DQ AM
BP NI KF LU BN RY UK NA KI OM WF SO OK KQ OA BL KL QA BL VK CK
HL MP TO AG QT PI HL TI NT CV EC IA SL LM YF RL HT IP PS CW CW
```

Figure 16-6 shows the sculpture. When Klaus learned about this cryptogram in 2015, it was still unsolved. According to the sculptor, the digraphs on the stone were a message encrypted using a Playfair cipher. However, he didn't remember the details of the encryption, let alone the key.

Figure 16-6: The Letter Stone, a sculpture located next to the GCHQ Headquarters in Cheltenham, UK, bears a Playfair-encrypted inscription, arrows, and letter pairs within each of the circles.

Klaus published an article about this cryptogram on his blog in September 2015.[28] After only a few hours, blog reader Dan Girard posted the solution, having broken it with his own hill-climbing program. It turned out that the keyword was **LECKHAMPTON**. Here's the beginning of the plaintext:

```
LECKHAMPTON CHIMNEY HAS FALLEN DOWN
THE BIRDS OF CRICKLEY HAVE CRIED IT IT IS KNOWN IN THE TOWN
THE CLIFXFS HAVE CHANGED WHAT WILL COME NEXT XTO THAT LINE
WATCHER OF WEST ENGLAND NOW THAT LANDMARK OAS FALXLEN . . .
```

Devil's Chimney is a rock formation at Leckhampton Hill, near Cheltenham.

Success story: Playfair world records

In Chapter 12, we mentioned that in 1936, the American cryptanalyst Alf Monge broke a thirty-letter Playfair message based on a keyword.[29] In 2018, Klaus wanted to know how short a Playfair cryptogram a codebreaker could solve if the matrix was not keyword based, meaning a dictionary attack wouldn't work. Thus, he presented a series of increasingly difficult Playfair challenges on his blog, along with corresponding solutions provided by readers. Most of the codebreaking work depended on hill climbing and simulated annealing.

As far as we are aware, the cryptanalysis results produced over the course of these challenges represent the best results of such an experiment. This means that they set world records, the last of which is still valid as of this writing. We and the challenge solvers published these codebreaking success stories in an article titled "How We Set New World Records in Breaking Playfair Ciphertexts," in *Cryptologia*.[30] In the following, we will present a summary of this article.

In April 2018, Klaus published on his blog a fifty-letter Playfair message not based on a keyword:[31]

```
MQ VS KP EV IS BA WK TP KP PN AU NU NE GL UZ TY UZ LY GC TZ KN KU
ST AG CT NQ
```

The challenge didn't remain a mystery for long; our colleague George Lasry solved it on the same day with a simulated annealing program of his own design. His fitness function used statistics about hexagraphs. Here's the plaintext:

```
WHILE IN PARIS I RECEIVED ORDERS TO REPORT X TO GENERAL FOSTER X
```

In December 2018, Klaus created another challenge, based on a plaintext with only forty letters:[32]

```
OF FC ER VU MW MO OM RU FI WC MA OG FV FX YB HG UX ZV EH
```

This time, German codebreaker Nils Kopal, the developer of CrypTool 2, was the one to post the solution on the same day. He had applied the same simulated-annealing algorithm written by George, including his hexagraph-based fitness function. The software delivered the following solution:[33]

MEET YOU TOMORROW AT FOUR TWENTY AT MARKET PLACE

Next, in April 2019, Klaus published a thirty-two-letter Playfair cryptogram based on a thirty-letter plaintext:[34]

SX CR ED BQ UG VZ RS MN DS IK RK WR SG NS NX VM

The challenge proved more difficult than the previous ones, as no solution popped up that day, week, or even month. However, five months later, in September 2019, Magnus Ekhall from Sweden deciphered the message with simulated annealing and again set a new record. His fitness function used the frequencies of five-letter groups (pentagraphs). The plaintext read as follows and included two **X**s as filler characters:[35]

TAKE THE LAST X TRAIN TO YORK ON SUNDAY X

In September 2019, Klaus created a new Playfair challenge—this time with twenty-eight letters:[36]

ZX LS EW HC HU CE LQ OE PN YR IW YC VQ LS

Again, Magnus Ekhall came up with the solution. The process, however, made it clear that a twenty-eight-letter Playfair message was considerably more difficult to break than one with thirty-two letters. Using simulated annealing, Magnus's software produced 100,000 solution candidates. Magnus then wrote an additional program to determine the correct candidate, reproduced here:[37]

STAY WHERE YOU ARE UNTIL THURSDAY

Continuing the experiment, Klaus published a twenty-six-letter challenge in November 2019:[38]

DB AQ IH KN RW VB KW NA DQ WR AM OQ IY

Four weeks later, the solution was posted by a person thus far unknown in the codebreaking community: Konstantin Hamidullin, from Riga, Latvia. Here's the plaintext:[39]

WAIT FOR FURTHER INSTRUCTIONS

Surprisingly, Konstantin (who has since become a working colleague of ours) had found this solution with neither a hill climber nor a simulated-annealing algorithm but with his own unique method, which performed a kind of dictionary attack against the first words of the plaintext. This attack required a list, or dictionary, of word groups that frequently appear at the beginning of English sentences. For instance, **ONCEUPONATIME** or **THEQUESTIONWEWILLDISCUSSTODAY** could appear in such a list.

As Konstantin couldn't find an existing collection that would suit his needs, he decided to create one. For this purpose, he turned to Project Gutenberg, a digital library that collects the full texts of tens of thousands of books in the public domain. He wrote a software program that worked through about 3,000 English-language books and generated a list of the most frequent word groups that appeared at the start of all the sentences.

Konstantin's codebreaking software then used the more frequent entries on this list as cribs for the beginning of the plaintext. Next, it checked whether a Playfair matrix existed that would lead from the crib to the corresponding ciphertext. In many instances, this was not the case: for example, the word group **THISIS** cannot encode to **DBAQIH**, as the repetition of **IS** would lead to a repetition in the ciphertext not present here. If, for a certain crib, a Playfair matrix existed, the software would extend the word group by another likely word—for instance, **ONCEUPONATIME** could become **ONCEUPONATIMETHERE**—and test again.

The breakthrough came when Konstantin's software received a positive result for the word group **WAITFOR** and successfully extended it to **WAITFORFURTHER**. When it added **INSTRUCTIONS** as the fourth word and rendered a positive result, the solution was found.

Lastly, Klaus published a twenty-four-letter challenge, which you can find in Chapter 12. As of this writing, the twenty-six-letter Playfair cryptogram solved by Konstantin is the shortest one ever deciphered. If you would like to try to break this record, try your luck at the twenty-four-letter one. To find out whether or not this challenge is still active, check out *https://codebreaking-guide.com/errata/*.

Solving machine ciphers with hill climbing

Hill climbing works not only for most substitutions and transpositions but also for the more sophisticated ciphers of the encryption machine era (which spanned roughly 1920 to 1970 and is discussed in Chapter 15). Most importantly, hill climbing proved extremely successful for breaking Enigma messages.

Success story: Breaking original Enigma messages

The exact number isn't known, but experts estimate that the Germans transmitted about a million Enigma messages during World War II.[40] For security reasons, radio operators usually destroyed any record of a ciphertext after decryption, which is why most original Enigma messages are lost today. Luckily, there are exceptions, and a few thousand Enigma messages from the war are preserved in archives, museums, or private collections. Of course, researchers may discover more of these messages in the future.

Over the last two decades, several Enigma enthusiasts have tried to break original Enigma cryptograms—with considerable success. We are aware of the following projects:

- *M4 Project*: This is an effort by German violinist Stefan Krah to break three original German Navy messages from World War II, which were encrypted with the four-rotor Enigma M4.[41] The goal was to find the solutions with the help of distributed computing. Thousands of people downloaded software that Krah had written for this purpose and provided CPU resources. The M4 project succeeded in breaking two of the messages in 2006. The third one was solved seven years later, in 2013.

- *Breaking German Wehrmacht Ciphers*: This is an ongoing project started by Geoff Sullivan and Frode Weierud in 2002.[42] Olaf Ostwald later joined the effort. Together, they have broken hundreds of original Enigma ciphertexts, including radio messages from the Flossenbürg concentration camp and Germany's Russia campaign (Operation Barbarossa).

- *Breaking German Navy Ciphers*: This is another ongoing project that aims to break original Enigma messages. It was started in 2012 by German schoolteacher Michael Hörenberg.[43] As of this writing, he and his cryptanalytic partner Dan Girard have succeeded in deciphering over sixty Enigma cryptograms.

The people involved in these projects have developed computer-based Enigma-breaking techniques that are much more powerful than the methods used by the British in Bletchley Park during the war. Many of these are based on hill climbing. Most of the original Enigma messages that are known to exist have been broken. The only exceptions tend to be very short messages or ciphertexts that likely contain errors.

17

WHAT NEXT?

Congratulations! If you have read this book up to this point and understood the main concepts we've explained, you have learned a lot about codebreaking. You're a considerable way along the path to becoming a skilled cryptanalyst. However, there is still a good deal more you can learn, and there are many more crypto challenges waiting to be solved. In the following sections, we will tell you how you can proceed on your codebreaking journey from here.

More unsolved cryptograms

In the first sixteen chapters of this book, we introduced dozens of unsolved cryptograms, such as the Voynich manuscript (Chapter 5) and the Beale ciphers (Chapter 6). Here are some more. Unlike the ones we have covered so far, these cryptograms cannot be assigned to a certain cipher type in an obvious way. After all, since they're unsolved, we don't even know how they were made!

The fourth Kryptos message (K4)

The sculpture *Kryptos*, created in 1990 inside CIA Headquarters in Langley, Virginia, bears an encrypted inscription divided into four parts (see Appendix A for details). While the first three parts have long been solved, number four (also known as K4) is still a mystery:

```
                     OBKR
    UOXOGHULBSOLIFBBWFLRVQQPRNGKSSO
    TWTQSJQSSEKZZWATJKLUDIAWINFBNYP
    VTTMZFPKWGDKZXTJCDIGKUHUAUEKCAR
```

Meanwhile, *Kryptos* creator Jim Sanborn has provided four different clues related to the K4 plaintext over the years. The first three were published in the *New York Times*, and the fourth was provided via email by the sculptor just shortly before the first edition of this book was published:

2010: The sixty-fourth through sixty-ninth positions of K4 are **BERLIN**.[1]

2014: The word **CLOCK** follows **BERLIN** in the K4 plaintext.[2]

January 2020: The word **NORTHEAST** appears at positions 26 through 34.[3]

August 2020: An additional word, **EAST**, appears at position 22.

The following diagram shows K4 along with the four hints. Note that, just because the plaintext starts at a certain position, it does not necessarily mean that there is a one-to-one mapping with the ciphertext. For all we know, there may also be some transposition involved.

OBKR

UOXOGHULBSOLIFBBWFLRVQQPRNGKSSO
EASTNORTHEAST

TWTQSJQSSEKZZWATJKLUDIAWINFBNYP
BER

VTTMZFPKWGDKZXTJCDIGKUHUAUEKCAR
LINCLOCK

Even with these four clues, as of this writing, nobody has been able to decipher K4.

The Rubin cryptogram

On January 20, 1953, the body of eighteen-year-old student Paul Rubin was found in a ditch near Philadelphia International Airport. As it turned out, the cause of his death was cyanide poisoning. It is unclear whether Rubin committed suicide or was murdered, but as a chemistry student, he certainly had access to the kind of poison that killed him. When his corpse was found, Rubin had a small box attached to his abdomen that contained an encrypted message (see Figure 17-1).

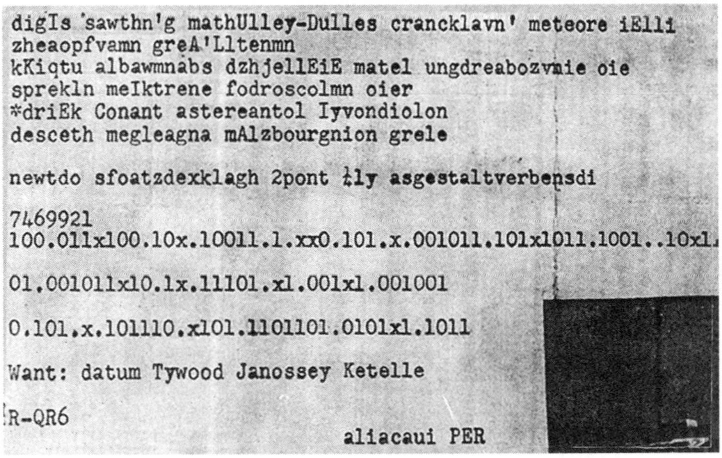

```
digIs 'sawthn'g mathUlley-Dulles crancklavn' meteore iElli
zheaopfvamn greA'Lltenmn
kKiqtu albawmnabs dzhjellEiE matel ungdreabozvnie oie
sprekln meIktrene fodroscolmn oier
*driEk Conant astereantol Iyvondiolon
desceth megleagna mAlzbourgnion grele

newtdo sfoatzdexklagh 2pont ily asgestaltverbensdi

7469921
100.011x100.10x.10011.1.xx0.101.x.001011.101x1011.1001..10x1.

01.001011x10.1x.11101.x1.001x1.001001

0.101.x.101110.x101.1101101.0101x1.1011

Want: datum Tywood Janossey Ketelle

R-QR6
                              aliacaui PER
```

Figure 17-1: Chemistry student Paul Rubin had this note with him when he was found dead in Philadelphia.

This cryptogram is unsolved to date, as is the criminal case. The best source about the Rubin case is Craig Bauer's book *Unsolved!*[4]

Ricky McCormick's encrypted notes

On June 30, 1999, police found a corpse in a cornfield near St. Louis, Missouri. After an investigation, they determined that he was a murder victim and identified him as forty-one-year-old Ricky McCormick. In one of his pockets, the investigators found two pieces of paper containing encrypted notes.[5] The FBI engaged its codebreaking department, the CRRU, to uncover the plaintexts, but none of the specialists could solve the encryption, which is unusual, considering that the CRRU claims to have a high success rate. Members of the American Cryptogram Association who tried to break the encryption were also unsuccessful.

On March 30, 2011, the FBI took the extraordinary step of publishing McCormick's two encrypted messages on the front page of the *https://www.fbi.gov* website, seeking the public's help either in solving the cryptograms or identifying any other encrypted text that looked similar. The cryptograms are reproduced in Figure 17-2.

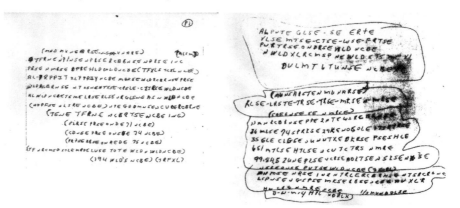

Figure 17-2: Murder victim Ricky McCormick left behind two encrypted notes. They have never been solved.

The McCormick cryptograms created tremendous interest but still remain unsolved.

The carrier pigeon message from World War II

In 1982, a man living in Surrey, United Kingdom, was cleaning his chimney and discovered the remains of a pigeon.[6] This bird turned out to be one of the carrier pigeons used in World War II and even had an encrypted message still attached to its leg (see Figure 17-3).

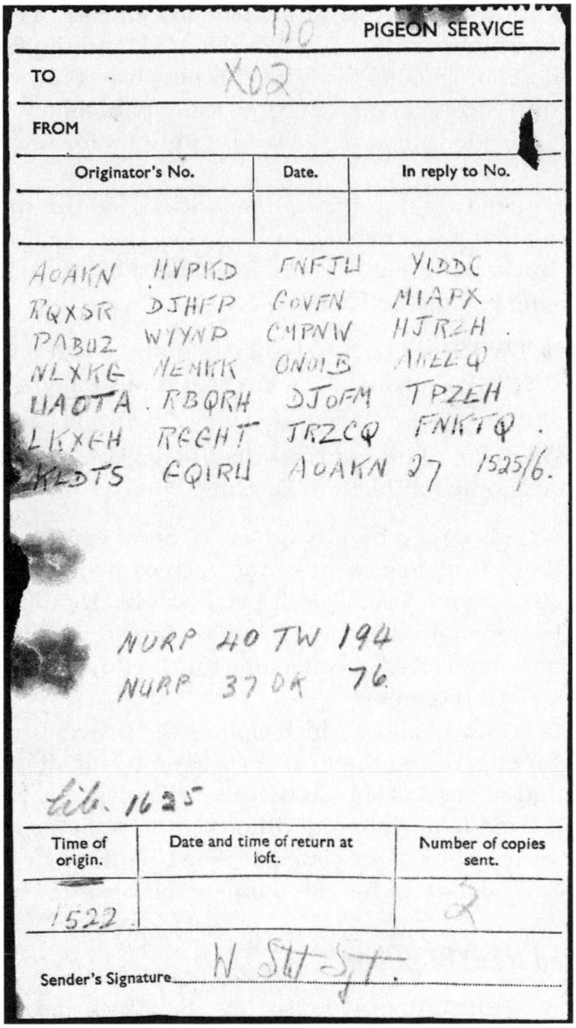

PIGEON SERVICE

TO X02

FROM

Originator's No.	Date.	In reply to No.

AOAKN HVPKD FNFJW YIDDC
RQXSR DJHFP GOVFN MIAPX
PABUZ WYYNP CMPNW HJRZH
NLXKG MEMKK ONOIB AKEEQ
UAOTA RBQRH DJOFM TPZEH
LKXGH RGGHT JRZCQ FNKTQ
KLDTS GQIRW AOAKN 27 1525/6.

NURP 40 TW 194
NURP 37 OK 76

Lib. 1625

Time of origin.	Date and time of return at loft.	Number of copies sent.
1522		2

Sender's Signature W Stt Sjt.

Figure 17-3: This message was transported by a carrier pigeon in World War II. After its publication, many tried to break the encryption, to no avail.

Here's a transcript:

```
AOAKN HVPKD FNFJW YIDDC
RQXSR DJHFP GOVFN MIAPX
PABUZ WYYNP CMPNW HJRZH
NLXKG MEMKK ONOIB AKEEQ
UAOTA RBQRH DJOFM TPZEH
LKXGH RGGHT JRZCQ FNKTQ
KLDTS GQIRW AOAKN 27 1525/6.
```

Little is known for sure about the pigeon's journey. The use of carrier pigeons was quite common in World War II, and the British Royal Air Force trained about 250,000 birds for this purpose. Typically, they dropped the pigeons into Nazi-occupied Europe, using parachutes. Agents picked them up and provided them to the British military for sending messages back home.

What we do know is that the pigeon that carried this message wore a ring indicating that it was banded in 1940. The message itself was carried in duplicate by two different pigeons. Each had a band from the National Union of Racing Pigeons (NURP):[7]

NURP 40 TW 194   The "40" indicates that the pigeon was banded in 1940. "TW 194" probably means that it was pigeon #194 in Twickenham.

NURP 37 DK 76   This indicates that the pigeon was banded in 1937 and that its home was likely in Dorking.

The message is signed by a "Sergeant W. Stot," which probably refers to Sergeant William Stott, age twenty-seven, who parachuted into Normandy on a reconnaissance mission. This dispatch was likely one of countless such messages transmitted around D-Day on June 6, 1944. The form said that its destination was X02, a codename for the Royal Air Force Bomber Command in High Wycombe.

Not much is known about which ciphers the British used at any particular time for encrypting their carrier pigeon traffic. It is therefore hard to say what kind of encryption was used for this message. Numerous codebreakers have tried to decipher it, without any luck. Some have suggested that the cipher used was a one-time pad (see Chapter 8), which would mean that the message will never be solved unless the key is found.

The encrypted NKRYPT pillars

NKRYPT is an art installation consisting of eight steel pillars located outside the Questacon Science and Technology Centre in Canberra, Australia (see Figure 17-4). Installed in 2013, *NKRYPT* was designed by Stuart Kohlhagen, a science educator and the director of science and learning at Questacon.

Each of the *NKRYPT* pillars is covered with two laser-cut ciphertexts consisting of letters, numbers, and symbols. Around the base of each pillar, a string of numbers runs in a circular pattern, which some have suggested may represent DNA sequences. The cryptograms are all discrete but interlinked, and solving one may provide a clue to solving others.[8] Additional challenges are located on and around the artwork, and the position and height of the columns have meanings, too.

Figure 17-4: NKRYPT *is an art installation located in Canberra, Australia. It displays a collection of encrypted messages, many of which are still unsolved.*

According to Kohlhagen, there are about sixty puzzles connected to *NKRYPT.* Some of them are hidden or only visible when others are solved, in a metapuzzle style. None of the cryptograms are based on modern crypto systems such as AES or RSA. The level of difficulty, at least of those that have been solved so far, varies considerably.

Two fan websites are dedicated to the sculpture: *NKRYPT* Sculpture by Melbourne-based computer scientist Glenn McIntosh[9] and DKRYPT by Greg Lloyd.[10] As the pillars don't have official names, we use Glenn's labels of A through H. Figure 17-5 shows a blueprint of the artwork, which Stuart Kohlhagen provided to us. The sequence is the same in both, but reversed.

Of the sixteen obvious *NKRYPT* cryptograms, nine have been solved by Glenn McIntosh, Bob Dovenberg, and others. Most of these ciphertexts consist of lines of twenty-six characters. They were encrypted using a simple binary code, a Caesar cipher, a pigpen system, a rotor cipher, and a scytale. In many cases, Kohlhagen employed an additional route transposition via an irregular pattern (or, at least, a pattern that does not yet seem to have a definable rule). On pillar A, for instance, the route looks like this:

```
3 5 2 4 8 6 1 4 9 1 6 3 5 3 5 4 7 1 0 1 4 9 0 9 7 4
2 4 7 2 5 3 9 1 5 0 9 4 1 4 8 9 2 5 3 3 7 3 1 9 4 1
1 4 9 0 9 5 7 3 5 2 2 6 8 1 4 9 0 3 6 7 3 5 3 6 3 6
4 1 6 3 5 3 5 3 2 1 3 1 9 4 1 1 6 4 3 5 3 4 6 7 0 9
8 1 4 9 1 0 4 0 3 5 3 1 8 0 1 4 9 0 9 2 6 3 5 3 7 7
```

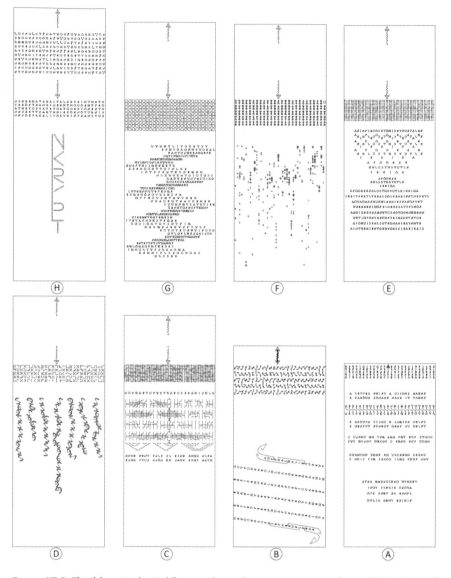

Figure 17-5: This blueprint by Kohlhagen shows the cryptograms on the eight NKRYPT pillars.

The plaintext begins at the top left-hand corner, **3527421491373** . . . This sequence of numbers represents latitude and longitude coordinates for locations around Canberra, in the following format: S 35.2742, E 149.1373; then, S 35.2984, E 149.1312; etc. The transposition paths on the other pillars look similar but are not the same. Kohlhagen has told us that once all eight are completed, they form a part of the sculpture's metapuzzle.

As a first example of an unsolved *NKRYPT* ciphertext, we'll look at the upper message on pillar G (see Figure 17-6). It consists of rounded figures with one angle (a symbol called a *squircle*), which form the aforementioned twenty-six-column pattern. Like all *NKRYPT* challenges, it doesn't have an official name, so we will simply call it the squircle cryptogram.

Figure 17-6: The squircle and PVL cryptograms are still unsolved.

The alphabet used in the squircle cryptogram consists of only four symbols, which McIntosh transcribes as 0, 1, 2, and 3. Here's his transcript of the message:

```
0111001101110102123133101 2
0203001332230333300020003 2
2122113310303232010200013 2
2312300212122300130113112 3
1010310001010120120122110 3
3021213103300020301111233 0
3010111121203213201221013 3
1330332302312022233332201 2
0000010102200120323131003 1
3011033320212011230211212 3
```

The squircle cryptogram consists of 260 characters but too few distinct symbols or even digraphs to encode twenty-six letters. Therefore, our guess is that Kohlhagen used tetragraphs (i.e., groups of four characters). A single tetragraph, with a range of 0000 to 3333, could represent 256 possible numbers. This is an ideal amount for encoding ASCII characters, including upper and lowercase letters, numbers, punctuation symbols, and so forth. The ciphertext message on the pillar consists of sixty-five tetragraphs, meaning that (if we are right) it could potentially lead to a plaintext of sixty-five ASCII characters.

Kohlhagen additionally pointed out to us that the cipher used for the squircle cryptogram includes a path transposition similar to the ones used for the other challenges. As all other known paths are based on a grid of single characters, independently of whether the cryptographic system uses digraphs or tetragraphs, one might have to form the tetragraphs after performing the transposition. Of course, the reverse could be true, as well!

Another unsolved *NKRYPT* ciphertext is depicted on pillar H. Again, each line consists of twenty-six characters, with ten lines in total and the letters P, V, and L written in a larger font. It has been called the PVL cryptogram. Here's the transcript that McIntosh provides on his website:

```
OXPUWAOEKZVCRLUYFMLXTPNATW
VGZTCGVGDAAXFDKOCRFRUOKAPW
LCMPTFPBTYXRSZKKQUBJAMHYUL
MZVSXXZHDLYHOKWWEJUXLXKRZU
PPESLBOEKOGRTAYDFOHRHVMPBN
DTEZBTYDXNMPXHVNKCIYEMJFVE
MNKDIQBOSUFFFWBVDNKHRTLIMZ
WRRQUFNNBGKUWNQCHDEFSTZZRQ
UIUDPTKGATPSJIFXXGGSNTWJLA
BRYVUCSBNPYAVSTTONZFWIUUNW
```

Kohlhagen told us that the PVL cryptogram forms a final code, meaning one can only solve it if one knows the solution of some other puzzles.

As far as encrypted sculptures go, *NKRYPT* has received considerably less attention in the crypto community than the famous *Kryptos*. If you want to try your hand at breaking an unsolved cryptogram, cracking one of the unsolved *NKRYPT* ciphertexts might be the easier goal!

Even more unsolved cryptograms

There are many more unsolved crypto mysteries you might want to explore. For instance, the Rayburn cryptogram,[11] the Nazi spy cryptogram,[12] the message in the 2010 movie *Fair Game*,[13] the Cylob cryptogram,[14] the D'Agapeyeff cryptogram,[15] the mLH cipher,[16] the Feynman Ciphers,[17] and the Rilke cryptogram[18] are all worth studying. There is also the *Rohonc Codex*, which we still list as unsolved. Gábor Tokai and Levente Zoltán Király proposed an interesting solution in 2018, but as of this writing, it has been challenged by other cryptologists.[19, 20, 21]

If you want to learn more about the world of unsolved cryptograms, check out Elonka's "List of Famous Unsolved Codes and Ciphers"[22] or Klaus's "Top 50 Unsolved Cryptograms" list,[23] which are both available online. You may also wish to check out Craig Bauer's 2017 book *Unsolved!*, as he also covers his own theories of how some of these messages could be cracked.[24] Or, if you can read German, try Klaus's 2012 *Nicht zu knacken* (Impossible to crack).[25] Another book about several unsolved cryptograms is *Can You Crack the Enigma Code?* by Richard Belfield.[26]

To our knowledge, the most comprehensive collection of (mostly unsolved) historical ciphertexts is available in the DECODE database operated by the University of Uppsala (*https://de-crypt.org/decrypt-web/RecordsList*). As of 2023, the university's list has over 4,000 entries.

Similar information about unsolved messages can be found in the Database of Cryptograms on the Portal of Historical Ciphers operated by Slovak cipher expert Eugen Antal (*https://cryptograms.hcportal.eu*).

Another site is The Cipher Foundation, a project by British cipher mysteries and Voynich manuscript specialist Nick Pelling (*https://cipherfoundation.org*), which provides detailed information about some thirty extremely interesting unsolved cryptograms.

Codebreaking tools

In Chapter 1, we introduced the codebreaking utilities CrypTool 2 (*https://cryptool.org*), dCode (*https://dcode.fr/en*), and Cipher Tools (*https://rumkin.com/tools/cipher/*). We used these tools in the previous chapters for tasks such as frequency analysis, letter pattern searches, and hill climbing. In the following, we list more software programs and web-based utilities (all free of charge) that provide useful codebreaking functions:

- The Multi-Dec website (*https://multidec.web-lab.at*), operated by Christian Baumann, presents some twenty-five useful codebreaking and decoding functions.
- Bion's Gadgets (*https://williammason.github.io/rec-crypt/Bions_gadgets_on_Github.html*) offers a large collection of codebreaking tools.
- Cipher Solving Assistants by Mary Ellen and John Toebes (*https://toebes.com/aca/*) is another codebreaking-tools website.
- Quipqiup is a cryptogram solver by Edwin Olson (*https://quipqiup.com*).
- CryptoPrograms (*https://www.cryptoprograms.com*), operated by Phil Pilcrow, provides numerous helpful encryption and text statistics tools, including the software CryptoCrack.
- The Litscape word-finder tools (*https://litscape.com/word_tools/pattern_match.php*) allow searching for words with a certain letter pattern.
- The Design 215 Word Pattern Finder (*https://design215.com/toolbox/wordpattern.php*), operated by Robert Giordano, is another letter pattern search tool.

Looking for more tools? There are many great utilities listed at Dave Oranchak's Zodiac Killer Ciphers wiki, such as Jarl Van Eycke's AZDecrypt (*http://zodiackillerciphers.com/wiki/index.php?title=Software_Tools*).

Other books about codebreaking

In our book, we have endeavored to introduce the most important techniques for breaking classical ciphers using both manual and computer-based methods. We believe our book is unique in that it is oriented toward the most frequent classical ciphers encountered in practice and introduces many genuine solved and unsolved cryptograms. We are not aware of another book with a similar scope, but of course, there are many other fine codebreaking books on the market.

The following ones were written decades ago and are therefore computer agnostic:

- Helen Fouché Gaines, *Cryptanalysis* (1939): This work is a classic and probably the most successful book about codebreaking ever written. Now outdated, as it was created before the computer age, it is still filled with valuable information for anyone interested in codebreaking techniques.

- André Langie, *Cryptography* (1922): This is a great book that explains the ciphers and codebreaking methods of its time in an easy-to-understand way.

- William Friedman, *Military Cryptanalysis, Parts I–IV* (ca. 1938): Friedman's widely used work delivers a scientific approach to codebreaking in over a thousand pages. Considered the most famous cryptologist in history, Friedman is also the person who coined the terms "cryptanalysis" and "index of coincidence."

- Andreas Figl, *Systeme des Dechiffrierens* (*Systems of Decipherment*) (1927): Written by a World War I–era Austrian codebreaker in German, this book, along with its sister book, *Systeme des Chiffrierens* (1926), is outdated. However, in addition to Gaines's *Cryptanalysis*, it is one of the best and most comprehensive codebreaking books of the pre-computer era.

- US Department of the Army, *Basic Cryptanalysis* (1990): This field manual about breaking simple substitution ciphers, polyalphabetic ciphers, and transpositions is available for free on the internet.[27]

- Solomon Kullback, *Statistical Methods in Cryptanalysis* (1976): This book focuses on codebreaking with statistics, such as frequency analysis and the index of coincidence.

- Parker Hitt, *Manual for the Solution of Military Ciphers* (1916): This compact codebreaking work is published by the Press of the Army Service Schools. It covers simple substitution, polyalphabetic ciphers, transpositions, and Playfair.

- Abraham Sinkov, *Elementary Cryptanalysis* (1966): This codebreaking book follows a mathematical approach.

- William and Elizebeth Friedman, *The Shakespearean Ciphers Examined* (1957): In a lighthearted style, the famous codebreaking couple goes back to their roots to thoroughly debunk the idea that there were hidden messages in the works of Shakespeare.

- Dermot Turing, *The Bombe: The Machine that Defeated Enigma* (2021): This book provides a very good description of the machine that was used by the British during World War II to break Enigma messages.

Codebreaking books that include computer-based techniques for solving historical ciphers are not as common:

- Robert Reynard, *Secret Code Breaker: A Cryptanalyst's Handbook* (1996): This ninety-page book has a very basic introduction to cryptanalysis and mentions a number of computer programs from the time, though few of them are still relevant today.

- George Lasry, "A Methodology for the Cryptanalysis of Classical Ciphers with Search Metaheuristics" (2018): This is George Lasry's PhD thesis about breaking manual and machine ciphers with hill climbing and other methods.[28]

- Al Sweigart, *Cracking Codes with Python* (2018): This work introduces many algorithms for implementing and breaking manual ciphers and also covers modern cryptography.[29]

In addition, there are many books that cover modern computer-based crypto algorithms, such as DES, AES, RSA, and Diffie-Hellman, but there are only a few that specialize in the cryptanalysis of those methods. *Applied Cryptanalysis: Breaking Ciphers in the Real World* (2007) by Mark Stamp and Richard M. Low and *Algorithmic Cryptanalysis* (2009) by Antoine Joux are good choices for anyone interested in cryptanalysis of modern systems.

Here are some other books that include information about codebreaking but do not focus on this topic:

- David Kahn, *The Codebreakers*, 2nd edition (1996): First published in 1967, this is the classic book about crypto history. As the title implies, it focuses more on the people who worked as codebreakers (and codemakers) than on codebreaking. Nevertheless, it is a must-read for everybody interested in cryptanalysis and the encryption methods of the last 4,000 years.

- Bernhard Esslinger and CrypTool team, *Learning and Experiencing Cryptography with CrypTool and SageMath* (2018): This free book contains interesting information about classical encryption systems and how they can be broken with free software.

- Craig Bauer, *Secret History: The Story of Cryptology*, 2nd edition (2021): This very interesting book combines the history of cryptology with mathematical descriptions of historical crypto algorithms. It is a good book for anyone who wishes to understand the mathematics of classical ciphers.

- Craig Bauer, *Unsolved!* (2017): This well-researched book is about famous unsolved cryptograms; it includes a great deal of information about potential approaches to these interesting codebreaking mysteries.

- Simon Singh, *The Code Book* (1999): This is a bestseller about the history of encryption. Some codebreaking techniques are explained.

- Simon Singh, *The Cracking Code Book* (2002): Based on *The Code Book*, this work provides an entry-level introduction to codebreaking, mainly for children. Some editions are titled *The Code Book for Young People*.

- Friedrich Bauer, *Decrypted Secrets* (2006): This classic was first published in 1997 and describes historical and modern encryption algorithms, along with cryptanalysis.

- Denise Sutherland and Mark Koltko-Rivera, *Cracking Codes & Cryptograms for Dummies* (2011): Despite the promise of the title, only about 10% of this book is actually about codebreaking, but it still can be of interest because it has a large number of puzzles to solve.

- A.J. Jacobs, *The Puzzler* (2022): Another bestseller, this was written by multiple-time TED speaker Jacobs in his entertaining point of view. He got in touch with experts (including us!), traveled to puzzle conventions, and even received an invitation from the CIA to see their encrypted *Kryptos* sculpture.

- Liza Mundy, *The Code Girls: The Untold Story of the American Women Code Breakers of World War II* (2017): This is an absorbing work about the thousands of young women who helped with the war effort and then took the secrets of their codebreaking adventures to their grave. We are glad to finally see their stories properly told.

- Benedek Láng, *Real Life Cryptology: Ciphers and Secrets in Early Modern Hungary* (2018): This book was published in both Hungarian and English, and the English version is available as a free download. It covers a variety of cipher types in medieval Europe in multiple languages.[30]

- John F. Dooley, *History of Cryptography and Cryptanalysis: Codes, Ciphers, and Their Algorithms* (2018): This is a textbook about the history of cryptology, from ancient Greek and early Arabic writings up through a bit of modern computer-based cryptography. Though it doesn't focus on computers, it includes more about modern encryption than other books of its kind.

- Herbert O. Yardley, *The American Black Chamber* (1931): One of the most famous books on cryptology ever published, this text was quite controversial in its time because it described the inner workings of an American governmental cryptography organization. Critics said it might even have given Japan an edge during World War II. Primarily, it covers stories about codebreaking without much focus on cryptanalysis, though there is some good information on frequency analysis and the breaking of a German transposition cipher.

- Tom Mahon and James J. Gillogly, *Decoding the IRA* (2008): This is an interesting read about Irish history in the 1920s, when the Irish Republican Army, a paramilitary organization, was fighting for independence from British rule and using ciphers in its communications. In the first chapter, Gillogly explains his deciphering methods.

Last, but definitely not least, we are pleased to see that codebreaker Elizabeth Friedman (1892–1980) has been receiving some long-overdue attention. Over the last few years, a documentary and multiple books about her (for both adults and children) have been released. We especially recommend the following:

- Jason Fagone, *The Woman Who Smashed Codes* (2017): This is a well-researched and very readable biography/adventure story about Elizabeth's life.

- G. Stuart Smith, *A Life in Code* (2017): This biography of Elizebeth Friedman was written by her great-nephew.
- Amy Butler Greenfield, *The Woman All Spies Fear: Elizebeth Smith Friedman and Her Hidden Life* (2021): Written for grades 8 and up, this is a Kirkus Best Book of the Year and a very readable biography.
- Laurie Wallmark (author) and Brooke Smart (illustrator), *Code Breaker, Spy Hunter: How Elizebeth Friedman Changed the Course of Two World Wars* (2021): This is an illustrated book about Elizebeth for young readers.

If you want to know about more books covering manual and machine-based encryption, check out *https://cryptobooks.org*. This website, operated by codebreakers Tobias Schrödel and Nils Kopal, describes over 500 titles from the last 600 years.

Websites about codebreaking

Here are some websites that provide further information about codebreaking:

- Klaus's *Cipherbrain* blog (*https://scienceblogs.de/klausis-krypto-kolumne/*): Klaus's blog was established in 2013 in German and then expanded with English translations in 2017. His site contains over a thousand reports on codebreaking and historical encryption, along with a very active community of readers who enthusiastically engage with each new blog post.
- Elonka's website (*https://elonka.com*): This contains, among other things, Elonka's list of famous unsolved codes and ciphers. Her website is also considered the gold standard for information about the CIA's encrypted sculpture *Kryptos*, as well as information about other famous solved cryptograms, such as the Friedman tombstone, the Smithy Code, and the *Cyrillic Projector*. It also includes a tutorial on how Elonka solved a hacker challenge (the PhreakNIC v3.0 Code) in 1999, which was the start of her codebreaking career.
- *Cipher Mysteries* (*https://ciphermysteries.com*): Nick Pelling, a London-based codebreaking expert, prolific author, and researcher, operates this exhaustive website that includes information about the Voynich manuscript and other encryption mysteries. He has hundreds of blog articles about topics ranging from the latest purported Voynich solutions to an analysis of research on the Somerton Man and Masonic ciphers.
- MysteryTwister (*https://mysterytwister.org*): This website, run by a group of German crypto-enthusiasts, including a few who are behind the CrypTool utility, has over 300 crypto puzzle challenges submitted from all over the world.
- CrypTool Portal (*https://cryptool.org*): This website not only provides the CrypTool software for download but also contains a great deal of interesting information about cryptography and codebreaking. In addition, there's a related YouTube channel, "CRYPTOOL 2: Cryptography for Everybody," which is operated by CrypTool developer Nils Kopal.

- Cryptiana (*http://cryptiana.web.fc2.com/code/crypto.htm*): Satoshi Tomokiyo from Tokyo, Japan, operates this great website about historical encryption techniques, old cryptograms, and solution methods.

- Cipher History (*https://cipherhistory.com*): This comprehensive website about vintage cryptography is operated by cipher-machine collector Ralph Simpson.

- American Cryptogram Association (*https://cryptogram.org*): The American Cryptogram Association, founded in 1930, is an organization dedicated to promoting the hobby and art of codebreaking. Its website provides tons of interesting information. The association runs an annual convention and publishes a bimonthly newsletter that contains a variety of cryptograms, along with a competition and a points system for solving them.

- *Kryptos* discussion group (*https://kryptos.groups.io*): Founded by Elonka and the late Gary Warzin on Yahoo! Groups and then moved to *https://groups.io*, this discussion board is co-moderated by Elonka, Chris Hanson, and Larry McElhiney.

- DECODE (*https://de-crypt.org/decrypt-web/RecordsList*): This website about historical ciphers is operated by scientists from the University of Uppsala, Sweden. It includes a large database of unsolved cryptograms.

- Portal of Historical Ciphers (*https://hcportal.eu*): This website about historical ciphers is operated by Eugen Antal from Slovakia. It features a database of unsolved cryptograms.

- Cryptograms & Classical Ciphers (Facebook group): Bart Wenmeckers, a New Zealand-based codebreaking expert, hosts this group.

- Christos's *Military and Intelligence Corner* (*https://chris-intel-corner.blogspot.com*): Operated by Greek crypto history and intelligence expert Christos Triantafyllopoulos, this blog covers historical cryptology, along with military and intelligence topics.

- Dave Oranchak's page (*http://www.zodiackillerciphers.com*): This page is run by Virginian Dave Oranchak, a member of the three-man team that solved the Z340 cipher. It mainly covers the Zodiac Killer and his cryptograms.

- Crypto Museum (*https://cryptomuseum.com*): This comprehensive website about cipher machines and crypto devices is operated by Dutch experts Paul Reuvers and Marc Simons.

- *Schneier on Security* (*https://schneier.com*): Bruce Schneier runs the gold standard of blogs about modern crypto systems, along with a monthly newsletter, *Crypto-Gram*. He also occasionally covers information about classical ciphers.

- National Puzzlers' League (*http://puzzlers.org*): Founded in 1883, this is the world's oldest puzzlers' organization. Cryptograms are one of their many topics.

- La Crittografia da Atbash a RSA (*http://www.crittologia.eu/*): This Italian site is operated by codebreaking expert Paolo Bonavoglia.

- Benedek Láng's website Rejtjelek, kódok, titkosírások (*https://kripto.blog.hu*): If you happen to speak Hungarian or can use Google Translate (or the German site DeepL), this page, whose title translates to "Codes, Ciphers, and Cryptograms," provides many interesting facts about codebreaking.

- Kryptografie (*https://kryptografie.de/*): This multilingual website by Oliver Kuhlemann contains a great deal of interesting information about cryptography and codebreaking. The timeline of different types of cryptography over the years is particularly well done.

- *Katkryptolog* (*https://katkryptolog.blogspot.com*): This interesting crypto history and codebreaking blog is written in a mix of Slovak and English by Hans Jahr.

Journals and newsletters

There are two main print publications that cover codebreaking and related issues:

- *Cryptologia*: Founded in 1977, this is a bimonthly academic journal primarily about crypto history. It includes many notable research papers about cryptanalysis, both historical and modern, along with the breaking of various cryptograms.

- *The Cryptogram*: This bimonthly publication was founded in 1932 by the American Cryptogram Association. Each volunteer-produced issue contains dozens of crypto puzzles, the vast majority of which are created by American Cryptogram Association members for their own competitions. The publication also occasionally covers some historical cryptograms.

Events

If you'd like to meet other people interested in codebreaking, listen to interesting talks about vintage crypto systems, give a talk yourself, or maybe even meet the authors of this book in person, you could try one of the following events:

- Symposium on Cryptologic History (*https://cryptologicfoundation.org*): This biennial event hosted by the NSA is the most important international event on historical encryption and codebreaking. It takes place near Fort Meade, Maryland (the location of NSA Headquarters), outside Washington, DC.

- ACA Convention (*https://cryptogram.org*): The American Cryptogram Association hosts a yearly convention, which takes placc at various locations.

- HistoCrypt (*https://histocrypt.org*): This annual European conference on the history of cryptology takes place in a different location every year.

- *Kryptos* Meeting (*https://groups.io/g/kryptos*): This biennial event gathers dozens of people interested in the *Kryptos* sculpture and its encrypted inscription (see Appendix A). Organized by Elonka via the *Kryptos* discussion group, this event always takes place in the Washington, DC, area on the Saturday after the Symposium on Cryptologic History.

- International Conference on Cryptology History (*https://www.crypto logichistory.org*): Founded in 2004 as "Crypto Collectors," this is an email forum for the discussion of cryptologic history. Online presentations on a variety of cryptologic topics are given approximately twice a month.

Other events that sometimes involve codebreaking topics (and where you might meet the authors of this book) are 44CON (London), Awesome Con or ShmooCon (Washington, DC), DEF CON (Las Vegas), HOPE (New York), Dragon Con (Atlanta), PhreakNIC (Nashville), HAM Radio (Friedrichshafen, Germany), and Worldcon (held at various locations).

A

KRYPTOS

Kryptos is a sculpture located at CIA Headquarters in Langley, Virginia.[1] It was created by Jim Sanborn, a local artist, in 1990. *Kryptos* bears an encrypted inscription, which has become the most famous crypto puzzle created in the last four decades (see Figure A-1).

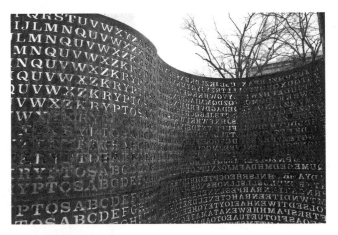

Figure A-1: Kryptos, a sculpture located at CIA Headquarters in Langley, Virginia, bears a four-part encrypted inscription. The fourth part is still unsolved.

In addition to *Kryptos*, Sanborn placed other pieces of art on the CIA grounds, such as a number of copper sheets bearing Morse code letters.[2] These messages, as well as their decoded counterparts, can be seen in Figure A-2. Here's a transcript of them:

```
eeVIRTUALLYe
eeeeeeINVISIBLE
DIGETALeee
INTERPRETATI
eeSHADOWee
FORCESeeeee
LUCIDeee
MEMORYe
TISYOUR
POSITION
SOS
RQ
```

We're unsure what these word fragments are supposed to mean, though Sanborn has said that they are related to the second part of the ciphertext. Note that there is an extra dash after INTERPRETATI, which could either mean that the final letter is a **U**, for **INTERPRETATU**, or, more likely, that the dash is the first character of the letter **O**, meaning that the entire word was intended to be **INTERPRETATION**. Similarly, T IS YOUR POSITION was probably originally **WHAT IS YOUR POSITION**. Sanborn has said he had longer messages on the sheets and then either cut the sheets in the middle of a message or allowed the messages to continue between the stone slabs.

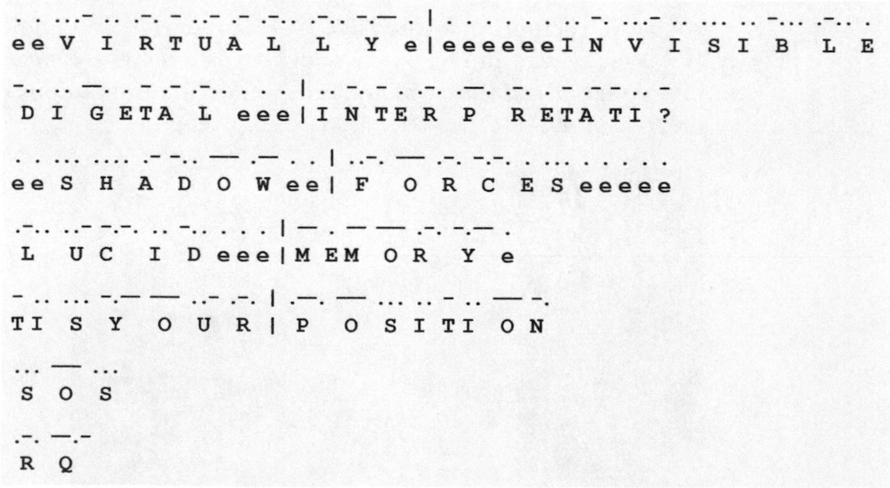

Figure A-2: Several copper sheets placed by Sanborn on the other side of the New Headquarters Building bear Morse code messages. Their decoded versions can be seen here.

The *Kryptos* inscription is divided into four quadrants. Two of these (the left ones when looking at the sculpture, as in Figure A-1) display a Vigenère-type tableau. The two other plates bear the actual ciphertext, which consists of at least four messages that are encrypted in different ways and are currently referred to in the crypto community as K1, K2, K3, and K4. In the following reproduction, we provide the entire ciphertext and indicate where each quadrant starts. (No such marks are present in the original.)

```
(K1)EMUFPHZLRFAXYUSDJKZLDKRNSHGNFIVJ
YQTQUXQBQVYUVLLTREVJYQTMKYRDMFD
(K2)VFPJUDEEHZWETZYVGWHKKQETGFQJNCE
GGWHKK?DQMCPFQZDQMMIAGPFXHQRLG
TIMVMZJANQLVKQEDAGDVFRPJUNGEUNA
QZGZLECGYUXUEENJTBJLBQCRTBJDFHRR
YIZETKZEMVDUFKSJHKFWHKUWQLSZFTI
HHDDDUVH?DWKBFUFPWNTDFIYCUQZERE
EVLDKFEZMOQQJLTTUGSYQPFEUNLAVIDX
FLGGTEZ?FKZBSFDQVGOGIPUFXHHDRKF
FHQNTGPUAECNUVPDJMQCLQUMUNEDFQ
ELZZVRRGKFFVOEEXBDMVPNFQXEZLGRE
DNQFMPNZGLFLPMRJQYALMGNUVPDXVKP
DQUMEBEDMHDAFMJGZNUPLGEWJLLAETG
(K3)ENDYAHROHNLSRHEOCPTEOIBIDYSHNAIA
CHTNREYULDSLLSLLNOHSNOSMRWXMNE
TPRNGATIHNRARPESLNNELEBLPIIACAE
WMTWNDITEENRAHCTENEUDRETNHAEOE
TFOLSEDTIWENHAEIOYTEYQHEENCTAYCR
EIFTBRSPAMHHEWENATAMATEGYEERLB
TEEFOASFIOTUETUAEOTOARMAEERTNRTI
BSEDDNIAAHTTMSTEWPIEROAGRIEWFEB
AECTDDHILCEIHSITEGOEAOSDDRYDLORIT
RKLMLEHAGTDHARDPNEOHMGFMFEUHE
ECDMRIPFEIMEHNLSSTTRTVDOHW?(K4)OBKR
UOXOGHULBSOLIFBBWFLRVQQPRNGKSSO
TWTQSJQSSEKZZWATJKLUDIAWINFBNYP
VTTMZFPKWGDKZXTJCDIGKUHUAUEKCAR
```

All four *Kryptos* ciphertext parts are covered in detail in this book: K1 and K2 in Chapter 8, K3 in Chapter 10, and K4 in Chapter 17. K1, K2, and K3 have been solved, but K4 is still a mystery. Parts 1–3 of the Kryptos ciphertext were solved by three different individuals or groups, all independently of each other. Here, we chronicle how they were solved.

Shortly after the sculpture was unveiled at CIA Headquarters in Langley, Virginia, a team of a dozen NSA employees in Fort Meade, Maryland, were invited "across the river" to the CIA to examine *Kryptos* and its related pieces. Then, in mid-1992, after the director of the NSA, Admiral William "Bill" O. Studeman, became deputy director at the CIA, he threw down the gauntlet to his NSA successor, Admiral Mike McConnell: "How come you hotshots haven't solved *Kryptos* yet?"

McConnell contacted Harry Hoover, the first chief of Z, a new organization consisting of cryptanalysts. Hoover tasked Ken Miller with being the head of the project. Miller assembled a team of three experts in "manual ciphers": Ed Hannon, a member of Hoover's team; Denny McDaniels, from Miller's team; and Lance Estes, a senior cryptanalyst from elsewhere in the agency. Hannon made the first breakthrough, solving K2. Estes solved K1, and McDaniels solved K3. After the team gave up on K4 in late 1992, Hoover said that they should not reveal their results until it was solved. But in June 1993, since that outcome did not look probable, Hoover directed Miller to write up a memo, which Hoover then sent to McConnell and, from there, to Studeman at the CIA. None of this was announced publicly.

In 1998, CIA employee David Stein derived the three solutions as well. This news was circulated internally at the CIA, and a brief, vague mention of it was made in the press, but nothing substantial was publicly revealed.[3]

In 1999, renowned codebreaker and American Cryptogram Association member Jim Gillogly cracked the three cryptograms, too. As both the NSA and the CIA had kept their codebreaking successes secret, the *Kryptos* encryption was still considered unsolved when Gillogly announced his achievement. So, he became celebrated internationally as the first one to break the first three parts.

Shortly after Gillogly's announcement, both the CIA and the NSA revealed that they had solved the three parts even earlier, though the NSA, in typical fashion, was cagey about who had done so and when. In 2004, Elonka obtained images of Stein's CIA report, which she published on her website.[4] In 2010, she filed a Freedom of Information Act request with the NSA to see their documents. After multiple follow-ups, this request was finally granted in 2013, when the NSA released documents that showed how their team had managed to solve the first three parts back in 1992. Shortly after that, the CIA released a redacted version of Stein's paper.[5] Both the redacted and unredacted versions are available on Elonka's website at *https://elonka.com/kryptos*.

All three codebreakers, and likely thousands of others around the world, have tried to decipher the fourth *Kryptos* part, to no avail.

K1

K1 is encrypted using a variant of the Vigenère cipher with the keywords **KRYPTOS** and **PALIMPSEST**. A *palimpsest* is a manuscript page from which the text has been scraped or washed off so that it can be reused for another text, in such a way that bits of the older message can be seen through the new.

Here is the Vigenère table Sanborn used; note the keywords **KRYPTOS** in the top row and PALIMPSEST in the first column:

```
KRYPTOSABCDEFGHIJLMNQUVWXZ
--------------------------
PTOSABCDEFGHIJLMNQUVWXZKRY
ABCDEFGHIJLMNQUVWXZKRYPTOS
LMNQUVWXZKRYPTOSABCDEFGHIJ
IJLMNQUVWXZKRYPTOSABCDEFGH
MNQUVWXZKRYPTOSABCDEFGHIJL
PTOSABCDEFGHIJLMNQUVWXZKRY
SABCDEFGHIJLMNQUVWXZKRYPTO
EFGHIJLMNQUVWXZKRYPTOSABCD
SABCDEFGHIJLMNQUVWXZKRYPTO
TOSABCDEFGHIJLMNQUVWXZKRYP
```

The K1 plaintext reads as follows. You can see that it includes a spelling error:

```
BETWEEN SUBTLE SHADING AND THE ABSENCE OF LIGHT LIES THE NUANCE OF
IQLUSION
```

When asked about the meaning of this plaintext, Sanborn replied that it is a sentence he wrote himself with "carefully chosen wording."

For more information about K1, check out Chapter 8.

Figure A-3: These original notes by sculptor Jim Sanborn show how the K2 plaintext was encrypted with the keyword **ABSCISSA**.

K2

K2 is encrypted in the same way as K1, though with a change to one of the keywords. This time, it used **KRYPTOS** and ABSCISSA (see Figure A-3). An *abscissa* is the *x*-coordinate of a point on a graph. We can decipher K2 with the following Vigenère table (see also Figure A-3):

```
KRYPTOSABCDEFGHIJLMNQUVWXZ
--------------------------
ABCDEFGHIJLMNQUVWXZKRYPTOS
BCDEFGHIJLMNQUVWXZKRYPTOSA
SABCDEFGHIJLMNQUVWXZKRYPTO
CDEFGHIJLMNQUVWXZKRYPTOSAB
IJLMNQUVWXZKRYPTOSABCDEFGH
SABCDEFGHIJLMNQUVWXZKRYPTO
SABCDEFGHIJLMNQUVWXZKRYPTO
ABCDEFGHIJLMNQUVWXZKRYPTOS
```

Here is the corresponding plaintext, which includes another spelling error, **UNDERGRUUND**:

```
IT WAS TOTALLY INVISIBLE HOWS THAT POSSIBLE? THEY USED THE EARTHS
MAGNETIC FIELD X THE INFORMATION WAS GATHERED AND TRANSMITTED
UNDERGRUUND TO AN UNKNOWN LOCATION X DOES LANGLEY KNOW ABOUT THIS?
THEY SHOULD ITS BURIED OUT THERE SOMEWHERE X WHO KNOWS THE EXACT
LOCATION? ONLY WW THIS WAS HIS LAST MESSAGE X THIRTY EIGHT DEGREES
FIFTY SEVEN MINUTES SIX POINT FIVE SECONDS NORTH SEVENTY SEVEN
DEGREES EIGHT MINUTES FORTYFOUR SECONDS WEST ID BY ROWS
```

The latitude and longitude coordinates in the message (N38° 57' 6.5" W77° 8' 44") point to a spot about 150 feet (forty-five meters) southeast of *Kryptos* itself, though there does not appear to be anything unusual there; it is part of a paved and landscaped area near the agency cafeteria. The location could have some connection to the other pieces of Sanborn's (the Morse code sections), which are located on the other side of the headquarters building. Sanborn has said that when he installed *Kryptos*, he made a point of checking the latitude and longitude from a nearby US Geological Survey marker to ensure that his coordinates were accurate.

In 2006, several years after the public solutions were made available, Sanborn indicated that the codebreakers had gotten the last three words of K2, **ID BY ROWS**, wrong.[6, 7] It turned out that there was a missing letter S in the last line of the ciphertext. Sanborn had intended it to end with the words **X LAYER TWO**. The codebreakers had not noticed the error, as, by mere coincidence, the expression **ID BY ROWS** seemed to make sense. So, the actual plaintext is the following:

```
IT WAS TOTALLY INVISIBLE HOWS THAT POSSIBLE? THEY USED THE EARTHS
MAGNETIC FIELD X THE INFORMATION WAS GATHERED AND TRANSMITTED
UNDERGRUUND TO AN UNKNOWN LOCATION X DOES LANGLEY KNOW ABOUT THIS?
THEY SHOULD ITS BURIED OUT THERE SOMEWHERE X WHO KNOWS THE EXACT
```

```
LOCATION? ONLY WW THIS WAS HIS LAST MESSAGE X THIRTY EIGHT DEGREES
FIFTY SEVEN MINUTES SIX POINT FIVE SECONDS NORTH SEVENTY SEVEN
DEGREES EIGHT MINUTES FORTYFOUR SECONDS WEST X LAYER TWO
```

For more information about K2, check out Chapter 8.

K3

K3 is encrypted with a transposition cipher. It can be solved in multiple ways. One method that Elonka came up with requires that the ciphertext be written in lines of forty-eight letters, not including the final question mark. The decryption begins at the **S** found at the last position of the fourth line:[8]

```
ENDYAHROHNLSRHEOCPTEOIBIDYSHNAIACHTNREYULDSLLSLL
NOHSNOSMRWXMNETPRNGATIHNRARPESLNNELEBLPIIACAEWMT
WNDITEENRAHCTENEUDRETNHAEOETFOLSEDTIWENHAEIOYTEY
QHEENCTAYCREIFTBRSPAMHHEWENATAMATEGYEERLBTEEFOAS
FIOTUETUAEOTOARMAEERTNRTIBSEDDNIAAHTTMSTEWPIEROA
GRIEWFEBAECTDDHILCEIHSITEGOEAOSDDRYDLORITRKLMLEH
AGTDHARDPNEOHMGFMFEUHEECDMRIPFEIMEHNLSSTTRTVDOHW
```

From there, the plaintext can be read with a simple rule: from the current position, go down four lines, and if you need to go beyond the last line, continue to the first one and go one position left. This rule gives us **L** as the second letter:

```
ENDYAHROHNLSRHEOCPTEOIBIDYSHNAIACHTNREYULDSLLSLL
NOHSNOSMRWXMNETPRNGATIHNRARPESLNNELEBLPIIACAEWMT
WNDITEENRAHCTENEUDRETNHAEOETFOLSEDTIWENHAEIOYTEY
QHEENCTAYCREIFTBRSPAMHHEWENATAMATEGYEERLBTEEFOAS
FIOTUETUAEOTOARMAEERTNRTIBSEDDNIAAHTTMSTEWPIEROA
GRIEWFEBAECTDDHILCEIHSITEGOEAOSDDRYDLORITRKLMLEH
AGTDHARDPNEOHMGFMFEUHEECDMRIPFEIMEHNLSSTTRTVDOHW
```

Next, **0** is the third letter:

```
ENDYAHROHNLSRHEOCPTEOIBIDYSHNAIACHTNREYULDSLLSLL
NOHSNOSMRWXMNETPRNGATIHNRARPESLNNELEBLPIIACAEWMT
WNDITEENRAHCTENEUDRETNHAEOETFOLSEDTIWENHAEIOYTEY
QHEENCTAYCREIFTBRSPAMHHEWENATAMATEGYEERLBTEEFOAS
FIOTUETUAEOTOARMAEERTNRTIBSEDDNIAAHTTMSTEWPIEROA
GRIEWFEBAECTDDHILCEIHSITEGOEAOSDDRYDLORITRKLMLEH
AGTDHARDPNEOHMGFMFEUHEECDMRIPFEIMEHNLSSTTRTVDOHW
```

Continuing with this method and adding a space when appropriate, the following plaintext appears:

```
SLOWLY DESPARATLY SLOWLY THE REMAINS OF PASSAGE DEBRIS THAT
ENCUMBERED THE LOWER PART OF THE DOORWAY WAS REMOVED WITH
TREMBLING HANDS I MADE A TINY BREACH IN THE UPPER LEFTHAND CORNER
AND THEN WIDENING THE HOLE A LITTLE I INSERTED THE CANDLE AND
```

PEERED IN THE HOT AIR ESCAPING FROM THE CHAMBER CAUSED THE FLAME
TO FLICKER BUT PRESENTLY DETAILS OF THE ROOM WITHIN EMERGED FROM
THE MIST X CAN YOU SEE ANYTHING Q

We can also derive this message using the following mathematical formula determined by crypto-enthusiast Ferdinando Stehle, in which x stands for the ciphertext position and y for the plaintext position in the transposition used:[9]

$$y = (192x + 191) \bmod 337$$

The text is a paraphrased excerpt from the diary of Howard Carter, the archaeologist who discovered the tomb of Pharaoh Tutankhamun ("King Tut") on November 26, 1922. His answer to the question, "Can you see anything?" was "Yes, wonderful things!"

Another interesting thing about K3 is that the letters DYAHR in the first line of the ciphertext are poorly aligned, as can be seen here:

EN DY A HR OHNLSR

We don't know what this means, but the artist says it has something to do with the first three parts. For more information about K3, check out Chapter 10.

Note that a question mark (?) appears between K3 and K4. For some time, codebreakers were unsure whether to interpret it as the last part of K3 or the beginning of K4, but Sanborn has said that it is not part of K4, which should be only ninety-seven characters long.

There are three other things of note about the *Kryptos* sculpture:

- There is an extra L in the Vigenère tableau. This character appears at the topmost line of one of the plates. Coincidentally (or maybe not), this is the same line where the out-of-alignment DYAHR letters appear on another plate (we have enlarged the letters Y, A, and R to indicate that they are raised). Instead of an L, this line should have ended with a J. When asked about this, Sanborn said he added the letter simply to keep things in balance, which might or might not be true, of course. Anything is possible! Some researchers have pointed out that the extra L might be there to draw the viewer's eye to the line, as a way of providing a subtle hint. With Sanborn, though, it's difficult to know one way or the other.

- There is an extra ABCD in the table. Normally, a Vigenère tableau uses a single alphabet of twenty-six letters, but in the case of *Kryptos*, Sanborn provided the extra letters for a total of thirty. Why? As usual, he offers no clear answer. Perhaps it was simply to keep things balanced or to align K3 with the ciphertext on the other two panels. Or perhaps there was some other reason?

- The reference alphabet along the top is a plain (unkeyed) A through Z. However, to perform the Vigenère encryption, Sanborn wouldn't have used a plain reference alphabet but a keyed alphabet instead. So, things are backward. This is especially interesting when we compare his Vigenère encryption to the encryption on the *Cyrillic Projector*. There, the reference alphabet was plain, but on the sculpture, the provided reference alphabet is keyed, so it's backward there, as well! To put it another way: the system that is carved into the *Cyrillic Projector* is the one used on *Kryptos*, and the system that is carved into *Kryptos* is the one used on the *Cyrillic Projector*. This could be a mistake or a deliberate act to make things more confusing. As Sanborn would say, "It's possible; anything's possible!"

K4

The ninety-seven characters of K4 are still a mystery:

```
                OBKR
UOXOGHULBSOLIFBBWFLRVQQPRNGKSSO
TWTQSJQSSEKZZWATJKLUDIAWINFBNYP
VTTMZFPKWGDKZXTJCDIGKUHUAUEKCAR
```

Between 2010 and 2020, *Kryptos* creator Jim Sanborn offered four clues with respect to K4 (see Chapter 17).

As of this writing, this thirty-year-old mystery remains unsolved. K4 has become one of the world's most famous unsolved cryptograms, often mentioned in the same breath as the Beale ciphers, the Voynich manuscript, and the Zodiac Killer messages. A worldwide community of *Kryptos* enthusiasts, co-founded and headed by Elonka, focuses primarily on finding the solution to K4. Elonka's *Kryptos* website has become the most important source for all things concerning K4, the sculpture, and the other three ciphertexts.[10]

USEFUL LANGUAGE STATISTICS

Letter frequencies

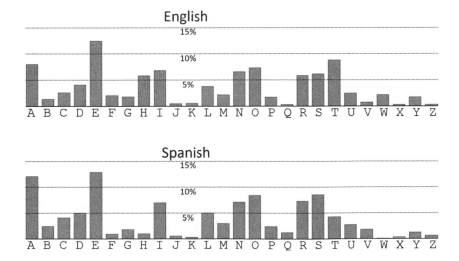

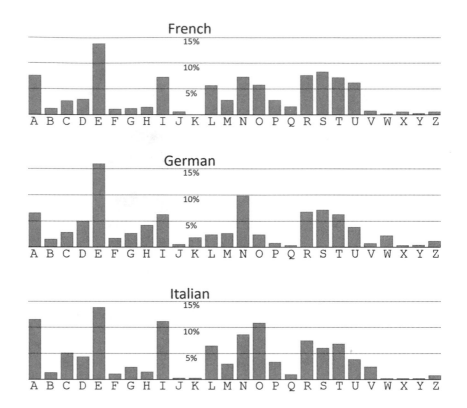

Letter frequencies from other languages are available in the Wikipedia article "Letter frequency."[1] The most frequent letters, ordered by frequency, can be memorized with nonsense words such as the following:

English: ETAOIN SHRDLU
Spanish: EAOSR NIDLT
French: ESAIT NRUOL
German: ENISR ATDHU
Italian: EAION LRTSC

Most frequent digraphs

	English	Spanish	French	German	Italian
1	TH	DE	ES	ER	ER
2	HE	ES	LE	EN	ON
3	IN	EN	DE	CH	DI
4	ER	EL	EN	DE	EL
5	AN	LA	ON	EI	ES

	English	Spanish	French	German	Italian
6	RE	OS	NT	TE	TE
7	ND	ON	RE	IN	EN
8	AT	AS	AN	ND	RE
9	ON	ER	LA	IE	AN
10	NT	RA	ER	GE	AL
11	HA	AD	TE	ST	RA
12	ES	AR	EL	NE	AR
13	ST	RE	SE	BE	NO
14	EN	AL	TI	ES	IN
15	ED	AN	UR	UN	LE
16	TO	NT	ET	RE	CO
17	IT	UE	NE	AN	DE
18	OU	CI	IS	HE	LA
19	EA	CO	ED	AU	NT
20	HI	SE	OU	NG	TA
21	IS	TA	AR	SE	NE
22	OR	TE	IN	IT	ED
23	TI	OR	IT	DI	IO
24	AS	DO	ST	IC	LL
25	TE	IO	QU	SC	RI

Most frequent doubled letters

	English	Spanish	French	German	Italian
1	LL	EE	EE	SS	LL
2	TT	AA	SS	NN	SS
3	SS	LL	NN	LL	TT
4	EE	RR	TT	EE	EE
5	PP	SS	MM	MM	CC
6	OO	CC	RR	TT	RR
7	RR	DD	PP	RR	AA
8	FF	NN	FF	DD	PP
9	CC	OO	CC	FF	II
10	DD	II	AA	AA	BB

Most frequent trigraphs

	English	Spanish	French	German	Italian
1	THE	DEL	ENT	ICH	CHE
2	AND	QUE	LES	EIN	ERE
3	THA	ENT	ION	UND	ZIO
4	ENT	ION	DES	DER	DEL
5	ING	ELA	EDE	NDE	QUE
6	ION	CON	QUE	SCH	ARI
7	TIO	SDE	EST	DIE	ATO
8	FOR	ADE	TIO	DEN	ECO
9	NDE	CIO	ANT	END	EDO
10	HAS	NTE	PAR	CHT	IDE

Most frequent words

	English	Spanish	French	German	Italian
1	the	de	de	der	non
2	of	la	il	die	di
3	and	que	le	und	che
4	to	el	et	den	è
5	a	en	que	am	e
6	in	y	je	in	la
7	that	a	la	zu	il
8	it	los	ne	ist	un
9	is	se	en	dass	a
10	I	del	les	es	per

Average word lengths in a text

Finnish: 7.6 letters

Russian: 6.6 letters

Italian: 6.5 letters

English: 6.2 letters

German: 6.0 letters

Swedish: 6.0 letters

French: 6.0 letters

Spanish: 5.8 letters

Index of coincidence

The *index of coincidence (IC)* is a statistical technique that can be used to glean information about a text or to compare two texts. After frequency analysis, the IC is the second-most important statistical tool for a codebreaker.

Unfortunately, several related but different definitions of the IC can be found in the literature. For this reason, one easily gets confused when reading about it in different sources. In this book, we define the index of coincidence as the probability that two randomly chosen letters from a particular text are the same. (We don't cover situations in which the two letters stem from different texts.)

As an example, let's look at the (quite short) text *AAB*. There are three ways to draw two letters from it: *AA*, *AB*, and *AB*. As only the first combination comprises two equal letters, the index of coincidence is 1/3, or 0.333, or 33.3%.

If we now look at the text *AABC*, we get six possible sets of two random letters: *AA*, *AB*, *AC*, *AB*, *AC*, and *BC*. Only one of them contains two equal letters, so the index of coincidence of *AABC* is 1/6, or 0.166, or 16.6%.

As is easy to see, the index of coincidence does not change when each letter is replaced by another one, such as when a simple substitution cipher is applied. *AABC* has the same index of coincidence as *XXYZ*. In addition, the index of coincidence stays the same when the order of the letters is changed, which happens when someone has applied a transposition cipher to it: *AABC* has the same index of coincidence as *ABCA*. Thus, the index of coincidence remains constant, no matter whether we are dealing with a message encrypted by simple substitution or by transposition.

The index of coincidence of a sufficiently long, completely random text created from an alphabet with twenty-six letters is always going to be close to 1/26, or 3.8%. A text written in any natural language, where the case does not matter, and not counting spaces, numbers, or punctuation marks, usually has an IC between 5% and 9%. One nice thing about this indicator is that every language has its characteristic IC. This means that a codebreaker can use the IC to detect the language of a text, even after a simple substitution cipher or a transposition has been applied to it.

The following list specifies the index of coincidence for the most common languages:

Czech: 5.1%

Russian: 5.3%

Polish: 6.1%

English: 6.7%

Danish: 6.7%

Swedish: 6.8%

French: 6.9%

Finnish: 7.0%

Turkish: 7.0%

Spanish: 7.2%

German: 7.3%

Italian: 7.4%

Portuguese: 8.2%

Calculating the IC without a computer is quite laborious. An IC calculator is available on the dCode website at *https://dcode.fr/index-coincidence*.

Apart from its use in determining a text's language, the IC has other applications in codebreaking. For an overview, we recommend the 1922 book *The Index of Coincidence and Its Applications in Cryptology* by William Friedman.[2]

Lastly, for our most thorough of readers, here is an example upon which to test the Dunin-Schmeh technique: `oottn vnhoc sgrah eertn aaoeo einms rpwtr nwnte tahot pihde aegis pctln edaip eoile snghr dhlwe guaep er`. (For a hint, begin at Chapter 11.)

GLOSSARY

Abbreviation cipher
A method that replaces each word of a text with its first letter or a different abbreviation of it.

American Cryptogram Association (ACA)
A nonprofit organization dedicated to promoting the hobby and art of codebreaking. The ACA publishes a bimonthly newsletter titled *The Cryptogram*.

Aristocrat
A simple substitution cipher where word divisions and punctuation are retained.

ASCII code
The acronym for American Standard Code for Information Interchange. ASCII is a standardized way of representing letters, numbers, and punctuation in binary digits, which are the zeros and ones that computers can understand. For example, the lowercase letter a is encoded as 01100001, and a capital A is encoded as 01000001. We can also represent these values in hexadecimal (base 16) for easier reading, such that a is 61 and A is 41.

Though ASCII is called a code, it is not really encryption; it is just a table of values, as is Morse code.

Baudot code
Another "table of values" system that is used primarily with teletypes/teleprinters and represents each character using a series of five bits. Using it, operators could punch holes into paper tape for each letter and rapidly feed rolls of the tape into any teletype, which would then convert the Baudot code into human-readable messages.

Caesar cipher
A cipher, created in Roman times, that shifts every letter in the alphabet by a fixed number of characters (originally three). Examples: **A ▶** D, **B ▶** E, **C ▶** F, **D ▶** G . . . Some sample ciphertext: `Pxvlfdo jurxs idprxv iru Olhjh dqg Olhi.`

Cipher
An encryption method that works on letters or letter groups. A properly constructed cipher system can encrypt any kind of plaintext because it works on the individual letters. For comparison, *see* Code.

Ciphertext
The result of an encryption.

Cleartext
An unencrypted text, specifically one that may be visible in an otherwise encrypted text that has unencrypted parts showing through. *See also* Plaintext.

Code
An encryption method that works on words or phrases. Codes generally involve codebooks with predefined words or word groups to be encrypted. Codes cannot easily be used to encrypt any random message. *See* Cipher.

Codebreaking
Another word for cryptanalysis. Note that the word *codebreaking* refers to the breaking of all kinds of encryption, including both ciphers and codes.

Codegroup
The number, letter group, or symbol that represents a word in a code. In a nomenclator, a codegroup may also represent a number, letter, or other character.

Columnar transposition
A transposition cipher that typically requires the plaintext to be written in lines of equal length and the columns to be shuffled. The ciphertext is then read column-wise. Usually, a keyword is used to carry out a columnar transposition. See Chapters 9 and 10 for the difference between complete and incomplete columnar transposition.

Crib

A word or phrase that a codebreaker knows or suspects to be in the plaintext. When breaking a cryptogram, it is usually helpful to know or guess a word that appears in the plaintext.

Cryptanalysis

In general, the craft of decoding a ciphertext without knowing the key. Also referred to as breaking (or trying to break) a cryptogram. Note that some cryptanalysts might also review an encryption system or analyze a message to determine the system being used without trying to recover the original message.

Cryptogram

An encrypted message (i.e., a ciphertext) that a codebreaker is trying to break.

Cryptography

The science of encrypting a message. From the Greek *kryptos* and *graphein*, meaning "hidden writing."

Cryptology

The entirety of the study of cryptography and cryptanalysis.

CrypTool

An open source project that develops a set of free software programs implementing over 400 encryption and codebreaking methods. These programs are CrypTool 1, CrypTool 2, JCrypTool (a Java-based tool), and CrypTool-Online. For the codebreaking tasks in this book, we mainly used CrypTool 2.

DCT

See double columnar transposition.

Decipher

To break a cipher, meaning to perform a successful cryptanalysis on it. Deciphering may be targeted at determining the key without determining the plaintext.

Decryption

The process performed by the intended recipient of a ciphertext. Decryption requires knowledge of the encryption method used and (usually) the key. Decryption should be contrasted with deciphering or breaking (also known as solving or cryptanalyzing) an encrypted message, which means that the key and/or the encryption method arc not known.

Digraph

A group of two letters (for instance, *SJ*, *IA*, *BD*, or *GG*). Also known as a bigram or a digram.

Digraph substitution

A substitution cipher that replaces letter pairs (digraphs). The Playfair cipher is by far the most popular method of this kind.

Double columnar transposition (DCT)

An encryption method that consists of two consecutive columnar transpositions in a row. Considered one of the best manual ciphers.

Dunin-Schmeh substitution

A substitution cipher that is often used to encrypt and hide metapuzzles in crypto books. Provides a level of security similar to double ROT-13 and the Duran-Fairport cipher. Often uses a Sheahan 1802 key. Example: `Ptmqt jetoq cforq wlqcl updkr tfbcq ylktt fbcqa loqyq ltfbc qaloq yqwlb jqmiu pqwlx.`

Enigma

A German encryption machine that is about the size of a typewriter and was used in World War II. Polish, French, and British cryptanalysts, along with other intelligence operatives, collaborated to break its cipher systems.

Exclusive-or (XOR) operation

A type of binary arithmetic in which a set of ones and zeros is added to another. The result, or sum, is considered to be 0 if both values are the same and 1 if they are different. For example, if 1111 is XORed with 0000, the result is 1111. If 1111 is XORed with 0010, the result is 1101. And if 1010 is XORed with 1110, the result is 0100. In cryptography, letters in words are sometimes converted to ASCII and XORed with the 1s and 0s of a predetermined key. The resulting binary stream is then transmitted to a receiver, who XORs them back to the original plaintext. If the binary key is random, we call this a Vernam cipher or a special case of a one-time pad.

Freemason's cipher

See Pigpen cipher.

Frequency analysis

The act of determining the frequency of letters in a message. An important tool for a codebreaker.

Heptagraph

A group of seven letters.

Hexagraph

A group of six letters.

Homophones

Multiple ciphertext letters or characters that stand for the same plaintext letter. *See* Homophonic cipher.

Homophonic cipher

A cipher that includes homophones. The user of a homophonic substitution can choose between several alternatives when encoding a certain letter.

Index of coincidence (IC)

The probability that two randomly chosen letters from a text are the same. An important analysis tool for a codebreaker.

Key

Some secret information that only the sender and receiver should know. In practice, most encryption methods have a key, though in some situations, knowledge of the method is the key. The intended recipient should be capable of easily decrypting a message if they know the key, whereas a third party should not be able to decipher a ciphertext without the key. (Note: Some simple systems, such as Aristocrats, can result in the ability to extract the plaintext without recovering the full key.)

Keyword

A representation of many keys (e.g., **BIRDHOUSE**) that is easier to memorize than, for instance, a number (e.g., **844708615**) or large table.

Manual cipher

An encryption method that can be applied with paper and pencil or simple cipher tools, as opposed to requiring the help of a complex cipher machine or computer.

Morse code

A system of dots and dashes or short pulses and long pulses that was developed to communicate messages via telegraph or radio. Though called a code, it is not an encryption system but a method of communication. (See Appendix D for a Morse code table.)

Nomenclator

An encryption method that combines a simple substitution or a homophonic cipher with a code. A nomenclator provides one or more numbers, letter groups, or symbols for each letter of the alphabet and for frequent words. This system is sometimes also called a nomenclature.

Null

A meaningless symbol included in a ciphertext for the purpose of confusing codebreakers. An integral part of many substitution ciphers, codes, and nomenclators.

Octagraph

A group of eight letters.

One-time pad

A substitution cipher that adds a random sequence (the key) to the plaintext. If used properly, meaning if the key is not guessable and only used once, a one-time pad is unbreakable. However, using a one-time pad requires large amounts of key material, which makes it impractical for many applications.

Patristocrat

A simple substitution cipher in which word divisions and punctuation are removed.

Pentagraph

A group of five letters. The most frequent pentagraph in the English language is *OFTHE*.

Pigpen cipher

A simple substitution cipher that replaces each letter of the alphabet with a symbol taken from a Tic-Tac-Toe-like grid. Also known as the Freemason's cipher, as it became very popular among Freemasons in the eighteenth century. There are many variants of it. Here is one example:

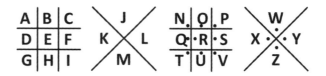

Plaintext

A message to be encrypted. Different from cleartext, which is unencrypted text that appears in an otherwise encrypted message.

Playfair cipher

An encryption method that replaces digraphs with other digraphs. Based on a square table and a number of simple substitution rules.

Polyalphabetic cipher

A substitution cipher based on several substitution tables. The application of each table follows some rule (for instance, table 1 might encrypt the first letter, table 2 might encrypt the second letter, etc.). A table can be constructed with a simple method, such as shifting each alphabet with a Caesar cipher.

ROT-13

A Caesar cipher that swaps each letter for the letter thirteen places away from it in a twenty-six-letter alphabet. The advantage of ROT-13 is that each letter, if encrypted twice, returns to its original form.

Shorthand

A writing method that increases the speed and brevity of writing. Sometimes used for (low-level) encryption.

Simple substitution

An encryption method based on a fixed, one-to-one substitution table. The Caesar cipher is one type of simple substitution cipher, though the cipher alphabet can also be keyed or random.

Steganography

The science of hiding information. Common steganographic methods include sympathetic (chemically reactive) ink, marked letters, word initials spelling out a message, and various digital systems that hide messages in the bits and bytes of some other file. While cryptography makes a message unreadable, steganography hides its very existence. Not to be confused with stenography.

Stenography

Another word for shorthand.

Substitution cipher

An encryption method that substitutes letters or letter groups, as opposed to a transposition cipher, which encrypts things by scrambling them.

Super-encryption

An encryption performed on a message that is already encrypted. Super-encryption is often used to enhance the security of a code. These methods are sometimes very simple; for instance, adding the current day of the month can cause a comparable shift to each letter of a message. See JN-25 in Chapter 7.

Tetragraph

A group of four letters, also known as a tetragram or a quadgram. The most frequent tetragraph in the English language is *TION*.

Transposition cipher

An encryption method that changes the order of the letters in a message. There are numerous transposition cipher variants, the most popular of which are turning grille ciphers and columnar transpositions.

Trigraph

A group of three letters, also known as a trigram. The most frequent trigraph of the English language is *THE*.

Turning grille

An encryption tool that consists of a square stencil with various holes cut into it. To encrypt a message, one turns the stencil by ninety degrees four times and writes letters in the holes at each orientation.

Vigenère cipher

A polyalphabetic substitution system once considered the "chiffre indéchiffrable," or the uncrackable cipher. Today, it is often solved quite quickly with modern codebreaking techniques.

MORSE CODE

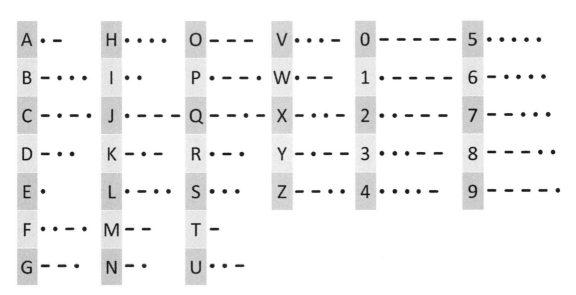

Figure D-1: The International Morse code table in use from 1900 through today

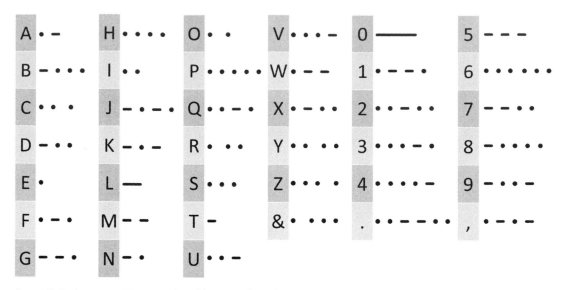

Figure D-2: American Morse code table in use from the 1850s to the 1950s

FIGURE SOURCES

Preface, uncaptioned

Photo of the authors, Elonka Dunin and Klaus Schmeh, in front of the wall mural at Beale's Beer restaurant in Bedford, Virginia, *https://www.bealesbeer.com*

Chapter 1, captioned

1-1. Encrypted postcard supplied by Karsten Hansky

Chapter 1, uncaptioned

Newspaper clipping

Chart created by authors

CrypTool 2 screenshot, created by authors

Codex compendium: Wellcome Library, London

Encrypted postcard from Charnwood Genealogy website, *http://www.charnwood-genealogy.com*

Encrypted postcard supplied by Tobias Schrödel

Excerpt of Manchester cryptogram, *Cryptolog* 109 (1987)

Turning grille cryptogram provided by Paolo Bonavoglia

Page from *Written Mnemonics: Illustrated by Copious Examples from Moral Philosophy, Science and Religion*

Freemason's mnemonic book in the Library and Museum of Freemasonry, London. Photograph by Klaus Schmeh.

Playfair message by Reginald Evans, courtesy of National Cryptologic Museum

Chapter 2, captioned

2-1. Telegram provided by Karsten Hansky

2-2. Composite: Photograph of disk by Hubert Berberich, 2013 (public domain). Photograph of slide by Klaus Schmeh

2-3. Diagram created by authors

2-4. Message provided by Gary Klivans

2-5. Excerpt from *Ciphergrams* by Herbert Yardley

Chapter 2, uncaptioned

Diagram created by authors

Diagram created by authors

Clipping from *The Times*, London, February 2, 1853

Clipping from *The Times*, London, February 11, 1853

Diagram created by authors

Clipping from the *Standard*, London, May 26, 1888

Message from Yudhijit Bhattacharjee's *The Spy Who Couldn't Spell*

Scene from 2006 film *The Prestige*. Credit: © Touchstone Films/courtesy Everett Collection/Mary Evans

Chapter 3, captioned

3-1. Photograph by Klaus Schmeh

3-2. Reproduction of encrypted title page created by Klaus, next to Klaus-created decipherment

3-3. 1909 postcard

3-4. Chart created by authors

3-5. Cryptogram from computer game *Call of Duty: Black Ops III* (2015)

3-6. Letter provided by Gary Klivans

3-7. Diary page by Beatrix Potter

3-8. Letter provided by Gary Klivans

Chapter 3, uncaptioned

Chapter 4, captioned

Chapter 6, uncaptioned

Chapter 7, captioned

7-9. Eighteenth-century nomenclator from *http://crypto-world.info*, Pavel Vondruška

7-10. Collage created by authors

    A. "Manchester cryptogram," *Cryptolog* 109 (1987)

    B. Letter from Nicolas de Catinat, 1702, Aargau Cantonal Library, Switzerland, *http://scienceblogs.de/klausis-krypto-kolumne/2016/05/01/wer-knackt-diesen-verschluesselten-brief-von-nicolas-de-catinat*

    C. National Cryptologic Museum, Kahn collection, 1898, *http://scienceblogs.de/klausis-krypto-kolumne/2017/10/22/an-unsolved-ciphertext-from-1898-who-can-break-it*

    D. 1911 telegram provided to Klaus by Frank Gnegel from the Museum für Kommunikation (Frankfurt, Germany), *http://scienceblogs.de/klausis-krypto-kolumne/2018/12/26/revisited-an-encrypted-telegram-from-german-south-west-africa*

7-11. Telegram provided by Karsten Hansky

7-12. Page from *The Science Observer Code*

7-13. Sixteenth-century nomenclator message from Albert Leighton's *A Papal Cipher*

7-14. Telegram provided by Karsten Hansky

7-15. Nomenclator by Mary, Queen of Scots; substitution table created by authors

7-16. Photographer credits: Klaus Schmeh; Norbert Biermann; Hiroko Tomokiyo

7-17. Bibliothèque nationale de France, *http://gallica.bnf.fr*, BnF fr. 2988 f.38

7-18. Chart created by Lasry, Biermann, and Tomokiyo

7-19. Chart created by authors

7-20. Telegram from *https://www.pinterest.co.uk/steelgoldfish/mount-everest/website*

7-21. Images courtesy of Sara Rivers-Cofield

7-22. Reproduction by Nicole Glücklich

7-23. "Manchester cryptogram," *Cryptolog* 109 (1987)

Chapter 8, captioned

8-1. Photograph by Klaus Schmeh. Metapuzzle license: qyaohlzlrzw

8-2. Chart created by authors

8-3. CrypTool 2 screenshot

8-4. Book cover courtesy of Penguin Random House

8-5. Screenshot from *https://dcode.fr*

8-6. Photos taken by authors

Chapter 8, uncaptioned

Reproduction of *Hitchhiker's Guide* challenge, created by Klaus

Excerpt of reproduction, created by Klaus

Excerpt of reproduction, created by Klaus

CrypTool 2 screenshot

CrypTool 2 screenshot

Reproduction of pigpen message from Diana Dors in documentary *Who Got Diana Dors' Millions?*

Chart created by authors

Chapter 9, captioned

9-1. Image from book *The Friedman Legacy*

9-2. Postcard from *http://www.postcardese.com/*, courtesy of Guy Atkins

9-3. Photograph by Klaus Schmeh

9-4. Reproduction of cryptogram created by Klaus on GCHQ website

9-5. Diary page kindly provided by Christopher Hill

9-6. Friedman notes courtesy of Jason Fagone, from scans taken in the Marshall Library, courtesy of the George C. Marshall Foundation, Lexington, Virginia

9-7. Challenge cipher published by Edgar Allan Poe; chart created by authors from sources at *https://www.eapoe.org/works/essays/gm41sw03.htm*

Chapter 9, uncaptioned

Chart created by authors

CrypTool 2 screenshot

Image from William Friedman's *Military Cryptanalysis IV*

Chapter 10, captioned

10-1. Photograph of Antonio Marzi diary by Filippo Sinagra, *cryptosite@yahoo.it*

10-2. Images courtesy of Jim Gillogly

Chapter 10, uncaptioned

Image courtesy of Tom Mahon and Jim Gillogly

Image courtesy of Tom Mahon and Jim Gillogly

Image courtesy of Tom Mahon and Jim Gillogly

Image courtesy of Tom Mahon and Jim Gillogly

Chart created by authors

Chapter 11, captioned

11-1. Collage of three images: (a) Photograph by Klaus Schmeh; (b) British National Archives, KV-2-62; (c) Photo by Klaus Schmeh at Günter Hütter collection

11-2. Holiday card created by authors

11-3. Chart created by authors

11-4. Ciphertext from Auguste Kerckhoffs's book *Cryptographie Militaire*

11-5. Birthday card created by authors

11-6. Chart created by authors

11-7. Birthday card created by authors

11-8. Turning grille cryptogram provided by Paolo Bonavoglia

11-9. Image from André Langie's book *Cryptography*

11-10. Image courtesy of the Royal Collection, The Netherlands

11-11. Reproduction of turning grille created by authors

11-12. Cover of the novel *Mathias Sandorf* by Jules Verne

11-13. Chart created by authors

11-14. Holiday card courtesy of the George C. Marshall Foundation, Lexington, Virginia

11-15. Challenge cipher created by Jew-Lee Lann-Briere and Bill Briere

11-16. Cipher from MysteryTwister

Chapter 11, uncaptioned

Chart created by authors

Chart created by authors

Chart created by authors

Chart created by authors

Chart created by authors

Chart created by authors

Chart created by authors

Chart created by authors

Image from André Langie's book *Cryptography*

Image from André Langie's book *Cryptography*

Image from André Langie's book *Cryptography*

Image courtesy of the Royal Collection, The Netherlands, with annotation by authors

Image courtesy of the Royal Collection, The Netherlands, with annotation by authors

Chapter 12, captioned

12-1. Table from *De furtivis literarum notis* by Giambattista della Porta

12-2. Chart created by authors

12-3. CrypTool 2 screenshots

12-4. Chart created by authors

12-5. Playfair message by Reginald Evans, courtesy of National Cryptologic Museum

12-6. CrypTool 2 screenshots

12-7. Cover of *Have His Carcase* by Dorothy L. Sayers

12-8. Top section: CrypTool 2 screenshot; Lower section: chart created by authors

12-9. Photograph from *Experimental Psychical Research* by Robert Thouless. Text excerpts from *A Test of Survival*, Proceedings of the Society for Psychical Research

Chapter 12, uncaptioned

Ciphertext created by authors from Porta symbols

Chapter 13, captioned

13-1. Ciphertext from *The Masonic Conservators* by Ray V. Denslow

13-2. All photographs taken by Klaus Schmeh at the Museum of Freemasonry, London; the New York Chancellor Robert R. Livingston Library and Museum; and from his private collection

13-3. Photograph taken by Klaus Schmeh at the Museum of Freemasonry, London

13-4. Scan courtesy of Walter C. Newman

13-5. Chart created by authors

13-6. Page from *Ecce Orienti!*

13-7. Page courtesy of JannaK on MetaFilter

13-8. Page from Oddfellows abbreviation cipher booklet

13-9. Chart created by authors, based on pages from Oddfellows book *Esoteric* and the related abbreviation cipher booklet

13-10. Birthday card created by Klaus, based on public-domain image from Pixabay

13-11. Somerton Man message

13-12. Encrypted postcards courtesy of anonymous donor

Chapter 14, captioned

14-1. Excerpt from *True Principles of the Spanish Language* by José Borras

14-2. Telegram from British National Archives, KV 2/2424

14-3. Cryptogram created by authors

14-4. Message courtesy of Louis Round Wilson Special Collections Library, University of North Carolina, Chapel Hill

Chapter 14, uncaptioned

Image courtesy of Dan Brown

Chapter 15, captioned

15-1. All photos by Klaus Schmeh: (a) from Günter Hütter's collection, Austria; (b) in the Heinz Nixdorf MuseumsForum, Paderborn, Germany; (c) in the National Cryptologic Museum, Fort Meade, MD; (d) at the Kryptologikum in Karlsruhe, Germany

15-2. Encrypted postcard courtesy of Dale Speirs

15-3. Shorthand plates by Winifred Kenna

15-4. Original image courtesy of Niedersächsisches Landesarchiv Abteilung Wolfenbüttel (Lower Saxonian State Archive, Wolfenbüttel section), 2 Alt (2837). Annotation added by authors

15-5. Image provided by New York State Archives

15-6. Photograph courtesy of John F. Kennedy Presidential Library and Museum

15-7. Photographs by Klaus Schmeh, with annotation

15-8. Page from the 1608 version of the third book of the *Steganographia*, pp. 166–167

15-9. Image designed by Cliff Johnson for David Blaine's book *Mysterious Stranger*

15-10. All photos taken by Klaus Schmeh: (a) Imperial War Museum (London); (b) Science Museum (London); (c) Fernmelde- und Informationstechnik der Bundeswehr (Feldafing, Germany); (d) Schreibmaschinenmuseum Beck (Pfäffikon, Switzerland)

15-11. Chart created by authors

15-12. Image courtesy of the US government

15-13. Chart created by authors

Chapter 15, uncaptioned

Chart created by authors

Excerpt from *The Shakespearean Ciphers Examined* by William and Elizebeth Friedman, p. 257

Chapter 16, captioned

16-1. Chart created by authors

16-2. Chart created by authors, simulated annealing

16-3. Image from *https://www.fbi.gov*

16-4. Sketch by San Francisco Police Department of the Zodiac Killer (left); Zodiac message Z408 (right)

16-5. CrypTool 2 screenshot

16-6. Photograph by Klaus Schmeh

Chapter 16, uncaptioned

Reproduction by Klaus Schmeh of drawing from *Curiosities of Olden Times*

IRA cryptogram courtesy of Jim Gillogly

Chart created by authors (matrix becoming 6 × 6 grilled)

Chapter 17, captioned

17-1. Note provided by Craig Bauer

17-2. Image from *https://www.fbi.gov*

17-3. Image from GCHQ

17-4. Photograph by Glenn McIntosh

17-5. Blueprint of *NKRYPT* sculpture by Stuart Kohlhagen

17-6. Close-up photographs of *NKRYPT* sculpture by Gregory Lloyd

Chapter 17, uncaptioned

Chart created by Glenn McIntosh at *https://www.meme.net.au/nkrypt/*

Appendix A, captioned

A-1. Photograph by Elonka Dunin

A-2. Chart created by authors

A-3. Chart courtesy of Jim Sanborn

Appendix A, uncaptioned

Chart created by authors

Appendix B, uncaptioned

Charts created by authors

Appendix C, uncaptioned

Chart created by authors

Appendix D, captioned

D-1. Chart created by authors

D-2. Chart created by authors

All cartoons created by Klaus Schmeh. Humor provided by both authors. Enjoy at your own risk.

REFERENCES

Chapter 1

1 Klaus Schmeh, "Ich glaub, mich tritt ein Pferd: Wer kann diese ver-schlüsselte Postkarte lösen?," *Cipherbrain* (blog), April 15, 2015, *http://scienceblogs.de/klausis-krypto-kolumne/2015/04/15/ich-glaub-mich-tritt-ein-pferd-wer-kann-diese-verschluesselte-postkarte-loesen/*.

2 Elonka Dunin, *The Mammoth Book of Secret Codes and Cryptograms* (New York: Carroll & Graf, 2006).

3 Jean Palmer, *The Agony Column Codes & Ciphers* (Gamlingay, UK: Bright Pen, 2005), 53.

4 Klaus Schmeh, "The Codex Compendium (Wellcome Library MS-199)," *Cipherbrain* (blog), 2013, *http://scienceblogs.de/klausis-krypto-kolumne/codex-compendium-wellcome-library-ms-199/*.

5 Simon Last, "1906 Postcard Lovers Secret Code!," *Charnwood Genealogy* (blog), January 6, 2016, *https://charnwoodgenealogy.wordpress.com/2016/01/06/1906-postcard-lovers-secret-code/*.

6 "Busman's Holiday: A British Cipher of 1783," *Cryptolog* 14, no. 4 (1987): 22–25, *https://www.nsa.gov/Portals/70/documents/news-features/declassified-documents/cryptologs/cryptolog_109.pdf*. For images, see "The

Manchester Cryptogram," *Cipherbrain* (blog), 2014, *http://scienceblogs.de/ klausis-krypto-kolumne/the-manchester-cryptogram/*.

7 Paolo Bonavoglia, "Two Cryptograms with 8×8 Grid," La Crittografia da Atbash a RSA, 2017, *http://www.crittologia.eu/storia/WW1/1916_griglia8x8 .html*.

8 "Written Mnemonics: Deciphering a Controversial Ritual," *Scottish Rite Masonic Museum & Library Blog*, October 1, 2013, *https://nationalheritage museum.typepad.com/library_and_archives/2013/10/written-mnemonics -deciphering-a-controversial-ritual.html*.

9 Joachim von zur Gathen, *CryptoSchool* (Berlin, Heidelberg: Springer, 2015).

10 Jean-Philippe Aumasson, *Serious Cryptography: A Practical Introduction to Modern Encryption* (San Francisco: No Starch Press, 2017).

11 Klaus Schmeh, *Kryptografie—Verfahren, Protokolle, Infrastrukturen* (Heidelberg: Dpunkt, 2016).

12 Bruce Schneier, "Memo to the Amateur Cipher Designer," *The Crypto-Gram*, October 15, 1998, *https://www.schneier.com/crypto-gram/archives/ 1998/1015.html#cipherdesign*.

13 Elonka Dunin, "Famous Unsolved Codes and Ciphers," Elonka.com, last modified December 8, 2022, *http://elonka.com/UnsolvedCodes.html*.

14 Klaus Schmeh, "The Top 50 Unsolved Encrypted Messages," *Cipherbrain* (blog), accessed March 31, 2023, *http://scienceblogs.de/klausis-krypto -kolumne/the-top-50-unsolved-encrypted-messages/*.

15 Ryan Garlick, "How to Know That You Haven't Solved the Zodiac-340 Cipher," University of North Texas, March 2014, *http://www.cse.unt.edu/ ~garlick/research/papers/Zodiac-340.pdf*.

Chapter 2

1 Klaus Schmeh, "Nicht schwierig: Wer löst dieses verschlüsselte Telegramm aus der Karibik?," *Cipherbrain* (blog), February 28, 2016, *http://scienceblogs.de/klausis-krypto-kolumne/2016/02/28/nicht-schwierig -wer-loest-dieses-verschluesselte-telegramm-aus-der-karibik/*.

2 Jean Palmer, *The Agony Column Codes & Ciphers* (Gamlingay, UK: Bright Pen, 2005), 15.

3 Herman Wuur, "Code in an 1888 Newspaper," Reddit, 2018, *https:// www.reddit.com/r/codes/comments/7fg4w1/code_in_an_1888_newspaper/*. Includes excerpt from *The Standard*, May 26, 1888.

4 Elonka Dunin, *The Mammoth Book of Secret Codes and Cryptograms* (New York: Carroll & Graf, 2006), 136.

5 Gary Klivans, "Cracking Gang Codes," Police1, *https://www.police1.com/ columnists/Gary-Klivans/*.

6 Gary Klivans, *Gang Secret Codes: Deciphered* (Santa Ana, CA: Police and Fire Publishing, 2016).

7 Gary Klivans, "Gang Codes: The Contraband Code," Police1, April 21, 2017, *https://www.police1.com/corrections/articles/gang-codes-the-contraband-code-BbG2vMguswZyCwYm/*.

8 Yudhijit Bhattacharjee, *The Spy Who Couldn't Spell* (New York: Berkeley, 2016).

9 Klaus Schmeh, "Who Can Break This Encrypted Journal from the Movie 'The Prestige'?," *Cipherbrain* (blog), January 7, 2018, *http://science blogs.de/klausis-krypto-kolumne/2018/01/07/who-can-break-this-encrypted-journal-from-the-movie-the-prestige/*.

10 Herbert Yardley, *The American Black Chamber* (Annapolis, MD: Naval Institute Press, 1931).

11 Herbert Yardley, *Ciphergrams* (London: Hutchison, 1932), 11.

12 Palmer, *The Agony Column Codes & Ciphers*, 182.

Chapter 3

1 David Kahn, *The Codebreakers* (New York: Scribner, 1996), 772.

2 Louis Kruh, "The Churchyard Ciphers," *Cryptologia* 1, no. 4 (1977): 372–375.

3 Oliver Knörzer, "The Book of Woo," Sandra and Woo, July 29, 2013, *http://www.sandraandwoo.com/2013/07/29/0500-the-book-of-woo/*.

4 Klaus Schmeh, "Decryption of the Book of Woo Soon to Be Published," *Cipherbrain* (blog), June 25, 2018, *http://scienceblogs.de/klausis-krypto-kolumne/2018/06/25/decryption-of-the-book-of-woo-soon-to-be-published/*.

5 Klaus Schmeh, *Codeknacker gegen Codemacher* (Dortmund, Germany: W3L, 2014), 177.

6 Edgar Allan Poe, "Secret Writing [Addendum III]," *Graham's Magazine*, December 1841.

7 René Zandbergen, "Text Analysis—Transliteration of the Text," last updated February 19, 2023, *http://www.voynich.nu/transcr.html*.

8 Klaus Schmeh, "An Unsolved Cryptogram Posted by a Reddit User," *Cipherbrain* (blog), September 25, 2018, *http://scienceblogs.de/klausis-krypto-kolumne/2018/09/25/an-unsolved-cryptogram-posted-by-a-reddit-user/*.

9 Klaus Schmeh, "Who Can Decipher This Encrypted Postcard from Wisconsin?," *Cipherbrain* (blog), August 29, 2017, *http://scienceblogs.de/klausis-krypto-kolumne/2017/08/29/who-can-decipher-this-encrypted-postcard-from-wisconsin/*.

10 Metapuzzle hint: mpx nful aporq mpx qrlaa npva mpx qrlaa zalf mpx qrlaa mavad mpx qrlaa qrlaa mpx qrlaa aporq mpx qrlaa mavad mpx nful qrlaa mpx nful qwf mpx nful fda mpx nful mpx mqaosdfolsjrps.

11 Federation of American Scientists, "Word and Word Pattern Tables," *Basic Cryptanalysis Field Manual* (Washington, DC: Department of the Army, September 13, 1990), appendix D, *https://fas.org/irp/doddir/army/ fm34-40-2/.*

12 Gary Klivans, *Gang Secret Codes: Deciphered* (Santa Ana, CA: Police and Fire Publishing, 2016).

13 Gary Klivans, "Gang Codes: Gang & Inmate Codes: Mistakes Don't Mean Failure" (PowerPoint presentation, Somerset, NJ, February 2015).

14 Kent Boklan, "How I Broke an Encrypted Diary from the War of 1812," *Cryptologia* 32, no. 4 (2008): 299–310.

15 Kent Boklan, "How I Decrypted a Confederate Diary: And the Question of the Race of Mrs. Jefferson Davis," *Cryptologia* 38, no. 4 (2014): 333–347.

16 Cara Giaimo, "Beatrix Potter's Greatest Work Was a Secret, Coded Journal She Kept as a Teen," Atlas Obscura, June 16, 2017, *https://www .atlasobscura.com/articles/beatrix-potter-secret-journal-code-leslie-linder.amp.*

17 Leslie Linder, *The Journal of Beatrix Potter: 1881 to 1897* (London: Frederick Warne, 1990).

18 David Kahn, *The Codebreakers* (New York: Scribner, 1996), 777.

19 Gary Klivans, "Gang Codes: The Sci-Fi Cipher," Police1, October 12, 2015, *https://www.police1.com/gangs/articles/gang-codes-the-sci-fi-cipher -H8qxcVICaOGlFAo8/.*

20 Klaus Schmeh, "Ten More Uses of the Pigpen Cipher," *Cipherbrain* (blog), October 10, 2016, *http://scienceblogs.de/klausis-krypto-kolumne/ 2016/10/10/ten-more-uses-of-the-pigpen-cipher/.*

21 Amanda Schnepp, "Aristocrats," *The Cryptogram* 1 (2019): 14.

22 Klaus Schmeh, "Can You Break This Encrypted Newspaper Ad from 1888?," *Cipherbrain* (blog), April 18, 2020, *http://scienceblogs.de/klausis -krypto-kolumne/2020/04/18/can-you-break-this-encrypted-newspaper-ad -from-1888/.*

23 Jean Palmer, *The Agony Column Codes & Ciphers* (Gamlingay, UK: Bright Pen, 2005), 292.

24 Craig Bauer, *Unsolved!* (Princeton, NJ: Princeton University Press, 2017), 155.

25 Ricardo Eugirtni Gomez, "Preliminary Report on Project MK-ZODIAC," April 2019, *http://mk-zodiac.com/DecipheringtheCelebrityCypher.html.*

26 Elonka Dunin, *The Mammoth Book of Secret Codes and Cryptograms* (New York: Carroll & Graf, 2006).

27 Klaus Schmeh, "Unsolved: An Encrypted Postcard from an Early Soccer Official," *Cipherbrain* (blog), February 28, 2021, *https://scienceblogs.de/klausis-krypto-kolumne/unsolved-an-encrypted-postcard-from-an-early-soccer-official/*.

Chapter 4

1 Tom Hays, "New Zodiac Letter: 'Sleep My Little Dad,'" *The Argus-Press*, August 6, 1994.

2 Klaus Schmeh, "Revisited: NSA's Unsolved Twitter Challenge from 2014," *Cipherbrain* (blog), December 28, 2017, *http://scienceblogs.de/klausis-krypto-kolumne/2017/12/28/revisited-nsas-unsolved-twitter-challenge-from-2014/*.

3 Liz Hull, "The Hitman Trapped by a Codebreaker: Gunman Convicted After His Secret Message from Jail Was Deciphered," *Daily Mail*, February 27, 2012, *https://www.dailymail.co.uk/news/article-2106384/Rapper-Kieron-Bryan-jailed-25-years-codebreaker-exposes-gangland-hitman.html*.

4 Klaus Schmeh, "Codeknacker auf Verbrecherjagd, Folge 9: Der Code des Gangster-Rappers," *Cipherbrain* (blog), March 30, 2014, *http://scienceblogs.de/klausis-krypto-kolumne/2014/03/30/codeknacker-auf-verbrecherjagd-folge-9-der-code-des-gangster-rappers/*.

5 Klaus Schmeh, "My Visit at the Cheltenham Listening Stones," *Cipherbrain* (blog), September 10, 2016, *http://scienceblogs.de/klausis-krypto-kolumne/2016/09/10/my-visit-at-the-cheltenham-listening-stones/*.

6 Klaus Schmeh, "Die Listening Stones von Cheltenham (Teil 2): Der Zahlenstein," *Cipherbrain* (blog), September 22, 2015, *http://scienceblogs.de/klausis-krypto-kolumne/2015/09/22/die-listening-stones-von-cheltenham-teil-2-der-zahlenstein/*.

7 David Kahn, *The Codebreakers* (New York: Scribner, 1996), 800.

8 Elonka Dunin, "Famous Unsolved Codes and Ciphers," Elonka.com, last modified December 8, 2022, *https://elonka.com/UnsolvedCodes.html*.

9 Klaus Schmeh, "The Top 50 Unsolved Encrypted Messages: 26. The Dorabella Cryptogram," *Cipherbrain* (blog), August 3, 2017, *http://scienceblogs.de/klausis-krypto-kolumne/2017/08/03/the-top-50-unsolved-encrypted-messages-26-the-dorabella-cryptogram/*.

10 Baxter, Robert, "POWELL, Dora Mary (1874–1964)," Archives in London and the M25 area, July 2001, *https://aim25.com/cgi-bin/vcdf/detail?coll_id=5702&inst_id=25*.

11 Craig Bauer, *Unsolved!* (Princeton, NJ: Princeton University Press, 2017), 127.

12 Bauer, *Unsolved!*, 462.

13 Bauer, *Unsolved!*, 472.

14 Mark Stamp, "Scanned Hamptonese Text," San Jose State University faculty pages, July 11, 2003, *http://www.cs.sjsu.edu/faculty/stamp/Hampton/pages.html*.

Chapter 5

1 Klaus Schmeh, "Zwei verschlüsselte Postkarten aus dem Jahr 1912: Wer kann sie knacken?," *Cipherbrain* (blog), August 25, 2013, *http://science blogs.de/klausis-krypto-kolumne/2013/08/25/zwei-verschlusselte-postkarten -aus-dem-jahr-1912-wer-kann-sie-knacken/*.

2 Klaus Schmeh, "From Russia with Love: An Unsolved Encrypted Postcard from 1906," *Cipherbrain* (blog), March 10, 2017, *http://science blogs.de/klausis-krypto-kolumne/2017/03/10/from-russia-with-love-an-unsolved -encrypted-postcard-from-1906/*.

3 André Langie, *Cryptography* (Walnut Creek, CA: Aegean Park Press, 1922), 78.

4 Nick Pelling, "La Buse's / Le Butin's Pirate Cipher (Part 1)," *Cipher Mysteries* (blog), April 15, 2013, *https://ciphermysteries.com/2013/04/15/ la-buse-le-butin-pirate-cipher*.

5 Nick Pelling, "La Buse's / Le Butin's Pirate Cipher (Part 2)," *Cipher Mysteries* (blog), April 20, 2013, *http://ciphermysteries.com/2013/04/20/ la-buses-le-butins-pirate-cipher-part-2*.

6 Klaus Schmeh, "Who Can Solve This Beautiful Encrypted Postcard?," *Cipherbrain* (blog), June 21, 2018, *http://scienceblogs.de/klausis-krypto -kolumne/2018/06/21/who-can-solve-this-beautiful-encrypted-postcard/*.

7 "Italy Police Decipher Coded 'Mafia Initiation Text,'" BBC News, January 9, 2014, *https://www.bbc.com/news/world-europe-25669349*.

8 Klaus Schmeh, "Ich glaub, mich tritt ein Pferd: Wer kann diese ver-schlüsselte Postkarte lösen?," *Cipherbrain* (blog), April 15, 2015, *http:// scienceblogs.de/klausis-krypto-kolumne/2015/04/15/ich-glaub-mich-tritt -ein-pferd-wer-kann-diese-verschluesselte-postkarte-loesen/*.

9 Klaus Schmeh, "Revisited: NSA's Unsolved Twitter Challenge from 2014," *Cipherbrain* (blog), December 28, 2017, *http://scienceblogs.de/klausis -krypto-kolumne/2017/12/28/revisited-nsas-unsolved-twitter-challenge-from-2014/*.

10 Klaus Schmeh, "Wer löst diese Verschlüsselung aus dem Jahr 1783?," *Cipherbrain* (blog), March 8, 2015, *http://scienceblogs.de/klausis-krypto -kolumne/2015/03/08/wer-loest-diese-verschluesselung-aus-dem-jahr-1783/*.

11 Klaus Schmeh, "Klaus Schmeh's Encrypted Books List," *Cipherbrain* (blog), 2023, *https://scienceblogs.de/klausis-krypto-kolumne/klaus-schmehs -list-of-encrypted-books/*.

12 Klaus Schmeh, "A Milestone in Voynich Manuscript Research: Voynich 100 Conference in Monte Porzio Catone, Italy," *Cryptologia* 37, no. 3 (2013): 193–203.

13 Elonka Dunin and Klaus Schmeh, "The Voynich Manuscript Compared with Other Encrypted Books," International Conference on the Voynich Manuscript, University of Malta, November 2022, *https://ceur-ws.org/Vol-3313/paper15.pdf.*

14 Gerry Kennedy and Rob Churchill, *The Voynich Manuscript* (London: Orion, 2004).

15 Raymond Clemens, *The Voynich Manuscript* (New Haven: Yale University Press, 2016).

16 Nick Pelling, *The Curse of the Voynich* (London: Compelling Press, 2006).

17 M.E. D'Imperio, *The Voynich Manuscript: An Elegant Enigma* (Laguna Hills, CA: Aegean Park Press, 1978).

18 Klaus Schmeh, "The Top 50 Unsolved Encrypted Messages: 7. The Cigaret Case Cryptogram," *Cipherbrain* (blog), July 5, 2018, *http://scienceblogs.de/klausis-krypto-kolumne/2018/07/05/the-top-50-unsolved-encrypted-messages-7-the-cigaret-case-cryptogram/.*

19 Klaus Schmeh, "Revisited: NSA's Unsolved Twitter Challenge from 2014," *Cipherbrain* (blog), December 28, 2017, *http://scienceblogs.de/klausis-krypto-kolumne/2017/12/28/revisited-nsas-unsolved-twitter-challenge-from-2014/.*

20 Klaus Schmeh, "The Top 50 Unsolved Encrypted Messages: 18. The Moustier Altar Inscriptions," *Cipherbrain* (blog), November 7, 2017, *http://scienceblogs.de/klausis-krypto-kolumne/2017/11/07/the-top-50-unsolved-encrypted-messages-18-the-moustier-altar-inscriptions/.*

21 National Security Agency, "Secret of the Altars," *Cryptolog* 1, no. 2 (1974): 10, 20, *http://cryptome.org/2013/03/cryptologs/cryptolog_02.pdf.*

22 Nick Pelling, "The Moustier Cryptograms," *Cipher Mysteries* (blog), April 2, 2013, *http://ciphermysteries.com/2013/04/02/the-moustier-church-cryptograms.*

Chapter 6

1 Craig Bauer, *Unsolved!* (Princeton, NJ: Princeton University Press, 2017), 440.

2 Pavel Vondruška, "Nápověda / soudobé nomenklátory," Crypto-World.info, 2013, *http://soutez2013.crypto-world.info/pribeh/napoveda.pdf.*

3 Vondruška, "Nápověda / soudobé nomenklátory."

4 Satoshi Tomokiyo, "Dumas' Cipher: Benjamin Franklin's Favorite Cipher," Cryptiana, August 24, 2008, *http://cryptiana.web.fc2.com/code/franklin.htm.*

5 Klaus Schmeh, "Als die Polizei einem Serienmörder ein Rätsel aufgab—Teil 2," *Cipherbrain* (blog), October 24, 2013, *http://scienceblogs.de/klausis-krypto-kolumne/2013/10/24/als-die-polizei-einem-serienmorder-ein-ratsel-aufgab-teil-2/*.

6 Bauer, *Unsolved!*, 155.

7 Dave Oranchak, "Let's Crack Zodiac - Episode 5 - The 340 Is Solved!," December 11, 2020, video, 13:02, *https://www.youtube.com/watch?v=-1oQLPRE21o*.

8 Nils Kopal, "Is David Oranchak's Zodiac Killer Cipher Z-340 Solution Correct???," December 11, 2020, video, 17:04, *https://www.youtube.com/watch?v=hIrOftXgibg*.

9 Nick Pelling, "Zodiac Z340 Is CRACKED!," *Cipher Mysteries* (blog), December 11, 2020, *https://ciphermysteries.com/2020/12/11/zodiac-z340-is-cracked*.

10 Joachim von zur Gathen, "Unicity Distance of the Zodiac-340 Cipher," Cyrptology ePrint Archive, December 14, 2021, *https://eprint.iacr.org/2021/1620*.

11 FBI San Francisco (@FBISanFrancisco), "#Breaking - Our statement regarding the #Zodiac cipher," Twitter, December 11, 2020, 11:21 a.m., *https://twitter.com/fbisanfrancisco/status/1337477701825925120*.

12 Sam Blake, "The Solution of the Zodiac Killer's 340-Character Cipher," *Wolfram* (blog), March 24, 2021, *https://blog.wolfram.com/2021/03/24/the-solution-of-the-zodiac-killers-340-character-cipher/*.

13 David Oranchak, "The Quest to Solve the Zodiac 340 Cipher," April 8, 2021, video, 64:10 (at 0:56 mark), *https://www.youtube.com/watch?v=iuNyQ44JYxM*.

14 Dave Oranchak, "Interpretations of the Seemingly Misplaced Words 'LIFE IS' and 'DEATH,'" Zodiackillerciphers.com, December 28, 2021, *http://zodiackillerciphers.com/wiki/index.php?title=Solution_to_the_340#Interpretations_of_the_seemingly_misplaced_words_.22LIFE_IS.22_and_.22DEATH.22*.

15 Thomas Ernst, "Die zifra picolominea: eine Geheimschrift der Habsburger während des Dreißigjährigen Krieges," *Mitteilungen des Instituts für Österreichische Geschichtsforschung* 129, no. 1 (2021), 124–147.

16 Klaus Schmeh, "Ungelöst: eine verschlüsselte Nachricht der Firma Theo H. Davies & Co.," *Cipherbrain* (blog), March 28, 2015, *http://scienceblogs.de/klausis-krypto-kolumne/2015/03/28/ungeloest-eine-verschluesselte-nachricht-der-firma-theo-h-davies-co/*.

17 Kristin Leutwyler, "A Cipher from Poe Solved at Last," *Scientific American*, November 3, 2000, *https://www.scientificamerican.com/article/a-cipher-from-poe-solved/*.

18 Edgar Allan Poe, "Secret Writing [Addendum III]," *Graham's Magazine*, December 1841, *https://www.eapoe.org/works/essays/gm41sw03.htm*.

19 *San Francisco Chronicle* map code letter from June 26, 1970, Zodiac Killer Facts Image Gallery, accessed March 31, 2023, *http://www.zodiackillerfacts.com/gallery/thumbnails.php?album=14*.

20 Nick Pelling, "Scorpion Ciphers," The Cipher Foundation, accessed March 31, 2023, *http://cipherfoundation.org/modern-ciphers/scorpion-ciphers/*.

21 Dave Oranchak, "Scorpion Ciphers," Oranchak.com, accessed March 31, 2023, *http://www.oranchak.com/scorpion-cipher.html*.

22 Bauer, *Unsolved!*, 195.

23 Cheri Farnsworth, *Adirondack Enigma* (Charleston: The History Press, 2010).

Chapter 7

1 David Kahn, *The Codebreakers* (New York: Scribner, 1996), 282.

2 John McVey, "Telegraphic and Signal Codes: 1911," last updated March 18, 2018, *http://www.jmcvey.net/cable/codescan_notes.htm*.

3 W.A. Sheahan, *Sheahan's Telegraphic Cipher Code* (Galesburg, IL: American Railway Association, 1892), *https://archive.org/details/ciphercodeofwor00shea/page/60/mode/2up*.

4 Ruth Selman, "'A Most Lamented Princesse': An English Princess at Versailles," *The National Archives* (blog), August 11, 2016, *https:/blog.nationalarchives.gov.uk/lamented-princesse-sudden-death-princess-henriette-anne-england/*.

5 Beryl Curran, *The Despatches of William Perwich* (London: Royal Historical Society, 1903), 96.

6 Gerhard Kay Birkner, "Briefe durch Feindesland. Die chiffrierte Post Wien-Istanbul um 1700," in Anne-Simone Rous and Martin Mulsow, *Geheime Post—Kryptologie und Steganographie der diplomatischen Korrespondenz europäischer Höfe während der Frühen Neuzeit* (Berlin: Duncker & Humblot, 2015).

7 Beáta Megyesi, ed., *HistoCrypt 2018: Proceedings of the 1st International Conference on Historical Cryptology* (Sweden: Linköping University Electronic Press, 2018), *https://ep.liu.se/ecp/149/ecp18149.pdf*.

8 Eugen Antal and Klaus Schmeh, eds., *Proceedings of the 2nd International Conference on Historical Cryptology, HistoCrypt 2019* (Sweden: Linköping University Electronic Press, 2010), *https://ep.liu.se/ecp/158/ecp19158.pdf*.

9 Rous and Mulsow, *Geheime Post*.

10 Peter Heßelmann, *Chiffrieren und Dechiffrieren in Grimmelshausens Werk und in der Literatur der Frühen Neuzeit* (Bern: Peter Lang, 2015).

11 Klaus Schmeh, "HistoCrypt 2018: A Video and Many Photos," *Cipherbrain* (blog), June 23, 2018, *http://scienceblogs.de/klausis-krypto -kolumne/2018/06/23/histocrypt-2018-a-video-and-many-photos/.*

12 Klaus Schmeh, "Revisited: A Terminology for Codes and Nomenclators," *Cipherbrain* (blog), October 7, 2018, *http://scienceblogs.de/klausis-krypto -kolumne/2018/10/07/revisited-a-terminology-for-codes-and-nomenclators/.*

13 Kahn, *The Codebreakers*, 107.

14 Kahn, *The Codebreakers*, 106.

15 James Madison to Edmund Randolph, August 1782, James Madison Papers at the Library of Congress, *https://www.loc.gov/resource/mjm .01_0693_0696/?st=gallery.*

16 Charles I, letter dated August 1, 1648, Harley MS 6988, f.208r, British Library, *http://www.bl.uk/manuscripts/Viewer.aspx?ref=harley_ms_6988 _fs001r.*

17 Klaus Schmeh, "Solved: The Encrypted Letters from Charles I to His Son," *Cipherbrain* (blog), May 5, 2021, *https://scienceblogs.de/ klausis-krypto-kolumne/solved-the-encrypted-letters-from-charles-i-to-his-son/.*

18 Kahn, *The Codebreakers*, 107.

19 Josef Šusta, "Eine päpstliche Geheimschrift aus dem 16. Jahrhundert," in *Mitteilungen des Instituts für Österreichische Geschichtsforschung*, Band 18, Heft 2 (1897).

20 Pavel Vondruška, "Nápověda / soudobé nomenklátory," Crypto-World.info, 2013, *http://soutez2013.crypto-world.info/pribeh/napoveda.pdf.*

21 Kahn, *The Codebreakers*, 190.

22 Helen Fouché Gaines, *Cryptanalysis* (New York: Dover, 1939), 1.

23 Abraham Sinkov, *Elementary Cryptanalysis* (Washington, DC: The Mathematical Association of America, 1967), 3.

24 Klaus Schmeh, "Eine ungelöste Verschlüsselung aus dem Jahr 1645," *Cipherbrain* (blog), March 20, 2015, *http://scienceblogs.de/klausis-krypto -kolumne/2015/03/20/eine-ungeloeste-verschluesselung-aus-dem-jahr-1645/.*

25 Klaus Schmeh, "Wer löst dieses verschlüsselte Telegramm aus Deutsch-Südwestafrika?," *Cipherbrain* (blog), January 15, 2016, *http://scienceblogs .de/klausis-krypto-kolumne/2016/01/15/wer-loest-dieses-verschluesselte -telegramm-aus-deutsch-suedwestafrika/.*

26 Klaus Schmeh, "Who Can Decipher These Encrypted Consular Messages?," *Cipherbrain* (blog), May 29, 2017, *http://scienceblogs.de/ klausis-krypto-kolumne/2017/05/29/who-can-decipher-these-encrypted -consular-messages/.*

27 Satoshi Tomokiyo. "Nonsecret Code: An Overview of Early Telegraph Codes," Cryptiana, September 25, 2013, *http://cryptiana.web.fc2.com/code/telegraph2.htm*.

28 John McVey, "Directory of Code Scans and Transcriptions," September 25, 2018, *http://jmcvey.net/cable/scans.htm*.

29 Klaus Schmeh, "Das verschlüsselte Telegramm eines Astronomen," *Cipherbrain* (blog), August 13, 2015, *http://scienceblogs.de/klausis-krypto-kolumne/2015/08/13/das-verschluesselte-telegramm-eines-astronomen/*.

30 John Ritchie, *The Science Observer Code* (New York: John C. Hartfield, 1885), *https://archive.org/stream/scienceobserverc13chanrich#page/n25/mode/2up*.

31 Peter P. Fagone, "The Solution of a Cromwellian Era Spy Message (circa 1648)," *Cryptologia* 4, no. 1 (1980): 1–4.

32 Albert C. Leighton, "A Papal Cipher and the Polish Election of 1573," in *Jahrbücher für Geschichte Osteuropas*, Band 17, Heft 1 (Stuttgart: Franz Steiner Verlag, 1969).

33 Paolo Bonavoglia, "The cifra delle caselle, a XVI Century Superencrypted Cipher," *Cryptologia* 44, no. 1 (2020): 39–52.

34 Klaus Schmeh, "21 Previously Unsolved Encryptions Solved," *Cipherbrain* (blog), July 30, 2022, *https://scienceblogs.de/klausis-krypto-kolumne/21-previously-unsolved-encryptions-solved/*.

35 Luigi Sacco, *Manuale di Crittografia* (Venice: Youcanprint, 2014), 111.

36 Klaus Schmeh, "Who Can Decipher This Encrypted Telegram from 1948?," *Cipherbrain* (blog), April 11, 2017, *http://scienceblogs.de/klausis-krypto-kolumne/2017/04/11/who-can-decipher-this-encryped-telegram-from-1948/*.

37 Klaus Schmeh, "Encrypted Telegram from 1948 Deciphered," *Cipherbrain* (blog), May 5, 2017, *http://scienceblogs.de/klausis-krypto-kolumne/2017/05/05/encryped-telegram-from-1948-deciphered/*.

38 Simon Singh, "The Black Chamber," accessed March 31, 2023, *https://simonsingh.net/The_Black_Chamber/maryqueenofscots.html*.

39 George Lasry, Norman Biermann, and Satoshi Tomokiyo, "Deciphering Mary's Lost Letters from 1578–1584," *Cryptologia* 47, no. 2 (2023): 101–202, *https://www.tandfonline.com/doi/full/10.1080/01611194.2022.2160677*.

40 Ashley Strickland, "Codebreakers Find and Decode Lost Letters of Mary, Queen of Scots," CNN, February 7, 2023, *https://www.cnn.com/2023/02/07/world/mary-queen-of-scots-lost-letters-scn/index.html*.

41 Ellen Gutoskey, "How Codebreakers Decrypted a Trove of Long-Lost Letters Written by Mary, Queen of Scots," Mental Floss, February 17, 2023, *https://www.mentalfloss.com/posts/mary-queen-of-scots-long-lost-letters-codebreakers*.

42 John Rabson, "All Are Well at Boldon: A Mid-Victorian Code System," *Cryptologia* 16, no. 2 (1992): 127–135.

43 Richard Collinson, *Journal of HMS Enterprise: On the Expedition in Search of Sir John Franklin's Ships by Bering Strait, 1850–55*, ed. T.B. Collinson (London: Sampson Low, Marston, Searle & Rivington, 1889), 337.

44 Michael Smith, *The Emperor's Codes* (New York: Arcade, 2000).

45 Kahn, *The Codebreakers*, 562.

46 Liza Mundy, *The Code Girls* (New York: Hachette, 2017), 80–81.

47 Peter Donovan, "The Flaw in the JN25 Series of Ciphers," *Cryptologia* 28, no. 4 (2004): 325–340.

48 Frederick D. Parker, *Pearl Harbor Revisited: U.S. Navy Communications Intelligence 1924–1941*, Series IV: World War II, Vol. 6, 3rd ed. (Fort Meade, MD: Center for Cryptologic History, National Security Agency, 2013), *https://www.nsa.gov/Portals/70/documents/about/cryptologic-heritage/ historical-figures-publications/publications/wwii/pearl_harbor_revisited.pdf*.

49 Ronald Clark, *The Man Who Broke Purple* (Boston: Little, Brown, 1977), 188.

50 Patrick D. Weadon, "The Battle of Midway," National Security Agency archive, accessed March 31, 2023, *https://www.nsa.gov/Portals/70/documents/ about/cryptologic-heritage/historical-figures-publications/publications/wwii/ battle-midway.pdf*.

51 Klaus Schmeh, "Revisited: An Encrypted Telegram from Mount Everest," *Cipherbrain* (blog), November 1, 2018, *http://scienceblogs.de/ klausis-krypto-kolumne/2018/11/01/revisited-an-encrypted-telegram-from -mount-everest/*.

52 Sara Rivers-Cofield, "Bennett's Bronze Bustle," *Commitment to Costumes* (blog), February 17, 2014, *http://commitmentocostumes.blogspot.com/2014/ 02/bennetts-bronze-bustle.html*.

53 Nick Pelling, "Ohio Cipher," The Cipher Foundation, *http://cipherfoundation .org/modern-ciphers/ohio-cipher/*.

54 Bryan Kesselman, *"Paddington" Pollaky* (Cheltenham, UK: The History Press, 2007).

55 Klaus Schmeh, "Sherlock Holmes and the Pollaky Cryptograms," *Cipherbrain* (blog), October 4, 2016, *http://scienceblogs.de/klausis-krypto -kolumne/2016/10/04/sherlock-holmes-and-the-pollaky-cryptograms/*.

56 Nicole Glücklich, "Sherlock Holmes & Codes," *Baker Street Chronicle* (Fall 2016), *https://sherlock-holmes-gesellschaft.de/baker-street-chronicle/*. Note that there are multiple newsletters with this title. This is the German-language edition.

57 "Busman's Holiday: A British Diplomatic Cipher of 1783," *Cryptolog* 14, no. 4 (1987), 22–25, *https://www.nsa.gov/Portals/70/documents/news*

-features/declassified-documents/cryptologs/cryptolog_109.pdf. For images, see "The Manchester Cryptogram," *Cipherbrain* (blog), 2014, *http://scienceblogs.de/klausis-krypto-kolumne/the-manchester-cryptogram/.*

Chapter 8

1 Klaus Schmeh, "Verschlüsselung auf Kryptos-Modell geknackt," *Cipherbrain* (blog), November 23, 2015, *http://scienceblogs.de/klausis-krypto -kolumne/2015/11/23/verschluesselung-auf-kryptos-modell-geknackt/.*

2 Bill Briere, "Highlights from My 'Cryppie Tour' Diary," October 2015, *http://tinyurl.com/2015CryppieTourDiary.*

3 "Cipher Types," American Cryptogram Association, accessed March 31, 2023, *http://www.cryptogram.org/resource-area/cipher-types/.*

4 David Kahn, *The Codebreakers* (New York: Scribner, 1996), 155.

5 Craig Bauer, *Secret History: The Story of Cryptology,* 2nd ed. (New York: CRC Press, 2021), 67–69.

6 Al Sweigart, "Hacking the Vigenère Cipher," in *Invent with Python* (self-pub., 2013), *https://inventwithpython.com/hacking/chapter21.html.*

7 Tobias Schrödel, "Breaking Short Vigenère Ciphers," *Cryptologia* 32, no. 4 (2008): 334–347.

8 Helen Fouché Gaines, *Cryptanalysis* (New York: Dover, 1939), 113.

9 Richard Hayes, "Solving Vigenères by the Trigram Method," *The Cryptogram,* June/July 1943.

10 Alexander Griffing, "Solving the Running Key Cipher with the Viterbi Algorithm," *Cryptologia* 30, no 4 (2006): 361–367.

11 Alexander Griffing, "Solving XOR Plaintext Strings with the Viterbi Algorithm," *Cryptologia* 30, no. 3 (2006): 258–265.

12 Klaus Schmeh, "Revisited: Diana Dors' Encrypted Message and Her Lost Millions," *Cipherbrain* (blog), April 9, 2018, *http://scienceblogs.de/ klausis-krypto-kolumne/2018/04/09/revisited-diana-dors-encrypted-message -and-her-lost-millions/.*

13 David D. Stein, "The Puzzle at CIA Headquarters," Elonka.com, 1998, *https://www.elonka.com/kryptos/mirrors/daw/steinarticle.html.*

14 Elonka Dunin, "Elonka's Transcript of the Cyrillic Projector," Elonka.com, June 13, 2003, *https://www.elonka.com/kryptos/cyrillic.html.*

15 Elonka Dunin, "Cyrillic Projector Solution," Elonka.com, 2003, *https:// www.elonka.com/kryptos/mirrors/CPSolution.html.*

16 Craig Bauer, *Unsolved!* (Princeton, NJ: Princeton University Press, 2017), 316.

17 Klaus Schmeh, "Richard Bean Solves Another Top 50 Crypto Mystery," *Cipherbrain* (blog), August 16, 2019, *http://scienceblogs.de/klausis-krypto -kolumne/2019/08/16/richard-bean-solves-another-top-50-crypto-mystery/.*

18 Jim Gillogly and Larry Harnisch, "Cryptograms from the Crypt," *Cryptologia* 20, no. 4 (1996): 325–329.

19 Elonka Dunin, "The Smithy Code," Elonka.com, April 28, 2006, *https://www.elonka.com/SmithyCode.html.*

20 Bauer, *Unsolved!*, 137.

21 History of Coast Guard Unit #387, 1940–1945, reviewed for declassification on October 2, 1980, National Archives and Records Administration, *http://archive.org/details/HistoryOfCoastGuardUnit387.*

Chapter 9

1 Center for Cryptologic History, *The Friedman Legacy: A Tribute to William and Elizebeth Friedman*, Sources in Cryptologic History No. 3 (Fort Meade, MD: National Security Agency, 1992, 2006), 13, *https://www.nsa .gov/Portals/70/documents/resources/everyone/digital-media-center/video-audio/ historical-audio/friedman-legacy/friedman-legacy-transcript.pdf.*

2 Klaus Schmeh, "The Top 50 Unsolved Encrypted Messages: 17. The Roosevelt Cryptogram," *Cipherbrain* (blog), December 8, 2017, *http:// scienceblogs.de/klausis-krypto-kolumne/2017/12/08/the-top-50-unsolved -encrypted-messages-17-the-roosevelt-cryptogram/.*

3 Guy Atkins, "Coded Love," *Postcardese*, March 21, 2010, *http://www .postcardese.com/2010/03/coded-love_21.html.*

4 Jean Palmer, *The Agony Column Codes & Ciphers* (Gamlingay, UK: Bright Pen, 2005), 264.

5 Palmer, *The Agony Column Codes & Ciphers*, 108.

6 Klaus Schmeh, "So hätten Sie der nächste James Bond werden können," *Cipherbrain* (blog), January 19, 2014, *http://scienceblogs.de/klausis-krypto -kolumne/2014/01/19/so-haetten-sie-der-naechste-james-bond-werden-koennen/.*

7 William Friedman, *Military Cryptanalysis IV* (Fort Meade, MD: National Security Agency, 1959), 11, *https://www.nsa.gov/Portals/70/documents/ news-features/declassified-documents/friedman-documents/publications/ FOLDER_452/41749819078904.pdf.*

8 Helen Fouché Gaines, *Cryptanalysis* (New York: Dover, 1939), 53.

9 Philip Aston, "A Decoded Diary Reveals a War Time Story," last updated October 21, 1997, *http://personal.maths.surrey.ac.uk/st/P.Aston/decode.html.*

10 Andro Linklater, *The Code of Love* (New York: Anchor Books, 2001).

11 Herbert Yardley, *The American Black Chamber* (Annapolis, MD: Naval Institute Press, 1931), 140–171.

12 Henry Landau, *The Enemy Within* (New York: G.P. Putnam's Sons, 1937).

13 David Bisant, "William Gleaves and the Capture of Lothar Witzke," *National Security Agency Newsletter* 47, no. 7 (1999): 4–6, *https://fas.org/irp/nsa/1999-07.pdf.*

14 David Kahn, *The Reader of Gentleman's Mail* (New Haven: Yale University Press, 2006), 42.

15 Donald McCormick, *Love in Code* (London: Eyre Methuen, 1980).

16 McCormick, *Love in Code*, 161.

17 Jason Fagone, *The Woman Who Smashed Codes* (New York: HarperCollins, 2017).

18 G. Stuart Smith, *A Life in Code* (Jefferson, NC: McFarland, 2017).

19 Ronald Clark, *The Man Who Broke Purple* (Boston: Little, Brown, 1977).

20 Palmer, *The Agony Column Codes & Ciphers*, 108.

21 Herbert Yardley, *Ciphergrams* (London: Hutchinson, 1932).

22 Satoshi Tomokiyo, "Solution of Tyler's Cryptograms Published in Poe's Article," Cryptiana, last modified February 18, 2015, *http://cryptiana.web.fc2.com/code/poe2.htm.*

23 "Oglaig Na h-Eireann," Headquarters Britain 69/44 (March 19, 1926), 262, no. 2 (email sent to authors by Jim Gillogly).

Chapter 10

1 Tom Mahon and James J. Gillogly, *Decoding the IRA* (Cork, Ireland: Mercier Press, 2008).

2 David D. Stein, "The Puzzle at CIA Headquarters," Elonka.com, 1998, *http://www.elonka.com/kryptos/mirrors/daw/steinarticle.html.*

3 Paolo Bonavoglia, "Encrypted/Decrypted Archive of Antonio Marzi 1945," La Crittografia da Atbash a RSA, accessed March 31, 2023, *http://www.crittologia.eu/critto/php/critMarzi.phtml.*

4 Tobias Schrödel, "Notes of an Italian Soldier," MysteryTwister, October 14, 2010, *https://mysterytwister.org/forum/forum/level-x-challenges-8/topic/challenge-notes-of-an-italian-soldier-20/.*

5 Moss Twomey Files, Headquarters Britain 69/44 (March 19, 1926), 262 (email sent to authors by Jim Gillogly).

6 Jean Palmer, *The Agony Column Codes & Ciphers* (Gamlingay, UK: Bright Pen, 2005), 93.

Chapter 11

1 Douglas W. Mitchell, "'Rubik's Cube' as a Transposition Device," *Cryptologia* 16, no. 3 (1992): 250–256.

2 Klaus Schmeh, "Rubik's Cube Encryption Challenge Solved," *Cipherbrain* (blog), March 17, 2019, *http://scienceblogs.de/klausis-krypto -kolumne/2019/03/17/rubiks-cube-encryption-challenge-solved/*.

3 Klaus Schmeh, "A Crossword Encryption Used by World War II Spy Wulf Schmidt," *Cipherbrain* (blog), July 4, 2017, *http://scienceblogs.de/ klausis-krypto-kolumne/2017/07/04/a-cross-word-encryption-used-by-world -war-ii-spy-wulf-schmidt/*.

4 Michael J. Cowan, "Rasterschlüssel 44—The Epitome of Hand Field Ciphers," *Cryptologia* 28, no. 2 (2004): 115–148.

5 "Cipher Types," American Cryptogram Association, accessed March 31, 2023, *https://www.cryptogram.org/resource-area/cipher-types*.

6 Auguste Kerckhoffs, "Cryptographie Militaire," *Journal des sciences militaires* 9 (January 1883): 161–191, *http://www.petitcolas.net/kerckhoffs/crypto _militaire_1.pdf*.

7 Paolo Bonavoglia, "Two Cryptograms with 8×8 Grid," *La Crittografia da Atbash a RSA*, 2017, *http://www.crittologia.eu/storia/WW1/1916_griglia8x8 .html*.

8 André Langie, *Cryptography* (Walnut Creek, CA: Aegean Park Press, 1922), 48.

9 Karl de Leeuw and Hans van der Meer, "A Turning Grille from the Ancestral Castle of the Dutch Stadtholders," *Cryptologia* 19, no. 2 (1995): 153–165.

10 Klaus Pommerening, "Commentary on Verne's Mathias Sandorf," Johannes Gutenberg-Universität Mainz, last updated January 14, 2021, *https://www.staff.uni-mainz.de/pommeren/Kryptologie/Klassisch/0 _Unterhaltung/Sandorf/Grille.html*.

11 Klaus Schmeh, "Who Can Solve These Encrypted Christmas Cards from the 1920s and 1930s?," *Cipherbrain* (blog), December 22, 2016, *http://scienceblogs.de/klausis-krypto-kolumne/2016/12/22/who-can-solve -these-encrypted-christmas-cards-from-the-1920s-and-1930s/*.

12 Lena Meier, "Grille Cipher," MysteryTwister, October 2011, *https:// mysterytwister.org/challenges/level-1/grille-cipher*.

Chapter 12

1 Giambattista della Porta, *De furtivis literarum notis* (1563), *https:// cryptobooks.org/book/112*.

2 David Kahn, *The Codebreakers* (New York: Scribner, 1996), 198.

3 Charles David, "A World War II German Army Field Cipher and How We Broke It," *Cryptologia* 20, no. 1 (1996): 55–76.

4 Klaus Schmeh, "Can You Solve This Bigram Challenge and Set a New World Record?," *Cipherbrain* (blog), July 13, 2019, *http://scienceblogs.de/ klausis-krypto-kolumne/2019/07/13/can-you-solve-this-bigram-challenge-and -set-a-new-world-record/*.

5 Kahn, *The Codebreakers*, 592.

6 Abbie Rowe, "AR6551-A. President John F. Kennedy Visits with A.R. 'Reg' Evans of New South Wales, Australia," May 1, 1961, *https://www .jfklibrary.org/asset-viewer/archives/JFKWHP/1961/Month%2005/Day%2001/ JFKWHP-1961-05-01-C*.

7 Helen Fouché Gaines, *Cryptanalysis* (New York: Dover, 1939), 198.

8 Parker Hitt, *Manual for the Solution of Military Ciphers* (Fort Leavenworth, KS: Press of the Army Service Schools, 1916), 76.

9 André Langie, *Cryptography* (Walnut Creek, CA: Aegean Park Press, 1922), 159.

10 Alf Monge, *Solution of a Playfair Cipher* (Fort Gordon, GA: US Army Signal Corps, 1936).

11 Robert Thouless, "A Test of Survival; Additional Note on a Test of Survival," *Proceedings of the Society for Psychical Research 1948*, Volume 48 (London: Society for Physical Research, 1946–1949), 253, 342, *http:// iapsop.com/archive/materials/spr_proceedings/spr_proceedings_v48_1946-49.pdf*.

12 Craig Bauer, *Unsolved!* (Princeton, NJ: Princeton University Press, 2017), 323.

13 Jim Gillogly and Larry Harnisch, "Cryptograms from the Crypt," *Cryptologia* 20, no. 4 (1996): 325–329.

14 Gillogly and Harnisch, "Cryptograms from the Crypt."

15 Klaus Schmeh, "Bigram 750 Challenge Solved, New World Record Set," *Cipherbrain* (blog), December 19, 2019, *http://scienceblogs.de/klausis -krypto-kolumne/2019/12/19/bigram-750-challenge-solved-new-world -record-set/*.

16 Klaus Schmeh, "Can You Solve This Playfair Cryptogram and Set a New World Record?," *Cipherbrain* (blog), January 27, 2020, *http://scienceblogs.de/ klausis-krypto-kolumne/2020/01/27/can-you-solve-this-playfair-cryptogram-and -set-a-new-world-record-3/*.

Chapter 13

1 Ray V. Denslow, *The Masonic Conservators* (Grand Lodge, MO: Ancient Free and Accepted Masons of the State of Missouri, 1931), 44.

2 Moses Wolcott Redding, *Cabala or the Rites and Ceremonies of the Cabalist* (New York: Redding, 1888).

3 Klaus Schmeh, "Unsolved: An Encrypted Freemason Document from the 19th Century," *Cipherbrain* (blog), September 19, 2017, *http://scienceblogs .de/klausis-krypto-kolumne/2017/09/19/unsolved-an-encrypted-freemason -document-from-the-19th-century/*.

4 Anonymous, *Ecce Orienti!* (New York: Redding, 1870).

5 Klaus Schmeh, "Who Can Decipher These Two Pages from a Freemason Mnemonic Book?," *Cipherbrain* (blog), November 21, 2017, *http://science blogs.de/klausis-krypto-kolumne/2017/11/21/who-can-decipher-these-two-pages -from-a-freemason-mnemonic-book/*.

6 Klaus Schmeh, "Holm-Kryptogramm: Eine Großmutter sprach in Rätseln," *Cipherbrain* (blog), February 6, 2014, *http://scienceblogs.de/klausis -krypto-kolumne/2014/02/06/holm-kryptogramm-eine-grossmutter-sprach -in-raetseln/*.

7 "'Action Line' Challenge," *Cryptologia* 2, no. 4 (1978): 368–370.

8 Klaus Schmeh, "Top-25 der ungelösten Verschlüsselungen—Platz 24: Das Action-Line-Kryptogramm," *Cipherbrain* (blog), June 7, 2013, *http:// scienceblogs.de/klausis-krypto-kolumne/2013/06/07/top-25-der-ungelosten -verschlusselungen-platz-24-das-action-line-kryptogramm/*.

9 Nick Pelling, "Action Line Cryptogram," *Cipher Mysteries* (blog), accessed March 31, 2023, *http://ciphermysteries.com/masonic-ciphers/action-line -cryptogram*.

10 Craig Bauer, *Unsolved!* (Princeton, NJ: Princeton University Press, 2017), 316.

11 Alan Yuhas, "Australia Exhumes the Somerton Man, and His 70-Year Mystery," *New York Times*, May 22, 2021, *https://www.nytimes.com/2021/ 05/22/world/australia/who-was-somerton-man.html*.

12 Daniel Keane and Gabriella Marchant, "Somerton Man Identified as Melbourne Electrical Engineer, Researcher Says," ABC News Australia, July 26, 2022, *https://www.abc.net.au/news/2022-07-26/somerton-man -identified-melbourne-born-engineer-researcher-says/101272182*.

13 Klaus Schmeh, "Die verschlüsselten Postkarten von Florence Maud Golding," *Cipherbrain* (blog), September 26, 2014, *http://scienceblogs.de/ klausis-krypto-kolumne/2014/09/26/die-verschluesselten-postkarten-von -florence-maud-golding/*.

Chapter 14

1 Herbert Yardley, *The American Black Chamber* (Annapolis, MD: Naval Institute Press, 1931), 120.

2 Ralph E. Weber, *Masked Dispatches* (Fort Meade, MD: Center for Cryptologic History, 1993), 101.

3 Jennifer Wilcox, *Revolutionary Secrets: Cryptology in the American Revolution Arnold Cipher* (Fort Meade, MD: Center for Cryptologic History, 2012), 24, *https://www.nsa.gov/Portals/70/documents/about/cryptologic-heritage/historical -figures-publications/publications/pre-modern/Revolutionary_Secrets_2012.pdf.*

4 "To Alexander Hamilton from Philip Schuyler, 11 June 1799," Founders Online, National Archives, January 23, 2002, *https://founders.archives.gov/ documents/Hamilton/01-23-02-0174.*

5 Weber, *Masked Dispatches*, 91.

6 Klaus Schmeh, "A German Spy Message from World War 2," *Cipherbrain* (blog), October 20, 2016, *http://scienceblogs.de/klausis-krypto-kolumne/ 2016/10/20/a-german-spy-message-from-world-war-2/.*

7 "Plain Language Code in Letters and Telegrams: Examples of Plain Language Codes and . . . ," KV 2/2424, 1942–1945, British National Archives, *http://discovery.nationalarchives.gov.uk/details/r/C11287845.*

8 André Langie, *Cryptography* (Walnut Creek, CA: Aegean Park Press, 1922), 88.

9 Langie, *Cryptography*, 138.

10 Martin Gardner, *Codes, Ciphers and Secret Writing* (New York: Dover, 1972).

11 Klaus Schmeh, "Verschlüsselte Zeitungsanzeigen, Teil 2: Eine mysteriöse Anzeigenserie," *Cipherbrain* (blog), November 15, 2014, *http://scienceblogs .de/klausis-krypto-kolumne/2014/11/15/verschluesselte-zeitungsanzeigen-teil-2 -eine-mysterioese-anzeigenserie/.*

12 Jean Palmer, *The Agony Column Codes & Ciphers* (Gamlingay, UK: Bright Pen, 2005), 38.

13 Klaus Schmeh, "Verschlüsselte Zeitungsanzeigen, Teil 2."

14 Weber, *Masked Dispatches*, 39.

15 Ralph E. Weber, *United States Diplomatic Codes and Ciphers* (Chicago: Precedent, 1979), 205.

16 Albert Leighton and Stephen Matyas, "The Search for the Key Book to Nicholas Trist's Book Ciphers," *Cryptologia* 7, no. 4 (1983): 297–314.

17 William Friedman, account of 1917 Hindu conspiracy and trial, January 21, 1920, George C. Marshall Research Library, *https://archive.org/details/ WFFHinduTrial1917/.*

18 David Kahn, *The Codebreakers* (New York: Scribner, 1996), 372.

19 Klaus Schmeh, "An Unsolved Message Sent to Robert E. Lee," *Cipherbrain* (blog), August 31, 2017, *http://scienceblogs.de/klausis-krypto -kolumne/2017/08/31/an-unsolved-message-sent-to-robert-e-lee/.*

20 Biff Hollingsworth, "8 April 1862: Cipher from Joseph E. Johnston to Robert E. Lee," *The Civil War Day by Day* (blog), April 8, 2012, *https:// blogs.lib.unc.edu/civilwar/index.php/2012/04/08/8-april-1862/.*

21 Satoshi Tomokiyo, "US Civil War Ciphers," Cryptiana, accessed March 31, 2023, *http://cryptiana.web.fc2.com/code/crypto.htm#SEC13.*

22 Klaus Schmeh, "A Dictionary Code Challenge," *Cipherbrain* (blog), October 29, 2018, *http://scienceblogs.de/klausis-krypto-kolumne/2018/10/29/ a-dictionary-code-challenge/.*

23 Palmer, *The Agony Column Codes & Ciphers*, 202.

24 Klaus Schmeh, "Two Unsolved Newspaper Ads from 1873," *Cipherbrain* (blog), September 30, 2019, *http://scienceblogs.de/klausis-krypto-kolumne/ 2019/09/30/two-unsolved-newspaper-ads-from-1873/.*

Chapter 15

1 Phwdsxccoh klqw, Dw wkh hqg ri brxu mrxuqhb, rqh zdb wr ilqg wkh sdvvzrug zloo eh wr frpelqh vrph ri wkh pxvlfdo nhbv zlwk wkh pdtxhwwh olfhqvh.

2 Craig Bauer, *Secret History: The Story of Cryptology*, 2nd ed. (New York: CRC Press, 2021), 4–5.

3 Luis Alberto Benthin Sanguino, "Analyzing Spanish Civil War Ciphers by Combining Combinatorial and Statistical Methods," Ruhr-Universität Bochum, 2014.

4 Klaus Schmeh, "M138 Challenges 1-4," MysteryTwister, accessed March 31, 2023, *https://mysterytwister.org/search/challenges/* (search for m-138).

5 Bauer, *Secret History*, 311–323.

6 J.V. Boone and R.R. Peterson, *The Start of the Digital Revolution: SIGSALY, Secure Digital Voice Communications in World War II* (Fort Meade, MD: National Security Agency, 2000), *https://www.nsa.gov/portals/75/documents/ about/cryptologic-heritage/historical-figures-publications/publications/wwii/ sigsaly.pdf.*

7 Dave Tompkins, *How to Wreck a Nice Beach* (Chicago: Stop Smiling Books, 2010).

8 Nathan Aaseng, *Navajo Code Talkers: America's Secret Weapon in World War II* (New York: Walker, 1992).

9 William C. Meadows, *The Comanche Code Talkers of World War II* (Austin: University of Texas Press, 2003).

10 "Navajo Code Talkers' Dictionary," revised June 15, 1945, and published April 16, 2020, online at *https://www.history.navy.mil/research/library/online -reading-room/title-list-alphabetically/n/navajo-code-talker-dictionary.html.*

11 Dale Speirs, "Secret Messages on Postcards," *The Canadian Philatelist*, March/April 2008.

12 *Encyclopaedia Britannica*, s.v., "Modern Symbol Systems," August 23, 1998, *https://www.britannica.com/topic/shorthand/Modern-symbol-systems*.

13 Charles Dickens, *A Christmas Carol*, printed in Gregg shorthand, with shorthand plates written by Winifred Kenna (New York: Gregg, 1918), *https://archive.org/details/AChristmasCarol-PrintedInGreggShorthand/page/n1/mode/2up*.

14 Gerhard Strasser, "Die Wissenschaft der Alphabete. Universalsprachen vom 16. bis zum frühen 19. Jahrhundert im Kontext on Kryptographie und Philosophie," in Anne-Simone Rous and Martin Mulsow, *Geheime Post—Kryptologie und Steganographie der diplomatischen Korrespondenz europäischer Höfe während der Frühen Neuzeit* (Berlin: Duncker & Humblot, 2015).

15 Niedersächsisches Landesarchiv Abteilung Wolfenbüttel WF: 2 Alt (2837), mid-seventeenth century, document provided to Klaus by Gerhard Strasser.

16 Klaus Schmeh, "Versteckte Nachrichten in Modezeichnungen, Grashalmen und Apfelbäumen," *Cipherbrain* (blog), May 21, 2015, *http://scienceblogs.de/klausis-krypto-kolumne/2015/05/21/versteckte-nachrichten-in-modezeichnungen-grashalmen-und-apfelbaeumen/*.

17 Klaus Schmeh, *Versteckte Botschaften—Die faszinierende Geschichte der Steganografie* (Heidelberg: Dpunkt, 2017).

18 Kristie Macrakis, *Prisoners, Lovers, and Spies* (New Haven: Yale University Press, 2014).

19 Jennifer Wilcox, *Revolutionary Secrets: Cryptology in the American Revolution* (Fort Meade, MD: Center for Cryptologic History, 2012), 13, *https://www.nsa.gov/Portals/70/documents/about/cryptologic-heritage/historical-figures-publications/publications/pre-modern/Revolutionary_Secrets_2012.pdf*.

20 Kat Eschner, "Why JFK Kept a Coconut Shell in the Oval Office," *Smithsonian Magazine*, August 2, 2017, *https://www.smithsonianmag.com/smart-news/why-jfk-kept-coconut-shell-white-house-desk-180964263/*.

21 "John F. Kennedy and PT 109," John F. Kennedy Presidential Library and Museum, accessed March 31, 2023, *https://www.jfklibrary.org/learn/about-jfk/jfk-in-history/john-f-kennedy-and-pt-109*.

22 David Mowry, *Listening to the Rumrunners* (Fort Meade, MD: Center for Cryptologic History, 2014).

23 Elonka Dunin, "Cipher on the William and Elizebeth Friedman Tombstone at Arlington National Cemetery Is Solved," Elonka.com, April 17, 2017, *https://elonka.com/friedman/FriedmanTombstone.pdf*.

24 Jason Fagone, *The Woman Who Smashed Codes* (New York: HarperCollins, 2017).

25 David Kahn, *The Codebreakers* (New York: Scribner, 1996), 882–884.

26 Kahn, *The Codebreakers*, 975.

27 Jürgen Hermes, "Textprozessierung—Design und Applikation" (PhD thesis, Universität zu Köln, 2012), *http://kups.ub.uni-koeln.de/4561/*.

28 Jim Reeds, "Solved: The Ciphers in Book III of Trithemius's Steganographia," *Cryptologia* 22, no. 4 (1998): 291–317.

29 Thomas Ernst, "Schwarzweiße Magie: Der Schlüssel zum dritten Buch der Steganographia des Trithemius," *Daphnis* 1 (1996).

30 Thomas Ernst, "The Numerical-Astrological Ciphers in the Third Book of Trithemius's Steganographia," *Cryptologia 22,* no. 4 (1998): 318–341.

31 Gina Kolata, "A Mystery Unraveled, Twice," *New York Times*, April 14, 1998, *https://www.nytimes.com/1998/04/14/science/a-mystery-unraveled-twice.html*.

32 Jürgen Hermes, "Die unbekannte Heldensage," *TEXperimenTales*, January 25, 2017, *https://texperimentales.hypotheses.org/1970*.

33 Schmeh, *Versteckte Botschaften*, 119.

34 Klaus Schmeh, "Der Trithemius-Code," *Skeptiker* 3 (2018).

35 Jeff Briden, "Deconstruction Deluxe," accessed March 31, 2023, *https://fools-errand.com/09-TH/solution-JB.htm*.

36 William Friedman and Elizebeth Friedman, *The Shakespearean Ciphers Examined* (Cambridge: Cambridge University Press, 1957).

37 Alan Mathison Turing, *The Essential Turing*, ed. B. Jack Copeland (Oxford: Oxford University Press, 2004), 236.

38 Gordon Welchman, "From Polish Bomba to British Bombe: The Birth of Ultra," *Intelligence and National Security*, January 1986.

39 US Army, *The US 6812 Division Bombe Report Eastcote 1944*, accessed March 31, 2023, *https://web.archive.org/web/20060523190750/http://www.codesandciphers.org.uk/documents/bmbrpt/bmbpg010.HTM*.

40 David Kahn, *Seizing the Enigma* (Boston: Houghton Mifflin, 1991).

41 Tom Perera and Dan Perera, *Inside Enigma* (Bedford, UK: RSGB, 2019), *https://enigmamuseum.com/iead.htm*.

42 Dermot Turing, *Demystifying the Bombe* (Stroud: Pitkin Press, 2014).

43 Kahn, *The Codebreakers*, 1.

44 Ronald Clark, *The Man Who Broke Purple* (Boston: Little, Brown, 1977), 138.

45 Stephen Budiansky, *Battle of Wits* (London: Penguin Books, 2000), 219.

46 Jerry Roberts, *Lorenz: Breaking Hitler's Top-Secret Code at Bletchley Park* (Stroud, Gloucestershire: The History Press, 2017).

47 Donald Davies, "The Lorenz Cipher Machine SZ42," *Cryptologia* 19, no. 1 (1995), 39–61.

48 Jerry Roberts, "How Lorenz Was Different from Enigma," The History Press, accessed March 31, 2023, *https://www.thehistorypress.co.uk/articles/how-lorenz-was-different-from-enigma/*.

49 Roberts, *Lorenz*.

50 "Intelligence," D-Day Revisited, accessed March 31, 2023, *https://d-dayrevisited.co.uk/d-day-history/planning-and-preparation/intelligence/*.

51 Thomas H. Flowers, "D-Day at Bletchley Park," in B. Jack Copeland, ed., *Colossus: The Secrets of Bletchley Park's Code-Breaking Computers* (Oxford: Oxford University Press, 2006), 80.

52 Roberts, *Lorenz*, 131.

53 Friedrich L. Bauer, *Decrypted Secrets: Methods and Maxims of Cryptology* (Berlin, Heidelberg: Springer-Verlag, 2007), 123.

54 Bauer, *Secret History*, 245.

Chapter 16

1 Sabine Baring-Gould, *Curiosities of Olden Times* (Edinburgh: John Grant, 1896), 17.

2 Klaus Schmeh, "An Unsolved Cryptogram Testing the Reader's Sagacity," *Cipherbrain* (blog), March 16, 2017, *http://scienceblogs.de/klausis-krypto-kolumne/2017/03/16/an-unsolved-cryptogram-testing-the-readers-sagacity/*.

3 Klaus Schmeh, "A Mird in the Hand Is Worth Two in the Mush: Solving Ciphers with Hill Climbing," *Cipherbrain* (blog), March 26, 2017, *http://scienceblogs.de/klausis-krypto-kolumne/2017/03/26/a-mird-in-the-hand-is-worth-two-in-the-mush-solving-ciphers-with-hill-climbing/*.

4 US Department of Justice, Federal Bureau of Investigation, "Case Study: Carlie Brucia Murder," in *Today's FBI: Facts & Figures, 2010–2011* (Office of Public Affairs, 2011), 48.

5 Federal Bureau of Investigation, *FBI Laboratory 2005 Report*, Publication No. 0357, *https://archives.fbi.gov/archives/about-us/lab/lab-annual-report-2005/fbi-lab-report-2005-pdf*.

6 Klaus Schmeh, "Codeknacker auf Verbrecherjagd, Folge 1: Wie das FBI den Code eines Kindermörders knackte," *Cipherbrain* (blog), February 26, 2014, *http://scienceblogs.de/klausis-krypto-kolumne/2014/02/26/codeknacker-auf-verbrecherjagd-folge-1-wie-das-fbi-den-code-eines-kindermoerders-knackte/*.

7 Nils Kopal, "Cryptanalysis of Homophonic Substitution Ciphers Using Simulated Annealing with Fixed Temperature," in *Proceedings of the 2nd International Conference on Historical Cryptology, HistoCrypt 2019,* ed. Eugen Antal and Klaus Schmeh (Sweden: Linköping University Electronic Press, 2009), 107–116, *https://ep.liu.se/ecp/158/ecp19158.pdf.*

8 Amrapali Dhavare, Richard M. Low, and Mark Stamp, "Efficient Cryptanalysis of Homophonic Substitution Ciphers," *Cryptologia* 37, no. 3 (2013): 250–281.

9 Mark Stamp, "Zodiac Cipher," MysteryTwister, July 2010, *https://www.mysterytwister.org/images/challenges/mtc3-stamp-03-zodiac-en.pdf.*

10 Tom Mahon and James J. Gillogly, *Decoding the IRA* (Cork, Ireland: Mercier Press, 2008).

11 Klaus Schmeh, "Top 25 Crypto Mystery Solved by Australian Codebreaker," *Cipherbrain* (blog), August 8, 2019, *http://scienceblogs.de/klausis-krypto-kolumne/2019/08/08/top-25-crypto-mystery-solved-by-australian-codebreaker/.*

12 George Lasry, "A Methodology for the Cryptanalysis of Classical Ciphers with Search Metaheuristics" (PhD thesis, Kassel University Press, 2017), *https://d-nb.info/1153797542/34.*

13 Otto Leiberich, "Vom diplomatischen Code zur Falltürfunktion—Hundert Jahre Kryptographie in Deutschland," *Spektrum der Wissenschaft* 6 (1999).

14 Rafael Sabatini, *Mistress Wilding* (New York: Grosset & Dunlap, 1910).

15 Klaus Schmeh, "Wettrennen der Codeknacker," *Heise,* January 9, 2008, *https://www.heise.de/tp/features/Wettrennen-der-Codeknacker-3416587.html.*

16 George Lasry, Nils Kopal, and Arno Wacker, "Solving the Double Transposition Challenge with a Divide-and-Conquer Approach," *Cryptologia* 38, no. 3 (2014): 197–214.

17 Paolo Bonavoglia, "Two Cryptograms with 8×8 Grid," *La Crittografia da Atbash a RSA,* 2017, *http://www.crittologia.eu/storia/WW1/1916_griglia8x8.html.*

18 Klaus Schmeh, "How Paolo Bonavoglia and Bart Wenmeckers Solved an Early 20th Century Cryptogram," *Cipherbrain* (blog), May 11, 2017, *http://scienceblogs.de/klausis-krypto-kolumne/2017/05/11/how-paolo-bonavoglia-and-bart-wenmeckers-solved-a-an-early-20th-century-cryptogram/.*

19 Klaus Schmeh, "Fleissner Challenge: Can This Cryptogram Be Broken?," *Cipherbrain* (blog), January 13, 2017, *http://scienceblogs.de/klausis-krypto-kolumne/2017/01/13/fleissner-challenge-can-this-cryptogram-be-broken/.*

20 Klaus Schmeh, "How My Readers Solved the Fleissner Challenge," *Cipherbrain* (blog), January 19, 2017, *http://scienceblogs.de/klausis-krypto-kolumne/2017/01/19/how-my-readers-solved-the-fleissner-challenge/.*

21 Klaus Schmeh, "Bigram Substitution: An Old and Simple Encryption Algorithm That Is Hard to Break," *Cipherbrain* (blog), February 13, 2017, *http://scienceblogs.de/klausis-krypto-kolumne/2017/02/13/bigram-substitution-an-old-and-simple-encryption-algorithm-that-is-hard-to-break/.*

22 Klaus Schmeh, "Can You Solve This Bigram Challenge and Set a New World Record?," *Cipherbrain* (blog), July 13, 2019, *http://scienceblogs.de/klausis-krypto-kolumne/2019/07/13/can-you-solve-this-bigram-challenge-and-set-a-new-world-record/.*

23 Klaus Schmeh, "Norbert Biermann Solves Bigram Challenge and Sets a New World Record," *Cipherbrain* (blog), August 13, 2019, *http://scienceblogs.de/klausis-krypto-kolumne/2019/08/13/norbert-biermann-solves-bigram-challenge-and-sets-a-new-world-record/.*

24 Klaus Schmeh, "Solve This Bigram Challenge and Set a New World Record," *Cipherbrain* (blog), October 7, 2019, *http://scienceblogs.de/klausis-krypto-kolumne/2019/10/07/solve-this-bigram-challenge-and-set-a-new-world-record/.*

25 Klaus Schmeh, "Bigram 1000 Challenge Solved, New World Record Set," *Cipherbrain* (blog), October 27, 2019, *http://scienceblogs.de/klausis-krypto-kolumne/2019/10/27/bigram-1000-challenge-solved-new-world-record-set/.*

26 Klaus Schmeh, "Solve This Bigram Challenge and Set a New World Record," *Cipherbrain* (blog), December 12, 2019, *http://scienceblogs.de/klausis-krypto-kolumne/2019/12/12/solve-this-bigram-challenge-and-set-a-new-world-record-2/.*

27 Klaus Schmeh, "Bigram 750 Challenge Solved, New World Record Set," *Cipherbrain* (blog), December 19, 2019, *http://scienceblogs.de/klausis-krypto-kolumne/2019/12/19/bigram-750-challenge-solved-new-world-record-set/.*

28 Klaus Schmeh, "Die Listening Stones von Cheltenham (Teil 2): Der Zahlenstein," *Cipherbrain* (blog), September 22, 2015, *http://scienceblogs.de/klausis-krypto-kolumne/2015/09/22/die-listening-stones-von-cheltenham-teil-2-der-zahlenstein/.*

29 Alf Monge, *Solution of a Playfair Cipher* (Fort Gordon, GA: US Army Signal Corps, 1936).

30 Elonka Dunin, Magnus Ekhall, Konstantin Hamidullin, Nils Kopal, George Lasry, and Klaus Schmeh, "How We Set New World Records in Breaking Playfair Ciphertexts," *Cryptologia* 46, no. 4 (2021): 302–322.

31 Klaus Schmeh, "Playfair Cipher: Is It Unbreakable, If the Message Has Only 50 Letters?," *Cipherbrain* (blog), April 7, 2018, *http://scienceblogs.de/klausis-krypto-kolumne/2018/04/07/playfair-cipher-is-it-unbreakable-if-the-message-has-only-50-letters/.*

32 Klaus Schmeh, "Playfair Cipher: Is It Breakable, If the Message Has Only 40 Letters?," *Cipherbrain* (blog), December 8, 2018, *http://science*

blogs.de/klausis-krypto-kolumne/2018/12/08/playfair-cipher-is-it-breakable
-if-the-message-has-only-40-letters/.

33 George Lasry, "Solving a 40-Letter Playfair Challenge with CrypTool 2," in *Proceedings of the 2nd International Conference on Historical Cryptology, HistoCrypt 2019*, ed. Eugen Antal and Klaus Schmeh (Sweden: Linköping University Electronic Press, 2019), 87–96, *https://ep.liu.se/ecp/158/010/ecp19158010.pdf*.

34 Klaus Schmeh, "Playfair Cipher: Is It Breakable If the Message Has Only 30 Letters?," *Cipherbrain* (blog), April 15, 2019, *http://scienceblogs.de/klausis-krypto-kolumne/2019/04/15/playfair-cipher-is-it-breakable-if-the-message-has-only-30-letters/*.

35 Klaus Schmeh, "Magnus Ekhall Solves Playfair Challenge and Sets a New World Record," *Cipherbrain* (blog), September 5, 2019, *http://scienceblogs.de/klausis-krypto-kolumne/2019/09/05/magnus-ekhall-solves-playfair-challenge-and-sets-a-new-world-record/*.

36 Klaus Schmeh, "Can You Solve This Playfair Cryptogram and Set a New World Record?," *Cipherbrain* (blog), September 10, 2019, *http://scienceblogs.de/klausis-krypto-kolumne/2019/09/10/can-you-solve-this-playfair-cryptogram-and-set-a-new-world-record/*.

37 Klaus Schmeh, "Magnus Ekhall Solves 28-Letter Playfair Challenge and Sets New World Record," *Cipherbrain* (blog), November 14, 2019, *http://scienceblogs.de/klausis-krypto-kolumne/2019/11/14/magnus-ekhall-solves-28-letter-playfair-challenge-and-sets-new-world-record/*.

38 Klaus Schmeh, "Can You Solve This Playfair Cryptogram and Set a New World Record?," *Cipherbrain* (blog), November 22, 2019, *http://scienceblogs.de/klausis-krypto-kolumne/2019/11/22/can-you-solve-this-playfair-cryptogram-and-set-a-new-world-record-2/*.

39 Klaus Schmeh, "Konstantin Hamidullin Solves 26-Letter Playfair Challenge and Sets New World Record," *Cipherbrain* (blog), December 12, 2019, *http://scienceblogs.de/klausis-krypto-kolumne/2019/12/21/konstantin-hamidullin-solves-26-letter-playfair-challenge-and-sets-new-world-record/*.

40 Jack Copeland, "Alan Turing: The Codebreaker Who Saved 'Millions of Lives,'" BBC News, June 19, 2012, *https://www.bbc.com/news/technology-18419691*.

41 Dirk Rijmenants, "Stefan Krah's M4 Project and the Story of U-264," Cipher Machines and Cryptology, last updated March 31, 2022, *https://www.ciphermachinesandcryptology.com/en/m4project.htm*.

42 Frode Weierud, "Breaking German Wehrmacht Ciphers," Frode Weierud's CryptoCellar, March 2006, *https://cryptocellar.org/bgac/index.html*.

43 Michael Hörenberg, "The Enigma Message Breaking Project," Breaking German Navy Ciphers, December 16, 2022, *https://enigma.hoerenberg.com*.

Chapter 17

1 John Schwartz, "Clues to Stubborn Secret in C.I.A.'s Backyard," *New York Times*, November 21, 2010, *https://www.nytimes.com/2010/11/21/us/21code.html?hp*.

2 John Schwartz, "A New Clue to Kryptos," *New York Times*, November 21, 2014, *https://www.nytimes.com/interactive/2014/11/21/science/new-clue-to-kryptos.html*.

3 John Schwartz, "This Sculpture Holds a Decades-Old C.I.A. Mystery. And Now, Another Clue," *New York Times*, January 29, 2020, *https://www.nytimes.com/interactive/2020/01/29/climate/kryptos-sculpture-final-clue.html*.

4 Craig Bauer, *Unsolved!* (Princeton, NJ: Princeton University Press, 2017), 289.

5 Bauer, *Unsolved!*, 308.

6 Gordon Corera, "WWII Pigeon Message Stumps GCHQ Decoders," BBC News, November 23, 2012, *https://www.bbc.com/news/uk-20456782*.

7 "Nick Pelling, "Dead WW2 Cipher Pigeon Timeline," *Cipher Mysteries* (blog), November 24, 2012, *https://ciphermysteries.com/2012/11/24/dead-ww2-cipher-pigeon-timeline*.

8 "NKRYPT," Questacon, July 7, 2022, *https://www.questacon.edu.au/whats-on/exhibitions/exhibits/nkrypt*.

9 Glenn McIntosh, "NKRYPT Sculpture," Meme, accessed April 2, 2023, *https://www.meme.net.au/nkrypt/*.

10 Gregory Lloyd, DKRYPT main page, last modified October 15, 2014, *https://www.dkrypt.org*.

11 Bruce Schneier, "Handwritten Real-World Cryptogram," *Schneier on Security* (blog), January 20, 2006, *https://www.schneier.com/blog/archives/2006/01/handwritten_rea.html*.

12 David Kahn, "German Spy Cryptograms," *Cryptologia* 5, no. 2 (1981): 65–66.

13 Klaus Schmeh, "The Top 50 Unsolved Encrypted Messages: 36. The Fair Game Code," *Cipherbrain* (blog), April 13, 2017, *http://scienceblogs.de/klausis-krypto-kolumne/2017/04/13/the-top-50-unsolved-encrypted-messages-36-the-fair-game-code/*.

14 Klaus Schmeh, "The Top 50 Unsolved Encrypted Messages: 50. The Cylob Cryptogram," *Cipherbrain* (blog), February 8, 2017, *http://scienceblogs.de/klausis-krypto-kolumne/2017/02/08/the-top-50-unsolved-encrypted-messages-50-the-cylob-cryptogram/*.

15 Nick Pelling, "D'Agapeyeff Cipher," The Cipher Foundation, accessed April 2, 2023, *http://cipherfoundation.org/modern-ciphers/dagapeyeff-cipher/*.

16 "The mLH Cipher," *The Cryptogram*, January/February 1978.

17 Nick Pelling, "Feynman Challenge Ciphers," The Cipher Foundation, accessed April 2, 2023, *http://cipherfoundation.org/modern-ciphers/feynman-challenge-ciphers/*.

18 Klaus Schmeh, "The Top 50 Unsolved Encrypted Messages: 15. The Rilke Cryptogram," *Cipherbrain* (blog), January 10, 2018, *http://scienceblogs.de/klausis-krypto-kolumne/2018/01/10/the-top-50-unsolved-encrypted-messages-15-the-rilke-cryptogram/*.

19 Klaus Schmeh, "Rohonc Codex: Top Ten Crypto Mystery Solved (Part 1 of 2)," *Cipherbrain* (blog), June 3, 2018, *http://scienceblogs.de/klausis-krypto-kolumne/2018/06/03/rohonc-codex-top-ten-crypto-mystery-solved-part-1-of-2/*.

20 Benedek Láng, *The Rohonc Code* (University Park: Penn State University Press, 2021).

21 Levente Zoltán Király and Gábor Tokai, "Cracking the Code of the Rohonc Codex," *Cryptologia* 42, no. 4 (2018): 285–315.

22 Elonka Dunin, "Famous Unsolved Codes and Ciphers," Elonka.com, last modified December 8, 2023, *https://elonka.com/UnsolvedCodes.html*.

23 Klaus Schmeh, "The Top 50 Unsolved Encrypted Messages," *Cipherbrain* (blog), accessed April 2, 2023, *http://scienceblogs.de/klausis-krypto-kolumne/the-top-50-unsolved-encrypted-messages/*.

24 Bauer, *Unsolved!*.

25 Klaus Schmeh, *Nicht zu knacken* (Munich: Hanser, 2012).

26 Richard Belfield, *Can You Crack the Enigma Code?* (London: Orion, 2006).

27 US Department of the Army, *Basic Cryptanalysis* (Washington, DC: US Department of the Army, 1990), *http://fas.org/irp/doddir/army/fm34-40-2/*.

28 George Lasry, "A Methodology for the Cryptanalysis of Classical Ciphers with Search Metaheuristics" (PhD thesis, Kassel University Press, 2017), *https://d-nb.info/1153797542/34*.

29 Al Sweigart, *Cracking Codes with Python* (San Francisco: No Starch Press, 2018).

30 Benedek Láng, *Real Life Cryptology: Ciphers and Secrets in Early Modern Hungary* (Amsterdam, Netherlands: Amsterdam University Press, 2018), *https://www.academia.edu/37205281/Real_Life_Cryptology_Ciphers_and_Secrets_in_Early_Modern_Hungary_Amsterdam_University_Press_Atlantis_Press_2018*.

Appendix A

1 Craig Bauer, *Unsolved!* (Princeton, NJ: Princeton University Press, 2017), 386.

2 John B. Wilson, "Kryptos: The Sanborn Sculpture at CIA Headquarters," *The Science Realm*, accessed April 2, 2023, *http://scirealm.org/Kryptos.html*.

3 Colin Bessonette, "Q&A on the News," *Atlanta-Journal Constitution*, November 16, 1998, A2.

4 David D. Stein, "The Puzzle at CIA Headquarters," Elonka.com, 1998, *https://www.elonka.com/kryptos/mirrors/daw/steinarticle.html*.

5 Kim Zetter, "Documents Reveal How the NSA Cracked the Kryptos Sculpture Years before the CIA," *Wired*, July 10, 2013, *https://www.wired.com/2013/07/nsa-cracked-kryptos-before-cia/*.

6 Elonka Dunin, "The Kryptos Group Announces a Corrected Answer to Kryptos Part 2," Elonka.com, April 19, 2006, *https://elonka.com/kryptos/CorrectedK2Announcement.html*.

7 Melissa Block, "Enigmatic CIA Puzzle 'Kryptos' May Be Flawed," NPR, April 21, 2006, *https://www.npr.org/templates/story/story.php?storyId=5356012*.

8 Elonka Dunin, "Elonka Dunin's Technique for Reading Part 3 of the Kryptos Sculpture," Elonka.com, May 23, 2003, *https://elonka.com/kryptos/part3.html*.

9 Elonka Dunin, "Kryptos Timeline," Elonka.com, accessed April 2, 2023, *https://www.elonka.com/kryptos/KryptosTimeline.html*.

10 Elonka Dunin, "Kryptos," Elonka.com, accessed April 2, 2023, *https://elonka.com/kryptos/*.

Appendix B

1 "Letter frequency," Wikipedia (January 21, 2020), *https://en.wikipedia.org/w/index.php?title=Letter_frequency&oldid=936795409*.

2 William Friedman, *The Index of Coincidence and Its Applications in Cryptology* (Laguna Hills, CA: Aegean Park Press, 1987).

INDEX